SHIELD AND SWORD

SHIELD AND SWORD

The United States Navy and the Persian Gulf War

Edward J. Marolda
and
Robert J. Schneller Jr.

Naval Institute Press
Annapolis, Maryland

Naval Historical Center
Washington, D.C.

Naval Institute Press
291 Wood Road
Annapolis, MD 21402

Originally published in 1998 by the Naval Historical Center. Naval Institute Press edition 2001.

ISBN 1-55750-485-7

Printed in the United States of America on acid-free paper ∞
08 07 06 05 04 03 02 01   9 8 7 6 5 4 3 2
First printing

to those who served

Contents

	Page
Foreword	xiii
Preface	xv
Acknowledgments	xvii

CHAPTER 1. Passage to Desert Shield ... 3

America and the Persian Gulf in the Early Years ... 4
Creation and Evolution of Central Command ... 13
Legacy of the Vietnam War ... 20
Rebirth of the Fleet and the Maritime Strategy ... 25
The Tanker War ... 32
End of the Cold War ... 40
The Iraq-Kuwait Crisis ... 43
The Invasion of Kuwait ... 52
Decision to Intervene ... 54

CHAPTER 2. Building the Shield ... 59

Holding the Line ... 59
Window of Vulnerability ... 66
The Naval Command ... 79
The Embargo ... 83
Sealift ... 96
Fleet and Shore-based Logistic Support ... 102
Shield in Place ... 110

CHAPTER 3. The Gathering Storm ... 111

Over to the Attack ... 111
Naval Deployments to the Gulf ... 121
Deployment of the VII Corps and the Phase II Buildup ... 131
Preparations for War ... 135
Continuing Operations ... 146
Life in the War Zone ... 153
Countdown to War ... 163

Page

CHAPTER 4.   Attack by Air and Sea 167

The Desert Storm Plan and Composite Warfare Doctrine 167
The Air Campaign: D-Day and D+1 170
Problems of the Air Campaign 183
The Great Scud Hunt 196
Deluge from Above 198
Fleet Defense and the Allied Right Flank 202
Storm in the Northern Gulf 210
Saddam Strikes Back 226
Bubiyan Turkey Shoot 229

CHAPTER 5.   Preparing the Battlefield 233

"First we're going to cut it off, . . . " 233
Interdiction 236
Kill Boxes 238
Gauging the Effectiveness of Phase III Air Attacks 241
The Strategic Air Campaign in February 245
The Right Feint 247
Ground Forces Move into Attack Positions 269
Eleventh Hour Measures 274

CHAPTER 6.   The Final Assault 277

Preliminary Operations 277
G-Day 282
Closing on the Iraqi Army in Kuwait 292
Rout of the Iraqi Army 297
An Aerial and Armored Blitz Ends the War 302
Temporary Cease-Fire 304

CHAPTER 7.   After the Storm 307

Defense of Kuwait 307
Safwan 309
The Prisoner Release 312
Reconstruction of Kuwait 314
Postwar Mine Countermeasures 320
Redeployment of Central Command Forces 325
Military Sealift Command Empties the Desert 329
The Welcome Home 331
Reorganization of NAVCENT 334
Enforcing the Peace 337

		Page
CHAPTER 8. Summary		355

Prologue to the War 355
Navy Shortcomings 358
Hardening the Shield 360
Increasing the Pressure on Saddam 362
Gearing Up for Battle 365
Littoral Combat in the Persian Gulf 369
The Air War 369
The Maritime Assault on Kuwait 376
Maintaining Peace and Learning from the
    Gulf War Experience 381

Abbreviations. 387

Notes 393

Bibliography 449

Index 491

Maps

Central Command Theater 6
Indian Ocean 15
Tanker War Operations 34
The Air Assault on Iraq 171
UN Naval Forces in the Persian Gulf, 17 January 1991 177
Iraqi Air Attack in the Gulf, 24 January 1991 206
Naval Operations in the Northern Gulf,
    17 January–2 February 1991 211
Kill Boxes in the KTO 239
Desert Storm Mine Clearance Operations 248
Disposition of Iraqi Ground Divisions, 23 February 1991 271
Ground Assault on Southern Kuwait, 24–28 February 1991 278
UN Naval Forces in the Persian Gulf, 24 February 1991 281
Liberation of Kuwait 291
Reopening of Kuwait 321

Tables

1. Iraq's Navy 68
2. NAVCENT Command Structure (18 August to 26 December) . . 84
3. Navy Special Warfare Forces in Desert Shield and Desert Storm 122
4. Port Security and Harbor Defense Command 124
5. NAVCENT Command Structure (26 December 1990 onward) . . 139
6. North Arabian Gulf Mine Statistics 324

Illustrations

Guided missile frigate *Taylor* in the Persian Gulf 4
Aircraft carrier *Dwight D. Eisenhower* in the Suez Canal 5
Oil platforms 10
Nuclear-powered guided missile cruiser *California* 14
Secretary of the Navy John F. Lehman Jr. 21
Guided missile destroyer *Coontz* and Soviet guided missile cruiser . 25
Battleship *Iowa* tests long-range naval guns 26
SPY-1A radar and other components of Aegis antiair
       warfare system 29
Reflagged Kuwaiti tankers in Operation Earnest Will 32
Guided missile frigate *Stark*, hit by Iraqi Exocet missiles 36
Captured Iranian mine layer *Iran Ajr* 37
American destroyer shells Iranian oil platforms 39
Iranian frigate *Sahand* burns after hits by Harpoons 39
"Saddam Hussein" 44
General Colin Powell briefs President Bush 55
Antietam, Reasoner, Jouett, and *Brewton* 60
British destroyer *York* 62
Muammar al-Qaddafi 63
Marine amphibious vehicle is unloaded from *Baldomero Lopez* 65
Marines board Military Airlift Command passenger plane 66
Vice Admiral Mauz and Lieutenant General Boomer 71
Armed Sea Raider utility craft patrols Manama harbor 72
Dutch heavy lift ship *Super Servant III, Avenger,* and *Adroit* 76
Navy MH-53E Sea Dragon mine countermeasures helicopter 76
P-3 Orion patrol plane 90
Goldsborough sailor trains his 50-caliber machine gun 92
British Royal Marines "fast rope" from Lynx helicopter 93
SEAL Team 8 in training mission 94
M1A1 Abrams main battle tank unloaded 96
A ship prepares to offload military vehicles 99
Sacramento refuels *Missouri* and *Wisconsin* 103
Gunner's mates attach cables to a 16-inch shell 104
Hospital ship *Comfort* 106
Lieutenant Susan Globokar (CEC) 108
Fleet Hospital 5 at al-Jubayl 109
Lieutenant General Charles A. Horner 115
Generals Norman Schwarzkopf and Colin Powell 119
Lieutenant Kelly Franke prepares to board her Sea King helicopter 125
Canadian Commodore Ken Summers 128
Battle Force Yankee 136

Page

Rear Admirals Riley D. Mixson and George N. Gee 140
HMAS *Brisbane* sailors arm a Phalanx 142
American and Dutch medical personnel 144
"The *Ibn Khaldoon* Peace Ship" 152
Saratoga chemical drill 155
Iraqi psychological warfare leaflets 158
Navy nurses 159
General Powell welcomed by *Wisconsin's* sailors 162
Comedian Jay Leno 162
A-7 Corsair II is catapulted from *John F. Kennedy* 169
Tomahawk land attack missile launch 169
"Tomahawk in Downtown Baghdad" 173
Carrier-based EA-6B Prowler 174
Air-to-surface missile launched by a Corsair 175
High-speed anti-radiation missile (HARM) 176
"A Hornet Stings" 179
Lieutenant Commander Mark Fox 180
Vice Admiral Stanley R. Arthur 182
An Air Force KC-135E and a Navy A-6E refuel Navy EA-6Bs 191
Submarine launched Tomahawk cruise missile 193
Precision guided munitions are readied on deck 195
An E-2C Hawkeye prepares to "catch a wire" 200
Iraqi concrete aircraft shelters 201
Commander John Leenhouts, Executive Officer of VA-72 201
Aegis guided missile cruiser *Bunker Hill* 204
HMAS *Brisbane* 210
Ranger refuels HNLMS *Jacob Van Heemskerck* 212
U.S. Army OH-58D Kiowa Warrior helicopter 213
"Seizure of the ad-Dorra Oil Platforms" 214
"A Navy LAMPS III Rescues a Downed American Pilot" 215
"The Lynx and Its Prey" 223
"The Liberation of Qaruh" 225
A-6E Intruder launches a Skipper laser guided bomb 228
Iraqi warship under attack during the "Bubiyan Turkey Shoot" . . . 228
An Iraqi FPB-57 lies dead in the water 230
Commanders Richard Cassara and Richard Noble 231
Superstructure of sunken Iraqi naval vessel 232
U.S. psychological warfare leaflet 238
Marine AV-8B Harriers 241
Aerial photo of al-Qaim 243
Beach defenses on the coast of Kuwait 249
Antipersonnel mines and wire entanglements 251
General Al Gray, Commandant of the U.S. Marine Corps 252

Page

Wisconsin's 16-inch gun shells Iraqi positions 257
Unmanned aerial vehicle 258
Captain Peter Bulkeley chalks a message to Saddam Hussein 259
American sailor on the lookout for Iraqi mines 261
Detonation of an Iraqi sea mine 262
Mine damage to *Tripoli* 268
Seabee earthmoving equipment 272
The al-Khanjar logistics support site 273
Marine M60A1 mine-clearing tank 282
"A Navy Corpsman and Marine Infantrymen on G-day" 284
Marines move captured Iraqi soldiers to the rear 287
Chinese-made Iraqi HY-2 Silkworm antiship missile 293
Naval medical personnel move a wounded marine 295
Destroyed Soviet-made Iraqi tank 298
Light armored vehicles secure Kuwait International Airport 299
M1A1 Abrams main battle tanks traverse the Iraqi desert 303
Jubilant coalition troops celebrate the liberation of Kuwait 306
"Iraqis on Faylaka Surrender to a UAV" 308
General Schwarzkopf and Saudi General Sultan at Safwan 311
Navy medical personnel tend to Air Force Captain William Andrews 313
Dead Iraqi swimmer 315
Navy EOD diver prepares to destroy a LUGM sea mine 316
British EOD divers return to shore 317
Opening the port of Ash Shuaybah 318
U.S. Army heavy lift vessel *Algiers* raises a destroyed
    Iraqi combatant 319
Rear Admiral Taylor briefs the press 323
UN coalition's postwar mine clearance flotilla 323
Cleaned Abrams tanks and plastic-encased Chinook helicopters .. 326
Honoring of Lieutenants Robert Wetzel,
    Lawrence Slade, and Jeffrey Zaun 332
Ticker-tape victory parade in New York City 332
Officers of *Thomas S. Gates* 333
Admiral Kelso confers with Rear Admiral Taylor 335
Kurds' winter encampment near Turkey 337
Amphibious assault ships *Wasp* and *Guadalcanal* 339
A Kurdish tent camp in northern Iraq 340
Crewmen of HMAS *Darwin* prepare to board Iraqi merchant ship . 341
Colonel Nasser al-Husainan receives medal 342
U.S.-Kuwaiti combined exercises 345
F-14 Tomcat in Operation Southern Watch 347
F/A-18 Hornet heads for a no-fly zone in Iraq 349
Carrier *Nimitz* and command ship *LaSalle* 351

Foreword

THIS VOLUME DESCRIBES IN DETAIL THE U.S. Navy's role in Operations Desert Shield and Desert Storm, one of the most successful campaigns in American military history. The work describes the contribution to victory of Navy men and women who served afloat in the carrier-based fighter and attack squadrons, the surface warships, amphibious and mine countermeasures vessels, submarines, and logistic and hospital ships. It also relates the activities of American sailors ashore or close inshore who protected the vital harbors of northern Saudi Arabia, provided Marine combat units with medical and construction assistance, flew vital supplies to forward areas, or coordinated all this activity on Navy and joint staffs. Overall, it is a story of Navy men and women, regular and reserve, who unselfishly answered their nation's call to arms when aggression threatened peace in the Persian Gulf.

The authors of this work are well qualified to present this naval history. Dr. Edward J. Marolda, the Center's Senior Historian and formerly head of the Contemporary History Branch, is a recognized authority on the modern operations of the U.S. Navy. He has written a number of books on the Vietnam War and overseen the preparation of many other Center publications relating to the naval service in the Cold War period. Dr. Robert J. Schneller, a member of the Contemporary History Branch, has published a highly regarded biography of the 19th century naval ordnance designer John Dahlgren and is currently writing a book on the integration of African Americans at the U.S. Naval Academy.

Many people, too numerous to name in this space, are responsible for the publication of this important work, including staff members of the Naval Historical Center; veterans of the Gulf War; members of the Center's Naval Reserve Detachment 206; the Joint, Army, Marine, Air Force, and Coast Guard historical offices; the Center for Naval Analyses; the Naval Historical Foundation; and scholars and professional colleagues in the United States and overseas. To the many deserving individuals go my sincere thanks.

As is true for all the histories published by the Naval Historical Center, the opinions and conclusions expressed in this work are solely those of the authors. They do not necessarily reflect the views of the Department of the Navy or any other agency of the U.S. Government.

William S. Dudley
Director of Naval History

Preface

I T HAS BEEN TEN YEARS SINCE Iraqi tanks rolled into Kuwait. Most accounts of the Persian Gulf War that have appeared in the past decade have highlighted the part played by air and ground forces in driving them back out.

This book focuses on the contribution of the United States Navy, warts and all, to the success of Desert Shield and Desert Storm. The Navy's ability to control the sea and project power ashore enabled the coalition to quickly construct a shield capable of defending America's Arab allies from further Iraqi aggression. It also allowed the coalition to concentrate the forces and resources necessary for a major counteroffensive. The Navy's warfighting capabilities proved vital to the coalition's victory over Iraq. Naval aviation played more than a minor role in the air campaign against Iraq, and naval surface operations proved important to the success of General Norman Schwarzkopf's famed "left hook."

This work also devotes considerable attention to the years before and after Desert Shield and Desert Storm, since the U.S. Navy's presence in the Persian Gulf has consistently served U.S. foreign policy objectives in the region. American naval support for friendly governments, especially during the Iran-Iraq War of 1980–88, paid dividends when the United States sought allies to counter Saddam Hussein's aggression in 1990. And although the confrontation with Iraq has slipped from public consciousness as this edition goes to press, the Navy is still engaged in daily operations to dampen Saddam's aggressive tendencies and prevent him from developing weapons of mass destruction. As of 18 August 2000, the tenth anniversary of the first maritime interception operation to enforce the UN embargo of Iraq, U.S. and UN naval forces have queried 29,307 merchant ships, boarded 12,763 of them, and diverted 748 to coalition ports for inspection. As of that same date, Navy carrier planes and other U.S. and UN aircraft have made 233,800 flights in support of Operation Southern Watch since its inception in August 1992.

This book stresses the U.S. Navy's involvement in joint and multinational operations. The Persian Gulf War was not the first conflict in which

American naval forces operated in conjunction with U.S. ground and air forces and those of its global allies, but the experience suggested that this would be true in most subsequent post–Cold War conflicts. Indeed, the experience in conducting joint and combined operations in the Gulf War has influenced military action in the recent conflicts in Bosnia and Kosovo.

This volume is written from the theater-level perspective, because General Schwarzkopf, Commander in Chief, U.S. Central Command, directed the operations of his subordinate naval, air, and ground components from his headquarters in Riyadh. As a result of the Goldwater-Nichols Act of 1986 and earlier bureaucratic decisions, the Chief of Naval Operations and other flag officers outside the theater were not part of the operational chain of command. Their involvement has been detailed only as it influenced decisions made in Riyadh and on board the flagship of Commander U.S. Naval Forces, Central Command.

The book is based on hundreds of action and operational reports, command histories, lessons-learned summaries, personal communications, and other documents held in the Navy's Operational Archives, the National Archives, and the Center for Naval Analyses; taped interviews conducted by the authors and by five captains of the U.S. Naval Reserve whom the Naval Historical Center dispatched to the gulf during Desert Shield and Desert Storm; the Defense Department's "Title V" report, the Center for Naval Analyses' previously classified, fourteen-volume Desert Storm Reconstruction Report, the Gulf War Air Power Survey, and other well-documented summaries and analyses; and the best secondary books and articles available.

Still, this book is not the last word on the U.S. Navy and the Gulf War. Ample documentary support exists for studies of individual operations; Navy-media relations; the employment of women in the combat theater; support provided by the home front and by the Navy's global logistic establishment; aircraft, ship, and ordnance performance; operational planning; intelligence support; and many other relevant subjects.

Historians sometimes cast a jaundiced eye on a history first published less than a decade after the event. Rear Admiral Samuel Eliot Morison, the late dean of American naval historians, appreciated that "no history written during or shortly after the event it describes can pretend to be completely objective or even reasonably definitive." Like Morison, however, we decided that there would be real benefit in providing U.S. Navy personnel, civilian policymakers, and the American public with a timely and reasonably well-documented narrative on the armed confrontation with Iraq that continues to this day.

Edward J. Marolda
Robert J. Schneller Jr.
September 2000

Acknowledgments

THE AUTHORS ARE GRATEFUL FOR THE GUIDANCE and support given by Dr. Dean C. Allard and Dr. William S. Dudley, successive Directors of Naval History, throughout the preparation of this volume.

We also deeply appreciate the thorough and insightful review of the entire manuscript by the following officers and scholars: General Colin L. Powell, USA (Ret.), former Chairman, Joint Chiefs of Staff; Admiral Stanley R. Arthur, USN (Ret.) and Rear Admiral Raynor A.K. Taylor, USN (Ret.), former Commanders U.S. Naval Forces, Central Command; Rear Admiral Thomas F. Marfiak, USN, and Captain Stephen R. Woodall, USN (Ret.), Gulf War veterans and knowledgeable analysts of naval operations; Dr. David A. Rosenberg, Chair of the Secretary of the Navy's Advisory Subcommittee on Naval History and a highly regarded scholar of 20th century naval strategy and policy; Marvin Pokrant, an expert on Desert Storm at the Center for Naval Analyses; Dr. Wayne Thompson and Dr. Frank N. Schubert, authors of works on the Persian Gulf War published by the historical offices of the U.S. Air Force and U.S. Army; Dr. Jack Shulimson, Major John T. Quinn, USMC, and Major Steven Zimmeck, USMC, Gulf War experts at the Marine Corps Historical Center; and Dr. Michael A. Palmer, Associate Professor of History at East Carolina University, author of two books on the Navy's activities in the Persian Gulf, and our former colleague at the Naval Historical Center.

Others commented on those portions of the manuscript for which they had direct knowledge or expertise, responded to our queries, completed interviews, or provided photographs for the work. They include Admirals Henry H. Mauz Jr., USN (Ret.), and Ronald J. Zlatoper, USN (Ret.); Vice Admirals Douglas J. Katz, USN, and John B. LaPlante, USN (Ret.); Rear Admirals William M. Fogarty, USN (Ret.), David S. Bill, USN, Robert Sutton, USN, Thomas A. Brooks, USN (Ret.), Daniel P. March, USN (Ret.), and Grant A. Sharp, USN (Ret.); Captains Peter W. Bulkeley, USN (Ret.), William C. Hunt, USN, Dennis G. Morral, USN (Ret.), Peter Bulkeley, USN (Ret.), David J. Grieve, USN (Ret.), and

Don A. Sharer, USN (Ret.); Colonel Joseph N. Purvis, USA (Ret.); Commanders Diana Cangelosi, USN, William Richards, USN, Michael R. Johnson (CEC), USN, Richard Cassara, USN (Ret.), and Greg Slavonic, USNR; Lieutenant Colonels Ronald J. Brown, USMCR, and Charles H. Cureton, USMC; Lieutenant Commanders Joseph T. Stanik, USN (Ret.) and Jeffrey Taylor, USN; Captain Douglas Kleinsmith, USMC; Dr. David B. Crist, Marine Corps Historical Center; Salvatore R. Mercogliano, East Carolina University; Major Mason P. Carpenter, USAF; and the following Gulf War authors and analysts at the Center for Naval Analyses: Laurie Trader, Dr. Peter Perla, Dr. Katherine McGrady, Dr. Michael Shepko, Mary Robin Holliday, and Dr. Ralph Passarelli.

We thank the staff members of the agencies mentioned above and those of other U.S. government and related offices who offered research, photographic, or general assistance: Brigadier General Edwin H. Simmons, USMC (Ret.), Colonel Michael F. Monigan, USMC, Benis M. Frank, Captain David A. Dawson, USMC, Lena Kaljot, and Danny Crawford, Marine Corps Historical Center; Robert K. Wright Jr., Center of Military History; Richard Hallion, Dr. Diane Putney, Dr. Perry Jamieson, Dr. Richard Davis, Thomas Y'Blood, and William Heimdahl, U.S. Air Force Historical Support Office; Dr. Robert Browning and Scott Price, U.S. Coast Guard Historical Office; Dr. John Partin and Michael Murphy, Special Operations Command History Office; Dr. James K. Matthews, Transportation Command; Jay Hines and David Rosmer, Central Command Historical Office; Walter Sansone, Military Sealift Command; Dr. Ronald Cole and Dr. Hans Paulisch, Joint Chiefs of Staff History Office; Janet A. McDonnell, U.S. Army Corps of Engineers History Office; Dr. Timothy Nenninger, National Archives and Records Administration; Dr. Dean Allen and Brian Shellum, Defense Intelligence Agency; David Hatch, National Security Agency; Captain Peter M. Swartz, USN (Ret.), Adam B. Siegel, and Dr. Thomas C. Hone, Center for Naval Analyses; Captain Rosario Rausa, USN (Ret.), *Wings of Gold* magazine; and PO Todd Stevens, Navy Office of Information Photo Service

We express sincere appreciation to our friends and colleagues overseas who helped make the point that the naval side of the Gulf War was truly multinational. They include Rear Admiral C. J. Oxenbould, RAN, Commander James Goldrick, RAN, Dr. Peter Dennis, David Stevens, Dick Sherwood, Joseph Straczek, Commander John Griffith, RAN, Dr. David Horner, Dr. Jeffrey Grey, and Michael Fogarty, Australia; Major Jean H. Morin, Lieutenant Commander Richard Gimblett, and Dr. Roger Sarty, Canada; Captain Philip Wilcocks, RN, Great Britain; Dr. Alan Lemmers and Dr. P. C. van Royen, Netherlands; Captain

Guillermo J. Montenegro, Argentine Navy (Ret.); General Tsujikawa and Dr. Hisashi Takahashi, Japan.

In one way or another, every staff member of the Naval Historical Center helped bring this project to fruition, but the following individuals deserve special mention: Captains Cletis F. Wise, William Vance, and Todd Creekman, successive Deputy Directors of Naval History, and staff members of the Administrative and Fiscal Branch, for their ready support for the processing and funding aspects of the project; our friends and colleagues of the Contemporary History Branch, Dr. Gary E. Weir, Dr. Jeffrey G. Barlow, Richard A. Russell, Robert J. Cressman, and Curtis Utz, for their informed and helpful critique of succeeding generations of the manuscript; Charles R. Haberlein Jr., Jack Green, and Ed Finney of the Curator Branch's Photographic Section for their assistance with the location and reproduction of suitable photographs; Jean Hort, Glenn Helm, David Brown, Tonya Montgomery, Young Park, Davis Elliott, Barbara Auman, and the late Paula Murphy of the Navy Department Library for their help locating and acquiring source materials; Bernard Cavalcante, Judy Short, Kathy Lloyd, Mike Walker, John Hodges, Ariana Jacob, Paul Breck, Regina Akers, and Kathy Rohr of the Operational Archives for their invaluable assistance exploiting the mountain of material gathered by the Navy on the Persian Gulf War; John Reilly, Timothy Francis, Ray Mann, and Kevin Hurst of the Ship's History Branch; and Roy Grossnick, Gwen Rich, Judith Walters, and Todd Baker of the Aviation History Branch, for their cogent advice on sources related to the Navy's surface warfare and aviation communities; Morgan Wilbur of the *Naval Aviation News* branch for the vivid and dramatic painting he accomplished for our book's dust jacket; Dr. Oscar P. Fitzgerald, Claudia Pennington, Susan Scott, and Dr. Edward Furgol of the Navy Museum; and Dr. Norman Cary and Mark Wertheimer of the Curator Branch for their expert advice on the characteristics of Navy Gulf War weapons and equipment; Ella Nargele for managing an especially expeditious security review of the manuscript by pertinent Navy and Defense Department agencies. As with many NHC manuscripts, this one benefited immensely from the processing efforts of Maxine Ware, the professional editorial and publication skills of Senior Editor Sandra Doyle, and the attention to detail by our indexer, Donna Packard. We gratefully acknowledge John Grier of the Government Printing Office and thank him for the many years he has provided professional design, typesetting, and layout for Center publications, including this work.

We also owe a debt of gratitude to Captains Steven U. Ramsdell, Douglas Bauer, William McClintok, and Michael Roberts of the Naval Historical Center's Reserve Detachment 206 for their wartime and early postwar taped interviews with naval personnel in the gulf. Captain

Harold S. Tiernan, USNR, prepared a history of the Military Sealift Command's role in Desert Shield and Desert Storm that was most helpful. Also deserving of high praise is Captain John Charles Roach, a renowned artist, who enhanced our text with expressive and informative illustrations.

Finally, we thank Admiral James L. Holloway III, USN (Ret.), Captain Kenneth L. Coskey, USN (Ret.), Commander David Winkler, USNR, and YNC Franke A. Arre of the Naval Historical Foundation for their intellectual encouragement and funding for audio tape transcription.

Grateful as we are for all the assistance provided us, we accept full responsibility for the conclusions drawn in this history and for any errors in fact.

Edward J. Marolda
Robert J. Schneller Jr.

The Authors

Edward J. Marolda is the Naval Historical Center's Senior Historian. He serves as the principal professional advisor to the Director of Naval History and supervises the Center's publications, oral history, fellowship/grant, and conference programs. He has been a member of the Center's professional staff since 1971. Between 1987 and 1996 he served as head of the Contemporary History Branch and in that capacity oversaw the creation of the Contributions to Naval History and The U.S. Navy in the Modern World narrative history series.

Dr. Marolda has authored, coauthored, or edited five books on the Vietnam War, including (with Dr. Oscar P. Fitzgerald) *From Military Assistance to Combat,* Volume 2 of *The United States Navy and the Vietnam Conflict,* and *By Sea, Air, and Land: An Illustrated History of the U.S. Navy and the War in Southeast Asia.* He has lectured on military and naval history in Australia, Japan, and the United States and published articles in the *Naval War College Review,* U.S. Naval Institute *Proceedings, Naval History, Journal of Strategic Studies,* and other scholarly journals.

Dr. Marolda holds the following degrees in history: a B.A. from Pennsylvania Military College, an M.A. from Georgetown University, and the Ph.D from George Washington University.

Robert J. Schneller Jr. is a historian in the Contemporary History Branch, where he has worked since joining the Naval Historical Center in 1991.

Dr. Schneller is the author of *A Quest for Glory: A Biography of Rear Admiral John A. Dahlgren* and editor of *Under the Blue Pennant, or Notes of a Naval Officer,* by John W. Grattan. He has given papers on American naval history in the United States and Canada, and has published articles and book reviews in the *Naval War College Review, American Historical Review, The North Carolina Historical Review, Naval Engineers Journal, Naval History,* and *American Neptune.*

Schneller holds an M.A. in history from East Carolina University and the Ph.D. in military history from Duke University.

SHIELD AND SWORD

CHAPTER 1

Passage to Desert Shield

I N THE EERIE GLOW OF FRIGATE *Taylor*'s combat information center, Commander Kevin P. Green, her skipper, gathered his thoughts for an address to the crew. The ship was moored in the inner harbor of Manama, Bahrain, taking on supplies and fuel. Commander Green had slept little since midnight, for his watchstanders had awakened him repeatedly with updates on the tense situation in Kuwait. Finally arising at 0400, he recorded a laconic entry in his personal daybook: "Iraq invades Kuwait." The date was 2 August 1990.

Green took the microphone. In his easy-going California manner, the captain told his crew that the state of affairs in the gulf might remain unsettled for weeks. But, he reassured them, their training and equipment would enable them to handle any situation. As he spoke, he watched a firecontrolman monitoring several unidentified aircraft tracks to the north on his weapons control console. Could these be Iraqi Mirage jets armed with deadly Exocet antiship missiles like the ones that nearly sank the frigate *Stark* (FFG 31) in 1987? The sailor's animated gestures bespoke confidence, however, not apprehension. *Taylor*'s crew, along with the rest of the men and women of the United States Navy, stood ready once more to fulfill their traditional role as America's shield and sword in the Persian Gulf.[1]

The Navy had formed the first line of defense for U.S. interests in the Persian Gulf region since the establishment of the Middle East Force in 1949. For that reason, forward deployed ships were available to respond immediately to the invasion of Kuwait. On 2 August, the ships of Joint Task Force Middle East—*Taylor* (FFG 50); cruiser *England* (CG 22); destroyer *David R. Ray* (DD 971); frigates *Vandegrift* (FFG 48), *Reid* (FFG 30), *Robert G. Bradley* (FFG 49), and *Barbey* (FF 1088); and venerable command ship *LaSalle* (AGF 3)—were on station in the central and southern waters of the gulf; carrier *Independence* (CV 62) and her eight-

USN DN-ST 92-06777

Guided missile frigate *Taylor* (FFG 50) passes an oil tanker in the Persian Gulf. *Taylor* and seven other warships of the U.S. Middle East Force were on station in the gulf when Saddam Hussein's forces invaded Kuwait on 2 August 1990.

ship battle group were cruising in the Indian Ocean near Diego Garcia; and carrier *Dwight D. Eisenhower* (CVN 69) and her nine escorts were steaming in the central Mediterranean in the last month of a regularly scheduled six-month deployment.

Soon after the Iraqi invasion, the Secretary of Defense authorized the *Independence* battle group to proceed to the Gulf of Oman and the *Dwight D. Eisenhower* battle group to move through the Suez Canal and take up position in the Red Sea. By 5 August *Independence* was close enough to the operational theater for aircraft from her 69-plane air wing to strike the advancing tank columns of Saddam Hussein's Iraqi army. The 71 aircraft of *Dwight D. Eisenhower*'s air wing were in range shortly afterward. By 7 August, the day that President George Bush launched Operation Desert Shield, the Navy was on hand in strength to back up U.S. policy in the region.[2]

America and the Persian Gulf in the Early Years

America's presence in the gulf traced its origins to the nineteenth century, when American merchant mariners made contact with local po-

USN

Aircraft carrier *Dwight D. Eisenhower* (CVN 69) steams through the Suez Canal enroute to the Red Sea in response to the Iraqi invasion of Kuwait.

tentates, established commercial connections, and traded goods. In the twentieth century, Middle Eastern oil deposits drew the attention of U.S. business interests. In the 1920s and 1930s, American companies obtained shares in British petroleum concessions operating in Iraq and Kuwait, took over the concession in Bahrain, and established the region's only all-American concession in Saudi Arabia.[3]

The region attracted little attention from the U.S. government until World War II, when America extended economic and military support, as part of the Lend Lease program, to Saudi Arabia and Iran. The latter country served as a major corridor through which supplies were transported to the Soviet Union. The U.S. Army presence in Iran during the war peaked at nearly 30,000 men, one of whom was Brigadier General H. Norman Schwarzkopf, whose son would later command all American forces in the region.

The government was also concerned about free access to Persian Gulf oil, which became a vital national interest during the war. Although the United States had produced about two-thirds of the world's oil in 1941, the country supplied roughly six of the seven billion barrels of oil consumed by the Allies during the war. Gloomy wartime forecasts, based on a downward curve in new discoveries and a decrease in drilling activ-

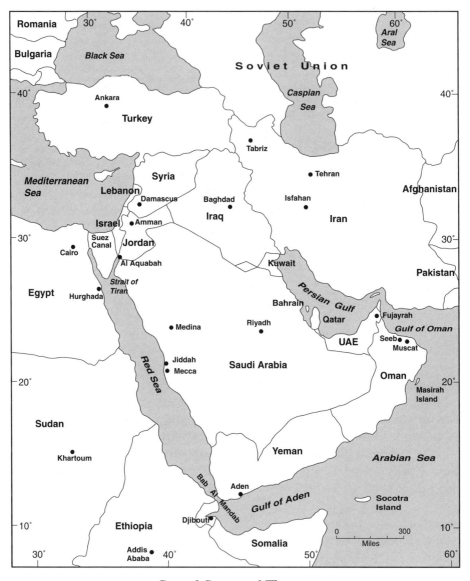

Central Command Theater

6

ity, persuaded American leaders that the United States might dangerously deplete its reserves.

Exploitation of Middle Eastern crude seemed to offer a way to conserve strategically vital domestic supplies. In November 1943, a mission headed by Everette Lee DeGolyer, a well-known oil geologist, estimated the proven and probable reserves in the Persian Gulf region—Iran, Iraq, Saudi Arabia, Kuwait, Bahrain, and Qatar—to be from 25 billion to 300 billion barrels of oil. For Saudi Arabia alone, estimates ranged from 5 billion to 100 billion barrels.[4] "The center of gravity of world oil production is shifting from the Gulf [of Mexico]-Caribbean area to the Middle East-to the Persian Gulf area," DeGolyer said, "and is likely to continue to shift until it is firmly established in this area."[5]

A new development soon joined oil in attracting American attention to the gulf. By the spring of 1946, U.S. leaders had concluded that Soviet dictator Joseph Stalin, their World War II ally, was bent not only on exporting Communist revolution worldwide, but advancing historical Russian interests along the USSR's European and Asian periphery. Determined to oppose this perceived threat to global peace, U.S. leaders adopted a strategy of "containment." The United States and its allies would oppose the encroachment of the Soviet Union and its allies wherever it might occur. By the summer of 1947, the "two-world assumption" had completely displaced any notions of cooperation resulting from the World War II fight against the Axis powers.[6]

The first crises of this new "Cold War" emerged in the Middle East and the Eastern Mediterranean. Between 1945 and 1947, the Soviets put political and military pressure on Iran, Turkey, and Greece. Stalin not only refused to withdraw his troops from Iran within six months of the end of World War II, as he had promised, but also set up the Communist Republic of Azerbaijan in northwest Iran. Under pressure from the United States and Britain, the Russians pulled out of Iran by the end of May 1946, and the Soviet-sponsored Azeri regime soon collapsed. The Iranian crisis, however, marked a major departure for America's postwar foreign policy.[7] President Harry S. Truman, who likened President Franklin Delano Roosevelt's negotiations with the Soviets to appeasement, grew tired of "babying" the Russians and decided that it was time to "get tough." He convinced Congress that the United States must "support free peoples who are resisting subjugations by armed minorities or by outside pressure."[8] Pundits dubbed this policy the "Truman Doctrine." Congress subsequently authorized $400 million in military and economic aid for Greece and Turkey.[9]

On 31 October 1950, in the wake of the Communist North Korean invasion of the Republic of Korea, Truman sent a letter to Saudi Arabian King Abdul Aziz Ibn Saud:

Our countries have been comrades in arms together and we have common cause in opposing the godless forces of Communism which are endeavoring to destroy freedom throughout the world. . . . I wish to renew to Your Majesty the assurances . . . that the United States is interested in the preservation of the independence and territorial integrity of Saudi Arabia. No threat to your Kingdom could occur which would not be a matter of immediate concern to the United States.[10]

Washington also feared threats to its interests in the Middle East from internal conflicts. It is a maxim that in the twentieth century the Middle East has suffered from chronic political and social instability. Authoritarianism, unequal distribution of wealth, class conflict, and other ills plagued the process of nation building among peoples with little tradition or experience in enlightened self-rule. Territorial, political, and ideological disputes erupted between Arab states, as did disagreements over the control of oil. Ethnic and religious strife was one thing that Arabs, Bedouins, Turks, Iranians, Kurds, Sunnis, Shiites, Christians, Jews, and everyone else who inhabited the region had in common. The creation in 1948 of the state of Israel, formerly the British protectorate of Palestine, led to a half century of confrontation between Arabs and Jews.

For some Arabs, pan-Arab nationalism, the belief that all Arabs could and must be unified in a single state, seemed an antidote to chaos. In its more radical formulations, pan-Arabism called for the total ejection of the West from Arab lands and the destruction of the state of Israel.[11] Some Arab nationalists hoped to use their oil resources to achieve political aims.

Despite the dire warnings of DeGolyer and others during the war, however, the oil industry's center of gravity remained in the United States. In the mid-1950s, for example, the United States produced twice as much oil as the Middle Eastern and North African oil states combined. The U.S. petroleum industry dealt with periodic disruptions in the flow of oil from the Middle East by increasing production elsewhere. Hence, such disruptions had little impact on the U.S. economy in this era.[12]

Nevertheless, American leaders recognized that the gulf's petroleum resources remained important to the United States, particularly to the U.S. Navy. Naval forces, forward-based in the Mediterranean and the Western Pacific after World War II, relied heavily on Persian Gulf petroleum for fuel. Accordingly, in January 1948 the Navy established a presence in the region when it created Task Force 126 to control the fleet tankers that plied gulf waters. The responsibility for managing U.S. warships and tankers steaming in the gulf assumed greater permanence on

16 August 1949, when the Navy established a locally based command, the Middle East Force.[13]

Successive American administrations also understood that the United States had important strategic interests in the Middle East, especially in the gulf, that demanded a strong political if not military presence. To limit Soviet encroachment, bolster pro-Western governments, and contain the damage from the bitter Arab-Israeli conflict, U.S. diplomats fostered the Baghdad Pact and its follow-on, the Central Treaty Organization (CENTO). These arrangements brought greater interaction between Iran, Turkey, Pakistan, Great Britain, and Iraq. Although the United States joined neither organization, its role in their formation was vital.

American diplomacy and the periodic employment of the Mediterranean-based U.S. Sixth Fleet played a major role in preventing the outbreak of region-wide, protracted war during the 1950s and 1960s. Washington helped limit the damage from Iran's nationalization of Western oilfields in the early 1950s, the Suez Crisis of 1956, the coup in Iraq in 1958, the Lebanon intervention of 1958, and the Arab-Israeli Six Day War of 1967.[14]

New variables entered the Middle East security equation in the wake of the Six Day War. In January 1968, Prime Minister Harold Wilson announced that Great Britain would end its defense commitments east of Suez, and would withdraw its forces from the Persian Gulf by 1971.[15] No longer could the United States rely on a British military presence in Kuwait, Oman, and elsewhere in the region to support Western policies.

The Soviets hoped to exploit Britain's pull-out. They had already made serious inroads into the region by providing diplomatic, economic, and military assistance to the anti-Western, anti-Israeli, and authoritarian regimes in Egypt, Syria, Iraq, and South Yemen. Moscow also had concluded cultural and trade agreements with Jordan, Kuwait, and Lebanon.

In the wake of Wilson's announcement, the Soviets stepped up efforts to increase their influence in the Middle East. Moscow sent a task force into the Indian Ocean and worked to secure permanent bases in countries in and around the Persian Gulf. The increasingly powerful Soviet navy maintained a continuous presence in the Indian Ocean throughout the 1970s.[16]

A logical American response to the British withdrawal and growing Soviet interest in the Middle East might have been to deploy U.S. military and naval forces to the region. But in 1968 the United States was fully embroiled in the Vietnam War. Forces based in Europe and in the United States had already been dangerously drawn down to support the all-consuming effort in Southeast Asia.

USN DN-SN 89-03128

The presence of huge oil reserves in the Persian Gulf and the world's dependence on the resource ensured high international interest in gulf affairs.

Because the American people elected Richard M. Nixon President in November 1968 on the pledge that he would turn the war over to the Vietnamese and bring American troops home, Nixon proved ill-disposed to commit the U.S. military to any new venture, particularly in the troubled Middle East. Instead, in speeches given in 1969 Nixon annunciated a new global policy regarding overseas commitments. To resist conventional aggression, a threatened ally would have to provide most of its own manpower, while the United States would supply air and naval power and war materiel. In his State of the Union Address of 22 January 1970, the President elaborated on what became known as the "Nixon Doctrine." "We shall be faithful to our treaty commitments," he said, "but we shall reduce our involvement and our presence in other nations' affairs." [17]

The Nixon Doctrine had a profound impact on American policy in the Persian Gulf. Nixon expected two local allies—Iran and Saudi Arabia—to provide security for the region. The "Twin Pillars" policy dovetailed neatly with the plans of the Shah of Iran who was determined to make his country the preeminent power in the gulf. Although the United States had long been supplying friendly Middle Eastern countries with arms, the Twin Pillars policy marked the first attempt to create a strong, pro-Western military bulwark in the region. For most of the decade, American military assistance flowed to Iran and, to a lesser extent, Saudi Arabia.[18]

By this time DeGolyer's prediction had finally come true. The discovery of additional petroleum deposits in the Persian Gulf sheikdoms of Qatar, Oman, Abu Dhabi, Dubai, and particularly Kuwait—its al-Burqan oilfield proved to be the largest oilfield in the Middle East—significantly enhanced the region's total resources. In 1971 the Middle East produced 32.4 percent of the world's oil.

By that time the relative position of the U.S. oil industry had declined dramatically. In the early 1970s, American wells accounted for only 19.1 percent of global production. U.S. domestic consumption rose from 15.1 million barrels per day in 1971 to about 18 million barrels in 1973. America's surplus capacity disappeared as the industry strained to keep up with the demand, dropping from 4 million barrels per day in 1963 to zero in March 1971. The United States needed more and more foreign oil to quench its thirst. By 1973 the amount of oil imported into the country had tripled from the previous decade. The center of gravity of world oil production had indeed shifted to the Persian Gulf.[19]

Two developments in the Middle East soon drove this fact home to the American people. The first was the growing power and collective action of Arab oil-producing states. By the early 1970s several Arab governments had wrested control of production from the Western oil companies on their soil and demanded more than 50 percent of the profits from oil sales. Moreover, in 1968 a number of Middle Eastern states founded the Organization of Arab Petroleum Exporting Countries (OAPEC). By 1970 its membership included Saudi Arabia, Kuwait, Libya, Algeria, Abu Dhabi, Bahrain, Dubai, and Qatar.

The second development stemmed from war. On 6 October 1973, Egypt and Syria launched a surprise attack on Israel, sparking the "Yom Kippur War." The Soviet Union supplied the Arab belligerents with munitions and diplomatic support and alerted its own military forces. The United States responded in kind with a Sixth Fleet buildup in the Eastern Mediterranean and the airlift to Israel of $2.2 billion worth of military hardware and munitions.

OAPEC retaliated by cutting off oil shipments to the United States and reducing the availability of oil worldwide. Arabs had been talking about using the "oil weapon" to achieve political objectives since the 1950s, but the United States had always shielded the West from the blow by increasing domestic production. But the disappearance of America's surplus capacity meant that the country could no longer increase production to compensate for disruptions to the flow of Middle Eastern oil. Although the Arab oil embargo removed no more than 10 percent of available petroleum from the world market, it provoked massive speculative buying by consumer countries, and oil firms worried about future shortages. As a result, the price of a barrel of oil skyrocketed by 400 percent in just a few short months.

This abrupt increase—what economists called a "price shock"—helped precipitate a worldwide recession, with all its inherent evils, including unemployment and dislocation of labor forces. The gross national product of the United States plunged 6 percent between 1973 and 1975, while unemployment doubled to 9 percent. Gasoline shortages and long lines at service stations during the embargo symbolized America's latent dependency on foreign oil. Perhaps for the first time, the American people realized that the Middle East was vital to their security and prosperity. Threats to stability and to U.S. interests in the Middle East henceforth commanded close attention.[20]

The next major threat was already developing. Emboldened by the surge in oil prices during the mid-1970s, Muhammad Reza Pahlavi, the Shah of Iran, had plunged his country into a pell-mell national modernization program that resulted in waste, inflation, and widespread corruption. Disgusted with the Shah's seeming disregard for traditional social and religious values, Iranians from all walks of life turned against him and his pro-American government. In 1978 labor strikes, street demonstrations, and riots spread across Iran with increasing frequency and violence. A revolution coalesced around fundamentalist Muslim Shiites led by the Ayatollah Ruhollah Khomeini, a charismatic cleric exiled to France years before. Embattled on all sides and stricken with cancer, the Shah left Iran on 16 January 1979, never to return. Soon afterward, Khomeini entered Tehran in triumph and established an anti-Western Islamic theocracy. He and his followers expressed the desire not only to spread Shiite extremism throughout the Persian Gulf but to expunge Western influence.

The Iranian revolutionaries harbored a particularly deep hatred for the United States, called the "Great Satan" by Khomeini, because Washington had been the Shah's principal benefactor. On 4 November 1979, Iranian zealots seized the U.S. embassy in Tehran and took its staff hostage, marking the beginning of a 444-day crisis.

The situation in the region worsened that December when Soviet forces invaded Afghanistan in support of indigenous Communists. Not since World War II had Moscow carried out such a large, bold, and strategically threatening military action. U.S. leaders feared that the Soviets hoped to capitalize on the American-Iranian crisis to secure a warm-water port on the Indian Ocean and to gain control of vital Persian Gulf oil resources.[21]

The Soviet invasion of Afghanistan, following hard on the heels of the Iranian revolution, galvanized support within the administration of

President James Earl Carter for a firm stand in the Persian Gulf. In his State of the Union message before Congress on 21 January 1980, Carter told the American people:

> In recent years as our own fuel imports have soared, the Persian Gulf has become vital to the United States as it has been to many of our friends and allies. Over the longer term, the world's dependence on Persian Gulf oil is likely to increase. The denial of these oil supplies—to us or to others— would threaten our security and provoke an economic crisis greater than that of the Great Depression 50 years ago, with a fundamental change in the way we live. Twin threats to the flow of oil—from regional instability and now potentially from the Soviet Union—require that we firmly defend our vital interests when threatened.[22]

As if to dispel any remaining doubt about his meaning, Carter told Congress two days later:

> Let our position be absolutely clear: An attempt by any outside force to gain control of the Persian Gulf region will be regarded as an assault on the vital interests of the United States of America, and such an assault will be repelled by any means necessary, including military force.[23]

This policy, dubbed the "Carter Doctrine," specifically committed American military forces, for the first time, to the defense of Persian Gulf oil.

Carter's successor, President Ronald Reagan, reaffirmed the Carter Doctrine. In a press conference held to diffuse fears that the United States might allow Saudi Arabia to go the way of Iran, Reagan said: "there is no way...that we could stand by and see [Saudi Arabia] taken over by anyone that would shut off the oil."[24] Subsequent statements by Reagan administration officials made it clear that the United States had committed itself to Saudi Arabian security, a pledge that became known as the "Reagan Corollary" to the Carter Doctrine. Reagan's Secretary of the Navy, John Lehman, put it best: "The Carter Doctrine, fully supported by the Reagan administration," highlighted "America's fundamental commitment to go to war to save Persian Gulf oil."[25]

Creation and Evolution of Central Command

Now that the U.S. government was committed to defense of America's interests in the Persian Gulf, the Department of Defense (DOD) needed to establish an appropriate military command structure and to give it substance with assigned forces.

Until the late 1970s, the U.S. global containment strategy placed primary emphasis on deterring or defeating Sino-Soviet bloc aggression

USN 1178473

Nuclear-powered guided missile cruiser *California* (CGN 36) and aircraft carrier *Nimitz* (CVN 68) return to the United States after a long deployment to the Indian Ocean in early 1980.

in Europe and the Western Pacific. Consequently, the two most important forward commands were the U.S. European Command and the U.S. Pacific Command, both multiservice or "joint" organizations. The European Command covered the Middle East, North Africa, and the Arabian Peninsula while the Pacific Command covered Pakistan and points east.

In reality, the Persian Gulf region lay on the divide in the U.S. global security structure. Washington's Europe-Far East focus, reliance on British forces to defend Western interests in the region, limited U.S. military resources, and post-Vietnam reticence about overseas military commitments resulted in only token presence of U.S. military forces in the Persian Gulf region throughout the Cold War. The Navy's three- to five-ship Middle East Force, consisting variously of seaplane tenders, destroyers, frigates, and amphibious transport ships, was hardly a major contingent. Pacific Fleet carrier task forces periodically steamed into the Indian Ocean, but remained in these waters only for brief periods. The

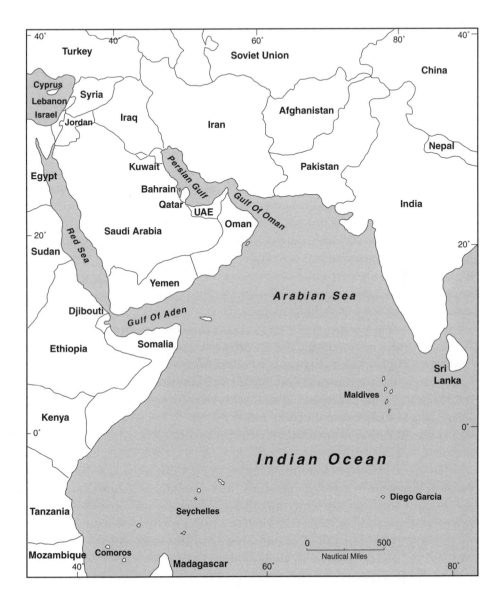

Indian Ocean

U.S. maintained an even more limited presence ashore. A small Administrative Support Unit (ASU) operated from Bahrain to provision the Middle East Force. After 1968 the Navy developed a modest base at Diego Garcia, a small, British-owned island in the Indian Ocean some 2,300 miles southeast of the Persian Gulf.

With the increased importance of the Persian Gulf to the United States during the 1970s, Washington began to develop a more energetic military approach in the region. Some senior U.S. officials speculated openly about the possibility of executing amphibious and airborne operations to secure critical oil-producing areas in the event of another embargo. Others maintained that the strategic importance of regions outside the Europe-Far East orbit demanded attention. In response to these concerns, President Carter created the Rapid Deployment Force. His Presidential Directive 18, signed on 24 August 1977, called for the establishment of a "deployment force of light divisions with strategic mobility for global contingencies, particularly in the Persian Gulf region and Korea."[26] On 1 March 1980, the Defense Department changed the name of the Rapid Deployment Force to the Rapid Deployment Joint Task Force (RDJTF). By definition, a joint task force was a temporary organization created for a specific purpose.

In July 1981 Admiral Robert L.J. Long, Commander in Chief, U.S. Pacific Command, assigned Rear Admiral (Select) Stanley R. Arthur, Assistant Chief of Staff, Plans and Policy, on the staff of Commander in Chief, U.S. Pacific Fleet (CINCPACFLT), additional duty as the naval component commander of the Rapid Deployment Joint Task Force. Long chose Arthur for the new billet primarily because of Arthur's involvement the year before with planning for the Iranian hostage rescue attempt.

Many of the Navy's senior leaders viewed the joint task force as an encroachment into the domain of the Commander in Chief, Pacific, traditionally a four-star admiral, and thus treated the new mission as a low priority. When Arthur, selected for flag rank but still a captain, reported to headquarters, located in a complex of trailers on the south side of MacDill Air Force Base near Tampa, Florida, he discovered that a three-star general led each of the other component commands. Moreover, Arthur had been assigned a lone lieutenant commander for his staff.

Soon convinced of the need for a joint, mobile task force for Middle East contingencies and the prospect that it would be expanded to a major unified command, Arthur repeatedly suggested to his Pacific Command superiors that they pay greater attention and devote more resources to his efforts. Their response was less than enthusiastic, some chiding him with the query, "what are they feeding you on these trips?"[27]

Indeed, the Defense Department concluded that the threat to the Persian Gulf region from the Iranian revolution and the Soviet occupation of Afghanistan demanded a reorganization of the U.S. global security structure. Hence, on 1 January 1983, the Defense Department established the U.S. Central Command (CENTCOM). Arthur, by then a rear admiral, became the first Commander U.S. Naval Forces, Central Command.[28]

The creation of Central Command, according to the organization's official history, reflected "the fact that the U.S. military community no longer looked upon this 'central' area of the world merely as an extension of either the Pacific basin or Europe."[29] CENTCOM's area of responsibility comprised 19 countries, including all those bordering on the Red Sea and the Persian Gulf. Its mission was to ensure Western access to oil, protect friendly nations from threats, and preserve regional stability. CENTCOM planners identified three principal threats: Soviet aggression, intraregional conflict, and internal unrest.[30]

The new command faced enormous difficulties. Critics of its predecessor had argued that the Rapid Deployment Force so depended on nonexistent air and sea transport capabilities that it was neither rapid, nor deployable, nor a force.[31] In its early days, Central Command was open to the same criticism. CENTCOM headquarters remained at MacDill Air Force Base, thousands of miles from the area of responsibility.[32] None of the countries in the Persian Gulf region allowed the United States to base ground forces or land-based air forces permanently on their soil. As a result, Central Command would have to draw on naval, air, and ground forces based in Europe, the Pacific, or the United States when a crisis arose. The logistical problems inherent in moving forces thousands of miles and then keeping them supplied would be formidable. U.S. military leaders knew they would have to deploy sizable, combat-ready forces to the Persian Gulf region in time to cope with an emergency. But how?

The solution they chose was "maritime prepositioning," a concept tested at the outset of the Vietnam War at the urging of Secretary of Defense Robert S. McNamara and refined thereafter.[33] In this approach, equipment, supplies, and vehicles were maintained on board Navy Military Sealift Command (MSC) ships that served as floating depots in forward areas. In an emergency, these ships would steam as close as possible to the crisis spot and unload their cargo, even at ports with only rudimentary facilities. Meanwhile, long-range transport aircraft of the Air Force's Military Airlift Command (MAC) would fly troops to an airfield near the ports where the men would "marry up" with their gear. Planners envisioned a virtual bridge of ships and airplanes to deploy strong forces to the theater and keep them supplied.

The Navy invested $7 billion in strategic sealift programs during the 1980s to make maritime prepositioning a reality. Thirteen specialized prepositioning ships were built or converted from existing hulls. These ships were divided into three maritime prepositioning ship (MPS) squadrons based in the Azores in the eastern Atlantic (MPS Squadron 1), Diego Garcia (MPS Squadron 2), and Guam (MPS Squadron 3). Each squadron contained the equipment and thirty days' worth of supplies for a Marine expeditionary brigade (MEB) of 16,500 men. The Army, Air Force, Navy, and Defense Logistic Agency stowed materiel in 11 other prepositioning ships based at Diego Garcia.[34]

The Defense Department invested in maritime prepositioning and sealift during the 1980s to improve America's warfighting ability in several potential theaters, not just in CENTCOM's area of responsibility. A Warsaw Pact attack on Western Europe requiring a massive U.S. transatlantic reinforcement and resupply effort remained the West's greatest concern. Accordingly, the Defense Department converted eight Sea-Land Corporation SL-7 class container ships into fast sealift ships (FSSs) capable of making 30 knots and able to load and unload their cargo quickly, even at unimproved ports. These ships were intended to embark a full U.S. Army mechanized division at East Coast ports, transport the unit to a global hot spot, and return to the United States for follow-on ground forces. Moreover, the Department of Transportation followed Navy Department recommendations and expanded its "Ready Reserve Force" (RRF) fleet from 36 to 96 cargo ships, tankers, and other auxiliaries. Planners expected to activate these vessels within 5, 10, or 20 days of notification, depending on the readiness status of each vessel.[35]

To test transportation and logistics capabilities for a variety of global contingencies, including a NATO-Warsaw Pact war, a Soviet attack on Iran, a regional conflict in Southwest Asia, and a simultaneous Soviet attack on Western Europe and the Middle East, the Defense Department conducted numerous exercises and studies during the late 1970s and early 1980s. To repair organizational flaws revealed by these tests and to improve coordination among the Military Sealift Command, Military Airlift Command, and the Army's Military Traffic Management Command, in 1987 the Defense Department created the joint U.S. Transportation Command, headquartered at Scott Air Force Base, Illinois. These measures went far to ensure swift deployment of combat-ready forces to Southwest Asia.[36]

Equally important to America's capability to defend its interests in the region was how Central Command would employ its multiservice forces once they arrived in the theater and in that regard, there was scant room for optimism. Theater command-control of multiservice forces had been a problem during the Iran rescue operation, the "peace-keeping" mission in Lebanon from 1982 to 1984, and the Grenada intervention of 1983. Confused command relationships, incompatible communications, inadequate intelligence sharing, and different service approaches to tactical problems persuaded military critics and, more important, key members of Congress that the military command organization needed restructuring. "The system is broke," declared Senator Barry Goldwater (R–Arizona), "and it must be fixed." Goldwater and Congressman William Nichols (D–Alabama) crafted a bill which, among other things, gave greater power to the unified commanders, or "warfighters." A major purpose of the legislation was to improve the planning, command-control, and execution of U.S. military operations. Supporters felt that these objectives could be achieved through greater "jointness," a term referring to interservice cooperation.[37]

Many Navy leaders disapproved of the Goldwater-Nichols legislation. Some naval officers and civilian policymakers raised the old argument that naval forces operated much more effectively when local commanders could seize the initiative and operate independently. The Navy had long emphasized decentralization and unit autonomy. This tradition dated from the age of sail, when during an emergency in some distant part of the globe a ship commander did not wait months to communicate with Washington, but took the initiative to protect U.S. interests. Secretary of the Navy John Lehman argued that the increased centralization embodied in the Goldwater-Nichols bill would lead to increased bureaucracy, separation of authority and responsibility, and diminished civilian control.[38]

Other Navy leaders objected to the Goldwater-Nichols proposal out of concern that an Army or Air Force commander in chief of a unified command would lack the doctrinal background to employ naval forces properly. They argued that naval warfare was fundamentally different in philosophy and practice from conflict on land or in the air. Ships depended less on bases, had different vulnerabilities, and relied more on mobility for defense than land or air forces.[39] Others suggested that the fleet, with its carrier and land-based air forces, marines, submarines, and surface ships, already followed a "joint" approach to warfare.[40] They contended that legislated jointness and centralized command of naval forces would be counterproductive. Still others resented Central Command for cutting into what had been the responsibilities of the Pacific Command, traditionally headed by a naval officer, and for potentially siphoning forces away from the Atlantic, Pacific, and Mediterranean.

Despite these objections, President Reagan signed the Goldwater-Nichols Department of Defense Reorganization Act of 1986 into law on

1 October of that year. Not only did the act enhance the ability of Commander in Chief, Central Command (CINCCENT) and other unified commanders to exercise operational control of the ground, air, and naval forces assigned to them, but also strengthened the authority of the Chairman of the Joint Chiefs of Staff (JCS).[41] The Chairman became the principal uniformed advisor to the Secretary of Defense and the President. Orders to the unified CINCs were channeled through the Chairman. He also oversaw a newly established Vice Chairman and a Joint Staff of more than one thousand officers. Furthermore, for officers hoping for promotion to flag rank, a stint at a joint service school, followed by a joint duty assignment became essential.[42]

Legacy of the Vietnam War

The events of the 1970s and early 1980s inspired greater focus on both the Navy's role in joint warfare and its ability to accomplish its basic missions. The Vietnam War and its aftermath profoundly influenced the naval service. Low morale affected all ranks for years afterward. Mid-level and junior officers and senior enlisted personnel had often endured two and even three grueling wartime tours. Many of the Navy's top officers believed that the civilian leadership had frittered away battlefield advantages and wasted lives and material resources in an ill-conceived and badly managed war effort.

Like American society in general, racial conflict troubled the naval service. Sometimes violent conflict between black and white sailors seriously hindered the operational performance of the Pacific Fleet's aircraft carriers *Kitty Hawk* (CVA 63) and *Constellation* (CVA 64) and oiler *Hassayampa* (AO 145) in 1972. The Navy's concerted efforts to deal with the social turmoil in its ranks helped alleviate some of the problems but caused others, including a breakdown in discipline and the traditional relationship between officers and enlisted personnel. Because of the various problems, some of the Navy's most experienced sailors left the service, prompting Admiral James L. Holloway III, Chief of Naval Operations, to complain that after 1975, "I didn't have the talent. I didn't have the petty officers needed to supervise, and I didn't have people who were technically trained [or experienced] to do the job."[43]

Sailors were subjected to longer and more frequent family separations during the 1970s as each administration continued to maintain overseas commitments with fewer ships and personnel. In addition, there were no raises in basic pay between 1973 and 1980, during which time inflation rose to nearly 20 percent. These developments virtually pauperized the enlisted career force. Consequently, enlisted retention

Secretary of the Navy John F. Lehman Jr. on the bridge of *Kitty Hawk* (CV 63) in April 1981. His advocacy of a "600-ship Navy" had much to do with the fleet buildup of the 1980s.

rates dropped in 1979 to the lowest ever recorded. Lehman, half in jest, observed that "the navy nearly had to resort to press-gangs."[44] Clearly, the Navy's personnel picture was not bright during the tumultuous 1970s.

The Vietnam War and its aftermath also had a severe impact on the size and combat readiness of the U.S. fleet. To provide the armed services with the bombs, missiles, aircraft, ammunition, construction material, and supplies they needed to fight the protracted war in faraway Southeast Asia, the Johnson and Nixon administrations put off or "stretched out" programs for the development and construction of new ships, aircraft, and weapons.[45] This development was especially troublesome, because by 1969 the more than 700 ships built in World War II or just afterward, which made up 58 percent of the fleet, were due for replacement. This "bloc obsolescence" would engage the attention of naval leaders throughout the 1970s.[46]

The fact that the government had expended great sums of money on an unsuccessful war effort without taking care of serious domestic needs upset many Americans. Accordingly, in the decade after 1968, defense budgets were drastically reduced to pay for ambitious social welfare programs begun by President Lyndon Johnson and often expanded by Richard Nixon. The gap between defense and nondefense outlays widened considerably.[47] In the 1968–1975 period, Congress routinely cut individual service budget proposals, especially the Navy's, by 15–20 percent. Between 1973 and 1980, the Navy budget declined 22 percent in real terms.[48]

The U.S. withdrawal from the struggle in Vietnam did not reverse the downward trend in warship construction. The fiscal year (FY) 1969 budget for ship construction was the smallest since 1956, but the following year, when the Defense Department suffered the largest reduction of its funding request since the end of the Korean War, the Navy had only $2.49 billion available for new ship construction.[49] The commissioning of *Nimitz* (CVN 68), the first ship in a new class of nuclear-powered aircraft carriers, was delayed for four years. A delay of four years also hit the next ship in the class, *Dwight D. Eisenhower*.[50] The Ford and Carter administrations continued to cancel or delay replacement vessels and closed two shipbuilding yards. In 1978 Carter reduced the Navy's five-year construction program from 159 ships to 70 and rejected Navy plans to build another *Nimitz*-class carrier.[51]

The Vietnam War was not the only reason for the shrinking of the surface fleet in the 1970s. The cost of deploying and maintaining the ballistic missile and attack submarine fleet also cut into Navy budgets. Because the ballistic missile firing submarines constituted a vital component of the nation's strategic nuclear deterrent force, the Navy routinely devoted a large portion of its shipbuilding budget for new or modernized undersea vessels. In addition, Rear Admiral Hyman G. Rickover, long-time "czar of the nuclear navy," used his considerable bureaucratic skills and strong congressional backing to push for nuclear reactors rather than less expensive propulsion systems both for new submarines and surface warships.[52]

The high cost for new, technologically sophisticated ships, weapons, and sensors also contributed to the shrinkage. Before Vietnam, the Navy could construct destroyers for $30 million each, but a new, *Spruance*-class ship of the 1970s cost $120 million.[53]

With few new surface ships being built and hundreds being decommissioned because of their advanced age, the U.S. fleet was halved from 976 ships in 1968 to 477 in early 1976. This included a 43-percent reduction in aircraft carriers, 59-percent reduction in amphibious assault ships, and a 72-percent reduction in cargo ships, tankers, and other auxiliaries.[54] Indeed, one historian suggests that from 1973 to 1980, the "U.S. Navy [suffered] its largest loss of ships in this short period of history," and none resulted from "enemy fire."[55]

The lack of adequate funding support for the maintenance and upkeep of naval vessels and their weapons systems, repair parts, and supplies after the Vietnam War hurt the readiness of the entire operating Navy. Admiral Holloway observed that on one occasion during the 1970s, when a group of five amphibious ships headed across the Atlantic bound for the Mediterranean, only one or two survived propulsion breakdowns to reach Gibraltar.[56] In 1974 Rickover publicly expressed his view that Navy ships were in the worst material condition in 50 years.[57] Furthermore, to conserve costly fuel stocks, the operational fleets cut back on steaming time and training time for their combatants.[58]

In the wake of the Vietnam War, many Americans were loath to consider U.S. involvement in other foreign ventures. The Nixon, Ford, and Carter administrations put greater reliance on America's existing alliance system, especially NATO, to help secure U.S. overseas interests. In addition, Carter hoped to resolve conflicts in the Third World through diplomacy rather than force or the threat of force, which he considered "interventionist" and therefore undesirable. Of course, the use of naval power in support of foreign policy objectives—"gunboat diplomacy"—had long been a vital function of the Navy. For example, the Navy served as the primary military instrument of U.S. foreign policy in more than 200 crises during the Cold War.[59]

This new approach did not augur well for the Navy. Even though Carter was a Naval Academy graduate, a number of naval leaders thought that he considered the Navy to be "of marginal utility." Harold Brown, Carter's Secretary of Defense, according to Lehman, "made no bones about his belief that the navy was of quite secondary utility."[60] Carter and his lieutenants stressed the importance to America's interests of NATO and Europe, almost to the exclusion of the other regions of the globe. Protecting the sealanes to Europe became the Navy's only real mission with any administration support.[61]

Concentration on the war in Southeast Asia, which involved operations with the other services and with allied forces, had clouded the Navy's other responsibilities, especially its blue-water, sea control mission. Parochial efforts during the 1970s by the Navy's air, submarine, and surface communities to acquire their shares of a shrinking resource pie obscured for many officers the Navy's overall purpose; its *raison d'etre*. According to Lehman, "with the navy leadership fully engaged in keeping the ship from sinking, there was no integrating vision."[62]

As the Navy and the other U.S. armed forces struggled to meet their commitments in the 1970s, the Soviet Union devoted enormous resources to its war-making establishment. The Soviets fielded thousands of mobile, intercontinental ballistic missiles armed with multiple independently targeted reentry vehicle (MIRV) warheads and other weapons of mass destruction. Moscow concentrated huge Soviet ground and air forces in Eastern Europe and positioned them to roll over the under-strength armies of the NATO alliance. Moreover, many observers believed that once the Soviet army had digested Afghanistan, it might move on the oil-rich nations of the Persian Gulf.

The growing power of the Soviet Union was not confined to the Eurasian land mass. Stung by their navy's seeming impotence during the Cuban Missile Crisis of 1962, Soviet leaders had overseen the construction from 1966 to 1970 of 209 modern surface warships, submarines, and amphibious ships. The Soviet navy flexed its muscles and moved aggressively into the oceans of the world, challenging both America's control of the sea and its overseas interests and influence. The Soviet navy marked its debut on the world stage with *Okean* 70, a peacetime naval exercise in which more than 200 Soviet warships carried out coordinated operations around the globe.[63]

During the Middle East crisis over Jordan in 1970 and the Yom Kippur War of 1973, the Soviet navy's powerful Fifth *Eskadra* deployed in strength to the Eastern Mediterranean, long the domain of the U.S. Sixth Fleet. The Soviet military presence clearly limited U.S. foreign policy options in these international confrontations. Indeed, Admiral Elmo R. Zumwalt Jr. gave Nixon and Henry Kissinger backhanded praise for pulling off "bluffs" in these crises.[64]

The Soviets repeated their 1970 performance with *Okean* 75, reaffirming the USSR's new global presence. Two hundred twenty ships and new, long-range bombers participated in mock strikes against the continental United States and its sea lines of communication. Thereafter, Russian ships continued to operate in all the world's major bodies of water, including the South Atlantic, the Indian Ocean, the Caribbean, and even the Gulf of Mexico. In classic examples of gunboat diplomacy during the 1970s, Soviet naval units backed up Moscow's involvement in the civil conflicts in Angola, Yemen, and Ethiopia. Another harsh spotlight was thrown on the changing naval balance when the Soviet navy began operating from the American-built base in Vietnam's Cam Ranh Bay.[65]

The ability to employ satellites that could locate ships at sea, computer command and control systems that could coordinate multidimensional naval attacks, low-observable or stealthy aircraft that were harder for radars to detect, "smart" antiship and antiradiation missiles, long-range lock-on-after-launch cruise missiles that came in fast and low from far away, and quicker, quieter nuclear-powered attack submarines made the Soviet navy a formidable opponent.

Just before he retired as CNO in 1974, Admiral Zumwalt observed that "the United States has lost control of the sea lanes to the Soviet Union."[66] He observed years later that "the odds are that we would have

Guided missile frigate *Coontz* (DLG 9) trails a Soviet guided missile cruiser during *Okean* 70, a worldwide Soviet naval exercise.

lost a war with the Soviet Union if we had to fight [during the mid-1970s]; the navy dropped to about a 35% probability of victory."[67]

His successor as CNO, Admiral Holloway, during whose tenure the fleet shrank to 459 ships, was less outspoken. However, he also expressed concern that the Navy's ability to hold the Mediterranean against a Soviet navy attack was "uncertain at best."[68] Just prior to his retirement, Holloway could only conclude that the U.S. Navy retained a "slim margin of superiority...in those scenarios involving our most vital interests."[69]

Rebirth of the Fleet and the Maritime Strategy

To cope with this growing military power of not only the navy but other components of the Soviet armed forces, the U.S. defense establishment concentrated on exploiting the West's technological edge. Supported by an increasingly alarmed electorate, the Reagan administration championed the development of space-based detection and weapons systems in the Strategic Defense Initiative (commonly called Star Wars) program; strengthened the strategic retaliatory forces with advanced B-1B bombers and D-5 warheads for Trident submarine-launched ballistic missiles; deployed Pershing II theater missiles to Western Europe; and beefed up American ground forces with new, sophisticated Abrams main battle tanks and Bradley armored fighting vehicles.

Lacking adequate resources in the post-Vietnam era to handle all of its extensive global responsibilities, the U.S. Navy focused on both

Battleship *Iowa* (BB 61) tests her powerful, long-range naval rifles during the mid-1980s, when the Reagan administration significantly strengthened the fleet. Combining 16-inch guns and new Tomahawk land attack missiles made *Iowa* and the other ships of her class, *Missouri* (BB 63), *New Jersey* (BB 62), and *Wisconsin* (BB 64), especially formidable warships.

proven and promising technologies, an investment that would pay huge dividends in the 1980s and early 1990s. Admirals Holloway, Thomas B. Hayward, and James D. Watkins, successive Chiefs of Naval Operations, for instance, did not accept a "high-low mix" of nuclear-powered *Nimitz*-class aircraft carriers and smaller, less capable ships, as advocated by the Carter administration and Admirals Zumwalt, Stansfield Turner, and others. Large-deck, *Nimitz*-class ships would be the only U.S. carriers to slide off the building ways in the 1980s. These ships displaced more than 90,000 tons fully loaded and embarked as many as 85 attack, fighter, and specialized aircraft.[70]

Countering the threat from Soviet land-based aircraft, especially the Backfire bomber armed with long-range air-to-surface missiles, demanded carrier battle groups equipped with powerful offensive and defensive tools. At least since 1890, when Alfred Thayer Mahan published his seminal work, *The Influence of Sea Power Upon History*, U.S. naval strategists had understood the importance of attacking the enemy before being attacked; of the primacy of offense over defense. According to a 1980s planning document, the battle group was expected to "strike—the earlier the better—at [the enemy's] capability to attack."[71]

To carry out this mission, the Navy armed the fleet with Tomahawk land attack missiles and Harpoon antiship missiles, the former of which could carry both nuclear and conventional warheads. The Tomahawks could be launched from surface ships and submarines and the Harpoon from these platforms and from aircraft. Also introduced to the fleet were advanced variants of the all-weather, day-night A-6 Intruder attack plane, new F/A-18 Hornet strike fighters, and EA-6B Prowlers. The four-seat Prowler carried comprehensive electronic countermeasures equipment to jam the enemy's communications and high-speed anti-radiation missiles (HARMs) to destroy his radars.[72] Ideally, these weapons systems would be employed against Soviet antiship missile batteries, both ashore and afloat, and airfields.

One naval historian has aptly observed that the arming of surface ships with cruise missiles produced a "synergistic relationship with the carrier navy." He added:

> The cruise missile made all ships an offensive threat and thus complicated the enemy's targeting problems. The cruise missile could hit enemy radar installations and command posts, thereby clearing the way for the carrier air strikes. If the tactical situation dictated, Harpoon and Tomahawk could carry a heavier portion of the offensive load, allowing the carrier to reduce its number of strike planes in exchange for more fighters. On the other side of the equation, the carrier helped the surface warships employ their cruise missiles [by verifying whether potential targets were friend or foe].[73]

U.S. leaders also anticipated the use of Navy-Marine amphibious task forces to eliminate Soviet airfields and naval staging bases. This mission prompted the construction of the *Whidbey Island* (LSD 41) and *Wasp* (LHD 1) classes of amphibious ships and landing craft air cushion (LCAC). To provide the marines with gunfire support and to deploy additional platforms for the Tomahawks, during the 1980s the Navy reactivated four *Iowa*-class battleships.[74]

It would not always be possible, however, to preempt an enemy strike against the fleet. Hence, American naval leaders considered it vital that the carrier battle group mount a strong defense. It was critical that the carrier battle group be able to discover and engage attacking aircraft and missiles at great distances. Naval leaders integrated advanced aircraft like the E-2C Hawkeye and shipboard radars and electronic systems into the fleet to handle such missions.[75] Once the fleet detected enemy aircraft, the paramount object was to destroy the "bandits" before they could launch missiles, or as Admiral James Watkins put it, "to shoot the archer before he releases his arrows."[76] Made responsible for this mission were the F-14 Tomcat fighter and the AIM-54C Phoenix air-to-air missile. The F-14 was a two-seat, twin-engine, air superiority fighter armed with 20mm cannon and as many as eight air-to-air missiles. The F-14's radar and weapons systems could detect targets at a range exceeding 200 nautical miles and conduct several engagements simultaneously.[77] The Phoenix missile, which only the Tomcat was equipped to carry, gave the plane a unique, long-range (100-plus nautical miles) air-to-air kill capability, prompting one Soviet pilot to lament, "how does one get near it?"[78]

If enemy aircraft survived the outer air battle and did launch their missiles, U.S. guided missile cruisers, destroyers, and frigates were charged with destroying the enemy's guided weapons.[79] With their SPY-1A phased array and other air search, surface search, and fire control radars, the Aegis guided missile cruisers became the battle group's principal antiair warfare ships when they entered service in the early 1980s.[80] The warships also boasted two sonar systems, a vertical-launch missile system, torpedo launchers, and two 5-inch guns.[81]

Enemy "leakers" that penetrated the battle group's area defenses then faced the point defense systems mounted on each ship, notably the Phalanx close-in weapons system (CIWS)[82] The CIWS, first installed on board ships in 1980, consisted of a multibarrel, 20mm gun capable of firing 3,000 depleted uranium rounds per minute at a target as distant as 1,500 yards from the ship. Its computer-assisted radars enabled the weapon to automatically track high-speed targets.[83]

Equally threatening to the carrier battle group was the Soviet attack submarine fleet, which by the late 1970s and early 1980s deployed some

USN DN-ST 84-01890

A SPY-1A radar and other components of the revolutionary Aegis antiair warfare system highlight the superstructure of *Ticonderoga* (CG 47), the first of a new class of warship.

of the most advanced undersea vessels in the world.[84] To counter this foe, the Navy brought into service the 3,650-ton *Oliver Hazard Perry* (FFG 7)-class guided missile frigate. This ship, as did the *Spruance*-class destroyer, embarked the especially capable SH-60B Seahawk Light Airborne Multipurpose System (LAMPS) helicopters.[85] Built around the Army Sikorsky UH-60A Blackhawk airframe, the LAMPS featured a search radar, underwater sonobuoy equipment, and torpedoes. Also focused on the antisubmarine effort was the two-seat, carrier-based, jet-powered S-3 Viking, which carried advanced detection and data processing equipment, including a high-resolution radar, forward-looking infrared, and a digital computer. The S-3 could also carry various combinations of bombs, naval mines, Harpoon missiles, and torpedoes.[86]

Despite the great range, speed, and lethality of the Navy's defensive weapons systems, in any major battle with Soviet units, a carrier group commander might have to cope with an attack by many bomb and gun-armed aircraft, high-speed missiles launched from air, surface, and sub-surface platforms, and torpedoes—all at once. A commander's ability to quickly and accurately process information provided by multiple subordinates and electronic sensors and then make the right decisions might determine the very survival of his force.

To enable its battle group commanders to manage such a defensive battle and also carry out strikes into the Soviet Union, the Navy developed the composite warfare commander (CWC) concept, adopted it as doctrine in 1981, and refined it in fleet exercises thereafter. In the organizational structure that this doctrine set forth, a CWC led a carrier battle group but assigned responsibility for major functions to subordinates. A strike warfare commander (STWC) managed those forces attacking enemy ships and bases beyond the defensive radius of the battle group. An antiair warfare commander (AAWC) monitored the airspace for hundreds of miles around the battle group and eliminated enemy planes and missiles that threatened it. An antisurface warfare commander (ASUWC) defended the battle group against hostile ships trying to penetrate its protective screen. And an antisubmarine warfare commander (ASWC) defended the group against the threat from below. Like the ships on which they sailed, these officers were responsible for a broad range of missions.[87]

Thus, convinced that its commanders could fight and protect forward-deployed battle forces operating in waters contiguous to the USSR, during the 1980s the Navy advocated scrapping the current strategic emphasis on protecting the sea lines of communication to Europe and the Far East—a defensive approach—in favor of an offensive "Maritime Strategy.[88]" Like Sir Basil Liddell Hart, the renowned British strategist of the pre-World War II years, U.S. naval leaders advocated an "indirect approach" strategy; exploiting the inherent flexibility and mobility of naval forces by hitting the enemy when and where he was most vulnerable.[89]

If the Soviet Union and its Warsaw Pact allies decided on war, U.S. naval strategists expected the enemy to launch a massive, combined-arms assault against Central Europe, hoping to achieve a quick, decisive, and one-front victory against the United States and its allies. Beginning in the mid-1970s, Admiral Thomas B. Hayward, in command of the Seventh Fleet and then the Pacific Fleet, and Admiral Robert Long, Commander in Chief, Pacific, pushed for a strategic approach that would undercut Soviet objectives by denying them a one-front war. These leaders, as did the officers who developed the Naval War College's Sea Plan 2000, persuaded Admiral Holloway, the CNO, that as soon as the Soviets opened an offensive in Europe, the U.S. Pacific Fleet should attack enemy forces afloat and ashore at Vladivostok and on the Kurile Islands and Sakhalin.[90]

The Maritime Strategy that followed from these initial efforts anticipated allied naval forces hitting the Soviets not only in their rear in the Far East but on their flanks in Europe. The most likely European scenario had the U.S. fleet denying the Soviets access to the North Atlantic, crossing the Greenland–Iceland–United Kingdom (GIUK) gap, and fighting its way into the Norwegian Sea. The carriers and their escorts would steam along the coast of Norway, fighting in and around the fjords to fend off waves of missile-firing Backfire bombers and ships, until they reached a position from which they could launch strikes against Soviet military forces on the Kola Peninsula. Marine air-ground task forces, operating with supporting battleship surface action groups, would also carry the fight to the enemy by landing in Norway and northern Russia. At the same time other allied naval forces would launch carrier and amphibious attacks against Soviet positions on the eastern Baltic or Black Sea coastlines.[91]

Throughout the 1980s, U.S. naval forces carried out numerous exercises with their allies in the Atlantic, Mediterranean, and Pacific to test and refine the Maritime Strategy, the composite warfare commander concept, and the new ships, aircraft, weapons, and equipment entering the fleet.[92]

While the Maritime Strategy was not formally adopted as a component of U.S. national strategy, its persuasive enunciation during the 1980s by Lehman, an especially energetic and media-wise Secretary of the Navy, and Admiral Watkins, a focused and intellectually gifted CNO, helped sell the American people on a "600-ship Navy." Moreover, their combined effort was "easily associated with, and indeed part of, the shift in national policy back toward putting pressure on the Soviet Union."[93]

With the support of President Reagan and the Congress, the Navy increased the production and deployment to the fleet of those ships, aircraft, weapons, and equipment that had been designed and developed in the lean budgetary years after the Vietnam War. Even though the Navy was short of the 600-ship target by two dozen vessels in 1990, cruising the oceans of the world was a powerful force of 15 carrier battle groups, 4 battleship surface action groups, 100 attack submarines, and scores more cruisers, destroyers, frigates, amphibious ships, and auxiliaries.[94] Vice Admiral John B. LaPlante, who led naval amphibious forces during the Persian Gulf War, later remarked that the Navy could not have accomplished in 1980 what it did in 1990 and 1991: "not on a bet; we got what we paid for in the Reagan years."[95]

A less tangible, but perhaps more important result of the Reagan buildup was the impact on the morale of service men and women. General Colin Powell, Chairman of the Joint Chiefs of Staff during the Persian Gulf War, spoke for many members of the armed forces when he later observed that, "the resurgence of the United States as a respected and credible military power, after the debacle of Vietnam and the fiasco of Desert One," ended the "long estrangement between the American people and their defenders." As a result of the Reagan buildup, "everyone in the military started standing taller."[96]

The Tanker War

A new crisis in the Persian Gulf region soon tested the revitalized fleet. Hard on the heels of the Iranian revolution and the Soviet invasion of Afghanistan came war between Iraq and Iran. In September 1980, Iraqi dictator Saddam Hussein launched his armed forces on a massive offensive into western Iran. He used Iranian-sponsored subversion of his regime as an excuse to grab territory. The Iraqi attack made great gains at first, but gradually bogged down in the face of fanatical resistance by Iran's Revolutionary Guards. The war soon degenerated into a stalemate featuring virtually stationary trench lines, human wave assaults, chemical attacks, and massive artillery bombardments reminiscent of World War I. Over one million Iraqis and Iranians died in the bloody conflict that dragged on for eight years.[97]

Since waging the war cost Iran and Iraq a total of more than $1 billion a month, each side hoped to break the deadlock by targeting the other's economic base.[98] Because oil was the lifeblood for both combatants, the contending armed forces struck at production and export facilities ashore, offshore platforms, and tankers underway in the Persian Gulf.

Reflagged Kuwaiti tankers, under escort by U.S. naval vessels in Operation Earnest Will, steam into the Persian Gulf.

USN DN-SC 88-03315

In the so-called "Tanker War,"[99] the United States and its allies became directly involved in the Iran-Iraq War. By 1987, surface-to-surface attacks by Iranian armed speedboats, land-based Silkworm missiles, and mines on neutral tankers plying the gulf alarmed Western leaders. These attacks threatened the safe passage through the Persian Gulf of oil, upon which the health of the world's economy hinged. Western leaders were also concerned that this offensive might lead to an Iranian victory, which raised the dreaded specter of revolutionaries flooding into the oil-rich Arabian Peninsula.

For these reasons, American leaders hoped to prevent an Iranian victory over Iraq. Washington recognized that Kuwait was devoting a significant proportion of its oil revenues to support Iraq's war effort. That support would dry up if Iran's increasingly damaging seaborne attacks on Kuwaiti-flag tankers shut down the gulf oil traffic. Kuwaiti officials came up with a solution. On 13 January 1987, they asked the U.S. government if their tankers could fly the American flag in the gulf and thus receive the same protection of the U.S. Navy as merchantmen under American registry. The Navy had been escorting U.S.-flagged ships in the gulf since the beginning of the war. Spurred to action by the prospect that the Soviet Union might agree to re-flagging and escort operations first, President Reagan authorized 11 Kuwaiti tankers to sail under U.S. registry.

Besides supporting Kuwait, the U.S. government considered it vital to protect the tankers that carried oil from the other gulf Arab states. The governments of Great Britain, France, Italy, Belgium, and Netherlands also grasped the importance of preventing Iranian depredations on oceangoing commerce, so they too dispatched ships to the gulf. Kuwait, Saudi Arabia, Bahrain, and the United Arab Emirates (UAE) contributed fuel to the effort and granted access to their port facilities and air bases.

Because American naval leaders remained uncertain about how Iran would respond, the U.S. Navy deployed a substantial task force, the largest naval contingent involved in escorting Kuwaiti tankers. By the end of 1987 the Navy had posted 13 warships inside the gulf, including ocean minesweepers, to carry out the operation, codenamed Earnest Will. A U.S. carrier battle group steaming in the Gulf of Oman increased the Navy's strength in the theater to between 25 and 30 warships.[100] "The carrier was there primarily in case the Iranians did something so formidable we had to retaliate against targets inside Iran," recalled the JCS Chairman, Admiral William J. Crowe Jr. The Navy, however, deployed the battleship *Missouri* (BB 63) instead of a carrier "in harm's way" in the Strait of Hormuz. *Missouri*, a widely recognized symbol of America's naval might, was less vulnerable than a carrier to Silkworm missiles and

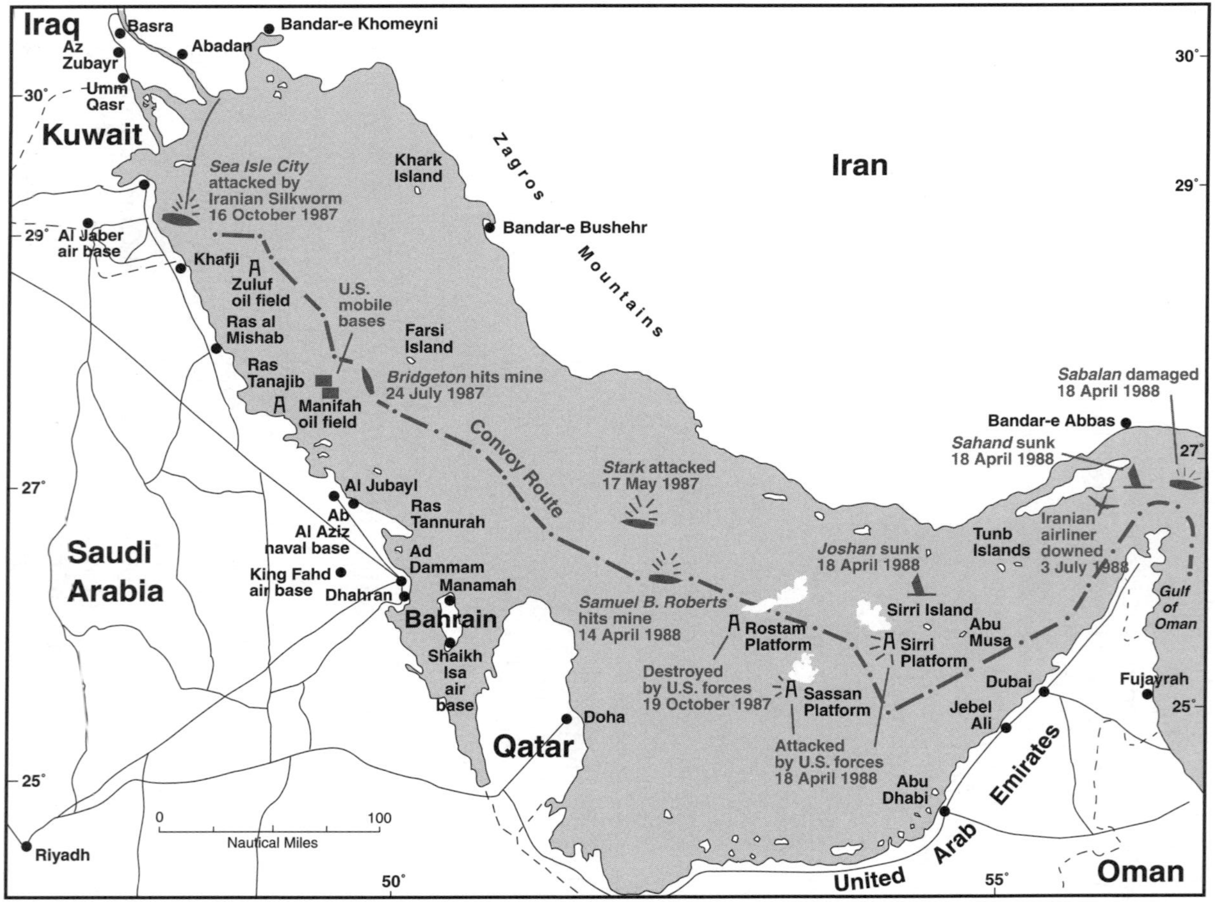

Tanker War Operations

Iran

Iraq
Basra
Az Zubayr
Umm Qasr
Abadan
Bandar-e Khomeyni

Kuwait
Al Jaber air base

Saudi Arabia

Sea Isle City attacked by Iranian Silkworm 16 October 1987

Kharg Island

Bandar-e Bushehr

Zagros Mountains

Khafji
Zuluf oil field
Ras al Mishab
Ras Tanajib
Manifah oil field
U.S. mobile bases
Farsi Island

Bridgeton hits mine 24 July 1987

Convoy Route

Al Jubayl
Ab Aziz
Al Aziz naval base
King Fahd air base
Dhahran
Ad Dammam
Ras Tannurah

Manamah
Bahrain
Shaikh Isa air base

Qatar
Doha

Stark attacked 17 May 1987

Samuel B. Roberts hits mine 14 April 1988

Destroyed by U.S. forces 19 October 1987

Rostam Platform

Sassan Platform
Attacked by U.S. forces 18 April 1988

Joshan sunk 18 April 1988

Sirri Island
Sirri Platform

Tunb Islands
Abu Musa

Abu Dhabi

Dubai
Jebel Ali

United Arab Emirates

Oman

Iranian airliner downed 3 July 1988

Gulf of Oman

Fujayrah

Bandar-e Abbas
Sahand sunk 18 April 1988
Sabalan damaged 18 April 1988

Riyadh

Nautical Miles
0   100

34

mines. With strong forces on either side of the Strait of Hormuz, Crowe "did not believe the Iranians were going to challenge us seriously." Still, he "wanted to make sure that if they did we could hit them with overwhelming power."[101]

The command and control of these forces hampered the effectiveness of the operation. Technically, Commander U.S. Naval Forces, Central Command (COMUSNAVCENT), established on 1 January 1983, should have directed the naval forces in the CENTCOM theater. But in 1987 COMUSNAVCENT was Rear Admiral (Select) Philip F. Duffy, headquartered in Pearl Harbor, Hawaii, far from the scene of the action.[102] In practice, Captain Duffy managed only the logistic and administrative support of naval forces in the gulf.[103] The Navy still regarded the Central Command theater as of much less importance than other operational areas of the globe, so the theater commander's requests for a more senior officer to be assigned to the COMUSNAVCENT billet made no headway in Washington. Hence, during the early stages of Earnest Will, CINCCENT Marine General George B. Crist simply did not have a senior naval officer on his staff with whom he could confer regarding naval issues.

The control of naval operations would pose special challenges. "Years of experience with military turf wars warned me that getting the right command structure was going to be troublesome," recalled Admiral Crowe.[104] The chief difficulty lay in the coordination of operations between the Middle East Force, operating inside the Persian Gulf under the jurisdiction of Central Command, and the carrier group steaming in the Gulf of Oman, which fell within the Pacific Command's area of responsibility. "That meant the operation would be taking place on the seam of [boundary between] two unified commands," noted Crowe, "a recipe for trouble."[105] Furthermore, the prospect that General Crist would direct a seagoing operation disturbed many Navy officers, who believed that only one of their own had the training necessary for such a mission. They wanted an admiral from the Pacific Fleet, long responsible for the Indian Ocean area, to take charge of the naval forces. But Admiral Crowe was persuaded by Crist that CINCCENT needed to have sole control of naval operations in the theater. As a result of their advocacy, on 20 September 1987 the Defense Department established the Joint Task Force Middle East (JTFME). Owing to the predominantly maritime nature of the mission, and "to satisfy the Navy's sensibilities," as Crowe put it, Rear Admiral Dennis M. Brooks, flying his flag with the carrier battle group in the North Arabian Sea, was designated Commander Joint Task Force Middle East. Brooks answered to Crist for operational and logistical direction.[106] Brooks, however, had considerable latitude in the way he ran the operation, since Crist was headquar-

USN DN-SC 87-06412

Stark (FFG 31) lists to port after being hit by two Iraqi Exocet air-to-surface missiles on 17 May 1987.

tered thousands of miles away in Florida. The command structure still did not function smoothly because Commander Middle East Force, Rear Admiral Harold J. Bernsen, retained some autonomy, and he and Brooks clashed repeatedly. To resolve this problem, Crowe finally combined Joint Task Force Middle East and the Middle East Force under Brooks' successor, Rear Admiral Anthony Less.[107]

U.S. naval forces operating in the gulf coped with another, more lethal problem. On 17 May 1987, an Iraqi Mirage F-1 pilot mistook the U.S. frigate *Stark* for an Iranian vessel and struck her with two French-made Exocet air-to-surface missiles. The attack killed 37 American sailors, but their surviving shipmates saved *Stark* from sinking with a dogged and skillful damage control effort.[108]

Then, on 24 July, during the U.S. Navy's first Earnest Will convoy escort mission, an Iranian-laid sea mine damaged the re-flagged tanker *Bridgeton*. The Navy's mine countermeasures forces in the area, which consisted of eight MH-53E helicopters and a small flotilla of ocean minesweepers, found and destroyed numerous mines during these and later operations in the gulf. Nonetheless, the aircraft were too few and the minesweepers too old, having seen almost 40 years of hard service, to accomplish the clearance mission adequately. American naval leaders

USN DN-SC 87-12581

Iran Ajr, with a U.S. landing craft alongside, the day after U.S. Army Sea Bat helicopters based on *Jarrett* (FFG 33) discovered the Iranian naval vessel laying mines in Persian Gulf shipping lanes.

hoped to compensate for this deficiency by employing a traditional mine warfare tactic—preventing the enemy from laying the weapons. In that regard, American forces in the gulf scored a major success on 21 September, when U.S. Army AH-6 Sea Bat helicopters, operating from the deck of frigate *Jarrett* (FFG 33), intercepted the Iranian vessel *Iran Ajr* in the act of dropping mines into the water. In a swift action, which included Navy SEALs and Marine helicopters, the joint team captured and then sank the minelayer. That October, Navy Mark III patrol boats and Seabats sank three speedboats when the Iranians opened fire on the aircraft near Middle Shoals Buoy.[109]

Undeterred, the Iranians struck and damaged the re-flagged tanker *Sea Isle City* with a Chinese-supplied Silkworm missile. In retaliation, the Navy, at Washington's direction, destroyed two Iranian oil platforms being used as military outposts. Then, on 14 April 1988, *Samuel B. Roberts* (FFG 58) struck an Iranian mine that blew a 22-foot hole in her side and wounded 10 sailors.

To drive home the point that the United States would not tolerate such attacks and meant to protect its allies and interests in the gulf, Navy and Marine forces launched another retaliatory strike, codenamed

Operation Praying Mantis, against Iranian forces. On 18 April, surface ships, carrier-based aircraft, and Marine helicopters based on mobile bases Wimbrown and Hercules destroyed two oil platforms in the gulf that the Iranian military was using. In this battle, U.S. naval forces sank or severely damaged half of Iran's operational navy. Even though a few Iranian fast attack craft continued to fire on American warships and merchantmen, Praying Mantis greatly reduced the threat to shipping. Then, on 3 July, guided missile cruiser *Vincennes* (CG 49) mistook an Iranian airliner for an attacking warplane and shot it down, killing its 290 passengers and crew.

This sad episode seemed to be the last straw for the Iranian people, reeling from almost a decade of revolution and war. Tehran's ground forces tottered on the brink of collapse under the weight of an Iraqi offensive. Antiwar demonstrations had broken out in Isfahan and Tabriz. The economy was in ruins, the treasury bankrupt. On 18 July, the Iranians agreed to accept a UN cease-fire proposal. The war with Iraq, and with it the Tanker War, soon came to an end.

The Navy's ships, aircraft, weapons, and personnel generally performed well in conducting littoral operations during Earnest Will. But, problems had arisen in two areas—mine warfare and command and control. Naval leaders recognized that the mine countermeasures force needed modernization badly and took steps to acquire new ships and equipment. They were less inclined to explore new approaches to melding theater and naval operations. If anything, naval leaders ascribed the difficulties that Commander Joint Task Force Middle East experienced with command-control of operations in the gulf to outside interference. While probably voicing an extreme and inaccurate view, former Secretary of the Navy John Lehman blamed Washington and the command structure for the "near-total loss of two new frigates and a civilian airliner." Other naval leaders, however, undoubtedly shared his views about the Navy-CENTCOM relationship. Said Lehman:

> The chief absurdity results as usual from the Washington obsession with "jointness." Although it is a naval operation 11,000 miles from the United States, Congress has created a "Unified" Central Command of 1,000 uniformed bureaucrats (850 army and air force, 150 navy/marine) to run the gulf operations; and for pork barrel reasons, located it in Tampa, Florida![110]

Despite these difficulties Operation Earnest Will had succeeded. The U.S. Navy-led Joint Task Force Middle East, working with America's European and Persian Gulf allies, accomplished the mission of protecting the vital gulf tanker traffic. Earnest Will also had the salutary effect of helping take some of the sting from Iran's revolutionary movement.

USN DN-SC 88-03384

In retaliation for Iran's attacks on tankers transiting the gulf, an American destroyer shells platforms used by Iranian military forces.

USN DN-SN 89-03122

Iranian frigate *Sahand* burns from stem to stern after being hit by three Harpoon anti-ship missiles fired by U.S. naval aircraft and guided missile destroyer *Joseph Strauss* (DDG 16). The disabled warship sank within hours of the attack.

Finally, the United States' stand in the gulf during 1987–1988 erased the negative images resulting from the failed Iranian rescue mission and withdrawal from Lebanon and persuaded the region's leaders that they could count on the United States. This last factor would soon prove beneficial when America's friends in the region faced a new menace to their very existence.

Meanwhile, relative quiet returned to the Persian Gulf. The United States gradually reduced its forces in the region. By the summer of 1990, only five naval vessels patrolled the gulf, the smallest contingent since the late 1970s.[111]

End of the Cold War

As the 1980s drew to a close, many observers of the international scene grew hopeful that they were witnessing the dawn of an era of world peace. The Soviet government withdrew its armed forces from Afghanistan, a process completed in February 1989. Impressed by the scope and sincerity of Soviet Premier Mikail Gorbachev's efforts to infuse the USSR's political, economic, and social structures with "Glasnost," or openness, President George Bush spoke of a "new breeze . . . blowing across the steppes."[112]

This spirit swept across the Soviet sphere in Eastern Europe with such intensity that between July and December 1989 the peoples of Poland, Hungary, Czechoslovakia, East Germany, Bulgaria, and Romania replaced their Communist regimes with governments that proclaimed adherence to democratic politics and market economics. East Germany capped the movement by opting for unification with West Germany. Instead of reversing this process, as it had in Hungary in 1956 and Czechoslovakia in 1968, the Soviet government, beset by a declining economy and internal unrest, began to withdraw its forces from Eastern Europe. The "evil empire," as Ronald Reagan had called it, that so influenced the post-World War II years, collapsed. World leaders anticipated a new era of U.S.-Soviet amity. President Bush spoke of moving beyond the strategy of containment "to welcome the Soviet Union back into the world order." The Cold War was over.[113]

The end of the Cold War had important strategic implications for the Persian Gulf. During the 1980s Central Command leaders ranked Soviet aggression as the number one threat to U.S. interests in the region. Their war plans focused on meeting a Soviet drive into Iran in the context of a global war. In light of the extraordinary events in Eastern Europe, in the fall of 1989 General Powell, the new Chairman of the

Joint Chiefs of Staff, directed his strategic planners to shift their focus from global to regional conflict.[114]

Powell, the cool "never let'em see you sweat"[115] and intellectually gifted son of Jamaican immigrants, was shaped by three prime factors: his long association with and love for the U.S. Army, his service in the Vietnam War, and direct involvement in the national security workings of the Reagan and Bush administrations. Because of the nature of the mission in Vietnam, of all the services the Army suffered the greatest number of casualties. Powell lost many close friends and longtime colleagues in the conflict. He later observed that "in Vietnam, we had entered into a halfhearted half-war, with much of the nation opposed or indifferent, while a small fraction carried the burden."[116] He concluded from this experience that American leaders should put the lives of the "nation's sons and daughters" in danger for only the most worthwhile reasons;[117] that "war should be the politics of last resort. And when we go to war, we should have a purpose that our people understand and support; we should mobilize the country's resources to fulfill that mission and then go in to win."[118] Secretary of Defense Caspar Weinberger, whom Powell served as a military advisor in the mid-1980s, expanded on these views in what came to be known as the "Weinberger Doctrine."[119] This approach to the use of American military forces was evident when Powell oversaw the removal from power of Panamanian dictator Manuel Noriega. Indeed, it became "the bedrock of my military counsel" for future threats.[120]

Sharing many of these views was General H. Norman Schwarzkopf Jr., USA, the new Commander in Chief, U.S. Central Command. Schwarzkopf's background had prepared him well for this assignment, giving him broad experience with combat and peacetime leadership, planning, joint operations, and foreign cultures. As an adolescent he spent a year in Tehran where his father headed the American advisory mission to the Imperial Iranian Gendarmerie. Over the years the general worked to enhance his knowledge of the governments and peoples of the Middle East.

He served two tours in Vietnam, first as an advisor to the South Vietnamese Airborne Brigade and then as commander of the 1st Battalion, 6th Infantry Regiment, 23d Infantry Division. Schwarzkopf was twice wounded. His leadership abilities and bravery in combat earned him two Silver Stars, three Bronze Stars, and the admiration of most of the men he served with. During a two-year tour at Pacific Command headquarters in Honolulu as an assistant staff officer for plans and policy, he learned about the planning and execution of naval operations. During the early 1980s he commanded the 24th Infantry Division (Mechanized), the Army's first armor-equipped division earmarked to fight in the Middle

East. He also served as deputy commander of the joint operation, Urgent Fury, to rescue American students on Grenada and restore the island to its people. Although Schwarzkopf preferred to be called "the Bear," perhaps because this moniker implied a warm and lovable disposition, officers who worked with him often used the nickname "Stormin Norman," a more accurate reflection of his temperament.

Powell felt that, like Dwight D. Eisenhower in World War II, Schwarzkopf's special gift was his "extraordinary ability to weld [a] babel of armies into one fighting force, without offending dozens of heads of state."[121]

Soon after taking command of CENTCOM on 23 November 1988, Schwarzkopf began to consider Iraq as the likeliest threat to U.S. interests in his theater. Rear Admiral Grant Sharp, Schwarzkopf's chief strategist (J-5 Plans and Policy) and the highest-ranking naval officer on the staff, suggested that Iraq should become the focus of their planning efforts. Schwarzkopf agreed and that same day they obtained JCS approval.[122]

By the end of the 1980s Iraq had replaced Iran as the preeminent power in the Persian Gulf. Baghdad then possessed the world's sixth largest air force with 733 fighters, attack planes, and bombers, and fielded the world's fourth largest army with nearly a million men. Many of these troops had endured years of grueling service in the war with Iran. Iranian forces, enervated after the conflict, could not effectively oppose the Iraqis, nor could the untested and minuscule military establishments of the gulf oil sheikdoms.

In the spring of 1990, the Central Command staff began to update a plan for defending the Arabian Peninsula in accordance with the new regional focus and threat perception. Named Operation Plan (OPLAN) 1002-90, the document had gone through two revisions by mid July. The staff intended to begin work on the Time-Phased Force and Deployment Data (TPFDD, pronounced "tipfid") segment of the plan in October. The TPFDD was a schedule that detailed the concentration of forces at U.S. air and sea ports, their embarkation in sealift vessels and airlift planes, and departure for the operational theater. A final deployment plan was slated for publication in April 1991, with supporting plans due out the following August.

OPLAN 1002-90 posited an attack by country "Red" (Iraq) into Kuwait and Saudi Arabia. Staff planners expected that a regional crisis would provide 19 days advance warning of an Iraqi offensive, during which time CENTCOM would begin deployment of forces, ideally in sufficient numbers to deter the attack. If deterrence failed, they expected to have nine more days to deploy forces before lead enemy elements reached the Saudi Arabian port of al-Jubayl, 130 miles south of the Kuwait border and one of three major ports of entry on the Persian

Gulf. The critical period of the campaign would be the first fortnight, during which the Iraqis were expected to drive south in an effort to overrun the ports and airfields needed to support an enemy's buildup. In the initial phase, U.S. air and naval forces would concentrate on achieving local air superiority and interdicting the enemy's vulnerable lines of communication.

Central Command held a command post exercise, codenamed Internal Look 90, during the last week of July. The exercise examined the feasibility of OPLAN 1002-90 and also the relationship between Central Command and its component commands. The evolution revealed at least one "significant deficiency" in the contingency plan. The Navy officers on hand were Rear Admiral (Select) Robert Sutton, COMUSNAVCENT, who traveled from Hawaii to Florida to take part in the exercise, and Admiral Sharp. They concluded that naval aircraft would not be able to contribute significantly to the defense of Saudi Arabia if the carriers operated in the Gulf of Oman east of the Strait of Hormuz. Sutton, however, was not prepared to recommend that the plan provide for the deployment of a carrier inside the Persian Gulf. He was concerned that there was not enough "maneuvering room" inside the gulf. Shortly after the Iraqi invasion of Kuwait, Sharp consulted Rear Admiral Anthony Less, the commander of Joint Task Force Middle East during the Iran-Iraq War, for his thoughts on the issue. Less, who in turn talked to the captains of carriers that had steamed periodically in the gulf during the 1970s and 1980s, observed that he "would never do it again." Sharp dropped the idea.[123]

Nonetheless, Internal Look 90 validated the plan's tactical concepts, logistics framework, and concept of air defense for Saudi Arabia. The exercise also indicated the need for a revised deployment list and a more mobile, armor-heavy force. Although the staff had not completed OPLAN 1002-90 when Iraqi tanks rumbled into Kuwait on 2 August 1990, the document became the foundation of the Defense Department's deployment order issued on 6 August.[124]

The Iraq-Kuwait Crisis

As 1990 dawned, Iraqi dictator Saddam Hussein seemed to have a bright future. His country had won what one observer termed the first "great war" of the Third World.[125] Although the war with Iran had cost Iraq dearly in human life and in economic terms, the country still possessed many strengths. With the world's second largest oil reserve, a dynamic, well-educated middle class, skilled workers, a fairly productive agricultural sector, and a stable, if repressed, society, Iraq had the potential to rebound vigorously.[126]

Unfortunately for Iraq, recovery depended on the leadership of its dictator. Saddam Hussein was born on 28 April 1937 to a poor peasant family near the village of Takrit on the Tigris River some 100 miles north of Baghdad. From the age of 10 he was raised by his maternal uncle Khayrallah Tulfah, whose pamphlet, entitled *Three Whom God Should Not Have Created: Persians, Jews, and Flies*, helped imbue his nephew with a sense of Iraqi nationalism and a hatred of foreigners.

"Saddam Hussein" by John Charles Roach

From 1959 to 1979 Saddam starred in Iraq's internecine power struggles, involving himself in assassinations, coups, and general mayhem. As head of the security arm of the anti-Western, ultra-Arab nationalist Baath Party, he earned a reputation for ruthlessness. He subsequently became a lieutenant general in the army, although he had never before served in the military. Throughout the 1970s, he systematically purged potential rivals, executed dissidents, and finally took complete control of the instruments of power.[127]

Saddam Hussein's rule in Iraq was a classic personality-cult dictatorship consciously modeled on that of his idol, Joseph Stalin. Saddam's images saturated town and country. To speak against the leader was to court death. Saddam ruled through fear and treated human beings as expendable pawns in pursuit of his own ambition. "Survival in power—with his dignity intact," as one scholar put it, was Saddam's "highest priority."[128]

Consequently, Saddam exercised absolute control over Iraqi society. For every thousand Iraqi citizens, 51 served in the Baath party militia, the army, or the police. Every person of significance was watched by three other people. If that individual did anything unusual, the "minders" were to report the deviation to the authorities. If two reported some transgression while the third failed to do so, the latter was subject to imprisonment or execution. And with relatives and others from his home town of Takrit holding the highest positions in the army and government, Saddam's regime resembled, in the words of one historian, "a family-run concern."[129]

Saddam was not content to rule only in Iraq. The dictator dreamed that his country would become the great power of the Arab world.[130] One expert explained Saddam's agenda thus:

> Since becoming president of Iraq in 1979, Saddam seems to have had a grand but simple design, beginning with gaining control of the Persian Gulf's oil. . . . Were Saddam to have succeeded in establishing a position from which he could dictate the fate of the Gulf's oil, the enthusiasm of Arab populations would likely have been such, at least in the Arab east, that governments would have had difficulty resisting calls for some form of unity under Saddam's leadership. That unity would have provided the base from which to lead a charge against Israel. And that, of course, is the old Arab nationalist dream. Saddam sought to carry it out.[131]

So, instead of rebuilding his country's economy after the war with Iran, Saddam continued to pour resources into his military machine. Although Iraq's population numbered only about 18 million people, he maintained a million men under arms, a force as large as that of sworn enemies Iran and Syria combined. Saddam also accelerated nuclear and biological weapons research programs and produced chemical weapons on a large scale. For example, the Iraqis developed and tested a binary nerve agent warhead for their Scud missiles and prepared anthrax and botulinum toxins for military use. Iraq's armaments industry developed the capability to produce most of the country's small arms and artillery munitions. All of this activity came at a high price. In 1990 Iraq's military machine consumed a budget of $12.9 billion, or $721 per citizen in a country where the average annual income was $1,950.

Iraq's economic situation stood as the greatest obstacle to Saddam's ambitions. His government had incurred a debt estimated as high as $80 billion during the war with Iran. Worse yet, he made no effort to pay off the debt. Foreign bankers came to regard Iraq as the world's greatest credit risk. By early 1990, the country faced bankruptcy.

Saddam resorted to international extortion to cure Iraq's economic woes. Rather than pay the $37 billion he owed his Arab neighbors, he demanded that they forgive the debt. After all, he reasoned, the Iraqis had incurred the debt defending their Arab brethren against the Persian onslaught. Saddam also demanded that the gulf states reduce their oil exports and allow his country a larger production quota.[132]

In February 1990 the leaders of Iraq, Yemen, Jordan, and Egypt held a summit gathering in Amman, Jordan, to mark the first anniversary of the Arab Cooperation Council, a regional common market. During a private meeting Saddam asked Jordan's King Hussein and

Egypt's President Hosni Mubarak to inform the gulf states that his country not only was adamant about a complete moratorium on its payment
of war loans, but urgently needed an additional $30 billion. "Let the gulf
regimes know that if they do not give this money to me," he said, "I
would know how to get it."[133]

In addition to debt, Saddam perceived U.S. power in the region as
a bar to his ambitions. At the opening of the Amman summit, he delivered a speech, alleging a U.S.-Israeli conspiracy against Arab interests,
suggesting that U.S. warships withdraw from the Persian Gulf, and declaring that the United States aimed to gain control over all of the gulf's
oil.[134] The Iraqi dictator also doubted U.S. staying power:

> We saw that the United States as a superpower departed Lebanon immedi-
> ately when some Marines were killed, the very men who are considered to
> be the most prominent symbol of its arrogance. . . . The United States has
> been defeated in some combat arenas for all the forces it possesses, and it
> has displayed signs of fatigue, frustration, and hesitation when committing
> aggression on other people's rights and acting from motives of arrogance
> and hegemony.[135]

He later told an American diplomat that "Yours is a society which
cannot accept 10,000 dead in one battle,"[136] implying that Iraqi society
could and had in fact done so during the war with Iran.

The Bush administration attached no specific significance to
Saddam's Amman speech, considering it a typical anti-American diatribe
that some Middle Eastern leaders used to curry favor with the masses.
Indeed, Washington policymakers believed U.S.-Iraqi relations had improved measurably since 1967, when Baghdad had severed diplomatic
relations because of American support for Israel. During the 1980s, with
Iraq fighting for its life against Iran, and Khomeini's hegemonic ambitions threatening Western access to Persian Gulf oil, the distance between Baghdad and Washington narrowed. The Reagan administration
pursued a balance of power approach toward Iraq, with the idea of
strengthening that country as a barrier against the spread of the Iranian
revolution. Accordingly, Washington restored diplomatic relations, supplied the Iraqi military with satellite intelligence of Iranian dispositions,
and subsidized hundreds of millions of dollars in grain purchases, enabling Iraq to become the world's largest importer of American rice.

The Bush administration, preoccupied with events in Russia and
Germany, followed its predecessor's diplomatic course with Iraq. Arab
experts in the U.S. State Department viewed Iraq as "the Arab country of
the future." As one writer observed, these "Arabists" pushed to maintain
the status quo: "a measure of engagement, a measure of appeasement."[137] The State Department concluded that Iraq had emerged from

the war with Iran prepared to play a more stable and constructive international role, and that normal relations with Baghdad would serve long-term American interests in the Middle East.

Bush's State Department operated on the assumption that U.S. political and economic incentives would curb Saddam's aggressive tendencies. John H. Kelly, Assistant Secretary of State for Near Eastern and South Asian Affairs, suggested that Saddam could be a "force for moderation" in the Middle East. Others, notably King Hussein and President Mubarak, shared this view.[138]

They were dead wrong. The Iraqi dictator proved anything but moderate during the spring and summer of 1990. Early in March, Baghdad hanged an Iranian-born British journalist on the trumped up charge of spying for Israel. Then, British customs officials seized steel tubes bound for Iraq that they suspected would be used to build a so-called Iraqi "supergun" capable of firing projectiles hundreds of miles. During the next few weeks, American, British, Greek, Italian, and Turkish customs officials seized other suspected weapon components, including triggers for detonating nuclear warheads.[139] In a 1 April public speech, Saddam denied that he was developing nuclear weapons but affirmed that Iraq possessed chemical weapons. He warned Israel not to attempt to "strike at some industrial metalworks," as it had against the Osirak nuclear facility in 1981. "By God," Saddam exclaimed, "we will make fire eat up half of Israel if it tried [anything] against Iraq."[140]

Both the White House and the State Department issued statements deploring Saddam's remarks.[141] Testifying before a House subcommittee on 26 April, Assistant Secretary of State Kelly proclaimed Washington's policy:

> If Iraq should seek to play a spoiler's role in the Middle East peace process, threaten the security of Israel and other countries in the area, and continue to violate human rights on a widespread scale, the United States and Iraq would become increasingly at odds. *We would take appropriate action on behalf of American interests.* If, however, Iraq plays an increasingly responsible role and cooperates with international efforts to control proliferation of nonconventional weapons, and improves its abysmal human rights record, the U.S.-Iraq relationship will improve, with benefits for both countries.[142]

The message was a variation on the old carrot-and-stick idea. If Iraq practiced moderation, it would get the carrot. If it misbehaved, it would get whacked with the stick.

Saddam apparently ignored the message. For, on 30 May, during the Arab League summit in Baghdad, the Iraqi dictator not only denounced Israel but, in a closed session with the visiting heads of state, accused Kuwait and the United Arab Emirates of waging "economic warfare" against Iraq by over-producing oil and thereby driving down prices. He then demanded that Kuwait pay billions of dollars to Iraq to compensate for his country's economic sacrifices during the war with Iran and that Kuwait grant Iraq territorial concessions. The Emir of Kuwait, Sheik Jabir Ahmed Sabah, flatly rejected these demands. Kuwait and the UAE finally agreed to abide by their oil quotas during the 10 July meeting of the Organization of Petroleum Exporting Countries (OPEC) in Jiddah, Saudi Arabia, but only after repeated warnings from Iraq and pressure from Saudi Arabia and Iran.[143]

It was too late. The evidence suggests that Saddam had already made the final decision to invade Kuwait. General Schwarzkopf later commented: "We pretty well have confirmed that [the Iraqis] had been planning the invasion of Kuwait for 2 to 4 years. . . . We know they had run computer simulations and war games for the invasion of Kuwait. A lot of information indicates they had similar plans for Saudi Arabia."[144] In mid-July, Iraqi troops rehearsed a heliborne assault on Kuwait City. A Kuwait army colonel who had served as an attache in Basrah claimed to have collected intelligence indicating that Saddam Hussein had made the decision to launch the invasion weeks before the actual assault.[145]

Despite the promise of Kuwait and the UAE to stop over-producing, on 16 July Iraqi Foreign Minister Tariq Aziz sent a letter to the Arab League reiterating the accusation that the two countries were involved in an American-inspired scheme to lower oil prices. The letter also said that Kuwait had illegally extracted oil from the al-Rumaila oilfield, which lay under both sides of the Iraq-Kuwait border. To make amends for these acts and to help the Iraqi economy recover from its defense of Arab homelands against Iran, Aziz demanded that Kuwait raise oil prices; cease the "theft" of oil from the al-Rumaila field and pay Iraq $2.4 billion to compensate for the "stolen" barrels; begin a moratorium on Iraq's wartime loans; and create an Arab "Marshall Plan" to reconstruct Iraq.[146] The next day, 17 July, Saddam made these demands public in a speech broadcast on Iraqi television. "If words fail," he concluded, "we will have no choice but to resort to effective action."[147]

The Emir of Kuwait sent to the Secretary General of the Arab League a memorandum expressing indignation, refuting Saddam's accusations, and refusing to accede to his demands. The emir tried to settle the dispute by offering Saddam a small, long-term loan; a gesture which some Arabs interpreted as an insult.[148]

Iraq then reasserted a historic claim to Kuwait's Warbah and Bubiyan islands. Kuwait rejected that claim. Saddam's objective was not to gain sovereignty over this territory, but to produce one more pretext for invading Kuwait, just as a dispute over the Shatt-al-Arab waterway had served as a pretext for the Iraqi invasion of Iran in 1980.[149]

Saddam's July diplomatic offensive was not mere bluster. On the 17th, while he threatened Kuwait on television, units of the elite Iraqi Republican Guard Forces Command began moving out of their garrisons around Baghdad. Three days later a Western military attache traveling along the six-lane highway from Baghdad to Kuwait City saw hundreds of Iraqi military vehicles heading south. On that same day U.S. intelligence analysts studying satellite photographs estimated that 30,000 Iraqi troops had taken up positions near the border with Kuwait. Iraq made no attempt to conceal the buildup.[150]

Between 21 July and 1 August, eight Republican Guard divisions— two armored, one mechanized, four infantry, and one special forces— took up positions between Basrah and the Kuwait border. This force, which included 140,000 troops and 1,500 tanks and infantry vehicles, was poised to strike into Kuwait on short notice.

Behind these forward units stood the entire Iraqi military establishment, by most measures a formidable fighting force. During the last six months of the war with Iran, the Iraqi army had conducted multi-axis, multi-corps, combined-arms offensives deep into hostile territory. Its staff had proven capable of long-range planning, coordination of air and artillery preparations, precise timing of armor-infantry attacks, and execution of complicated logistics operations. Iraqi combat engineers had proven expert in the construction of sophisticated defensive fortifications.

Iraq's senior military echelon was the General Headquarters, dominated by ground force officers. The headquarters integrated operations of the Republican Guard, the army, navy, air force, air defense forces, and the paramilitary Popular Army.

Iraq possessed more than 5,000 main battle tanks, 5,000 armored infantry vehicles, and 3,000 artillery pieces larger than 100mm. The Republican Guard, Iraq's most loyal and capable military arm, comprised almost 20 percent of the ground forces. Its highly trained divisions fought with Iraq's best equipment, including Soviet-produced T-72 main battle tanks, Soviet BMP armored personnel carriers, French GCT self-propelled howitzers, and Austrian GHN-45 towed howitzers. The regular army consisted of more than 50 divisions and additional special forces units. Most of these troops were infantry, but the army included several armored and mechanized divisions equipped with 1960s-vintage Soviet and Chinese equipment. The training, equipment readiness, and fighting quality of the army units varied greatly. The Popular Army numbered 250,000 poorly trained and equipped Baath Party militiamen.[151]

Cognizant of Saddam's increasing bellicosity and fully aware that Iraqi army units were on the move, the Bush administration reaffirmed U.S. interest in Persian Gulf stability. On 23 July, the President placed the Navy's Middle East Force on alert and directed its commander, Rear Admiral William Fogarty, to help execute a combined exercise requested by the UAE shortly after Saddam's 17 July television speech. U.S. Air Force Brigadier General Buster Glosson, Deputy Commander of the Joint Task Force Middle East, coordinated the operation, codenamed Ivory Justice. The exercise involved one U.S. Air Force C-141 cargo transport and two KC-135 tankers, which practiced aerial refueling with UAE jet fighters in an effort to discourage Iraqi attacks against UAE oil installations, both ashore and in the gulf. Frigates *Reid* and *Taylor* supported the exercise, which was the first combined operation between U.S. and UAE forces in history. Although a Kuwaiti tanker refueled *Reid* on 29 July, that emirate's government decided against a formal role in the exercise, fearing that it might provoke rather than discourage an Iraqi attack.[152]

On the 24th, State Department spokesman Margaret Tutwiler told the press that although the United States did "not have any defense treaties with Kuwait, we . . . remain strongly committed to supporting the individual and collective self-defense of our friends in the Gulf with whom we have deep and longstanding ties."[153]

Washington considered backing its rhetoric with a show of force to deter Iraqi aggression. High-level Defense Department civilian officials and Admiral David E. Jeremiah, Vice Chairman of the JCS, discussed speeding up movement of a carrier to the North Arabian Sea and deploying the Diego Garcia-based MPS ships to the gulf. Unlike sending American ground and air units to the region, dispatching naval forces did not require the permission of local governments. Powell thought that the deployment toward the gulf of the *Independence* carrier group and the maritime prepositioning squadron would be only "token moves" and questioned their impact on Saddam. In addition, Powell, who was known for his caution regarding commitments of American forces overseas, and the Secretary of Defense "were reluctant to get out in front of the White House" about "warning Iraq."[154]

Administration officials did not want to raise the U.S. military profile because they remained hopeful that Egyptian President Mubarak and other friendly Arab leaders could mediate the dispute. On the 24th, Saddam assured Mubarak that he intended only to frighten the emir into complying with oil production quotas and raising oil prices, not to invade Kuwait. He agreed to Mubarak's offer to set up a 1 August meeting in Jiddah, Saudi Arabia, so Iraq and Kuwait could iron out their differences.[155]

On the 25th, the Iraqi dictator summoned April Glaspie, the U.S. Ambassador to Iraq, to his office. Saddam spoke at length about his country's economic plight and grievances against the gulf states and the United States. Holding Tutwiler's statement and the announcement of the combined U.S.-UAE exercise in his hand, he accused the United States of pressuring Iraq. He threatened terrorist action against the United States should it continue its hostile policy.

Glaspie assured Saddam of the President's good will toward Iraq. She added, however, that while border disputes were not U.S. business, it was emphatically U.S. business that they be resolved without violence. The ambassador stressed that the United States would defend its interests in the area and would not countenance threats or intimidation.

A telephone call from Mubarak interrupted the discussion. Upon returning, the dictator told Glaspie about the coming Jiddah meeting and stated that Kuwait had nothing to worry about if it negotiated in good faith. Glaspie left Saddam's office convinced that Ivory Justice had caught his attention. She cabled Washington that "he does not want to further antagonize us."[156]

Her cable came as no surprise at the State Department where the prevalent view held that Saddam was "sabre rattling," and that once the Kuwaitis made some concessions he would relent. Moreover, Glaspie's colleagues believed that she had communicated to the Iraqi dictator the message that the United States would not tolerate a challenge to its interests in the gulf.

The leaders of the nations neighboring Iraq shared the view that Saddam would not attack another Arab country. They understood that super-heated rhetoric was the norm in inter-Arab politics, not the use of force. Mubarak, King Hussein of Jordan, and Saudi King Fahd assured President Bush that Iraq would not commit aggression.[157]

Not everyone agreed. On 25 July, U.S. Central Intelligence Agency (CIA) analysts concluded that Iraq planned to invade Kuwait. The evidence suggested that Iraqi forces were not just maneuvering for show but deploying for battle. CIA analysts believed that the Iraqis intended to seize only disputed territory along the border, not all of Kuwait.[158] Admiral Sharp, Schwarzkopf's head of plans and policy, later stressed that "the ability of our intelligence community to correctly assess Saddam Hussein's intentions was totally inadequate; totally inadequate."[159] Rear Admiral Thomas Brooks, Director of Naval Intelligence, put the issue in perspective. He observed that "anybody who will try to predict the intentions of Saddam Hussein is nuts, because I'm not certain Saddam Hussein knows on Monday what he will do on Tuesday."[160]

On 31 July and the next day, Schwarzkopf presented deployment options based on OPLAN 1002-90 to Powell, Secretary of Defense Richard B. Cheney, the National Security Council, and President Bush.

On 1 August, new information led the CIA and Central Command to conclude separately that Iraq would invade Kuwait within 24 hours. Staff officers in Tampa monitored their intelligence reporting equipment in rapt attention as Iraqi tanks and infantry massed on the Kuwaiti border. Republican Guard divisions in the desert south of Basrah were acting like the "Red" forces had in the Internal Look exercise. Watching this unfold "was something like the Twilight Zone," said Central Command intelligence officer Major John Feely, USA. That same day the JCS issued a Threat Condition 1 message, a warning that hostilities were imminent.[161]

As the world held its breath, Iraqi and Kuwaiti representatives met in the Saudi city of Jiddah on the Red Sea. Would it be peace or war once more in the strife-ridden Middle East? The Iraqi representative brusquely repeated Saddam's recent demands. Having already yielded on oil production quotas and price increases, the Kuwaitis refused to concede more. The talks collapsed. Saddam Hussein now had his final pretext for war.[162]

The Invasion of Kuwait

At 0100 local time on the morning of 2 August, three Iraqi Republican Guard armored and mechanized divisions stormed across the Kuwaiti frontier. A half hour later, special operations forces launched amphibious and heliborne assaults against key government facilities in the capital, Kuwait City, and landed to the south on the coastal highway to Saudi Arabia. After daylight, Republican Guard tank units linked up with the special forces contingent in Kuwait City, while other formations moved south of the capital to establish blocking positions on the main avenues of approach from Saudi Arabia.[163]

Largely caught in garrison, Kuwait's 20,300-man military establishment, consisting of 5 army brigades, 23 small naval coastal combatants and patrol craft, 35 fixed-wing aircraft, and 18 armed helicopters, proved no match for the 100,000 Iraqi invaders. Kuwait's armed forces had gone on full alert after Saddam Hussein's 17 July speech but stood down a week later. The Kuwaiti government hoped that the stand-down would mollify the Iraqi dictator.

Hard fighting erupted near Dasman Palace as Iraqi commandos tried to capture Sheik Jaber al-Ahmed al-Sabah. The palace guard sacrificed themselves in a brave stand to protect the emir, whose younger brother died in the fighting. The palace guard's heroism and the warning provided by a balloon-mounted radar set up near the border enabled most of the royal family to escape to exile in Saudi Arabia.

Most other Kuwaiti forces offered only sporadic and short-lived resistance. A few ground units managed a fighting retreat across the border into Saudi Arabia; Kuwaiti air force planes flew a number of sorties against the attackers before Iraqi units overran their two bases and forced them to withdraw to Saudi Arabia; and several Kuwaiti naval vessels fired on Iraqi tanks ashore as they fought their way out to sea and safety. Despite these efforts, during the next two days Iraqi forces captured all of Kuwait and began massing on the Saudi border.[164]

Until Saddam Hussein's records and those of the Iraqi government are open to public scrutiny, one can only speculate on his motivation for seizing Kuwait.[165] Whether paranoia, delusions of grandeur, desperation to redress Iraq's economic woes, or a combination of these and other reasons drove him to act, he clearly believed that it was the moment to strike.

The invasion was Saddam's biggest gamble, and he was betting that the world would let it stand. He seemed to believe that after Vietnam the United States possessed neither the will nor the ability to go to war in Southwest Asia. While a U.S. air campaign might punish Iraq, he doubted that it would be powerful enough to make him abandon his objectives in the gulf. Nor was he afraid that the heterogeneous United Nations organization, the militarily weak Persian Gulf sheikdoms, or the Arab powers would contest his action. What Arab country would sanction infidel Western troops deploying to the sacred soil of Islam? Moreover, he calculated that few Arabs would lament the passing from power of the rich and arrogant Sabah family of Kuwait. Indeed, he counted on the support of the routinely anti-Western governments of Libya, Yemen, and Sudan, and the Arab masses throughout the Muslim world.[166]

Saddam was not all wrong. Jordanians and Palestinians signed up in Amman to fight alongside the Iraqis. The governments of Jordan, Libya, Yemen, and Sudan and the Palestine Liberation Organization voiced moral support for Iraq's bold action.

The rest of the world, however, roundly condemned Saddam's brutal and callous invasion of Kuwait and, more importantly, lined up to reverse his action. The United States found itself at the helm of an international coalition of nearly 50 countries, including the Soviet Union, the Western allies, many Arab states, and many nations of the Third World. All told, Saddam Hussein had badly miscalculated the odds.

Hours after Saddam's troops crossed the border, the UN Security Council passed Resolution 660 denouncing the aggression and demanding the complete and unconditional withdrawal of Iraqi forces from Kuwait. Shocked by the invasion, which violated all the principles of honor, integrity, and neighborliness that lay at the heart of Arab culture, 14 of the 21 members of the Arab League supported a similar resolution a week later. The United States, Great Britain, and France froze Iraqi and Kuwaiti assets in their respective countries. The USSR halted weapons sales to Iraq. On 3 August, the United States and the Soviet Union issued an unprecedented joint condemnation of the invasion. On the 4th, the European Economic Community imposed economic sanctions on Iraq. Even Switzerland abandoned its traditional neutrality and joined the coalition forming against Iraq. On the 5th, Japan banned oil imports from Iraq and Kuwait. On the 6th, the UN Security Council passed Resolution 661, which imposed an economic and military embargo on Iraq.

Decision to Intervene

On the morning of 2 August (Washington time), President Bush held the first of several meetings with top advisors, including CIA Director William Webster, Secretary of Defense Richard Cheney, Under Secretary of Defense for Policy Paul Wolfowitz, and White House Chief of Staff John Sununu, to discuss the implications of the Iraqi invasion and the options available to the United States. They considered the possibility of further Iraqi aggression, particularly against Saudi Arabia. Intelligence analysts warned that the Iraqi forces inside Kuwait were much larger than needed to occupy the tiny sheikdom. Despite Saddam Hussein's announcement of a forthcoming withdrawal, additional forces were pouring into Kuwait and massing on the border with Saudi Arabia. By the 6th, Iraq had elements of 11 divisions inside Kuwait, a force amounting to more than 200,000 troops. This army was certainly capable of overwhelming Saudi Arabia's ill-equipped and trained 40,000-man army. Despite Saddam's assurances to the contrary, the Iraqis seemed on the verge of invading Saudi Arabia. The CIA was predicting as much.[167]

The prospect of Saddam Hussein establishing hegemony over the oil-rich nations on the Arabian Peninsula frightened the Bush administration. The President told the American people: "Our jobs, our way of life, our own freedom, and the freedom of friendly countries around the world would all suffer if control of the world's great oil reserves fell into the hands of that one man, Saddam Hussein."[168]

Bush, Cheney, Powell, Schwarzkopf, and members of the National Security Council once again met at Camp David to discuss U.S. options in the crisis. After Powell and Cheney recommended a military response, Schwarzkopf briefed the President on OPLAN 1002-90. According to Admiral Sharp, who was present at the meeting, Schwarzkopf made a

OSD

At a meeting in the Pentagon, General Colin Powell, Chairman of the Joint Chiefs of Staff, briefs the President on the Persian Gulf crisis. Also at the table are General H. Norman Schwarzkopf, Commander in Chief, Central Command (far left), and Richard Cheney, Secretary of Defense.

persuasive "case for the readiness of the United States military to defend Saudi Arabia."[169]

Bush felt that a naval blockade of Iraq and Kuwait alone would not deter Saddam from driving further south. The Navy's carriers could launch strikes against targets in Iraq or against Iraqi troops in Saudi Arabia, but aircraft flying from staging areas in the Red Sea and North Arabian Sea would be operating at extreme range. Moreover, Iraq's 733 fighters, attack planes, and bombers would seriously outnumber a few 80-plane carrier wings. Air Force bombers based far from the theater would face even greater operational difficulties. Bush concluded that the best way to deter further Iraqi aggression, or to stop an attack should one materialize, was to deploy ground, air, and naval forces to Saudi Arabia—in short, to implement Plan 1002-90.[170]

But first the Bush administration had to persuade King Fahd to request the deployment of American troops to his kingdom, site of the cities of Mecca and Medina and the most sacred soil in Islam. This object could be accomplished through Article 51 of the United Nations charter, which provided that any member nation could invite any other member nation to bring military forces to its aid in time of crisis.

Accordingly, Bush dispatched Cheney and Schwarzkopf to Saudi Arabia to lay out the proposal to King Fahd.

On 5 August, the President revealed the direction of his thinking to the press. "This will not stand," he said, "this aggression against Kuwait." A reporter asked what the United States could do to prevent the installation of a puppet government in Kuwait. Bush replied emphatically, "Just wait, watch and learn."[171]

The American delegation joined King Fahd and a select few from his inner circle in Jiddah on the evening of 6 August. Cheney and Schwarzkopf described the thrust of OPLAN 1002-90 without mentioning the plan by name. Schwarzkopf pointed out that the size of the Iraqi force in Kuwait was much larger than necessary to hold the tiny emirate. He affirmed that within four months of initial deployment, American forces in Saudi Arabia would be able to handle anything the Iraqis could throw at them. Cheney promised that U.S. forces would stay as long as needed and, of equal importance, would leave at Fahd's request. The king reflected on his country's long relationship with the United States and fondly recalled his father's meeting with President Roosevelt on board the U.S. heavy cruiser *Quincy* (CA 71) in Egypt's Great Bitter Lake in 1945. After sharply admonishing one of his advisors who raised a concern, Fahd agreed to welcome American forces into Saudi Arabia, in concert with forces from friendly Arab countries.

Soon after Cheney communicated the king's positive response to Washington, the President ordered immediate execution of OPLAN 1002-90.[172] The initial deployment order was issued at 2150 Eastern Daylight Time, 6 August. The stated U.S. military objectives were to establish a force in the region capable of deterring further Iraqi aggression, to build and integrate forces sent by other nations, to enforce United Nations sanctions against Iraq, and to defend Saudi Arabia from an Iraqi attack.

The President announced his decision to the American people from the Oval Office two days later. Bush enumerated the goals of the U.S. deployment: (1) the immediate, unconditional, and complete withdrawal of all Iraqi forces from Kuwait; (2) the restoration of Kuwait's legitimate government; (3) the maintenance of security and stability in the Persian Gulf; and (4) the protection of the lives of American citizens abroad. In a news conference later that day, he emphasized that the immediate purpose of the deployment was to prevent further Iraqi aggression. As he put it, "a line has been drawn in the sand."[173]

Central Command began to deploy combat forces to the operational theater on 7 August. This marked the beginning—Commencement Day or C-Day in military parlance—of the implementation of

OPLAN 1002-90. The next day, Powell and Schwarzkopf discussed possible titles for this deployment. They were looking for a catchy name to emphasize the defensive nature of the operation. They came up with several alternatives, including "Crescent Shield" and "Peninsula Shield." On 9 August, they informed the unified and specified commanders of the name they had chosen: "Operation Desert Shield."[174]

CHAPTER 2

Building the Shield

S ADDAM HUSSEIN'S RUTHLESS INVASION OF Kuwait galvanized global opinion against him and inspired UN political action to reverse his aggression and defend Saudi Arabia and the gulf states. Now it was up to the United States and its allies to back the UN resolutions with military force.

Holding the Line

"Having decided on the deployment of U.S. forces," Secretary of Defense Cheney noted in a statement to Congress:

> we rejected the idea of a gradual, calibrated buildup. We also rejected the concept of a modest trip wire force, since we did not want to send just enough troops to provoke an Iraqi attack without being able to defend against it. We intended to present a credible deterrent and to convey to Saddam Hussein that we were serious.[1]

Although not initially so conceived, Operation Desert Shield unfolded in two phases. The first—a defensive phase—extended from 7 August to 31 October 1990. The second—preparation for an offensive—lasted from 1 November 1990 to 16 January 1991, the eve of war. Central Command's Operation Plan 1002–90, while not yet complete on 2 August 1990, served as the overall guide for the buildup of coalition forces in the theater and the defense of Saudi Arabia during the first phase. Its objectives included deterring Saddam from attacking Saudi Arabia and defending the desert kingdom if deterrence failed.

Appropriately, Schwarzkopf directed Sharp, who remained in Riyadh after the meeting with King Fahd, to organize the multinational defense of Saudi Arabia based on the plan with which the admiral was thoroughly familiar. He shared this responsibility with General Yousef

59

Madani, the operations chief on the Saudi Joint General Staff. American and Saudi staff planners worked side by side in Riyadh.[2]

OPLAN 1002-90's concept of operations featured deployment of mobile ground forces to the Arabian Peninsula backed by naval power and land-based air power. The plan called for the eventual deployment of a Marine expeditionary force, an Army airborne corps, various special operations forces, three aircraft carrier battle groups, one surface action group formed around a battleship, and nine Air Force wings. First, light airborne, infantry, and special warfare forces would secure critical ports and airfields to enable the buildup ashore of heavier ground units, land-based air forces, materiel, and munitions. Once this lodgement had been secured, armor-heavy forces would expand the perimeter and beef up defenses on the likeliest avenues of approach for an enemy attack. A strong mechanized reserve would also enable U.S. forces to counterattack the invading Iraqi army. Central Command planners continued to refine the plan's basic concepts and operational approaches throughout Desert Shield.[3]

A critical premise of OPLAN 1002-90 was that Central Command would have several weeks to deploy forces to the theater before Iraqi forces went on the offensive. But Iraqi tanks rolled into Kuwait on 2 August

USN DN-SC 92-05664

Guided missile cruiser *Antietam* (CG 54), followed by frigate *Reasoner* (FF 1063), guided missile cruiser *Jouett* (CG 29), and frigate *Brewton* (FF 1086), steam from Diego Garcia for the Persian Gulf soon after the Iraqi invasion of Kuwait.

1990, and the National Command Authorities had not yet deployed any major forces to the region. Moreover, U.S. intelligence had concluded that the Iraqis meant to seize only a small portion of northern Kuwait. But when Saddam's army grabbed the entire country and seemed ready to continue the offensive, General Schwarzkopf concluded that heavy armored and regular infantry units would have to be rushed to the region faster than anticipated in order to deter or fend off an Iraqi attack down the Arabian Peninsula.[4] Accordingly, he revised the deployment approach embodied in 1002-90 and adopted a "shooters first" strategy, deploying primarily combat units during August and September and deferring the movement of certain special warfare and logistic support units until later.

The force ultimately fielded by the United States during Phase I of Desert Shield was both larger and somewhat different in composition than that proposed in the original plan. In addition, combat forces from other coalition nations, particularly Egypt, Syria, France, and the United Kingdom, soon joined U.S. and Saudi forces on the ground, at sea, and in the air.[5]

Fortunately, coalition naval forces were already on hand in the region to deter or, if that failed, combat an Iraqi thrust by sea or air against the Persian Gulf coast. On 7 August, the first day of Operation Desert Shield, U.S. cruiser *England*, destroyer *David R. Ray*, frigates *Vandegrift*, *Reid*, *Taylor*, *Robert G. Bradley*, and *Barbey*, and command ship *LaSalle* of the Joint Task Force Middle East, and British destroyer *York* (D 98) and Royal Fleet Auxiliary oiler *Orangeleaf* (A 110) of the Armilla Patrol, formed a first line of defense in the central gulf. Behind these warships and defending the inshore approaches stood several hundred frigates, missile corvettes, fast attack craft, patrol boats, and other armed coastal vessels of Saudi Arabia, Bahrain, Qatar, the UAE, and Oman.[6]

U.S. carriers were close enough not only to launch aircraft against Iraqi forces attacking in the gulf, but also to defend the airfields ashore that were vital to the buildup of allied ground forces and ground-based air forces. Carrier *Dwight D. Eisenhower* passed through the Suez Canal on 7 August and took up station in the Red Sea. Her air wing and that of *Independence* stood ready to cover the approaches to airfields on the Arabian Peninsula, many of which lay near the Red Sea and Persian Gulf coasts.[7]

Besides protecting the coalition's airlift, naval forces ensured the security of sealift operations, which would prove the key to establishing and maintaining the UN military presence in the theater. The ships of the U.S. Middle East Force, whose steadfastness at sea during the Tanker War helped favorably resolve the Iran-Iraq conflict, continued to inhibit any Iraqi or Iranian hostile action in the Persian Gulf. A carrier[8] and nu-

USN DN-ST 91-02612

British destroyer HMS *York* in the Persian Gulf. British and French combatants had bolstered the naval power of the UN coalition since the earliest days of the gulf crisis.

merous cruisers, destroyers, attack submarines, and other warships of the 30-ship[9] U.S. Sixth Fleet, long deployed in the Mediterranean, guarded that vital segment of the sea lines of communication from the U.S. East Coast and Western Europe. Other naval forces of the North Atlantic Treaty Organization, including those of Germany whose government decided against dispatching units to the Persian Gulf, contributed to the international effort by standing watch over the waters of the Eastern Mediterranean.

The presence of friendly naval forces in these waters and in the Red Sea not only reassured Arab members of the coalition, but also restrained those governments and peoples along the sea route who supported Saddam Hussein and might otherwise have provided him with war materiel and reinforcements. Naval leaders were particularly concerned that Libya's Colonel Muammar al-Qaddafi would order his merchant ships to sow mines in the Gulf of Suez as he had in 1984. Furthermore, the Libyan armed forces included over 500 MiG, Mirage, and other combat aircraft; six Soviet-made Foxtrot submarines; 34 surface combatants armed with Styx and Ottomat antiship missiles; and nine mine warfare vessels. The Sudanese and Yemeni air and naval forces operated over 100 fighters and attack planes and 10 missile and

The unpredictable Libyan dictator Muammar al-Qaddafi. Without the presence of strong coalition naval forces in Middle Eastern waters, the pro-Iraqi leader might have been tempted to use his military forces against the unarmed merchant ships of the Desert Shield sealift effort.

torpedo-firing naval vessels. Fast boats loaded with terrorists and explosives also had the potential to wreak havoc with the sealift ships navigating the several narrow "chokepoints" along the route to the Persian Gulf. With powerful coalition naval and air forces positioned just off their shores, however, these nations wisely refrained from any outwardly hostile acts.

Fortunately for the coalition, President Mubarak granted permission for U.S. warships to transit the Suez Canal. He also gave U.S. merchant ships supporting the coalition priority passage through the canal. Otherwise, the coalition would have had to ship its reinforcements and supplies around the African Continent, adding more than 3,000 miles to the journey.[10]

With the air and sea routes to Saudi Arabia thus secured, on 8 August Air Force transport planes landed advanced elements of the Army's 82d Airborne Division at Dhahran, a Saudi city on the gulf coast approximately 180 miles south of the Kuwait border. The day before, two F-15 fighter squadrons of the 1st Tactical Fighter Wing and five E-3 Airborne Warning and Control System (AWACS) aircraft from the Ninth Air Force had flown into Riyadh, the Saudi capital.[11]

Also on 8 August, Maritime Prepositioning Ship Squadrons 2 and 3 sailed from Diego Garcia and Guam, respectively. The ships of these units carried the equipment and 30 days of supplies for the 7th Marine Expeditionary Brigade based in Twentynine Palms, California, and for the 1st MEB based in Hawaii. The marines of both MEBs were airlifted to the gulf, as was the case for almost all other U.S. troops.

Critics have observed that the MPS squadrons should have left port on 2 August, given the vital importance of putting troops on the ground as quickly as possible and signaling American intent. Some attributed the six-day delay to General Powell, who wanted to "avoid an ill-considered use of force."[12] Another suggested that Washington "simply let the matter slip through the cracks," since "when the White House thought about deploying forces," it did not give much attention to the "floating warehouses in the Indian Ocean."[13] In support of this idea, Admiral Sharp later related that the issue of moving the MPS ships forward never came up at meetings in Riyadh during that first frantic week of August 1990 and added, "I guess it was an oversight, in retrospect."[14] A third reason for the delay was Central Command's lack of authority over the MPS squadrons. The vessels "belonged" to the Atlantic Command and the Pacific Command. The Defense Department orders had not allocated the vessels to Central Command, so General Schwarzkopf had to specifically request deployment of the MPS squadrons.[15] This delay might have been lethal had the Iraqis struck before the first prepositioning ships reached al-Jubayl.[16]

By 14 August more than 12,000 soldiers from all three brigades of the 82d Airborne Division and over 200 Air Force combat aircraft had deployed to Saudi Arabia.[17] Nonetheless, from mid-August to early September, naval forces afloat and ashore comprised the bulk of allied military power facing Saddam Hussein. By 1 September the coalition had assembled a powerful armada in the Persian Gulf, the Indian Ocean/Arabian Sea, and the Red Sea that included U.S. carriers *Independence* and *Saratoga* (CV 60), 319 carrier and shore-based Navy and Marine aircraft,[18] battleship *Wisconsin* (BB 64), 7 cruisers, 7 destroyers, and 11 frigates, some of them armed with Tomahawk land attack missiles. (*Saratoga* replaced *Dwight D. Eisenhower* in the theater on 27 August.) Royal Navy warships included guided missile destroyer *York* and frigates *Jupiter* (F 60) and *Battleaxe* (F 89). Operating primarily in the Red Sea from the protectorate of Djibouti were French carrier *Clemenceau* (R 98),[19] guided missile destroyers *Suffren* (D 602) and *Dupleix* (D 641), and four frigates. Finally, the Kuwaiti missile boats *Istiqlal* (P 5702) and *Al Sanbouk* (P 4505), which had fought their way out of Kuwait harbor on 2 August, steamed with the coalition's naval contingent.[20]

The first three ships of MPS Squadron 2 reached al-Jubayl on 15 August. Tanks, light armored vehicles (LAVs), assault amphibian vehicles (AAVs), and artillery pieces rumbled directly onto the pier from these container roll-on/roll-off, or CON/RO, ships. At the same time, Navy cargo handlers and the men of Amphibious Construction Battalion 1, the first Seabees to arrive in Saudi Arabia, used the ships' cranes to unload hundreds of steel containers loaded with food, supplies, ammunition, and equipment. Marines of the 7th MEB, who had begun to arrive at al-Jubayl's air facilities the previous day, soon "married up" with their ship-delivered equipment. On the 25th, Major General John I. Hopkins, the 7th MEB commander, reported to Schwarzkopf that his

A Marine amphibious assault vehicle is unloaded from maritime prepositioning ship *Baldomero Lopez* (T-AK 3009) in a Saudia Arabian port.

brigade, by then numbering 15,248 marines, 123 tanks, and 124 aircraft, had established a blocking position north of al-Jubayl. Marine shore-based F/A-18 Hornets took over responsibility for a round-the-clock combat air patrol (CAP) of the northern Persian Gulf, which freed the carriers operating in the more distant North Arabian Sea from long-range missions.[21]

Operation Desert Shield confirmed the wisdom of stationing fully loaded and ready to go merchant ships in regions of the world where U.S. military action seemed likely. Prewar exercises had established planning goals of about 250 strategic airlift sorties to deploy a MEB's troops; the 7th MEB actually took 259. Ships of MPS Squadron 2 equipped the 7th MEB marines in the anticipated time of 10 days. These and later deployments owe much of their success to Saudi Arabia's superb, up-to-date port facilities and airfields and the willing support of the Saudi people. But, superior Navy–Marine Corps planning and training was the primary reason. Constant practice had enabled the Marines to avoid the confusion normally expected when troops and their equipment do not deploy together. It also ensured that equipment emerged in good shape from the temperature- and humidity-controlled storage holds of the MPS vessels. The spread-loading concept—loading each vessel with a

USAF DF-ST 92-10021

U.S marines stream onto a Military Airlift Command passenger plane that will carry them to Saudia Arabia, where they will "marry up" with armored vehicles, weapons, and equipment delivered there by the Military Sealift Command.

variety of equipment and supplies rather than placing the entire complement of a given type in one ship—proved another sensible approach. Aside from motor oil and batteries, the Marines did not lack key supply items, and indeed transferred some munitions to less well-provisioned Army airborne units. A difficulty encountered during the initial deployment of 7th MEB was the insufficiency of aerial refueling support for Marine fixed-wing aircraft flying from the United States. There were simply not enough tankers to go around.[22]

Despite this relatively minor problem, the Desert Shield experience validated the maritime prepositioning idea. Many U.S. military leaders shared General Powell's conclusion that it was "a most successful concept."[23]

Window of Vulnerability

The first U.S. forces to arrive in Saudi Arabia found themselves outnumbered and outgunned by the large Iraqi army that poured into Kuwait and southern Iraq. By late August, Iraqi forces in Kuwait numbered an estimated 265,000 troops, most of them from elite Republican Guard outfits.

Central Command also faced a robust, combat-tested Iraqi air force of more than 700 fighters, attack planes, and bombers, many of them Soviet, Chinese, and French models. These aircraft carried a wide range of weapons, including French AM-39 Exocet antiship missiles, the AS-30L laser guided smart missile, and Beluga bomblet dispensers; Soviet AA-6 and AA-7 air-to-air missiles; and French Magic and R-530 air-to-air missiles. Iraqi aircraft operated from 24 modern airfields and 30 dispersal bases located around the country.[24]

Coalition ships in the northern Red Sea and Persian Gulf faced potential attack from aircraft-launched Exocet missiles or shore-launched Silkworm missiles. The Chinese-made Silkworm, a direct copy of the Soviet Styx missile, used an active-radar or infrared seeker, depending on variant, and had a maximum range of 68 miles. It pushed a 1,131-pound warhead at a speed of Mach 0.9. Iraq had approximately 50 Silkworm missiles and seven launchers. The French-built Aerospatiale Exocet, perhaps the best-known Western antiship missile, carried a 364-pound warhead at a speed of Mach 0.93. The Exocet employed an active-radar seeker and had a maximum range of 96 miles. Analysts compared its punch to that of a 13.5-inch shell fired by battleships, and its unexpended solid fuel had been known to start serious fires after impact. Throughout the war with Iran, Iraqi jets had flown deep into the gulf to strike at Iranian ports and oil platforms, and had damaged hundreds of tankers and sunk others. Furthermore, an Iraqi Mirage almost sank *Stark* with two Exocet missiles.[25] U.S. naval commanders were especially concerned that Iraqi jets would fly down the valleys parallel to Iran's coastal mountain range, undetected by Iranian or coalition air search radars, and then pop out over the central gulf to strike the fleet or ports on the southern shore.

On the other hand, U.S. intelligence did not credit Iraqi pilots with great flying and fighting skills. Their training was considered subpar by Western standards. Even the Soviets, who had overseen development of the Iraqi air force, were not impressed. Soviet flight instructors referred to their Iraqi students as "stoneheads."[26]

The allies had relatively less to worry about from Iraq's navy. The most potent threat from its largely obsolescent inventory of about 165 naval craft came from 13 missile boats, including 7 ex-Soviet *Osa* boats armed with Styx antiship missiles and 1 FPB-57 and 5 TNC-45 Exocet missile boats captured from Kuwait. The Styx, the first Soviet sea-based antiship missile to enter service, was a radar- or infrared-homing, fire-and-forget weapon with a speed of Mach 0.9, an effective range of 16 to 45 miles, depending on variant, and a 1,100-pound warhead (Table 1).

Table 1

IRAQ'S NAVY

quan.	type	disp. (tons)	length (ft.)	speed (kts.)	crew	armament
Missile Boats						
1	FPB-57	398	191	36	39	4/Exocet 1/76mm 2/40mm AA
5	TNC-45	259	147	41.5	32	4/Exocet 1/76mm 2/40mm AA
5	*Osa II*	240	127	36	30	4/Styx 4/30mm AA
2	*Osa I*	215	127	36	30	4/Styx 4/30mm AA
Mine Warfare Ships						
2	T-43	570	190	14	77	4/37mm AA 8/mg
3	*Yevg.*	90	86	11	10	2/25mm AA
4	*Nestin*	78	89	15	17	5/20mm AA
Amphibious Ships						
3	*Polno.*	1,150	268	18	42	4/30mm AA 2/122mm rockets
3	*Zahraa*	5,800	348	15.5	35	—

The bulk of Iraq's naval craft ranged in length from 30 to 100 feet and carried 20mm or smaller guns.

Iraq's navy included 5,000 personnel.

SOURCE: Bernard Prezelin, ed., *The Naval Institute Guide to Combat Fleets of the World 1990/91: Their Ships, Aircraft, and Armament*, trans., A.D. Baker III (Annapolis: Naval Institute Press, 1990), 261–64; *The Military Balance 1990–1991* (London: Brassey's, 1990), 106.

Except for a training frigate, which was not assessed as a serious threat, the rest of Iraq's navy consisted of small patrol boats, a few hovercraft, amphibious landing ships, and auxiliary vessels, including Soviet S.O. 1 and *Zhuk* patrol boats; Soviet *Polnocny-C* class tank landing ships; and a *Spasilac*-class salvage ship. Most analysts thought that the best this flotilla could do was to "harass" coalition warships. Iraqi mine warfare vessels, including Soviet T-43-class fleet minesweepers and *Yevgenya*-class inshore minesweepers as well as Yugoslav *Nestin*-class river minesweepers, also posed a threat to allied vessels operating in the gulf.[27]

Saddam's main naval base at Basrah remained cut off from the Persian Gulf by debris and unexploded ordnance left over from the war with Iran. His other principal naval bases at az-Zubayr and Umm Qasr lay along the banks of the az-Zubayr River, Iraq's only open outlet to the Persian Gulf.

The Iraqis could mount harassment operations throughout the northern Persian Gulf. They could station targeting teams on any of the hundreds of oil platforms, large mooring buoys, navigation buoys, and small islands dotting those waters. The oil platforms and islands could also be used as bases for surprise attacks against coalition combatants and merchant vessels. Iraqi missile boats had the potential to dart out from such hiding places, launch their missiles, and inflict severe damage on coalition naval vessels, merchantmen, and port facilities. These fast attack craft could also disrupt coalition coastal operations.[28]

Nevertheless, Central Command assessed the overall operational capability of Iraq's navy as "poor." Its performance in the Iran-Iraq War had been undistinguished. The readiness and training of Iraqi naval personnel were so low that the vessels retreated to their bases during the war's first days and remained in port for the duration.[29] "The [Iraqi] navy," concluded a CENTCOM operations order, "is an aging force of limited capability hampered by an inadequate maintenance program, a lack of trained career officers, and unit inactivity."[30]

Although Central Command leaders believed they had little to fear from most conventional Iraqi forces and weapons, they felt otherwise about Saddam's chemical and biological arsenal. From the top leaders to the troops, the worst nightmare was a chemical or biological attack. Numerous reports suggested that Iraq was developing weapons systems to carry botulinum, cholera, and typhoid bacteria. Even more concrete intelligence indicated that Iraq possessed some 2,000–4,000 tons of blister-causing mustard gas, as well as nerve agents Sarin and Tabun. The Iraqis could deliver these chemicals with aerial bombs, artillery shells, rockets, aircraft-mounted spray tanks, and surface-to-surface ballistic missile warheads. Moreover, Saddam Hussein had already used chemical weapons against enemy troops and civilians during the war with Iran and against his own Kurdish countrymen afterward. From these experiences, the Iraqis adapted training and developed relevant battlefield doctrine.

To prepare for possible Iraqi chemical and biological attacks, U.S. and allied units trained and operated frequently in Mission-Oriented Protective Posture (MOPP) gear. It was no mean feat, for wearing MOPP gear during the scorching summer days in the desert proved quite uncomfortable and debilitating.[31]

In short, the Iraqi armed forces posed a threat to coalition forces at sea, in the air, and especially on the ground.

One of the few "major disagreements" between the Americans and Saudis planning for the ground defense of Saudi Arabia related to the main line of resistance. Not unlike the Germans, who had hoped to stop Soviet ground forces before they rolled over much of the Federal Republic of Germany in a NATO–Warsaw Pact war, the Saudis were determined to fight for every inch of their soil in northern Saudi Arabia. The Americans, conscious of the weakness of the defending forces, wanted to trade space for time by deploying arriving Army and Marine units around critical ports and airfields many miles behind the frontier. After several weeks of disagreement, capped by an eight-hour meeting between Schwarzkopf, Sharp, General Khalid Bin Sultan (Saudi commander in chief), and others, the conferees compromised and decided that Saudi forces would defend strong points on the border while the American Army and Marine combat divisions concentrated to their rear.[32]

U.S. commanders deemed the six-lane highway stretching along the coast from Kuwait to Dhahran as the likeliest enemy avenue of approach, for along that road lay some of Saudi Arabia's most important oil, water, and industrial facilities as well as the crucial ports and airfields. Another likely attack route, this one defended by allied Arab troops, was the inland highway that led to Riyadh.[33]

Schwarzkopf believed that an armored force more powerful than originally planned would be necessary to defeat a determined Iraqi drive. However, shortages of fast sealift vessels with roll-on/roll-off capability, crucial to unloading armored vehicles quickly, prevented him from deploying heavy forces as fast as he would have liked. Coalition ground commanders dubbed the weeks that passed until the armor arrived the "window of vulnerability" for allied forces in Saudi Arabia and the "window of opportunity" for Saddam Hussein.[34]

Officers and enlisted men and women alike appreciated the gravity of the situation. U.S. leaders did not believe that the few Saudi trip-wire units stationed on their northern border or the remainder of the 40,000-man Saudi army would deter an Iraqi attack. "From our perspective," noted Lieutenant General Walter E. Boomer, Commander Marine Forces, Central Command, and the highest-ranking Marine officer ashore, "it made sense for the enemy to attack."[35] Marine and Army units fully expected to fight as they rushed from transport aircraft to defensive positions around Dhahran and al-Jubayl. Some units were issued ammunition before deploying in case they landed during an attack. Aircrews who had ferried aircraft into Saudi air bases found themselves flying patrols or placed on strip alert within hours of their arrival. Airmen, soldiers, and sailors worked furiously to clear ports and airfields of arriving supplies and equipment to minimize loss in case of attack. There were numerous alerts and often hasty defensive preparations.[36]

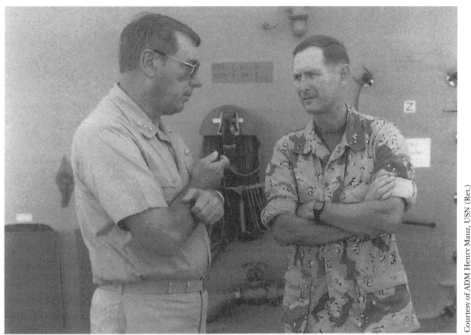

Courtesy of ADM Henry Mauz, USN (Ret.)

Vice Admiral Henry H. Mauz Jr., Commander U.S. Seventh Fleet/Commander U.S. Naval Forces, Central Command, and Lieutenant General Walter E. Boomer, Commanding General, I Marine Expeditionary Force/Commander U.S. Marine Forces, Central Command.

The Iraqis could attack Bahrain, al-Jubayl, and ad-Dammam not only from the land or sky, but also from the sea. The ports were potentially vulnerable to assault by hard-to-detect mine-laying boats, explosives-laden swimmers, missile-armed fast attack craft, or saboteurs. Exploding ammunition ships and tankers would have wrought havoc in these harbors. The loss of any of the three ports might have doomed an allied defense of Saudi Arabia, or at least frustrated military operations.[37] The loss of *LaSalle*, command ship of the Middle East Force and long a symbol of U.S. presence in the gulf, might have had serious military and political consequences. On 2 September, the I Marine Expeditionary Force staff received the sobering if exaggerated report, presumably referring to al-Jubayl harbor, that "our weakest point right now is the water. At night we have only one boat from the Navy."[38]

The Navy acted quickly to shore up the seaward defenses of the three ports. Detachments of SEAL (sea, air, and land) naval commandoes and special boat units of Naval Special Warfare Group 1 were airlifted into the theater on 10 August and immediately began nightly patrols of the harbor and terrain surrounding al-Jubayl.[39] In September the Pacific Fleet deployed detachments from its Explosive Ordnance

Disposal (EOD) Mobile Unit 5 to deal with any sea mines or limpet mines that threatened port operations. Eventually, detachments from EOD Mobile Units 3 and 9 reinforced the first contingents.[40]

Vice Admiral Henry H. Mauz Jr. was named Commander U.S. Naval Forces, Central Command on 16 August. Mauz promptly selected the former COMUSNAVCENT, Rear Admiral Sutton, as Commander U.S. Naval Logistics Support Force (COMUSNAVLOGSUPFOR), with the task designator of Commander Task Group 150.3. Sutton and thirty members of his Pearl Harbor-based staff established the logistics headquarters at Administrative Support Unit, Bahrain, the Navy's permanent support facility in the theater. Mauz also designated Sutton as Commander Harbor Defense Command (CTG 150.9) under Commander Middle East Force.

USN DN-SC 91-08343

An armed Sea Raider utility craft, crewed by U.S. Coast Guard reservists, patrols the harbor of Manama, Bahrain, to prevent waterborne attacks on *LaSalle* (AGF 3) and other coalition vessels in port.

Sutton, a veteran of combat on the coast of Vietnam, knew the importance of protecting vital ports from waterborne threats.[41] Headquartered in Bahrain, the admiral established three subordinate Port Security–Harbor Defense (PSHD) groups, with PSHD Group 1 in Bahrain's port of Mina Sulman, PSHD Group 2 in al-Jubayl, and PSHD Group 3 in ad-Dammam. That same month, MAC aircraft transported to the gulf the San Diego-based Commander Naval Mobile Inshore Undersea Warfare Group 1, his staff, and Mobile Inshore Undersea Warfare Units (MIUWUs) 103 and 105. The entire contingent consisted of members of the Naval Reserve, 6,300 of whom were called up during Desert Shield. Then, the U.S. Coast Guard dispatched Port Security Units (PSUs) 303 and 301, staffed by men and women of the Coast Guard Reserve.[42]

Despite these measures to defend Saudi Arabia and the Gulf Cooperation Council (GCC) nations, some questioned whether coalition forces could have fended off a full-scale Iraqi sea, air, and ground assault in August 1990. Opinions differed, even among military officers who were in the theater at the time. CENTCOM and NAVCENT staff officers who separately studied the question in August 1990 concluded that with the limited forces at hand, the U.S. command "could not successfully defend the key facilities along the coast."[43] "Had Saddam come south in the early days," Admiral Mauz later recalled, "we would have had a hard time stopping him. He might have reached the oilfields less than 200 miles [from the Kuwait-Saudi border], but he probably could not have sustained significant forces there for a protracted period because of logistics constraints. He could have done a hell of a lot of damage in a short time, though."[44] Lieutenant General Gary E. Luck, commander of the Army's XVIII Airborne Corps, believed that if Saddam had launched an armored attack, the deployed light infantry element of his 82d Airborne Division, which was short of artillery and antitank ammunition, would have been a mere "speed bump."[45] Schwarzkopf held a similar view, describing the 82d as "nothing more than a trip-wire force."[46] But other Army officers contended that the ground force "was no mere speed bump" and that the coalition's air forces, "with open terrain and clear weather... would have badly mauled any armored force, particularly if it were tied to the main coastal road."[47] During the early days, however, Air Force squadrons lacked critical supplies of ordnance, fuel, and repair parts. Admiral Sharp observed after the war that "the only thing we really had was carrier air [because] the Air Force could get airplanes out there, but all they had was air-to-air munitions; they didn't have any air-to-ground munitions positioned... where we could bring them to bear in any intensity on the battlefield.... That was a major deficiency."[48] The carriers, however, were short of precision guided munitions.[49]

Rear Admiral Fogarty; Rear Admiral Thomas C. Lynch, commander of the *Dwight D. Eisenhower* battle group; and Rear Admiral Jerry L. Unruh, commander of the *Independence* battle group, were also worried about the lack of adequate procedures for coordination between Navy and Air Force units, as well as among U.S., Saudi, United Arab Emirates, and Bahraini air forces. "*If* we were directed by LGEN Horner (CENTCOM forward) to attack Iraqi forces headed south into Saudi Arabia during those first few weeks with U.S. Navy air forces," Fogarty noted after the war, "the danger of 'blue on blue' [accidental collisions and attacks] was sobering to say the least."[50] In a postwar study, an Air Force analyst contended that the Iraqi army in Kuwait outmatched the coalition's ground forces. If air power could not stop the Iraqi forces, he argued, "they simply could not be stopped."[51]

General Hopkins, Commanding General, 7th MEB, was more sanguine. He felt that the Marines' M60A1 tanks (even though less capable than the Army's M1A1), attack aircraft, helicopters, and self-propelled artillery of his air-ground task force, roughly the size of an Army division, were far superior to anything in the Iraqi inventory. Had the Iraqis attacked, he would have executed a fighting withdrawal from as far forward as possible into a defensive position in front of al-Jubayl and ad-Damman roughly analogous to the Pusan perimeter of the Korean War. His objective would be to

> delay and attrit the Iraqis with air power, then defend in a main battle area along what became known as "cement ridge." The Iraqis had two possible attack routes. We thought they'd either come down the coast or use a route a little bit to the west, but both these routes come together at a junction near the cement factory [located 40 miles north of al-Jubayl].[52]

"If they kept coming," Hopkins emphasized, "we had drawn a line in the sand by the cement factory. We were going to stay there."[53] General Boomer agreed that "we could have stopped [Saddam]" but admitted that "it would have been one hell of a fight."[54]

"Hussein missed his chance in not attacking in the first couple of weeks," Boomer later observed, because the dictator's window of opportunity narrowed as coalition forces poured into Saudi Arabia and the gulf states.[55] On 25 August, 1st MEB marines stepped off air transports in al-Jubayl and the next day married up with the arms and equipment that MPS Squadron 3 had just delivered to the port.[56]

Also on the 26th, the Commander in Chief, U.S. Central Command, and soon to be the *de facto* commander of the coalition's military forces, arrived at his forward headquarters in Riyadh. During his first meeting with the press corps, General Schwarzkopf stated that he believed the period of greatest danger had passed, even though he could not guarantee the outcome if the Iraqis invaded Saudi Arabia.

On 3 September, Lieutenant General Boomer established the I MEF. The general was a 52- year-old North Carolinian whom General Sir Peter de la Billière, overall commander of British forces in the theater, described as "a tall, gangling man, quiet and likeable."[57] Boomer was commissioned in the Marine Corps following graduation from Duke University in 1960. He earned two Silver Star Medals for bravery during his two tours in Vietnam. He formed I MEF by "compositing" or fitting together the 1st and 7th MEBs, now organized into the the 1st Marine Division under Major General James M. Myatt, the 3d Marine Aircraft Wing led by Major General Royal N. Moore, and the 1st Force Service Support Group under Brigadier General James A. Brabham. Major General Hopkins became Deputy Commander I MEF.

The Navy-Marine Corps team added a new dimension to the defense of Saudi Arabia when the five ships of Amphibious Squadron 5, carrying the 13th Marine Expeditionary Unit (MEU), Special Operations Capable (SOC), and the 13 amphibious vessels of Amphibious Group 2, with the East Coast-based 4th MEB embarked, steamed into the North Arabian Sea in mid-September.[58] The 2,300-man 13th MEU(SOC) was specially trained for special warfare missions.

General Schwarzkopf kept these units afloat because he recognized the advantage of having an amphibious force to strike at the flank and rear of the Iraqi army if it advanced against al-Jubayl along the vulnerable coastal road. It also gave him a mobile offshore reserve force.[59]

Just before Schwarzkopf's return to Washington in early August, he met with Sharp in Jiddah. The admiral recommended that CINCCENT push for the deployment to the Saudi ports on the gulf of Navy mine countermeasures forces "as soon as possible," because he feared Iraqi mining of the waters off Kuwait "at any time." [60] In mid-August the Navy began dispatching mine countermeasures (MCM) resources to the gulf. On 1 October, the Dutch heavy lift ship *Super Servant III* delivered *Avenger* (MCM 1), a newly commissioned mine countermeasures ship, and the 1950s-vintage ocean minesweepers *Adroit* (MSO 509), *Impervious* (MSO 449), and *Leader* (MSO 490). Captain David J. Grieve, Commander U.S. Mine Countermeasures Group, arrived on the 3rd. The next day, huge MAC C-5 Galaxy and C-141 Starlifter transport planes delivered Helicopter Mine Countermeasures (HM) Squadron 14. The unit, a veteran of operations in the Red Sea and the Persian Gulf during the 1980s, flew six MH-53E Sea Dragon mine countermeasures helicopters.[61]

Captain Grieve faced difficult challenges right from the start. Since no hard evidence surfaced early in Desert Shield that the Iraqis were planting sea mines, Admiral Mauz accorded MCM a low priority. Furthermore, in the admiral's eyes the MCM forces "were not well trained, their equipment was not reliable, and they lacked confidence." [62]

Mauz also harbored doubts about the utility of MCM helicopters in the waters off Kuwait, so he did not request their deployment to the gulf. Washington dispatched HM-14 over his objections. Mauz then faced the problem of where to put the squadron. MCM helicopters operated best from an amphibious ship, but the admiral decided against stationing HM-14 afloat because he did not want to deprive the amphibious task force (ATF) of a platform essential for its aerial assault forces.[63]

Moreover, Mauz did not want the squadron displacing combat aircraft—"shooters"— at the airfields and ports near Kuwait. Mauz eventu-

Dutch heavy lift ship *Super Servant III* partially submerges to float mine countermeasures ship *Avenger* (MCM 1) and ocean minesweeper *Adroit* (MSO 509) after a long passage from the United States to Manama, Bahrain.

A Navy MH-53E Sea Dragon mine countermeasures helicopter operates minesweeping gear in the Persian Gulf.

ally agreed to Grieve's proposal to base HM-14 on a five-acre site at Port Zayed in Abu Dhabi.

Captain Grieve considered Abu Dhabi an excellent location for his MCM group, designated Task Unit 150.3.1 under Admiral Sutton and then Task Unit 150.4.1 under Admiral Fogarty.[64] His ships and helicopters did not have to compete for berthing or runway space as did the naval units stationed further north. In addition, the government of Abu Dhabi imposed fewer restrictions on foreign forces than its neighbors. Grieve needed this freedom of action to properly prepare his forces, since they were not ready for MCM operations upon arrival in the gulf. Because the Navy assembled an MCM force only when it needed it, and manned it with temporarily assigned active duty personnel and reservists on a short-term basis, the units had not trained together before reaching the theater.

Preparation of the MCM force for combat operations did not go as smoothly as it should have. For instance, because of its low priority, the MCM group did not rate a communications van, so staffers had to drive 15 miles to an Air Force communications station to send and receive messages. Logistics proved unnecessarily complicated because the Navy lacked a doctrinal framework for incorporating MCM forces into a battle group or amphibious task force. For these and other reasons, not until early November was the MCM group properly trained, equipped, and organized for battle.[65] Admiral Sharp later observed that "we should have done a better job deploying our MCM forces" and "in future [they] should be prepared to go up where the mines are going to be."[66]

The British also dispatched a mine countermeasures flotilla. *Hunt*-class mine hunters *Cattistock* (M 31), *Hurworth* (M 39), and *Atherstone* (M 38), supported by survey ship *Herald* (A 138), entered the CENTCOM theater on 7 September. *Dulverton* (M 35) and *Ledbury* (M 30) joined them later. In many ways the British flotilla was more modern and capable than the U.S. force. The five British mine hunters, with Lynx and Sea King helicopters used as mine spotters, carried some of the most advanced mine countermeasures equipment then available and reflected the longstanding focus on mine warfare of the Royal Navy. British expertise in mine countermeasures was second to none.[67]

Ground forces poured into the theater. By 23 September, the Military Sealift Command had delivered the last units of the Army's 24th Infantry Division (Mechanized) to Dhahran. For weeks the advanced M1 tanks rolled off the Navy's fast sealift ships and moved forward. The division from Ft. Stewart, Georgia, took up positions alongside I MEF north and west of al-Jubayl, establishing a line of U.S. mechanized forces across the two likeliest Iraqi avenues of approach into eastern Saudi Arabia. At the same time, MAC brought in Army Patriot air defense missile units.

Central Command's Army component, ARCENT, deployed batteries of the as-yet untested Patriot missiles in defensive arcs around Dhahran, al-Jubayl, ad-Dammam, Riyadh, and the coalition's other vital logistic and command centers.

Admiral Mauz realized that "if the Navy was going to be relevant to the war and the air campaign," he would have to operate carriers in the constrained waters of the gulf.[68] To determine the feasibility of operating in those waters, the admiral considered a short-term deployment there of the *Independence* battle group at the end of September. When Mauz broached the idea with Admiral Unruh and his staff during a visit to the carrier in mid-September, they exclaimed: "Hot Damn! We were thinking the same thing."[69] The staff broke out charts showing desired operating areas in the gulf. Carrier aircraft flying from the central gulf rather than from more distant staging areas east of the Strait of Hormuz could double the battle group's strike sorties.

The Persian Gulf's geography and environment presented numerous difficulties. At first glance, its 450-by-130-nautical-mile expanse seemed quite large enough for flight operations. However, shallow water and navigational obstacles reduced the available space considerably. Most of the deeper water (more than 100 feet deep) lay in the gulf's eastern half, much of it within the Iranian Exclusion Zone. The western shoreline and southern elbow were heavily shoaled. Oil platforms, small islands, and isolated shallows studded the waters throughout the gulf. The Strait of Hormuz offered the only escape or reinforcement route. Apart from occasional winter storms, the gulf was usually clear and calm. Wind direction and velocity varied with the seasons. But summer temperatures could drive the mercury over 110 degrees Fahrenheit, and the ubiquitous airborne sand had great potential for creating ship and aircraft maintenance problems. And high temperatures and low wind speeds would require carriers to generate more speed for launches, or to launch planes with partially empty fuel tanks. All in all, the gulf could be an unfriendly place for flattops.

On the first day of October, the *Independence* battle group began a highly visible, three-day deployment into the Persian Gulf. An after action report concluded that "extended operations within the Arabian Gulf are feasible from a sea room and air space perspective. . . . Traffic density, oilfield platforms, water depths, and air space management require close attention but CV operations are clearly doable."[70] It soon became clear to friend and foe that the fleet could readily buttress the defense of Saudi Arabia and the gulf states.[71]

By early October, Schwarzkopf had little doubt that the forces on hand could defend the Arabian Peninsula successfully. At that time the *Saratoga, John F. Kennedy* (CV 67), and *Independence* battle groups, each with five to seven escorts, operated in contiguous waters. The *Midway* (CV 41) battle group was enroute from her home port, Yokosuka, Japan. The battleship *Wisconsin* plowed through the warm waters of the Persian Gulf, ready for action. Eighteen amphibious ships, loaded with Marine infantry, helicopters, and Harrier vertical/short take-off and landing (V/STOL) aircraft, stood by near the Strait of Hormuz or inside the gulf. In all, 52 Navy combatants then sailed in the CENTCOM theater.

Ashore, the Army's 101st Airborne (Air Assault) Division, 3d Armored Cavalry Regiment, and 12th Aviation Brigade had joined the 82d Airborne Division, the 24th Infantry Division, and the 1st Marine Division. Lead elements of the 1st Cavalry Division had begun to arrive. Combat aircraft of the Air Force's 1st, 4th, 35th, 37th, 48th, and 366th Tactical Fighter Wings prepared to clear the sky of any Iraqi planes that crossed into Saudi air space. Five squadrons of F-16C Falcons and four squadrons of A-10 Thunderbolts, armed with deadly accurate Maverick missiles and 20mm rapid-fire cannon, awaited the chance to pounce on enemy tank columns. The 3d Marine Air Wing weighed in with four squadrons of F/A-18s, two squadrons of AV-8Bs, one squadron of A-6s, and three squadrons of Cobra attack helicopters armed with TOW anti-tank missiles. In short, Central Command had slammed shut Saddam Hussein's window of opportunity.[72]

The Naval Command

The Navy was fortunate that Iraq did not attack in the early days of Desert Shield, because its command structure for operations in the Central Command theater was in a state of flux. The set-up when Saddam's forces crossed the Iraq-Kuwait border on 2 August reflected the Navy's long-standing focus on meeting threats from the Soviet Union, and later, Iran. Because of the latter's long coastline on the Persian Gulf and proximity to the narrow Strait of Hormuz, U.S. naval strategists had rightly concluded that routinely operating the main body of the fleet in the confines of the gulf was fraught with danger.

The naval flag officers who commanded Joint Task Force Middle East during the Earnest Will tanker escort operation in 1987 had reported to CINCCENT but exercised the control of fleet units from a carrier deployed east of the Strait of Hormuz. Some naval forces of necessity operated in the Persian Gulf, as they had since 1949 under Commander Middle East Force. Considering the air threat from Iran manageable, Washington in February 1988 authorized the consolidation of both staffs under one admiral, who broke his flag in command ship *Coronado* (AGF 11) deployed inside the gulf. The Navy, however, saw the

JTFME as a special, ad hoc response to the peculiar circumstances and limited scope of the tanker escort operation.

For a large-scale conflict in the region, naval leaders expected the fleet to operate from the broad expanse of the North Arabian Sea, where carrier task forces could take advantage of their inherent mobility and flexibility. Responsibility for that body of water fell to the U.S. Pacific Command. The Navy anticipated that that command would provide both the fleet and fleet commander for combat operations in the CENTCOM area.[73] Stanley Arthur, CENTCOM's first naval component commander, later said, half in jest: "There was a stone tablet that I was given [by higher command] that said, 'We the Navy operate in support of. That is our way of operating, and we're never going to change. And don't you dare' [give away this philosophy]."[74] Admiral Mauz concurred, later recalling, "From the Navy's point of view there had been sentiment toward being 'in support' rather than part of CENTCOM's command structure . . . mainly because of [area of responsibility] tug of wars and doubt that CENTCOM was competent to command naval forces. Being located in Florida instead of its assigned [area of responsibility] cost CENTCOM credibility. Officers assigned to that staff never went anywhere. And so on."[75]

Moreover, with a long tradition of independent blue-water operations, the Navy abhorred the idea of surrendering control of its forces, particularly its carriers, to an Army general. Indeed, the naval service had successfully resisted repeated attempts by General William C. Westmoreland, Commander U.S. Military Assistance Command, Vietnam, to gain control of Seventh Fleet carriers during the Vietnam War.

Hence, the Navy downplayed its connection to CENTCOM. The permanent billet of Commander U.S. Naval Forces, Central Command, the CENTCOM naval component, had been in existence since 1983, but the incumbent was not of flag rank, had a small staff, and conducted business from Hawaii, thousands of miles from either Tampa or Riyadh. In theory, COMUSNAVCENT should have exercised operational control of all U.S. naval forces assigned to Central Command. In practice, COMUSNAVCENT yielded operational control to the Commander Middle East Force/Commander Joint Task Force Middle East, a more senior Navy flag officer. Admiral Sharp stated the obvious when he observed that the arrangement was "awkward."[76] COMUSNAVCENT did, however, exercise the naval component commander responsibilities for long-range planning, brief naval units deploying to the Middle East Force, maintain a naval intelligence appraisal of the countries in the Central Command region, participate in CENTCOM joint exercises, and provide logistics, administrative, and personnel support to all naval forces in the Central Command theater.

The scenario used in Internal Look 90, the CENTCOM command post exercise held in late July to test Operation Plan 1002-90, involved three carrier battle groups and a battleship group, and assumed that command of naval forces would be exercised from a forward post co-located with CINCCENT. Neither Admiral Mauz nor his staff participated because they had not yet been assigned to Central Command and the exercise was not held in the Seventh Fleet's area of responsibility. Although Internal Look 90 suggested the need to restructure the Navy's command and control relationships in the Persian Gulf region, the Navy had taken no relevant actions when Iraq invaded Kuwait.[77] This was unfortunate, because shortly after the war, Schwarzkopf observed to Admiral Kelso that "integrated operations of the other services [went] more smoothly because I had three star component commanders with whom I had exercised and who had played key roles in the development of our OPLANS." He regretted that "the Navy commander [Mauz] was not there for the practice sessions and only arrived after the balloon went up."[78] Rear Admiral Sutton was COMUSNAVCENT when Iraq invaded Kuwait.[79]

The scope of the crisis and the immediate need for strong forces to deter or fight Iraqi aggression persuaded General Schwarzkopf and the Department of Defense that CINCCENT should be able to make use of all available U.S. military resources. Accordingly, on 2 August, DOD issued an order directing the Commander in Chief, U.S. Central Command to assume operational control of the *Independence* battle group when it entered his area of operations.[80] To enhance Schwarzkopf's ability to use his carrier forces, Washington transferred operational responsibility for the Gulf of Oman and the Gulf of Aden from the Pacific Command to the Central Command.[81]

The scale of the Iraqi invasion and the planned U.S. response to it convinced General Powell, Admiral Frank B. Kelso II, the other Joint Chiefs, General Schwarzkopf, and Admiral Huntington Hardisty, CINC-PAC, that the commander of CENTCOM's naval component should be a three-star flag officer, on par with the other component heads, and an experienced fleet commander.[82] Accordingly, the JCS designated Vice Admiral Mauz, then Commander Seventh Fleet, U.S. Pacific Fleet, as COMUSNAVCENT. Mauz continued to direct the Seventh Fleet.[83]

"Hank" Mauz was one of the Navy's best officers. Following graduation from the U.S. Naval Academy in 1959, he served in destroyers *John A. Bole* (DD 755) and *Blue* (DD 744). Mauz learned hard lessons of combat as a river patrol boat officer with River Squadron 5 in Vietnam, earning the Bronze Star with Combat V. Following that experience, he filled increasingly challenging billets in the surface warfare community and in the Pentagon, including the Strategy and Concepts Branch (OP-603) in the Office of the Chief of Naval Operations, Chief of the Operations and Readiness Branch of Supreme Headquarters, Allied Powers, Europe, and Deputy Chief of Staff for Operations and Plans, U.S. Pacific Fleet. In 1986, as Commander Battle Force Sixth Fleet, Mauz planned and conducted joint strikes against Libya in Operation El Dorado Canyon. In November 1988, he received command of the Seventh Fleet, traditionally a plum assignment.[84]

Admiral Mauz could not tackle his new responsibilities in the gulf in August 1990 as quickly as he wanted, however. Naval leaders in the Pacific remained reluctant to part with their major combat fleet. CINCPAC insisted on formal transfer authority. Hardisty directed Mauz to delay his arrival in the CENTCOM theater until a message order appointing him COMUSNAVCENT arrived from Washington. Mauz spent 14 August waiting on Diego Garcia. On the 16th, one day after reaching Bahrain by air with part of his staff, Mauz took command of U.S. Naval Forces, Central Command.[85] Until the arrival of his Seventh Fleet flagship *Blue Ridge* (LCC 19) on the 1st of September, he directed operations from *LaSalle*, the Persian Gulf veteran.

Because of "overriding operational demands," Mauz decided to remain on board his flagship and not establish NAVCENT headquarters in Riyadh, as did his Army and Air Force counterparts. He elaborated:

> The maritime intercept operations, the steady Iraqi air operations over the northern Persian Gulf (posing a threat to our ships), the need to coordinate Navy air [operations] and plans, the need to work with GCC countries, and the complete lack of C3 in Riyadh all made going there a nonstarter. Sure, ARCENT was there—he was mostly a support provider, an area commander with little operational [responsibility]. Horner was there, but it took him *months* to establish adequate C3. Boomer was in the field. So was NAVCENT.[86]

Admiral Mauz spent about two days each week visiting ships, shore bases, air heads, field hospitals, logistics facilities, and other naval activities. "If you don't get out and around," Mauz noted, "you can't understand the impact of what you are asking your people to do, you can't get their feedback and you can't assess combat readiness and morale." He also visited the GCC countries to discuss operations, plans for future activity in the gulf, logistic support, and port visits of U.S. naval units. Public relations duties and visits from President and Mrs. Bush, General Powell, and other VIPs absorbed a significant amount of Mauz's time.[87]

For liaison with CENTCOM headquarters, Mauz created the subordinate billet of NAVCENT Riyadh, headed initially by Commander Carrier Group 3, Rear Admiral Timothy W. Wright. He also dispatched to the Saudi capital a Fleet Coordinating Group, under Captain Raymond Francis J. Sullivan, to work with the staff of Air Force Lieutenant General Charles Horner, dual-hatted as Commander U.S. Air Forces, Central Command (COMUSCENTAF) and Commander Ninth Air Force.

General Schwarzkopf designated Horner the Joint Force Air Component Commander (JFACC), making him responsible for coordinated employment of all U.S. and allied air forces. The primary responsibility of the JFACC staff was to develop the CENTCOM air campaign plan. Although the naval officers of the Fleet Coordinating Group had not previously interacted with any of General Horner's staffs, they had often worked with other Air Force staffs in the Western Pacific.[88]

The agreement between General Schwarzkopf and Admiral Kelso that made Admiral Mauz Central Command's naval component commander also reorganized the structure of NAVCENT. It gave Mauz operational control of all naval forces assigned to Schwarzkopf, including the battle forces in the Red Sea and Persian Gulf, the Middle East Force, and the shore facilities of the Administrative Support Unit, Bahrain. Admiral Sutton, under the title COMUSNAVCENT Pearl Harbor, retained responsibility for sealift coordination, naval logistics, and naval personnel support throughout Desert Shield and Desert Storm. Because Schwarzkopf exercised joint command, the Joint Task Force Middle East title was no longer needed. Rear Admiral Fogarty, the former JTFME commander, then reported to Mauz exclusively as Commander Middle East Force (Table. 2).[89]

The Embargo

As the Navy tightened its organizational structure, the UN coalition instituted an embargo of Iraqi overseas trade. The strangulation of Iraqi commerce, a blockade[90] in all but name, provided the UN with the means to bring direct and immediate pressure on Saddam.

On 6 August, the UN Security Council passed Resolution 661, which prohibited export of cargo originating in Iraq and Kuwait, and forbade import of cargo, except medical supplies and, under "humanitarian circumstances," food. The embargo had two goals: to degrade Iraq's military capabilities by denying the country access to vital foreign-produced supplies, spare parts, and equipment; and, more ambitiously, to compel Saddam to withdraw his forces from Kuwait. Coalition leaders

Table 2

NAVCENT COMMAND STRUCTURE

(18 August to 26 December)

Commander U.S. Naval Forces, Central Command (CTF 150)
    Vice Admiral Henry H. Mauz Jr.
Commander Middle East Force (CTG 150.1)
    Rear Admiral William M. Fogarty
Commander U.S. Maritime Interception Force (CTG 150.2)
    Rear Admiral Fogarty
Commander U.S. Naval Logistics Support Force (CTG 150.3)
    Rear Admiral Robert Sutton
Commander Carrier Battle Group North Arabian Sea (CTG 150.4)
    Rear Admiral Jerry L. Unruh
    Rear Admiral Daniel P. March
Commander Carrier Battle Group Red Sea (CTG 150.5)
    Rear Admiral Thomas C. Lynch
    Rear Admiral George N. Gee
    Rear Admiral Riley D. Mixson
Commander U.S. Amphibious Task Force (CTG 150.6)
    Rear Admiral John B. LaPlante
Commander U.S. Maritime Prepositioning Force (CTG 150.7)
    Rear Admiral Stephen S. Clarey
Commander U.S. Landing Force (CTG 150.8)
    Major General Harry W. Jenkins Jr., USMC
Commander Carrier Battle Group Mediterranean (CTG 150.9)
    various

SOURCE: Marvin L. Pokrant, *A View of Desert Shield and Desert Storm as Seen From COMUSNAVCENT* (Alexandria, VA: Center for Naval Analyses, 1991), 2–8; Michael Shepko, Sandra Newett, and Rhonda M. Alexander, *Maritime Interception Operations* (Alexandria, VA: Center for Naval Analyses, 1991), 6.

---

considered the embargo a strong incentive, for Iraq derived 95 percent of its income from the sale of oil abroad. Many hoped that these UN economic sanctions would persuade Saddam to relinquish Kuwait, but because political and military alliances have often proven fragile, others feared that the UN coalition would disintegrate before an embargo forced Iraq to yield.[91]

But Saddam Hussein's actions served to strengthen rather than weaken the international effort. On 8 August, the dictator announced the annexation of Kuwait as Iraq's nineteenth province. Two days later, he called for a holy war—a *jihad*—against the coalition, exclaiming that Islamic holy sites had been "captured by the spears of the Americans and the Zionists." On the 12th, he tried to rally Arab support by asserting that Iraq would not withdraw from Kuwait until Israel withdrew from the West Bank and Gaza Strip. Meanwhile, refugees from occupied Kuwait reported widespread arrests, looting, rape, and torture by the invaders. Saddam subsequently rounded up Japanese and Western nationals in Kuwait and Iraq and kept them hostage at power plants, factories, and military installations, hoping that these "human shields" would deter attacks on the sites. He also set a deadline for closure of foreign embassies in Kuwait. On the eve of that deadline, the dictator staged a televised interview with hostage families, including frightened children, in an attempt to thwart coalition efforts to reverse his aggression.[92]

The torrent of rage and scorn that these acts precipitated indicated that Saddam Hussein had miscalculated yet again. The UN Security Council responded to his "diplomacy" by declaring the annexation of Kuwait null and void (Resolution 662) and calling for the immediate release of foreign nationals (Resolution 664).[93]

The Navy took the lead in what became a multinational blockade of Iraq. On 16 August, President Bush directed Central Command to begin enforcing an embargo of Iraqi trade and the following day the U.S. Navy began maritime interceptions.[94]

The U.S. Navy was no stranger to this kind of operation. The naval quarantine of Cuba in the fall of 1962 was a model for such open ocean surveillance operations. The patrol aircraft and surface combatants of the U.S. Atlantic Fleet monitored Soviet naval and merchant ship movements so successfully that Premier Nikita Khrushchev's options were severely limited in the crisis. Without firing a shot, the Navy helped enable President John F. Kennedy to achieve his strategic objective of removing Soviet ballistic missiles and other offensive weapons systems from Cuba.[95]

The Navy's prowess in modern maritime patrol operations was also related to its experience in the Vietnam War. In Operation Market Time, which lasted from 1965 to 1972, the U.S. Navy, U.S. Coast Guard, and the Vietnam Navy patrolled the 1,200-mile coast of the Republic of Vietnam and much of the South China Sea. Their mission was to limit the enemy's use of the sea to infiltrate munitions and supplies into South Vietnam. Patrol planes, warships, and patrol vessels, tied in with a sophisticated command, communications, intelligence, and radar network, destroyed or otherwise frustrated 48 steel-hulled Communist trawlers attempting to evade the blockade during the eight-year operation.[96]

The U.S. naval forces under Admiral Mauz, a veteran of Operation Market Time, and Admiral Fogarty, whom Mauz named Commander Maritime Interception Force, put their embargo patrol skills to use on 18 August. A boarding party from cruiser *England* carried out the first MIO when they inspected the cargo and manifest of Chinese freighter

Heng Chung Hai. Later, guided missile destroyer *Scott* (DDG 995) ordered the Cypriot merchantman *Dongola* away from the Jordanian Red Sea port of al-Aqabah after her master admitted that the ship carried cargo bound for Iraq.[97]

That same day Iraqi merchantmen *Khanaqin* and *Baba Gurgur* tested the blockade's effectiveness by steaming right past the U.S. fleet. The masters of these empty tankers refused to slow or stop their vessels, even when U.S. frigates *Reid* and *Robert G. Bradley* fired warning shots across their bows. The captain of another tanker, this one fully loaded, also ignored warning shots. Following existing guidance, which authorized gunfire to "damage only non-vital parts of the intercepted ship, such as the rudder,"[98] Admiral Mauz prepared to direct his ship captains to disable the latter merchantman. Washington vacillated, giving him the go-ahead to disable the vessel and then withdrawing it. General Schwarzkopf saw this as a "classic illustration of what happens when Washington tries to direct combat operations from afar," as it had during the Vietnam War. In this instance, however, CINCCENT did not object. He, like his superiors, recognized that a hostile act at sea could precipitate hostilities with Iraq and neither the United States nor the UN was ready for war. The Iraqi ship was allowed to proceed to Aden, Yemen, where it anchored. Washington suspended MIO interceptions while the coalition decided how to enforce its will.

Operations resumed on 25 August when the UN Security Council passed Resolution 665, which explicitly authorized coalition naval units to employ force to uphold the embargo. Even with this authority, the American command proceeded more cautiously. New procedures, developed by Admiral Sharp and Colonel Burton R. Moore, USAF, Schwarzkopf's planning and operations staff directors, stipulated that "if disabling is necessary, prior approval from the [National Command Authorities] is required."[99]

Resolution 665 also invited all UN member nations to participate in the naval blockade. Eventually, 60 warships from Argentina, Australia, Belgium, Canada, Denmark, France, Greece, Italy, the Netherlands, Norway, Spain, and the United Kingdom took part in maritime interception operations. Although Gulf Cooperation Council navies did not participate in high-seas interceptions, they patrolled inshore waters to prevent merchantmen from evading the blockade.[100] Maritime interception operations provided an opportunity for nations leery of a ground commitment on the Arabian Peninsula to join in the international effort. The multinational nature of the blockade sent a clear signal to Saddam Hussein that the global community was unified in its determination to end his occupation of Kuwait.[101]

Since the UN lacked a permanent military organization and staff, the United States took the lead in developing a command and control system for maritime interception operations. At the behest of General Schwarzkopf, Admiral Mauz organized the effort. On 9 and 10 September, and almost every month thereafter, Mauz convened a conference in Bahrain of naval representatives from the nations taking part in the embargo patrol. This group became known as the "coordinating committee." Under the guidelines set forth in UN Security Council Resolutions 661 and 665, the committee developed procedures for intercepting merchant ships bound to and from Iraq, Kuwait, and the Jordanian port of al-Aqabah, except those transporting medicines. Al-Aqabah was included because King Hussein's government permitted overland transshipment of cargo to Iraq from that port.[102]

Although each coalition naval contingent followed rules of engagement laid down by its home government, the coordinating committee established common interception procedures, delineated patrol sectors covering over 250,000 square miles of ocean, and shared operational assignments. At the first meeting, the member navies recognized that some central direction of the blockade was necessary. Most agreed that as the traditional leader of many post-World War II combined operations and the largest naval force in the theater, the U.S. Navy should serve that function.[103]

A representative from the French foreign office, however, disagreed with Admiral Mauz's suggestions for operational coordination and pressed for a separate role for the naval units of the Western European Union (WEU) nations. Only the Italian naval representative lent some support to the French diplomat. The British felt that "political games were going on which had less to do with efficient execution of the blockade and rather more to do with eroding American domination of NATO and the newly formed Coalition."[104] The British and the naval representatives from other nations, particularly the Netherlands, Canada, and Denmark, followed the American lead. To resolve the problem, according to Mauz, "we simply assigned the [WEU] countries a separate operating area, off the UAE where there was almost no intercept action." He added, "they were happy and the rest of us got on with the program."[105]

The command arrangements for the maritime interception operation, best characterized as "loose association," worked so well that Admiral Mauz decided against pushing for formal establishment of a combined command. Subsequent monthly meetings handled practical issues like command-control-communications, intelligence sharing, boarding techniques, and rules of engagement.[106] Schwarzkopf later observed that "in a perfect world, all military operations would have unity of command." He recognized, however, that "national pride, politics and public perception play as large a role in determining relationships as military requirements." He concluded, "in coalition warfare where several nations temporarily unite against a common enemy we may be obliged to seek an informal command relationship which will work."[107] This was certainly the case with the maritime interception operations during 1990 and 1991.

Coalition naval forces carried out interception operations in the Persian Gulf (U.S., British, Norwegian, Italian, and Danish), the Gulf of Oman and the Gulf of Aden (U.S., Argentine, Belgian, Australian, Canadian, Dutch, French, and Spanish), and the Red Sea (U.S., French, Spanish, and Greek). The outstanding geographical features of these waters were the Strait of Hormuz separating the Persian Gulf from the Gulf of Oman, the Bab al-Mandab between the Gulf of Aden and the Red Sea, and the Strait of Tiran off al-Aqabah. The success of maritime interception operations depended upon close surveillance of these narrow "choke points."

The senior naval officer present in each patrol sector coordinated combined operations in that sector. A U.S. carrier battle group commander was usually responsible for overall coordination of the patrols in the northern Red Sea, Persian Gulf, and northern Arabian Sea.[108] The carrier battle group commander generally delegated interception responsibility to the commander of his destroyer escort squadron. Eventually, the destroyer squadron commanders carried out independent interception operations and reported directly to Admiral Fogarty.[109]

These commanders faced an enormous task. In August 1990, Iraq's merchant fleet numbered some 140 vessels, of which 20 tankers, 3 roll-on/roll-off (RO/RO) vessels, and 19 miscellaneous cargo vessels were suitable for overseas shipping. Several of the ships were underway when the coalition began the embargo patrol, but the others had to put to sea from Iraq's only two ports, Umm Qasr and az-Zubayr, via narrow waterways emptying into the northern reaches of the Persian Gulf. Captured Kuwaiti ports afforded additional access to the gulf. Dispatching tankers from the major ocean terminal at Mina al-Bakr was Iraq's only way to export large amounts of oil after Saudi Arabia and Turkey shut down the pipelines across their lands at the outset of the crisis.

Although most of the merchant ships plying the waters around the Arabian Peninsula were not headed to or from prohibited ports, each local coordinator had to locate, track, and identify all merchant ships in his patrol area and had to assign vessels to check those he thought likely to be carrying prohibited cargo.[110]

Shared experience in combined operations during the Tanker War and during years of NATO, Australia–New Zealand–U.S., and bilateral exercises enabled U.S. Navy commanders and their coalition partners to develop workable procedures for the embargo patrol.[111] An Australian historian, for example, noted that the Royal Australian Navy (RAN) "had not exercised at any length with the Dutch Navy, but because of the RAN's contact with the US and Royal Navies, the Australian ships found it very easy to operate with the Dutch task group."[112] With some irony, the commanding officer of the Spanish frigate *Vencedora* observed that his navy's "coordinated operations [with the European navies of] Holland, the U.K., [and] France" had occurred since 1960, but the training was "neither . . . as frequent nor intense" as with the U.S. Navy.[113] It is instructive to note that in 1989 and 1990 alone, the U.S. Navy carried out exercises around the globe with 16 of the 18 navies that eventually took part in the embargo patrol and with the armed forces of another 34 nations.[114] The upshot was that the Royal Australian Navy, and most of the other coalition navies employing similar rules of engagement and standard operating procedures, were able to "cooperate closely and effectively in joint interdiction operations" with the U.S. Navy.[115]

The commanders gathered information from all available sources, including intelligence reports, international shipping registers, radar and visual reports, and satellite imagery. To facilitate fast and accurate decision making, the information was processed by computerized systems. The Joint Intelligence Liaison Element deployed on board flagship *Blue Ridge* was a key link between the external intelligence agencies and the fleet.

The Navy Operational Intelligence Center, located in Suitland, Maryland, provided merchant shipping analyses directly to interdiction forces. The center also provided an inspection checklist for boarding teams, as well as lists of companies suspected of trading with Iraq or in behalf of Iraq. Rear Admiral Thomas Brooks, Director of Naval Intelligence, considered the group at Suitland the "unheralded, unsung heroes" of the intelligence effort.[116]

Interception operations followed a general pattern. Maritime patrol aircraft searched the waters surrounding the Arabian Peninsula. U.S. Navy P-3 Orions flying from Masirah, Oman, and Jiddah, Saudi Arabia, Royal Navy Nimrods operating from Seeb in Oman, and French Navy Atlantique patrol planes based at Djibouti on the Horn of Africa located merchant vessels and directed coalition warships to them.[117]

Normally, two coalition combatants operated together. After intercepting a merchantman, the warships queried the vessel's master by radio. They requested the ship's identity, point of origin, destination, and cargo. If the vessel proved not to be heading to or from a port in Iraq, Kuwait, or Jordan, she was allowed to proceed unhindered.

The coalition patrol directed suspicious merchantmen to stop for inspection. The allies would then dispatch a boarding party. Boarding

A P-3 Orion patrol plane investigates a vessel transiting the Persian Gulf. Patrol aircraft were critical to the effectiveness of the maritime interception operation mounted against Iraq.

parties preferred using the few available rigid-hull inflatable boats (RHIBs), rather than the Navy's standard motor whaleboats, because the inflatable boats possessed superior seakeeping ability, speed, and durability. The inspection team normally consisted of one Coast Guard officer (the team leader), a naval officer, three U.S. Coast Guard enlisted specialists, and five Navy bluejackets. The coastguardsmen were members of law enforcement detachments (LEDETs). Six LEDETs operated in the Red Sea and four in the Persian Gulf. The LEDETs had been created as a result of the Coast Guard's hard-earned experience with the Navy in Caribbean drug interdiction operations. The expertise of these Coast Guard seamen in boarding techniques, small-arms handling, smugglers' tactics, and the intricacies of shipping documentation and maritime law proved invaluable in foiling Iraqi attempts to evade the embargo.[118] To impart some of the knowledge they had gained in past operations, on 28 September coastguardsmen from *Brewton* (FF 1086) boarded HMAS *Success* and presented relevant briefings and lectures to the visit and search parties of HMAS *Success*, HMAS *Darwin*, and HMAS *Adelaide*.[119] One foreign observer considered the LEDETs to be the "most experienced boarding and search parties in the world."[120]

For the first two months of the embargo, Admiral Mauz paid close attention to the interceptions. Sometimes he spent the better part of a day and night trying to stop a recalcitrant Iraqi tanker. In such cases, he and General Schwarzkopf maintained close telephone contact. "He had a phone in each ear, one to me and one to [General Powell], during contentious intercepts," the admiral recalled. "I also had two phones— my other one was to a commander at sea."[121]

On 4 September, *Goldsborough* (DDG 20) intercepted and challenged the Iraqi cargo ship *Zanoobia*. Several days earlier, the merchantman had departed Colombo, Sri Lanka, bound for Iraq. *Goldsborough's* skipper, Commander James A. Reid, offered the Iraqi master the choice of being boarded and inspected or of making port someplace other than Iraq or Kuwait. The master chose the former. The boarding team found the ship loaded with tea, a cargo prohibited by UN resolution. Lieutenant (jg) John Gallagher, the Coast Guard officer in charge of the boarding party, suggested the master direct his ship to a non-Iraqi or Kuwaiti port. The master refused. As a result, on Gallagher's orders, Navy Seaman David Lee Handshoe took the helm and steered *Zanoobia* to Muscat, Oman.[122]

In another instance, on 14 September, U.S. and Australian warships communicated for 24 hours with the Iraqi ship *Al Fao* to induce her to stop for inspection. The merchantman slowed only when U.S. frigate *Brewton* and HMAS *Darwin* fired warning shots across her bow, allowing coastguardsmen and crew members from both men-of-war to board.

When the boarders found that *Al Fao* was empty, the coalition ships allowed her to proceed to the Iraqi port of Basrah.[123]

Searching merchantmen was risky business. "We didn't know if . . . someone would be waiting for us," noted a boarding team member from *Brewton*.[124] If the boarding party found prohibited cargo, like military equipment or chemicals, or discovered bookkeeping discrepancies, improper designation of consignees, or other irregularities in the ship's manifest, the sector commander would divert the ship to a coalition or other port.[125] Admiral Fogarty advised his units to "assume the vessel is attempting to deceive the boarding officer and act accordingly. . . . Guilty until proven innocent is a good thought process in trying to detect evasion attempts."[126]

The Iraqis used various tactics to circumvent the embargo and to frustrate the interception force. Saddam threatened violence against the family of any master whose ship stopped to allow a coalition boarding. On different occasions, Iraqi captains and crews ignored verbal challenges, delayed responding to radio queries, disregarded warning shots, released water on decks to make them slippery, refused to cooperate

A sailor on board guided missile destroyer *Goldsborough* (DDG 20) trains his 50-caliber machine gun on Iraqi merchantman *Zanoobia* as his shipmates prepare to board the ship.

Courtesy of Royal Australian Navy

British Royal Marines, covered by a Royal Australian Navy Squirrel helicopter, "fast rope" from a Lynx helicopter onto Iraqi ship *Tadmur*. A British naval officer was the on-scene commander for this operation on 8 October 1990 that also involved *Goldsborough*, HMS *Brazen*, and HMAS *Darwin*.

with coalition officers, hid cargo in hard-to-reach spaces, and headed for a different port than directed.

The coalition's countermeasures usually foiled these attempts at evasion. Thorough scrutiny of holds and manifests usually discovered cargo improperly labelled as crew food or papers falsely prepared. An Orion's radar and infrared detection set enabled its crew to spot Iraqi lettering under freshly painted false Egyptian markings on the Iraqi merchant vessel *Zanoobia*. In most cases an intercepted ship's master cooperated once assured he could inform his government that he had been forced to comply.[127]

Occasions arose when the Navy's rules of engagement permitted intercepting warships to use disabling fire to stop a recalcitrant Iraqi merchantman, but Admiral Mauz never allowed them to shoot. Critics suggested that not doing so may have given Saddam the impression that the coalition lacked resolve. "The way I saw it," recalled Mauz,

> was that no significant cargo got in or out of Iraq, and that to shoot up one of those unarmed ships was an extreme act that bordered on the fool-hardy. There was no military value to the act, it would have been a public

USN DN-SC 93-03388

Fully armed and equipped for the mission, men of SEAL Team 8 engage in a bridge-seizure training exercise on board USNS *Joshua Humphreys* (T-AO 188).

relations nightmare, and we would have "bought" the ship—i.e. had to rescue survivors, tow the ship, find a port, clean up the oil spill, and so on. As it turned out, we throttled Iraq's trade, promoted coalition unity, didn't have any casualties, and did some fine work at sea.[128]

If a merchantman refused to stop, the intercepting force used helicopters to insert armed teams which took temporary control of the ship. Such operations were called "vertical insertions." Since any attempt to board a ship that had refused to stop could meet with a hostile reception, coalition naval units mustered overwhelming force. Usually three or four warships surrounded a defiant merchantman while an SH-60 helicopter stood by to give covering fire as SH-3 helicopters moved in above the target vessel. Then, heavily armed special warfare teams "fast roped" (rappelled) to the deck to seize control of the ship. U.S. vertical insertion teams typically consisted of 16 Navy SEALs or marines, the latter from the 4th MEB and 13th MEU(SOC). Once the team secured the bridge and gained control of the vessel, small boats from the surrounding warships brought additional people alongside to inspect the merchantman. Vertical insertions enabled the coalition to prevent violations of the embargo while avoiding the potential political problems associated with using naval gunfire to disable a merchant vessel.[129]

Two such operations occurred during October. On the 8th, *Reasoner* (FF 1063), HMS *Battleaxe,* and HMAS *Adelaide* (F 01) intercepted the Iraqi merchantman *Al Wasitti* in the Gulf of Oman. The master refused to stop his ship despite warning shots fired across the bow. Finally, Royal Marines fast-roped onto the merchantman from British Lynx helicopters and compelled the captain to bring the vessel to a stop. The ship was allowed to proceed when a law enforcement detachment from *Reasoner* saw the empty cargo holds.[130]

Then, on the 28th, HMAS *Darwin* intercepted the Iraqi oil tanker *Amuriyah* off the coast of Oman near Masirah. The Iraqi master initially refused to answer *Darwin*'s radio queries. Soon *Reasoner, Ogden* (LPD 5), and HMS *Brazen* (F 91) steamed onto the scene. Hoping to stop the merchantman, *Darwin* towed a spar across her bow at high speed. Then an F-14 Tomcat and an F/A-18 Hornet from *Independence* made six low subsonic passes over her. *Reasoner* and *Darwin* fired warning shots ahead of the ship. The Iraqi ship did not stop. Finally, 21 marines of the 13th MEU(SOC) fast-roped from helicopters onto the merchantman. The leathernecks encountered no resistance, but still the uncooperative master refused to muster his crew. The marines radioed *Ogden* to dispatch a party of SEAL reinforcements.

Although to no avail, the Iraqis wet the deck with a water cannon to try to prevent the SEALs from boarding. A party of U.S. Coast Guard, U.S. Navy, and Royal Australian Navy sailors, known locally as the "A-Team" (Australian-American), then boarded the vessel. One Iraqi crewman in the engineering spaces tried to attack one of the Americans with an axe, but the marines disarmed and restrained him. The Americans believed that throughout the episode the master received detailed guidance by radio on how to interfere with boarding operations. Despite repeated Iraqi attempts to obstruct the coalition's mission, the inspection turned up no prohibited cargo. The on-scene commander allowed the merchantman to proceed. Clearly, on both 8 and 28 October, the Iraqis were testing the embargo patrol.[131]

Despite several tense moments, most operations involved routine interceptions of hundreds of merchantmen from many nations innocently plying their trade in Middle Eastern waters. About 100 ships steamed in and out of the Persian Gulf every day, so most radio queries of merchantmen occurred in these waters. A great majority of the boardings by coalition forces took place in the Red Sea, even though only 2 to 14 merchant vessels operated each day in the Gulf of Aqabah off Jordan. Vertical insertions of Iraqi ships occurred mostly in the Gulf of Oman and the North Arabian Sea.[132]

The embargo proved effective. The sanctions not only demonstrated Iraq's international isolation, but also denied Saddam access to world markets, eliminated his main source of income—oil exports—and stopped the resupply of his war machine. In December 1990, Generals Powell and Schwarzkopf testified before Congress that sanctions could weaken Saddam's military, particularly his air force. By then the lack of spare parts needed to maintain Iraq's foreign-made equipment had already begun to debilitate its armed forces.[133]

Sealift

While U.S. and other coalition combat forces tightened the noose around Iraq, the United States mounted a monumental operation to move hundreds of thousands of military personnel and millions of tons of equipment and supplies almost half-way around the world.

Charged with managing this operation was the U.S. Transportation Command (TRANSCOM) under Air Force General Hansford T. Johnson. His three major components, the Air Force's Military Airlift Command, the Army's Military Traffic Management Command, and the Navy's

USN DN-ST 91-00372

An M1A1 Abrams main battle tank is driven onto fast sealift ship USNS *Regulus* (T-AKR 292) in Savannah, Georgia.

Military Sealift Command oversaw the movement across land, air, and sea of the troops, vehicles, equipment, supplies, and fuel that General Schwarzkopf needed to fight and win in the Persian Gulf.

The Military Sealift Command, led by Vice Admiral Francis R. Donovan, operated a fleet of ships that deployed and sustained U.S. forces around the globe. Civilian merchant mariners manned Donovan's ships, which were organized into three major components. The Naval Fleet Auxiliary Force operated oilers, ammunition ships, stores ships, surveillance ships, and ocean tugs that provided direct support to combatants, enabling them to remain on station for long periods of time. The Special Mission Support Force controlled ships that conducted oceanographic research, missile tracking, and cable laying and repairing. The Strategic Sealift Force handled the 25 ships of the Afloat Prepositioning Force (12 cargo ships or tankers carrying Air Force, Army, and Navy materiel and 13 MPS ships), the eight fast sealift ships, and hospital ships *Comfort* (T-AH 20) and *Mercy* (T-AH 19).

With the Secretary of the Navy's approval, the Military Sealift Command's Strategic Sealift Force was also empowered to activate the 96 Ready Reserve Force ships maintained by the Department of Transportation's Maritime Administration and could charter merchantmen owned by U.S. and foreign commercial firms. The Ready Reserve Force vessels included roll-on/roll-off vessels, breakbulk cargo ships,[134] tankers, and barge carriers. During peacetime the Maritime Administration kept them ready to respond to overseas emergencies on 5, 10, or 20 days' notice. The Maritime Administration also controlled two Marine Corps aviation-support ships.

Central Command was responsible for working with TRANSCOM to determine the troops, supplies, and equipment that would be needed for likely contingencies in the CENTCOM theater. Operation Plan 1002-90 was nearing completion when Saddam invaded Kuwait, but the part of the document that laid out CENTCOM's transportation requirements and deployment schedule—the time-phased force and deployment data—had not been finished. Hence, information on the size and composition of forces to be deployed, their needs for cargo space, ports of embarkation, and methods of transportation was incomplete. But U.S. military personnel were well trained. MSC and the other components of General Johnson's command had conducted numerous peacetime exercises like Team Spirit, the crisis reinforcement of U.S. forces in South Korea. The men and women of TRANSCOM were able to respond to the crisis in the gulf with great ingenuity and flexibility.[135]

MSC's most important task during Phase I of Desert Shield was to move the tanks and armored personnel carriers, wheeled vehicles, guns, ammunition, and field gear of four Army divisions from ports in the

United States to ports in the Persian Gulf. A single mechanized division deployed with more than 100,000 tons of cargo, and once overseas, needed more than 1,000 additional tons of supplies, ammunition, and spare parts each day to operate.[136]

The stars of the sealift effort were MSC's fast sealift ships.[137] In the 1980s, the Navy bought these container ships from the Sea-Land Corporation, an American civilian shipping company, and civilian shipyards converted them to roll-on/roll-off ships, so they could quickly load and unload wheeled and tracked vehicles. The 946-foot-long ships could accommodate 700 Army vehicles, including M1A1 Abrams main battle tanks, Bradley armored fighting vehicles, troop transporters, and fuel trucks.[138] An FSS had a crew of 40 merchant seamen and a top speed of 33 knots.

On average, one fast sealift ship carried more cargo per voyage than any two chartered vessels. Five of these ships completed three deliveries each to the gulf during Phase I, a feat unmatched by any other type of ship. The seven operational fast sealift ships delivered almost 20 percent of Central Command's unit equipment and related support during Phase I.[139]

Despite this outstanding performance, the fast sealift ships suffered from a number of problems during Desert Shield. During peacetime the vessels were kept in an inactive status at several U.S. ports, where their nine-member skeleton crews were hard pressed to maintain shipboard machinery. Inevitably, during activation of the ships, engineering problems surfaced that caused delay in the departure and ocean passage of the vessels. The Navy expected to get the ships underway in four days after they were alerted for a mission, but it usually took about six days. In addition, during Phase I the FSS's averaged only 23 knots because of bad weather and such things as speed limitations in the Suez Canal.[140]

Although atypical of the FSS performance, the transatlantic travails of USNS *Antares* (T-AKR 294) attracted the most attention during Desert Shield.[141] Earlier, the ship had suffered an engine room fire while returning from an exercise in Korea. Repairs were made but a complete overhaul was postponed for lack of funds. When the crisis broke in August, the Navy decided that the need for the ship warranted the risk of sending her to sea. Unfortunately, *Antares* suffered an engineering breakdown in the middle of the Atlantic and had to be towed to Spain. Once there, *Altair* (T-AKR 291) took on her vital cargo, M1A1 tanks of the Army's 24th Mechanized Infantry Division, and delivered it to Saudi Arabia, three weeks later than scheduled.

Most of the ships of MSC's Ready Reserve Force accomplished their missions during Desert Shield, the first-ever wartime use of this fleet, but many of them did not perform as expected. Normally, when the RRF

USMC DN-SC 91-12023

A ship chartered by the Military Sealift Command prepares to offload military vehicles and equipment at al-Jubayl, Saudi Arabia.

ships received their activation orders, tugs towed them to nearby ship-yards for mechanical preparation, and crews were drawn from the ranks of the U.S. Merchant Marine. Then the ships were turned over to MSC for operations. Admiral Donovan activated 44 RRF ships during Phase I. Only 12 of them were ready for operations on time. Twelve others were one to five days late, and the remaining 20 were six or more days late. These ships had been tied up at Norfolk, Virginia, Beaumont, Texas, and in California's Suisun Bay for as long as 13 years, so delays in their activation should have come as no surprise.[142]

Even though Secretary Cheney and General Johnson were disap-pointed with the readiness of the RRF, once activated and turned over to Military Sealift Command, its ships maintained a 93 percent reliability rate and delivered about 30 percent of the unit equipment and related support in Phase I.

Another problem of the sealift effort was the initial shortage of enough skilled American merchant mariners to crew the mobilized mer-chant fleet. Enthusiastically answering the call to service, veterans of Vietnam, Korea, and even World War II, cadets from the Merchant Marine Academy, and union-recruited seamen joined the sealift effort. There was a special need for engineers to operate the outdated steam propulsion plants in 20–45-year-old ships. One such marine engineer who reported for duty was 83 years old.[143]

Although these seamen were well paid by most standards, they earned their pay when they faced many of the same risks from Iraqi mines, antishipping missiles, and aircraft as their comrades in the fleet. Almost 10,000 merchant mariners went to sea during the Persian Gulf War, even though they were not guaranteed the same return rights offered to military reservists who left their civilian jobs. More than half of them served in the war zone and were entitled to the Transportation Department's U.S. Merchant Marine Expeditionary Medal.[144] Still, there were not enough specially trained American mariners available to crew all the ships needed for the sealift mission.

It soon became apparent that the older breakbulk ships could not accommodate big armored vehicles and helicopters, and that MSC needed to supplement its fleet of 17 RO/RO ships. These vessels had spacious holds and were easier to load and unload, thereby reducing their time in port. They carried nearly twice as much combat and support equipment in Phase I as all other ship types combined.

To alleviate this shortage, not only of RO/RO ships but of other merchantmen, MSC chartered numerous U.S.-flagged ships.[145] As a rule, it took several fewer days for a chartered ship to reach a port of embarkation after receiving her charter than it took for a RRF ship to activate and deploy. Moreover, while it cost $1.6 million to activate an RRF ship and $40,000 each day to operate her, it cost only an average of $23,000 a day for chartered roll on/roll off ships and $10,000 for breakbulk ships. Chartered ships carried some 30 percent of the combat and support equipment during Phase I.[146]

MSC officials arranged with certain U.S. carriers a "Special Middle East Support Agreement" that provided U.S. flag container ships to deliver dry cargo (excluding ammunition) to the gulf. Each of these ships sortied from U.S. ports with as many as 2,700 40-foot containers, which cargo handling equipment could quickly load and unload, thus reducing turnaround time. Although MSC did not directly control these ships, they represented, as one analyst put it, a "little recognized, but crucial, contribution of the U.S. merchant marine to the success of Desert Shield/Desert Storm."[147]

MSC also chartered foreign-flag ships. As in past international confrontations, members of the U.S. maritime establishment criticized the government's heavy reliance on foreign-flag shipping. However, the Persian Gulf War was truly an international effort the likes of which had not been seen since the Korean War.[148] As some defense analysts have observed, "complaints about foreign flags seem especially strange in a war for which foreign contributions of any type were eagerly solicited."[149]

The establishment early in Desert Shield of a new headquarters to coordinate in-theater operations helped improve control of the sealift effort. When MPS Squadron 2, under Commander Richard Crooks, discharged its cargo at al-Jubayl in August, the Navy redesignated the staff as Military Sealift Command, Southwest Asia and set up the headquarters at Administrative Support Unit, Bahrain.[150]

MSC turned in an impressive performance during Phase I of Desert Shield. The command delivered 1,034,900 tons of equipment, 135,100 tons of supplies, and 1,800,000 tons of petroleum products to the Persian Gulf region. Of the 173 ships involved, 124 were U.S.-flag vessels, and these accounted for 85 percent of the tonnage. During the first three weeks of Desert Shield, MSC carried more tonnage to the Persian Gulf region than had been transported to South Korea during the first three months of the Korean War. Even though Phase I ended formally on 5 December, virtually all of Schwarzkopf's planned requirements had been satisfied by 11 November.[151]

Many factors helped make the sealift and airlift a success. Saudi Arabia boasted some of the most modern seaports and airports in the world and readily made them available to coalition military forces. The Saudi government had spent a monumental $650 billion on these transportation facilities and roadways in the decade before the invasion of Kuwait. Saudi Arabia and the other GCC member states also provided U.S. and other coalition forces with truck transportation, port and airfield services, cargo handling equipment, large warehouses, and great quantities of fuel free of charge. As a result, sealift vessels unloaded at modern piers, not out in the stream, and the huge Air Force C-5 transport planes landed on smooth 12,000-foot runways.[152]

Many of the arrangements for support from Saudi Arabia and the other gulf states resulted from the hard work of U.S. State Department officials. They negotiated critical status of forces agreements with host nations and obtained their permission for the use of basing, staging, and enroute fueling sites.[153] Other members of the international coalition supported the sealift with their own merchant vessels. Japan, South Korea, Kuwait, and Denmark provided $72 million worth of shipping, measured in the number of days their merchantmen were at sea. Japan's contribution accounted for almost half of the total.[154]

"Murphy's alive out there and there has [sic] been a lot of little problems," General Schwarzkopf said of sealift, "but there have been no show stoppers at all."[155] General Johnson partly attributed the success of his operation to Saudi Arabia's superb facilities and host nation assistance, the international support for the military buildup in the gulf, and Saddam's decisions not to attack coalition maritime traffic or the ports of Saudi Arabia.[156] But the performance of the Military Sealift Command certainly proved crucial. According to initial estimates, 300 shiploads were required to deploy and sustain U.S. forces in the CENTCOM theater. Although to General Johnson this figure seemed "staggering," MSC actually "moved 459 shiploads" during the Persian Gulf crisis.[157]

Fleet and Shore-based Logistic Support

In addition to deploying and sustaining sizable U.S. ground and air forces in the theater, the U.S. Navy's logistic establishment kept the operating fleet on line. The Navy had maintained combat fleets in the Western Pacific, the Mediterranean, and other waters along the rim of the Eurasian land mass since 1945.

Throughout the long Vietnam War, the Pacific Fleet's Service Force enabled the 100-ship Seventh Fleet to operate continuously in the Gulf of Tonkin and the South China Sea, over 7,000 miles from the United States. Navy logisticians refined the "connected replenishment" method, by which logistic ships transferred supplies and fuel to combatants while underway, via lines and hoses strung between the ships. The "vertical replenishment" approach, in which helicopters transferred supplies between ships, was inaugurated during the conflict in Southeast Asia. As a result of the Vietnam experience, extended operations in the Indian Ocean during the 1970s and early 1980s, and the tanker escort mission in the gulf in 1987–1988, the Navy's logistic establishment was well prepared to support the 120 ships of Naval Forces, U.S. Central Command deployed to the theater by January 1991.[158]

Most ships deployed to the CENTCOM theater with enough supplies to last at least 90 days.[159] Before *John F. Kennedy* departed Virginia in August, the Naval Supply Center at Norfolk loaded the battle group's ships—in record-breaking time—with two million eggs, 185,000 pounds of hot dogs, 250,000 pounds of chicken, 400,000 pounds of hamburger, and 300,000 pounds of french fries.[160]

Shipboard stores were not the fleet's sole source of supply, however. Integral to the Sixth Fleet in the Mediterranean and the Seventh Fleet in the Western Pacific were Logistics Task Forces 63 and 73. The Combat Logistics Force (CLF) ships of Task Force 63 supported U.S. naval forces in the Red Sea while Task Force 73 units operated in the other seas of the region.[161]

The workhorses of the CLF fleet were combat stores ships (AFSs), fast combat support ships (AOEs), oilers (AOs), replenishment fleet tankers (AORs), and ammunition ships (AEs). Routinely, individual

USN DN-SN 91-09310

Fast combat support ship *Sacramento* (AOE 1), a veteran of underway replenishment operations in the Vietnam War, refuels battleships *Missouri* and *Wisconsin* in the Persian Gulf.

stores, tanker, and ammunition ships supported an assigned carrier task group, but they also supplied other task groups and individual ships if the need arose. Other CLF units moved independently about the Red Sea and the Persian Gulf and North Arabian Sea or operated as ship-to-shore shuttles. In the Persian Gulf and North Arabian Sea, replenishment normally took place by the "delivery boy" method, in which a CLF ship brought supplies to a warship at the latter's station. Thus, combat units could remain on the line. In the Red Sea, the CLF used the "gas station" method, in which combatants rotated off the line and sought out a tanker in "gas alley," to the rear of the operating areas. By whichever method, fighting ships normally received fuel, ammunition, and stores about every three or four days.[162] Four CLF vessels were deployed in August and eight were on station by mid-November.[163]

Each week combat stores ships spent an average of two days loading supplies and provisions at the forward logistic support sites and five days distributing them to warships at sea. Carriers usually were replenished once a week. Oilers refueled other men-of-war every three days to maintain their fuel tanks at a minimum of 60 percent capacity.[164]

The experience of combat stores ship *Sylvania* (AFS 2) exemplified CLF operations. The ship spent seven months in the Red Sea. In filling

30,000 requisitions for supplies, she transferred 20,500 tons of material to combatants. Detachment 4 of Helicopter Support Squadron 6 embarked in *Sylvania* transferred to her customers via vertical replenishment 915 passengers, 31,000 pounds of mail, and 5,000 tons of supplies.[165]

The U.S. Navy not only supplied its own forces at sea but supplemented the logistic support provided by coalition navies to their own deployed forces. For instance, the MV *Overseas Valdez,* under contract to the Military Sealift Command, topped off HMAS *Success* with diesel and aviation fuel soon after the Australian ship arrived in the Gulf of Oman in November.[166] On one occasion, Commander L. G. Cordner, RAN, captain of HMAS *Sydney*

USN DN-ST 92-02359

To stow the ordnance below deck, Gunner's Mate 1st Class William Dokman (left) and Gunner's Mate 2d Class Terodney Russell attach lifting cables to a 16-inch shell.

(F 03), expressed the view that the delivery of 27 pallets of supplies in only 19 minutes by USNS *Spica*'s CH-46 helicopter was "a most impressive evolution."[167] Another time, Captain C. A. Ritchie, Commanding Officer of HMAS *Brisbane* (D 41), characterized a simultaneous CONREP and VERTREP evolution as "an impressive and efficient operation which typified the American logistic support" in the gulf crisis.[168] Not only the U.S. Navy, but each coalition navy, depending on its means, shared supplies and fuel.

While the fleet depended primarily on its own sources of supply, shore facilities were necessary to speed the delivery of critical repair parts, specialized supply items, and naval personnel. The Administrative Support Unit, Bahrain served as the Navy's principal headquarters ashore for logistics support in the Central Command theater.

In addition to sealift, port security and harbor defense, and medical support responsibilities, Rear Admiral Sutton served as Commander Naval Logistics Support Force (CTF 150.3). From his headquarters in Bahrain, he oversaw all naval logistics in the theater. His specific charge was to ensure that the forces afloat received optimum shore-based support.

To do this task, during Desert Shield Sutton established port and airfield facilities, named forward logistics support sites (FLSSs). Coalition member states readily provided these shore-based sites. A site at Jiddah, Saudi Arabia, served naval forces in the Red Sea. The ports and air heads at Bahrain and Jebel Ali in the UAE supported fleet units operating in the Persian Gulf. The harbor and air facilities of the logistics site at Fujayrah, UAE, speeded the flow of supplies to ships involved in both Persian Gulf and North Arabian Sea operations. The air head of Masirah in Oman served the amphibious task force during Desert Shield.[169]

Admiral Sutton's job also included ensuring the air delivery to naval forces in the theater of new or replacement personnel, mail, critical repair parts, and other special cargo. The Military Airlift Command transported passengers and cargo from the Cubi Point Naval Air Station in the Philippines to Fujayrah. MAC flights originating at the Atlantic Fleet base in Norfolk delivered sailors and materiel to the logistics site at Bahrain International Airport.[170]

Another of Sutton's responsibilities was to coordinate medical support for Navy and Marine forces. After the start of Desert Shield, he ensured that the naval establishment did its part to meet the goal of 7,350 beds in the theater set by Central Command's chief surgeon.

The Navy's long planning and preparation to provide medical support in an overseas emergency paid off. Afloat prepositioning ship MV *Noble Star* steamed from her readiness station at Diego Garcia on 9 August and 12 days later arrived in the gulf with equipment and supplies stowed in 431 containers for Fleet Hospital 5. Simultaneously, MAC airlift transports enplaned the unit's Naval Reserve medical and support personnel in Norfolk, Virginia, and delivered them to the airport in al-Jubayl.

At General Boomer's insistence, the Navy established the hospital at al-Jubayl near his marines rather than Dhahran as originally planned. The site change caused some disruption during the installation process because the hospital lacked essential fleet support of personnel and supplies.[171]

Nevertheless, by the end of the month the medical staff and two Seabee units had transformed the shipping containers into the forward-deployed Fleet Hospital 5, complete with operating rooms, intensive care units, and radiological facilities.[172]

Hospital ships *Comfort* and *Mercy* embarked their crews, medical staffs, and supplies and departed ports in the United States five days after being alerted for duty. Entering service in the mid-1980s, these hospital ships carried modern equipment and reflected the operational experience of their Vietnam War predecessors, *Repose* (AH 16) and

The 1,000-bed hospital ship USNS *Comfort* (T-AH 20) carries out a connected replenishment operation with Australian logistic support ship HMAS *Success*.

Sanctuary (AH 17). Each of the new hospital ships boasted 12 operating rooms, 4 x-ray rooms, 500 acute care beds, and 500 minimal care beds. Of greater importance, a crew of about 70 civilian merchant mariners and 1,190 well-trained and dedicated health care professionals of the Navy's Medical, Medical Service, Dental, and Nurse corps were embarked in *Mercy* and *Comfort*. Most were naval reservists recalled to duty. The two ships arrived in the Persian Gulf in mid-September.[173]

Complementing these medical facilities, every ship in the fleet included a medical department, and each of the amphibious assault ships of the Amphibious Task Force had a 300-bed hospital ward. Fleet tenders, such as *Acadia* (AD 42) carried medical and dental facilities including pharmacies, laboratories, operating rooms, and a full range of x-ray and other diagnostic equipment. Daily health care service to the fleet prepared the Navy medical and dental staffs to handle a surge of battle casualties.

Ashore, Navy medical corpsmen served with every Marine unit and other naval personnel staffed aid stations and medical battalions. Medical personnel from the San Diego Naval Hospital's Surgical Team 1 and the Portsmouth Naval Hospital's Surgical Team 2 employed their skills at a 350-bed hospital run by the government of Bahrain. The Navy

Dental Corps used a specially modified, extended-bed, five-ton truck dubbed "Drills on Wheels" to bring dental care to marines at the front. Field hospitals established by the other services, host-country hospitals, and the approximately 25,000-bed fixed military facilities in Germany and the United States backed up these Navy medical services.

Conscious of the fact that in the Korean and Vietnam Wars disease and non-battle injury caused more military casualties than combat, early in Desert Shield the Navy deployed to Saudi Arabia a preventive medicine team, made up of personnel from the Navy Medical Research Institute. A number of these professionals had been stationed in Cairo, Egypt, where they had studied first-hand the negative impact on military effectiveness of such desert-related problems as heat stroke, diarrhea, skin rashes, respiratory ailments, irritated eyes, fevers, and psychological disorders. The team set up a system to keep close watch over the water, food, and sewage handling systems of Marine and Navy units ashore and to identify any outbreaks of infectious diseases. A team also stood guard against biological agents, which U.S. intelligence knew Iraq had developed.

Early in the deployment, U.S. medical personnel faced an outbreak of diarrhea that affected 40 percent of the people deployed ashore. "There is no question [that the epidemic] lowered our combat readiness," noted one medical officer. "If war had been forced on us in early September, we would have had a significant number of troops with diarrhea, which makes it difficult to drive a tank, fly a plane and be in the infantry."[174] The medical teams identified strains of diarrhea-inducing bacteria peculiar to the region that were resistant to the usual antibiotics but not to ciprofloxicin. The medical commands rushed the drug to the troops and prevented an outbreak of the disease. In fact, by December, such measures reduced the rate of disease and non-battle injuries below that of the Korean and Vietnam conflicts and below the rate predicted by epidemiologists for the gulf crisis.[175]

As they had in every war since 1942, Navy Seabees deployed ashore with the Marines. Airlifted into the theater early in Desert Shield from their stations around the globe were Naval Mobile Construction Battalions (NMCBs) 4, 5, 7, and 40 and Construction Battalion Units 411 and 415. These Seabee units served under Captain Michael Johnson (CEC), Commander 3d Naval Construction Regiment, who soon became a valued member of General Boomer's staff.

The Seabees quickly got to work widening taxi-ways and aircraft parking areas, building ammunition storage sites, and improving habitability for the marines awaiting Saddam's forces in the desert northwest of al-Jubayl. The naval construction men and women also built tank barriers and fighting bunkers, paved roadways, unloaded MPS ships, built portside storage facilities, erected tent cities, drilled wells for water, and installed electrical systems.

This new generation of Seabees used innovative construction techniques and equipment to erect buildings as much as 80 percent faster than by conventional means. Automatic building machines produced "K-span" arches, while fabric membranes stretched over steel frames formed "sprung instant" and "clamshell" structures that were then emplaced atop concrete slabs. Within weeks, Seabee-built hut and tent cities covered the landscape around al-Jubayl.

The two construction battalion units, headed by Lieutenants Susan Globokar (CBU 411) and Lynn Bever (CBU 415), were instrumental in the swift installation of Fleet Hospital 5 at al-Jubayl. In remembrance of Steelworker Second Class Robert Dean Stethem, a Seabee murdered by Lebanese Shiite (Hezbollah) terrorists in Beirut in 1985, NMCB 5 named the cantonment they built near al-Jubayl airport Camp Stethem.[176]

Responsibility for the logistic support of General Boomer's I MEF fell to the Marine 1st Force Service Support Group (FSSG). This command moved supplies from the ports forward to the troops. One of the most critical items handled by 1st FSSG was ammunition, which had to

USN DN-ST 91-07188

Lieutenant Susan Globokar (CEC) was charged with overseeing the work of 80 Seabees constructing Fleet Hospital 5 during the early days of Desert Shield.

USN

Fleet Hospital 5 at al-Jubayl.

be offloaded from the MSC ships, transported from the port, and stored in open-air ammunition supply points as close to Marine front lines as was safe. Since a 30-day supply of ammunition for a Marine division totaled 265,000 tons, this was a difficult task.[177]

Providing adequate supplies of water to the troops in the desert proved even more demanding. The units that reached Saudi Arabia in August and September experienced daily temperatures as high as 120 degrees Fahrenheit. A marine required many gallons each day for drinking, cooking, washing, and hygiene. Local water sources, bottled water, and reverse osmosis water purification units that made seawater potable satisfied most of the water needs of I MEF.[178]

Marine Corps doctrine stated that a MEF would deploy with 60 days' supplies. Joint doctrine and service agreements specified that the Army and Air Force would support the Marines thereafter. However, Schwarzkopf's "shooters-first" decision delayed the deployment of Army and Air Force logistics units, with the result that the Marines had to sup-

port themselves longer than they had anticipated. Nonetheless, gener-
ous host nation support compensated for most shortages.[179]

Shield in Place

During Phase I of Operation Desert Shield, the United States deployed 60 naval vessels, more than 1,000 ground-based aircraft, and
some 240,000 men and women to the Middle East. By the end of
October the 12 ships of the *Midway* carrier battle group had joined the
warships already on station in the region. Among the troops deployed
were nearly 42,000 marines—close to one-quarter of the corps' total active duty strength and a fifth of the total U.S. force in the theater. The
31,000-marine I MEF stood ready in Saudi Arabia to defeat an Iraqi invasion. The 13,000 marines of the 4th MEB and the 13th MEU(SOC)
awaited orders offshore in the ships of the amphibious task force. The
Air Force had dispatched over 31,000 people, many from Air Force
Reserve and Air National Guard units, and about 700 fighters, bombers,
tankers, transports, and other aircraft to the CENTCOM area of responsibility. Also ashore in the theater were the Army's 82d Airborne
Division, 24th Mechanized Infantry Division, 101st Airborne (Air
Assault) Division, 1st Cavalry Division, 3d Armored Cavalry Regiment,
and other elements totaling more than 115,000 soldiers. These units
were equipped with 700 tanks, 1,000 armored personnel carriers, 145
AH-64 Apache helicopters, and 294 155mm self-propelled howitzers.[180]

At the start of Desert Shield, Generals Powell and Schwarzkopf informed President Bush that they would not finish deployment of sufficient forces to hold Saudi Arabia against a major Iraqi assault until early
December. But, on 1 November, Powell reported to the President that
"Schwarzkopf had advised us that he believed he had the combat capability in place, in the region, to successfully defend against any Iraqi
attack."[181] Despite problems, the U.S. armed forces had quickly and efficiently built a formidable shield in the water and sky surrounding the
Persian Gulf states and ashore in the Saudi Arabian desert.

CHAPTER 3

The Gathering Storm

THROUGHOUT THE FALL OF 1990, a torrent of allied troops, vehicles, aircraft, ammunition, and supplies flooded the deserts of Saudi Arabia and the other GCC countries. Meanwhile, coalition leaders grappled with various measures to induce or compel Saddam Hussein to relinquish his hold on Kuwait. Given the Iraqi dictator's record of intransigence, the Bush administration concluded that the coalition would ultimately have to use military force to eject his army of occupation from the emirate.

Over to the Attack

Almost immediately after Iraqi forces invaded Kuwait, U.S. military leaders began to think of counterstrokes. Meeting with the President at Camp David on 4 August, General Schwarzkopf suggested that an offensive campaign might be necessary, although he believed that it might take as much as a year to deploy and prepare sufficient ground, air, and naval forces.[1] At the same time, General Horner and his CENTAF staff at MacDill Air Force Base were considering the feasibility of air strikes against targets in Iraq if Saddam employed chemical weapons against allied forces. But in these early days of the crisis, as Air Force tactical squadrons and Navy aircraft carrier wings converged on the theater, military planners concerned themselves much less with retaliatory strikes than with using air power to defeat Iraqi forces should they invade Saudi Arabia.

Generals Schwarzkopf and Powell did foresee the need for a comprehensive plan encompassing offensive air operations. Since Schwarzkopf did not want to distract his own staff from their round-the-clock efforts to deploy forces to the gulf, however, on 8 August he asked the Air Force staff in Washington to help out.[2]

111

The Air Force assigned the task to a group in the lower regions of the Pentagon already planning offensive operations. Colonel John A. Warden III, the Air Staff's Deputy Director for Warfighting, and five other Air Force officers of the so-called "Checkmate" group had begun working on an air campaign plan shortly after the invasion of Kuwait.[3] An intellectual descendant of Italian General Giulio Douhet, American Colonel Billy Mitchell, and other theorists, Warden believed that air power by itself could reverse Saddam's aggression and restore Kuwait to its people.[4]

On 10 August, Warden and his group flew to Tampa and briefed General Schwarzkopf on the group's operational concept, which they dubbed "Instant Thunder." General Powell received the same briefing the next day. The resemblance of the Instant Thunder label to the Rolling Thunder Campaign of the Vietnam War was no accident. Air Force planners, many of whom had witnessed first-hand the failure of the "graduated response" approach to air warfare in Southeast Asia, anticipated instead an all-out, one-week operation to hit 84 critical targets in Iraq and Kuwait.[5]

Although Schwarzkopf liked the concept, he later admitted being "leery" of Warden, whom he characterized in his autobiography as a member of the "Curtis LeMay school of Air Force planners—guys who think strategic bombing can do it all and that armies [and navies] are obsolete."[6]

At this point, Schwarzkopf still saw Instant Thunder as a "retaliation plan" for dealing with some "crazy" act by Saddam like using chemical weapons against Israel.[7] In contrast, General Powell felt that something more than the one-week retaliatory campaign might be needed to chasten the Iraqi leader. "I don't want them to go home," said the Chairman. "I want to leave smoking tanks as kilometer fence posts all the way [back from Kuwait] to Baghdad."[8] Powell also felt that planning air operations called for a broader, multiservice approach. Hence, he requested that Army, Navy, and Marine Corps planners join the Checkmate group. The plan soon included the use of Navy Tomahawk land attack missiles and Navy and Marine Corps aircraft and identified Iraqi naval ports as a "target set." Powell also put this campaign planning function under the Joint Staff. Despite these changes, the Air Force Checkmate group still dominated the process.[9]

But General Horner, whom Schwarzkopf would charge with directing the aerial blitz against Iraq, strongly disliked the concept when Warden briefed him in Riyadh. The general considered the plan "seriously flawed in its operational aspects and disapproved of its relative neglect of the Iraqi forces in Kuwait."[10] He reportedly kept asking, "what about the Iraqi army?" which was answered with, "don't worry about it, they'll surrender." Horner later observed that he "did not believe that assurance because of my reading of history" and he "certainly knew that Schwarzkopf would not buy it."[11]

Consequently, Horner established his own planning group under Air Force Brigadier General Buster C. Glosson, who "soon became the engine that drove the Desert Storm air campaign."[12] Glosson, who had been serving as the Deputy Commander Joint Task Force Middle East and had been stationed on board flagship *LaSalle* when Saddam's forces stormed Kuwait, was familiar with the strategic picture. Glosson's staff was officially called the Special Planning Group but soon became known as "The Black Hole" for the isolated and closely guarded spaces they occupied in the Royal Saudi Air Force headquarters building in Riyadh. His group eventually totaled 30 U.S. Air Force, Navy, Marine Corps, Army, British Royal Air Force, and Royal Saudi Air Force planners. General Horner, who served as CENTCOM Forward until Schwarzkopf deployed to the theater and then was "dual-hatted" as Commander Central Command Air Forces and Joint Force Air Component Commander, closely monitored the work of the special planning group as did Schwarzkopf.[13]

In terms of strategic targets and objectives, Glosson's eventual plan differed little from Warden's. But because of Powell and Schwarzkopf's views, the Instant Thunder concept became the first phase of a larger, four-phase air, sea, and land campaign plan codenamed "Desert Storm."[14]

On 25 August, Schwarzkopf flew to Washington and presented the Desert Storm plan to Secretary Cheney and General Powell. Phase I embodied a strategic air offensive against Iraq and isolation of the Kuwait Theater of Operations (KTO) (all of Kuwait and Iraq south of 31 degrees, north latitude, which encompassed Kuwait and southeastern Iraq). Strategic targets included the command-control-communications network that Saddam needed to direct his forces; nuclear, biological, and chemical storage facilities; the electrical power system; oil refineries; railroads, bridges, and ports; air defense radars, fixed surface-to-air and surface-to-surface missile sites, and airfields; operational air and naval forces; and the Iraqi army.

Phase II entailed the establishment of air supremacy against Iraqi air forces in the KTO; Phase III involved the destruction of Iraqi ground forces in Kuwait, particularly the Republican Guard armored and mechanized divisions; and Phase IV called for a ground offensive into Kuwait to eject Saddam's army from the country. The objective of the entire campaign was to paralyze Iraq's leadership, degrade the military capabilities of its armed forces, and neutralize its soldiers' will to fight.[15]

General Horner approved the operation order for the Phase I strategic air offensive in early September. Shortly thereafter, coalition air forces in the theater became strong enough to carry it out. A number of U.S. leaders, including General Michael A. Dugan, the Air Force Chief of Staff, believed that air power alone could drive the Iraqi invaders from Kuwait, without resort to a costly ground campaign.[16] Secretary Cheney relieved Dugan for airing his strategic views to the press, but other Air Force officers shared his belief.[17]

Other American and coalition leaders, however, knew that the results promised by air power advocates in World War II, Korea, and Vietnam had never materialized. Generals Powell and Schwarzkopf and former Chairman of the JCS, Admiral William Crowe, Vietnam veterans all, understood the dangers of overestimating American military power and underestimating that of even a "Third World" country.[19]

When briefed on the budding air campaign plan, Marine and Navy commanders argued that coalition aircraft attacking the Iraqi capital before Saddam's air defenses had been neutralized would take heavy losses and achieve limited results. Major General Royal N. Moore Jr., commander of General Boomer's air wing, and Admiral Mauz pressed for an alternative, "rollback" approach in which allied air power would systematically unhinge the enemy's forward defenses before tackling fortress Baghdad. They failed, however, to persuade the air planners to change the approach.[19]

Mauz and Horner also disagreed on command and control of air power. In his first meeting with the general, Mauz suggested dividing the airspace above the theater into separate sectors to be patrolled independently by Navy and Air Force aircraft. "We were faced with the problem of using air power from disparate locations to deal with an Iraqi attack south," Mauz later recalled.

> These units had never even met each other, much less trained together. In these circumstances I thought it wise to keep things as simple as possible. Having different aircraft over the same target area at the same time without having trained together or coordinated C3, etc., was *not* a simple way to do it. I suggested to Horner that, at least in those early days, assigning Navy and Air Force tacair [tactical air forces] to certain geographical areas could minimize confusion. Later on we could get more sophisticated and mix strike and support aircraft from the two services if it made sense.[20]

The admiral's suggestion—akin to the establishment of Vietnam-era "route packages"—immediately raised Horner's ire. According to Mauz, the general shouted "Fuck that! Don't ever talk to me about it again, because we're not going to do it! I'll resign first." Although Mauz later noted that he and Horner "got along OK," this confrontation cre-

Lieutenant General Charles A. Horner, USAF, Commander U.S. Air Forces, Central Command/Joint Force Air Component Commander.

ated a gulf between the two commanders that they were never quite able to bridge.[21] As one pundit put it, Horner and Mauz "utterly failed to connect," and route packages were not established.[22]

Whatever the approach to air operations by his subordinates, Schwarzkopf saw no viable alternative to a complementary ground offensive. Official military estimates of casualties from ground combat ran as high as 20,000, including 7,000 dead,[23] and he had little confidence that an independent air campaign or the UN embargo of Iraq would induce Saddam to withdraw his army from Kuwait, certainly not in the near term.[24]

CENTCOM planners made one significant alteration to the overall campaign plan by placing greater emphasis on neutralizing the Republican Guard, Iraq's elite military formation and the military muscle Saddam employed to rule. Schwarzkopf saw the guard as not only the greatest threat to his ground forces but the "heart and soul" of Saddam's regime. The general wanted the guard destroyed.[25]

Schwarzkopf intended to soften up the Republican Guard and the enemy army in Kuwait with air power, then launch the cross-border offensive to deliver the knockout blow. A ground assault into Kuwait had been under consideration soon after the Iraqi occupation. Admiral Sharp, Schwarzkopf's staff planning chief, related that when the general arrived in Saudi Arabia in August, he carried with him the only existing copy of an offensive plan. Instructed by CINCCENT to refine it, Sharp responded that he was too fully committed to preparation of the defensive plan. The admiral suggested instead assigning the task to a group of "top-notch" planners.[26] Hence, Schwarzkopf set up another secret planning cell in Riyadh, this one made up of four field grade Army officers hand-picked from the staff of the School for Advanced Military Studies at Fort Leavenworth, Kansas. Led by Lieutenant Colonel Joseph H. Purvis, these officers called themselves the "Jedi Knights." Schwarzkopf charged this group with evaluating CENTCOM's attack options based on the forces available upon completion of the deployment of allied forces by airlift and sealift.[27]

On 25 September, Colonel Purvis' planning cell laid out an estimate of ground attack options for Admiral Sharp and then on 6 October for Schwarzkopf. An offensive with the single available corps-sized contingent was risky. The armor-weak force would have to make a frontal assault into the teeth of Iraqi fortifications on the Saudi-Kuwait border. Purvis and other Army leaders feared that a one-corps attack would produce heavy friendly casualties, especially if the enemy used chemical weapons as everybody expected. Worse, it might bog down short of the objective, raising the specter of a protracted war in the desert. The lack of sufficient combat forces or logistic support resources seemed to rule out flanking or other alternative maneuvers.[28] Schwarzkopf asked Purvis, "What would you need to really do this and guarantee a win?" CENTCOM planners had also considered a two-corps assault, in which an armored corps would swing west around the Iraqi right flank while an infantry-heavy corps pushed straight north. The colonel replied, "You need another corps." Having already reached the same conclusion, the general added, "I agree."[29]

On 11 October, Major General Robert B. Johnston, USMC, the CENTCOM Chief of Staff, speaking for General Schwarzkopf, briefed the President, Cheney, Powell, and other top officials on the one-corps offensive plan to liberate Kuwait. The risks immediately became obvious to most of the participants at the Washington meeting. But Deputy National Security Advisor Robert Gates, who believed that CINCCENT already had all the necessary forces, equated Schwarzkopf with Civil War General George B. McClellan for his lack of aggressiveness. Apparently, Gates' criticism only annoyed Schwarzkopf, for if there was one thing that he and other officers who had served in Vietnam had learned from that experience, it was the importance of attacking an opponent with overwhelming force, not merely with what might be considered sufficient force.[30]

President Bush and Secretary Cheney agreed with Schwarzkopf's sobering assessment of the one-corps attack. The next day they ordered preparation of alternative plans for a ground advance into Kuwait and dispatched General Powell to Riyadh to determine what CINCCENT needed to carry it out. At that point the President stood ready to give Schwarzkopf whatever forces he needed to do the job.[31]

In addition to one- and two-corps options, CINCCENT and his staff considered a Navy-Marine amphibious landing in Kuwait or southern Iraq in support of the main ground thrust. Purvis' group studied several amphibious scenarios, including an assault by the 4th Marine

Expeditionary Brigade across marshy Bubiyan Island and onto the mainland near the Kuwait-Iraq border. After running several manual and computer-assisted simulations, the planners found that attacking Bubiyan would present serious problems. The enemy's offshore and coastal defenses were expected to be lethal; it would take too long to re-inforce and strengthen the beachhead; the Marine force ashore would lack a strong armored contingent; and Republican Guard armored and mechanized divisions deployed just north of the Iraq-Kuwait border would be able to reach the landing site in only a few hours. Taken to-gether, these problems forcasted heavy Marine casualties and a possible debacle. Consequently, as Colonel Purvis put it, "our assessment from early on was that an [amphibious landing] was not feasible in support of the main attack."[32] During the 11 October meeting at the White House, according to Purvis, "some of the civilian members present did ask about an Inchon-like amphibious option, which the military leaders were quick to oppose."[33]

For Admiral Mauz, the geographical aspects of Kuwait and its ad-jacent waters ruled out a large scale assault. "I supported the idea in principle," Mauz recalled, not only because it would conform to the principles of maneuver warfare and because he saw the war as a "defin-ing point in carving out roles and missions among the Services for the post-Cold War era." He added: "The Air Force and Army had seen their primary Central Region [of Europe] focus melt away and were after the expeditionary missions of the Navy and Marine Corps. The trouble was, there was no good place to do a landing."

Mauz considered a landing on the al-Faw Peninsula to fix enemy troops in the area, but dismissed the idea when he considered the diffi-culties of landing troops, supplying them, and enabling them to break out of the beachhead. The proximity of the operating area to Iran was another problem. He also contemplated a landing near Ras al-Qulayah if Saddam struck toward the Saudi oilfields. To the admiral, however, the most important role of the amphibious forces was to serve as a strategic reserve, and to "pose a threat in Saddam's mind and cause resources to be diverted from other areas."[34]

Rear Admiral John LaPlante and Major General Harry Jenkins, leaders of the Navy–Marine Corps amphibious team, concluded that there were too many drawbacks to a major landing in Kuwait or south-eastern Iraq. Since a channel would have to be dredged to enable his forces to land on Bubiyan or on the mainland near Umm Qasr, LaPlante "didn't take any of that crap seriously; it was a non-starter." Amphibious forces could deploy ashore north and south of Kuwait City, but, accord-ing to the admiral, poor hydrographic conditions and beach gradients there and in the Bay of Kuwait would make it especially difficult for the follow-on "sustainment forces."[35]

The changing balance of forces also worked against the Americans. During the fall of 1990, as Saddam prepared his army to repel a coalition assault, the Iraqi forces and defenses in Kuwait got stronger and stronger while the strength of the U.S. amphibious contingent remained constant. LaPlante and Jenkins controlled only the 4th MEB, with its weak force of 17 M-60 tanks. The amphibious commanders were concerned that if they had had to launch an amphibious landing in December or January, before they were reinforced with the 5th MEB and the 13th MEU(SOC), "we would get our ass kicked."[36]

Lieutenant General Bernard E. Trainor, USMC (Retired), a former Marine Deputy Chief of Staff for Operations and an informed commentator on national security affairs, concluded that Schwarzkopf ruled out an amphibious assault because there was no powerful or persuasive advocate in the theater to lobby for a landing.[37] General Boomer, the I MEF commander, focused his attention on the future operations of his Marine units ashore and did not command NAVCENT's afloat amphibious force in any case. Unlike the Air Force and the Army, the Marine Corps did not set up planning cells to analyze amphibious options until months after the Iraqi invasion. Finally, Trainor observed that Admiral Mauz "discouraged any thought of an amphibious attack."[38] Another source reported that COMUSNAVCENT "was unwilling to run a high risk if the landing was not vital to the ground campaign. Indeed, having a single ship hit a mine was deemed unacceptable if the landing was not vital."[39]

General Schwarzkopf loathed the risk of heavy casualties that, even in the best of circumstances, an amphibious landing could incur. Thus, after the end of this initial phase of the planning process, there is no indication the general seriously considered an amphibious landing on Kuwaiti or Iraqi shores. He did, however, incorporate the Navy–Marine Corps amphibious force into his campaign plan. Schwarzkopf also denied Mauz's insistent and repeated requests to halve the number of amphibious ships in the theater. Shortly after the war, CINCCENT related to General Powell and his fellow commanders in chief that "high priority was placed on deception from the outset of the crisis" in that "we worked very hard to convince the Iraqis that coalition forces would attack directly into Kuwait supported by amphibious operations." He added that this strategic deception succeeded because he enforced a "strict need to know within the CENTCOM staff, the components, and the JCS" and that this "compartmentalized approach to campaign planning helped ensure our efforts were not compromised."[40]

Having dispensed with the one-corps and amphibious options, CENTCOM planners concentrated on the two-corps attack. Ideally, the second corps would swing around the Iraqi right flank through the desert of southern Iraq, but terrain analysts worried that the area might be impassable for tracked vehicles. Operating in great secrecy lest they compromise the budding offensive concept, CENTCOM staff officers and a few Saudi officers reevaluated the available intelligence, questioned Bedouins and oil company employees, and drove vehicles in the desert west of the Saudi-Kuwait border. They found the area to be hard and flat, like a tabletop. On 18 October, Purvis' group affirmed for Admiral Sharp that with additional combat units and logistic resources, the coalition could mount a grand offensive through the desert to envelop and cut off the Iraqi army in Kuwait. Then, air strikes and artillery fire could destroy the trapped army with minimum allied losses.[41]

On 22 October, General Schwarzkopf presented the new two-corps option to General Powell when the JCS Chairman arrived in Riyadh. In the ensuing discussion this option clearly emerged as the optimum approach, for it would enable the coalition to make its main thrust against weaker enemy forces and less sophisticated defenses in southern Iraq, west of Kuwait. Schwarzkopf believed that a powerful armored fist would be the best weapon for punching through the enemy line. Upon departing Saudi Arabia, Powell told Schwarzkopf that he would enlist support

Courtesy of CDR Greg Slavonic, USNR

In October 1990, General Schwarzkopf (left) recommended that heavy U.S. armored forces be deployed to Saudi Arabia for the liberation of Kuwait. General Powell endorsed that proposal to the President.

from the President and the Secretary of Defense for the deployment to the theater of major reinforcements, especially the Army's VII Corps.

U.S. military leaders had good reasons to choose the VII Corps. Consisting of the 1st Armored Division, a brigade-size unit of the 2d Armored Division, 3d Armored Division (reassigned from the V Corps), and 2d Armored Cavalry Regiment, the VII Corps would provide exactly the kind of mailed fist that Schwarzkopf envisioned. Because it had trained in close proximity to potential enemy forces in Germany since the end of World War II, the corps had high combat readiness and familiarity with large-unit maneuvers. Furthermore, VII Corps operated the most advanced armored vehicles and aircraft in the world, including the M1A1 Abrams main battle tank, the Bradley armored fighting vehicle, and the Apache attack helicopter. Finally, the corps was closer to the Persian Gulf theater than comparable U.S.-based formations.[42]

President Bush readily endorsed the recommendations of his civilian and military advisors to substantially increase the forces at Schwarzkopf's disposal. On 31 October, he decided to deploy an additional 200,000 U.S. soldiers, sailors, marines, and airmen to the Persian Gulf region. The reinforcements included the Army's VII Corps and 1st Infantry Division; the Marine Corps' 2d Marine Division, 2d Force Service Support Group, 5th MEB, and squadrons from the 2d Marine Air Wing; 410 Air Force warplanes and support aircraft; and from the Navy, three more carrier battle groups and a battleship.[43] U.S. leaders expected to complete this additional deployment, designated Desert Shield, Phase II, by 15 January. A joint Egyptian-Syrian corps and a force made up of GCC units were slated to join U.S. forces in the Saudi desert.[44] Clearly, this was the overwhelming force that the Vietnam veterans leading the U.S. armed services deemed essential for a quick, decisive victory.

On 8 November, the President held a news conference to make public his intentions. "From the very beginning," said Bush,

> we and our coalition partners have shared common political goals: the immediate, complete, and unconditional withdrawal of Iraqi forces from Kuwait; restoration of Kuwait's legitimate government; protection of the lives of citizens held hostage by Iraq both in Kuwait and Iraq; and restoration of security and stability in the Persian Gulf region.
>
> After consultation with King Fahd and our other allies, I have today directed the Secretary of Defense to increase the size of U.S. forces committed to Desert Shield to ensure that the coalition has an adequate offensive military option should that be necessary to achieve our common goals.[45]

These words made it crystal clear that the United States would go to war in order to throw Iraqi armed forces out of Kuwait.

Naval Deployments to the Gulf

As the United States led the United Nations in applying diplomatic pressure on Saddam, the Navy bent to the task of doubling its forces in the theater. The President made this possible by increasing personnel strength. On 14 November and again on 1 December, the Secretary of Defense executed his orders to authorize the call-up of additional reserves. The authorization eventually totaled 365,000 men and women, with the Navy's portion amounting to 44,000. Many of those called up during Phase II consisted of National Guard, reserve combat support, and reserve combat service support personnel.[46]

The naval forces converging on the CENTCOM theater from mid-November to mid-January represented a sizable segment of the U.S. fleet. Carrier *Midway*, which had departed Yokosuka, Japan, on 2 October, relieved *Independence* in the North Arabian Sea on 1 November. Twelve days later, battleship *Missouri* (BB 63) departed Long Beach, California, and headed for the Persian Gulf on what was to be her last overseas deployment. On the first day of December, *Tarawa* (LHA 1), *Tripoli* (LPH 10), *New Orleans* (LPH 11), and 10 other amphibious ships and 3 MSC ships of Amphibious Group 3, with the troops, vehicles, and aircraft of the 5th Marine Expeditionary Brigade embarked, steamed from California ports. A week later, on the 8th, Pacific Fleet aircraft carrier *Ranger* (CV 61) and her escorts got underway from San Diego and cruiser *Horne* (CG 30) and frigate *Jarrett* departed Long Beach. Then, on 10 December, the bulk of the 2d Marine Division, 2d Marine Aircraft Wing, and 2d Force Service Support Group headed out to the gulf from Camp Lejeune, North Carolina, on board MAC aircraft and the ships of MPS Squadron 1. Ten days later the Navy Helicopter Combat Support Squadrons (HCSs) 4 and 5, operating HH-60H strike rescue helicopters and manned exclusively by naval reservists, were airlifted from naval air stations in California to Saudi Arabia. The units were responsible for combat search and rescue (CSAR), that is the rescue of survivors from downed aircraft or sunken ships. The units also transported SEALs on their missions at sea or on land.[47]

Three days after Christmas, Atlantic Fleet carriers *Theodore Roosevelt* (CVN 71) and *America* (CV 66) and the 15 cruisers, destroyers, frigates, oilers, and ammunition ships of their battle groups sortied from Norfolk and four other East Coast ports. The two battle groups passed through the Suez Canal in mid January. *America* took up battle stations in the Red Sea and *Roosevelt* steamed for a staging area in the North Arabian Sea.[48]

On 12 January 1991, Amphibious Squadron 5, with the 13th MEU(SOC) embarked, steamed back into the gulf after completing a deployment to the Philippines.[49] Amphibious Group 3, carrying the 5th MEB, completed its long ocean passage from southern California. The entire amphibious task force then consisted of 31 amphibious assault ships, 7 Military Sealift Command ships, and the assault elements of two Marine expeditionary brigades and a smaller Marine expeditionary unit.

Besides reinforcing its forces afloat, the Navy deployed additional naval special warfare units to Saudi Arabia. These forces, in conjunction with similar Army and Air Force units, served under the operational control of Special Operations Component, Central Command (SOCCENT), led by Colonel Jesse Johnson, USA, and they supported Schwarzkopf's Navy and Marine components as well. COMUSNAVCENT directed the separate naval special warfare forces based at sea. These forces worked with the fleet on embargo patrols, mine clearance, combat search and rescue, and in support of amphibious operations.

SOCCENT's 256-man Naval Special Warfare Task Group Central (Naval Special Warfare Group 1), led by Captain Ray Smith, consisted of six detachments (Table 3). From September to mid-January, SEALs and special boat unit personnel helped train 100 Kuwaiti marines and 124 Kuwaiti sailors, the latter from the patrol ships *Istiqlal* and *Sambouk*, and barge *Sawahil*. SEALs and Army Special Forces men worked together to train Saudi troops and sailors in such skills as small unit tactics, demolition, diving, and high-speed boat operations. Beginning in mid-October,

---

Table 3

**NAVY SPECIAL WARFARE FORCES IN DESERT SHIELD
AND DESERT STORM**

Naval Special Warfare Group 1

    SEAL Team 1 (two platoons)

    SEAL Team 5 (two platoons)

    Swimmer Delivery Vehicle Team 1 (one platoon)

    Special Boat Unit 12 (one High Speed Boat Detachment and one Rigid
        Inflatable Boat Detachment)

    Naval Special Warfare Development Group (one High Speed Boat
        Detachment)

    Mobile Communication Team

SOURCE: U.S., Department of Defense, *Conduct of the Persian Gulf War: Final Report to Congress* (Washington: Government Printing Office, 1992), 525.

SEAL platoons and Saudi naval forces carried out patrols of the Saudi Arabia–Kuwait border from a post north of the coastal town of Khafji. The SEALs carried out hydrographic surveys, beach reconnaissance, and deception operations, and trained their counterparts in calling in air and naval gunfire. Despite a language barrier, the SEALs and their Army and Air Force comrades greatly improved the integration of Arab forces into the coalition.[50]

Naval forces also helped defend vital Persian Gulf ports from potential Iraqi attack. At the peak of Phase II in January, the "bottleneck of personnel and equipment at the ports presented an incredibly rich target."[51] Coalition naval and air forces had already established a formidable first line of defense out in the gulf. In all likelihood, these forces would have destroyed most, if not all, Iraqi aircraft and naval vessels bent on attacking the ports. Furthermore, the Saudi, Bahraini, and UAE navies had deployed hundreds of patrol boats and small defense craft to coastal waters and ports. Nonetheless, ships in the harbors and port facilities remained vulnerable to explosives-laden small boats, swimmers, and saboteurs. Vice Admiral Stanley Arthur, who would replace Vice Admiral Mauz as COMUSNAVCENT on 1 December 1990, later observed that "we were unthwarted by any acts of terrorism, yet very vulnerable to even single determined acts."[52]

Consequently, in mid-November, MAC aircraft transported the New Hampshire reservists of Mobile Inshore Undersea Warfare Unit 202 from the Atlantic Fleet's Naval Inshore Undersea Warfare Group 2. At the end of the month Coast Guard Port Security Unit 302, staffed by reservists from Cleveland, Ohio, flew to the gulf. These units joined the port security harbor defense units already operating at Bahrain, al-Jubayl, and ad-Dammam. At each port a naval officer from the MIUWU community served as the joint port security harbor defense group commander and exercised operational control of the Navy MIUWUs, Coast Guard PSUs, and explosive ordnance disposal units assigned to him (Table 4).

At strategic locations on piers in each of the ports the MIUWUs parked vans housing radars, sonars, radios, and day and night-vision aids. Around the clock, the sailors in these units kept watch over ships in the harbor by monitoring electronic systems designed to sense any presence around and under these vessels. If a unit detected a suspicious contact, the MIUWU officer in charge directed the Coast Guard patrol boat force to investigate. The PSUs manned small boats powered by outboard motors and armed with a 50-caliber machine gun forward and an M-60 machine gun aft. The craft, equipped with a surface-search radar and communications gear, were manned by Coast Guard men and women and a

Table 4

PORT SECURITY AND HARBOR DEFENSE COMMAND

Bahrain:	Port Security and Harbor Defense Command/CTG 151.9
Bahrain:	PSHDGRU ONE/CTU 151.9.1 MIUWU 202, PSU 302, EODMU elements
al-Jubayl:	PSHDGRU TWO/CTU 151.9.2 MIUWU 103, MIUWU 112, PSU 301 EODMU 3, EODMU 5
ad-Dammam:	PSHDGRU THREE/CTU 151.9.3 MIUWU 105, MIUWU 108, PSU 303, EODMU 5, EODMU 9

SOURCE: Ltr, Sutton to Marolda, 12 Apr 1996, Authors' Files, OA.

Saudi or Bahraini representative. On occasion, SEALs and Special Boat Unit 12 sailors reinforced the harbor patrol effort.[53]

Like other reserve and regular units deployed to the gulf, the port security units discovered operational deficiencies. Inadequate training created problems, as did interaction with the Navy's harbor defense units and personality conflicts among some commanding officers. But greater difficulties arose from the lack of familiarity of many Coast Guard and Navy officers with the small boat tactics, harbor defense doctrine, and operational capabilities of the other service. "It's a good thing we didn't get off the plane and walk into the middle of a war," observed one Coast Guard officer.[54]

But these proved minor difficulties, and the services carried out their joint responsibility with increasing effectiveness. Coast Guard Commander Vince Lombardi, Executive Officer of PSU 302, noted that with the tempo of operations increasing and war approaching "our response time got faster and faster."[55] By the start of Desert Storm, the Navy–Coast Guard teams were well integrated, with the MIUWUs acting as the "eyes and ears of the operation" and the PSUs as "the teeth."[56]

To support the additional combatants and shore-based naval forces during Phase II of the buildup, the Navy increased its overseas logistics resources. With permission from the Egyptian government, the Navy established a forward logistics support site at Hurghada on the Red Sea. Living in hastily erected tent cantonments, sailors soon put inactive runways into operation for fixed-wing aircraft and helicopters.

The number of Combat Logistics Force ships on station in the theater almost tripled from 8 in mid-November to 22 on 17 January. The latter figure represented over 40 percent of all CLF ships in the Navy.

USN DN-ST 91-11225

Lieutenant Kelly Franke of Helicopter Combat Support Squadron 2 prepares to board her SH-3G Sea King helicopter, which operated from Bahrain.

MSC also provided 20 U.S. and foreign charter tankers, stores ships, ammunition ships, and fleet ocean tugs.[57]

Having requested and received more resources, NAVCENT took steps to improve the management of the logistics establishment. The command recognized that Admiral Sutton was already fully engaged with supplying the fleet and managing the Navy's construction, diving and salvage, explosive ordnance disposal, mine countermeasures, search and rescue, harbor defense, medical support, control of shipping, and sealift units based ashore or operating from theater ports. COMUSNAVCENT also understood that the Red Sea and Persian Gulf were distinct operational areas, each with several unique requirements. Hence, in December COMUSNAVCENT decentralized logistic support responsibilities. He directed his two battle force commanders to designate logistics coordinators in each carrier battle group, the Amphibious Task Force, and the Middle East Force. These coordinators scheduled the afloat replenishment of combatants.[58]

Once the command and control structure changed and additional resources arrived, the logistics situation improved. Eventually, Sutton managed a fleet of C-9 planes and SH-3 and CH-53 helicopters for intra-theater support of naval forces ashore and at sea. He also coordinated the scheduling of C-2 carrier on board delivery (COD) planes for the battle group commanders. The C-2s were normally based at the Fujayrah or Jiddah airheads and made available for intra-theater lift when not in support of the parent carrier. The C-2s and helicopters flew between air heads in the theater and the carriers and logistics "hub" ships of the fleet. From these vessels CH-46 Sea Knight helicopters delivered to the surface combatants new personnel, electronic parts, helicopter rotor blades, and of greatest importance to the sailors, letters and packages from home. At the Navy's request, MAC C-130 aircraft flying regular shuttle routes augmented intra-theater airlift.[59] Captain Joseph S. Mobley, Commanding Officer of *Saratoga* in the Red Sea, observed, with only slight exaggeration, that the "logistics have been better than they've ever been any place else in the world, I think. We were getting parts [from Norfolk] sometimes three days after [we requested them.]"[60]

The Navy's tenders and repair ships provided yeoman service in the theater. Destroyer tender *Acadia* set up shop at various times in Fujayrah, Dubai, Jebel Ali, and anchorages in the gulf. The destroyer tender's repair staff of 650 men and women issued thousands of spare parts, ran a ship's store the size of a state-side "mini-mall," and repaired most fleet vessels, from small patrol boats to large cruisers.[61] Repair ship *Jason* (AR 8) operated at Masirah Island in support of the amphibious task force. Atlantic Fleet tenders *Vulcan* (AR 5) and *Yellowstone* (AD 41) anchored near the Red Sea exit of the Suez Canal and later in the Saudi port of Jiddah. The men and women of *Yellowstone*'s skilled crew accomplished over 10,000 repair jobs for 30 U.S. and allied ships.[62]

The Pacific Fleet deployed a ship repair unit to Bahrain where its skilled personnel coordinated with U.S.-based naval commands and commercial firms to obtain technical assistance. The governments of Bahrain and the UAE made available the Arab Shipbuilding and Repair Yard and the Dubai Drydock Company to handle war damaged U.S. naval vessels.

The salvage forces on hand for Persian Gulf operations included Navy salvage ship *Beaufort* (ATS 2) and contracted oceangoing tugs SMIT *New York* and SMIT *Madura*. The Navy also dispatched six officers and one enlisted master diver from the office of the Supervisor of Salvage and from the Atlantic Fleet and Pacific Fleet salvage commands, all of whom served with the Ship Repair Unit, Bahrain Detachment (CTG 151.12). One of the officers' functions was to advise a diving detachment based at ad-Dammam and al-Jubayl of 47 soldiers, whom the Army posted to the gulf for harbor clearance duties.[63]

Even in peacetime the fleet's repair and salvage units had their hands full. On 30 October, tragedy struck when a main steam line in *Iwo*

Jima (LPH 2) broke away. Ten sailors died from the sudden release of super-hot steam. By the outbreak of hostilities, however, *Acadia*'s crew had the ship back on the line. The second day of 1991, the fleet oiler USNS *Andrew J. Higgins* (T-AO 190) grounded south of Masirah Island. The tug SMIT *New York* and the salvage ship MV *Courier* successfully freed the vessel and dispatched her to a repair yard.

Three days before the onset of Desert Storm, fleet salvers faced a major challenge when destroyer *Harry W. Hill* (DD 986) and oiler *Kansas City* (AOR 3) collided while engaged in an underway replenishment operation in the North Arabian Sea. *Kansas City* remained operational but *Harry W. Hill* sustained serious damage to one of her bulkheads and a sonar dome. Even though the warship had to depart the theater for repairs, divers from submarine tender *McKee* (AS 41) and *Cape Cod* (AD 43) completed underwater repairs that prevented further damage.[64]

The only significant problem that consistently hindered naval logistic operations in the theater was the lack of reliable U.S. communications. For instance, because of inadequate communications, Sutton's shore-based headquarters lost numerous chances to use aircraft of the other services or of allies to transport supplies from the logistics sites out to the fleet.

But in general, the Navy's logistic support of the fleet in the Central Command theater was a success story. The system provided repair parts so efficiently that naval aviation units routinely had 90 percent of their aircraft operational, an improvement over peacetime rates. This advance resulted largely from the establishment of direct satellite communication between the carriers and their parts support office in Philadelphia. For the amphibious force, even though the lack of state-of-the-art communications gear caused minor delays, repair parts generally reached the ships in a timely fashion.[65] And ships' material readiness remained consistent with pre-crisis rates.[66] In fact, Admiral LaPlante felt that his amphibious ships "came back in better material condition than when they went out."[67] Problems with mail delivery, however, seemed to defy solution. With letters normally taking 12 and sometimes 20 days to reach sailors, Admiral Arthur exclaimed after the war that "mail service has never been worse."[68]

Plain old hard work certainly accounted for much of this overall success, but luck also played a part. The ample time between Saddam's invasion of Kuwait and the start of Desert Storm enabled naval leaders to plan and execute an efficient logistics support program. Moreover, the proximity of modern ports and airfields on the Arabian Peninsula to the task force operating areas enhanced the Navy's ability to keep its combatants on line.[69]

The Americans could count on ample logistic support from U.S. logistic support ships and shore facilities as well as from other coalition navies. Throughout Desert Shield and Desert Storm, sharing of resources was the rule among coalition navies. For example, on 4 January HMAS *Success* refuelled American frigate *Nicholas* (FFG 47) and shortly afterward her helicopter transported an Australian sailor to *Comfort* for medical treatment.[425] Later in the month *Success* replenished HMS *Gloucester*, HNLMS *Jacob Van Hermsherk*, HMAS *Sydney*, HMAS *Brisbane*, and U.S. warships *Midway*, *Mobile Bay* (CG 53), *Marvin Shields* (FF 1066), and *Fife* (DD 991).[71]

The Royal Canadian Navy's contribution to the logistic support effort in the Persian Gulf stood out from the rest because of the actions of Commodore K. J. "Ken" Summers, Commander Canadian Joint Forces Middle East. He told Admiral March that while the Canadian destroyer *Athabaskan*, frigate *Terra Nova*, and replenishment tanker *Protecteur* lacked the weapons and defensive equipment to fight in the northern gulf with American, British, Australian, and Dutch forces, the task group was strong enough, with the protection of U.S. Aegis cruisers, to operate in the central gulf. Summers also argued that the Canadian navy's com-

ISC91-4118 CFPU, Courtesy of Canadian Directorate of History

Commodore Ken Summers, Commander Canadian Joint Forces Middle East, discusses operations with his Chief of Staff, Colonel Dave Bartram (left) and Commander Jean-Yves Forcier on 15 January 1991.

patible communications equipment, skilled staff officers, and experience convoying and escorting NATO forces and supplies to Europe made it uniquely qualified to manage an important task—the naval logistics effort in the gulf. What he did not tell March was that he wanted his three ships to operate together so they would bring special recognition to Canada's role in the war.

There was need for better coordination of underway replenishment in the gulf, because the staffs of Admirals March and Fogarty, feverishly preparing for combat operations, could not give adequate attention to the complex underway replenishment schedules. Consequently, in January Admiral March accepted Commodore Summers' offer that a Canadian naval officer serve as Coordinator of a Combat Logistics Force operating in the southern gulf.[72] Thereafter, Captain Duncan E. "Dusty" Miller, RCN, chosen because of his familiarity with U.S. and NATO operating procedures, was charged with coordinating the underway replenishment of more than 60 ships that included March's four carriers, flagships *Blue Ridge* and *LaSalle*, and hospital ships *Mercy* and *Comfort*. He made sure that merchant ships and coalition auxiliaries were protected and escorted through the Strait of Hormuz into the logistics staging area—nicknamed the "Pachyderm Palace" for the behemoths that frequented those waters—and on to the northern gulf or the ports on the southern littoral.[73]

U.S. naval logistics in the Persian Gulf region also entailed the support of U.S. and allied forces ashore by naval construction forces and medical units. By the end of December, Reserve Naval Mobile Construction Battalions (RNMCBs) 74 and 24 relieved NMCB 4 and NMCB 7 and joined NMCB 5 and NMCB 50 at their main camps in Bahrain and near the I MEF headquarters at al-Jubayl.[74] RNMCB 74 moved into the existing Seabee Camp Tom Orr in Bahrain and completed construction for the Navy's Administrative Support Unit, Bahrain. The unit also improved the tarmac at Shaikh Isa Air Base for Marine Air Group 11 and Bahrain Defense Force units. Seabee battalions 5 and 40 continued work begun soon after their introduction to the sands of Saudi Arabia in the early months of Desert Shield. NMCB 40 installed tank barriers, extended air strips, and established water supply points for Fleet Hospital 5 and British and Saudi forces near al-Jubayl. Both units moved mountains of earth to establish ammunition supply points and erected a 15,000-man base camp for newly arriving Marine forces.[75]

On 12 November, General Schwarzkopf asked his component commanders to enhance their medical resources to handle the casualties expected in a ground offensive. Schwarzkopf directed COMUSNAVCENT to increase the capacity of each hospital ship, *Mercy* and *Comfort*, from 500 to 1,000 beds. Furthermore, CINCCENT called for an additional

1,000 Navy beds ashore. To handle these requirements, the Navy called up 10,500 medical and non-medical reserve personnel, a figure representing 50 percent of the overall Naval Reserve callup. Many of these reservists filled billets at facilities in the United States vacated by personnel deployed to the gulf.[76]

The allies pitched in as well. By the start of Desert Storm, a medical task group of 40 Australian surgeons, anesthetists, nurses, and aides from the navy, army, and air force operated as an integral part of *Comfort's* medical staff. A Canadian medical team was embarked on *Mercy*. The Poles also dispatched a hospital ship to the gulf.[77]

In December men and women of the 500-bed Fleet Hospitals 6 and 15 completed two weeks of training at Fort Dix, New Jersey, in such subjects as the use of chemical-biological-radiological gear, medical management of chemical casualties, burn life support, and trauma care. The trainees also studied the lessons learned by Fleet Hospital 5, which had been in the operational theater at al-Jubayl since August 1990.

Where to establish the fleet hospitals proved a more difficult question. Admiral Sutton and the NAVCENT surgeon thought that the medical facilities could function most effectively in Bahrain, where they would be closely linked to the logistic support resources of the fleet. General Boomer, whose battle casualties these hospitals would handle, believed otherwise. "If the battle is in Kuwait," he said at a staff meeting, "a fleet hospital in Bahrain is too damn far."[78] The general wanted all three hospitals located near al-Jubayl, close to his troops. Ultimately, Admiral Arthur directed Fleet Hospital 6 to deploy from Japan and join Fleet Hospital 5 in the desert with the Marines north of al-Jubayl. Fleet Hospital 15 was airlifted from a storage site in Norway and set up at Awali, Bahrain.[79]

Like other commands, the medical establishment in the gulf lacked adequate communications equipment. Other concerns arose from too few people trained to handle helicopter operations and the lack of some supplies, including chemical protective and decontamination gear for personnel, patients, and facilities. In regard to the latter, it was difficult to protect a fleet hospital that covered about 28 acres of ground or a hospital ship with the square footage of a ten-story building. The fleet hospitals used sealants to keep airborne chemical agents from seeping through the canvas of their tents, but no one had an answer for sealing air conditioners, essential for patient care in a desert environment. The crew of *Comfort* rigged plastic PVC piping around the exterior of the ship as a chemical washdown system. Fortunately, the need for decontamination never arose because this system never worked properly.

Another problem developed from the shortage of helicopters to operate between medical facilities ashore and afloat. U.S. leaders solved the problem by assigning 12 Army UH-60 transportation helicopters and their crews to the Navy's medical establishment, a good example of interservice cooperation that characterized most gulf operations. The Navy was lucky that Desert Shield lasted as long as it did, because several such problems were not worked out until the eve of war.

Nonetheless, by the start of coalition ground operations in February, both ships, the three fleet hospitals, and the other facilities were fully staffed. At that point the Navy operated 3,500 of the 18,530 hospital beds in the theater. During the entire Persian Gulf deployment, the Navy's medical establishment managed 6,613 inpatient admissions and 53,433 outpatient visits. Fleet Hospital 5 handled the heaviest load with 4,347 inpatients and 28,942 outpatients.[80]

Deployment of the VII Corps and the Phase II Buildup

While the Navy completed its medical preparation, the U.S. Army's VII Corps moved from the mountains and forests of Germany to the deserts of Saudi Arabia. This enormous enterprise succeeded because of the cooperation among Navy, Army, and Air Force personnel at all levels, and also because of their common sense, ability to improvise, and hard work. And once again, America's NATO allies provided critical assistance.

The management of this major deployment benefited from 24 years of experience with the "Reforger" exercises, which entailed U.S. reinforcement by sea and air of NATO forces on the frontier with the Warsaw Pact. Vice Admiral Leighton W. Smith Jr., Director of Operations on the European Command staff in 1990, later observed that because of Reforger, "we knew what the [port] storage capacity was like, and we knew what the routes to get into those ports were like and how much of a problem we were going to have moving those forces into those port areas. We also knew how to . . . call on the relationships that had been previously developed in working the trains, the roads system, the barge system throughout those northern countries."[81] The Military Airlift Command, which managed the massive air lift in Phase II, also used the network of sophisticated air facilities developed in Europe for the NATO mission.[82]

Operating from European air facilities and other staging bases around the globe, MAC delivered 99 percent of American military personnel and 6 percent of the petroleum products and dry cargo moved into the operational theater in Phase II. In a single day at the peak of the Desert Shield deployment, 124 MAC-controlled transport planes landed in Saudi Arabia. Passenger planes contributed by 34 U.S. airline companies to the Civil Reserve Air Fleet; aircraft provided by South Korea, Japan, Kuwait, Italy, and even tiny Luxembourg; and U.S. Navy transport aircraft moved over 500,000 coalition troops and 544,000 short tons of dry cargo into the theater during Desert Shield and Desert Storm.[83]

The Navy planes came from U.S. Naval Reserve units. The day after Christmas, the Navy activated four transport squadrons (VRs) in California, Texas, and Florida. Five days later the units took station in Sembach and Bitburg in Germany and Sigonella in Sicily. Of the 700 missions flown by the four squadrons, 209 supported the Transportation Command's global airlift. Each squadron of 12 C-9 cargo aircraft transported passengers to Turkey, bombs and fuses for B-52 bomber operations to Moron, Spain, and supplies and personnel to Hurghada, Egypt, and Jiddah, Saudi Arabia. During their three months of operation, the C-9s moved some 18,000 passengers and almost 4,000 tons of dry cargo.[84]

As important as the airlift was, however, sealift remained absolutely vital to allied success in this phase. In Phase I, much of the equipment, vehicles, and weapons of the relatively lightly armed airborne and special warfare forces had been airlifted into the combat zone. But only ships could transport all the heavy tanks and armored fighting vehicles of the Army's VII Corps in a reasonable amount of time.

Alerted in October to the possibility that the VII Corps would be sent to Saudi Arabia, Admiral Donovan and the staff of Military Sealift Command immediately began preparations for a second phase of the buildup. As a result of this advance planning, during Phase II MSC controlled 7 fast sealift ships, 4 maritime prepositioning ships, 6 afloat prepositioning ships, 39 Ready Reserve Force ships, and 45 merchant charter ships. Its tanker fleet more than doubled.[85]

The Military Sealift Command began to execute a massive movement of armored fighting vehicles, equipment, and supplies in early December following Phase I. Scores of ships braved the heavy winter weather and rough waters of the North Atlantic to reach European ports. In 128 of 178 instances, ships arrived in port before cargo was ready for loading.

Nonetheless, problems similar to those that afflicted the Phase I sealift exacerbated the transportation of VII Corps from Europe. "Movement priorities and ship capabilities seldom seemed to mesh," observed an Army logistics plans officer.[86] As before, delays resulted from difficulties in activating Ready Reserve Force ships and from the disparity in the age, cargo capacity, and speed of the various types of MSC ships. Of the 26 RRF ships called up for service during Phase II, only 3 reported on time, 6 took at least five days to get ready for operation, and the remaining 17 took more than five days to gear up.[87]

Planners had to improvise the movement of the VII Corps to a much greater degree than Phase I deployments. The U.S. military establishment had contingency plans for putting a corps into Europe, but not for getting one out. The result, as one Army officer put it, was that "management of strategic sealift remained a daily exercise in crisis management."[88] The Army's units, equipment, and ammunition stocks were dispersed throughout Germany. Transportation planners initially intended to move the VII Corps' 40,000 pieces of equipment and 24,000 tons of ammunition by train to Bremerhaven, Rotterdam, Antwerp, and other ports of embarkation. They soon discovered, however, that the move would require not only rail resources but all the trucks and barges they could obtain.[89]

To move the VII Corps from European to Saudi ports, Army and joint transportation planners estimated first that 55 ships would be needed, then 62 ships, and finally 120. It actually took 111 vessels.[90] As a rule, when a ship arrived in port, cargo handlers loaded it with whatever was ready to go. As a result, some Army equipment and ammunition got dispersed throughout the sealift fleet. For example, the week before the ground campaign began, the Army had stockpiled in Saudi Arabia 50,000 155-millimeter artillery shells without necessary propellant charges and 50,000 mortar rounds without fuses.

To meet these challenges and to coordinate the massive lift by sea, air, and land, the MSC, Military Traffic Management Command Europe, Military Airlift Command, and the Army's 21st Theater Army Area Command refined transportation and loading schedules, found cargo handling and stowage materials, and obtained barge, train, and truck transport. Lieutenant General Frederick M. Franks Jr., Commanding General VII Corps, also set up 50-person action teams and dispatched liaison officers to Riyadh, where they coordinated plans with CENTCOM staffs.[91]

The governments and peoples of Germany, Belgium, and the Netherlands enthusiastically assisted in the corps' deployment, even though some questioned the legality of support for a non-NATO mission. There were other oddities. An Army officer, conscious of the irony involved, noted that "heads turned in amazement as former East German Tatra military tractor trailers moved U.S. Army equipment down the autobahns. Hundreds of containers of supplies were loaded by former East German soldiers using Warsaw Pact sideloaders."[92]

Problems cropped up in European ports. The RRF ship *Cornhusker State*, loaded at the German port of Cuxhaven with 1st Armored Division elements, became, according to one observer, "the logisticians' 'Flying

Dutchman' as it toured scenic repair facilities"[93] before finally heading for the open sea.

Other problems arose when ships neared the theater. For political, religious, or other reasons, some foreign crewmen on 12 of the 206 commercial ships chartered for the operation refused to enter the war zone.[94] Switching crews, transloading ships, and unloading ships at alternative ports minimized delays caused by these "balkers."

Navy cargo handling and control of shipping units, with the help of Marine and Army units, unloaded ships arriving at ad-Dammam and al-Jubayl. General Alfred M. Gray Jr., Commandant of the Marine Corps, observed that these modern ports "looked like they were designed for sailors, marines, soldiers and airmen."[95] Lieutenant General William G. "Gus" Pagonis, Schwarzkopf's chief logistician, tried to adhere to the policy that "when a ship is unloaded, *nothing* sits on the dock."[96] Nevertheless, VII Corps units had difficulty clearing the ports. A given unit's equipment might be spread among as many as eight ships, which arrived in port at different times. Furthermore, the troops arrived from Germany by air at locations separate from their equipment. The integration of troops and equipment was no easy task in crowded eastern Saudi Arabia.

VII Corps units then had difficulty moving from the ports to the front hundreds of miles to the northwest. The Army had only 112 heavy equipment transporters (HETs) in the theater to carry tanks and other armored vehicles to the front. General Boomer's I MEF had another 34 HETs. To save time and fuel and to reduce wear and tear on tracked vehicles and Saudi roads, General Pagonis assembled a fleet of 1,300 heavy equipment transporters and tractor trailers provided by Saudi Arabia, Egypt, Germany, and several of the United States' former Warsaw Pact adversaries. Still, when Desert Storm began, 30,000 VII Corps soldiers remained at Saudi ports and airfields awaiting transportation forward. One Army general reported in mid-January that the "backlog at the [Saudi] ports is considerable and growing."[97] Like the French "Taxicab Army" in the World War I Battle of the Marne, many troops went to the front in a motley assortment of military and civilian trucks, rental cars, buses, and more than 200 Japanese four-wheel-drive vehicles.

Despite these difficulties, in little over three months the U.S. armed forces and their coalition partners deployed 122,000 personnel and 50,500 pieces of equipment from one theater to another. On 23 February, the VII Corps, General Schwarzkopf's "Sunday Punch," stood armed and ready for battle on the Saudi frontier.[98]

Heavy combat forces from other coalition nations also streamed into the theater during Phase II. During late December and early January, the 4th Egyptian Armored Division joined the 3d Egyptian Mechanized Division and the 9th Syrian Armored Division in the Saudi desert. British merchantmen and Royal Navy logistic landing ships rein-forced Britain's 7th Armoured Brigade with the 4th Armoured Brigade to form the 1st Armoured Division. Additional forces brought the French 6th Light (Daguet) Armored Division up to full strength.[99]

As in Phase I, the Military Sealift Command transported combat forces to the theater along with the supplies, ammunition, and fuel they would need. Admiral Donovan's seven fast sealift ships dramatically re-duced their previous transit times, averaging 27-knot speeds on the pas-sage between Savannah, Georgia, and ad-Dammam, Saudi Arabia. This small contingent of the MSC fleet carried an impressive 10 percent of all the cargo delivered to the theater. Several of these ships made seven round-trips during Phase II.

The FSSs were the work horses of the sealift effort, but Admiral Donovan's other ships carried the bulk of the supplies. On New Year's Eve, 85 of the 217 ships under MSC control were loading material in the United States and Europe, discharging cargo in the operational area, or returning for more. At the same time the other 132 merchantmen were steaming fully loaded for the Persian Gulf. With an average of one ship every 50 miles from Savannah to the gulf, the MSC fleet formed a verita-ble "steel bridge" across the sea.[100]

The sealift produced impressive results. In Phase II, MSC-con-trolled ships delivered 1,270,300 short tons of equipment, 235,400 more than in the earlier effort. The 404,700 tons of supplies delivered in Phase II almost tripled that of Phase I. Finally, MSC delivered to theater forces 3,500,000 short tons of fuel, 1,700,000 more than in Phase I.

Preparations for War

Although the Phase II mobilization suggested the probability of war in the immediate future, the Navy only slowly adjusted to the new situa-tion. On 14 November, during a meeting in Dhahran, General Schwarzkopf revealed the Desert Storm plan in its entirety for the first time to 22 of his top generals and admirals, including Mauz. The admi-ral later stated that the briefing reinforced his belief that the crisis in the gulf would lead to war.[101] Nevertheless, Admiral Kelso and his staff in Washington did not demonstrate a conviction that the coalition would resort to force to eject Saddam's army from Kuwait, at least not in the near term. One consequence was that the three carrier battle groups dis-patched to Southwest Asia in Phase II arrived in the CENTCOM theater the week before Desert Storm, with little time to prepare for combat operations. Indeed, Commander Maurice Smith, who represented the Red Sea battle force (Battle Force Yankee) in Riyadh, noted that instead

Carriers *Saratoga* (CV 60) (in the van), *John F. Kennedy* (CV 67) (foreground), and *America* (CV 66) (background) and the other combatants of Battle Force Yankee in the Red Sea.

of readying *America*'s air wing for the air campaign, "higher authority" had the aviators planning a peacetime exercise for the Mediterranean.[102]

In addition, neither the naval command in Washington nor Admiral Mauz acted to free COMUSNAVCENT of his Pacific Command responsibilities, thus preventing him from focusing totally on the coming war. Believing that his duty lay with the afloat naval forces, Mauz continued to exercise command from his flagship, *Blue Ridge*, tied up at Mina Sulman, Bahrain, rather than from Riyadh, the Central Command headquarters. "I never had the slightest inclination to relocate to Riyadh," Mauz later recalled.[103]

The admiral saw Schwarzkopf during weekly meetings of senior commanders convened by the general to discuss the evolving Desert Storm campaign plan. CINCCENT visited Mauz and the fleet in early October when *Independence* entered the gulf. Even so, Mauz never developed as close a working relationship with Schwarzkopf as did his counterparts, Generals Boomer, Horner, and John Yeosock. CINCCENT later remarked that "the geographic separation prevented us from planning and conferring with all component commanders on a regular basis and made coordination between components more difficult."[104] This proved to be a significant problem, since it became clear that Schwarzkopf would provide strong direction of the air, ground, and naval campaign from his command center.[105]

Even if he had developed closer ties with Schwarzkopf and his staff, Mauz was not going to take part in the war, for Washington had long before scheduled him for another job. Vice Admiral Stanley Arthur replaced Mauz as Commander U.S. Naval Forces, Central Command and Commander Seventh Fleet on 1 December 1990. According to Arthur's description of the debate in Washington, Admiral Kelso and his staff asked rhetorically, "what are we going to do? Are we going to leave Mauz there or are we going to send Arthur out?" Eventually, they concluded that "this thing [Desert Shield] may go on forever, it may not be anything, lets go ahead [with the relief]."[106] Moreover, Kelso wanted Mauz to relieve another flag officer on the naval staff so that the latter could take up a command in the Pacific Fleet.[107]

Washington did not seem concerned that Arthur would take the helm as COMUSNAVCENT only six weeks before the onset of combat. The new commander would be hard-pressed to prepare NAVCENT for war, direct the ongoing maritime interception operations, and manage the massive naval buildup in the theater.

Fortunately, Admiral Arthur had attributes that likened him to the great leaders in U.S. naval history. General Schwarzkopf considered him "one of the most aggressive admirals I'd ever met."[108] General Boomer concurred that Arthur was a "fighter." "This time, folks," Boomer said to his staff, "we got a guy who is willing to fight, and that's a tremendous—well, that's an improvement; lets put it that way."[109]

Arthur had long been a warrior. His service in naval aviation spanned three decades and included several tours in Vietnam, where he logged 500 hours in aerial combat. During that time he earned the Distinguished Service Medal, Legion of Merit, Distinguished Flying Cross, and numerous other awards and decorations. The admiral brought experience to the job in carrier operations, campaign planning, and logistics. His previous tour as COMUSNAVCENT in the early 1980s was particularly relevant to the new job.

Shortly after Admiral Arthur's helicopter landed on board *Blue Ridge* on 1 December 1990, Mauz took him into his quarters to brief him on the overall situation and the planning for naval operations. Mauz admitted that he had gotten off to a rocky start with General Horner, but believed that NAVCENT was responding well to Central Command's needs. Arthur realized that to Mauz, a surface warfare officer who knew what Aegis could do, the idea of establishing separate patrol sectors for the various air forces had seemed logical. But as a veteran of air combat in Vietnam, Arthur also understood Horner's aversion to anything that remotely smacked of "route packages." Arthur made smoothing over any remaining rough edges with Horner a top priority.[110] When he called on Schwarzkopf shortly thereafter, Arthur quickly realized that war was near. At the same time, Arthur, according to British Commodore Chris Craig, who had lunch with him on board *Blue Ridge*, was "frustrated and disappointed to find [NAVCENT's] war planning immature."[111]

Schwarzkopf shared this view. In an "eyes only" message to Admiral Kelso shortly after the war, the general observed: "Simply stated, the naval forces were not totally integrated in the battle plan prior to the execution of the campaign" and that "I, as a CINC, must confess that I do not feel I got the maximum benefit from the large number of naval vessels deployed over here."[112]

Arthur was also upset at not being headquartered in Riyadh. As COMUSNAVCENT under Generals Paul X. Kelly, USMC and Robert Kingston, USA, Arthur had always operated by their side. He briefly considered moving his headquarters to the Saudi capital, where he could make the Navy's presence felt, and putting one of his aggressive battle force commanders in charge of fleet operations, but time was too short. He did not want "to get caught in a headquarters shift at about the time we start shooting." That would have been "disastrous."[113]

Nonetheless, the dynamic naval officer made the best of his situation and took action. To inspire a warlike mentality in his command and to simplify the task force numbering system, Admiral Arthur reorganized NAVCENT the day after Christmas (Table 5). He also beefed up

Table 5

NAVCENT COMMAND STRUCTURE

(26 December 1990 onward)

Commander U.S. Naval Forces, Central Command (CTF 150)
   Vice Admiral Stanley R. Arthur

Commander Middle East Force (CTF 151)
   Rear Admiral William M. Fogarty

Commander Maritime Interception Force (CTF 152)
   Rear Admiral Fogarty

Commander Naval Logistics Support Force (CTG 150.3)
   Rear Admiral Robert Sutton

Commander Battle Force Zulu (CTF 154)
   Rear Admiral Daniel P. March

Commander Battle Force Yankee (CTF 155)
   Rear Admiral Riley D. Mixson

Commander Amphibious Task Force (CTF 156)
   Rear Admiral John B. LaPlante

Commander Landing Force (CTF 158)
   Major General Harry W. Jenkins Jr., USMC

Commander Mediterranean Strike Group (CTG 150.9)
   Rear Admiral Mixson

SOURCE: Michael Shepko, Sandra Newett, and Rhonda M. Alexander, *Maritime Interception Operations* (Alexandria, VA: Center for Naval Analyses, 1991), 6.

the staffs of NAVCENT Riyadh and the Fleet Coordinating Group, both posted in the Saudi capital.[114]

For the most part, U.S. and coalition naval forces made good use of the time Desert Shield afforded to train for the coming war. Five of the six air wings that took part in the air campaign against Iraq rehearsed strike operations at the Navy's range near Fallon, Nevada, before departing for the theater. Captain Dean M. Hendrickson, Commander Carrier Air Wing 17, in *Saratoga*, considered this training helpful in preparing his squadrons for later operations over Iraq and Kuwait.[115] Homeported

USN DN-SC 91-04752

Rear Admiral Riley D. Mixson (left), Commander Battle Force Yankee, and Rear Admiral George N. Gee, a subordinate battle group commander, share a lighter moment during Desert Shield. Intensive prewar training involving Red Sea naval aviation units and Air Force units helped limit problems during later combat operations.

in Yokosuka, Japan, *Midway* was unable to benefit from this training. In addition, *Midway, Saratoga, Theodore Roosevelt,* and *Ranger* completed predeployment tactical and integrated battle force exercises.

Unlike *Theodore Roosevelt, Ranger,* and *America, Saratoga, John F. Kennedy,* and *Midway* had plenty of time to operate in the theater before the start of Desert Storm. Naval air units trained in Saudi, Omani, and Egyptian skies on a daily basis. The carriers also completed a number of two- and three-carrier "mirror-image" strike exercises with U.S. Air Force and coalition air units. In most ways these exercises closely resembled the missions that allied air forces would fly in Desert Storm.[116]

The carrier squadrons practiced low-level strikes, which would prove to be the wrong approach in Desert Storm. As a result, naval aircrews were not as well prepared as they should have been to locate, identify, and hit ground targets from altitudes above 20,000 feet.[117]

From October to January, Navy units conducted surface warfare and antiair warfare exercises with the Royal Navy, the Royal Air Force, Canadian air and naval forces, the Royal Saudi Naval Forces, and the Qatar air force. On several occasions, allied officers boarded U.S. cruisers *Mobile Bay* and *Bunker Hill* (CG 52) for briefings by American antiair warfare commanders on the Aegis system's capabilities and the overall scheme for the fleet's defense against air attack.[118] Central Command naval forces also practiced intercepting high-speed terrorist boats with UAE naval, air, and coast guard units.

Missouri and *Wisconsin* began conducting naval gunfire support exercises in December. Skilled crewmen from both battleships also went ashore to coordinate future calls for fire with Marine air and naval gunfire liaison personnel.[119]

Desert Shield afforded coalition naval forces enough time to prepare for the coming war in other ways besides training. The Persian Gulf was the site of more than 10,000 anomalies, such as dense dust clouds and oil rigs, which made it a problem-ridden area for communicating. Fleet leaders not only used the time to solve many of these problems, but also to refine command relationships and communications connections with allied navies and shore installations. Australia, Great Britain, Canada, the Netherlands, and Italy placed their naval task forces in the Persian Gulf under March's tactical control. Years of cooperation among the NATO navies considerably eased this process. Indeed, one American officer declared that the "NATO system was a godsend [because] it's the way we do business." [120]

U.S. naval forces used the Desert Shield period to gather information on the Iraqi armed forces and to study the Navy's past operational experience in the theater. NAVCENT units pored over "lessons learned" during the Tanker War's convoy escort, mine clearance, and other naval operations. Damage control personnel studied the experience of the sailors whose quick thinking, training, and courage saved the badly damaged frigates *Stark* and *Samuel B. Roberts.*

The Navy's MCM group spent much of Desert Shield training for under-fire mine clearance in support of amphibious landings. The forces assigned to Captain Grieve had a lot to learn, for their previous training had focused largely on breaking out of mined ports. The MCM group practiced joint helicopter, ship, and explosive ordnance disposal operations; trained against mine emulators, which they had not done in the United States; and conducted combined exercises with the Royal Navy and Royal Saudi Naval Forces. Because he lacked naval craft to support his EOD divers, Grieve obtained civilian tugs. He also supervised efforts to repair his ships and reduce their magnetic "signatures." Grieve remarked after the war that putting *Avenger* "in the fray" was a "bad idea," because as a test ship she was not yet ready for wartime operations. Grieve had to put four new engines and a new sonar in her. His command's low priority status compelled Grieve to work harder than he

Courtesy of Royal Australian Navy

HMAS *Brisbane* sailors arm their U.S.-supplied Phalanx close-in weapon system for operations in the Persian Gulf. The ship's sides have been draped with radar-absorbing "RAM panels."

should have to obtain the GPS navigation systems crucial for accurately marking cleared lanes through minefields.[121]

Also preparing for the coming offensive campaign were the U.S. intelligence agencies, whose actions were significantly influenced by the Goldwater-Nichols Act. Just as the military chiefs of staff did not direct the field operations of the individual services, the armed forces' intelligence departments did not provide sole-service support. The focus of effort in Washington was centered in the Joint Staff's J-2 and the Pentagon's Joint Intelligence Center.[122] Although he did not have statutory authority to do so, the Director Defense Intelligence Agency, Lieutenant General Harry E. Soyster, USA, "for the first time attempted to exercise the role of director of military intelligence"[123] with the Military Intelligence Board. Its members included the heads of the service intelligence departments. A prominent unofficial member was the head of the National Security Agency, Admiral William O. Studeman. According to Rear Admiral Thomas Brooks, the Director of Naval Intelligence during the Gulf War, this ad hoc arrangement worked because of the good leadership skills of Soyster and Studeman and their productive relationships with Brooks and his counterparts.[124]

One action taken by the board was to dispatch intelligence teams to Saudi Arabia to augment the existing staffs, which were underpowered owing to CENTCOM's prewar status as a "backwater command." Ultimately, around 1,200 personnel handled intelligence matters in the theater.[125]

Working through the joint structure, the Office of Naval Intelligence focused some of its effort on providing timely and relevant intelligence for anticipated amphibious operations. One analysis group at Suitland, with a surface warfare captain as the head and an intelligence officer as his deputy, provided the amphibious forces with information needed for executing amphibious operations in the Persian Gulf. Admiral Brooks later remarked that because of good cooperation between Navy and Marine intelligence teams, the amphibious forces probably received the "best intelligence they have ever had."[126] Admiral LaPlante agreed that during Desert Shield, the "intelligence was great," except that there was perhaps "too damn much of it."[127]

The most noteworthy accomplishment of naval intelligence during the Gulf War, however, was its support for the air war. After American intelligence officers debriefed Soviet and French trainers who had worked with Iraqi pilots and aircraft, "we knew exactly how the Iraqis would fly them." By training with aircraft known to be in the Iraqi inventory against U.S. planes, American air crews learned how to defeat their aerial adversaries. Naval intelligence also carried out several "very highly effective deception operations" and "information warfare" actions against the enemy's electronic air defense network.[128]

Some of the most valuable information came from the Naval Intelligence Command's Strike Projection Evaluation and Anti-Air Warfare Research (SPEAR) group. The Navy had created SPEAR to help carrier forces deal with the sophisticated land-based air defense systems of the Soviets and other potential foes. The sea service did not want a repeat of the embarrassing 1983 mission over Lebanon, when the Syrians shot down two carrier planes, killed one air crewman, and captured another. In December 1990, Captain Michael Johnson, a veteran of air combat in Vietnam, headed the SPEAR group. Reinforced with analysts from each of the armed services, his team explored ways for the coalition to breach Saddam's air defense shield. They concluded that radar guided, surface-to-air missiles, not interceptor aircraft, were Iraq's "logical choice as the primary air defense weapon." Accordingly, strike planners and air crews concentrated their training on neutralizing the systems that controlled the SAMs. As the postwar Gulf War Air Power Survey put it, SPEAR's analysis "remains perhaps the best assessment of the Iraqi air force and air defense system."[129]

American and Dutch medical personnel share information on board the Netherlands fast combat support ship HNLMS *Zuiderkruis.* The international naval contingents worked especially well together during Desert Shield and Desert Storm.

The SPEAR group also gave Admiral Mauz, before his departure from the gulf, and his air staff the ammunition they needed to argue that the coalition should not use the Vietnam-era A-6 Intruders in the initial strikes on Baghdad, as Glosson's Black Hole team planned. Concerned about the potential for high casualties, SPEAR recommended against sending the aging bombers into the lethal air defense environment of the Iraqi capital. Mauz was not prepared to accept high losses among pilots and air crews when pilotless and stealthy Tomahawk missiles were available.

TLAMs, however, had never before been used in combat, and non-naval leaders such as Glosson, Schwarzkopf, and Powell were relatively unfamiliar with them. Moreover, Air Force officers on the JFACC staff remained uncertain about the reliability of Tomahawk missiles and their launchers and the likelihood that TLAMs would reach and destroy their targets. One observer to the planning process described a "long and sometimes contentious fight . . . required to get Air Force planners to accept the missile and its capabilities." [130] A computer simulation directed by Glosson, however, predicted that about half of the non-stealthy planes would be lost in the initial attacks. So, despite continuing concerns, planners incorporated the Navy's Tomahawks into the plan. The Navy spent the last months of Desert Shield ironing out problems with the weapons' navigational and targeting systems, but by 17 January the fleet was ready for the debut of its ship-launched, land attack missile.[131]

As always in war, no system operates flawlessly, and the intelligence system was no exception. In some cases, collection of intelligence was a problem. Having retired the venerable RF-8, RA-5C, RA-3B, and other photographic reconnaissance aircraft, the Navy did not have enough F-14s equipped with TARPs available for tactical intelligence gathering. Admiral Brooks has cogently observed that "we had better tactical intelligence support available in Vietnam than Stan Arthur had available to him in the Gulf War."[132]

Brooks also concluded that "where we had a serious failure, serious breakdown . . . was in our ability to disseminate the intelligence [from satellite imagery] rapidly, reliably, in the format required, to the place required, and when required."[133] Lack of suitable equipment was one reason. For instance, the carriers were not capable of receiving all of the product electronically. Admiral March, the Battle Force Zulu commander, later stressed "there was a real problem getting the pictures that we needed. . . . There were boxes and boxes of pictures sitting in Riyadh that never got out" to the ships.[134] Admiral Brooks later related that some Suitland-based intelligence personnel had to pack their bags with images and analysis, fly with it out to the carriers via MAC and then COD aircraft, and then return to Washington for more.

Another reason was bureaucracy. Brooks observed that "CENTCOM for the most part did not provide useful intelligence to the carriers at sea at least partially because they were fighting an Army war; an Army general, and an Army J-2 fighting an Army war."[135] Schwarzkopf conceded that because of poor "inter-service interoperability . . . the timely passage of intelligence data between CENTCOM and the components was cumbersome and hindered component capability." Had it not been for the time afforded by Desert Shield to develop "work arounds . . . lack of interoperability of intelligence systems could have jeopardized mission success."[136]

Bureaucratic imperatives also influenced intelligence analysis in Washington. Since the Chief of Naval Operations and his intelligence advisor were out of the operational "loop," they often did not have a "need to know" regarding certain information. For instance, other than knowing that the United States had a stealth program, Brooks was in the dark about the F-117's capabilities and planned central role in the campaign plan. He also felt that interservice politics limited his access to the workings of Colonel Warden's Checkmate group in the Pentagon.[137] As a result, in Brooks view, the prewar campaign analysis provided by the

Military Intelligence Board to CENTCOM was inadequate. Rather than overestimating the Iraqi capacity for resistance, the intelligence advisors underestimated the precision, reliability, and destructiveness of a host of American weapons systems and the skill with which the U.S. military would employ them.[138]

Continuing Operations

Admiral Arthur's fleet continued to conduct defensive operations while it prepared for war. Indeed, the threat of attack from Iraqi aircraft, missile boats, and Silkworm missiles added a strong sense of realism to the preparations. Many commanders knew that during the Iran-Iraq War Iraqi aircraft had attacked hundreds of merchant ships in the gulf, sometimes at night and far from Iraq. Until late 1990, friendly forces in the northern gulf consisted of *Bunker Hill*, an Aegis cruiser, *Worden* (CG 18), a new threat upgrade (NTU) cruiser, and a frigate. The cruisers and the frigate served as "gate guards" for the fleet, or more formally, as the units in the positive identification radar advisory zone (PIRAZ), an early warning and air control concept developed in the Vietnam War.[139] EP-3 electronic warfare planes from VQ-1 Detachment Echo based in Bahrain flew a "race-track" patrol pattern off the coast of Kuwait to detect emissions from Iraqi radars and other electronic systems.[140]

Also covering the northern and central gulf, in 24-hour combat air patrol sectors Whiskey 1 and Whiskey 2, were a squadron of shore-based Marine F/A-18 Hornets of Marine Air Group 11[141] and a squadron of Canadian CF-18s. The latter unit, Colonel Philip Engstad's Canadian Air Task Group, Middle East, deployed to Doha in Qatar in October and was assigned to COMUSNAVCENT, since the government in Ottawa hoped its aircraft would fly cover for Canadian warships. Mauz, however, badly needed these planes to stiffen his air defenses over waters that the Canadian surface combatants would not steam in for months. He placed the CF-18s under the tactical control of Admiral Fogarty and through him the antiair warfare commander in Aegis cruiser *Antietam* (CG 54). To their surprise, the Canadian pilots, air force officers to a man, found themselves in a "setting dominated by sailors."[142]

Despite these resources, U.S. naval leaders were not comfortable during the latter months of 1990 with Horner's command-control-communications system for air defense of the gulf. According to Captain Thomas F. Marfiak, Antiair Warfare Commander during much of Desert Shield, the Navy's northernmost defensive ships had a data link with only one Air Force AWACS plane and Marine shore stations. The voice communications picture was somewhat brighter, especially after additional circuits and frequencies were brought on line, but that took time. "In hindsight," Mauz recalled after the war, "there were vulnerabilities that Saddam could have exploited."[143]

Throughout the fall of 1990, Iraqi air forces did probe into gulf airspace. "I think Saddam was testing our defenses and making a statement about being able to threaten our forces at sea," Mauz noted. "The [northern Persian Gulf] was also a good ingress route for Iraqi air should Saddam go after northeastern Saudi Arabia or the oilfields."[144] On 14 October, *Antietam* warned a pair of Canadian CF-18s patrolling at CAP station Whiskey 2 that two Iraqi jets were headed out to sea. When the Canadians maneuvered to intercept, the Iraqis quickly turned back, prompting Admiral Fogarty's staff in *LaSalle* to radio the allied aviators, "Way to go, Canada!"[145]

On 6 November, 12 Iraqi MiG-23s and F-1 Mirages entered gulf airspace from the northwest and headed for *Worden*, which had arrived on station only a few days earlier.[146] Commander William Richards, *Worden*'s Executive Officer, later remarked that the incident "was a good thing for us because it gave us a big slap in the face and got us into the ball game very quickly."[147] During later months as many as 18 Iraqi aircraft sortied in formation over the gulf. Because of these incursions, Captain William Hunt, *Worden*'s Commanding Officer, felt "sure the war was going to start earlier" and that the Iraqis "were either going to make a move Christmas Day, . . . right around New Year's," or just before all the carriers arrived in the gulf in January.[148] During the latter months of 1990, Hunt and other commanders in the northern gulf harbored concerns that the carriers operating in the North Arabian Sea were not close enough to support them if the Iraqis attacked.[149] Lieutenant Commander Diana Cangelosi, Assistant Officer in Charge of VQ-1 Detachment Echo and a naval flying officer, was also concerned during Desert Shield that there were too few air defense aircraft in position to protect her unarmed planes flying a necessarily repetitive, "easily targetable" pattern just off Kuwait.[150]

But Admirals Mauz and March were more concerned about the threat to their carriers from Exocet-armed Iranian planes. The Battle Force Zulu commander later observed that the Iranians "weren't exactly friendly neutrals." He added that he was "just never comfortable with the situation in Iran. It kept me up at nights."[151] Indeed, at times Iranian vessels and combat aircraft operated uncomfortably close to coalition naval forces. Consequently, other than for short periods, these U.S. naval leaders did not deploy carriers into the Persian Gulf. Initially, Arthur shared these concerns. But a few weeks after he took over as COMUS-

NAVCENT, Arthur decided that the carriers were needed in the central gulf and that they could operate there in relative safety.[152]

The naval command also feared that an allied reaction to these Iraqi actions might prematurely trigger the war. Marine F/A-18 aircraft intercepted the Iraqi formation involved in the 6 November probe and then pursued the jets as they retired toward Kuwait. When Iraqi fire control radars locked onto the Hornets, the Marine pilots concluded that their contacts had hostile intent and requested permission to shoot them down. Officers controlling the antiair operation from *Worden* denied the marines authority to engage.[153] General Boomer at first felt that "the [Iraqi] testing would stop"[154] if his Hornets took out their aircraft, but after a few days' reflection, he told his staff, "We don't want to start the war next week; we are not quite ready yet."[155] Clearly, however, war could occur at any time.

Iraqi naval forces also conducted operations in the gulf during late 1990. Captain Hunt received information that Iraqis periodically rehearsed operations in which 16 to 18 small craft practiced coordinated attacks on a target from many different directions. Alerted by this information, American sailors trained hard with their deck-mounted, 25-millimeter "chain guns" and .50-caliber machine guns.[156]

Evidence of an even more ominous Iraqi naval threat soon emerged. In late November and December, while operating in the northern reaches of the gulf, Captain Hunt witnessed hour upon hour of Iraqi helicopter activity. He concluded that the Iraqis were laying mines, and so informed naval intelligence. But, according to Hunt, the response was, "Captain, you're crazy." "I told them two or three times," he recalled, "[but then] I stopped telling them."[157]

Actually, as early as 10 August 1990, the Navy had asked the Defense Intelligence Agency for intellience of Iraqi mining activity. The naval command had received information from several sources that the Iraqis were laying mines in gulf waters. Saudi fishermen, who went about their business despite the Iraqi invasion, reported that the Iraqis were dumping "objects" offshore. Reports surfaced in September that they were mining Kuwait harbor and nearby waters. In early November, the *Washington Times* reported that Iraqi ships had planted Soviet-made mines in the northern gulf. On another occasion intelligence photographs showed soldiers on a pier transferring large spherical objects from a truck to a mine warfare vessel.

Still, indisputable evidence of a systematic Iraqi mining effort remained absent. At the end of November one intelligence officer on the I MEF staff observed that "NAVCENT has tried to come up with a way to be able to discern mining" but was "unsuccessful in that."[158] General

Boomer lamented that "the U.S. Navy is impotent when it comes to mines, almost, and we are very close to it on the ground side."[159]

Evidence mounted as Desert Storm drew nearer. On 21 December, Royal Saudi mine countermeasures forces operating in the Zuluf oilfield discovered a drifting Iraqi mine, the first of many such sightings to come. By the second week of January, U.S. mine countermeasures units had spotted another 12 Iraqi mines adrift in the gulf. On the 9th, U.S. intelligence photographs showed sea mines stowed on the decks of an Iraqi T-43 minelayer and a Spasilac vessel. That same day, U.S. special warfare forces operating on the coast near Khafji spotted these two vessels 10 miles out to sea with crewmen throwing objects into the water for about an hour. This constituted the first confirmed evidence of mines on a ship and mining activity.[160]

Unfortunately, the Navy could do little to monitor the waters of the northern gulf more closely, because General Schwarzkopf had prohibited aircraft, even unmanned aerial vehicles (UAVs), from flying nearer than 55 miles from the Kuwait-Saudi border (or above 27 degrees, 45 minutes north) and his naval forces from steaming within 72 miles of that border (or above 27 degrees, 30 minutes north). Washington shared his fear that operations any closer to occupied Kuwait might trigger a war before the coalition was ready, politically and militarily.[161] Rear Admiral Raynor A.K. Taylor, who became COMUSNAVCENT after Desert Storm, has suggested that if the Navy had participated fully in the theater planning process before the war, and had demonstrated that its forces were skilled, disciplined, and fully subordinated to CENTCOM control, General Schwarzkopf would have granted the fleet greater freedom of action in the northern gulf.[162] As it turned out, Arthur's pleas for authority to eliminate the Iraqi mine-laying vessels or at least operate patrol aircraft over the northern gulf fell on deaf ears in Riyadh and Washington.[163]

Iraq was not the only problem. Iran—certainly no friend of the United States—dominated the Persian Gulf's northern coast. Coalition leaders could not predict what actions that country might take. Indeed, at one point an Iranian religious figure called for a Muslim "jihad" or holy war against the United States. Iran could field hundreds of modern jet aircraft and naval vessels, all of which moved actively about Iranian airspace and in the waters surrounding offshore oil rigs and coastal islands. An Iranian plane would not even have to cross the coastline before launching an antishipping missile against the coalition fleet.[164]

The uncertainty surrounding Iran also complicated the problem of what to do with the amphibious forces afloat in the Persian Gulf. Having virtually ruled out a large-scale landing, General Schwarzkopf faced the question of whether to disembark the amphibious forces and use them ashore, or to keep them afloat for some other purpose. Army planners in his headquarters favored the former option.[165] But Schwarzkopf seized upon the idea of using Admiral LaPlante's Amphibious Task Force and General Jenkins' Landing Force to focus Saddam's attention on the Iraq-Kuwait coastline and waters offshore. It would prove a masterful use of strategic deception.

To foster the impression that he was planning an assault from the sea, Schwarzkopf ordered the execution of a number of Navy-Marine amphibious exercises.[166] From 15 to 21 November, the ATF mounted Exercise Imminent Thunder on the Persian Gulf coast of Saudi Arabia. Imminent Thunder involved over 60,000 U.S., Saudi, British, Kuwaiti, Canadian, and French forces. Navy amphibious ships and craft pushed through a rough surf to put marines ashore. At the same time Marine and allied ground-based air squadrons and air units from *Midway*, which for this exercise made the second carrier foray into the gulf since September, practiced coordinated strike operations. The amphibious exercise was one of several "operations carefully designed to deceive the Iraqi command as to the direction of the Coalition's ground attack."[167] Admiral LaPlante characterized Imminent Thunder as "beating our chest for the press, saying 'see what amphibious warfare can do.'"[168] Imminent Thunder worked so well, in fact, that a Kuwaiti who escaped to Saudi Arabia reported that during the exercise "some Iraqi forces stationed on the border fled their positions in fear of being attacked, thereby allowing [him] and some 600 Kuwaiti refugees to get across the border."[169] On the negative side, LaPlante and Jenkins were concerned that they were revealing too much about how the Navy and Marine Corps conducted amphibious warfare. A detailed description of such operations published in *Newsweek* magazine a few weeks before the start of the ground war, according to the admiral, "just blew us away."[170] The amphibious forces subsequently mounted practice landing exercises Sea Soldier III and Sea Soldier IV.[171]

Few in the U.S. command knew that General Schwarzkopf had already ruled out an amphibious assault into Kuwait. Absolute secrecy was vital to the success of the strategic ruse. Arthur later revealed: "I knew that neither he [Schwarzkopf] nor the chairman [Powell] wanted to have an amphibious landing. That was the last thing that they wanted to have happen. And there was never an occasion where an amphibious landing was going to be necessary to conduct the war the way they wanted to."[172] Conversely, neither Admiral LaPlante nor General Jenkins were "in the loop" until just before the onset of the ground campaign.[173] Judging from the nature of his remarks to the I MEF staff, General Boomer might have been privy to Schwarzkopf's real intentions, but other marines were not. On 15 December, the day after a meeting with

Schwarzkopf in Riyadh, General Boomer and his staff gathered to weigh possible options for the ground offensive. Major General John I. Hopkins, Boomer's deputy, suggested that the Marine Corps' amphibious warfare mission could be at risk if the offensive plan did not include a seaborne assault. "I think there has to be a major amphibious operation," he said, "or else we will get looped, [on] the political side."[174] Boomer assured Hopkins that possible "raids [and] deceptions" were "very much on the table and I think will play a critical part" of the offensive plan. Indeed, General Schwarzkopf did consider raids on islands off Kuwait and other amphibious operations to be feasible.

While amphibious and other allied air, sea, and ground forces prepared for battle, the coalition's maritime interception forces kept the pressure on Saddam Hussein. This complemented the diplomatic pressure from the United States and the United Nations. With operational procedures, the division of inspection sectors, and other matters worked out by the beginning of November, coalition naval leaders focused on improving the effectiveness of the embargo. As of 15 December, 50 ships of 13 non-U.S. coalition navies patrolled in the Persian Gulf, Strait of Hormuz, Gulf of Oman, Gulf of Aden, and the Red Sea. By late 1990 most interceptions were routine.

On 13 and 14 December, however, boarding parties dispatched from U.S. naval vessels patrolling off the Jordanian port of al-Aqabah discovered unusual cargo on board two departing merchantmen. Sailors from cruiser *Mississippi* (CGN 40) and guided missile destroyer *Sampson* (DDG 10) found motor vehicles that had been stolen in Kuwait. The patrol force compelled the freighters to return to port.[175]

Another atypical interception occurred on 26 December, when naval units intercepted the Iraqi-flagged ship *Ibn Khaldoon*, enroute to Iraq from Algeria. The vessel's master did not respond to instructions radioed to him from the Australian frigate *Sydney*, so the on-scene commander ordered helicopter-borne SEALs and marines of the 4th MEB to board and stop her. The boarding party encountered a phalanx on deck of 60 women, including a congressional staff member and an American lawyer, who linked arms and barred access to the bridge. Several of the women tried to seize team members' weapons and even knocked down one of the men. It was no coincidence that the activists were women, that the action took place during the week between Christmas and the New Year, and that the cargo turned out to be food, which was allowed into Iraq under strict UN supervision. Saddam Hussein was attempting to provoke an incident that he could use to discredit the embargo. The SEALs and marines rose to the occasion. Using warning shots and smoke grenades, and without bloodshed, they subdued the protestors and took control of the ship. Reinforced by Australian sailors from *Sydney*, British

"The Ibn Khaldoon Peace Ship" by John Charles Roach

sailors from *Brazen,* and American bluejackets from destroyers *Oldendorf* (DD 972) and *Fife,* the allied contingent kept that ship's cargo from its destination.[176]

On 4 January 1991, Spanish and American naval forces discovered Soviet merchant ship *Dmitriy-Furmanov* enroute to al-Aqabah with an unmanifested cargo of tank parts, detonators, and rocket launchers. Six days later sailors from *Mississippi* and the Spanish frigate *Diana* boarded *Dmitriy-Furmanov* and once again found the unmanifested cargo. Since it was clear that no munitions had been offloaded, the patrol force allowed the vessel to leave the Red Sea by way of the Suez Canal.[177]

By the start of Desert Storm the maritime interception force in the Red Sea was making 50 at-sea contacts each day, down from 200 per day in August 1990. During the same period the number of merchantmen entering or leaving the Jordanian port of al-Aqabah fell from 30 to 50 ships each day to three or four ships each day.[178]

The embargo was not airtight. Some war materiel was smuggled across Iraq's borders, and two outbound Iraqi merchant ships might have slipped through the maritime patrol in the Persian Gulf and made it out to sea, but the evidence is not conclusive. However, such evasions of the embargo patrol proved rare.[179]

The maritime interception operation between early November and mid-January succeeded from several standpoints. It severely curtailed the flow of shipping to and from Iraq and Kuwait. It put teeth in the UN Security Council actions to punish Iraqi aggression at a time when direct measures were needed to back up diplomatic pressures; the world's moral outrage was not sufficient. As Admiral David E. Jeremiah, Vice Chairman of the Joint Chiefs of Staff, observed, "the naval enforcement of U.N. sanctions against Iraq was a major factor in demonstrating to the world that the allies could form an effective military coalition."[180]

Once the coalition decided to oust the Iraqi armed forces from Kuwait, the embargo prevented the future enemy from importing replacement parts for his sophisticated weapons systems and from building up stocks of munitions. Vice Admiral William D. Smith, a U.S. representative to NATO, credited the maritime interception operation with diverting one million tons of shipping carrying "surface-to-air missile systems, command-and-control equipment, early warning radars, weapons, ammunition, repair parts, foodstuffs, and general supplies required to maintain Iraq's industrial base."[181] Speaking to the press in mid-February, General Merril A. McPeak, Air Force Chief of Staff, said that the embargo had been "spectacularly successful. . . . The Navy has been very quietly going about that job in a professional way." He added with only slight exaggeration that "nothing has gone in or out of Iraq since [the UN] imposed that embargo. And it may well be that is a very, very important thing in the long run, that we have shut off those supplies."[182] General Schwarzkopf phrased it most succinctly, crediting the multinational naval force with forming a "steel wall around the waters leading to Iraq."[183]

Life in the War Zone

Life was not easy for the American sailors and marines deployed to the sands of the Arabian Peninsula and the waters that washed its shores. Once President Bush announced the massive buildup of combat forces, most service members realized that there would be war. They understood that the enemy was much more powerful than the foes they faced in Grenada and Panama. Military pundits reinforced the perception that war with Iraq's million-man armed forces could mean many months of bloody combat under a blistering Middle Eastern sun. After a mid-December U.S. intelligence briefing, which apparently "sobered" members of the NAVCENT staff, one officer said it "sounded as though we were getting into another war we had no chance of winning, like Vietnam." [184]

To provide sailors and marines with some understanding of the nature of modern combat, Admiral LaPlante had Michael Thornton, a SEAL serving with the amphibious force and a Vietnam War Medal of Honor recipient, share his experiences during visits to fleet units. The admiral also aired on the internal video systems of his ships Ken Burns' moving, if chilling, *Civil War* documentary. LaPlante remarked that his men were "riveted" to their screens because of the obvious parallel to their own situation. [185] As General Powell observed in his memoirs, "thanks to Burns' artistry," Americans "understood that, yes, you went to war for high principles, but you should not go into it with any romantic illusions." [186]

What American service personnel feared most was an Iraqi attack with weapons of mass destruction. Intelligence reports made it clear that the Iraqis possessed large stocks of chemical and biological agents and the weapons to deliver them. Saddam's gassing of thousands of Iranian civilians during the Iran-Iraq War made it clear that he had no moral compunctions about using them. [187] Remembrance of the thousands of soldiers killed, blinded, or otherwise permanently disabled by gas during World War I haunted the Western allies. Captain Hunt said that the greatest fear of *Worden*'s crew was that Iraqi aircraft or missiles would release chemical or biological agents over the ship. Sailors standing topside watches felt especially vulnerable. And the men were not sure their gas masks were up to the task. [188] Finally, there remained the possibility, however slight, that Saddam possessed an operational nuclear weapon. [189]

Still, American sailors were no strangers to the danger inherent in naval operations, even peacetime naval operations. Death struck the Navy's Middle East contingent even before the start of hostilities. To give the crew of *Saratoga* some well-deserved liberty before they began final preparations for war, the naval command authorized the ship to make a port call at Haifa, Israel. On 21 December, an Israeli-chartered ferry returning over 100 sailors to the carrier from liberty ashore capsized in the harbor. Twenty-one crewmen drowned in this tragedy. Rear Admiral George N. Gee, Commander Cruiser Destroyer Group 8, on board "Sara" at the time, said that "the crew had a difficult time in dealing with the incident, because it hit like a bolt of lightning or an earthquake" and "all the men who perished were young." Nonetheless, after a memorial service at sea, *Saratoga*'s sailors realized that "they still had a job to do, that they had to press forward, and they did so." [190]

Along with mental stress, many naval personnel had to deal with the physical hardship of living and working in the Saudi desert or the

USN DN-SC 91-05918

Saratoga's primary flight control personnel, wearing protective masks, carry out their duties during a Desert Shield chemical warfare drill.

waters around it. During a typical summer day the temperature reached as high as 120 degrees Fahrenheit. High humidity increased the misery factor along the Persian Gulf and Red Sea coasts and out to sea. The temperature in battleship *Wisconsin*'s un-airconditioned engine and boiler room spaces routinely topped 100 degrees. "We had a real problem with heat stress then," said Lieutenant Greg Clark, a *Wisconsin* engineering officer. "You just couldn't stand it down [there] more than two hours at a stretch."[191]

The Navy's experience in the Persian Gulf during Earnest Will and the peacetime training of other commands in Egypt and California highlighted the importance of water consumption to survival in the desert. Central Command officers repeatedly stressed that people were to drink lots of water, sometimes as much as four gallons a day. American military personnel were importuned to remember the Golden Rule of the Desert: "If your urine is dark, you need water!"[192] As a result of this advice, sailors and marines with water bottles pressed to their lips became a common sight during Desert Shield.

The wind sometimes brought welcome relief from the heat, but just as often brought sandstorms and dust that choked people and fouled weapons, vehicles, and equipment, even out to sea. Because of microscopic dust, crewmen on board the ships of Admiral Arthur's fleet put gauze over all air intakes, even though the intakes already had filters. The same problem afflicted naval units ashore. The Marine helicopter fleet suffered a variety of problems owing to sand ingestion and erosion of turbine engines and rotor blades. Still, the Marines had at least one advantage over their Army comrades. The flexible seals on Marine aircraft, weapons, and equipment, which had been designed to keep out salt water, helped somewhat against sand intrusion.

Amphibious Task Force ships had embarked more marines and equipment for Desert Shield than they would have for a normal peacetime deployment. The unusually crowded conditions, coupled with the heat and humidity of the region and uncertainty about the length of the deployment, heightened the potential for "explosive and dangerous situations," according to Admiral LaPlante. To diminish tension between sailors and marines, he recommended that his skippers emphasize the joint nature of the mission and discourage terminology such as "blue side" and "green side." He told his men, "only together are we the most versatile and flexible fighting force in the world." [193]

LaPlante reminded his commanding officers that the marines embarked on their ships had lots of time on their hands. He recommended integrating the marines as much as possible into routine shipboard duties and encouraging physical training. The admiral observed that, "the more you put your Sailors together with their Marine shipmates in working and recreational situations, the less likely they will be to get into confrontational ones." [194]

The heat of summer soon gave way to the chill winds and rough seas of winter. During the early months of 1991, nighttime temperatures sometimes dipped close to the freezing mark. The periodic heavy rain and wind made daytime little better for coalition personnel on topside watches at sea and in bunkers, fighting holes, and tents ashore.

On occasion, naval personnel in the desert shared their habitat with other living things. Sailors and marines received warnings about cobras, puff adders, several varieties of viper, scorpions, and poisonous spiders, which "love cool, dark places, like boots, rucksacks, helmets, and sleeping bags," as a handbook issued to the troops explained. As if that were not enough, the Americans and their allies also had to contend with lice, mice, wasps, mosquitoes, and flies. A particularly loathsome creature was the sheep botfly, which deposited live maggots in the eyes of a number of marines. [195]

Along with the discomfort from the climate and pests, naval men and women ashore had to cope with working and living in austere facilities. Ensign Cheryl Blanzola, a Navy nurse assigned to Fleet Hospital 5 in al-Jubayl, had the typical experience of working 12-hour shifts, six days a week, for months at a time. Blanzola and her shipmates, as she recalled, "had to build [their] own tents, help build bunkers [with Seabees], fill sandbags and set up the hospital." [196]

Although most American service men and women in the theater were prepared to endure these hardships, they commonly expressed the desire to get on with the job so they could return home. This was especially true of naval reservists who had families and civilian jobs waiting for them in the United States. After visiting Saudi Arabia, noted sociologist and military manpower analyst Charles Moskos said that "not once did any soldier mention waiting out the effects of the embargo on Iraq." [197] For all their concerns about combat, American military personnel wanted to carry out their mission with dispatch so they could resume their peacetime pursuits.

American personnel had another reason for wanting to get on with the job. "Almost to a person," noted Moskos, "the troops believe that the longer they stay in the Gulf without action, the greater the erosion of home front support. Vietnam lies close to the surface for today's American soldier. The troops in Desert Shield are already alert to and upset by the sporadic anti-military protests at home." [198]

Hoping to exacerbate these concerns, Baghdad radio warned American troops that the desert sand dunes "have swallowed up many people and they will swallow you [too]." Like their fathers and grandfathers who listened to "Hanoi Hanna," "Tokyo Rose," and "Axis Sally," Gulf War sailors and marines sometimes tuned their radios to "Baghdad Betty." "Remember what the petrol emirs are doing with American girls," she would say in all seriousness. "Do you want to defend them?" [554] U.S. leaders had little to fear from these ludicrous Iraqi attempts at psychological warfare. Indeed, the periodic comic relief provided by Baghdad radio probably improved the morale of coalition personnel.

The potential for clashes between Western and Arab cultures, however, posed a credible threat to the war effort. This was particularly true in Saudi Arabia, home to the most socially conservative Arabs in the region and the holy cities Mecca and Medina and the coalition's most important host nation. The Saudis wanted neither their culture nor their religion contaminated by Western influence. At worst, a culture clash could escalate to a point where the Saudis would feel compelled to withdraw permission for the Western military presence on their soil. U.S. leaders worked hard to prevent such an occurrence.

Each service man and woman received a handbook, which included general information on Arab culture. Sailors, marines, soldiers, and airmen learned in 15 pages of "dos and don'ts" that to offer one's left hand to an Arab was considered an insult, and that to sit with legs crossed so that the sole of one's foot was pointing at an Arab was consid-

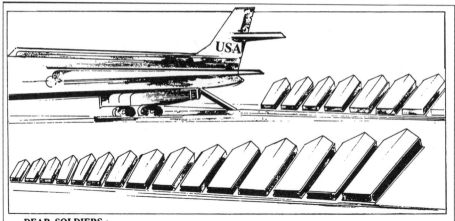

DEAR SOLDIERS :
YOUR COMMANDERS HAVE SAID THAT   THE WAR WILL TAKE FEW DAYS WERE
THEY CORRECT ?   AND CONVINCED YOU THAT LOSES WILL BE MINIMUM IN THE
GROUND COMBAT, WE ASSURE THAT THEY WONT BE CORRECT

BEWARE , DONT STEP FORWARD , IRAQI FIRE IS FATAL

Iraqi psychological warfare leaflets.

ered "offensive." The Americans learned not to take offense if an Arab
invaded one's "body space" by moving in close on an elevator, bus, or
park bench. American women were advised to "always keep their legs
covered, and be conservative in posture, dress, and speech." Forbidden
topics of conversation included religion, politics, and Israelis. Muslims
also frowned upon pictures of men and women embracing and "sensual
advertisements" for perfume or blue jeans.[200] The point of these stric-
tures, according to General Schwarzkopf, was to make the Arabs aware
that "all Americans aren't religious infidels, gangsters, or drug-addicted

young people." It was a facetious remark, but one that underscored the importance of proper decorum to the war effort.[201]

The Saudi government, in turn, made concessions to Western culture in recognition of the sacrifices being made in their defense. They allowed American service women on official duty to drive vehicles, a privilege denied their own females. Moreover, the Saudis did not require non-Arab women to be fully covered in public. Riyadh frowned on foreign flags being flown in the kingdom, but took no action to stop the practice within U.S. cantonments and out of sight of the Saudi citizenry. Saudi authorities permitted the U.S. Armed Forces Radio and Television Service to broadcast 24 hours a day, provided the broadcasts were inoffensive. During the first months of Desert Shield, the Saudis forbade the mail delivery to Americans of religious items, but in December they relaxed this restriction. Initially, the Saudis insisted that American chaplains be referred to as "morale officers," but later shelved that requirement as well. Indeed, U.S. chaplains quietly and discreetly carried out their religious responsibilities for the hundreds of thousands of service men and women in the theater. Finally, Saudi and U.S. officials arranged

USN DN-ST 91-11543

Surrounded by tents, which shielded them from outside view, Navy nurses of Fleet Hospital 15 enjoy a few moments of sun and relaxation. American military personnel made great efforts to respect the ultra-conservative religious, cultural, and social mores of Saudi Arabia.

visits to the holy city of Mecca for Americans who followed the Muslim faith. While the situation might have changed if the Western military presence in Saudi Arabia had lasted longer than it did, few Saudi-American social, religious, or political incidents occurred.[202] Motivated by the common desire to throw Saddam out of Kuwait, Americans and Arabs generally developed friendly relationships.

Of course, ships far out to sea were beyond any country's jurisdiction, so crews set up shipboard radio stations that played the same music heard in the United States and closed-circuit TV that featured the latest American-made films. Many ships set aside compartments for weight lifting and exercise.

For the men and women of the fleet, however, this was not a normal overseas deployment. With danger close by and war imminent, bluejackets served "port and starboard" watches; that is, 12 hours on duty and 12 hours off in a 24-hour period. And during their "off watch" time, they were expected to carry out their routine duties, maintain their equipment, shower, eat, and catch a few precious hours of sleep. With aircraft being launched and recovered on the carriers, hatches being slammed shut, and equipment being operated all day and night, however, restful sleep at sea was a sometime thing.

Despite the irritants and difficulties of military life in the theater, the morale of the Navy's men and women remained high throughout Desert Shield. Officers and enlisted people commonly expressed confidence in the superiority of their ships, weapons, and training. The knowledge that they were part of a global coalition determined to defeat the adventurism of Saddam Hussein, whom many saw as evil, enhanced their morale. According to LaPlante, there were few morale or disciplinary problems because the sailors and marines believed that their mission was important. He observed that, "they knew that the whole consciousness of America was focused on them; they knew that and they appreciated it."[203] Many officers and enlisted people asked Admiral Mauz, "when are we going to attack?"

The people of the United States also boosted their morale. Just before the Christmas holiday, American corporations, schools, civic organizations, and millions of private citizens dispatched to the Middle East over 400 tons of mail and "care packages" loaded with cookies, decorations, and personal items. Throughout Desert Shield, Americans sent hundreds of thousands of books, audio tapes, video games, and video tapes along with several thousand televisions and video cassette recorders to the gulf. Captain Mobley noted that *Saratoga* got

> ten gazillion letters. Every school in the United States, I think, has written to *Saratoga*. Obvious exaggeration, but we have had tremendous support,

organizations sending us things. Saratoga County, New York, sending us VCRs and movies and games. I mean, they've spent lots of money on the Christmas party for our families back home. The Children had a wonderful Christmas party, all expenses paid, including a very nice Christmas present, compliments of the citizens of Saratoga, New York.[204]

Moreover, the Red Cross processed thousands of messages between service personnel and their families relating to such matters as birth announcements and emergency leave. Commercial communications companies worked with CENTCOM headquarters to install telephones in the field so personnel could talk to loved ones at home.

Back in the States, Navy Family Service Centers and community support groups helped families while their fathers, mothers, and other relatives were overseas. The Navy's Bureau of Personnel and Office of Information set up emergency communications center "hotlines" to handle emergency situations for family members and to answer questions about the course of the war. The outpouring of support by naval personnel in the United States mirrored that of the American public for a cause in which the vast majority wholeheartedly believed.[205]

The Defense Department also worked hard to ease the strain on personnel in the operational theater by dispatching a contracted cruise ship to the gulf. The day before Christmas the *Cunard Princess* put in at Bahrain. For almost a year the ship served as a home away from home for thousands of American service men and women. Designated the Armed Forces Reserve Center to accommodate local sensibilities, *Cunard Princess* provided a four-day, three-night program of rest and recreation (R&R) for 900 service personnel. Soldiers, sailors, airmen, and marines could enjoy the dining, sports, and exercise facilities on board, experience a little privacy in one of the two- or three-person cabins, and take a guided tour of Bahrain. Furthermore, 350 Jewish personnel were able to celebrate a Passover Seder on board the ship. Between December and June more than 50,000 Central Command people spent time in *Cunard Princess*, even though they represented only a small proportion of the half-million American troops in the theater.[206]

Central Command took other actions to improve morale, including hosting visits by President Bush, Vice President Daniel Quayle, Secretary Baker, Secretary Cheney, General Powell, General Gray, and a succession of congressmen. On Thanksgiving Day, President and Mrs. Bush flew out to amphibious ship *Nassau* (LHA 4), bringing holiday cheer to American sailors who thronged around the pair. Miles out to sea, they could also celebrate a religious service. These visits demonstrated to service men and women that their leaders were behind them. They also served as a necessary link between the troops and the American people.[207]

USN DN-SC 91-07155

General Powell, Chairman of the Joint Chiefs of Staff, responds to the warm welcome from *Wisconsin* sailors during his visit to the ship in September 1990.

USN DN-SC 91-03461

Comedian Jay Leno entertains sailors and marines of amphibious assault ship *Iwo Jima* (LPH 2) in Bahrain.

As in World War II, Korea, and Vietnam, the United Services Organization (USO) sponsored visits by entertainers, but because of Arab sensitivities there were no extravaganzas of sight and sound in the gulf. Nevertheless, comedian Bob Hope spent his forty-eighth Christmas overseas with American service personnel. Fellow comedians Jay Leno and Steve Martin put on impromptu performances in the Saudi desert, usually atop sandbagged bunkers, or on board ships plying the waters around the Arabian Peninsula. TV actors Delta Burke and Gerald McRaney also did their part to boost morale. Because social restrictions were less rigid on the island of Bahrain, not only Bob Hope but Ann Jillian, Marie Osmond, and the Pointer Sisters entertained American military personnel there. General Schwarzkopf noted wryly that these performances "were a whole lot less austere than the one I saw" in Saudi Arabia.[208]

R&R for the great majority of men and women in the theater took the form of volleyball games and other diversions set up by their own commands. During the Christmas season, for example, *Wisconsin* hosted the "Operation Desert Shield Holiday Sports Festival," in which sailors and marines from the battleship, command ships *Blue Ridge* and *LaSalle*, cruiser *Bunker Hill*, destroyer *Macdonough* (DDG 39) and frigate *Nicholas*, and the staff of Commander Middle East Force took part in boxing, weightlifting, and wrestling competitions.[209]

Coalition naval forces often found ingenious ways to strengthen morale. On Christmas Day, the British destroyer *Brazen*'s helicopter lowered down to the surprised crewmen of *Worden* a specially baked holiday cake. Not to be outdone, the Canadians had one of their SH-3 Sea King helicopters, painted red for the occasion, circle *Worden*. A Canadian sailor dressed as Santa Claus hung out the door waving a Christmas greeting. Finally, he was lowered to the deck of the cruiser to deliver to the appreciative Americans a big bag of ice-cold Molsen beer.[210]

Countdown to War

Even as the United States and the other member nations of the UN coalition built up forces for offensive action against Iraq, President Bush increased pressure on Saddam Hussein to relinquish his hold on Kuwait. Bush and his advisors doubted that anything short of armed force would prompt the Iraqi dictator to pull out, even though they would have welcomed a voluntary withdrawal.

The administration knew that a war against Iraq would have to be quick and decisive. Neither the international community nor the American public would support a war that left Saddam's power intact, produced excessive allied casualties, or dragged on interminably. The Saudis and the other Arabs would not stand for a long-term Western presence on the ground in the region.

The timing of a military offensive to oust the Iraqis, however, depended upon numerous military, diplomatic, and political considerations. The most obvious military consideration was that the deployment of forces for the offensive would not be completed until mid-January. Furthermore, by that time, nearly one-third of the active U.S. armed forces, including one-half of the Marine Corps, was deployed to the gulf. Six of the Navy's 14 carriers were in the region. There was no draft in place. These factors raised the question of rotation of forces home, for the United States could not realistically expect its service men and women to remain in the theater indefinitely.

If the war began in the spring, it might interfere with the June pilgrimages to the Muslim holy cities of Mecca and Medina. Furthermore, the weather became unbearable in the summer. In addition, world leaders feared that the cost of the war and the impact on the world's economic stability would only get worse if the crisis dragged on.

But Bush could not launch an attack until the American public, America's allies in the UN, and the pro-Western Arab nations were convinced that other options had been exhausted. Hence, the administration hinted that while the international embargo had cut off Iraq's prime resource, oil money, and critical munitions for its armed forces, it probably would not by itself cause Saddam to back down. Even though by late 1990 the maritime interception operation was functioning efficiently, the dictator publicly belittled the international effort. In late 1996, long after the war, by which time the continuing UN embargo patrol had intercepted tens of thousands of merchant vessels, neither the Iraqi state nor Saddam Hussein's regime stood in danger of collapse.

Saddam's own actions helped convince the world that war was necessary. Contrasted with his release of Western hostages before Christmas was the brutalization of Kuwait by his forces. Sources as diverse as the Kuwaiti resistance and Amnesty International circulated reports of Iraqi troops and police torturing and summarily executing Kuwaiti citizens, raping women, removing babies from hospital incubators, and systematically looting the country. Although some of these reports later proved false, many instances of Iraqi atrocities were confirmed.

Saddam's unwillingness to compromise helped enable the United States to gather support in the United Nations for war. The Bush administration's personification of Saddam, and not the Iraqi people, as a threat to world peace facilitated that effort. World leaders remained concerned about the Iraqi dictator's outright invasion of a sovereign Arab nation, ill treatment of foreign civilians held captive, and development of nuclear, chemical, and biological weapons, and they expressed outrage over Saddam's brutal occupation of Kuwait. On 29 November, the UN Security Council passed Resolution 678, empowering UN member nations to "use all necessary means" to oust Iraqi forces from Kuwait, unless they withdrew voluntarily on or before 15 January 1991. Thus, the UN sanctioned war.[211]

Saddam seemed unfazed. That same day, he expressed his disdain for American military power. On 2 December, his forces tested three surface-to-surface missiles.

Nevertheless, President Bush gave the dictator every opportunity to avoid the approaching maelstrom. Six days before the UN deadline, Secretary of State James Baker met with Iraqi Foreign Minister Tariq Aziz in Geneva, Switzerland. Despite the mountain of evidence to the contrary, Saddam, according to Aziz, believed that he might still compel the UN coalition to back down. The meeting made it clear to all that the confrontation in the Persian Gulf would not be resolved short of war.

It remained for Bush to obtain affirmation from the American people before launching the attack. For American leaders, Vietnam had reinforced a basic strategic precept, codified by Secretary of Defense Casper Weinberger, that U.S. armed forces had to have political support before they could enter combat. Saddam's continued intransigence, the manifest international unity, and the fact that a large American expeditionary force was now in the field, persuaded the great majority of Americans that war was the most logical course of action. On 12 January 1991, the U.S. Congress resolved to authorize the President to use military force against Iraq. There would be war.[212]

CHAPTER 4

Attack by Air and Sea

AT 0141 ON 17 JANUARY 1991, GMG2 Joseph Palisano stood on the deck of destroyer *Paul F. Foster* (DD 964), watching the first Tomahawk missile fired from the Persian Gulf against Iraq blast off from his ship. "There it goes," he exclaimed, "we just started a war!"[1] Later that morning, speakers on board *Ranger* blared the "William Tell Overture" as the ship's catapults hurled A-6 Intruders, EA-6B Prowlers, and F-14 Tomcats into the predawn darkness over the gulf, where they joined scores of aircraft from three other U.S. carrier battle groups.[2]

From his bridge on board the Australian guided missile destroyer *Brisbane*, Commodore C. J. Oxenbould, RAN, watched as the U.S. ships launched wave after wave of Tomahawk missiles and aircraft. He found it "altogether a most incredible and unforgettable sight, which imposed stunned silence in the operation room as we listened to the calm, measured tones of the US commanders unleashing their well planned strike on Iraq."[3] Operation Desert Storm had begun.

The Desert Storm Plan and Composite Warfare Doctrine

Central Command's comprehensive, four-phase Desert Storm plan served as the blueprint for the allies' 43-day war against Iraq. The plan's official title, "Combined OPLAN for Offensive Operations to Eject Iraqi Forces from Kuwait," reflected one of the coalition's two major objectives.[4] The other was to destroy Iraq's capacity for future aggression. The basic thrust of the plan had changed little since October 1990, when President Bush and his advisors concurred that a massive offensive would be required to accomplish the coalition's political goals.

U.S. air power served as the principal combat arm in Phases I, II, and III of Desert Storm. Phase I was a strategic air campaign aimed at decapitating Saddam's military power by rendering his forces blind, deaf, and immobile. To accomplish these goals, allied warplanes would strike the twelve strategic target sets identified by General Horner's air planning staff: leadership command facilities; electricity production facilities; telecommunications and C3 nodes; air defense system; military depots and storage facilities; nuclear, biological, and chemical weapons research, production, and storage facilities; air forces and airfields; railroads and bridges; Scud missile launchers and production and storage facilities; oil refineries and distribution facilities; naval forces and port facilities; and ground forces, especially the Republican Guard.[5]

In Phase II, allied forces would establish air superiority in the KTO. In Phase III, air and naval power would prepare the battlefield by isolating and reducing enemy forces in the theater. If Saddam refused to capitulate, the coalition would launch Phase IV, a multinational ground offensive supported by air and naval forces aimed at removing the Iraqis from Kuwait. General Schwarzkopf would not begin the ground attack, however, until allied air power had cut the combat effectiveness of Iraqi forces in half.[6]

Phases I–III of the theater plan—strategic attack, air superiority, and battlefield preparation—comprised the air campaign. Originally, the phases were planned for sequential execution, with Phase I lasting 6 to 10 days, Phase II roughly a day and a half, and Phase III about 2 to 3 weeks. But President Bush's doubling of the combat force in November 1990 had provided Horner with enough aircraft to execute all three phases simultaneously, in compliance with Schwarzkopf's wish to begin attacking enemy ground forces on day one. As it turned out, the aerial campaign mostly involved strategic bombing and air superiority missions during January and battlefield preparation missions in early February.[7]

Naval forces played a key role in Desert Storm. Admiral Arthur had two primary missions: 1) to support the air campaign, and 2) to convince Saddam that the allies intended to launch an amphibious assault on his left flank. Even if General Schwarzkopf had no intention of doing so, a credible amphibious threat would pin substantial Iraqi forces to the coast.[8]

In 1991 the Navy found itself in a regional, "green-water" war against Iraq. Naval leaders had long reasoned that if the fleet could take on the Soviets, it could also handle Third World powers. The naval service has long regarded its weapons, ships, and tactics as flexible instruments that could be modified to meet the needs of a particular armed confrontation. During the Gulf War, the Navy adapted the composite warfare commander concept to the littoral nature of the conflict. The strike warfare commanders supported General Horner, the JFACC, and followed his air tasking order (ATO) for CENTCOM air operations

USN

An A-7 Corsair II is catapulted from *John F. Kennedy* in the Red Sea to attack targets hundreds of miles inland in Iraq.

USN

A Tomahawk land attack missile is launched from a Battle Force Zulu combatant at the start of Desert Storm.

in Iraq and Kuwait. The antiair warfare commander concerned himself not only with fleet defense, but with protecting the entire right flank of the coalition. Admiral Arthur found that the composite warfare commander concept worked well in fighting Iraq, enabling him to give his warriors the latitude they needed to fight and win.[9]

Rear Admiral Daniel March, Commander Carrier Group 5 and Commander Battle Force Zulu, served as both the composite and strike warfare commander for the U.S. naval forces in the Persian Gulf. In the Red Sea, Rear Admiral Riley D. Mixson, Commander Carrier Group 2, led Battle Force Yankee. Like March, Mixson served as composite and strike warfare commander for his battle force.[10]

The Air Campaign: D-Day and D+1

The Tomahawks and aircraft heading for Iraq and Kuwait in the early hours of 17 January 1991 formed the vanguard of the biggest air strike since World War II. At approximately 0130, 90 minutes before H-Hour, U.S. warships had begun launching Tomahawk missiles toward targets in Iraq. Aegis cruiser *San Jacinto* (CG 56) had fired the first TLAM from the Red Sea, followed 11 minutes later by *Paul F. Foster* in the Persian Gulf. In all, U.S. ships successfully fired 122 missiles on the first day.

Soon after launch, the 20.5-foot missiles dropped their rocket boosters, deployed wing and tail surfaces, fired up their jet engines, and accelerated to a cruising speed of approximately 480 knots. Gyroscopic inertial guidance systems kept the TLAMs on course over water. Terrain contour matching (TERCOM) systems guided the Tomahawks over land by comparing the terrain below with images carefully prepared and installed in their memory systems, enabling them to bob and weave toward Baghdad at altitudes between 100 to 300 feet. Cruise missile support activities in Norfolk and Hawaii had provided mission planning and flight path programming, using data supplied by the Defense Mapping Agency. Each mission required 80 hours to develop because of the detailed intelligence and geographic information required. Once over the Iraqi capital, the missiles used on-board video cameras to literally read the map of the city to find their targets.[11]

The first wave of aerial attackers heading for Iraq included not only TLAMs but 30 Air Force F-117A stealth fighters of the 37th Tactical Fighter Wing. Allied leaders relied heavily on F-117s and Tomahawks against the enemy seat of government because they feared that the Iraqis would be ready for conventional aircraft over the capital, especially after former Air Force Chief of Staff Dugan's imprudent public dis-

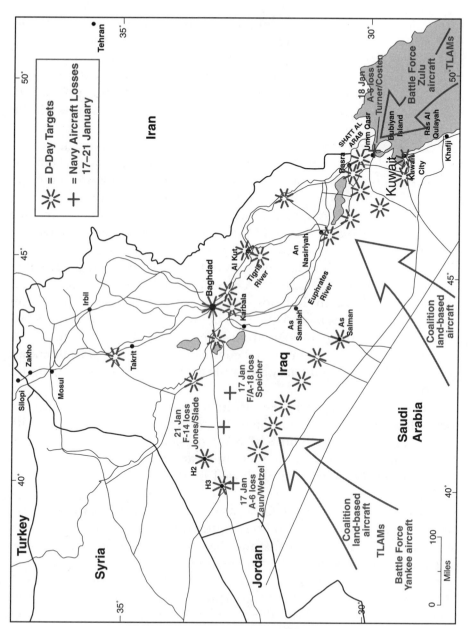

The Air Assault on Iraq

cussion about winning the war in "downtown Baghdad." However, non-stealth aircraft, including F-16s and F/A-18s, attacked targets in Baghdad, particularly during the first week of Desert Storm.[12]

Altogether, 668 aircraft from the U.S. Air Force, Navy, Marine Corps, and 11 other allied nations would strike that first night.[13] Dozens of B-52 bombers winged toward their targets. More than 160 aerial tankers refueled the coalition aircraft enroute to Iraq. Reconnaissance and airborne early warning aircraft stood by to provide intelligence coverage and air control for the coming battle. As H-Hour approached, fighters led electronic warfare planes and tactical bombers through the clear, moonless night into Iraq.

The coalition's approaching aerial armada faced a sophisticated integrated air defense system that Air Force officials would later claim was far more imposing than that developed by the Soviets in Eastern Europe at the height of the Cold War. Saddam's "layered" system used a mix of Soviet and Western equipment, including advanced radars, interceptor aircraft, surface-to-air missiles (SAMs), and antiaircraft artillery (AAA). Saddam's forces boasted some 7,000 radar and optically guided antiaircraft guns and 16,000 radar and infrared guided surface-to-air missiles, including the Soviet SA-2, SA-3, SA-6, SA-7, SA-8, SA-9, SA-13, SA-14, and SA-16; Franco-German Rolands; and American HAWKs captured in Kuwait. The AAA was most dangerous below 15,000 feet, while the SAMs provided overlapping coverage from near ground level to about 40,000 feet. A French-built, computerized command and control system known as "Kari" ("Iraq" spelled backwards in French) tied all of these weapons together.

The Iraqis organized their air defenses in three components. The first, a highly centralized national system, protected key airfields with fighters and fixed SA-2 and SA-3 SAM sites. The second, operated by the Republican Guard, defended nuclear, biological, and chemical warfare facilities. The third, deployed by the Iraqi army, covered the battlefield.[14]

Because the Iraqi air defense system had the potential to seriously damage if not thwart the coalition's entire offensive campaign, the most important objectives of the first two days' strikes were to clear the skies of enemy aircraft and, as Air Force Chief of Staff General Merrill A. McPeak put it, "disintegrate [Iraq's] integrated air defense setup."[15] "The systematic destruction of Saddam's eyes and ears," noted Commander William J. Luti, Executive Officer of *John F. Kennedy*'s VAQ-130, "was the one precondition necessary to implement the remaining phases of the air campaign."[16] Once the coalition accomplished these goals, Iraq's armed forces and warmaking infrastructure would be vulnerable to the full weight of air attack.[17]

"Tomahawk in Downtown Baghdad" by John Charles Roach

Minutes before H-Hour, 0300, F-117s dropped the first bombs on Baghdad.[18] Soon after, Tomahawk missiles began to rain down on heavily defended targets in and around the enemy capital, destroying or damaging a Scud missile plant, the Baath Party headquarters, the Presidential Palace, command and control installations, and electrical power facilities.[19] On the balcony of Baghdad's al-Rashid Hotel, a British cameraman's jaw dropped as a Tomahawk screamed past his window and slammed into the Iraqi Ministry of Defense, inflicting severe damage.[20] Nearby, CNN correspondents Bernard Shaw, John Holliman, and Peter Arnett were broadcasting live while air-raid sirens wailed and antiaircraft fire crisscrossed the sky. Air Force and Navy officers watching television hundreds of miles away in General Horner's Riyadh office cheered wildly when their screen suddenly went blank. CNN Baghdad had just gone off the air (albeit temporarily).[21]

A storm of AAA fire greeted allied aviators inside Iraq. Solid streams of tracers arced and twisted in the sky above Baghdad like red ropes. Pilots spotted dense flak over the capital from over 100 miles away. "It was an overwhelming amount," noted Commander John Leenhouts, Executive Officer of VA-72, a *John F. Kennedy* A-7E squadron.

USN DN-ST 91-04251

Carrier-based EA-6B Prowlers were critical to coalition efforts to "disintegrate Iraq's integrated air-defense system."

"It looked like the fireworks display at Disney World multiplied by a hundred."[22]

But this show was deadly. That night Hornets from *Saratoga*'s VFA-81 participated in a strike on Iraqi air defenses near Baghdad. During the attack, Commander Michael Anderson spotted the afterburner trail of a MiG-25 and reported the contact to the nearby AWACS, seeking clearance to fire. Before the AWACS could verify the contact, Lieutenant Commander Michael Scott Speicher's Hornet disintegrated in midair. It is unclear whether the MiG shot down the F/A-18 or collided with it, but Speicher was the first coalition aviator killed in combat.[23]

The second wave of attacking aircraft struck some 20 minutes after the first. Its 70 planes included Navy and Marine Hornets, Intruders, and A-7 Corsairs armed with high-speed anti-radiation missiles, and Navy EA-6B Prowler and Air Force F-4G Wild Weasel and EF-111 Raven electronic countermeasures (ECM) aircraft, all flying suppression of enemy air defenses (SEAD) and electronic warfare (EW) missions. These aircraft located enemy radar installations and then either jammed their electronic signals or attacked them with HARMs. In this manner, the coalition began to neutralize Iraq's surface-to-air missiles, large-caliber antiaircraft artillery pieces, and the command and control centers that

USN

Launched from a Corsair attack plane, the air-to-surface missile will soon descend toward a target in Iraq.

operated them. In the first 48 hours of the war, naval aviators accounted for 60 percent of the coalition's SEAD sorties.[24]

During the initial attacks Navy and Marine Corps planes also released tactical air-launched decoys (TALDs), which mimicked the radar signature of strike aircraft. The 92-inch-long decoys caused the defenders to waste expensive, hard-to-replace SAMs on what they thought were enemy bombers. The Air Force did not have a suitable decoy, but by the start of Desert Storm, the staff at the Naval Air Station, Point Mugu, California, had trained an Air Force team in the use of the Navy's BQM-74 drone.[25]

According to one source, the Iraqis fired as many as nine SAMs every time they detected one of the decoys overhead.[26] This tactic also fooled the enemy into turning on their radars, revealing their locations and rendering them vulnerable to HARM attack. Iraqi radar operators soon learned that switching on their equipment was tantamount to suicide. To avoid HARM, SAM crews fired their missiles ballistically—that is, without radar guidance—severely curtailing their effectiveness. Neutralization of Iraq's radars carved out medium- and high-altitude sanctuaries from which allied aircraft could attack strategic targets with virtual impunity. However, strike groups still needed SEAD aircraft to

USN

A high-speed anti-radiation missile (HARM).

defeat the numerous local point-defense missiles operated by the Republican Guard and Iraqi Army.[27]

Scores of Navy and Marine aircraft hit strategic targets throughout the theater that first night. Planes from *John F. Kennedy*'s Carrier Air Wing 3 and *Saratoga*'s Carrier Air Wing 17 together with U.S. Air Force and Royal Air Force planes struck targets near Baghdad and heavily defended airfields in western Iraq. *America*'s Carrier Air Wing 1 conducted defensive air operations over the northern Red Sea and western Saudi Arabia. Navy F-14s and Marine Corps F/A-18s joined Air Force F-15s in flying combat air patrol and fighter sweep missions. *Midway*'s Carrier Air Wing 5, *Ranger*'s Carrier Air Wing 2, and Marine Aircraft Group 11, based ashore at Shaikh Isa Air Base, Bahrain, along with other coalition air forces struck airfields, port facilities, the Umm Qasr naval base, and air defenses in southeastern Iraq.[28]

Carrier-launched strikes covered enormous distances. If a map of North America were superimposed over the KTO, Battle Force Zulu would appear near Richmond, Virginia, Baghdad near Detroit, and Battle Force Yankee near Little Rock, Arkansas. During the first two days of Desert Storm, *Midway* and *Ranger* operated from a position roughly 85 nautical miles east of Bahrain and 280 nautical miles south-

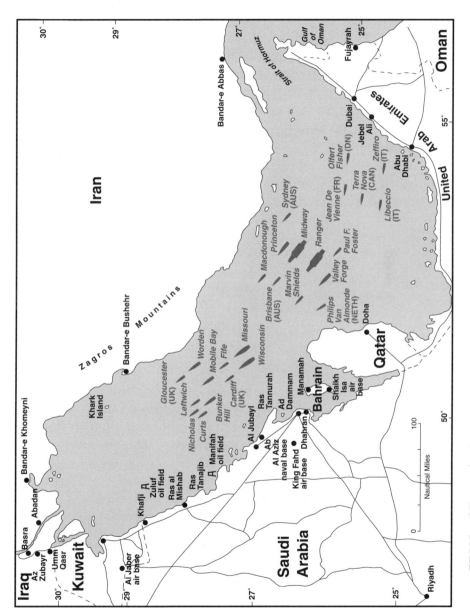

UN Naval Forces in the Persian Gulf, 17 January 1991 (position of ships approximate)

177

east of Kuwait City. Battle Force Yankee operated some 120 nautical miles south-southeast of the tip of the Sinai Peninsula and 420 nautical miles from the Iraq-Saudi border. Planes from Battle Force Yankee routinely flew missions involving round-trip distances of 1,400 miles. Nevertheless, the Red Sea carriers were closer to key targets in western Iraq than were many of the principal Air Force land bases, while carriers in the gulf were positioned closer to targets in Kuwait than the majority of land-based aircraft.[29]

Within the first few hours of the war, the coalition effectively gained air superiority—defined as the dominance by a group of aircraft in a given time and space without prohibitive interference by the opposing force. By severing the Iraqi air force from its leadership, destroying its aircraft on the ground, and cratering its runways, allied aircraft largely preempted their Iraqi counterparts from fighting. As a result, few Iraqi interceptors rose to meet the attackers.[30]

Iraqi pilots who did get aloft seemed confused. During one bombing run, Commander Leenhouts saw one group of Iraqi MiG-21 fighters zooming back and forth between his strike group and another. "I don't think they had a very clear picture of exactly who was out there," he noted. "We expected them to have their fighter aircraft more regimented, more uniform in their attacks, but they were truly random."[31]

Saddam's airmen also proved inept. On 17 January, an Iraqi MiG-29 pilot shot a missile that destroyed his own wingman. Then, perhaps mesmerized by the resulting fireball, he flew his own plane into the ground.

As the Naval Intelligence Command had forecast, Saddam chose to risk only a few of his aircraft in aerial combat with the coalition. The Iraqi command handled those few badly. "Any of my captains could have run [Saddam's] air force and caused much more trouble than he did," said General Horner.[32] In contrast to more than 2,000 missions flown on the first day by the allies, the Iraqis sortied only 24 combat aircraft, nine of which never returned.[33]

Two of these fell to Lieutenant Commander Mark I. Fox and Lieutenant Nick Mongillo, F/A-18 pilots from *Saratoga*'s VFA-81. These Hornets and two others were flying four abreast into western Iraq at approximately 30,000 feet at mach .9[34] with their radars in the air-to-ground mode in preparation to bomb an airfield. About 35 miles out from the target, an E-2C Hawkeye early warning plane from *Saratoga* radioed an alert: "Hornet, bandits on your nose, 15 miles." Two Iraqi MiG-21s were flying straight toward the F/A-18s, closing fast.

Fox immediately switched his radar to the air-to-air mode and selected a heat-seeking Sidewinder missile. He locked onto the MiG on the right and fired. The Sidewinder appeared not to track the target, so he fired a radar-seeking Sparrow missile. Just after the Sparrow left its rail,

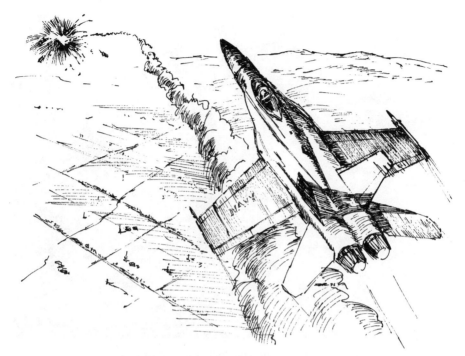

"A Hornet Stings" by John Charles Roach

the Sidewinder slammed into the MiG with a bright flash, a brilliant orange flame, and a puff of black smoke. Three or four seconds later the Sparrow struck the flaming MiG, which plummeted to earth. Mongillo radioed, "splash one." At the same time Mongillo locked onto the second MiG and fired a Sparrow at it. The missile pulled a hard right turn and hit the MiG almost abeam of Mongillo's F/A-18. "Splash two," said one of the other carrier pilots. Two other Iraqi aircraft had converged on the area, but fled when the Hornets' radars locked onto them. Only 40 seconds had elapsed since the Hawkeye's warning.

Switching their radars back to the air-to-ground mode, the four pilots prepared to execute their bombing run. Amid popcorn-like bursts of antiaircraft shells and corkscrew streaks from hand-held SAMs, the F/A-18s rolled in and released their bombs.[35] "Jinking" to avoid the SAMs, Fox watched his 2,000-pound Mark 84 general purpose bombs walk through a hangar, then lit his plane's afterburner and headed south. The other aircraft scored hits on fuel stores and a control station. To Fox and Mongillo, the bombing run seemed much easier than taking on the two MiGs.[36]

For a variety of reasons, these were the Navy's only victories over Iraqi fixed-wing aircraft during the war. Navy fighter pilots flew most of

USN DN-SN 91-06493

Lieutenant Commander Mark Fox, the first coalition pilot to shoot down an Iraqi MiG, poses in the cockpit of the F/A-18C he flew during the mission (another pilot's plane).

their sorties on combat air patrol above allied ships. In fact, CAP missions accounted for 21 percent of the sorties flown by carrier aircraft during the Gulf War. With the Iraqis attempting a mere 100 air-to-air sorties in the first three days of Desert Storm, and only one operation over water during the entire war, Navy fighter pilots had few opportunities to shoot down an Iraqi plane.[37]

The primary factor in the paucity of Navy air-to-air victories, however, proved to be limitations of the equipment on board Navy fighters. Most of the coalition's air-to-air kills occurred with clearance to fire anti-air missiles beyond visual range. CINCCENT rules of engagement, structured to minimize the possibility of one coalition aircraft shooting down another, required that allied planes be able not only to pick up distant contacts on radar but to determine from at least two sources if they were friend or foe. Intended to operate in the crowded air space over Central Europe, the Air Force F-15 could handle both tasks. Designed to form the fleet's first line of defense, the Navy F-14's radars and 100-mile-range Phoenix air-to-air missiles were ideally suited to destroying distant threats. But when at war far out to sea, the Navy normally considered any contacts approaching the battle group as hostile. Hence, the F-14 had less capable IFF equipment than the F-15. Although Navy and

Marine F/A-18s possessed enhanced IFF equipment, the "short-legged" aircraft were built to operate close to the fleet. As a result, General Horner limited the employment of Navy fighters in the congested air space over Iraq.

"I didn't feel that the rules of engagement were structured against the Navy," Lieutenant Commander Fox later noted. "They just took advantage of the technical capabilities of the F-15."[38] Admiral Arthur, however, protested that the Navy's aerial resources were not being fully exploited. When the issue arose in Riyadh, Schwarzkopf, who by then had established a close working relationship with Horner, told the Air Force general to handle it as he saw fit.[39] Horner sent his deputy, Brigadier General Buster Glosson out to *Blue Ridge* to work out a solution. Arthur argued that the F-14s were equipped to operate safely with the Air Force air defense fighters. According to March, Glosson, "had blinders on; we couldn't convince him." The admiral considered Glosson a "real blue suit asshole all the way; he was not joint."[40] Finally, Arthur and Glosson agreed that the JFACC could establish CAP stations over those areas of Iraq where the F-14s could operate without undue risk to coalition aircraft. But, according to Arthur, "they never did."[41]

On the second day of Desert Storm, carrier forces mounted an aerial mining operation for the first time since the Vietnam War.[42] Hoping to isolate Iraqi naval combatants operating in the northern Persian Gulf from the port facilities and bases at Basrah, az-Zubayr, and Umm Qasr as well as to prevent enemy boats in these ports from entering the gulf, four A-6 Intruders supported by another 14 planes from *Ranger* made a low-level drop of 42 Mark 36 Destructor mines at the mouth of the az-Zubayr River. The Iraqis fought back, shooting down one of the A-6s and killing its pilot and bombardier-navigator, Lieutenant Charles Turner and Lieutenant William Costen of VA-155. This loss prompted Admiral Arthur to cancel further mine-laying missions. Arthur later recalled that he "did not like that operation,... didn't think we needed it," and since numerous Iraqi-laid weapons were already in the northern gulf, he felt that the Navy "didn't need to put any [more] mines up there."[43] For lack of adequate post-attack battle damage assessment—a recurring problem for all the services in Desert Storm—the naval command could not directly evaluate the results of the mission.[44] But analysts who studied the operation after the war concluded that, based on subsequent enemy naval activity in the northern gulf, the minefield had little effect on Iraqi naval operations.[45]

That same day carrier aircraft also attacked Iraqi naval installations near Umm Qasr and hit hangars and parking ramps at the Ash Shuaybah and al-Jaber air facilities in Kuwait while Tomahawks struck 17

USN DN-ST 91-08572

Vice Admiral Stanley R. Arthur, Commander U.S. Seventh Fleet/Commander U.S. Naval Forces, Central Command. Arthur, a veteran of aerial combat in the Vietnam War, was a dynamic and clear-sighted naval leader in Desert Storm.

oil, electric, and leadership targets. By the second day's end aircraft from Battle Forces Yankee and Zulu had flown 1,100 combat sorties and Navy warships had fired 216 Tomahawks.[46] Attack submarine *Louisville* (SSN 724), operating in the Red Sea, fired several of these missiles. *Pittsburgh* (SSN 720), a Mediterranean-based submarine, later joined the attack on Iraq.[47] This opening salvo of the Gulf War marked the consummation of a weapons development project that traced its origins to the Navy's Regulus land attack missile program of the late 1950s.[48]

The allied success had a price; during the first 48 hours of Desert Storm, the Iraqis shot down ten coalition aircraft, including three U.S. Navy planes. The loss of several of these planes during low-level attacks reminded Admiral Arthur of past combat experience. He addressed his air commanders:

> Gentlemen far be it for me to dictate specific combat tactics but I must inject my early observations relative to the age-old argument of low altitude delivery versus high. With a quick look at what has happened to the multinational air forces to date, one cannot escape the fact that current AAA environment makes the low altitude delivery a non starter. I want you to take a very hard look at how your air wings are handling the issue. We learned a hard lesson in Vietnam relative to AAA and then later many told us we learned it wrong—I think not. There is a place and time for low altitude delivery and it usually involves surprise. We can no longer count on surprise. That went away shortly after [midnight on D-Day].[49]

In addition to the F/A-18 and A-6 mentioned above, the enemy shot down an A-6 from *Saratoga*'s VA-35 and captured its crew, Lieutenant Jeffrey Zaun (pilot) and Lieutenant Robert Wetzel (bombardier-navigator).[50] The world watched in horror as the Iraqis paraded the bruised and dazed-looking Zaun before their cameras. Many Americans now knew that the Iraqis would mistreat captured aviators, as had the Korean and Vietnamese communists before them.

Fortunately, Saddam Hussein was well on the way to defeat. Allied attacks had severed him from his armed forces and driven his regime underground. His country's command-control-communications and intelligence network, integrated air defense system, and power-generating infrastructure lay in shambles.[51] "The war was won within the first 48 hours," Rear Admiral Gee later noted, "because of a well designed campaign plan which was executed throughout the chain of command to win."[52]

Problems of the Air Campaign

Ultimately, prosecution of the air campaign by means of the Joint Force Air Component Commander and air tasking order system was a stunning testament to America's military prowess. But, on the road to victory, numerous problems arose in planning and executing the aerial assault on Iraq.

Long before the invasion of Kuwait, General Schwarzkopf intended to organize Central Command's air forces under a JFACC in the event of a war in his area of responsibility. Operation Plans 1002-88, 1002-90, and all of the Desert Shield and Desert Storm plans specified this arrangement. From the first days of Desert Shield, Schwarzkopf made it clear to his component commanders that General Horner, his Riyadh-based JFACC, would have significant control over Air Force, Navy, and Marine Corps air units assigned to CENTCOM.[53] Horner concurred with this top-down control, and his staff of 2,000 personnel handled both JFACC and CENTAF responsibilities. Most of these people were Air Force officers from the Ninth Air Force staff, with a sprinkling of representatives from Military Airlift Command and Strategic Air Command, and "liaison officers" from the other services.[54] But Horner's authority was far from absolute. He did not exercise operational control of most U.S. helicopter forces, the Air Force tankers, or the Air Force wing operating from Turkey (although he did direct the daily combat missions of the latter two).[55]

The Navy disliked the JFACC tasking of carrier aircraft committed to the air campaign. Captain Robert L. Johnson, chief of operations on the NAVCENT staff, attributed this attitude to a "difference of philosophy" between Navy and Air Force combat doctrine. "We train our people to be able to operate independently," he observed, "and that's inconsistent with top-down type of control."[56] The Navy had resisted a single manager for air operations in Korea and Vietnam. While the air campaigns in those wars suffered from innumerable shortcomings, most naval officers blamed political mismanagement for American failings, not the lack of joint control of air resources. Some naval officers doubted that the JFACC would make optimum use of carrier aircraft and Tomahawk missiles.[57] Others feared that the Desert Storm experience would set a precedent that would have long-term negative effects on the Navy's wartime operational flexibility and peacetime budgets. Indeed, Colonel Brian E. Wages, the Air Force liaison officer to Admiral Arthur's staff, commented that in the months before Desert Storm, "NAVCENT was still looking for ways to disestablish the JFACC."[58]

Since the Air Force did not have a standard system for strike planning and no approved joint air tasking procedures, General Horner used the system familiar to his Ninth Air Force.[59] The ATO itself was a large, detailed, computer-generated document, often numbering more than 300 pages and weighing as much as six pounds, prompting Admiral

Arthur to quip that "trees were big losers in Desert Storm."[60] The JFACC produced an updated ATO for every day of the war. Each document provided precise information on the target, mission, SEAD and aerial tanker support, and weapons for almost all of the 2,000-plus strike sorties planned for that day.

To naval officers raised in the tradition of independent operations and flexible doctrine, the system seemed complex and rigid.[61] The ATO "overwhelmed us, overwhelmed the Navy, almost overwhelmed everybody," noted General Boomer.[62] "We assumed it would never work," said Captain Harry Stanbridge, Rear Admiral Mixson's air operations officer.[63] Many NAVCENT staff officers felt that the system would be unable to cope with the fast pace and complexity of the air campaign, forcing General Horner to adopt the geographical area, or route package, approach used in Vietnam.[64] However, because of his own experience as a combat airman in Vietnam, Horner said that "we will have route packages over my dead body."[65] The general later discussed how he felt that system had created problems in Southeast Asia:

> The air campaign in Vietnam was divided into "route packages," because the Air Force and the Navy couldn't agree on a single commander. It was stupid. Rather than have a coordinated effort, we used geographic areas to separate our operations. I'll never forget flying toward my route package and looking down at a Communist resupply convoy. But we couldn't go after it because it was in the Navy's route package.[66]

The issue resolved itself when the pace of Desert Storm outstripped the ability of Navy strike planners to keep up. After the first two days of the war, NAVCENT never again attempted multiple-carrier strikes because they proved too difficult to organize. Unlike the Air Force, which had been planning for a massive, centrally controlled air war in Europe, the Navy's bread and butter in recent years had been small-scale contingency operations. Consequently, the Navy had no system for planning and directing sustained air campaigns, and even lacked a mechanism to plan integrated strikes from more than one carrier.[67] "I found that my staff was not adequately trained in strike planning," Admiral March lamented in a postwar report to Admiral Arthur.[68] With no viable alternative, NAVCENT had to adapt to the ATO system.

Generally, JFACC strike planners began work on a given day's air tasking order two to three days in advance. Officers selected targets, based on the latest intelligence, and submitted them to CENTAF's consolidated targeting board. General Horner and one of his legal advisors reviewed each target approved by the board. Aware that even one errant bomb could have a devastating moral or political impact, they made every effort to minimize civilian casualties and avoid damaging mosques, museums, archaeological sites, religious shrines, schools, and hospitals. Once targets received Horner's approval, the staff assigned aircraft to attack them and entered the information into the ATO.[69]

Navy input into strike planning came from NAVCENT Riyadh and the carrier battle forces. Before his departure from the theater, Admiral Mauz had merged the NAVCENT Riyadh and Fleet Coordinating Group staffs, which he and Admiral Arthur beefed up with additional officers, including former carrier air wing commanders. The new NAVCENT Riyadh organization was modeled on the long-standing and successful Seventh Fleet liaison units attached to the headquarters of Commander in Chief, Combined Forces Command and the Seventh Air Force in Korea. These, in turn, had been based on Commander Seventh Fleet's Detachment Charlie, established at MACV Headquarters near Than Son Nhut Air Base during the Vietnam War. Historically, these liaison units coordinated air operations with the other services, but did not plan them.[70]

The first COMUSNAVCENT Riyadh, Rear Admiral Timothy W. Wright, Commander Carrier Group 3, brought considerable experience to bear on the problems of strike planning. Wright and Mauz spoke to one another several times each week. Most often they discussed the status of the JFACC strike plan. Wright and his staff also maintained a close working relationship with the strike planners on board the carriers. However, Wright had taken the COMUSNAVCENT Riyadh job with the understanding that after three months he would return to his battle group.[71] In November a surface warrior, Rear Admiral Conrad C. Lautenbacher, Commander Cruiser Destroyer Group 5, replaced him as COMUSNAVCENT Riyadh. One observer noted that "this change entailed a significant reduction in the degree of flag-level Navy expertise in strike warfare available to the CINCCENT staff."[72] Captain Stephen U. Ramsdell, a naval aviator and historian who conducted extensive interviews with top naval officers during the war, observed that Lautenbacher "had little or no credibility with the Air Force people [because] he is not an aviator and they know he is not an aviator."[73] Captain Stanbridge, Mixson's air operations officer, felt that Lautenbacher made up for his lack of aviation expertise by selecting Captain Lyle Bien, a former Top Gun instructor and battle-tested air wing commander, to head up a Navy JFACC strike cell charged with helping to prepare the daily air tasking orders.[74]

Admiral March later remarked that since he was not an aviator, "Lautenbacher was not the right guy" to have in Riyadh. March added that he "really felt that [Lautenbacher] didn't play as strong a game as he could have there."[75] March, an aviator and Commander Battle Force Zulu, might have made a difference in Riyadh, but he visited

Schwarzkopf and Horner in the Saudi capital only once during Desert Storm. He later concluded that, "if I were to do things over again, I think right from the git-go I would have spent a little bit more time on the beach with Horner and some of those people and at least tried to cement, at a flag level, a pretty good understanding of our capabilities. I think Riley [Mixson] did an extraordinarily good job of that."[76]

The Navy JFACC strike cell consisted of seven aviators and two intelligence officers.[77] Although these men were competent and experienced commanders, they were too few in number and too junior in rank to exert influence in proportion to the Navy's participation in the air campaign.[78] In the so-called "Black Hole," the JFACC's targeting group for Iraq, U.S. Air Force officers predominated numerically, held all of the key positions, and dominated day-to-day decision-making processes.[79] According to an official Air Force history, the staff, headed by an air force officer, "usually...gave priority to Air Force F-16s and A-10s for daytime operations and to F-111s and F-15Es for nighttime ones." In addition, the Navy was even less successful than the Marine Corps in getting tank-busting assignments in the ATO.[80]

By January 1991, only two of the 48 officers serving in the JFACC were from Bien's strike cell: Commander Donald W. "Duck" McSwain represented the Persian Gulf carriers; Commander Maurice "Fast Eddie" Smith represented the Red Sea carriers.[81] The Navy's under-representation in Riyadh and lack of experience in campaign-level strike planning along with Navy and Air Force parochialism created friction between the services. According to Colonel Wages, NAVCENT staffers assumed that "every CENTAF action and policy position had a secret underlying motive with adverse intent for the Navy," while Air Force officers on the JFACC staff "tended to project a smug attitude," declaring to their naval counterparts that "this is the way it's going to be; play or don't play at your own choice."[82] As Admiral March later observed: "I got the feeling as things started to go that they [JFACC] were never going to bend over backwards to accommodate the Navy; that it was really an Air Force air war. We were assets to be used but we were not major players."[83] It did not help relations that JFACC directives were sometimes issued on Ninth Air Force stationery.[84] One NAVCENT Riyadh officer noted that Air Force planners "usually" were not "malevolent," but, as another naval officer described it, Navy–Air Force relations in Riyadh sometimes resembled "trench warfare."[85] Admiral Mauz recalled that CENTAF "thought we were from the moon, and it took a long time to get in the door."[86] Admiral Arthur concluded that the Navy would have fared better in Riyadh if it had placed "enough people in position of the right flavor and the right qualifications."[87]

Input from the battle forces into the strike planning process came from two echelons. Each carrier organized a "strike cell" staffed by representatives of the battle group commander, the embarked air wing, and the ship's company. This scheme enabled each carrier to operate as a single combat team. At the next echelon, each battle force established a cell, led by the strike warfare commander, to coordinate the individual carrier cells. Normally, three days before a proposed operation, the carrier strike cells passed their target nominations through their respective battle force cells to NAVCENT Riyadh. An amphibious task force targeting cell, composed of Navy and Marine staff officers, also recommended missions for the ATO.[88]

Disseminating the daily air tasking orders to the fleet, according to Admiral Arthur, Admiral March, and Captain Bien, proved to be the Navy's "biggest problem" with the ATO system.[89] The preferred means by which the JFACC staff transmitted the air tasking order to the various air units was the Computer-Aided Force Management System (CAFMS). This was a Ninth Air Force system, although not an Air Force-wide system. The carriers lacked CAFMS, as did several Air Force units, particularly those based in Turkey.[90] Even if the carriers had installed the system, they would have had to dedicate a portion of their communications capacity to it, and they had none to spare. The Navy and Air Force tried several alternate methods for transmitting the ATO electronically, but none proved satisfactory, owing largely to equipment limitations. Transmitting the 200–500-page ATOs could clog communications circuits for hours. As an expedient, the Navy employed a "pony express" of aircraft to fly hard copies of the ATO out to each carrier every day. This hand-delivery method proved a hardship for Navy air sortie planners, particularly for AAW controllers on board Aegis cruisers, which received the ATO by helicopter from the carriers, but no other viable solution could be found during Desert Storm.[91]

Battle Forces Yankee and Zulu had different experiences in adapting to the ATO system. Having exercised regularly and at length under the system during Desert Shield's "mirror-image" strike rehearsals, the air wings of *Saratoga* and *John F. Kennedy* in the Red Sea quickly established a routine that worked well throughout the war. As Admiral Gee said, "we rapidly became believers."[92] Since Battle Force Yankee—unlike Battle Force Zulu—had minimal concerns about defending against enemy air or surface threats, Admiral Mixson committed almost all of his daily sorties to the air campaign in Iraq.[93] General Horner said that Mixson "had a detailed knowledge of how the [control of air operations] worked, and he always got whatever he wanted. We always functioned well together. It was really a very, very smooth operation."[94]

Battle Force Zulu's accommodation to the ATO system proved more difficult.[95] Only *Midway* had operated in the region for any length of time before the war, but her air units flew most often over the North Arabian Sea, Persian Gulf, or Gulf of Oman, all of which lay outside JFACC control. Hence, Admiral March had his units train with the ATO, but did not make it a regular feature of Battle Force Zulu's air strike rehearsals. *Ranger*, which had steamed into the gulf only two days before Desert Storm, had even less time to exercise with the ATO process before hostilities began. *Theodore Roosevelt* arrived on station four days after Desert Storm began. March admitted that the Navy should have been better prepared to operate with the ATO system, and that he spent "an awful lot of time trying to integrate into the strike plan when that time could be better spent doing other things."[96]

Battle Force Zulu and CENTAF's mutual lack of familiarity bred bitter disputes over the legitimacy of allocating aircraft for fleet defense and concerns about striking maritime targets or targets of importance to the amphibious task force. Admiral March "really felt that the Navy was getting screwed in terms of sorties and targets."[97] To the JFACC staff, it seemed that aviators from Persian Gulf carriers too often hit alternate rather than primary targets. This perception, along with naval aviators' occasional improper use of ATO-specified call signs, led some of Horner's staff to regard the gulf carriers as unpredictable and unreliable.[98]

On the other hand, the JFACC staff and the ATO process did not always recognize or accommodate Battle Force Zulu's operating requirements. The Persian Gulf was not only the coalition's right flank, but also its jugular, through which flowed the troops and materiel necessary to defeat Saddam Hussein and to liberate Kuwait. Early in the war, Iraq's air and naval forces, particularly Exocet-armed aircraft and missile boats, still had the potential to mount attacks against allied ships.[99] Uncertainties about Iran's intentions required naval forces to keep watch over the gulf's entire length. Moreover, missions ordered by the JFACC staff did not always reflect an understanding of the weapons capacity, range, and communications characteristics of naval aircraft.[100]

Other difficulties stemmed from the air tasking system itself. Its effectiveness in managing the daily average of 2,500 sorties flown by allied air forces during Desert Storm and in preventing coalition aircraft from accidently shooting each other down was beyond question. But the 48-hour cycle needed to prepare an ATO did not permit quick response to mobile targets, such as Iraqi missile boats underway, or to potential sudden attacks by Iranian forces. Although the system included procedures to handle requests for immediate, unplanned action, the Persian Gulf carrier staffs found them unwieldy.[101] Admiral Arthur noted after the war:

> We've had many examples of us bringing back real time intelligence, fleeting moments of opportunity, without being able to get back to them. We had an enemy that crumpled on us this time, but if we had an enemy that was very tough and a lot smarter, we can't let those little windows of opportunity ever disappear.[102]

Even Air Force officers recognized that the "ATO document itself was cumbersome to work with due to the inability to format products flexibly to meet different user needs."[103]

In order to resolve these interservice disputes, the Navy retained control of air-to-air and air-to-surface sorties for fleet defense. This enabled Battle Force Zulu to plan and conduct fleet defense and maritime strike missions outside the air tasking order process, within the composite warfare commander framework. Thus, JFACC controlled air operations over land while Battle Force Zulu controlled air operations over the gulf. The Marines reached a similar arrangement. General Boomer designated missions to be flown by Marine aircraft in the U.S. Marine Forces, Central Command (MARCENT) area of operations while General Horner handled the external missions. Horner did not press the doctrinal issue and accommodated the Marines' desires to emphasize strike missions in the KTO rather than "downtown Baghdad."[104]

Aerial refueling proved to be another problem. The long distances between the carriers or allied airfields and their targets meant that aircraft usually had to refuel at least once during a strike mission. Each carrier air wing included three to five KA-6 aerial refueling planes, but they were not enough to carry out sustained, large-scale operations at the distances required. As a result, the Navy depended on the Air Force's land-based KC-135 tankers. One historian has aptly described these tankers as the "single most important aircraft type in the theater."[105]

This dependence created technical difficulties, because long before the Gulf War each service had developed equipment and fuel best suited for its particular mission. To help minimize the danger of fire on board carriers, the Navy normally used JP-5, a jet fuel with a higher combustion temperature than that used by the Air Force. Fire presented a far graver danger to crowded carriers than to air bases where the ordnance, planes, and fuel could be dispersed over a wide area. The conflagration touched off accidentally on board *Forrestal* (CV 59) in July 1967 in the Gulf of Tonkin, for example, put the ship out of action and killed more naval aviators than any air operation of the Vietnam War.[106] Additionally, Air Force tankers used a boom system to pump "gas" to thirsty aircraft, while Navy refuelers did so with hose and drogue equipment. To solve

An Air Force KC-135E and a Navy A-6E refuel Navy EA-6Bs enroute to targets in Iraq.

these problems, the Navy reluctantly accepted the increased fire hazard and allowed its aircraft to take on Air Force JA-1, while the Air Force fitted basket adapters to the KC-135s assigned to refuel Navy planes.[107]

Navy, Marine, and other allied tankers flew 4,000 refueling sorties during the war while Air Force tankers flew more than 15,000. Roughly 16 percent of the latter supported naval operations, a figure slightly less than the Navy's proportion of coalition strike aircraft in the theater. The Center for Naval Analyses (CNA) concluded that its evaluations did "not indicate that the Navy was unfairly treated with regard to land-based tanker sortie allocation," but some naval aviators, particularly those in the gulf, felt slighted by the JFACC's aerial tanker sortie allocation.[108]

Despite interservice differences over control of the air campaign, the ATO system, tanker allocations, and related issues, Navy and Air Force planners and commanders managed perhaps the most successful air campaign in military history. Their goal was to achieve victory while minimizing loss of coalition lives and resources, so they often argued their cases passionately. But most of the men and women on the various staffs routinely accommodated other views and operational approaches. For instance, Captain Edward P. O'Connell, an Air Force intelligence officer who helped with strike planning on board *Saratoga* during Desert

Shield, observed that his Navy counterparts were especially cooperative and welcomed his insight on targeting.[109] Admiral Sharp related that his liaison with General Glosson's target planning group, an Air Force colonel, reported that he "didn't think the plan for the employment of Tomahawk [was] robust enough . . . and there's a lot more that could be done." With the admiral's approval, the colonel worked successfully to improve integration of the TLAMs into the air operations plan.[110] Moreover, Admiral Arthur's relations with General Horner remained cordial, mutually respectful, and professional.[111] As Arthur put it, "from General Horner and my level . . . it was a straight up-and-down operation."[112] Horner explained how the services worked out their differences: "You do common sense things. And don't worry about doctrine. Doctrine is bull shit."[113] Even the critical Colonel Wages concluded that despite friction between the Navy and Air Force, "there were no show stoppers and the joint air campaign was conducted to exceptional effect."[114]

There was also some Army-Navy friction. Arthur later observed that the Army-heavy CENTCOM staff had "not a clue" about mine warfare and other aspects of naval warfare. He also believed that Generals Powell and Schwarzkopf ordered him in mid-February to cease firing Tomahawks, not just to conserve the expensive missiles, but to end the "good publicity" that the Navy was receiving from the videotaped launches. Moreover, Arthur said that Schwarzkopf ordered him to "stop firing the goddam [16-inch guns of the] battleships" for the same reason.[115]

Tanker sinkings in the gulf also produced joint fireworks. On 23 January, carrier aircraft attacked the oil-laden supertanker *Amuriyah* at Kuwait's Mina al-Bakr oil terminal, listed on the ATO as a target. Admiral March related that the ship was deliberately attacked, because U.S. intelligence learned that the Iraqis on board were reporting on coalition flight operations. The admiral asked for and got permission to destroy the merchantman. He emphasized that the ship was a "legitimate hit," because the "son of a bitch was passing information."[116] The resulting blaze eventually consumed most of the tanker's cargo and sank the ship. The next day, two of *Ranger's* A-6 Intruders attacked and set fire to what had been identified as a *Spasilac* minelayer tied up at Kuwait's offshore Sea Island Ocean Terminal. The ATO also listed the terminal as a target.[117]

Conscious of Iraq's expressed intention to defeat the allied offensive with "rivers of fire," Admiral Arthur regarded tankers as threats to his naval forces. Exploding tankers and oil-covered waters posed obvious dangers to surface ships and landing craft loaded with marines. Better to eliminate those threats long before any amphibious operations. During

USN

A Tomahawk cruise missile, as viewed through the periscope of attack submarine *Pittsburgh* (SSN 720), breaks the surface of the sea and begins its long journey from the Eastern Mediterranean to a target in Iraq.

Desert Shield, Schwarzkopf had concurred with Arthur's evaluation of Iraqi tankers as valid wartime targets and even directed the Navy to "sink every goddam Iraqi ship in sight" once hostilities began.[118]

Washington, however, did not wish to incur the political and environmental costs associated with oil spills in the gulf. Consequently, the CENTCOM staff sent Arthur a message on 17 January rescinding authority for attacking tankers in the gulf. Because the message went out on communications circuits that were overloaded with ATO data, the fleet only received it on the 24th.[119]

On the night of 26 January, two days after Admiral Arthur learned that Schwarzkopf had prohibited attacks on tankers in the Persian Gulf, however, naval patrol aircraft discovered two such ships in a river north of Bubiyan Island. Arthur determined that since these vessels had not yet entered the gulf, they were fair game. Attack aircraft from Battle Force Zulu soon zeroed in on the two ships.[120] According to Arthur, the general reacted by "going berserk" and "yelling and screaming."[121]

Nevertheless, this episode was an exception to the generally good relationship Arthur had with Schwarzkopf. The general was "a good guy to work for," Arthur later said.

> He's a very volatile guy. A lot of it's theatrical. He's like a lot of people. You get to him one on one, and tell him what your problem is, if he's got confidence in you, he's going to let you do it. Try to get him in the heat of battle when there's a lot of people around, and he's just going to unload, and go like gang busters. Hence the "Stormin Norman."[122]

Arthur concluded that "there were a couple of little incidents along the way, but . . . there was never a time that I couldn't get to him one on one and not resolve the problem. Never."[123]

Besides operational problems with the other services, the Navy dealt with internal issues during the air campaign. One set of difficulties arose from the inadequate preparation of air crews. According to one analyst, the Navy's prewar "training emphasis on low-level attack tactics proved detrimental to Desert Storm operations."[124] The carrier squadrons were not well prepared for dropping ordnance from higher altitudes, where the absence of enemy air defenses offered coalition air units a virtual sanctuary. Until the crews adjusted operations to the unfamiliar higher altitudes, the accuracy of bomb drops suffered. Furthermore, inadequate preparation prevented Navy units from employing the Maverick air-to-ground missile, and the Marine Corps squadrons did so with limited success.

The naval air forces also experienced performance problems with some of their aircraft, ordnance, and equipment. The F/A-18s, for all their versatility and maneuverability, could carry only a small bomb load, lacked the capability to operate effectively in foul weather and at night, and could not fly great distances without aerial refueling. The Vietnam-era A-6 Intruders had none of these drawbacks, but their need for 60 hours of maintenance for every sortie reflected their long years of service. Because the Marine AV-8 Harriers could deliver their ordnance with precision only at lower altitudes, they had to face Iraqi air defense weapons where they were most lethal. Enemy hand-held surface-to-air missiles shot down four Harriers which, unlike the Hornets, were less able to survive missile hits.[125] Except for the A-6, Navy and Marine air-craft lacked laser designators for directing laser guided bombs (LGBs) to the targets.

Moreover, the naval services found that they needed warheads that would enable their Tomahawk and standoff land attack missiles and general purpose bombs to penetrate the enemy's thick, concrete-encased aircraft and communications shelters. In addition, Rockeye bombs did not perform as well as they might have had airplanes dropped them from the lower altitudes for which they had been developed. Many Rockeyes proved to be duds because the bomb canisters failed to open at higher altitudes. As a result, naval air units had to drop three bombs when one should have been sufficient to hit a target. Coalition ground

Courtesy of *Wings of Gold* magazine

Precision guided munitions are readied on *John F. Kennedy*'s flight deck.

troops would later discover thousands of unexploded Rockeye bomblets littering the ground in Kuwait and southern Iraq.[126] The LGBs, Forward-Looking Infrared (FLIR) and Global Positioning System (GPS) sets, chaff, flares, electronic decoys, and other specialized equipment that the naval air units employed worked especially well, but in-theater stocks of these essential items were too low to support extended operations. Although the supply effort was generally efficient and responsive, Navy and Marine logisticians were unable before war's end to supply AH-1 Cobra helicopter units with Sidearm antiradar missiles and fighter squadrons with upgraded versions of the Sidewinder air-to-air missile. Each of the American military services shared their stocks of aerial munitions with the others, but as one analyst put it, "in general, the services' weapons systems and their associated support structures are different enough to preclude true interoperability—even in the case of ostensibly multiservice weapons like Maverick."[127]

The Great Scud Hunt

One aspect of the air campaign that was more of an embarrassment than a demonstration of military prowess, at least on the tactical level, was the effort to destroy Iraq's ballistic missile capability. With its small warhead and poor accuracy, the Soviet-designed Scud was little better than a World War II German V-2 rocket, and it posed only a limited military threat. General Horner called it "a lousy weapon."[128] But long before Desert Storm began, coalition leaders feared that Saddam Hussein would attack Israel with the missiles in order to draw the Jewish state into the war. Officials in Washington worried that if that happened, several Arab members of the UN coalition might bolt.[129]

With precisely that end in mind, Saddam began to launch volleys of Scuds from western Iraq into Israeli cities on the second day of the war. The missiles killed and wounded dozens of Israeli citizens and terrorized many more, who, mindful of Saddam's prewar threat to "make fire eat up half of Israel," feared that incoming Scuds might bear chemical warheads. The Israeli government tottered on the brink of retaliation. "The Israelis nearly came into the war today," General de la Billiere wrote his wife Bridget on 19 January. "We may have the greatest difficulty keeping them out tomorrow and it will be impossible if there is another Scud attack on them."[130] At one point Israel had strike groups of F-16s airborne, and only intense international pressure kept them from attacking Iraq.[131]

To prevent the disintegration of the coalition that he had worked so hard to create, President Bush ordered the rapid deployment of U.S.

Patriot antimissile batteries to Israel. In addition, his diplomats persuaded Tel Aviv not to respond militarily to the attacks by promising that U.S. aircraft would destroy Iraq's Scud production and storage facilities and hunt down the individual mobile launchers that dotted the vast Iraqi desert. For the first time in its history, Israel entrusted another country with its own defense.

On D-Day, allied air forces flew the first missions of what soon became known as "the great Scud hunt." U.S. intelligence estimated that as of early January, Iraq possessed some 64 fixed launching sites in the western portion of the country and almost 30 mobile erector-launcher vehicles, which were the size of medium trucks.[132] Air Force and Navy aircraft patrolled day and night, scanning the ground for an erector-launcher in the open, or for the telltale plume of a missile launch. The erector-launchers proved elusive targets. Their crews kept them constantly on the move, hiding them by day and bringing them out at night to fire missiles from positions whose distances to the targets had been preplotted. The rugged terrain of western Iraq where many of them operated featured numerous ravines, culverts, and highway underpasses in which to hide. As little as 10 minutes after firing a missile, a launcher crew could pack up and drive the vehicle anywhere within a five mile radius of the launch site.

The Iraqis also positioned launchers in the eastern part of their country, from where they sent Scuds streaking toward Riyadh, cities in eastern Saudi Arabia, and Bahrain. The Arab populations in these nations suffered the same trauma as the Israelis. In fact, Iraq fired more Scuds at Saudi Arabia than at Israel. On 15 February, one of these missiles hit the water (but failed to explode) only a few score yards from the main pier at al-Jubayl. Eight ships were docked there, including *Tarawa* and the Polish hospital ship. Moreover, some 5,000 tons of 155-mm artillery shells were stacked on the pier. One can imagine what would have happened had that missile struck those shells. Only one Scud actually hit a military target during the war. On 25 February, a single missile struck a barracks in Dhahran, killing 28 U.S. soldiers and wounding almost 100 more. In all, Scuds killed 42 and wounded 450 people and damaged or destroyed 10,750 homes and buildings in Israel and Saudi Arabia, and they precipitated considerable psychological, military, and political repercussions.[133]

Because of this impact, by day four General Horner had diverted a significant proportion of sorties from other assigned targets to the Scud chase. "We certainly employed many, many more assets toward keeping the Scuds inhibited than we originally thought we'd have to," Horner later noted.[134] Ultimately, the allies mounted 1,460 strikes against mobile launchers, suspected hiding places for the launchers, fixed launch sites, and missile and fuel production facilities, most of them during the war's first three weeks.[135]

Conceivably as a result of the allied effort, Scud launches fell from an average of 4.7 per day in the first week of the war to an average of only 1.5 per day during the last 36 days. Nevertheless, coalition air power did not stop the launches and destroyed at best a few of the mobile launchers because of the limited capability of allied airborne sensors and the effectiveness of Iraqi decoy tactics.[136] "The Scud was the most effective weapon in the Iraqi inventory," concluded the Gulf War Air Power Survey. "It drew off significant numbers of Coalition air sorties that could have found more productive utilization in other areas."[137] As Horner put it, the Scud patrols were "a high price to pay to kill a pain in the ass."[138]

Despite the coalition's tactical failure, the great Scud hunt proved a strategic success. The energy and seriousness of allied aerial search operations, along with the Patriot antimissile deployments, kept Israel out of the war and thereby helped preserve the coalition.[139]

Deluge from Above

In the first few days of Desert Storm, the allied aerial armada had won air superiority and fragmented Saddam's strategic air defenses and command-control-communications network. For the rest of January the coalition focused the bulk of its air power against strategic targets. Allied warplanes pursued the destruction of Iraq's known nuclear, biological, and chemical production and storage facilities; airfields and hardened aircraft shelters; oil production and refining installations; and lines of communication with Kuwait. Coalition aircraft also meted out increasing punishment to enemy ground and naval forces.

Operations settled into a routine for the Persian Gulf and Red Sea battle forces. With three carriers, Battle Force Yankee operated on a four-day-on, two-day-off cycle. Each carrier spent two days in each of three operating areas, or "boxes," rotating from the south box to the north box to a logistic support box, where they conducted replenishment operations during their two days "off."[140] Admiral Mixson's carriers conducted a demanding 15 to 18 hours of flight operations daily. This entailed launching two major strike formations, providing aircraft for SEAD support to coalition partners, and continuously maintaining combat air patrol stations.[141]

Air operations for the carriers in the Persian Gulf normally lasted 15 hours each day. *Ranger* and *Theodore Roosevelt*'s on-duty periods occurred during opposite segments of the day, with three hours of concurrent operations during turnovers. *Midway*'s on-duty period centered roughly on one of these turnovers. The gulf carriers operated closer to their targets, enabling them to launch more sorties of shorter duration than their Red Sea counterparts.[142]

A Navy "strike package" assigned to a major bombing mission usually numbered about 25 aircraft: 8 F-14 fighter escorts; 4 EA-6B or other aircraft for SEAD missions; and 13 F/A-18s, A-6s, or A-7s for the bombing attack. Normally, Navy E-2Cs provided direct command and control for the strike while Air Force E-3 AWACS planes supplied a radar picture of Iraqi airspace.[143]

A typical strike group launched from the Red Sea flew into Saudi skies, rendezvoused with tankers about 300 nautical miles south of the Iraqi border, then headed north. The tankers turned back at a point some 50–75 miles south of the border. The strike group, led by fighters ready to engage enemy interceptors, entered Iraqi airspace at high altitude and high speed. Once in the target area, the SEAD aircraft jammed enemy air defense radars and launched HARMs against them while the bombers rolled in on their runs. Generally, the aircraft refueled again during the return flight to the carriers.[144]

One exception occurred on 21 January, when an enemy SAM shot down a *Saratoga* Fighter Squadron 103 F-14A Tomcat flying a combat air patrol mission over Iraq. Before the pilot, Lieutenant Devon Jones, and his radar intercept officer (RIO), Lieutenant Larry Slade, could react, the missile emerged from the clouds below them at supersonic speed and exploded just aft of their plane. When the badly damaged Tomcat went into an uncontrollable spin, Jones pulled the ejection lever and both men "punched out." As their parachutes descended through the dark sky, the Navy fliers lost sight of one another and Jones could not raise Slade on his emergency radio. In keeping with his training, as soon as Jones set down on the desert floor he buried his chute, concealed himself, and signaled for help. Several Air Force A-10 "Warthogs" operating in the area picked up the signal and called in search and rescue helicopters. The next morning the A-10s strafed enemy troops who were feverishly trying to find the naval aviator, hidden in a shallow trench that he hacked out of the desert sand with his survival knife. Meanwhile, a pair of Air Force Pave Low helicopters flew more than 160 miles into Iraq, and one of them swooped down and picked up the pilot. Three days later Lieutenant Jones was once again flying naval aircraft.

Lieutenant Slade, the "backseater," had also landed safely, but the Iraqis soon captured him. Watching a CNN broadcast from Baghdad on

An E-2C Hawkeye prepares to "catch a wire" on board *Saratoga*. These aircraft were vital components of the fleet's airborne early warning system during the Gulf War.

their carrier's video system several nights later, Slade's squadron mates in Air Wing 17 were surprised but happy to see that he too was alive.[145]

Unfortunately, Slade's experience proved more typical of downed air crews than Jones'. Despite the brave and determined efforts of the rescue forces, the Iraqis captured most surviving aviators after they parachuted to the desert floor. Many of these air crewmen ejected near heavily defended enemy positions, deep inside Iraq, making capture a far more likely prospect than rescue. Exacerbating the problem, most coalition aviators lacked advanced hand-held survival radios like the PRC-112, and special forces units would not launch CSAR missions without reasonable prospect of locating a survivor. Accordingly, although the coalition lost 38 aircraft to enemy action during the war, special forces units launched only seven CSAR missions, and of these, only three resulted in the recovery of allied aviators.[146]

Meanwhile, Navy and Marine Corps aircraft continued to make an essential contribution to the success of the 43-day air campaign. The 600 aircraft that these naval services operated accounted for 26 percent of the coalition's 2,300-plane armada and flew an average of 650 sorties per day.[147] At the beginning of the war, the Navy dedicated about 70 percent of its sorties to support missions, particularly combat air patrols and

Iraqi concrete aircraft shelters clearly show the effects of hits by coalition precision guided munitions.

A smiling Commander John Leenhouts, Executive Officer of VA-72, in the cockpit of his A-7 Corsair II on the return leg of a strike into Iraq. The camels stenciled on the fuselage indicate he has completed ten successful missions.

fighter sweeps; approximately 10 percent to bombing inland targets; and 20 percent to SEAD missions, many in support of Air Force and allied strikes. The Navy figured prominently in the SEAD campaign because it supplied about a quarter of the coalition's tactical electronic warfare aircraft, and because EA-6B Prowlers from Battle Force Yankee were closer to targets in western Iraq than the Air Force's electronic warfare aircraft, all of which were based in eastern Saudi Arabia or Bahrain. Moreover, the EA-6B proved so effective at suppressing enemy defenses that, according to one analyst, "none of the strike packages—not even the British—would go unless they had an EA-6B Prowler EW aircraft to escort them and do the jamming." [148]

The percentage of the Navy's inland bombing sorties increased steadily throughout the campaign to about 45 percent of the Navy total by the end. The Red Sea battle force dedicated 40–50 percent of its sorties to inland bombing and SEAD missions throughout the war. Battle Force Zulu flew 30–50 percent of its sorties on combat air patrols and maritime strikes during the first half of Desert Storm, but its proportions of fighter escort and maritime strike missions decreased as the allies neutralized the Iraqi air threat and destroyed the Iraqi navy. By war's end its percentage of theater strike missions had quadrupled. [149]

Phase II operations ended on 8 February. Iraqi air defenses retained the ability to react piecemeal to allied strikes, but could no longer coordinate defensive actions. Although Phase I operations continued throughout the war, by early February the weight of the allied air attack had shifted from strategic targets in Iraq to the army and Republican Guard forces in the KTO. [150]

Fleet Defense and the Allied Right Flank

At the outset of Desert Storm, the possibility of aerial attack by Iraqi jet aircraft armed with antiship missiles especially concerned naval commanders and the captains of coalition warships in the Persian Gulf. As an Argentine commanding officer observed, the picture of the American frigate *Stark*, which two Iraqi Exocets had almost sunk in 1987, "always entered the minds of the commanders." [151] Captain Johnson, Admiral Arthur's operations officer, later said that "had [Saddam Hussein] chosen to come down here with any kind of force, he would have sunk ships." [152] Admiral March elaborated on that idea: "I think we were lucky . . . that they didn't use their air assets properly [because] there was significant potential for them to get through with a couple of assets, suicidal or whatever, with some Exocets. . . . I think we would have taken some losses." [153] Iraqi air power also threatened unarmed merchantmen loaded with fuel, ammunition, and supplies for the allied expeditionary force and the vital ports of al-Jubayl, ad-Dammam, and Bahrain. Admiral Arthur took his flank guard responsibility "very seriously." [154]

But the Iraqis would not have had an easy time of it, for the coalition put up a formidable defensive umbrella against aerial attack. The primary objective of Battle Force Zulu's antiair warfare commander was to ensure coalition air supremacy over the waters of the Persian Gulf, the Gulf of Oman, and the North Arabian Sea, and to provide air defense for allied ships operating in those waters. To carry out this mission, antiair warfare units continuously monitored the airspace over the area and kept combat air patrol fighters, aerial refuelling planes, and strike aircraft on the hunt for Iraqi warships. The AAW mission involved "delousing;" the identification of enemy planes that might try to trail behind a coalition formation returning from a strike ashore and use it for cover. The antiair warfare units also focused on the "deconfliction" of aircraft over the gulf. This involved keeping track on radar of all aircraft in flight to prevent accidental collisions or shootdowns—so-called "blue-on-blue" incidents. Not only the *Stark* episode but also cruiser *Vincennes*' destruction of an Iranian airliner during the Iran-Iraq War were remembered by coalition sailors. In the words of Commodore Craig, "everyone afloat, and many more aloft, were very edgy at the prospect of a recurrence." [155]

Because the Aegis cruiser was the Navy's most capable antiair platform, Rear Admiral March designated Captain Thomas Marfiak, Commanding Officer of *Bunker Hill,* as Battle Force Zulu's primary AAWC, and Captain Stephen R. Woodall, Commanding Officer of *Mobile Bay* (CG 53), as alternate AAWC. Marfiak retained that responsibility until *Bunker Hill*'s departure for duty with the *Ranger* task group in mid-February 1991. For the rest of Desert Storm, Woodall served as the primary AAWC.[156] Rear Admiral Gee, Commander Cruiser Destroyer Group 8, served as Battle Force Yankee's antiair warfare commander throughout Desert Storm.

Marfiak later stressed that it was the fleet's weapons systems that gave punch to the antiair defensive structure. He observed: "Data alone would not have been sufficient. Communications alone would not have sufficed. Electronic warfare and intelligence circuits . . . would have been merely supportive but not determinant in the absence of long-range, overland sensors coupled to weapon systems capable of engaging low-altitude, high-speed threats." [157]

Because aircraft standing ready on carrier decks or at airfields ashore would have precious little time to react to an enemy attack, Admiral March and Captain Marfiak established forward-positioned com-

From this warship, the Aegis-equipped guided missile cruiser *Bunker Hill* (CG 52), Captain Thomas Marfiak directed the air defense of Battle Force Zulu, one of whose four carriers is visible behind her.

bat air patrols. For most of the war, Battle Force Zulu maintained three round-the-clock CAP stations in the central and northern Persian Gulf manned by sections of two fighters each.[158] Canadian CF-18s supplemented these patrols while Marine Corps F/A-18s manned a CAP station off the coast of Saudi Arabia. Just before the ground war started, the Navy established a CAP station over southeastern Iraq to intercept Iraqi aircraft attempting to flee to Iran. Battle Force Zulu and Battle Force Yankee shared the responsibility for manning this station. On 7 February, an F-14 from *Ranger*'s Fighter Squadron 1 patrolling there shot down an Iraqi Mi-8/17 HIP helicopter with an AIM-9M Sidewinder missile. Owing to the minimal threat in the Red Sea, Battle Force Yankee operated only one round-the-clock CAP station. The Navy devoted 3,720 sorties to combat air patrol during Desert Storm, a figure amounting to 21 percent of the total number of sorties flown by carrier planes during the war. Battle Force Zulu accomplished about 70 percent of these sorties.[159]

Battle Force Zulu kept at least one E-2C Hawkeye airborne early warning plane aloft continuously during Desert Storm. Each carrier maintained a single E-2C on 30-minute deck alert when none from that ship was flying. The Hawkeyes' primary mission was to control the strike formations flying to and from the mainland. The E-2Cs also warned the fleet of approaching "bogies," provided limited CAP air control, and helped patrolling aircraft communicate with the carrier battle groups.[160]

Many of the surface ships operating in the Persian Gulf stood watch against air attack and performed air control and deconfliction duties. By mid-February, for example, 21 of the ships operating in the Persian Gulf, excluding the carriers, were partially or totally devoted to antiair warfare, including 9 U.S. cruisers and 12 U.S., British, Australian, Dutch, and Italian destroyers and frigates. *Mobile Bay* spent most of the war as the northernmost antiair warfare picket. The NTU cruisers *Worden*, *Richmond K. Turner* (CG 20), and *Wainwright* (CG 28) took station in international waters close to the Iranian coast because their radars had better detection capabilities over land. Each carrier had an Aegis cruiser serving as "shotgun." As often as possible, another Aegis cruiser occupied a position between the carrier operating area and the northern AAW picket. These dispositions provided the fleet with effective air control and overlapping radar coverage from the carriers to the northern CAP stations.[161]

Mines were a greater concern to the crews of AAW picket ships than enemy air attack during Desert Storm. "I could make [an Iraqi] airplane a memory," said Captain Woodall, but "the most appreciable threat to us [was] just hitting a mine." Because of this threat, COs of the coalition ships posted at least one lookout on the bow specifically to watch for mines. Some mines stayed only slightly under the water. In one instance, a lookout on *Mobile Bay* spotted eight mines chained together, drifting along just below the surface. If the lookout had not seen that one, recalled Woodall, it would have made *Mobile Bay* "a monument."[162]

Radar operators and tactical action officers on board the AAW units were also charged with ensuring the flying safety of allied aircraft in the air space above the waters surrounding the Arabian Peninsula. Each day in the Persian Gulf and the Red Sea, air controllers tracked an average of 1,200 coalition aircraft, including strike group fighters and attack planes, CAP aircraft, early warning planes, maritime patrol aircraft, and fixed-wing and helicopter units searching for enemy surface vessels.[163]

Air control and deconfliction eventually became the primary AAW tasks during Desert Storm, for Saddam's air force tested the fleet's air defenses only once. At approximately 0850 on 24 January, four to five Iraqi aircraft took off from al-Kut, southeast of Baghdad, and headed for the coast of Kuwait in a high-low split. The high-flying planes turned back before going "feet wet," but two low-flying F-1 Mirages continued southeast just seaward of the Kuwaiti shore, trailing returning American strike planes. The Iraqis might have been heading for the critical Saudi oil complex at Ras Tannurah.

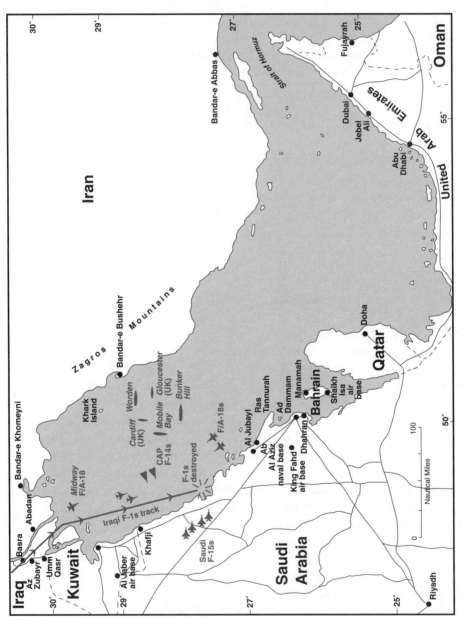

Iraqi Air Attack in the Gulf, 24 January 1991

Whether by accident or design, the Mirages flew near the boundary between U.S. Air Force and U.S. Navy air defense sectors. American air and naval radar systems overlapped the area, but their equipment sometimes failed to produce a consolidated air picture. As *Mobile Bay*'s skipper later said, "we were never able to affect a sustainable, good direct link with the AWACS."[164] As a result, the Iraqis survived longer than they would have had they flown straight for the fleet or the northern land border of Saudi Arabia. An Air Force AWACS tracked the F-1s as they winged down the gulf at 550 to 600 knots. The E-3 did not provide *Worden, Bunker Hill,* or *Mobile Bay* with its tracks of the enemy fighters. However, the AWACS reported the Mirages' position and bearing to the ships by voice. The E-3 directed the nearest patrolling fighters under its control, four Saudi F-15s, to intercept the Mirages.

Meanwhile, at 0920 a *Midway* F/A-18 providing fighter cover east of Bubiyan Island for a strike group returning from Iraq picked up the F-1s on its forward-looking infrared system and began tracking them. Five minutes later, the Hornet's pilot determined that the Mirages were not threatening the strike group and disengaged. At about the same time, Commander Bill Richards, Tactical Action Officer on board *Worden,* vectored two *Theodore Roosevelt* F-14s from Navy CAP station "Whiskey 4" toward the F-1s. *Worden*'s own radar system did not hold a track on the Iraqi planes, nor could the ship verify them as hostile, so the Tomcats could not attack. *Mobile Bay* detected the Mirages and identified them as hostile, but lost them before she could engage.

By this time, three different groups of coalition fighters were closing in on the F-1s: the Saudi F-15s from the west, the Tomcats from the northeast, and F/A-18s from the southeast.[165] According to Commander Richards, the enemy "turned into the F-15s. If he had turned the other way, he'd have gotten a faceful of F/A-18. If he stayed where he was going to go, in another 14 seconds he was going to get shot down by F-14s who were moving into position and doing their last pre-fire checks before they let those weapons loose."[166] As it turned out, at approximately 0934, Royal Saudi Air Force pilot Captain Ayedh al-Shamrani shot down both F-1s with Sidewinder missiles.[167]

"Believe me, we were all pretty shocked when we received the final AWACS report on the Splash position and plotted it," recalled Lieutenant Kevin E. Pollock, Tactical Action Officer on board *Bunker Hill.* Before Captain al-Shamrani destroyed them, the F-1s had reached a point west of the Manifah oilfield off the northern Saudi coast and 60 nautical miles from *Mobile Bay,* within Exocet range of the ship.[168]

The AWACS had maintained continuous coverage of the Mirages after they went feet wet, but the antiair ships had held only intermittent contact, owing to the limits of their radar horizon. Navy aircraft flying

CAP missions in the gulf usually monitored AWACS control frequencies, but *Theodore Roosevelt* had just arrived in the theater and her air wing was still unfamiliar with these procedures, so the Tomcats did not learn the location or composition of the F-1 flight as quickly as they could have. As one analyst suggested, because "USS *Bunker Hill*, USS *Mobile Bay*, and USS *Worden* were the primary controllers for the CAP, time was wasted while the surface ships tried to build their picture from fragmentary radar intercepts and voice calls."[169] The F-1 incident "was obviously a thorn in our side," concluded Lieutenant Pollock, "and brings to the forefront some important joint operation problems. However, if you get right down in the weeds of AAW management," in Desert Storm it was a resounding success.[170]

Indeed, despite adverse weather conditions and a high density of electronic and other interference, coalition antiair warfare units operating in the gulf detected, tracked, and identified more than 65,000 air sorties during Desert Storm without a single blue-on-blue incident.[171] Although there were some close calls, Captains Marfiak and Woodall never directed attack on an allied aircraft, even if it failed to identify itself or "squawk" when it was supposed to, or if its Identification Friend or Foe (IFF) system malfunctioned. "We could not have done the Gulf War with *Belknap*-class cruisers trying to do the air picture on scope heads," Woodall said after the war.[172] The AAW effort during Desert Storm was an especially great victory for the Aegis system.

In contrast, the performance of the Iraqi air force during Desert Storm was abysmal. Saddam's warplanes downed only one coalition aircraft, Lieutenant Commander Speicher's Hornet, while losing 42 aircraft in air-to-air engagements. After nine days of combat, Saddam's fighter pilots abandoned their attempts to intercept allied aircraft, thereby acknowledging the coalition's absolute mastery of the air. His attack pilots fared even worse, failing to inflict any damage on coalition forces. Lieutenant Larry DiRita, Weapon and Combat Systems Officer on board the Aegis cruiser *Leyte Gulf* (CG 55), spoke for many in the allied camp when he later observed:

> Given the almost comical and certainly cowardly way in which the Iraqi air force carried itself during the war, it is today hard to remember that we anticipated an aggressive, experienced air threat from relatively sophisticated fighters equipped with some of the most advanced versions of the Exocet air-to-surface missile in the world.[173]

The coalition's destruction of the Iraqi command and control system and shootdown of the few bold pilots who ventured skyward took all the fight out of an enemy already inclined to surrender air control. Then, Saddam ordered his air force to avoid battle. In all probability, he hoped to preserve as many planes as possible to bolster his regime after the war. Initially, he dispersed aircraft among hundreds of hardened shelters. On 23 January, however, coalition aircraft began piercing the shelters with special ordnance and destroying the planes inside. The allies eventually eliminated an estimated 141 Iraqi aircraft that way. Saddam also tried to protect his aircraft by scattering them singly and in pairs among residential buildings, archaeological sites, and previously bombed installations. These planes survived the war because the coalition sought to minimize non-military damage and civilian casualties, but their operational value was nil.[174]

Still, allied commanders grew concerned on 26 January when a large number of Iraqi combat planes began to brave the allied gauntlet and fly to airfields in neighboring Iran. Iraq's entire fleet of Su-24 strike aircraft and an assortment of Mirage F-1s and MiG-29s, the "flower of the air force," made this mass exodus. After 15 days, more than 120 Iraqi aircraft had touched down at airfields in Iran. Tehran's passivity in this aerial migration fueled speculation among allied leaders that Saddam had reached some arrangement with Iran to use Iran as a staging area for an "Air Tet"—an all-out aerial attack against the Western-led coalition or the nations of the GCC, friends of neither Iraq nor Iran.

The sudden movement of Iraqi aircraft to Iran, as Admiral March related, "really heightened my threat awareness."[175] He remained concerned because he could not get the U.S. intelligence community to provide him with timely satellite photos that would show if there were stockpiles of ordnance or aircraft support equipment at Iranian airfields.[176]

Admirals Arthur and March were particularly concerned that hostile aircraft might emerge from a gap in Iran's Zagros Mountains and within minutes be over the carriers now operating far forward in the gulf. March deployed HMAS *Brisbane* and HMAS *Sydney* to the north of his ships as the "Zagros Gateguard." Australian Commodore Oxenbould felt that "this tasking demonstrated considerable trust by the USN in RAN capabilities."[177] The gulf naval leaders could ill afford to take this potential threat to coalition naval forces and the gulf ports lightly. Hence, for much of Desert Storm, they had to ensure that the surface and air screen in the gulf remained strong and ready.[178]

For the Iraqi air force, however, the exodus to Iran symbolized its utter defeat. It proved nothing more than a desperate attempt by Saddam to preserve his beaten and harried air arm. A number of Iraqi planes ran out of fuel and crashed; Air Force F-15s blasted others out of the sky. The Iranian government promptly seized the surviving aircraft and holds them to this day.[179]

Courtesy of Royal Australian Navy

HMAS *Brisbane,* fitted for Desert Storm with the Phalanx close-in weapon system and cloth-like, antiradar "RAM Panels," moves swiftly through gulf waters. Because of their advanced defenses and communications, and compatibility with American systems, Australian warships served as the "Zagros Gateguard" for Battle Force Zulu.

On 27 January, General Schwarzkopf announced that the coalition had won air supremacy over Iraq and Kuwait. The Iraqi air force was no longer capable of seriously interfering with the allied war effort.[180]

Storm in the Northern Gulf

While naval air forces did their part to rid the sky of Iraq's air force and dismantle the infrastructure of its war machine, Admiral Arthur carried out his mission of convincing Saddam that the allies intended to launch an amphibious assault on Iraq's left flank. To achieve this objective, Arthur planned a two-stage maritime campaign: 1) establish air and sea control in the northern gulf to enable coalition naval forces to operate there; and 2) conduct inshore operations in the northern gulf—air strike, mine countermeasures, naval gunfire, special warfare, and amphibious—to allow the coalition to mount or to threaten a seaborne in-

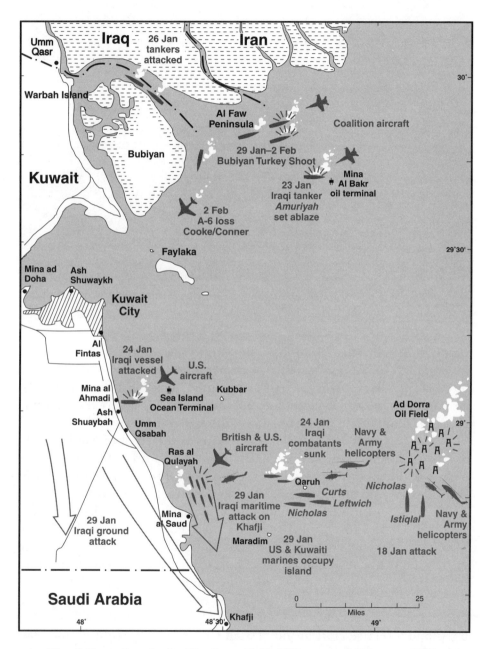

Naval Operations in the Northern Gulf, 17 January–2 February 1991

USN

Carrier *Ranger* (CV 61) refuels one of the ships of its air defense screen, the Dutch guided missile frigate HNLMS *Jacob Van Heemskerck.*

vasion of Kuwait. Inauguration of the second stage depended on success-ful completion of the first. In that respect, the maritime campaign dif-fered from General Horner's air campaign. The staging areas for allied air forces were in friendly hands at the outset of Desert Storm while those for naval forces in the northern gulf had to be seized.[181]

The first step involved clearing a path to the coast of Kuwait along Saddam Hussein's seaward flank. The obstacles in Admiral Arthur's way included the Iraqi navy, enemy troops posted on oil platforms and is-lands in the gulf, and mines. Removing the first two fell to Battle Force Zulu's antisurface warfare commander. Initially, Captain J. W. Parker, Commander Destroyer Squadron 15, embarked in *Midway* with Admiral March, served in that capacity. Parker promulgated three antisurface warfare objectives: maintaining accurate surface surveillance in the gulf, establishing sea control, and conducting offensive operations.[182]

The maritime campaign kicked off on the second day of the war. On 18 January, aircraft from *Ranger* and *Midway* damaged two Iraqi gun-boats and a service craft in the Persian Gulf some 22 nautical miles east of Bubiyan Island.[183]

Coalition forces assigned to combat search and rescue duty also experienced combat in the northern gulf on the 18th. The day before,

USN

A U.S. Army OH-58D Kiowa Warrior of B Troop, 4th Squadron, 17th Aviation Regiment, which operated with U.S. Navy SH-60B Seahawk LAMPS Mark III helicopters from frigates *Nicholas* (FFG 47), *Curts* (FFG 38), and *Jarrett* (FFG 33).

Commander Dennis G. Morral led a three-ship flotilla, including guided missile frigate *Nicholas* and the Kuwaiti guided missile patrol boats *Istiqlal* and *al-Sanbouk*, into the northern gulf. *Nicholas* was equipped with a Kingfisher mine avoidance sonar; an upgraded antiair warfare system; a 25mm chain gun; and a mast-mounted sight with night vision capability. To reduce the ship's radar signature, naval engineers had applied a layer of special rubberized material to the superstructure, antennae, and masts. The ship carried a SEAL detachment, a Coast Guard Law Enforcement Detachment, and two Navy SH-60B Seahawk LAMPS Mark III helicopters of Detachment 8, HSL 44. Also on board were two U.S. Army OH-58D Kiowa Warrior helicopters and support personnel from the Army's B Troop, 4th Squadron, 17th Aviation Regiment.[184]

The 4th Squadron, in 1991 commanded by Lieutenant Colonel Bruce E. Simpson, USA, was a veteran of service with the Navy in the Persian Gulf. During Operation Earnest Will, the "Sea Cavalry" helicopter detachment, then known as Task Force 118, flew thousands of hours on over-water armed reconnaissance and tanker escort duty. More than half of the men who served in the gulf in 1987 and 1988 were still part of the unit during Desert Storm, which made it a truly veteran unit. The OH-58s were armed with Hellfire missiles, launchers for 2.5-inch rockets, and .50-caliber machine guns. The aircraft also carried a mast-mounted sight, night vision goggles, radar warning receivers, and jamming equipment.[185]

Commander Morral planned to "hide" his ships among the nine oil platforms of the ad-Dorra oilfield, located only 40 miles off the coast of Kuwait. Morral knew that his ships were well within range of Iraqi Silkworm missile batteries and aircraft and fast attack vessels armed with Exocet missiles and he wanted to make it hard for enemy radar operators to distinguish his ships from the platforms. The ad-Dorra field would also be a good site from which Morral's helicopters could operate to rescue downed pilots.

As his surface flotilla steamed toward the objective on the evening of 17 January, Morral sent the two OH-58Ds and a LAMPS helicopter ahead to determine if there was an enemy presence on the previously abandoned platforms. To Morral's surprise, the LAMPS crew picked up radar emissions from the site. Colonel Nasser al-Hussainan, commander of the Kuwaiti naval contingent, and a U.S. naval officer serving as a liaison on board *Istiqlal* also reported that tracer fire had emanated from

"Seizure of the ad-Dorra Oil Platforms" by John Charles Roach

"A Navy LAMPS III Rescues a Downed American Pilot" by John Charles Roach

the platforms. Then, the Army pilots saw through their night vision goggles that men and antiaircraft weapons occupied the platforms. Unseen by their prey, the Army helicopters videotaped the human activity on the platforms. Later, when Colonel Nasser and another Kuwaiti naval officer boarded *Nicholas* and viewed videotape made by the Army aircraft, Nasser exclaimed, "that's not Saudi; that's not Kuwaiti; that's Iraqi!"[186] Soon after reporting this information up the chain of command, Morral received orders to return south.

Morral and his superiors recognized that these enemy troops were a threat to allied ships and planes in the vicinity. The Iraqis could also warn their comrades ashore of coming coalition air strikes. Since Morral's flotilla could not operate safely near the enemy-garrisoned platforms, the commander requested and received permission to neutralize the sites.[187]

On 18 January, as *Nicholas* and *Istiqlal* headed once more for the ad-Dorra oilfield and Morral prepared for his nighttime attack, a LAMPS helicopter was dispatched for a daylight reconnaissance of the platforms. A LAMPs unit from *Nicholas* and a Lynx H.A.S. Mk. III helicopter from HMS *Cardiff* approached the ad-Dorra platforms close enough to observe one or two individuals on two separate platforms waving their arms and white cloths, which could be regarded as an attempt to surrender. One of the American pilots later stated, however, that "he still was not sure what the individuals were trying to do [and that] the wave may have just been a form of greeting."[188] The LAMPS crew reported their observations to *Nicholas.* The ship's executive officer and tactical action officer thought that this information might indicate Iraqi willingness to surrender the platforms. They strongly suggested that their commanding officer obtain guidance from higher authority.

Morral, unaware that the helicopter got as close as 100 yards to the platforms without drawing fire, discounted the importance of the LAMPS crew's observations. He felt that even if a few individuals wanted to surrender, there was no indication that their officers or fellow soldiers were of the same mind.[189] What also made an impression on Morral was the observation of the Kuwaiti naval officers that Iraqi troops often used the waving of white cloths as a ruse to fool their enemies. Feeling that with every passing minute the threat to his ships increased, Morral decided not to make a potentially time-consuming request for advice from his superiors or even apprise them of the LAMPS report. Planning for the attack went forward.[190]

That evening, as coalition warships once again closed the ad-Dorra platforms, Morral ordered his LAMPS and OH-58D helicopters aloft. The Army aircraft approached the platforms low so the sounds of the sea masked the noise of their engines. When the Army helicopters came within range, Morral gave them the order to fire, and they opened up on two platforms with Hellfire laser guided missiles. Then, *Nicholas* and *Istiqlal* moved in and opened up with shellfire and rockets on seven other oil rigs. The Hellfires proved more effective than the other weapons because they struck gun emplacements and other laser-designated targets with pinpoint accuracy. Because of the darkness and open structure of the platforms, Morral had difficulty determining the effect of the rockets and gunfire.[191]

As he monitored the attack from the bridge, the commander heard a chilling report over *Nicholas'* bridge speaker system: "Missile inbound." Morral told his bridge team to hit the deck, ordered all ahead flank speed, and directed the helmsman to make a sharp turn. The ship fired off chaff. Morral bounded out to the bridge wing, where he saw a big ball of fire descending on *Nicholas.* Only then did he realize that the contact was not hostile. Apparently, a Navy plane, heading back to its carrier after a mission ashore, had mistaken the flashes from *Nicholas'* guns as enemy antiaircraft fire. Because *Nicholas* was operating in a so-called "no attack zone," the aircraft had not engaged the ship. The pilot instead had dropped flares to divert possible heat-seeking SAMs away from his jet engine and the lookout on *Nicholas* had mistaken the burning flare for the plume of a missile. Good fire discipline all around had prevented a potentially tragic "friendly-fire" incident.[192]

Meanwhile, *Nicholas* and *Istiqlal*'s attack had stunned the Iraqi soldiers on the oil platforms. "These guys never had a chance," Morral said after the war.[193] Not only were they unaware of the attackers' presence until coalition munitions started ripping through their sandbag and plywood shelters, but their antiaircraft artillery and shoulder-launched surface-to-air missiles lacked the capability to lock onto targets at night. The Iraqi soldiers, five of whom were killed, did not return fire and most quickly surrendered.

For some of the soldiers and sailors on the scene, the action brought home for the first time the cruel reality of war. Lieutenant Colonel Simpson, who had joined his men in time for the night action, later remarked: "I could just see it on a lot of their faces—the excitement of doing all this all of a sudden turned into reality, because here were the guys that they had just shot and some of them were messed up pretty bad. . . . I figured it had an effect on us when they saw what those weapons do. You know, it's kind of like a video game in a way until you see what it did." [194]

Nicholas and *Istiqlal* spent the rest of the night picking up enemy prisoners and retrieving or destroying Iraqi equipment from the platforms. U.S. Navy SEALs and Kuwaiti sailors, operating in motor whaleboats and rigid-hull inflatable boats, found a variety of weapons and equipment such as a long-range radio, shoulder-launched SAM missiles, 23mm antiaircraft guns, high explosives, and diving gear.[195]

As *Nicholas* steamed through the ad-Dorra oilfield, she captured six Iraqi soldiers who had escaped from one of the platforms in a rubber raft. The Coast Guard law enforcement detachment, with the help of Navy Seaman Apprentice Mahdi Abd-al-Ayala, an American citizen who was born and raised in Kuwait,[196] immediately searched the prisoners, using standard procedures developed for drug smuggling operations in the Caribbean. The prisoners became visibly upset when the coastguardsmen had the first man kneel down on a mat, apparently thinking he would be killed with a bullet through the back of the head. Only when the American sailors assured them that their lives were not in danger did the prisoners relax. At dawn Morral discovered that there were still Iraqi soldiers on one of the platforms. *Nicholas* and *Istiqlal* moved in and the Kuwaiti patrol boat, captained by Commander al-Ansari, fired warning shots with its 40mm antiaircraft gun. The Iraqis soon surrendered.[197]

In all, *Nicholas* and *Istiqlal* captured 23 Iraqi soldiers, the Gulf War's first enemy prisoners of war (EPWs). That morning *Istiqlal* transferred her prisoners to *Nicholas.* Commander Morral's medical staff, which had been beefed up in anticipation of treating downed coalition fliers, patched up the wounded Iraqis. Morral credits Lieutenant Commander Robert Culligan, a Navy doctor, with saving the lives of at least two badly wounded Iraqi EPWs. ASU Bahrain "Desert Duck" helicopters transferred the EPWs ashore on the 19th and 20th. Thus ended the war's first surface engagement.[198]

These Iraqi prisoners were an eye-opener for the Americans. Some of the prisoners had been tough-looking men who were clearly unhappy about having been captured. A few were Baath Party officials who, like Soviet commissars in the old days, were probably there to keep the others in line. But most of the prisoners, in poor physical condition and ill-clothed, were quite happy about their internment. One soldier even tried to kiss his Navy captor. These were not the battle-hardened Iraqi soldiers many Americans expected to face. Commander Morral noticed a SEAL standing next to an Iraqi conscript. The contrast could not have been more striking between the "well-trained, well-fed, well-equipped, [and] highly motivated" SEAL and the "poorly-equipped, starving, beat-up conscript." Morral concluded that "this may not be quite the force we think it is."[199] Hence, even before the battle of Khafji, there were clear indications that the Iraqi armed forces were anything but "ten feet tall."

Nicholas and her embarked helicopter units carried out the first at-sea rescue of the war on 23 January, when they pulled from the water, several miles off the coast of Kuwait, Major John R. Ball, USAF, a downed F-16 pilot. Ball later presented Morral with a framed expression of appreciation, signed by the major and his squadron mates, that gave "thanks to the men of the USS *Nicholas* for saving a fighter pilot's ass."[200]

Despite the success of Morral's operations, coalition naval forces did not pursue the maritime campaign aggressively during Desert Storm's early days. In messages exchanged on 20 January, two of the commanding officers operating in harm's way in the northern gulf, *Wisconsin's* Captain David S. Bill III and *Mobile Bay's* Captain Woodall, described the antisurface effort in the northern gulf to that time as "awful." They and others believed that the situation warranted dedicating more ships and aircraft to the operation, and to improving the ASUW command and control structure.[201] One problem was that the U.S. naval command had to adapt a tactical approach developed for war on the open sea—the composite warfare commander concept—to the littoral conditions of the Gulf War. In blue water, the antisurface warfare commander was responsible for maintaining a protective ring around the battle group and destroying any enemy forces or weapons entering this area, not for hunting enemy warships in distant waters or in port.[202]

But more significant, the American antisurface warfare commander did not have enough ships and planes at his disposal to mount a full-scale offensive. For operations in the northern gulf, Captain Parker could only count on U.S., British, Canadian (air only), Kuwaiti, and Saudi Arabian forces. Numerous political and military considerations restricted the naval forces of Argentina, Australia, Denmark, Netherlands, France, Italy, Norway, Spain, and the GCC to patrol and defensive operations in the central and southern gulf.[203] And with only two carriers, Battle Force Zulu had few planes left after meeting its commitment to the air campaign for hunting enemy surface vessels. Furthermore, at this early stage of the air campaign, Arthur had trouble getting Iraqi vessels entered into the JFACC target list. As a result, initial operations to seize control of the northern gulf moved at a slow pace.[204]

Something had to be done. On 20 January, Vice Admiral Arthur, Rear Admiral March, Rear Admiral David E. Frost (Commander Carrier Group 8), and Rear Admiral Ronald J. "Zap" Zlatoper (Commander Carrier Group 7) gathered on board *Midway* to discuss the campaign. Intelligence revealed that the enemy was strengthening his defenses on Faylaka Island and deploying mines off Kuwait. The admirals decided to mount a more aggressive, faster-paced effort to destroy the Iraqi navy, particularly its surface-to-surface missile vessels, and thereby win control of northern gulf waters. Then, coalition naval forces would move up to conduct mine countermeasures, bombardment, and amphibious operations. Moreover, Admiral March's carriers could move closer to the enemy coast for their strikes against inland targets, enabling them to decrease their dependence on Air Force aerial tankers, increase their sortie rate, and reduce the wear and tear on their air crews and machines.[205]

A flag officer was present with each of the carrier battle groups assigned to Admiral March's Battle Force Zulu. Indeed, as March observed after the war, "I had too many flags and not enough assignment tasks."[206] Consequently, he assigned them new responsibilities within the CTF 154 composite warfare commander framework. On 21 January, Admiral Zlatoper relieved Captain Parker as the antisurface warfare commander in the gulf. Zlatoper expeditiously selected his chief warfighters—his local antisurface warfare (LASUW) commanders: Captain G. T. Forbes, Commander Destroyer Squadron 7, embarked in *Paul F. Foster*, got the mission of clearing the enemy navy from the northern gulf; Captain Ernest E. Christensen Jr., Commanding Officer of *Ranger*, became responsible for defense of coalition ships in the central and southern gulf; and Commodore Ken Summers, commander of the Canadian task group, continued to protect the coalition's logistic support ships in the central gulf. *Mobile Bay* served as the primary air control unit in the northern gulf for antisurface missions.[207]

Reinforcements entered the gulf that day. The arrival of *Theodore Roosevelt* and her air wing on 21 January provided Admiral March with enough aircraft both to execute General Horner's strike missions ashore and to prosecute the maritime campaign.[208]

Naval leaders worked quickly to improve the conduct of antisurface warfare in the gulf. On the same day that *Theodore Roosevelt* joined the other carrier groups, Captain Forbes sent Admiral Zlatoper a message about what he thought the Iraqi fleet's intentions were and how to defeat it. Forbes opined that the Iraqi navy was "executing a layered bastion defense along classic Soviet lines." The Iraqis knew that "U.S. forces will come to dinner, and they are setting the table." Forbes surmised that the Iraqis did not intend to use their missile boats until they believed that the Amphibious Task Force was approaching the coast of Kuwait for a landing. Meanwhile, the Iraqis were using their coastal craft to place observers on offshore oil platforms to watch for the ATF.

Forbes argued that "we need to recalibrate our ASUW posture" to keep coalition naval forces "leaning forward and on the offense." He recommended easing the criterion for identifying a seagoing craft as hostile, making better use of signals intelligence, increasing the number of surveillance aircraft on patrol over the northern gulf, repositioning the British destroyers *Gloucester* and *Cardiff* farther north to better exploit their Lynx helicopters, and refining the tactics used to attack Silkworm missile sites. "Bottom line here, Admiral," said Forbes in closing, "is your northern exposure is ready to reach out and *carpe* Saddam's *diem.*"[209]

Admiral Zlatoper agreed with Captain Forbes' assessment of the Iraqi navy's defensive posture. The "apparent Iraqi tactic to keep [their missile boats] out of sight until the Gators [amphibious vessels] arrive is most feasible," Zlatoper told Forbes, "and further emphasizes our need to conduct aggressive anti-small boat [operations] now."[210]

In order to eliminate the Iraqi naval threat before 1 February, when mine countermeasures operations were slated to begin off Kuwait, Zlatoper devised an aggressive "rollback" concept. This entailed neutralizing Iraqi naval vessels and troops posted on oil platforms and islands.[211] Zlatoper aimed not only to defend the fleet from attack—standard antisurface warfare doctrine—but to seek out and destroy enemy naval forces at sea, along inland waterways, and in port. His surface ships, warplanes, and armed helicopters would, as naval forces had in World War II, Korea, and Vietnam, go "boat hunting."[212] The admiral even changed the operational jargon to reflect his more aggressive approach. As he later noted, "we cast aside the defensive-sounding 'Surface

Combat Air Patrol (SUCAP)' and 'Surface Search Coordinator (SSC)' monikers for the terms 'Armed Surface Reconnaissance (ASR)' for A-6s and F/A-18s and 'Armed Scouts' for S-3s."[213]

In Admiral Zlatoper's offensive antisurface warfare scheme, U.S. P-3 Orion and British Nimrod patrol planes flew round-the-clock search patterns over the northern gulf, Kuwaiti coastline, and Iraqi ports, on the lookout for enemy warships. Carrier-based A-6 Intruders, F/A-18 Hornets, and S-3 Vikings, the latter normally responsible for locating hostile submarines, cruised at low altitudes on armed surface reconnaissance and armed scout missions to search for and engage Iraqi units. The cruisers and destroyers of the antiair "picket" force coordinated the air-sea operation.[214]

Ship-based U.S. Navy LAMPS III and Royal Navy Lynx helicopters also flew antisurface missions to pounce on and destroy Iraqi ships. Borrowing from the Army's experience in the Vietnam War, the American and British aviators worked during Desert Shield to refine the so-called "T-bone" tactic, in which helicopters acted as a "hunter/killer" team. In Desert Storm, a LAMPS helicopter, which Commander Morral called the "AWACS of the helicopter force,"[215] swept the waters with its long-range sensors to locate a target and then called in a Lynx to attack with its two Sea Skua air-to-surface missiles. The Sea Skua, a 460-pound radar guided antiship weapon with a range of approximately five miles and the punch of a 6-inch shell, had been designed to fight small Soviet bloc combatants in the confined waters of northern Europe.[216]

U.S. Army OH-58D Kiowa Warrior helicopters armed with Hellfire missiles also operated with the LAMPs units in hunter/killer teams.[217] The AGM-114 Hellfire was the Army and Marines' standard helicopter-launched, laser guided air-to-ground missile. This 100-pound weapon had a shaped-charge warhead and a range of five miles.[218]

Nighttime hunter-killer operations were the forte of the LAMPs III/OH-58D, ship-based team. In the apt words of Lieutenant Colonel Simpson, "nighttime is our friend. . . . The night masks us, you know. Its our hill, its our tree line."[219] Routinely, the LAMPS III picked up a contact with its long-range radar and then guided a pair of Kiowa Warrior helicopters to it. After the Army aviators confirmed the identity of the contact through their night vision goggles and onboard video equipment, they sought the OK of higher authority via the LAMPS to engage the target. On receipt of that permission, the Kiowa Warrior helicopters opened up on the normally unsuspecting prey with their lethal array of missiles and guns.

Iraqi combatants were difficult to track down. Before the war Saddam had dispersed his vessels, most of which were relatively small, fast, and maneuverable boats, and after the shooting started kept them constantly on the move.

A typical antisurface engagement began when the sensors on board a patrol aircraft detected a vessel and reported the contact to an air controller, who then vectored in helicopters or fixed-wing aircraft flying antisurface missions in the area. Positive visual identification was an absolute necessity because not only Iraq, but Iran and GCC countries operated similar types of small combatants in the gulf's congested waters. "There were actually Iranian ships bumping around up there in the northern gulf watching the show," recalled Captain Woodall after the war, "and you had to distinguish between the Iranians and Iraqis before you sank something."[220] The visual identification requirement also helped sort out the true contacts from spurious electronic emissions, oil well heads mistaken for ships, and, as Captain Forbes labeled them, "Saddam's famous radar reflectors," which mimicked the radar signature of small vessels.[221] Obtaining positive visual identification of a vessel in darkness, rain, or fog, however, proved particularly difficult.[222]

Occasionally, a trailing aircraft running low on fuel had to break contact with a suspicious vessel because it did not receive timely permission to fire. This resulted from the six-link chain of command for ASUW engagements. According to Captain Woodall, a "Mother may I?" request to fire had to pass from the trailing attack aircraft to the *Mobile Bay* as air control unit, to Captain Forbes as local antisurface warfare commander, to Admiral Zlatoper as Battle Force Zulu ASUWC, to Admiral March as composite warfare commander in the gulf, and finally to Admiral Arthur as COMUSNAVCENT. Permission to fire then had to travel back through each link to the aircraft on the scene. Woodall found this procedure to be "frustrating" and "agonizingly slow."[223] He elaborated:

> It took a lot of aggressive pursuit [by the aircraft]. Almost every one of those kills involved some kind of dance of death with the permission system. It made sense during the war. I'm not arguing against the need to get permission because it was very important not to kill an Iranian. But the point is that it was awkward.[224]

Indeed, communications problems, at least twice cost ASUW forces the opportunity to engage the enemy. Admiral Zlatoper blamed it on "the extremely poor quality of [the] KY-75 encrypted circuit [which] makes it unusable for we oldtimers and the consummate challenge for younger ears."[225] At such times, or when aloft antisurface aircraft were unavailable or out of ammunition, or when the situation warranted extra force, Captain Forbes requested launch of aircraft standing by on carriers. He could also divert Navy planes from combat air patrol or ATO-specified missions.

"The Lynx and Its Prey" by John Charles Roach

When COMUSNAVCENT confirmed a contact as hostile, the allied aircraft attacked. At that point the enemy was practically helpless, for Iraqi naval personnel lacked adequate combat training and their defensive systems proved woefully inadequate. Fire-control radars on board radically maneuvering enemy vessels could not track the highly agile allied helicopters or fast-moving planes. Conversely, the coalition's sophisticated missiles usually left an Iraqi vessel dead in the water after a few minutes of action. For an expenditure of 26 Sea Skuas, the British sank 12 Iraqi vessels. U.S. Army OH-58D helicopters also accounted for several Iraqi vessels with Hellfire missiles. The Sea Skuas and other helicopter-launched missiles lacked the explosive punch to sink a larger vessel, but follow-on attack jets had no difficulty finishing the job with cluster bombs.[226] From 22 January through the end of the month, allied aircraft flying offensive antisurface missions hit Iraqi port facilities, Silkworm missile sites, or naval craft on a daily basis.

Mines remained foremost in everyone's thoughts during the effort to eliminate the Iraqi navy. Admiral Arthur and his staff pondered several schemes for obtaining good intelligence on the location of Iraqi minefields. Arthur considered as too risky the suggestion that a special forces team raid Ras al-Qulayah to capture Iraqi minelayers at the pier. He believed, however, that seizing a minelayer at sea was possible and might yield invaluable information. On 21 January, Arthur designated the capture of enemy minelayers as the task force's number one priority. For the same purpose, he and his staff began planning operations to take three small islands, Qaruh, Maradim, and Kubbar, located off the coast of Kuwait.[227]

Early on the morning of the 24th, the COMUSNAVCENT staff gathered to discuss the progress of the plans. Arthur had originally intended to launch a raid on Qaruh and Maradim that night, but cancelled the operation because CENTCOM's special operations command could not provide the needed SEALs. He then considered using Amphibious Squadron 5 and the 13th MEU(SOC) to take the three islands. Events soon overtook the plans.[228]

Around 0650 that same morning a patrol aircraft reported a possible Iraqi minesweeper at the pier at tiny, barren Qaruh Island located roughly halfway between the ad-Dorra oilfield and the coast of Kuwait. Captain Forbes dispatched a pair of Intruders from *Theodore Roosevelt*'s Attack Squadron 65 to investigate. At 0700 the Intruders positively identified the vessel at the Qaruh dock as an Iraqi Yevgenya-class minesweeper. Forbes ordered the Intruders to wait until the minesweeper put out to sea and then disable it.

The Iraqi minesweeper departed the pier around 0915. When the vessel reached a point some two miles from Qaruh Island, the Intruders pounced, bombing and strafing it. The A-6s reported the minesweeper disabled and life rafts in the water. The guided missile frigate *Curts* (FFG 38), patrolling nearby in an oilfield with *Nicholas* and *Leftwich* (DD 984), was ordered to move in, capture the crew, and gather information useful for intelligence from the minesweeper. *Curts* and her LAMPS helicopter sped towards the stricken vessel. Soon, the helicopter spotted a floating mine 1,000 yards off *Curts*' starboard bow and sank it with machine gun fire. Then the aircraft spotted the minesweeper and an Iraqi patrol boat nearby. While maneuvering to avoid aerial attack, the patrol boat struck a drifting Iraqi mine and sank. *Curts*, meanwhile, launched her two embarked Army helicopters of the 4th Squadron, 17th Cavalry, under Chief Warrant Officer Dudley C. A. Carver, to cover the LAMPS. As the frigate drew near the minesweeper, her bridge team saw Iraqi sailors on board the ship attempt to destroy equipment and documents. The LAMPS strafed the vessel to stop this activity and the crew abandoned ship. *Curts* dispatched a party of SEALs and other sailors in a motor whaleboat. After the team boarded the minesweeper and removed everything of intelligence value, *Curts* sank her with 76mm gunfire. The frigate picked up 22 survivors of the short fight.[229]

During the operation the OH-58D helicopters took small arms fire from Qaruh Island. The aircraft moved in and engaged several bunkers and antiaircraft emplacements on the island with rockets and .50-caliber weapons, killing two Iraqis. At one point CWO Carver reviewed the videotape from his onboard equipment and discovered an Iraqi hoisting a white flag. Then, the OH-58 crews spotted two dozen Iraqi soldiers with their arms raised in surrender. When Carver passed on this information, *Curts'* captain had a composite SEAL platoon from elements embarked on *Curts, Leftwich,* and *Nicholas* land on the island. The group captured twenty-nine more enemy prisoners. A search of the island yielded night vision goggles, a cache of small arms, a .50 caliber machine gun, SA-7 missiles, and rocket-propelled grenade launchers.

At 1707, SEAL Ensign John Pugh raised the flags of Kuwait and the United States on Qaruh Island.[230] "The high point for me," recalled Commander Glenn H. Montgomery, *Curts'* captain, "was when I saw the Kuwaiti flag flying over its own territory."[231]

The operation not only reclaimed the first piece of Kuwait captured by Iraq, but also yielded information on Iraqi minelaying activity and minefields in the area. The intelligence indicated that the Iraqis had positioned a minefield below Maradim island, farther south than

"The Liberation of Qaruh" by John Charles Roach

Arthur and his staff had expected it to be. Moreover, a few of the enemy prisoners admitted setting several mines adrift.[232]

Admiral Arthur now set his sights on Maradim Island. Intelligence had originally indicated that an Iraqi infantry company manned a radar and listening post there. The crew of an aircraft returning from a strike mission reported observing "SOS we surrender" spelled out in rocks on the island. Arthur ordered Admiral LaPlante and General Jenkins to assault Maradim on 29 January. At 0300 on the appointed day, the amphibious ship *Okinawa* (LPH 3) rendezvoused with *Mobile Bay, Caron* (DD 970), *Leftwich*, and *Curts*. Between 0810 and 0836, two CH-53 Sea Stallion and four CH-46 Sea Knight helicopters, with troops embarked, took off from *Okinawa*. Meanwhile, an Intruder from *Midway* made two high-speed passes over Maradim and reported no activity. Then, a section of AH-1 Sea Cobra helicopter gunships from *Okinawa* and two Army helicopters from *Curts* overflew the island. They also reported no activity below. At 0900, the Sea Stallions landed on the northern end of Maradim and disgorged 60 U.S. and Kuwaiti marines. The landing force, finding the island deserted, raised the Kuwaiti flag and conducted a thorough search. They discovered some cases of ammunition and explosives, 2 heavy mortars, 15 SA-7 surface-to-air missiles, 2 complete radar systems, and other weapons and equipment. The landing party recovered some of this war materiel and destroyed the rest. They also retrieved 25 pounds of documents. Around 1200 Admiral March reported 15 to 17 Iraqi small craft in the vicinity of Ras al-Qulayah, heading southeast at high speed. LaPlante and Jenkins ordered the landing force to withdraw. The helicopters embarked the marines and lifted off at 1215. Although the operation failed to net any enemy prisoners, the captured documents yielded intelligence.[233]

Saddam Strikes Back

Saddam Hussein struck back late in January. Perhaps as early as the 19th, the dictator ordered his military command to pump oil stored at Kuwait's Mina al-Ahmadi facility into the Persian Gulf. That same day five loaded tankers positioned off the Kuwait coast released their cargoes.[234] Eventually, a 20-mile-long slick containing some 400 million gallons of oil spread into the gulf and along the coastline. The oil slick threatened to close Saudi desalinization plants on which coalition troops and Saudi civilians depended for potable water. But Kuwaiti resistance personnel and American air power once again frustrated the dictator. Kuwaitis working in the oil facilities "secretly closed a valve the Iraqis didn't know about and, to fool them, changed the valve indicator to 'open'."[235] On the 27th, Air Force F-111 fighters destroyed pipeline pumping equipment at Mina al-Ahmadi with laser guided bombs. These measures stemmed the flow of oil into the gulf.[236]

Soon after the allies discovered the spill, President Bush dispatched to Saudi Arabia experts from the U.S. Coast Guard, Environmental Protection Agency, National Oceanic and Atmospheric Administration, Army Corps of Engineers, and Navy Supervisor of Salvage. The team set up shop in Dhahran and went to work advising GCC officials about cleanup techniques.[237] Admiral Arthur assisted this effort with aircraft patrols, nicknamed "oil CAP" by his pilots, that monitored the composition and drift direction of the oil slick.[238] Meanwhile, Saddam had stepped up his campaign of environmental terrorism. On the 25th, he ordered his engineers to dynamite the 600 working oil wells in Kuwait.

On 29 January, the Iraqi dictator mounted a much more serious counterstroke. Under a full moon, just after midnight, elements of his 3d Armored Division and 5th Mechanized Division mounted three separate attacks south across the Kuwait border into Saudi Arabia. At this writing, Saddam has not revealed his reasons for launching these attacks. One analyst contends that a coalition deception operation simulating an attack might have caused the Iraqi leader to "jump the gun."[239] Others suggest various motives: that he hoped to trigger the ground war before the allies were ready for battle, raise the morale of his troops, capture prisoners to discover allied intentions, inflict casualties on the Americans, foment antiwar sentiment in the U.S., and humiliate the Saudis.[240]

One contingent of Iraqi forces entered Saudi Arabia at Observation Post No. 6, located some nine miles south of al-Manaqish, Kuwait; another group crossed the border at a point approximately 55 miles west of the Saudi Arabian coastal town of Khafji.

The most successful enemy force, composed of two armored/mechanized brigades, drove toward Khafji, entering the deserted city by 2315. Although Khafji's population had long since left for safer rear areas, King Fahd felt that the action defiled his kingdom. The attack cut off a few good men of the Marine 1st Surveillance, Reconnaissance, and Intelligence Group, who holed up in an abandoned house. For two days these "leathernecks" directed Marine artillery and close air support aircraft against a confused enemy in the streets outside.

The Iraqi attack on Khafji involved naval forces as well. On 29 January, just as U.S. and Kuwaiti marines were mopping up on Maradim, 15 to 17 Iraqi fast patrol boats sped south from Ras al-Qulayah, a point along the southern Kuwait coast, in an apparent attempt to land commandoes below Khafji, where they would sow confusion in the Saudi rear. They

The A-6E launches a 1,000-pound Skipper laser guided bomb.

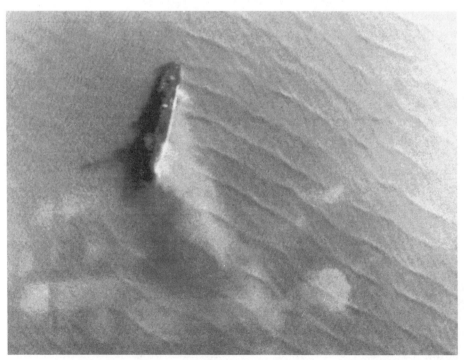

An Iraqi warship under attack during the "Bubiyan Turkey Shoot."

never made it. Royal Air Force GR-1A Jaguar jets spotted the formation, then Lynx helicopters from British warships *Brazen, Cardiff,* and *Gloucester* and Saudi naval units attacked, sinking or damaging several and scattering the rest with missiles and guns. Other allied aircraft subsequently destroyed or damaged the survivors.

That night coalition aircraft detected other elements of the two Iraqi divisions inside Kuwait positioned for what looked like attack. Although the JFACC had reacted tardily to the Iraqi offensive, General Horner soon rectified the lapse. For the next eight hours, allied aircraft attacked and decimated these units. In one mission, F/A-18s from *Saratoga* dropped 100 Mark 83, 1,000-pound bombs on an Iraqi army target in Kuwait. Daybreak on the 31st found the Iraqis retreating in disarray. Meanwhile, Saudi and Qatari armored forces rumbled into Khafji. These troops, Marine Cobra attack helicopters, and other allied aircraft killed many of the Iraqis, captured several hundred enemy prisoners, and drove the rest back into Kuwait.

By midday on 31 January the battle of Khafji had passed into Marine Corps history. Whatever Saddam hoped to achieve by this assault, it revealed that his armed forces fought poorly. Conversely, Khafji boosted the confidence of the coalition, for it demonstrated that Arab and American ground forces could fight and win as a team. It also helped focus Iraqi attention away from their desert flank.[241]

Bubiyan Turkey Shoot

Even before the issue was settled at Khafji, coalition naval forces had begun the battle that would destroy the Iraqi navy as a viable threat. Late in the evening of 29 January, Commanders Richard Noble and Richard Cassara, pilot and bombardier/navigator of an A-6 Intruder from *Ranger*'s VA-145, completed their attack on a Silkworm missile site at Umm Qsabah in Kuwait. As they began a patrol along the coast of Bubiyan Island, Cassara picked up a huge return on his radar just off Iraq's al-Faw peninsula. As the plane drew closer, the large blip dissolved into four distinct objects in a line. Cassara could tell from his forward-looking infrared sensor that these were combatant vessels heading east at 15 to 18 knots.[242] Noble angled the jet down to 10,000 feet for a closer look and the crew tentatively identified three of the contacts as an FPB 57 and two TNC 45s—Exocet missile boats that Iraq had captured from Kuwait. The vessels were speeding towards Iranian coastal waters with their lights out.

Cassara's report of the sighting seemed to confirm Captain Forbes' estimate of two days earlier that the Iraqi navy would attempt a mass exit to Iran, just as the air force had done. Forbes had placed special emphasis on the allied air and sea patrol of the waters between Iraq and Iran and it had paid off. An E-2C Hawkeye, to which he assigned control of Noble's A-6, relayed the authorization from Captain Forbes to attack the vessels. The Intruder hit two of the boats with 500-pound laser guided bombs. Using the "buddy bomb" tactic, in which Cassara used his plane's laser designator to guide the 500-pound bomb of his VA-155 wingman's plane toward the target, the Americans hit a third boat. All three of the boats caught fire and went dead in the water. The last Iraqi boat continued to speed toward Iranian waters, but both A-6s were now low on fuel. Forbes then assigned two Canadian CF-18s piloted by Major David W. Kendall and Captain Stephen P. Hill, who were on a combat air patrol mission, to the Intruders. Under a bright, full moon, the CF-18s strafed the fourth boat, a Soviet-made *Osa II,* with 20mm guns. The lucky Iraqi vessel was later spotted in an Iranian port, but it had sustained substantial damage to its superstructure. This action marked the opening of

Courtesy of CDR Richard Cassara, USN (Ret.)

An Iraqi FPB-57, which tried to flee to Iraq, lies dead in the water, and abandoned.

Bombadier/navigator Commander Richard Cassara (left) and pilot Commander Richard Noble of VA-45 pose in front of their Rockeye-armed A-6E Intruder on board *Ranger*.

what became known as the "Battle of Bubiyan Channel" or the "Bubiyan Turkey Shoot."[243]

The next day a large force of Iraqi combatants based at the az-Zubayr and Umm Qasr naval bases, which naval aircraft had struck repeatedly since the start of the war, sortied on a high-speed dash for Iran. Saddam himself issued the sailing orders hoping, as with his air force, to preserve armed forces for the postwar era. Coalition forces detected the movement and attacked the fleeing vessels for the next 13 hours. In 21 separate engagements, coalition naval aircraft destroyed or damaged 7 missile boats, 3 amphibious ships, a minesweeper, and 9 other Iraqi vessels in the shallow waters between Bubiyan Island and the Shatt-al-Arab marshlands. At the climax of the battle Royal Navy Lynx helicopters touched down on British destroyers only to refuel, then lifted off again to rejoin the fight. Navy Combat Search and Rescue units fished 20 Iraqis out of the water. Only one missile boat and one amphibious ship, both shot up, made it to Iranian waters. The Iranians promptly seized the remains of Saddam's navy, as they had his air force.[244]

By 2 February coalition forces had destroyed or disabled all 13 enemy missile boats and many other less-threatening combatants, "[driving] Saddam's navy into Neptune's soggy arms," as Captain Forbes phrased it.[245] The surface threat to the coalition was eliminated. Six days later Admiral Arthur declared that the coalition had established sea control in the northern Persian Gulf.[246] The successful conclusion of the coalition's offensive antisurface operation, in less than two weeks, made it possible for the second phase of the maritime campaign to begin. Free from the enemy's surface threat, the fleet prepared to move forward for operations right off Saddam's eastern flank.

USN DN-ST 92-06819

Only the superstructure of this Iraqi naval vessel sunk by an HMS *Gloucester* Lynx helicopter shows above the shallow water of the Persian Gulf.

CHAPTER 5

Preparing the Battlefield

P HASE III OF OPERATION DESERT STORM—battlefield preparation—pitted allied air and naval power against the Iraqi armed forces in the Kuwait Theater of Operations. Throughout February, coalition aerial attacks and, to a lesser extent, naval gunfire, methodically reduced the fighting power of the enemy army. Meanwhile, allied armored, mechanized, and naval forces moved into position for Phase IV, the final assault to liberate Kuwait.

"First we're going to cut it off, . . . "

Throughout Desert Shield and the initial phases of Desert Storm, the Iraqis strengthened their defenses in Kuwait. Iraqi combat engineers, highly touted for their performance during the Iran-Iraq War, built extensive fixed defenses, particularly the so-called Saddam Line, two major defensive belts that paralleled the border with Saudi Arabia. The first belt, roughly three to nine miles inside Kuwait, consisted of a continuous line of minefields varying in depth from 100 to 200 yards and featured barbed wire, antitank ditches, earthen berms, and oil-filled trenches situated along key avenues of approach. The minefields contained both antitank and antipersonnel mines. Platoon and company-sized infantry formations covered these obstacles.

The second belt constituted the main defensive line. It began on the coast some 20 miles north of the Saudi border, ran west to a point north of the al-Wafrah oilfield, and then turned northwest, converging with the first line near al-Manaqish. Mutually supporting infantry brigades, dug into trench lines and strong points on slight rises, overlooked obstacles and minefields on the lower ground to their front. Numerous revetted tanks and artillery pieces reinforced the infantry. Twenty-five of the 43 divisions that Iraq had deployed to Kuwait manned the Saddam Line, with the remaining 18 held in strategic reserve, including eight Republican Guard Forces Command armored, mechanized, and infantry divisions arrayed north and west of Kuwait, to counter any coalition penetrations.[1]

"Our strategy for dealing with this army is very, very simple," General Colin Powell told reporters on 23 January 1991. "First we're going to cut it off, then we're going to kill it."[2] In Phase III, the coalition sought to reduce the effective combat strength of Iraq's fielded military forces by cutting off their supplies and destroying their command and control, largely by aerial attack.[3]

From General Schwarzkopf's perspective, Phase III was intended to soften up enemy ground forces in preparation for Phase IV. The plan for the final assault envisioned the main attack as a "left hook" by armor-heavy units, wheeling around the enemy western flank, cutting off Iraqi forces in Kuwait, and destroying the Republican Guard. Admiral Arthur's operations were intended to divert enemy attention from the main thrust and pin down enemy forces along the coast. Supporting attacks by I MEF and Arab units along the Kuwait-Saudi border would fix and destroy Iraqi forces in Kuwait and liberate Kuwait City. General Schwarzkopf would launch Phase IV when he believed that coalition troops were ready, sufficient munitions and supplies were on hand, the weather favored a broad offensive, and the combat capabilities of enemy ground forces in the KTO had been sufficiently reduced by Phase III attacks.[4]

Despite the fact that there was no separate air plan, only a single theater plan involving air power, many Air Force planners believed that air power alone could defeat Saddam Hussein, rendering a ground offensive unnecessary.[5] "We are not '*preparing* the battlefield,'" declared Lieutenant Colonel David Deptula, director of the strategic planning cell in Riyadh, "we are *destroying* it."[6] General Horner, however, did not share this view. He understood that victory would be the product of a fully integrated and complementary air, ground, and naval effort.

Throughout Phase III, U.S. Navy, Marine, and Air Force aviators along with the coalition's European, Canadian, and Arab airmen mounted round-the-clock strikes against the Iraqi army in the KTO. Most Air Force units operated from bases throughout the Arabian Peninsula, although many B-52 bomber flights originated from Diego Garcia, Great Britain, Spain, and even Louisiana.[7] Marine air units were based afloat in amphibious assault ships and ashore at such locations as Saudi Arabia's Abd al-Aziz Naval Base. Marine planes rearmed and refueled at forward operating facilities at al-Jubayl, Tanajib, and Ras al-Mishab in northern Saudi Arabia. In addition, the leathernecks established a helicopter base, named "Lonesome Dove" after a popular television mini-series, in the Saudi desert south of the "elbow" of Kuwait. These forward bases enabled Marine air units to respond quickly to mission requests. For example, AV-8 Harriers could rearm and refuel within 17–25 minutes at Tanajib, an Arab-American Oil Company facility 35 miles south of the Kuwait border, and return to the combat area over southern Kuwait in 5–7 minutes.[8]

While Battle Force Yankee operated from the same area in the Red Sea throughout the war, Battle Force Zulu moved farther north in the Persian Gulf as the campaign progressed. Between 4 and 14 February, Admiral March's carriers operated from a position 75 nautical miles northeast of Bahrain and 250 nautical miles southeast of Kuwait City. On the latter date, his flattops steamed 65 nautical miles northwest to a position 80 nautical miles north-northeast of Bahrain and 185 nautical miles southeast of Kuwait City, where they remained for the rest of the war.[9]

Some critics have contended that Admiral March waited too long to move his carriers forward in the gulf. He responded that he was "caught between a rock and a hard place—a balance between trying to be aggressive and support and not be too aggressive." He explained that the "last thing we really needed to do was have a carrier run into a mine and be knocked out of action, because that would just give ammunition to the newspapers."[10]

On 8 February, Admiral Arthur ordered the *America* battle group to join Battle Force Zulu in order to concentrate more naval firepower in the eastern KTO. In six days the carrier and its escorts steamed approximately 2,000 miles around the Arabian Peninsula, taking up station in the Persian Gulf late in the afternoon of the 14th. *America* began strike operations the next morning.[11]

Both battle forces maintained a steady tempo of operations during Phase III, hitting strategic as well as battlefield preparation targets. For most of February, each carrier launched an average of between three and three and a half strike packages per day.[12] Despite *America*'s arrival in the gulf, Admiral March usually operated only three carriers at a time during Phase III. Between 4 and 23 February, Battle Force Zulu mounted attacks from all four carriers on only two days, the 15th and 22d of February.[13] *Midway* suspended air operations between the 16th and 21st to resurface her flight deck. *Ranger* suspended operations during the 23d and the morning of the 24th to conduct general maintenance. Upon *America*'s departure from the Red Sea, Battle Force Yankee initiated a new carrier rotation schedule for flight operations which produced approximately the same number of sorties as before.[14]

According to March, he and Arthur moderated the pace of air operations because they wanted to conserve their resources. Commander Battle Force Zulu "didn't want to burn out ... air assets prematurely."

March remarked, "if you would have asked me if the [ground] war would be over within three days, I would have said no way, Jose. I figured our guys were going to have a hell of a time beating their way up through Kuwait [and] be in there fighting for a long time." The admiral added that "with the benefit of hindsight, it [slower pace of operations] was not a good decision." [15]

Interdiction

Phase III aerial attacks fell roughly into two categories: interdiction missions against enemy lines of supply and direct strikes against enemy units. Interdiction operations aimed at cutting the flow of supplies into and within the KTO, and to stop the movement of enemy forces throughout the theater. Naval and other air units hit railroad marshaling yards, fuel depots, supply concentrations, and highway interchanges. In addition, strike aircraft flew armed reconnaissance missions along sections of the main highways leading into the KTO, seeking and destroying truck convoys.

Perhaps the most critical targets were 40 Tigris and Euphrates river bridges that air planners had identified as key links in the Iraqi transportation system.[16] Planes from the Red Sea carriers hit bridges deep inside Iraq. Admiral March's units struck bridges clustered around Basrah in southeastern Iraq. Battle Force Zulu carried out 45 of the 64 Navy "bridge busting" missions.

With little prewar preparation or training for high-altitude delivery of ordnance, and plagued by foul weather, Navy attack squadrons were relatively ineffective against the bridges assigned them. Air Force units did little better. Normally, the one bomb that each of the attacking planes delivered did not destroy a bridge. At the end of January, General Horner added Royal Air Force units to the bridge destruction mission. Profiting from the American experience, the British routinely launched four GR-1 Tornado bombers, each armed with three 1,000-pound laser guided bombs, against each bridge. The Tornados generally released all 12 weapons against a single bridge, targeting aimpoints at opposite ends of the structure. Because they launched far more laser guided bombs per strike than the Navy, Marine, or Air Force units, the RAF planes knocked out over 63 percent of the bridges they attacked.[17]

Iraqi communications cables ran across some of the bridges between Baghdad and the KTO. Bombing these spans severed Iraqi supply lines and important connections in the military communications network. By mid-February communications between corps and division headquarters and their subordinate units along the Kuwait-Saudi border had become sporadic, forcing many Iraqi commanders to rely upon messengers. Ultimately, coalition aircraft severely damaged or destroyed approximately 75 percent of the bridges between central Iraq and the KTO.[18]

Often, large Iraqi convoys jammed up on the approach roads behind knocked out bridges. Coalition aircraft bombed and strafed the trapped vehicles. By the third week in February, the Iraqis largely restricted resupply operations to the night hours, hoping to cloak their vehicles in darkness. The ability of allied aircraft to operate at night undercut the effectiveness of this measure. The Iraqis also shifted from convoys to single trucks in an attempt to evade detection. The loss of military transport vehicles forced the Iraqis to use civilian vehicles, even garbage trucks, to run the gauntlet of allied aircraft in the attempt to resupply forward troops.

But the Iraqis were not totally helpless in the face of the allied aerial onslaught. They too gained insight from the Vietnam War. They managed to counter coalition operations against their transportation system on numerous occasions by rerouting traffic to still-standing bridges, ferrying supplies and equipment across the water, and spanning rivers with pontoon bridges and earthen causeways.[19]

Despite these efforts, allied aerial interdiction reduced the flow of supplies to the Iraqi army in the KTO and disrupted its logistic system. Some units, notably the Republican Guard divisions in the rear areas, enjoyed an overabundance of supplies. Iraqi soldiers in other units, particularly those in the front lines, suffered from malnutrition. Because allied air attacks had deprived them of food, water, and other basic necessities, their morale plummeted and the desertion rate increased.[20]

To exacerbate these effects of interdiction, allied forces conducted psychological warfare operations. The best known effort was the dissemination of printed leaflets. Between 30 December 1990 and 28 February 1991, Air Force MC-130 cargo planes, B-52 bombers, and F-16 fighters, Navy F/A-18s, and Marine Corps A-6s showered Iraqi soldiers and civilians with 29 million leaflets.[21]

One such leaflet related directly to the amphibious deception. It depicted a tidal wave about to inundate Iraqi soldiers on a Kuwait beach. The wave incorporated the image of a leatherneck uttering the Marines' fierce battle cry, "ooh-rah!", and ready to strike a fear-stricken Iraqi soldier with a K-Bar combat knife. Ships and aircraft in motion behind the wave completed the impression of an assault from the sea. Ten thousand of these leaflets were sealed into empty plastic water bottles, which a local smuggler released near the Kuwait coast. Psychological operations officers believed that the bottles began washing ashore toward the end

This leaflet, dropped by the thousands over Iraqi troops on the coast, reinforced enemy fears that U.S. naval forces would storm ashore to liberate Kuwait.

of February. Air Force F-16s subsequently dropped another 200,000 "Tidal Wave" leaflets onto Iraqi defensive positions along the coast.[22]

In general, psychological warfare leaflets emphasized that the coalition opposed Iraq's national policy, not the Iraqi people, blamed the war on Saddam Hussein, stressed the futility of resistance, and encouraged Iraqi soldiers to desert their units or to surrender. Many of the Iraqis who surrendered did so clutching a leaflet, which they said had influenced their decision to give up.[23]

Kill Boxes

Daily pounding by coalition aircraft provided perhaps the greatest impetus to surrendering Iraqis. Allied air planners organized direct strikes against enemy ground units by means of "kill boxes." A kill box was a geographical area measuring 30 miles by 30 miles, subdivided into four 15-by-15-mile squares. Air planners superimposed a grid of such boxes over a map of Iraq and Kuwait. The air tasking order assigned a flight of aircraft to a kill box quadrant for a specified period of time. Sometimes the ATO designated specific targets, but more often it authorized aircraft to attack targets of opportunity, including moving targets like tanks, armored personnel carriers, and trucks and fixed targets such as artillery sites, buildings, bunkers, and revetments. The kill box system reduced the danger of mid-air collision and fratricide arising from the large numbers of allied aircraft crisscrossing the constricted airspace over the KTO, and from the limited visibility caused by bad weather and

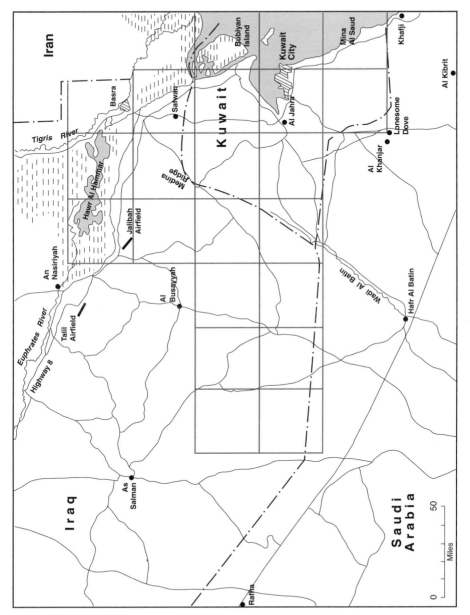

Kill Boxes in the KTO

239

smoke from burning oil wells. Kill boxes also prevented redundant strikes by different allied units on the same targets.

Admiral March requested that each carrier air wing be assigned to the same kill box, reasoning that familiarity with the terrain, enemy air defenses, and other critical features of a given area would enhance air unit effectiveness. The JFACC assigned Battle Force Zulu air wings to a few contiguous kill boxes, but changed the assignments each day, perhaps to avoid any semblance of Vietnam-era route packages.[24]

The Persian Gulf carriers launched their first kill box mission on 25 January, followed four days later by the ships in the Red Sea. The carriers averaged 48 kill box missions apiece during Desert Storm. In a typical Battle Force Zulu kill box mission, between 3 and 13 planes entered an assigned quadrant, searched the area below with their radars, made two to three passes during a 25-minute time-on-target period to inspect potential targets, and then dropped their ordnance at 7,000–10,000 feet. Because of allied success against the Iraqi field army's antiaircraft defenses during January, by early February coalition aircraft were fairly safe attacking all but the heavily defended Republican Guard forces from these relatively low levels.[25]

Allied aircrews found that some of their advanced weapons were ideally suited to the desert battlefield. During Desert Shield, the Air Force began practicing medium altitude strikes against individual vehicles, utilizing their forward-looking infrared systems. At sunset the FLIR could detect half-buried tanks, because metal cooled more slowly than the surrounding sand. The allies incorporated this discovery into a new tactic, nicknamed "tank plinking." F-111F crews located individual Iraqi tanks with their FLIRs and destroyed them with GBU-12, 500-pound laser guided bombs. A-6s and F-15s also adopted this tactic. The AGM-65 Maverick missile, fired by AV-8s, F/A-18s, and other allied planes, were effective against tanks as well. The upshot, according to one captured Iraqi officer, was that many tank crews left their vehicles and lived in trenches a hundred yards away. The operational readiness of enemy armored units suffered accordingly.[26]

Kill box missions became almost routine. During one nighttime mission, Lieutenant Paul Mackley and Lieutenant (jg) Christopher Saito, an Intruder crew from *Ranger*'s VA-145, flew into a kill box in Iraq. Saito, the bombardier/navigator, found a long line of Republican Guard emplacements on his forward-looking infrared. He immediately called for Mackley and the pilot of an accompanying A-6 to "pickle off" their bombs. The tape from the imaging system on board Mackley's aircraft showed two lines of explosions stitched neatly across the revetments. A few nights later, Mackley and Saito surprised a convoy of free rocket over ground (FROG) launchers and destroyed two of them.[27]

The AV-8 Harriers of Marine squadron VMA-331 on board *Nassau* joined the fray against Saddam's ground forces on 20 February. This marked the first time in history that American vertical/short take-off and landing planes conducted combat missions from a landing helicopter assault ship. By war's end the AV-8s had flown 243 interdiction and close air support missions, as many as 47 a day. In all, coalition air forces flew more than 35,000 sorties against KTO targets, including more than 5,600 against the Republican Guard. The Navy expended more ordnance against kill box targets than any other kind.[28]

Gauging the Effectiveness of Phase III Air Attacks

Allied leaders surmised that their air attacks were hurting Iraqi forces in Kuwait, but they disagreed on the extent of the damage. The question was particularly thorny for General Schwarzkopf, who needed to determine when Phase III had sufficiently reduced the combat effectiveness of the enemy's forces in Kuwait for him to inaugurate Phase IV.[29] "We couldn't afford distorted assessments," he recalled. "Too much optimism could prompt us to launch the ground war too soon, at the cost of many lives; too much pessimism could cause us to sit wringing our hands and moaning that the enemy was still too strong."[30] At Glosson's suggestion, Schwarzkopf and his senior commanders deter-

USAF DF-ST 92-07395

Marine AV-8B Harriers of Marine Attack Squadron 513 fly in formation over Saudi Arabia.

mined that the final assault should not be launched until the combat capabilities of Iraqi ground forces had been cut in half.[31]

How to measure the reduction of Iraqi combat effectiveness proved to be a controversial question. Initially, CENTCOM planners used equipment attrition as the criterion, which meant that Phase III operations would have to destroy half of the enemy's 10,000 to 11,000 tanks, armored personnel carriers, and artillery pieces. Army, Marine, and other coalition ground force commanders also wanted to eliminate a significant number of the enemy's command posts, supply and ammunition depots, communications sites, and troop concentrations.[32]

The allies used a wide variety of resources to gather information on the damage being done by the bombing campaign, including satellites, manned reconnaissance aircraft, unmanned aerial vehicles, signals intelligence systems, gun camera imagery, forward observation posts, ground-based reconnaissance patrols, counterintelligence operations, and enemy prisoner of war debriefings. The Defense Intelligence Agency, Central Intelligence Agency, foreign agencies, and CENTCOM's component commands all provided bomb damage analysis to General Schwarzkopf. NAVCENT, for example, supplied intelligence on Iraqi naval facilities and vessels. CENTCOM's components, in turn, received support from their own intelligence organizations. The Seventh Fleet intelligence staff on *Blue Ridge* supported NAVCENT while the 1st Surveillance, Reconnaissance, and Intelligence Group supported MARCENT.[33] Gauging the effectiveness of the aerial attacks on Iraqi ground forces ultimately boiled down to battle damage assessment (BDA),[34] a perennial problem in the application of air power.[35]

As in any war, enemy efforts exacerbated the problem. Iraqi combat engineers proved adept at protecting and concealing equipment. Tanks, for example, were often dispersed, dug in up to their turrets, and surrounded by earthen berms. Except from low altitude, allied pilots had great difficulty spotting dug-in tanks and artillery pieces, and found it almost impossible to distinguish empty revetments from occupied revetments.[36]

To compound the difficulty, Iraqi engineers tried to paint a false picture of the battlefield using decoys and other techniques. They deployed dummy Scud launchers, artillery pieces, tanks, and SAM and Silkworm missile sites, and literally painted "holes" in airfield runways to simulate bomb damage. By night, they placed burning tires near the decoys to simulate heat signatures in order to fool FLIR sensors in allied aircraft. By day, they placed smoke canisters or containers of burning diesel oil on operational tanks to create the impression that they had already been hit.[37]

Equipment limitations further complicated the BDA problem. Many of the weapons systems used in Desert Storm lacked sensors and cameras to record the effects of the munitions. Reconnaissance satellite cameras generally could not penetrate a heavy overcast, and clouds covered the KTO for half of the war. Of course, no satellite camera could see inside enemy tanks, bunkers, and buildings. It was almost impossible to confirm destruction of dug-in targets until coalition ground forces arrived to see for themselves. Accordingly, the allies missed some targets and hit others that were already destroyed.[38]

Little timely BDA information from satellites and other national intelligence sources trickled down to Battle Force Yankee. Satellite imagery usually arrived on the Red Sea carriers three to five days after the pictures were taken, and 90 percent of the images depicted the Persian Gulf coast rather than Battle Force Yankee's inland operating areas. Admiral Mixson had to rely almost entirely on air crew debriefs and mission recorder film to evaluate damage to targets and the effectiveness of his units' tactics.[39]

For Battle Force Zulu, information from national sensors was more useful for prewar planning than for Desert Storm operations.

The Tactical Air Reconnaissance Pod System (TARPS) of a Navy F-14 Tomcat captured this aerial photo showing bomb damage to the Iraqi superphosphate fertilizer plant at al-Qaim.

Hence, the Tactical Area Reconnaissance Pod System (TARPS) imaging equipment hung under F-14 aircraft became especially vital to wartime strike, amphibious, and marine ground operations. TARPS aircraft, however, were few in number. The Navy's tactical intelligence staffs on board the carriers also lacked enough trained personnel and some specialized equipment.[40]

Schwarzkopf assigned the responsibility for tracking the attrition of Iraqi equipment to ARCENT's G-2 (intelligence directorate), which based the tally of destroyed equipment on pilot reports and aerial photography. Intelligence agencies in Washington expressed strong reservations about this method and the rapidly mounting count of kills it produced. CIA and DIA analysts believed that pilots overestimated their accomplishments. In late February, the Central Intelligence Agency reported to President Bush that CENTCOM was grossly exaggerating the damage inflicted on the Iraqis.

The lack of BDA doctrine was the core of the problem. Intelligence professionals in Washington generally refused to count a tank as out of action unless it had been blown apart or had landed upside-down, but many tanks disabled by bombs or missiles appeared intact in aerial photographs. Similarly, no one had reliable means for assessing situations in which an Iraqi unit remained in position, but might have been so severely deprived of food, water, communications, and respite from round-the-clock air strikes that its combat power was nil.[41]

The upshot was that General Schwarzkopf was unhappy with much of the analysis he received. Shortly after the war he told Powell and the other commanders in chief that "incisive, accurate, and predictive analysis of Iraqi capabilities and intentions . . . was either lacking, erroneous, contentious or caveated to the point of being unusable at the theater level."[42] He reiterated these points to the Senate Armed Services Committee during postwar hearings:

> I think it is fair to say that although the fundamental intelligence facts that we had were helpful, that the analysis we received was unhelpful. It was unhelpful because it ended up being so caveated—there were so many disagreements within the intelligence community themselves [*sic*], there were so many disclaimers, that by the time you got done reading many of the intelligence estimates you received, no matter what happened they would have been right, and that is not helpful to the guy in the field.[43]

In his memoir Schwarzkopf quipped that "if we'd waited to convince the CIA, we'd still be in Saudi Arabia."[44]

In the end General Schwarzkopf rethought the practice of tying Iraqi unit effectiveness directly to equipment attrition. Instead, his intelligence officers developed a methodology for gauging the effectiveness of Phase III attacks based on several different kinds of information, including equipment attrition assessments, national intelligence, and deserter reports. This methodology was relatively successful in estimating the percentages of Iraqi equipment destroyed during Phase III.[45]

CENTCOM intelligence officers soon had firsthand evidence to confirm their intelligence estimates. For example, one source picked up the following conversation between two Iraqi soldiers:

Callsign 13: When are we getting our next issue of rations?

Callsign 16: In three days' time.

Callsign 13: What are we supposed to eat in the meantime? Rocks?[46]

During February increasing numbers of enemy soldiers braved the wire and mines on the Kuwait frontier to surrender to allied forces. They told their captors that their comrades on the front lines were receiving little food or water, were exhausted from the incessant aerial attacks, and had little desire to die for Saddam. In some divisions as many as 50 percent of the soldiers had deserted their units. Ibrahim al-Hamas, commander of a Saudi reconnaissance unit who handled a number of Iraqi prisoners, remarked that "they no longer believe in what they are doing."[47]

On 23 February, CENTCOM estimated that coalition forces had destroyed 1,772 Iraqi tanks, 948 armored personnel carriers, and 1,477 artillery pieces, which ultimately proved to be a fairly accurate assessment. Even though Phase III attacks had knocked out less than half of the enemy's tanks and armored personnel carriers in the KTO, the allies had come close to 50 percent attrition of Saddam's artillery. Enemy prisoner of war reports indicated that many Iraqi units in the KTO were demoralized, immobilized, unable to communicate, and virtually isolated from their chain of command. General Schwarzkopf concluded that six weeks of incessant aerial attack had severely eroded the Iraqi leadership's ability to mount an effective defense and had destroyed the Iraqi soldier's will to fight.[48]

The Strategic Air Campaign in February

Meanwhile, allied air units continued mounting Phase I strikes against strategic targets in Iraq. But this effort lost much of its punch as the coalition devoted increasing attention to preparing the battlefield in the KTO. The intensity of the attacks on Baghdad and related target areas also diminished as Washington cut short operations. Following the enemy's 1 February shootdown of a number of Tomahawks fired against sites in Baghdad, General Powell decided that the results no longer justified the cost of using the expensive weapons. At Powell's direction, Schwarzkopf called off further Tomahawk launches. By then, the Navy had successfully launched 282 Tomahawks from 2 battleships, 9 cruisers, 5 destroyers, and 2 submarines operating in the Persian Gulf, Red Sea, or Eastern Mediterranean.[49] Admiral Arthur raised no objections to the halt in TLAM operations because not only did he dislike the JFACC's targeting methods, but he had only 180 TLAMs left in the theater.[50] Thus ended the coalition's only daytime air operation against Baghdad.

Washington's concern with maintaining both the political cohesion of the coalition and the American people's support for the war effort also influenced the strategic air campaign. From the first days of Desert Storm, General Horner's planners had taken pains in their targeting and the use of precision guided weapons to limit civilian casualties and damage to non-military structures. As late as five weeks into the six-week war, Baghdad radio reported the relatively low figure of 1,100 Iraqi civilian deaths. Responsible observers such as John G. Heidenrich, formerly a military analyst with the DIA, estimated that the total of Iraqi civilian deaths during Desert Storm numbered fewer than 1,000. Given the scope and intensity of the aerial campaign, allied air men and women at all levels, from General Horner's staff down to individual pilots and air crews, exercised restraint during Desert Storm.[51]

Unfortunately, aerial attacks that destroy non-military structures and kill innocent civilians are virtually impossible to prevent in war. Only two such bombing sites were available for Iraqi propagandists to display to international reporters during the war. American intelligence described the first building as a well-guarded, well-camouflaged chemical munitions plant. The negligible casualties caused by the raid and the crudely handwritten signs posted among the ruins, which read "baby milk factory," failed to convince many observers that the Iraqis were telling the truth.[52]

The other structure the Iraqis touted as an example of indiscriminate American bombing was the al-Firdos bunker located in the Amiriya district of Baghdad. U.S. intelligence had concluded that the partially camouflaged bunker was an operational military command center, and, as it turned out, senior Iraqi security and intelligence personnel were indeed working there. Unbeknownst to allied air planners, Iraqi authorities had permitted several hundred civilians to shelter there. On the night of 13–14 February, two F-117s destroyed the bunker with a pair of 2,000-pound laser guided bombs designed to penetrate thick concrete casements. At least 100 men, women, and children were killed that night. Even though Washington understood that the al-Firdos bunker was a valid military target, the tragedy received so much unfavorable media attention that Defense Secretary Cheney and General Powell severely curtailed bombing in downtown Baghdad after 16 February.[53]

Despite the al-Firdos tragedy, the Iraqi people realized that the allies sought to spare them. Milton Viorst, a reporter for the *New Yorker* who traveled around Iraq after the war, found most Iraqis "remarkably tolerant of the allied bombs that had destroyed homes or killed civilians. They referred to them as 'mistakes'—conceding, in effect, that American pilots had occasionally missed their aim but had not deliberately sought out civilian targets."[54] CNN's Peter Arnett, present in Baghdad during the height of the bombing, observed that "after the first few days the Iraqis were not afraid of our bombs. They knew we were only going after military targets."[55] All but a tiny fraction of Iraq's shops, offices, hospitals, schools, religious and cultural sites, and homes emerged from the war untouched.[56]

The Right Feint

While allied aircraft prosecuted the air campaign, naval forces prepared the battlefield from the sea. Having neutralized the Iraqi surface vessel and air threat in the northern gulf, U.S. and allied ships now executed the next phase of Admiral Arthur's maritime campaign. To use a boxing analogy, while coalition ground forces set up the left hook, naval forces jabbed with the right. In February, as allied ground units moved into position to knock out Saddam's army with a powerful attack against its western flank, naval forces steamed into the northern Persian Gulf to conduct combat operations designed to fix Iraqi attention on the coast. These operations included clearance of enemy sea mines from offshore waters and air and surface bombardment of troops, coastal fortifications, artillery sites, and Silkworm missile batteries ashore.

Although the purpose of these operations was to enhance the credibility of the strategic feint, the danger inherent in conducting them was very real, for in the six months after the invasion of Kuwait, Iraqi vessels had used the cover of night to create formidable offshore and coastal mine defenses. The outermost minefield covered approximately 24 percent of the northern Persian Gulf and consisted of more than 1,200 mines laid out in a two-belt, 150-mile arc stretching from Bubiyan Island to the Saudi border. The outer belt, which featured several types of mines laid in four rows, bulged out 30 miles into the Persian Gulf almost to the 49 degrees, 15 minutes east longitude. The inner belt consisted of bottom-moored mines deployed in one row. These belts contained eleven different types of sea mines, including moored contact mines such as the Myam and the Soviet M-08, advanced bottom weapons like

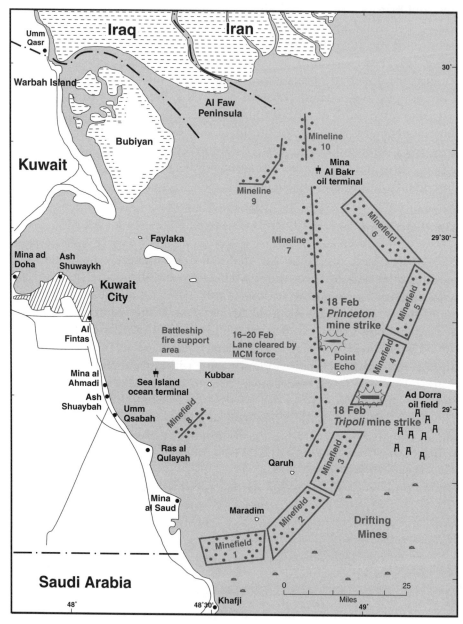

Desert Storm Mine Clearance Operations

the Italian Manta acoustic/magnetic mine, the Soviet UDM acoustic influence mine, and the Iraqi-produced Sigeel acoustic influence mine. About 75 percent of the mines that the Iraqis laid were LUGM-145 types, a moored three-horned chemical contact mine with a 300-pound explosive charge. Although the design of these latter weapons dated from before World War I, they were powerful enough to sink modern ships. Influence mines contained acoustic or magnetic equipment designed to detonate an explosive charge when it detected the sound or magnetic field of a passing ship. Influence mines could be set to explode after several ships had passed over them, with the idea that mine countermeasures ships would miss them and they would explode under higher value targets such as warships or cargo vessels.[57]

The coast of Kuwait resembled Normandy's Omaha Beach on the eve of D-Day in World War II. On likely landing beaches Iraqi combat engineers had emplaced antiboat and antipersonnel mines, thickets of stakes called "hedgehogs," underwater electric cables, barbed wire entanglements, and other obstacles meant to sink or ensnare landing craft and kill marines trying to reach the shore. To cover the beach, the enemy had erected Silkworm batteries, dug trenches, and built bunkers. The latter were spaced 25 to 50 yards apart and surrounded by chain link fences to

Courtesy of CDR John Griffith, RAN

After the war coalition troops inspect a camouflaged and dug-in Iraqi tank that was part of the enemy's formidable beach defenses on the coast of Kuwait.

deflect rounds from direct-fire weapons. From Ash Shuaybah northward, the Iraqis fortified high-rise condominiums and other buildings which overlooked the beach. Earthen berms, land mines, antitank ditches, dug-in tanks, and barbed wire obstacles blocked the likely exits from the beach. Elements of four enemy infantry divisions guarded the coast between Kuwait City and the Saudi border. At al-Ahmadi the tanks and infantry of the Iraqi 5th Mechanized Division stood by in reserve to blunt any breakout from the beach area. In short, Saddam's generals clearly expected the U.S. Marines to storm ashore in Kuwait.[58]

The Amphibious Task Force was certainly sizable enough for such an operation. The ATF included 24,000 marines of the 4th MEB, 5th MEB, and 13th MEU(SOC), under General Jenkins, embarked on Admiral LaPlante's 31 amphibious assault ships. The ATF also operated 17 landing craft air cushion and 13 landing craft utility (LCU). Six combat logistics ships, one repair ship, and seven commercial ships supported the assault units. The leathernecks' equipment included tanks, antitank vehicles, light amphibious vehicles, 19 Harriers, 136 helicopters, and 115 assault amphibian vehicles.[59]

At best, however, Admiral LaPlante had enough CH-53 helicopters and LCACs to execute a moderate-size operation. The ATF lacked sufficient specialized engineering equipment for a large-scale assault. Most of the Marine Corps' mine and obstacle-clearing equipment had been allocated to the I MEF for breaching the Saddam Line.[60]

Also slated to take part in an amphibious landing was the 23-man Australian Clearance Diving Team 3. The unit's officer in charge, Lieutenant Commander John R. Griffith, RAN, concluded that neither the Navy SEALs nor Marine personnel were properly trained to carry out beach reconnaissance or to remove mines and obstacles from the invasion site. He was also disturbed that American plans did not provide for the suppression of enemy fire that would emanate from the defensive works overlooking the beach. "With the feasibility of the amphibious operation seriously compromised," he later noted, "CDT withdrew from the planning process."[61]

Over a month earlier, on 30 and 31 December, Admiral Arthur held an amphibious planning conference on board *Blue Ridge*. Most of the Navy and Marine flag officers in the theater attended. General Boomer suggested that I MEF might need a port on the Kuwaiti coast as a forward resupply base to relieve the strain on the Marines' logistic system if the ground campaign became protracted. The flag officers were discussing only a landing to reinforce and sustain the coalition's ground offensive, however, not an operation to strike the enemy in flank or cut their lines of communication as at Inchon.

Antipersonnel mines and wire entanglements were part of the enemy's coastal defenses near Ras al-Qulayah.

General Gray and other Marine Corps leaders, who had consistently pressed for a major amphibious operation, redoubled their efforts. Major General John J. Sheehan, whom LaPlante describes as "Al Gray's guy," was posted to the NAVCENT staff to oversee amphibious planning and lobby for a landing.[62]

At the gathering on board *Blue Ridge* in December, Captain Grieve delivered a briefing, prepared several days before at Admiral Fogarty's direction, on mine countermeasures in preparation for a landing. Grieve presented several options for clearing a fire support area (FSA) off southern Kuwait, from which the battleships could provide gunfire support to coalition forces ashore. In the option requiring the shortest time, Grieve estimated that it would take 13 days to achieve 60 percent clearance in the FSA; in other words, a probability that 60 percent of the mines had been cleared from a minefield. "When I finished," Grieve recalled after the war, "I sensed that it was quite sobering to the Flags; especially when I noted that the non-MCM forces would do the remaining 40 percent of the clearing."[63]

Despite the difficulties, in early January LaPlante developed a plan, codenamed Operation Desert Saber, for an amphibious assault north of Ash Shuaybah. The object of this landing was to pin down and destroy enemy forces along the coast and seize port facilities for sustained logistic support of the I Marine Expeditionary Force.

A key feature of the plan was the employment of naval "logistics-over-the-shore" forces. Under Admiral Sutton's direction, the Navy loaded a number of non-combatant ships with fuel, water, and ship-to-shore refueling equipment and assembled for the operation a contingent of 1,200 sailors from Naval Beach Group 2, Naval Cargo Handling Battalions 3 and 13, and MPS Squadron 1.[64]

General Schwarzkopf approved the concept for a landing at Ash Shuaybah, scheduled to kick off four days after the start of the general ground of-

USMC

General Al Gray, Commandant of the U.S. Marine Corps, lobbied hard for an amphibious landing on the coast of Kuwait.

fensive, but his refusal to authorize certain operations to prepare for a landing suggested that he really had no intention of ordering an amphibious assault. Admiral LaPlante had requested the bombing and destruction of a liquified natural gas plant that would pose a threat to marines in the landing area, but Schwarzkopf denied the request because he feared damage to nearby Kuwaiti industrial facilities. Similarly, CINCCENT prohibited destruction of numerous waterfront high-rise apartment buildings and condominiums, which afforded the enemy excellent defensive positions from which to oppose the assault. LaPlante was no more successful acquiring intelligence gathered by Navy SEALs on the coast of Kuwait. He and Jenkins began to ask, "who the hell is preparing our battlefield?"[65]

Mine countermeasures issues also complicated the preparations for amphibious operations. The mine countermeasures helicopters needed a "mother" ship from which to operate, and the likely candidates steamed with the ATF. An LPH could embark not only all six of the Navy MH-53E Sea Dragon AMCM helicopters of HM-14, but a number of Marine AH-1 Sea Cobras and logistic support helicopters. Naturally, Admiral Arthur's amphibious force commanders did not want to relinquish one of their valuable, multipurpose LPHs. In addition, the proposed action would entail the shifting of 1,000 naval personnel and much equipment and supplies among six ships. Instead, LaPlante and Jenkins recommended for the mission use of an amphibious transport dock ship (LPD). That type of ship could embark only three or four helicopters, however. In the end, Arthur directed that *Tripoli* be assigned to the mine countermeasures force.[66]

Early in January Admiral Fogarty's staff intensified planning for MCM operations in connection with the possible landing at Ash Shuaybah. The MCM group would have to clear a sea echelon area (SEA) for the amphibious ships, fire support areas for the battleships, and lanes to the beach for the amphibious assault vehicles. Since time was a critical factor, the MCM staff planners considered reducing the area to be cleared or accepting a lower probability of complete clearance, which of course increased the risk to the amphibious vessels.

Another critical consideration was the threat to the unarmed minesweepers from Iraqi Silkworm missiles and artillery and Exocet-armed fixed-wing aircraft and helicopters. Admiral Fogarty tasked Captain David Bill, skipper of the battleship *Wisconsin*, with coordinating protection of the mine countermeasures and naval gunfire support forces.[67]

Despite the crucial role envisioned for Royal Navy forces in the mine countermeasures operation, as late as mid-January no one had involved British officers in the MCM planning. Only when Commodore Chris Craig, RN, commander of British naval forces in the gulf, asked Fogarty for information about the mine clearing operation was he invited to participate in a conference slated for the 26th on board *Tripoli*.[68]

On the appointed day, Craig and his MCM staff, headed by Commander John Scoles, RN, joined Captain Grieve, relevant U.S. ship captains, and Fogarty's staff in the wardroom of the LPH. Fogarty was absent due to ill health. The plan presented by the Americans envisioned a combined force of MCM ships, battleships, and escorts moving into the northern gulf as early as 4 February. AMCM helicopters would sweep a path to within two miles of the beach and a rectangular fire support area. On the first pass the Sea Dragons would deploy wires to cut moored mines and on a second pass tow a sled to detonate influence mines. The MCM ships would follow, searching for mines that the helicopters missed. A battleship, and if necessary antiair cruisers and destroyers, would then move into the FSA and cover the minesweepers as they cleared additional fire support and sea echelon areas.[69]

Captain Grieve observed to the group that the operation would take 16 to 20 days, unless the MCM forces discovered that the Iraqis had deployed the especially worrisome Sigeel mines known to be in their arsenal, in which case the operation might take 43 days.

Commodore Craig was "unpleasantly surprised" to learn that the Americans had developed an MCM plan to which the British had not been privy and which he considered suicidal. He later remarked that the American concept seemed "so ill-conceived and immature" that he "could not believe that the USN had been their architect." To the assembled officers he expressed grave doubts about the American assertion that attack helicopters and battleship gunfire would adequately suppress the Iraqi defenses throughout the approach to the beach. Craig refused to risk his mine-hunting ships unless the naval coalition provided stronger defensive forces.[70]

Then, the focus of the amphibious plan changed. On 2 February, Generals Schwarzkopf and Boomer joined Admiral Arthur on board *Blue Ridge* to discuss the contemplated assault on Ash Shuaybah. Naval planners told the assembled leaders that it would take at least 10 days of mine countermeasures operations to clear a lane to shore and three to five days of naval and aerial bombardment to neutralize Iraqi beach defenses in preparation for the landing. Schwarzkopf and Arthur voiced concern about the possible wholesale destruction of Kuwaiti property on the invasion coast, something which Kuwaiti officials wanted desperately to avoid.[71] In an obvious allusion to Vietnam, the admiral later testified before Congress that "we were not about to destroy Kuwait to save Kuwait."[72] At the same time the trio of American leaders knew that Seabees and Marine engineers had been steadily improving the overland transportation routes in northern Saudi Arabia, rendering a coastal supply base near the border with Kuwait increasingly unnecessary. Schwarzkopf asked Boomer point blank: "Walt, can you accomplish your mission without an amphibious assault?" After a long pause, the marine answered that he could as long as the naval deception operation kept the enemy's coastal defense units pinned to the shore. Schwarzkopf ended consideration of a major amphibious landing on the mainland.[73]

As an alternative to a large-scale assault, Admiral Arthur suggested an amphibious attack on Faylaka Island, where intelligence sources believed the enemy had posted a 2,500-man brigade. A raid or an assault on Faylaka had been under consideration since Desert Shield. Schwarzkopf liked the Faylaka option, for it promised to distract Iraqi attention from his left hook maneuver, minimize collateral damage to Kuwait, and require less MCM preparation. He told Arthur to begin preparations for the Faylaka operation, codenamed Desert Slash.[74] The amphibious operation would be timed to support the ground attack. In a subsequent message to Arthur, Schwarzkopf emphasized that "an amphibious assault into Kuwait, *or the credible threat to execute one,* is an integral part of the overall campaign plan for Operation Desert Storm."[75]

In accordance with the evolving plan for northern gulf naval operations, Admiral Fogarty relieved Captain Bill of the responsibility for defending the mine countermeasures and naval gunfire forces. The admiral assigned operational control of the MCM and naval gunfire support units to Commander Task Group 151.11, Captain Douglas M. Armstrong (Commander Destroyer Squadron 22).

On its face, the decision to assign Armstrong and his staff to this critical responsibility was curious. Armstrong had been fully occupied until late January investigating the tragic accident involving *Saratoga* in Haifa, Israel. Moreover, he was scheduled for routine return to the United States in mid-February. Furthermore, the Destroyer Squadron 22 staff had entered the combat theater as part of the *Theodore Roosevelt* battle group only two weeks before.

Soon after Armstrong and his subordinates joined Captain Grieve's staff in *Tripoli*, the two officers visited Admiral March on board his flagship, *Midway*. Armstrong and Grieve hoped to gain operational control over the carrier aircraft and surface combatants slated to protect Task Group 151.11 as it moved into the northern gulf, then cleared the water approaches to Faylaka, and bombarded the island. March, however, made it clear that he would exercise control over the protective forces through Fogarty, Commander Task Force 151; and Captain Woodall, the antisurface and antiair warfare commander. In short, March, the Battle Force Zulu commander, would exercise significant control over the operations of Task Group 151.11.[76] The command and control of coalition mine countermeasures, naval gunfire support, and amphibious operations in the gulf was becoming too involved.

During Desert Shield, Admiral Mauz had essentially divided responsibility for naval operations in the gulf. In theory, the battle force commander, March, controlled all naval activities in the gulf, but in reality he focused on air operations while Fogarty, with an inadequate flagship and staff, handled everything else.[77] This division of labor continued under Admiral Arthur. Try as he might, March "could never get Fogarty put into a subordinate role to me as the battle force commander." March later argued that "there's gotta be one war-fighting commander at sea, with all the assets."[78]

Other naval leaders agreed, but contended that March, because of the aviator's focus on carrier air operations, would not have been the best candidate for that job. Admiral LaPlante concluded that both the Battle Force Zulu staff and the NAVCENT staff paid little attention to his concerns because they were preoccupied with "getting theirs" in the competition with the Air Force, and the threat to the fleet posed by Iran.[79]

Commodore Craig described March as "an imposing man: young, fit, alert, [and] utterly self-confident," but "single-mindedly absorbed in aircraft-carrier operations" and showing "little interest in any likely coastal surface action."[80] Craig implied that since the primary task of coalition naval forces in the gulf was to threaten Saddam's seaborne flank by "eliminating Iraqi surface vessels, minefields, and coastal defenses," another commander would have been better suited.[81]

Compounding the command and control problem was the constant rotation of U.S. commanders who were charged with the coastal operations. Craig was amazed at the "US Navy's zest for replacing warfare commanders with great rapidity in mid-combat."[82]

Preparations for naval gunfire support also ran into trouble. To help the Marines secure a lodgement on Faylaka, a battleship bombardment was intended to soften up defending enemy forces. Naval shelling of targets along the Kuwait coastline and on enemy-occupied islands would also lend credibility to amphibious deception operations by simulating preparatory fire. General Schwarzkopf also expected the Navy to provide immediate, mobile, and accurate fire support to the Marines and GCC troops during the ground campaign.

The U.S. Navy was fortunate that former Secretary of the Navy John Lehman had pushed for recommissioning the *Iowa*-class battleships in the 1980s, because without them naval gunfire support for troops ashore might not have been available during the Gulf War. The shallow water all along the Kuwait coast and far out to sea prevented warships from closing within range of their 5-inch guns, the main battery of every surface combatant in Admiral Arthur's fleet, save two—*Missouri* and *Wisconsin*. The eighteen 16-inch naval rifles on these historic ships, first commissioned in 1944, could hurl their 2,700-pound shells more than 17 miles with great accuracy. In addition, the heavily armored behemoths could absorb a great deal of punishment from enemy surface and air weapons.

The underwater threat to these venerable men-of-war was another story. Initially, Arthur did not want to risk the battleships in mine infested waters without good cause. But after the battle of Khafji in late January, the admiral decided that the need for heavy firepower offshore justified the risk. Between 4 and 9 February he stationed the battleships near the Kuwait border and within several miles of the Saudi coast. Captain Albert L. Kaiss, *Missouri*'s skipper, served as fire support unit coordinator in the gulf. As such he coordinated the gunfire of the battleships and other warships in the area. *Missouri* and *Wisconsin* took turns bombarding Iraqi troops, command-control-communications bunkers, artillery emplacements, radar sites, naval vessels, and other targets in southern Kuwait. On one occasion, the Iraqis shot back at *Missouri*. The rounds, perhaps 40mm, splashed into the water near the bow, causing no damage but getting the rapt attention of the crew.

USN

One of battleship *Wisconsin*'s 16-inch guns, which dwarfs the .50-caliber machine gun in the foreground, lofts a shell toward Iraqi positions on the littoral of Kuwait.

The battleships hit preselected targets and targets of opportunity, and responded to calls from marines ashore. Marine OV-10 Bronco observation aircraft and unmanned aerial vehicles found targets and spotted the fall of the shells. Until the beginning of the final assault, the battleships remained on seven-hour alert to General Boomer in case the Iraqis mounted another offensive.[83]

The UAVs added a new dimension to naval gunfire. They were first tested in combat during the Vietnam War, with mixed results because of technical flaws.[84] The UAVs of 1991, however, enabled commanders afloat to spot targets ashore on shipboard TV monitors, "walk" shells onto those targets, and observe the extent of destruction, without risking the life of a pilot or wasting costly ordnance. These small, pilotless airplanes weighed about 400 pounds, had a wingspan of 17 feet and a length of 14 feet, and were powered by a noisy, two-cycle engine. The unit was launched from the ship with the assistance of a rocket-powered booster and recovered in a net strung between two poles on the fantail. During *Missouri*'s operations off Khafji, Master Chief Fire Controlman Mark Snedeker and other American sailors on the battleship watched the UAV's TV monitor with great interest; they observed an enemy truck as it moved from one well-camouflaged position to the next, delivering food to Iraqi soldiers. Soon after the truck departed each site, shells cascaded down on the unsuspecting enemy units.

The two battleships used UAVs for 52 percent of their spotting missions during the war and for virtually all of the BDA missions. In one instance, a UAV's unblinking eye detected a well-concealed enemy command and control facility established in a walled villa. *Wisconsin's* guns soon reduced it to rubble. On another occasion, one of the battleship's five UAVs spotted the fall of her projectiles on a staging basin that had been used by Iraqi small boats to raid the Saudi coast.[85]

When Admiral Fogarty, Captain Armstrong, Captain Grieve, and Commodore Craig gathered on board *LaSalle* on 4 February, General Schwarzkopf's intended use of the amphibious armada was known only to him and perhaps a few chosen intimates. What the naval officers did know was that there were no serious efforts underway by coalition air forces to destroy Iraqi defenses and Silkworm batteries on the coast of Kuwait. Craig was especially concerned, because he was much more willing to hazard his forces in a full-fledged amphibious assault than a deception operation.

Nevertheless, the confidence that had developed between Armstrong and Craig and their staffs fostered completion of a minesweeping plan for the Faylaka raid. The combined MCM forces would begin clearing a

USN DN-ST 91-02639

An unmanned aerial vehicle (UAV) is launched from *Wisconsin's* fantail for a surveillance mission in Iraqi-occupied Kuwait.

15-mile-long, 2,000-yard-wide approach lane to Faylaka from a point they believed to be well east of the Iraqi minefields. They would then clear a 10-by-3-mile fire support area from which the battleships could bombard the island. After achieving 80 percent clearance of the approach lane and the FSA, the force's helicopters and surface ships would open additional inshore waters for the battleships. Confident in Armstrong's ability and satisfied with this plan, Craig finally committed the British mine hunters to the northern gulf operation. While retaining operational control of his mine-hunting ships, Craig transferred tactical control of the British units to Grieve.[86]

Before this happened, however, a change in U.S. naval commanders once again complicated the command-control picture. Captain Peter Bulkeley was slated for the routine relief of Armstrong as Commander Destroyer Squadron 22 on the 15th. On 7 February, five days after Bulkeley came on board *Tripoli,* Armstrong turned over operational control to the newly arrived officer. The next day, Admiral Fogarty informed Bulkeley that he was to lead the Anglo-American force into the northern gulf on the 13th. The captain spent the next five days feverishly preparing himself and his task group for the impending combat mission.[87]

Captain Peter Bulkeley chalks a message to Saddam Hussein on one of *Missouri's* huge shells.

Courtesy of CAPT Peter Bulkeley, USN (Ret.)

Early in the morning of 13 February, Captain Bulkeley's 31-ship MCM/NGFS (mine countermeasures/naval gunfire support) task group departed the UAE for the northern gulf. Helicopters patrolled above the 13-mile-long formation on watch for mines. Besides the two battleships, Task Group 151.11 included the flagship *Tripoli*, 9 U.S. and British mine hunters and minesweepers, and 19 U.S. and British cruisers, destroyers, frigates, and support ships. The ships carried 32 Navy, Marine Corps, Army, and Royal Navy helicopters; SEALs; and U.S., British, and Australian naval explosive ordnance disposal teams.[88]

Early in the afternoon of 15 February, as the task group entered the northern gulf, a British Lynx helicopter sighted a mine on the surface. *Curts* launched an SH-60 helicopter, whose embarked EOD team destroyed the mine with an explosive charge. This was the first of many floating mines spotted by Task Group 151.11. It mattered little whether these mines were left over from the Iran-Iraq war, had broken free of their tethers, or were deliberately set adrift by the Iraqis; they all posed a lethal threat to allied ships.

Tension mounted as the force closed to within range of Iraqi missiles and aircraft. The Royal Fleet Auxiliary *Argus* (A 135), an aviation support ship configured as a hospital ship, Royal Fleet Auxiliary *Olna* (A 123), an oiler, and a couple of frigates broke off from the formation and purposely took station near the ad-Dorra offshore oilfield. Inbound enemy missiles would have to pass through numerous oil rigs to get to the ships, and they would probably lock on a platform instead of their intended targets. The ships served as "lilypads" for refueling helicopters operating in the northern gulf. The ad-Dorra oilfield was aptly dubbed "gasoline alley." *Wisconsin* left the formation to resume her station off Khafji.[89]

On 16 February, as Task Group 151.11 moved further into the northern gulf, Captain Bulkeley deployed UAVs over Faylaka, 35 miles away. Through the robot unit's camera, Bulkeley saw Navy strike planes returning from missions on the mainland drop leftover bombs on a suspected Silkworm battery on the island. He could see that these high-altitude drops failed to destroy the site. Bulkeley concluded that it would take too long to lay on a strike from Admiral March's carriers, so around 2100 he dispatched *Jarrett*'s LAMPS helicopter and two Army helicopters to attack the suspected battery. The OH-58Ds scored two direct Maverick missile hits on what proved to be a dummy battery, but the action confirmed the absence of an enemy threat from that quarter.[90]

Meanwhile, the combined mine countermeasures force began to search waters that needed to be free of mines before the battleships could bombard Faylaka Island. MCM operations not only involved destroying mines, but also verifying the absence of mines in a given area.

An American sailor, on the lookout for Iraqi mines, mans a watch station at the bow of an American warship in the Persian Gulf.

Although one could never be certain that an area was entirely free of mines, the confidence level increased with each pass of an MCM helicopter or ship.[91]

The U.S. Navy conducted mine countermeasures with an integrated system of helicopters and surface ships. The Navy's MH-53E helicopters were specifically adapted for airborne MCM operations.[92] To counter moored mines, the MH-53Es towed a mechanical device through the water to cut the mooring cables so that naval gunners or EOD divers could destroy the mines on the surface. To counter influence mines, the helicopters towed acoustic or magnetic sleds, which simulated a ship's propeller noise or magnetic signature to set off the weapons. Although an MH-53E covered only a relatively narrow swath of water compared to an MCM ship, the helicopter could cover more ground because it conducted influence sweeping at 25 knots, compared to the ship's 7 or 8 knots.[93]

The MH-53Es made initial, or "precursor," sweeps through a suspected minefield to reduce the risk to the MCM ships that followed.[94] Mine countermeasures ships either swept mines or hunted them. To sweep mines, an MCM ship towed cable cutters or influence gear. The vessels used a GPS receiver to plot cleared areas and mark the position of mines. Surface ships were especially valuable at night or in bad weather, when the helicopters could not fly. Neither the ships nor the helicopters could sweep for both influence and moored mines at the same time. To hunt mines, an MCM ship searched the seabed with its sonar array. Divers or unmanned, remotely operated vehicles (ROVs) destroyed mines revealed by sonar. Since ROVs could not operate in low-visibility conditions, Navy divers often had to find their "prey" by touch in murky water.[95]

The U.S. Navy's mine countermeasures ships that served in Desert Storm included *Avenger* and ocean minesweepers *Impervious, Leader,* and *Adroit.* The Royal Navy deployed HMS *Herald* (AGSH 138), which acted as a mine countermeasures command and support ship, a capability the U.S. Navy lacked, and five *Hunt*-class ships able to both sweep and hunt mines.[96]

Since contact mine clearance had been a major responsibility of the British during the Cold War, they had devoted considerable attention and resources to their MCM forces. The Royal Navy's *Hunt*-class vessels were the most sophisticated coastal mine-hunting ships in the world. Each *Hunt* carried an EOD team, a highly trained crew, and state-of-the-art equipment for finding and destroying mines. Each ship was constructed with glass-reinforced plastic and nonmagnetic metals to mini-

EOD personnel operating from guided missile frigate *Curts* destroyed this Iraqi sea mine.

mize its magnetic field, or "signature," and the propulsion system was designed for minimal noise. The magnetic hull signatures of the *Hunt*-class ships were so low that the Royal Navy considered them invulnerable to Iraqi mines in depths greater than 30 feet.[97] "The British are well ahead of us," noted Lieutenant Commander David Jackson, Commanding Officer of *Impervious*. "Not only are their *Hunt* class . . . superior platforms for MCM, but they have an excellent logistics system to support them."[98]

Despite the Korean War, Vietnam War, and Earnest Will experiences,[99] the U.S. Navy had neglected mine warfare for decades. American MCM forces were ill-prepared to support amphibious operations during Desert Storm. When Iraq invaded Kuwait, the Navy had neither a separate mine warfare support command in the United States nor a permanent, deployable staff. Even by the end of Desert Storm, the staff of the MCM Group consisted of 22 officers and sailors from 15 different commands, few of whom had worked together before. Furthermore, EOD personnel were not permanently assigned to American MCM ships.

American MCM ships were generally inferior to the British *Hunt*-class ships. The magnetic hull signature of *Avenger*, the only modern mine countermeasures ship in the American fleet, was significantly higher than that of a *Hunt*. *Avenger* had been designed for operations in deep ocean waters, so low hull signature was less important. The magnetic hull signature of two of the 40-year-old ocean minesweepers was lower than *Avenger*'s, but still higher than that of a *Hunt*. Furthermore, sonar and engine problems plagued the American MCM flotilla during Desert Storm.[100] After the war Admiral Arthur said that "everybody in the world had better minesweepers out there than I did."[101] General Schwarzkopf recalled that the Navy's "very, very antiquated mine-sweeping fleet . . . frankly, just could not get the job done."[102]

When the British *Hunt*s and American helicopters led Task Group 151.11 into the northern gulf in mid-February 1991, the naval command lacked a solid understanding of the location, dimensions, and composition of the enemy's minefields. An underwater search for mines in early February by a SEAL delivery vehicle (SDV) in a 27-square-mile area near Qaruh, Maradim, and Kubbar islands found no moored mines. General Schwarzkopf had prohibited air and surface patrols of the northern gulf during Desert Shield because he feared that such operations would spark a war prematurely. This decision troubled Admiral Mauz: "If you let your enemy put mines in the water," he observed, "it will take a long time to clear them, no matter how good at MCM you are."[103] Admiral Arthur had also protested Schwarzkopf's decision, arguing that Iraqi mine laying in international waters, of which he had some intelligence, should at least be observed if not countered. But since Schwarzkopf had not budged, allied naval forces could only guess where the Iraqis had planted their mines. "We [had] heard that there was a crescent[-shaped] mine field from intelligence," Captain Bulkeley recalled after the war, "but we didn't know where it was, or how far out, or how big it was."[104]

Captain Grieve began sweeping the approach lane at "point Echo," located at 29 degrees, 7 minutes north latitude/48 degrees, 53.15 minutes east longitude, about 30 miles off the coast of Kuwait. Determining where to start had been a difficult decision. To begin clearing the lane, the surface MCM forces would have to slow down from their transit speed to the optimum mine-hunting speed of three knots. The farther out they started, the longer it would take to clear the approach lane. Admiral Fogarty's staff had felt that point Echo was too far from the coast. The available intelligence, based on scattered and uncorrelated reports of enemy mine laying, indicated no mine threat in the transit route and immediate vicinity of point Echo. As it turned out, point Echo actually lay between the outer and inner belts. The *Hunts* made the entire transit into the northern gulf with their mine avoidance sonars in operation to discover drifting or moored mines, but detected no mines when they passed through the outer belt.[105]

As night fell on 17 February, Captain Bulkeley received an intelligence report that the Iraqis intended to fire a Silkworm missile at the task group. As a result, the mine hunters and sweepers pulled back behind the escorting AAW ships. Bulkeley did not request an air strike because he was unsure of the Silkworm launch site. The Aegis cruiser *Princeton* (CG 59), commanded by Captain Edward B. Hontz, the local antiair warfare commander, was operating nearby. Responding to Bulkeley's request for protection, *Princeton* hurriedly took on fuel from HMS *Olna* in the ad-Dorra oilfield, raced westward, and placed herself between the Kuwaiti coast and the MCM ships.[106] "In that position," noted Hontz, "we would be able to shoot down any Silkworm missile fired at the minesweepers."[107]

The mine countermeasures force resumed operations at 0240 the next morning. At 0435, after operating for 11 hours in an undetected minefield, *Tripoli* struck a mine. Sitting at his desk, Captain Bulkeley felt a little jerk and heard an "ugly" groaning sound. The explosion lifted the bow of the ship and tore a 20-by-30-foot hole, 10 feet below the waterline just forward of the starboard beam. The blast carried up through several decks, blowing hatches off their openings and twisting steel plating. The explosion vaporized hundreds of gallons of JP-5 fuel in a tank and paint stored in a paint locker, filling the entire forward section of the ship with volatile fumes which, had they ignited, could have destroyed the bow. Water flooded compartments on three decks and the ship lost communications. Miraculously, not one sailor was killed and only four were injured.

Quick action by *Tripoli*'s damage controlmen and other sailors contained the flooding and restored communications. The crew's training and ability to remain calm saved the ship.[108] At first, *Tripoli*'s officers thought the ship had hit a drifting mine. But when they established the location of the hole, they figured that she had struck a moored contact mine, probably a LUGM-145. Fortunately for *Tripoli*, the weather was moderate. Captain G. Bruce McEwen, *Tripoli*'s Commanding Officer, felt that had the sea gotten rougher, the ship would have gone to the bottom.[109]

Even though the sound of the explosion carried far over the water, for a time U.S. ships continued to move about. With the ocean minesweepers leading the way, *Tripoli* tried to leave the minefield by the same route she had come in. But the minesweepers kept making mine-like contacts, so Captains Bulkeley, Grieve, and McEwen decided to anchor until they could sort things out.[110]

Meanwhile, less than 10 nautical miles away, *Princeton* had been steaming unwittingly along a line of Manta mines in the inner minefield. She was almost due east of Kuwait City and closer to the Kuwait coast than any other coalition vessel. "The ship was . . . barely maintaining steerageway," recalled Captain Hontz, "in order to allow maximum reaction time if a mine was spotted."[111]

At 0715, just as Hontz was telling his crew to be especially vigilant in light of *Tripoli*'s misfortune, a Manta mine exploded under *Princeton*'s stern on the port side. The quarterdeck reared up into the air. I-beams providing the ship with structural integrity bent and snapped. High-tensile steel deck plating buckled and tore. The force of the explosion caused a whiplash motion along the keel, much like a fiberglass fishing pole, flinging the stern lookout into the sea and throwing the bow lookout 10 feet into the air. Three seconds later, shock waves from the explosion set off another mine about 350 yards off *Princeton*'s starboard bow. The second blast imparted a horizontal force against the side of the ship, adding a side-to-side motion to the longitudinal whiplash and tossing sailors around like rag dolls. The violent action lasted 6–7 seconds and almost tore the ship in two.

After the motion subsided, Hontz and the boatswain's mate-of-the-watch sounded General Quarters. The explosions had damaged the rudder and propeller shaft and ruptured the stern fire main, which doused a major electrical box and created a serious fire hazard. Internal fuel tanks had also burst, forcing damage control parties to work in pools of volatile fuel and dirty water. Automatic sprinklers that activated with the explosion aggravated the flooding. Surprisingly, the blast killed no one, but seriously injured three sailors.[112]

While damage control teams on board *Princeton* and *Tripoli* fought to save their ships, *Impervious*, *Leader*, and *Avenger* marked the positions of additional mines and searched for sailors thrown overboard. The salvage ship *Beaufort* steamed from her position in the ad-Dorra oilfield toward the stricken ships. After *Beaufort*'s executive officer and master diver determined that *Tripoli* needed no immediate assistance, the salvage ship prepared to follow *Adroit* toward *Princeton*. Just before the pair got underway, a sailor stationed in *Beaufort*'s bow spotted a moored contact mine about five feet below the surface on the port side. *Beaufort* reached the cruiser after maneuvering slowly and carefully through the minefield.[113]

Within two hours of the mine explosion, *Princeton*'s crew had reduced the danger from fire and flooding and had begun to bring the ship's radars back on line. The ship's combat systems, however, were not fully functional.[114] As the day wore on, Captain Hontz grew increasingly concerned that his ship's loss of maneuverability might cause it to drift into another mine. At his request, *Beaufort* took *Princeton* in tow. With *Adroit* in the lead, locating and marking mines with flares, the salvage ship towed the stricken cruiser out of danger. *Princeton* remained on antiair duty for 30 hours, until relieved by *Valley Forge* (CG 50). Escorted by Canadian destroyer *Athabaskan*, *Princeton* was towed to Bahrain for repairs.[115]

Task Group 151.11 spent the rest of 18 February pulling out of the minefield. Captains Bulkeley and Grieve selected a new anchoring site on the northern edge of the ad-Dorra oilfield, reasoning that the Iraqis had not mined the area because of the difficulty of working near the drilling platforms. The AMCM helicopters swept the new box and found it clear of mines, except in the southwest corner. At Bulkeley's direction, *Impervious* and *Leader* led *Tripoli* and the other ships clear of the dangerous area, maneuvering them around several mines on the way out.

With *Tripoli* safely anchored in the new box, Captains Grieve and Bulkeley revised the mine countermeasures plan. The immediate goal became clearing an area off Faylaka from which *Missouri* could bombard the island. They selected a new starting point about 24 miles east of point Echo, and plotted a new channel to the area that the MCM group had already cleared. Grieve estimated that it would take 43 days to sweep the new channel plus the previously planned areas. Bulkeley knew from prior discussions with Admiral Fogarty that Schwarzkopf would soon launch the ground offensive. The captain realized that the original MCM concept was infeasible if the battleships were to support the forces ashore. Bulkeley and Grieve decided to concentrate on sweeping a 31-

mile-long, 1,000-yard-wide channel that would enable a battleship to fire on Faylaka and maneuver if it came under attack.[116]

The MCM group soon resumed channel clearing operations, working westward from the newly identified outer edge of the minefield. Because of the ever-present potential for attack by enemy aircraft, artillery, or missiles, Sea Cobra gunships escorted the AMCM helicopters while AAW missile ships covered the surface vessels. Fighter, early warning, and patrol aircraft also kept watch over the task group.[117]

For almost a week, *Tripoli* remained on station and continued to serve as the Task Group 151.11 command ship and the floating base for the airborne mine countermeasures unit. During that time, however, the hole in the hull grew larger, and the ship's aviation fuel supply ran low. The ship needed to make port for repairs and resupply. On 23 February, when *Missouri* joined *Tripoli*, Captain Bulkeley and his staff transferred temporarily to the battleship.

That same day, as the result of a turnover planned long before, Rear Admiral Raynor A.K. Taylor relieved Fogarty as Commander Middle East Force and Commander Task Force 151/152. Taylor immediately conned *LaSalle* into the northern gulf and relieved *Tripoli* of her on-site MCM duties.

Even after *Tripoli* put in at al-Jubayl for repairs, HM-14 continued to operate, but at a considerable disadvantage. "Mission completion," in the words of the squadron's command history, "involved having two crews fly from [al-Jubayl] to the 'lily pad,' [*LaSalle*] disembark one crew, refuel, fly one mission, hot seat and hot refuel, fly the second mission, refuel, pick up the second crew and finally fly the hundred-or-so miles back to the TRIPOLI."[118]

On the 24th, in yet another routine change of command, Captain David Vail relieved Grieve as Commander U.S. Mine Countermeasures Group.[119] That same day *Tripoli* transferred her AMCM units to a shore facility at Ras al-Mishab and headed for Bahrain.[120]

Despite the damage suffered by *Tripoli* and *Princeton*, the coalition got off relatively lightly in Saddam's minefields. Before disaster struck those two vessels, several other allied ships had been operating unknowingly in the minefields. Fortunately for the allies, the Iraqis had failed to activate many of the weapons and chose not to cover the minefields with aircraft, naval vessels, artillery, or missiles. More expertly laid and defended mines would have sunk ships and killed sailors and marines.[121]

The Iraqi ineptitude in mine laying had another effect. "Since [U.S. helicopters] were sweeping to explode the mines," Captain Grieve noted after the war, "they needed to work for us to show success. Inert mines don't explode. . . . So we ended up with the perception that the helos did not contribute much to the effort."[122]

USN

The magnitude of the mine damage to *Tripoli*, in drydock at Bahrain, is clear in this photo.

The coalition's wartime MCM effort, however, was a disappointment. As Admiral Arthur later stated, "Iraq successfully delayed and might have prevented an amphibious assault on Kuwait's assailable flank, protected a large part of its force from the effects of naval gunfire, and severely hampered surface operations in the northern Arabian Gulf, all through the use of naval mines."[123]

As it was, by 23 February, on the eve of the coalition's ground offensive into Kuwait, the MCM group had cleared a 31-mile-long, 1,000–2,000-yard-wide swath of water, enabling *Missouri* to close with Faylaka and commence bombardment of enemy positions on the island.[124]

As the final assault drew near, the right feint seemed to be working. While the MCM forces were clearing a path for *Missouri*, the Defense Intelligence Agency and CENTCOM's intelligence directorate began to receive indications that the Iraqis were preparing to repel an amphibious assault against Faylaka Island. Since the primary objective of Admiral Arthur's maritime campaign was to fix Saddam's attention on the coast of Kuwait, the coalition's amphibious, mine countermeasures, and naval gunfire units were indeed accomplishing their mission.[125]

Ground Forces Move into Attack Positions

While coalition air and naval forces prepared the battlefield, five major allied ground formations moved into position for Phase IV, the final assault on Saddam's army in Kuwait. On the right stood General Boomer's I Marine Expeditionary Force, Joint Forces Command East (JFC-E), and Joint Forces Command North (JFC-N). The latter forces consisted of combat units from Egypt, Syria, Saudi Arabia, Kuwait, Qatar, Oman, Bahrain, the UAE, Pakistan, Bangladesh, Morocco, Senegal, and Niger. The three corps-sized formations took up positions that extended from the Persian Gulf to the western-most portion of Kuwait, with JFC-E on the coast, I MEF in the center, and JFC-N on the left. The VII Corps and the British 1st Armoured Division fell in to the left of Joint Forces Command North, while the XVIII Airborne Corps and the French 6th Light Armoured Division took the western-most position on the allied line.[126]

During Phase IV, the XVIII Corps and VII Corps were to launch the main attack, driving deep into the desert west of the main Iraqi defensive line, then turning east to envelop the Iraqi army in Kuwait and destroy the Republican Guard. The Marines and Islamic coalition forces were to launch attacks designed to support the left hook.

General Schwarzkopf gave the I MEF a tough assignment. Boomer's marines were to prevent Iraqi forces in southeastern Kuwait from reinforcing enemy units facing the coalition's main attack to the west, block the retreat of the enemy troops along the coast, and help Arab units liberate Kuwait City. The Army's 1st Brigade (Tiger Brigade), 2d Armored Division would fight with the 2d Marine Division on the left of the I MEF line.[127]

The Iraqi III Corps and elements of IV Corps occupied the area of southeastern Kuwait opposite I MEF and the Islamic coalition forces. Five Iraqi infantry divisions defended the two obstacle belts southwest of Kuwait City. Another four infantry divisions faced the sea. The 5th Mechanized Division, located near the Burqan oilfield, and the 3d Armored Division, deployed about ten miles north of al-Jaber Air Base, stood by in reserve. The 1st Mechanized Division and the 6th Armored Division defended the al-Jahra road intersections and the adjacent Mutla Ridge.

The Iraqis positioned their artillery brigades so the D20 152mm howitzers could shell targets 5,000 to 10,000 yards south of the outer belt. Brazilian-made rockets and Soviet-designed FROG unguided missiles augmented the artillery. General Boomer considered these indirect fire weapons to be the greatest threat to his troops, because the enemy had deployed so many of them and because they could deliver chemical-filled projectiles.

The Iraqi tactical plan for ground combat aimed at slowing attacking forces at the first belt, trapping them in prearranged killing zones between the two belts, and destroying them with pre-registered artillery fire before they could penetrate the second belt.[128] "The nightmare scenario," as General Schwarzkopf observed, "would have been to go through, get hung up . . . and then have the enemy artillery rain chemical weapons down on troops that were in a gaggle in the breach."[129]

In the original concept, I MEF was to attack straight into the teeth of Iraqi defenses through a single breach in the defensive lines between the al-Wafrah oilfield and the coast. To carry out this mission, early in January the I MEF moved north from its defensive positions in and around the so-called "Triangle" in northern Saudi Arabia. Brigadier General James M. Myatt's 1st Marine Division deployed to an area 40 miles west of Ras al-Mishab and south of al-Wafrah. Major General William M. Keys' 2d Marine Division moved into position just northwest of the "Old Breed" Marines of the 1st.[130]

To support I MEF's attack, Brigadier General Charles C. Krulak, Commanding General Direct Support Command, established a logistics base in the desert about 33 miles south of the border and 36 miles west of Ras al-Mishab. The Marines named the base al-Kibrit after a tiny Bedouin settlement nearby. Before the I MEF moved north, the Seabees of Naval Mobile Construction Battalions 5, 40, and 74 and Marine engineers widened the two-track dirt road from Ras al-Mishab to al-Kibrit to eight lanes and improved an adjacent dirt airstrip so that it could handle C-130 Hercules transport aircraft. Between 28 December and 6 February, General Krulak's command concentrated 1.8 million gallons of fuel and 15,800 tons of ammunition at al-Kibrit. In addition, the Navy-staffed 1st Medical Battalion set up a 470-bed hospital there.[131]

In mid-January the top Marine commanders and their staffs conducted map exercises and war games to test their assault plans. The Iraqis expected the coalition to launch its main attacks north along the coastal road and from the Saudi border area lying closest to Kuwait City, and had positioned their forces accordingly. The war games and exercises indicated that if General Boomer's units followed the original avenue of approach, they would hit the enemy's strongest concentration of forces. Therefore, Boomer shifted the point of attack westward to the area between the al-Wafrah and Umm Gudair oilfields in the "heel" of Kuwait. This new avenue would enable the leathernecks to bypass the bulk of the defenders in southern Kuwait.[132]

Shortly after this change of plans, I MEF received enough additional engineering equipment to carry out another breaching operation.

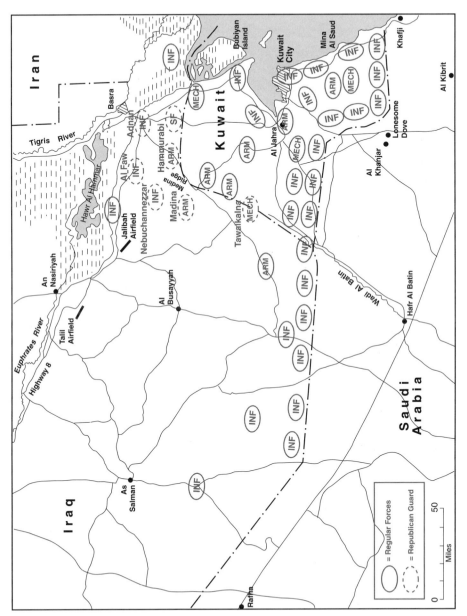

Disposition of Iraqi Ground Divisions, 23 February 1991

271

On 6 February, Boomer modified the assault plan to include a second point of attack. Two breaches would allow the Marine divisions to advance abreast and support one another, avoid the vulnerability inherent in traversing the Saddam Line along only one avenue of attack, and heighten the enemy's confusion. The 1st Marine Division would penetrate the Saddam Line northwest of al-Wafrah, while the 2d Marine Division would breach the twin obstacle belts near the Umm Gudair oilfield.[133]

To support this new concept of operations, General Krulak shifted the Marines' primary logistics base from al-Kibrit to a flat expanse of desert 23 miles southwest of the northern corner of the heel of Kuwait. Krulak's staff dubbed the place "al-Khanjar," an Arabic word for a type of short sword, to the delight of the Arab officers attached to the Marines. Between 6 and 20 February, Marine engineers and NMCBs 5, 24, 74, and 40 of Captain Michael Johnson's 3d Naval Construction Regiment built a dug-in complex covering 11,280 acres and stockpiled supplies there. When they had finished, al-Khanjar featured more than 24 miles of blast-wall berms, the largest ammunition supply point in the history of the Marine Corps, five million gallons of fuel, one million gallons of water, two 5,700-foot dirt airstrips capable of handling C-130s, and a

Earthmoving equipment of Naval Mobile Construction Battalion 5 prepares the ground before Seabees erect a tent camp in the Saudi desert.

USN DN-ST 91-05511

Courtesy of CAPT Frederick M. Burkle Jr. (MC), USNR

Marine combat engineers and Navy Seabees developed this logistics support site almost overnight in the Saudi desert, and named it al-Khanjar.

naval hospital with 14 operating rooms established by the Marines' 2d Medical Battalion.[134]

To help mask the move to the west of General Boomer's combat formations, Marine Task Force Troy and Naval Mobile Construction Battalion 74 mounted an operation to deceive the enemy. Much as the Allies had done in England before the Normandy invasion of World War II, the Marine-Navy team created a "phantom army" (albeit a small one) in front of Iraqi lines. The Seabees fabricated, from wood and canvas, 35 mock tanks and artillery pieces and with Task Force Troy emplaced them in the dark of night on the Saudi-Kuwait border. The Iraqis soon spotted what they believed was a Marine heavy unit in the desert to their front and during the week before G-Day concentrated artillery and mortar fire on the bogus position.[135]

General Boomer was impressed by the Seabees' overall performance. To his staff, he remarked that Seabees were "doers." "They don't talk a lot of bull shit," he added, "they just go out and do the job."[136]

While Seabees and Marine engineers were building al-Khanjar, I MEF's 60,000 leathernecks began advancing into their tactical assembly areas. The 2d Marine Division moved to a position south of al-Manaqish, while the 1st Marine Division took up a position west-southwest of al-

Wafrah.[137] Like their great-grandfathers in World War I, these marines braced themselves for a fight that many observers told them would involve crossing flat ground covered by enemy machine guns and artillery, penetrating rows of barbed wire entanglements, and seizing enemy-held trenches and redoubts. They also expected to have to fight through clouds of lethal gas.

Meanwhile, General Yeosock's Army Forces Central Command set up General Schwarzkopf's "left hook" or "Great Wheel" flank attack. From its assembly area just east of the Wadi al-Batin, the armor-heavy VII Corps rumbled west for more than 150 miles. Simultaneously, the XVIII Airborne Corps deployed almost 300 miles inland and around VII Corps to take up position on the far left of the allied line.

This shift westward, involving approximately 270,000 troops and 65,000 vehicles, was one of the largest such maneuvers in military history. Day and night, from 20 January to the third week of February, American, British, and French tanks, trucks, and soldiers moved into position for battle. The operation required detailed planning and precise execution. Every minute, an average of 18 trucks passed by highway checkpoints. Every seven minutes for thirteen days, Air Force C-130 transport planes supporting the movement took off or landed at King Fahd International Airport. The Iraqis could not penetrate the aerial umbrella over Saudi Arabia in what one analyst characterized as a "war between the seeing and the blind."[138] As a result, Saddam was ignorant of the enormous army gathering on the exposed flank of his doomed forces in Kuwait.[139]

Eleventh Hour Measures

During the third week of February, General Schwarzkopf selected a date for G-Day, when he would begin Phase IV. ARCENT forces were due to complete moving into their attack positions on the 20th. Despite CIA estimates to the contrary, Central Command intelligence concluded that attrition of Iraqi front-line tanks and artillery pieces would reach 50 percent on the 21st. Schwarzkopf and his commanders wanted good weather and a dark night, with a minimum of moonlight, for launching the ground campaign, and meteorologists were predicting favorable conditions between 21 and 24 February. As everything fell into place, Schwarzkopf settled on 24 February as G-Day.[140]

Saddam Hussein hoped to end the war before the allies launched the scheduled onslaught. Seeking to preserve as much of his army as possible, and having failed thus far to gain any positive results from his military actions, the Iraqi dictator took another stab at diplomacy. His former Soviet ally gave him an opening. Even though Moscow opposed Iraq's seizure of Kuwait, Soviet General Secretary Mikhail Gorbachev made several attempts to broker a cease-fire, hoping that success would oblige the world to continue regarding his troubled nation as a great power. On 9 February, Gorbachev issued a statement expressing concern that the coalition's military actions might be exceeding the UN mandate and calling for a political settlement based on Security Council Resolution 660, which demanded the complete and unconditional withdrawal of Iraqi forces from Kuwait. Two days later, he dispatched Yevgeny Primakov to Baghdad as his "personal emissary." Primakov met with Saddam on 12 February and advised the dictator that if he did not end the war soon, an allied ground attack would complete the destruction of his forces in Kuwait.

On the 15th, Baghdad radio announced that the Revolutionary Command Council was now prepared "to deal with Security Council Resolution 660, with the aim of reaching an honorable and acceptable solution, including withdrawal [from Kuwait]." But, Saddam apparently regarded the Primakov mission as a sign of American weakness, so he also issued a set of demands: an immediate cease-fire; an end to the embargo; an Israeli withdrawal from Palestine, the Golan Heights, and southern Lebanon; cancellation of all relevant UN resolutions subsequent to 660; cancellation of Iraq's $80 billion foreign debt; and economic reconstruction of Iraq by the coalition. In short, with a major attack only days away, the Iraqis were still trying to negotiate a compromise.[141]

President Bush denounced the statement as a "cruel hoax" and called for the Iraqi people "to force Saddam Hussein, the dictator, to step aside, and to comply with the United Nations resolutions and then rejoin the family of peace-loving nations."[142] The United States' coalition partners, particularly the Arab states, also rejected the demands.

Moscow, however, pressed forward with its peace initiative. As a result of meetings between Gorbachev and Iraqi foreign minister Tariq Aziz, Baghdad accepted a new eight-point peace plan and agreed to pull out of Kuwait after a cease-fire. Once again, however, Iraq tried to wrangle concessions from the allies. All UN resolutions would cease to be in effect upon completion of the withdrawal. There would be no postwar embargo and Iraq would not have to pay reparations. But Saddam did concede to two major U.S. demands: no linkage between Kuwait and the Palestine issue, and the release of allied prisoners of war (POWs) immediately after the cease-fire.

Bush and his advisors agreed that Iraq's acceptance of the Soviet plan represented a step forward. But it did not go far enough. There was no reference to the thousands of Kuwaitis interned in Iraq since the invasion. The timetable of the withdrawal was unclear. Iraq would not be required to renounce its claim to Kuwait as specified by Resolution 662. Worst of all, a cease-fire would enable Saddam to withdraw his army from Kuwait with much of its offensive power intact. If that occurred, the Iraqi dictator would continue to pose a threat to the United States and its regional allies. Bush saw little reason to grant concessions to Saddam when the coalition stood on the threshold of victory. The President insisted on unconditional Iraqi withdrawal from Kuwait.[143]

On 22 February, Bush presented the Iraqi dictator with an ultimatum. Saddam had until noon (Washington time) on 23 February to begin pulling his troops out of Kuwait, with full withdrawal to be completed within a week. The lack of time would force Iraqi units in the KTO to abandon most of their heavy equipment, particularly their tanks and artillery. The ultimatum implied that any breach of its terms would precipitate the ground campaign. The deadline came and went with no movement from Saddam's forces.[144] Since the Iraqis had refused to quit Kuwait voluntarily, the UN coalition would launch the final phase of Desert Storm to compel them by force to leave. The climax of the Gulf War was at hand.

CHAPTER 6

The Final Assault

THE FINAL OFFENSIVE TO FREE KUWAIT began on 24 February 1991. While Admiral Arthur's naval forces carried out diversionary operations to draw the enemy's attention to the Persian Gulf, General Boomer's two-division I MEF and the two combined Islamic formations, the Joint Forces Command East and Joint Forces Command North, crashed through the Saddam Line. Meanwhile, to the west, the U.S. Army's XVIII Airborne Corps and the armor-strong VII Corps, accompanied by French and British armored divisions, drove deep into the Iraqi desert toward a confrontation with the enemy's elite Republican Guard Forces Command.[1]

Preliminary Operations

I MEF's mission during Phase IV was to destroy Iraqi forces in its sector, prevent enemy units from escaping to Iraq, and help liberate Kuwait City. Toward these ends, the 1st Marine Division was to capture Kuwait International Airport while the 2d Marine Division was to seize key crossroads near Mutla Ridge and the town of al-Jahra.[2]

But first, General Boomer's marines had to breach the Saddam Line. The coalition's airborne intelligence-gathering resources had produced a broad, general picture of these fixed defenses. Only first-hand human surveillance of enemy positions and reconnaissance of the terrain, however, would provide the ground-hugging rifleman with crucial information not evident on aerial photographs, such as gaps in the enemy's defenses and the kinds of mines he would face. Accordingly, beginning on 17 February, small Marine reconnaissance teams infiltrated into Kuwait and reported on such information via satellite, high frequency radio, and other means.

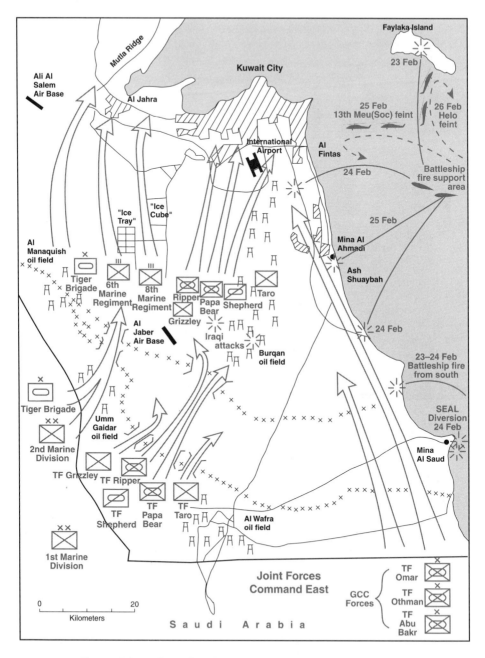

Ground Assault on Southern Kuwait, 24–28 February 1991

Meanwhile, Navy Seabees of the 3d Naval Construction Regiment and Marine engineers began bulldozing channels through the berm that defined the border. Then, on the 21st, Task Forces Taro and Grizzly[3] of General Myatt's 1st Marine Division and the 2d Light Armored Infantry (LAI) battalion of General Keys' 2d Marine Division began moving into Kuwait to establish forward positions from which they would support breaching operations.

Iraqi artillery fired sporadically on these units as they advanced. Devastating return fire from Marine artillery, attack helicopters, and fixed-wing aircraft induced increasing numbers of Iraqi soldiers to surrender. This experience suggested the depth to which Iraqi morale had plummeted. When enemy soldiers walked southward to surrender, they revealed the unmined areas through which the Marine main body could cross the Saddam Line. By nightfall on the 23d, task forces Grizzly and Taro and the 2d LAI had advanced as far as 12 miles into Kuwait, and most of the artillery of the two Marine divisions had established positions just south of the first defensive belt from which to support breaching operations on G-Day.[4]

At 0800 on the 23d, the 16-inch guns of *Wisconsin*, operating from a fire support area a few miles off the northern gulf coast of Saudi Arabia, opened an intense bombardment of targets in Kuwait. The battleship's unmanned aerial vehicle spotted the fall of its enormous projectiles, which rained down on Iraqi artillery and infantry positions, ammunition storage facilities, and logistics sites. This bombardment supported the Joint Forces Command East, slated to advance north along the coast road the following morning.[5]

Naval gunfire also lent credibility to Admiral Arthur's maritime deception. As Arthur later remarked:

> [*Wisconsin* and *Missouri*] were my leading element of trying to hold in place the threat of the amphibious landing. I knew that the Iraqis always expected to see a battleship since we had them there associated with amphibious landings. All I had to do was start moving the battleships . . . and then line General Jenkins and his fine marines and our amphibs up behind them, and there was no doubt in anybody's mind that we were coming.[6]

Missouri, inside the fire support area east of Ash Shuaybah, began shelling Faylaka Island at 2315. *Missouri* destroyed antiaircraft guns, mortar and artillery batteries, ground-launched missile sites, and troop bunkers on the island to reinforce the enemy perception that a landing was coming. Before sunrise on the 24th, the battleship shifted her fire to the Kuwaiti coast to freeze Iraqi mobile reserves in position.[7]

The night before Arthur had cancelled the amphibious raid on Faylaka, Operation Desert Dagger/Slash, scheduled for G-Day. This resulted from a briefing on the plan that Admiral LaPlante and General Jenkins had provided Arthur and Schwarzkopf eight days earlier. The latter officers agreed that the raid had strategic and tactical merit, but Schwarzkopf said there was little enthusiasm for it outside the theater. Indeed, during their visit to Riyadh on 8 and 9 February, Secretary Cheney and General Powell expressed concern that the operation would produce casualties for only marginal gain. Arthur, who shared this view, decided that air strikes, naval gunfire, and feints were sufficient for deception.[8]

Naval air and special forces units also conducted operations designed to keep enemy eyes trained on the coastline. Throughout 23 February, aircraft from *America, Midway,* and *Theodore Roosevelt* struck targets on Faylaka Island and on the coast of Kuwait.[9] Since late January, SEALs, and on one occasion Kuwaiti commandos, had operated with their boats along the coast of Kuwait or come ashore as part of the deception effort. This activity reached a climax on the night of 23 February. A few hours after dark, four high-speed boats carrying a SEAL platoon from Task Force Mike arrived at a point nine miles off the Kuwait coast near Mina al-Saud. Then, 15 Navy commandos led by Lieutenant Thomas Dietz dropped three Zodiac rubber assault craft into the water, loaded them with 20-pound demolition charges and navigational marker buoys, and pushed off. At a point only 500 yards offshore, six swimmers slipped into the water and kicked toward the beach. The men designated lanes through the water with the marker buoys, as they would for an amphibious landing, and sowed the explosive charges. After recovering the swimmers, two speedboats moved in closer to the beach. The charges exploded at 0100. At the same moment, the SEALs and special boat unit sailors on the speedboats called in air strikes and laced enemy bunker complexes ashore with machine gun and grenade launcher rounds.[10] These actions would help persuade the Iraqis that the long anticipated American amphibious assault had begun.[11]

Meanwhile, individual leathernecks quietly made their own final preparations in the last hours before the start of the general advance into Kuwait. Amid darkness, blowing sand, cold rain, and dense smoke from burning oil wells that swept over their positions, the men donned chemical protective suits, swallowed nerve agent pills, and readied their gas masks and gloves, preparing for the worst. Marine commanders and Navy chaplains offered them last-minute words of encouragement and comfort.[12]

Two schools of thought dominated the Marines' vision of the final assault. One held that the enemy army in Kuwait was so brittle that it would shatter at the first blow from coalition ground forces. The air campaign had destroyed enemy command and control systems, pre-

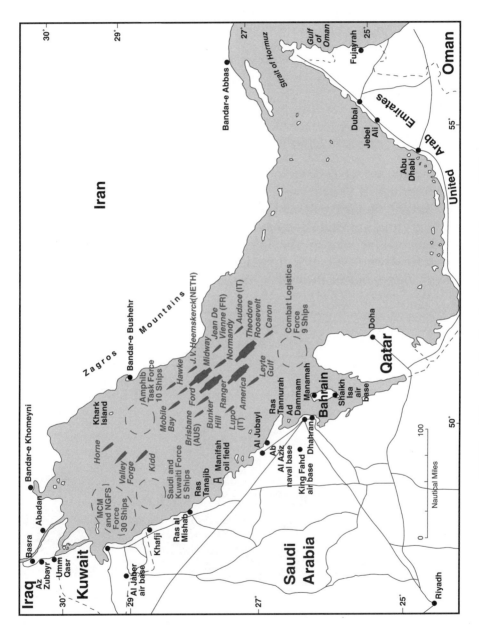

UN Naval Forces in the Persian Gulf, 24 February 1991

vented resupply of forward units, and weakened morale of Iraqi troops, most of whom were poorly trained, equipped, and motivated to begin with. The other school had braced itself for a bloody and perhaps prolonged battle. Boomer and his staff firmly believed that the enemy intended to launch chemical weapons and strong armored counterattacks against his forces.[13] Some of the men expected to die. The combat engineers assigned to breach the Saddam Line ahead of the main forces considered themselves "walking dead." Many leathernecks felt that the first 24 hours of the assault would settle the question, one way or the other.[14]

G-Day

At 0400 on 24 February 1991, the 1st Marine Division's armored task forces began to penetrate the Saddam Line near the al-Wafrah oil-field. At each obstacle belt, tanks, artillery, aircraft, and infantrymen provided covering fire while combat engineers launched single- and triple-shot line charges across the minefields. Detonation of the charges blasted yard-deep, V-shaped trenches into the sandy soil and exploded many of the mines in their path. Before the dust settled, M60A1 tanks

USMC DM-ST 91-11590

A Marine M60A1 tank, equipped with reactive armor and mine-clearing rollers and plows, prepares to lead a column of assault amphibian vehicles through the heavily fortified Saddam Line.

equipped with mine plows and mine rakes "proofed" and widened the trenches into lanes almost six feet in width, enabling waiting armored and mechanized forces to stream through.

Not all of the lanes were cleared easily. About a third of the line charges failed to detonate. When this happened, tank plow crews pressed forward despite the danger. Fortunately, exploding mines disabled only a few vehicles. At some locations, marines entered the minefields on foot to detonate charges which had failed to go off or to hand-carry unexploded mines out of the way. The 1st Marine Division's combat engineers opened 14 lanes through the Saddam Line that day.[15]

By mid-afternoon the bulk of the division had passed through both obstacle belts. As they cleared the second barrier and drove northwest along the edge of the al-Burqan oilfield, the Marine task forces encountered and destroyed enemy T-55s and T-62s. Individual oil wells were burning fiercely, like giant flares. "The black smoke in the air was unbelievable," recalled Lieutenant Colonel Ray Cole, General Myatt's assistant operations officer. "I wear glasses, and it covered my glasses in a matter of a half hour to 45 minutes. You were constantly having to clean them off. We were all covered with oil, and as we found out later, ingesting all that oil."[16]

The last hours of G-Day found General Myatt's task forces Ripper, Shepherd, and Papa Bear maintaining a defensive posture near al-Jaber Air Base and preparing to resume the attack at daylight. "Like a snake getting ready to strike," as the 1st Marine Division historian put it, "[General Myatt] began building combat power for the next day's attack on Kuwait International Airport."[17]

General Keys' 2d Marine Division kicked off its attack at 0530, and in much the same way as Myatt's division, quickly breached the Saddam Line. In the face of light to moderate opposition from Iraqi mortar, tank, and artillery fire, Keys' troops pressed forward through the first obstacle belt. The men of the 6th Marines were spurred on when they heard the strains of the Marines' Hymn over the thunder of artillery and the crack of small arms, compliments of a loudspeaker-equipped Army psychological warfare unit attached to the regiment.[18]

This exhilaration turned to anxiety at 0656, when one of the division's German-made Fuchs or "Fox" chemical reconnaissance vehicles detected traces of a "possible nerve/mustard" blister agent, which the Marines initially thought had come from a chemical mine.[19] Another Fox sent to the site picked up a "trace of mustard gas." It appeared that every leatherneck's worst nightmare was about to come true. Two marines in the area who failed to don their gas masks and gloves fast

"A Navy Corpsman and Marine Infantrymen on G-Day" by John Charles Roach

enough received blisters on their exposed skin. This prompted both Marine divisions to order an immediate, high-priority, mission-oriented protective posture (MOPP 4). Many leathernecks remained in their hot, stifling MOPP suits for the next 72 hours of combat. Fortunately, the mercury never rose above 70 degrees Fahrenheit. Several more times during the campaign the sensitive gear on the Fox vehicles picked up toxic chemical traces, most likely from oil well fires. While the enemy maintained stores of chemical weapons at or near the front, it appears that the Iraqi high command never ordered their use. Uncertainty over how President Bush would retaliate quite possibly deterred the Iraqi dictator from that possibly suicidal action.[20]

Despite continued concern about the enemy's potential for chemical warfare, the 2d Marine Division pressed the attack and breached the Saddam Line by noon. The rapidly advancing marines encountered only sporadic enemy resistance and found hastily abandoned fighting positions, artillery emplacements, arms, ammunition, and equipment. That afternoon the Army's armored Tiger Brigade crossed the Saddam Line and swung northwest toward the al-Manaqish oilfield, a likely staging area for enemy tank units planning a counterattack. During the evening, General Keys' forces consolidated their positions and prepared to advance the next morning toward their primary objective, the critical al-Jahra crossroads.[21]

During the hours of darkness, Marine helicopter and truck units resupplied both Marine divisions with ammunition, fuel, and equipment, while Marine engineers improved lanes through the breaches. Navy Seabees worked on the main supply route.[22]

Throughout G-Day, Saddam's vaunted artillery had fired only intermittent, limited, and ill-directed barrages. The enemy's fire planning methods, techniques for attacking targets of opportunity, and targeting equipment were rudimentary. Moreover, the coalition's pre-G-Day focus on destroying enemy artillery had paid off. The high volume of Iraqi fire that Boomer and other allied leaders feared never materialized.

The Iraqi armored forces deployed forward with the infantry also proved to be less dangerous than expected. Enemy tanks almost always missed their targets. "It was as if we were up against the 'Gang That Couldn't Shoot Straight,'" said Lieutenant Colonel Jim Mattis, Commanding Officer of 1st Battalion, 7th Marines.[23] In contrast, the leathernecks' return fire routinely hit targets on the first round.[24] Marine M1A1 and M60A1 tanks, LAVs, high-mobility multipurpose wheeled vehicles (HMMWVs, or "humvees") armed with TOW antitank missiles, and heavy artillery destroyed hundreds of Iraqi T-55 and T-62 tanks and other armored vehicles during the ground campaign.[25]

Allied aircraft also exacted a heavy toll of enemy forces opposite I MEF. Because Marine units had fewer armored vehicles and artillery tubes than comparable Army units, the leathernecks depended heavily on air support.

As they had in Korea and Vietnam, Marine commanders in the Gulf War insisted upon controlling aircraft operating within their area of responsibility. The leathernecks believed that only controllers trained in Marine operational techniques could safely and accurately call down strikes against enemy forces close to friendly units.

Within I MEF's operational area the 3d Marine Aircraft Wing directed all planes and helicopters flying close air support (CAS) missions requested by the division commanders or their subordinates. Close air support was defined as air attacks against enemy forces conducted short of the fire support coordination line (FSCL) on the map. Fixed-wing aircraft operated under a "Push CAS" system instituted by General Moore. Planes entered designated areas near the front lines at fixed intervals. If the ground commander requested support, forward air controllers directed the aircraft onto the desired targets. If no unplanned attacks were needed, the planes hit targets in kill boxes forward of the fire support coordination line while others took their place behind the line. Moore designed Push CAS to provide virtually continuous close air support for frontline troops, but for most of the ground campaign, bad weather and smoke from the oil well fires hampered the operation of fixed-wing aircraft.[26]

Attack helicopters could operate more effectively in adverse conditions than fixed-wing aircraft. Oftentimes when bad weather and smoke prevented their high-flying comrades from carrying out their missions safely, Marine Cobras would zoom in "close to the deck" above advancing marines, then "pop up" and destroy their targets with guided missiles or gunfire.

Although no U.S. Navy or non-U.S. coalition fixed-wing aircraft flew close air support missions during the ground campaign, they did fly interdiction missions to support the Marines. In fact, most allied air sorties flown during the ground campaign involved interdiction targets— those that lay beyond the fire support coordination line.[27] Marine airborne forward air controllers orchestrated the interdiction attacks of Marine aircraft as well as of Navy F/A-18 Hornets and A-6 Intruders and Air Force F-16 Falcons and A-10 Thunderbolts. Their missions aimed at disrupting Iraqi armored counterattacks and preventing enemy units from retreating.

Weather and smoke hindered interdiction operations as much as they did close air support. Nevertheless, allied aircraft destroyed hundreds of Iraqi armored vehicles and artillery pieces with cluster-munitions, high-explosive bombs, and missiles throughout Phase IV.[28]

As the ground campaign gained momentum and the marines overran enemy positions, the trickle of surrendering Iraqi soldiers became a flood. "Those guys came out of bunkers dancing, skipping, and singing with their thumbs up," recalled Lieutenant William Delaney, who served with Task Force Ripper.[29] "The amount of EPWs [enemy prisoners of war] coming my way reminded me of [Dodger] Stadium after a Dodgers home game in Los Angeles," said Lieutenant John Anderson of the 7th Marines.[30] Many Iraqis were waving air-dropped surrender leaflets, which the marines called "get out of Kuwait free cards." In some cases, the surrendering soldiers produced a stack of leaflets, as if they were currency, in the belief that the more leaflets they had, the better treatment they would receive.[31]

In General Schwarzkopf's words, "a great deal of the failure of the Iraqi Army to fight [can be attributed to] their own leadership. They committed them to a cause that they did not believe in. [The enemy prisoners] are all saying that they didn't want to be there; they didn't want to fight their fellow Arab; they were lied to; they were deceived, and when they went into Kuwait they didn't believe in the cause."[32] "The heart wasn't in this fight," General Boomer told a reporter. "They were someplace they didn't want to be and about to die for something they didn't want to die for."[33]

While the Iraqis who surrendered were elated to be alive after enduring six weeks of air attack and the Marine assault, many of them were malnourished, exhausted, and louse-ridden. Some suffered from wounds which had gone untreated for days. The poor physical and mental condition of these men testified to the effectiveness of the allied aerial and ground campaign.[34]

On the lighter side, there were a number of amusing incidents in the Marine effort to remove enemy prisoners from the operational area. On one occasion, a young Marine reserve sergeant and a security guard by themselves delivered 200 enemy prisoners, via flatbed tractor trailer, to the headquarters of the Direct Support Command. When the commanding general of the logistics command, Brigadier General Charles Krulak, approached the truck and looked up at its 200 frightened occupants, the sergeant loudly sang out, "Old McDonald had a farm." In one voice, the Iraqis replied "E-I-E-I-O."[35]

On another occasion, a Tiger Brigade medic, Staff Sergeant Ryan Welch, and his men got separated from their unit on a rainy, misty night. Rather than risk driving over a land mine or encountering enemy forces in the darkness, Welch parked their ambulance for the night on a

A U.S. marine moves captured Iraqi soldiers to the rear.

small hill. When they awoke the next morning, they found themselves perched atop an Iraqi brigade command post and surrounded by multiple rocket launchers, antiaircraft guns, and nearly 100 Iraqi soldiers. Unsure what to do next, the Americans stared wide-eyed until the enemy soldiers slowly raised their hands in surrender.[36]

Many Iraqis feared surrendering to marines, whom they had been told were so fierce that they had to kill a close family member in order to join the Corps! The leathernecks' firm but decent treatment of prisoners soon calmed most Iraqis. Indeed, more than 8,000 enemy soldiers put aside their dread to surrender to I MEF on G-Day. Although pleased about bagging so many prisoners, the leathernecks found them to be a logistical headache, threatening to slow their advance. Pundits had a field day, however, describing Saddam's "mother of all battles" as the "mother of all retreats" and the "mother of all surrenders."[37]

The Joint Forces Command East also took numerous Iraqi prisoners during the first day of its attack. The combined Arab and Islamic command[38] moved out at 0800, penetrated the Saddam Line, and advanced north along the coast road to Kuwait City.

Naval aircraft and gunfire from *Wisconsin* provided invaluable support to the Joint Forces Command East. The Marines' 1st and 2d Air/Naval Gunfire Liaison Companies coordinated gunfire, air, artillery, and communications support for the Islamic unit.

Wisconsin soon demonstrated the value of her 16-inch shells to the JFC-E. Early in the advance, the newly formed Royal Saudi Marine Battalion approached a key road junction that the Saudis expected the enemy would fight hard to hold. U.S. Marine Captain Douglas Kleinsmith of the 1st ANGLICO offered to "prep" the area by calling in a few rounds from the unseen American battleship offshore. The Saudi battalion commander, a colonel, looked at him incredulously. "You can call in the battleships?" he asked. "Yea," answered Captain Kleinsmith, "that's why we're here." Kleinsmith contacted *Wisconsin* and the battleship opened fire. The captain heard the muted roar of her 16-inch guns through his radio. The 43 seconds required for the first shell to reach its target seemed an eternity. Kleinsmith was beginning to wonder if he had transmitted the wrong coordinates when projectiles began to fall precisely where he wanted them. The Saudi marines stared in amazement as the 2,700-pound shells lifted whole houses into the air. "You can do this any time?" asked the Saudi battalion commander. Kleinsmith replied in the affirmative. "Ah," exclaimed the colonel, "we can win now."[39] Indeed, the combined Islamic force met no enemy resistance until it was out of range of *Wisconsin*'s guns. This situation enabled the JFC-E to accelerate its attack timetable. By the end of G-Day, the Joint Forces Command East had taken its primary objectives and captured large numbers of Iraqi troops.[40]

While *Wisconsin* supported the JFC-E during the final assault, *Missouri* supported I MEF and the Amphibious Task Force. Direct support missions such as the one Captain Kleinsmith called in were certainly dramatic, but they accounted for only 6 percent of the two battleships' fire during the campaign. In part, the swift allied advance and lack of determined resistance precluded more frequent calls for fire. Moreover, I MEF, more heavily engaged than JFC-E, only came within range of the battleships' weapons the day before coalition forces seized Kuwait City. The shallow water and uncleared mines off Kuwait prevented *Missouri* from moving closer to the shore. Accordingly, most of the battleship's 16-inch rounds fell on pre-planned point and area targets, like artillery and mortar positions, ammunition storage sites, supply dumps, Silkworm batteries, and entrenchments.[41]

As I MEF and JFC-E attacked north into Kuwait on 24 February, the 13 ships of Rear Admiral Stephen S. Clarey's Amphibious Group 3 brought in reinforcements, Brigadier General Peter J. Rowe's 7,400-man 5th Marine Expeditionary Brigade. From waters near the northern Saudi border, amphibious assault ship *Tarawa* (LHA 1) launched the 5th MEB's helicopter-borne battalion landing team, which took up a blocking position south of al-Wafrah. Meanwhile, LCACs landed the brigade's two remaining battalion landing teams on the beach near Ras al-Mishab. The men then moved 40 miles to the north near al-Kibrit to serve as the I MEF reserve. Support units worked feverishly to make Ras al-Mishab into a forward supply base and, despite shortages of transport vehicles and cargo handling equipment ashore, completed deploying the entire 5th MEB in only 70 hours. Even though the dramatic success of the Marine offensive into Kuwait did not necessitate the 5th MEB's insertion into the line, the brigade executed mop-up operations and helped control the thousands of enemy prisoners streaming south.[42]

When the sun's last rays faded on 24 February, the I Marine Expeditionary Force and Joint Forces Command East had overrun both Iraqi defensive lines, advanced as much as 20 miles into Kuwait, and eliminated the better part of three enemy infantry divisions. Despite some difficulties and the ever-present danger from enemy mines, the breaching operations had gone exceedingly well. The first reports were "better than we dared hope," noted General Schwarzkopf. The marines "had encountered no impassable minefields, no walls of flame, no murderous gas barrages, and very little resistance."[43] Coalition forces found Saddam's defenses less sophisticated than expected and his soldiers largely unwilling to fight.[44] "My assessment is that it's cracking," General

Boomer told his staff that evening. "The Iraqi army is cracking and it's cracking pretty quickly."[45]

Meanwhile, far to the west of I MEF, the left flank units of the Army's XVIII Airborne Corps had advanced far into Iraq. At 0400 the French 6th Light Armoured Division and the U.S. 82d Airborne Division, which had been involved for more than a week in cross-border infantry and helicopter raids on the enemy, pushed up the only hard-surface road in the area. By nightfall the Franco-American force had surrounded the Iraqi 45th Infantry Division at as-Salman, a key desert crossroads. Heliborne forces of the 101st Airborne Division (Air Assault) set up their night defensive positions 170 miles into Iraq and just south of Highway 8, the main line of communications between Baghdad and the KTO. The division's AH-64 Apache attack helicopters scoured the hard-surface road in search of Iraqi reinforcement and supply convoys.[46]

The early success of the XVIII Airborne Corps on the left and I MEF on the right led General Schwarzkopf to accelerate the pace of the coalition advance. Early in the afternoon of 24 February, Schwarzkopf called General Boomer and expressed his concern that I MEF's rapid progress might expose the Marine left, since the Army's VII Corps and the XVIII Corps' 24th Infantry Division (Mechanized) were not slated to open their attack along that flank until the next morning. When Boomer suggested launching their assault that day instead, Schwarzkopf agreed.[47]

Accordingly, the VII Corps and the 24th Division crossed the line of departure at 1500 and the neighboring Arab Joint Forces Command North one hour later. Concerned about an Iraqi counterattack, the 3d Egyptian Mechanized Division, the JCF-N's lead unit, stopped short of its initial objectives and dug in for the night.[48]

As with the I MEF, the VII Corps had already softened up enemy forces in its path. Like Boomer, Lieutenant General Frederick Franks Jr., the VII Corps commander, was "most concerned about the danger posed by Iraqi artillery." Air Force bombing had failed to destroy many Iraqi batteries.[49] Accordingly, beginning on 7 February, the corps had launched helicopter and artillery raids to destroy the enemy's indirect fire weapons and to fool the Iraqis into thinking that the force meant to attack up the Wadi al-Batin rather than farther west. By G-Day the VII Corps' artillery had destroyed 83 out of 100 revetted guns of the Iraqi 48th Infantry Division, while air strikes had accounted for only 17.[50]

Hence, when the coalition's armed might punched into Iraq on G-Day it faced light enemy opposition. On the far left, the XVIII Corps' 24th Mechanized Infantry Division with the 3d Armored Cavalry Regiment pressed north at 25 kilometers per hour. By midnight the mechanized formations were three-quarters of the way to the

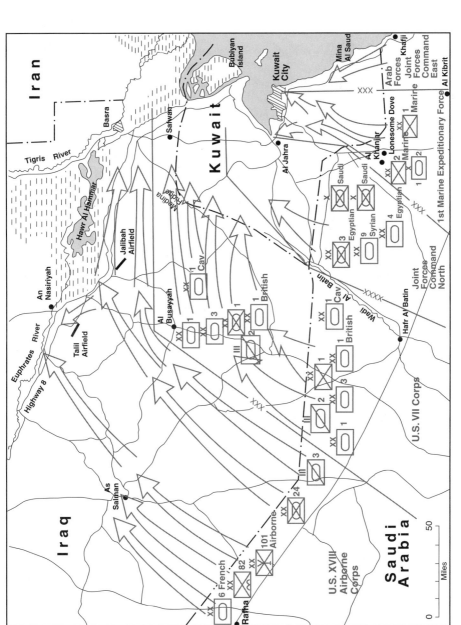

Liberation of Kuwait

Euphrates River. The VII Corps advanced on a broad front across the Saudi-Iraq border. General Franks' armored goliath quickly smashed through the already devastated Iraqi frontline units, halted for the night, and prepared for the next day's advance, designed to envelope Saddam's field army.[51]

Closing on the Iraqi Army in Kuwait

Toward the end of G-Day, Schwarzkopf directed LaPlante and Jenkins, through Arthur, to make an amphibious demonstration just north of the Kuwait port of Ash Shuaybah before dawn the next day. With the ground forces advancing faster than anyone had anticipated, the general hoped that the demonstration would pin the Iraqi forces located south of Kuwait City to the coast and dissuade them from reinforcing units under attack by I MEF or JFC-E.

At 0100 on 25 February, amphibious ships *Okinawa* and *Portland* (LSD 37) broadcast over their radios recordings of amphibious operations. At 0300, the naval rifles on *Missouri* began hurling 16-inch shells, one every 45 seconds, toward enemy targets near Ash Shuaybah. Two hours later her fire reached a crescendo of one round every five seconds, simulating the final preparatory fire for an assault. Huge explosions ripped through Iraqi fuel and ammo dumps, command posts, artillery emplacements, and fortifications.

At about 0400, ten helicopters of the 13th Marine Expeditionary Unit took off from *Okinawa* (LPH 3) and headed for al-Fintas, a Kuwaiti coastal town just north of Ash Shuaybah. The helicopters closed to within three miles of the coast, clearly within sight of enemy forces ashore. In addition, the ships of the amphibious force increased the use of their communications equipment to enhance the credibility of the feint. Then, at about 0450, the helicopters turned away sharply and flew back to the ship.

Two developments marked the operation a success. First, none of the Iraqi divisions on the coast south of Kuwait City redeployed on 25 August, but remained in place to meet the feared attack. Second, the Iraqi command used a weapon they had taken special efforts to husband and defend from coalition air attack—the Silkworm antiship missile.

As *Missouri* poured fire into Kuwait from some 17 nautical miles offshore, she steamed along a 1,000-yard gunline within a one-square-mile box at the extreme western edge of the fire support area. The battleship, escorts *Jarrett*, HMS *London* (F 95), and HMS *Gloucester* (D 96), and five British mine-hunting ships operated within range of enemy Silkworm missile batteries and heavy artillery. On several occasions, when detec-

USN DN-ST 92-00829

A Chinese-made Iraqi HY-2 Silkworm antiship missile seized by coalition forces after the war.

tors suggested the presence of chemicals in the air, the group went to maximum defensive posture. As was the case on land, fumes from the oil well fires probably set off the detectors.[52]

The fact that Iraqi targeting radars frequently "painted" these ships as they carried out their mission heightened concern among the crews about potential enemy surface-to-surface missile attack. Their anxiety peaked at 0452, two minutes after LaPlante's helicopters turned away from the beach, when an Iraqi Silkworm battery near al-Fintas fired two missiles at the bombardment group.[53] One of the Silkworms splashed harmlessly into the sea soon after it was launched. The other, traveling 375 feet above the water at 605 knots, continued pushing its half-ton warhead toward *Missouri. Jarrett* and *Gloucester* were then east of the battleship. Radar systems on the British warships detected and tracked the missile. Lookouts on the mine hunters, escorts, and the battleship saw the Silkworm as a huge fireball speeding by to the north. *Missouri, Jarrett,* and a Seahawk helicopter flying above them fired "chaff" (thousands of thin, radar-reflecting metal strips), "torch" (flares), and "ducks" (multiple decoys) to confound any radar or heat-seeking guidance systems on the Silkworms.

Gloucester's defense system had locked onto the real Silkworm. As the enemy weapon hurtled past *Missouri* and her escorts, Petty Officer

John Roberts, RN, launched two of *Gloucester*'s Sea Dart surface-to-air missiles. They destroyed the Silkworm in a spectacular explosion. For a terrifying moment, *Missouri*'s after lookout thought that *Gloucester* had blown up.

Captains Bulkeley and Kaiss immediately launched an unmanned aerial vehicle that retraced the missile's path from shore. When the aerial vehicle reached the beach, its camera spotted an old burned out missile site, so the operator directed the UAV to the south. It was a fortuitous choice, for about a thousand yards from the old site, the camera spotted two launchers, a control truck, and Iraqi soldiers milling about. *Missouri* fired about 30 rounds at the position, neutralizing the battery and marking the first time in history that a battleship put counterbattery fire onto a surface-to-surface missile launcher.[54]

While Anglo-American naval forces parried the Iraqi Silkworm thrust at sea, both divisions of General Boomer's I MEF beat back enemy attacks on land. Under cover of darkness, fog, and smoke from hundreds of oil well fires, an Iraqi armored brigade and an armored/mechanized brigade concentrated in the al-Burqan oilfield for a counterattack. Unfortunately for the Iraqis, they revealed their intentions to allied intelligence, so the 1st Marine Division was ready for them.[55]

At 0515 the enemy struck the division's right flank. For the next three hours, Marine and Iraqi units fought one another at close quarters. At one point enemy armored vehicles came within 300 yards of Myatt's command post. The contest, however, was one-sided. Without losing a single marine, Cobras, Harriers, tanks, artillery, and TOW-equipped light armored vehicles fended off every enemy thrust and in the process destroyed or disabled 75 Iraqi armored vehicles and captured at least 300 enemy soldiers. After weathering the Iraqi counterattacks, the 1st Marine Division moved forward to the northeast. Driving toward Kuwait City, marines overran numerous Iraqi artillery batteries whose guns were pointed out to sea. The tracks that the gunners made as they tried to turn their weapons around at the last minute remained visible in the sand, clear indication that the amphibious deception had worked, at least in that sector. By day's end, the "Old Breed" leathernecks had fought their way to within 10 miles of Kuwait City.

Meanwhile, Myatt's units had come within range of *Wisconsin*'s big guns. While no spotters were available on the ground to call in fire close to marine riflemen, the battleship's guns shelled Kuwait International Airport, site of the last Iraqi armor concentration in front of Kuwait City and the 1st Marine Division's final objective. Marines spotting fire for the battleship via UAV cameras observed the 16-inch bombardment ripping apart hangars, terminals, and enemy armored vehicles. When they could, Iraqi crewmen fled from their vehicles. The bombardment pre-

USN DN-SC 91-09957

Naval medical personnel move a wounded marine from a helicopter to an emergency station of Fleet Hospital 5.

pared the way for the 1st Marine Division's assault the next morning on Saddam's remaining tanks and mechanized vehicles at the airport.[56]

The Iraqis fared no better against the 2d Marine Division on 25 February. Long before dawn penetrated the smokey darkness over the battlefield, elements of the Iraqi III Corps formed up south of Kuwait City for a counterattack on General Keys' division. But before the Iraqis could launch their ill-fated attack, Marine and Air Force aircraft reduced the enemy force to less than brigade strength. Then the division's tankers got into the action.

Around 0530 Corporal Brad Briscoe, on watch as his comrades caught a few hours of sleep, spotted enemy T-72 tanks through the thermal-imaging system in his tank, an Abrams M1A1. Briscoe's unit, Company B, 4th Tank Battalion, was attached to the 8th Marines. The company was the only Marine reserve unit equipped with this superb armored vehicle. Briscoe jumped from his tank and ran over to inform two of his officers, Captains Alan Hart and "Chip" Parkison. Hart told the corporal not to worry: "Probably just our own amtracs [amphibious tractors] running around in front of us again." A moment later the three men heard engine noises—not the high-pitched squeal of amtracs, but the deep rumbling of T-72 diesels. As he raced for his own tank, Hart yelled to his marines to get ready for battle.

Unaware of the presence of the Marine M1A1s now drawing a bead on their vehicles, a long column of T-72s was preparing its own ambush of a nearby Marine truck convoy. But before the Iraqis could shoot, the Marine M1A1s opened fire. TOW-equipped vehicles soon joined the fray. In a matter of minutes, marines destroyed 34 of the 35 enemy tanks engaged. Other 2d Marine Division units soon beat back the rest of what Keys' men dubbed the "Reveille Counterattack," and then continued their advance.[57]

Early that afternoon the 2d Marine Division began its attack on the "Ice Tray," a built-up area so-named because of its appearance on Marine maps, and the "Ice Cube," a walled area northeast of the Ice Tray that contained Kuwait's radio and television transmitters. The two fortified positions dominated the surrounding terrain. Marines spent the rest of the day and most of the night methodically clearing each building and bunker in the area. Then, the 2d Marine Division and the Tiger Brigade prepared for the morning's seizure of the al-Jahra crossroads, control of which would cut off all Iraqi forces still in southeastern Kuwait and Kuwait City.[58]

Far to the west on 25 February, Lieutenant General Gary Luck's XVIII Airborne Corps secured the coalition's left flank in Iraq, Arab formations of Joint Forces Command North pushed slowly into southwestern Kuwait, and the VII Corps drove deep into the Iraqi desert. Army historians described the going:

> The weather, already miserable, was growing worse. What had been one of the hottest spots on earth only weeks earlier was now near freezing. Earlier fog had turned into intermittent rain that by afternoon had increased in intensity. Howling gusts of wind mixed fine powered sand with blowing rain and propelled the infernal muddy concoction against windshields, vision blocks, and map boards, and into every exposed corner of every vehicle on the march. Visibility dropped to near zero.[59]

As they groped their way forward, the coalition tank, mounted infantry, and attack helicopter formations encountered several enemy armored and mechanized brigades, which they soon dispatched with their concentrated, accurate fire. As the day wore on, the VII Corps units began to execute their part in the "Great Wheel," Schwarzkopf's grand maneuver to hit Saddam's army in the flank and to destroy it.[60] Observers likened the 90 degree turn to the east of the 1st Armored Division's 6,000 vehicles to an intricate naval maneuver in which Abrams tanks, Bradley armored fighting vehicles, and humvees assumed the roles of battleships, cruisers, and destroyers.[61] With Franks' mighty armada swinging to the east like the spoke of an enormous wheel and Boomer's marines closing on the capital city, victory in the battle for Kuwait seemed certain.

Rout of the Iraqi Army

As early as 2000 on 25 February, both I MEF and Central Command sensors began to detect large numbers of vehicles on the move near Kuwait City. Army and Air Force Joint Surveillance and Target Attack Radar System (JSTARS) aircraft and the Kuwaiti resistance soon confirmed reports that enemy units were heading away from the battle front opposite I MEF and the Arab joint forces commands.[62]

About 10 hours later Saddam announced over Baghdad Radio that "on this day, our valiant armed forces will complete their withdrawal from Kuwait."[63] President Bush called the dictator's broadcast an "outrage." "He is not withdrawing," declared Bush, "his defeated forces are retreating. He is trying to claim victory in the midst of a rout, and he is not voluntarily giving up Kuwait. He is trying to save the remnants of power and control in the Middle East by every means possible."[64]

To try to delay the evacuation of enemy forces from the coastal reaches of Kuwait, Admiral Arthur ordered amphibious feints against Bubiyan and Faylaka Islands. In the early hours of 26 February, 23 Marine helicopters lifted off from amphibious assault ships *Nassau, Guam,* and *Iwo Jima,* rendezvoused with carrier-based A-6 Intruders and EA-6B Prowlers, and approached the enemy-held islands. When they got within range, the aircraft hit the Iraqi defenders with machine gun fire, rockets, and bombs. Just as suddenly, the naval aircraft turned and disappeared over the horizon.[65]

Meanwhile, Central Command directed Navy, Air Force, and Marine aircraft to attack enemy forces retreating north on the only major road between Kuwait City and Basrah. This stretch of superhighway lay within the kill box assigned to *Ranger*'s Air Wing 2. Responding to the call, the aviators found themselves overlooking what they described as "an attack pilot's dreamscape" and "the mother of all target opportunities."[66] Hundreds of military and civilian vehicles laden with loot from Kuwaiti homes and businesses clogged the road in a pell-mell bid to escape. The fleeing Iraqis were "basically just sitting ducks," noted Commander Frank Sweigart, Commanding Officer of VA-155.[67]

After dropping aerial mines to stop the northbound traffic, the naval and other aircraft worked over the trapped vehicles. Despite low clouds and persistent smoke from burning oil wells, coalition aviators attacked throughout the day. The scene on the ground quickly degenerated into total chaos. In a panic, Iraqi drivers steered their vehicles into the desert on either side of the highway, only to have them bog down in sand. Hundreds of others tried futilely to negotiate the mass of burning, wrecked, and abandoned buses, trucks, and automobiles on what reporters soon dubbed the "Highway of Death" or "Highway to Hell." These ominous sounding monikers were actually misnomers, however, for journalists who later arrived at the scene counted only 200 to 300 dead scattered among the approximately 1,400 destroyed vehicles that analysts identified in aerial photos.[68] Most of the enemy soldiers had fled the destruction on foot into the desert.[69]

While the enemy ran, I MEF continued its attack into Kuwait. At about 0630 on the 26th, Myatt's 1st Marine Division resumed its northward advance. At first smoke from oil well fires that blotted out the sun was more troublesome than Iraqi soldiers, who surrendered in droves. That afternoon the "Old Breed" began its final drive on Kuwait International Airport. Reports indicated little activity there after the previous night's pounding by *Wisconsin*. But, as Task Forces Ripper, Papa Bear, and Shepherd approached the perimeter of the airport, they encountered sizable Iraqi armored and mechanized units. Here the enemy put up more of a fight, but they met the same fate; death or capture. By

A Soviet-made Iraqi tank destroyed by allied arms near Kuwait City.

the early morning hours of 27 February, Myatt's forces had secured the airport, the 1st Marine Division's final objective in Desert Storm. The first rays of light fell upon the remains of some 320 Iraqi tanks and other armored vehicles destroyed by the combined fire from Marine ground and air forces and the battleship.[70]

As the 1st Marine Division began its attack on Kuwait International Airport, the I MEF staff realized that the Iraqis were in full retreat. General Boomer and General Keys were eager for the 2d Marine Division to seize blocking positions astride Mutla Ridge and on al-Jahra's superhighway intersections before Iraqi forces slipped out of the noose tightening around them. Also realizing the importance of the position, the Iraqi command attacked Keys' 2d Marine Division early in the day. At 1200, after defeating the enemy's thrust, the 2d Marine Division, with the Tiger Brigade on the left, launched its own attack. As intended, the Army's heavy unit made the main effort. With two battalions of Abrams tanks in the lead and one battalion of Bradley fighting vehicles right behind, the Tiger Brigade raced across the desert on the enemy's flank. Colonel John B. Sylvester's armored force then stormed Mutla Ridge, knocked out scores of Iraqi tanks and BMPs in its path, and cut the six-lane highway, the enemy's last exit from Kuwait City.

USAF DF-ST 92-08209

Light armored vehicles of the 1st Marine Division secure the Kuwait International Airport for use by the CH-53 Sea Stallion and CH-46 Sea Knight helicopters behind them.

From atop Mutla Ridge, the highest point of land for hundreds of miles in any direction, the soldiers beheld the awesome spectacle of thousands of smoking, ruined vehicles of all descriptions stretched for miles along the "Highway to Hell." A marine who witnessed this scene recalled a verse from the Koran: "He that does good shall be rewarded with that which is better. But he that does evil shall be requited with evil."[71] General Keys' other forces quickly overcame the sporadic resistance of the Iraqi troops to their front and by nightfall had firm control of the freeway between al-Jahra and Kuwait City.[72]

Last light on 26 February found the Joint Forces Command East, after a day of steady advance north on the coastal road, in position to enter Kuwait City in the morning. Assigned to the command was Marine First Lieutenant Brian G. Knowles' platoon from the 2d Force Reconnaissance Company, 1st Surveillance, Reconnaissance, and Intelligence Group. Knowles decided that the way was open for his unit and a Saudi force, so he enlisted members of the Kuwaiti resistance to guide them into Kuwait City. Knowles and his men decided to liberate the embassy on their own initiative; they received no specific orders to do so. As the 1st SRIG after action report concluded: "Force RECON Team Piglet 2-1 ordered to assume fire support responsibilities for 2/8. They abandon their posts and begin a series of grandstand plays to race for the Embassy. Fortunately none are killed by friendly fire."[73]Knowles' force quickly secured the American Embassy compound, whereupon one of his marines raised the "Stars and Stripes." A dying comrade had given the flag to the leathernecks during the 1968 Tet offensive in Vietnam. After completing this act, a fitting symbol of the U.S. military's journey from defeat in Vietnam to victory in Kuwait, Knowles declared the embassy secure at 2210.

The 3d Special Forces Group and Navy SEALs had been assigned the mission of liberating the embassy, and had been training for the operation for weeks. Despite Knowles' presence, the Green Berets and SEALs flew to the embassy as planned and "fast roped" from helicopters onto the embassy rooftop. At the same time British and French special forces liberated their own embassies.[74]

By daybreak on 27 February, the I Marine Expeditionary Force had secured all of its objectives. Both divisions consolidated their positions and began to mop up the last pockets of enemy resistance. Organized Iraqi action within Kuwait City ceased. All forward lines of I MEF were now in, or adjacent to, built-up areas. A key phase of the liberation of Kuwait had come to an end. The marines held their positions and awaited the arrival of Arab forces, to whom fell the honor of liberating the capital.

At about 0400 on the 27th, a Joint Forces Command East composite battalion of officers and troops from Saudi Arabia, the UAE, Qatar, Oman, Bahrain, and Kuwait passed through Task Force Shepherd's position east of Kuwait International Airport and entered the capital. To the west, Egyptian and Syrian units of Joint Forces Command North passed through 2d Marine Division's lines near Ali al-Salem Air Base. Later that day elements of the two Arab commands met in Kuwait City near its landmark water towers.[75]

General Boomer and his command group drove into the capital behind the Arabs and headed for the American Embassy. Flag-waving Kuwaiti citizens flashed "V" signs and greeted the Americans with shouts of "*Allahu Akbar!*" (God is great) "USA! USA!" and "God bless George Bush!" "It was one of the greatest experiences of my life," Boomer later recalled.

> The joy on the faces of the people as we drove by [was] indescribable. Citizens of all ages were crying tears of happiness. They streamed down to the sides of the highway to cheer as they saw and heard us approaching and showered us with candy. Scenes of the liberation of France came to mind constantly as we progressed.[76]

The leathernecks' greatest concern now became the live rounds that exuberant Kuwaitis were firing into the air, an Arab tradition.[77]

While Kuwaiti citizens celebrated their liberation, special warfare teams searched government buildings for remaining enemy soldiers. SEALs entered the Kuwait police headquarters and confiscated numerous Iraqi documents. Boomer and his staff entered another building and found a veritable gold mine. An elaborate sand table stood in the middle of one room. It contained a full-color relief map of Kuwait that showed the position of Iraqi forces along the coast before the final assault. Large red arrows pointing from the sea indicated where the enemy had expected an amphibious attack.[78]

The naval deception had worked. As General Myatt later observed:

> They were concerned from day one about a threat from the sea. When you get down and you look at the really fine engineering effort that was done on defense of the beaches and defense in-depth against an attack coming from the sea, it tied up at least six [70,000 to 80,000 troops] of the 11 Iraqi divisions that were facing I MEF. I would say that probably 40% to 50% of the Iraqi artillery pieces were pointed to the east in defense of this perceived real threat—an attack from the Gulf. . . . I think [the amphibious feints] saved a lot of Marine lives.[79]

An Aerial and Armored Blitz Ends the War

But the war was not over. Even though Arab and American forces had entered Kuwait City, much hard fighting remained before the international coalition achieved its objectives. For Saddam's army was on the run north of the city and General Schwarzkopf was determined to destroy it as an offensive force.

Allied aircraft pressed their attack to prevent an orderly retreat of the enemy army. Intruders, Corsairs, and Hornets flying from *Midway*, *Ranger*, *America*, and *Theodore Roosevelt* flew over 600 combat missions on 27 February alone. Marine aircraft continued to attack Iraqi units in northern Kuwait.[80]

Meanwhile, allied ground forces administered the *coup de grace* to Saddam's army in the largest tank battles fought since World War II. To meet General Franks' oncoming juggernaut, the Iraqi high command had repositioned five Republican Guard and regular armored and mechanized divisions in and around northwest Kuwait. Around 1600 on 26 February the 2d Armored Cavalry Regiment smashed into the Republican Guard's Tawalkalna Mechanized Division, opening what came to be know as the Battle of Wadi al-Batin.[81] Abrams tanks and Bradley fighting vehicles furiously exchanged fire with T-72s and BMPs, but the contest was one-sided. With superior night-vision technology and training, the American gunners almost always hit their target on the first round, while the Iraqis shot at the muzzle flashes of American tanks that had fired on the move and had already pressed on. From beyond the range of the enemy's weapons, the U.S. gunners destroyed one Iraqi target after another.[82] A captured Iraqi tank battalion commander later told his interrogators that "when the air operations started I had 39 tanks. After 38 days of the air battle I had 32 tanks. After 20 minutes against the 2d Armored Cavalry Regiment, I had 0 tanks."[83]

As Franks' armor and mechanized units battled it out with the Republican Guard, hordes of Apache attack helicopters from Colonel John Hitt's 11th Aviation Brigade flew deep into the enemy rear and pulverized the Iraqi 10th Armored Division, then in reserve just west of the Basrah–Kuwait City highway. Through their night-vision devices, Hitt's Apache crews spotted hundreds more enemy tanks and BMPs heading north out of Kuwait, but the Army aviators were helpless to stop them. The targets lay beyond the VII Corps fire support coordination line; that is, in an area regulated by the ATO process. Before the VII Corps commander could obtain permission from Riyadh to strike the lucrative but fleeting targets, they were gone. According to an Army history, "the missed opportunity frustrated Franks and the 11th Aviation Brigade pilots. Franks had lost a chance to attack in depth by synchronizing

USA

M1A1 Abrams main battle tanks of the Army's VII Corps traverse the Iraqi desert.

maneuver and air power. As for the pilots, they had had to pass up an attack pilot's dream."[84]

Meanwhile, the American and British armored divisions rolled on, relentlessly destroying Republican Guard and regular army units in their path. As the sun rose in the sky on the morning of the 27th, 350 Abrams tanks of General Griffith's U.S. 1st Armored Division, in formation abreast, rumbled over the crest of a ridge and came face to face with the Republican Guard's Medina Armored Division. From beyond the range of the enemy's guns, the American tankers methodically eliminated their foe. In the words of one tanker, "each crewman was grimly killing Iraqi tanks with calm, mechanical regularity. Excitement could be heard on the radio, but no panic—just an occasional shouted warning or a correction, or perhaps a muttered word of encouragement. It was a scene of uncanny discipline and phenomenal human control in the midst of hell."[85] The Battle of Medina Ridge, in which the Americans destroyed 300 enemy armored vehicles, mirrored the success that day of the entire VII Corps, its attached British 1st Armoured Division, and Major General Barry R. McCaffrey's 24th Mechanized Division, the latter fighting on the south bank of the Euphrates River.[86]

At 1700 on 27 February, Central Command headquarters notified the VII and XVIII corps that the suspension of offensive operations was imminent. In the remaining hours of the final assault, allied ground forces pushed as far east as possible, aiming to complete the encirclement of the Republican Guard in what became known as the "Basrah pocket."[87]

Temporary Cease-Fire

On the afternoon of 27 February, General Powell briefed President Bush in the Oval Office on the military situation in the KTO. Allied forces had reduced Saddam's ballistic missile threat to Saudi Arabia and Israel; destroyed his known nuclear, biological, and chemical weapons facilities; eliminated his ability to direct military operations; and bloodied his once-vaunted Republican Guard. Iraqi forces were fleeing Kuwait. General Schwarzkopf had reported that Saddam no longer possessed the military capability to threaten his neighbors. In short, the coalition had achieved its military and political objectives. As a result, the President ordered that offensive operations cease at 0800 on 28 February 1991 (Persian Gulf time), exactly 100 hours after the final assault had begun.[88]

Powell phoned Schwarzkopf to discuss the President's decision. Schwarzkopf had originally intended to press the attack through 28 February and had remarked that the campaign would probably go down in history as the "Five-Day War."[89] The Chairman of the Joint Chiefs said that policymakers in Washington were getting "nervous" about the damage being inflicted on the fleeing enemy and asked CINCCENT what he thought about stopping the offensive at 0800. "I don't have any problem with it," Schwarzkopf replied. As he later recalled,

> I'd have been happy to keep on destroying the Iraqi military for the next six months. Yet we'd kicked [Saddam Hussein's] butt, leaving no doubt in anybody's mind that we'd won decisively, and we'd done it with very few casualties. Why not end it? Why get somebody else killed tomorrow? That made up my mind.[90]

Because significant Iraqi forces survived as a result, President Bush's decision to end the final assault after 100 hours later precipitated a storm of controversy. Numerous individuals castigated the President for not advancing to Baghdad and finishing off Saddam and his army. But the UN mandate authorized coalition forces to eject the Iraqis from Kuwait; it did not call for the occupation of Iraq or the overthrow of the Iraqi regime, although many coalition political leaders would have liked to have seen Saddam fall. Allied military leaders generally felt as did General Keys, who concluded:

> In retrospect, it is clear that we could have done a lot more damage to the Iraqi forces if we had pressed on. . . . But at the time it would not have made sense to expose our forces to counterattacks by overextending ourselves, under the assumption that the enemy would never fight. That's how it looked at division level, anyway. Overall, I tend to agree with the President: If we had pursued the retreating forces into Iraq, we'd still be in Iraq now—and would probably be there for the next hundred years. We didn't manage to nail the major culprit in all of this, but we did what we had set out to do.[91]

Admiral Arthur thought that the ground war should have been ended twelve hours earlier! He reasoned that with the enemy on the run and Kuwait on the verge of liberation, it made no sense for the coalition to destroy even more Iraqi forces. The admiral did not want the United States and its Western allies to make martyrs of the Iraqis, for in the future the Islamic world might say that the "Christians . . . butchered us."[92]

At 9:02 on the evening of 27 February (Washington time), the President announced his decision in a speech broadcast on national radio and television:

> Kuwait is liberated. Iraq's army is defeated. Our military objectives are met . . . at midnight tonight eastern standard time, exactly 100 hours since ground operations commenced and 6 weeks since the start of Desert Storm, all United States and coalition forces will suspend offensive combat operations. It is up to Iraq whether this suspension on the part of the coalition becomes a permanent cease-fire.[93]

"I had to hand it to them," Schwarzkopf later quipped. "They really knew how to package an historic event."[94]

Bush emphasized that the suspension of military operations was not an absolute cease-fire, but was contingent upon specific conditions. Iraq had to release all coalition prisoners of war, third country nationals, Kuwaiti detainees, and the remains of coalition dead; inform Kuwaiti authorities of the nature and location of all mines in their country and adjacent waters; and comply fully with all relevant UN Security Council resolutions. That included renouncing the annexation of Kuwait and compensating the emirate for the loss, damage, and injury caused by Iraqi aggression. Iraqi forces were not to fire on coalition forces, nor could they launch Scud missiles against any other country. If Saddam violated these latter terms, coalition forces would be free to resume military operations. Bush called on the Iraqi government to designate military commanders to meet with their coalition counter-

USN DN-ST 91-05842

Jubilant coalition troops wave the Saudi, Kuwaiti, British, and U.S. flags as they liberate Kuwait City from the brutal Iraqi occupation.

parts within 48 hours to work out military arrangements for a permanent cease-fire.[95] The Iraqi government agreed to the meeting.

At 0800 on 28 February 1991, the coalition ceased offensive military operations. Allied forces at sea, in the air, and on land stood by to resume the attack if necessary. At this time Central Command and the Defense Intelligence Agency assessed 33 Iraqi divisions as combat ineffective. Most Iraqi army units had surrendered, had been destroyed, or were in flight.[96] The coalition's ground, air, and naval offensive of 24–28 February had killed 14,000 to 34,000 Iraqi troops and destroyed 2,000 tanks, 500 other armored vehicles, and 1,500 artillery pieces. More than 86,000 Iraqi soldiers had entered coalition EPW enclosures. The final assault had ended just as many observers had expected it would—in victory for the coalition.[97]

After the Storm

IN BELIEVING THAT HIS ARMY COULD PROLONG the land campaign by killing large numbers of allied troops and thereby forcing the coalition to accept a settlement short of its stated political objectives, Saddam Hussein made the mother of all miscalculations.[1] Instead, the Iraqi army suffered a devastating defeat, at relatively little cost to the coalition. After the cease-fire, U.S. and allied forces held their ground in the Kuwait Theater of Operations until it became clear that Saddam's army posed no immediate threat to the victorious coalition. Then, President Bush began to withdraw U.S. service men and women from the region.

The United States Navy played a key role in redeploying U.S. forces, aiding in the reconstruction of Kuwait, providing humanitarian aid to Iraqi Kurd and Shiite refugees, and in implementing U.S. postwar policy in the Persian Gulf region. These missions engaged the Navy's ships, planes, and sailors in the Central Command area of responsibility long after the Gulf War.

Defense of Kuwait

The cessation of offensive operations and the temporary cease-fire did not immediately bring peace to the KTO. Although the cease-fire had gone into effect at 0800 on 28 February, violent clashes continued to kill and wound Iraqis, Americans, and others in succeeding days. The Navy maintained a defensive posture during this tense period, albeit at a dramatically reduced tempo of operations. Navy and Marine aircraft flew combat air patrol, counter-air, reconnaissance, Scud reaction, and resupply missions. Surface forces conducted mine countermeasures, surface surveillance, and maritime interception operations. Submarines stood

"Iraqis on Faylaka Surrender to a UAV" by John Charles Roach

ready with their TLAMs and reported on merchant traffic in the theater. All U.S. forces stood ready to resume combat, if necessary.[2] "Until [a] formal agreement [is] signed," Captain Bulkeley warned his task group, "pockets of resistance may still exist in the KTO. Terrorist low-slow fliers and small boats [are] considered feasible. Be vigilant."[3]

The naval command was unsure whether the Iraqi 440th Marine Brigade dug in on Faylaka Island would give up without a fight. On 1 March, the battleship *Wisconsin* dispatched its unmanned aerial vehicle over the island. The Iraqi garrison, having suffered under several days of battleship bombardment during the ground campaign, knew full well that a UAV flying overhead meant that 16-inch shells would soon follow. American sailors observing the scene transmitted back to their shipboard video monitor by the UAV's camera stared in amazement as Saddam's soldiers emerged from their trenches, waving white flags. For the first time in military history, enemy troops were trying to surrender to a robot! Two days later, Navy CH-46 helicopters equipped with loudspeakers flew over the island to tell the Iraqi marines how to surrender. At 0800 on 4 March, a U.S. Marine company from the 13th MEU(SOC) landed on the island and began dispatching to the amphibious ship

Ogden over 1,400 prisoners, including one brigadier general, five colonels, and 100 other officers.[4]

But not all of Saddam's soldiers remaining in the battle zone gave up so readily. On the morning of 2 March, elements of the U.S. Army's 24th Mechanized Infantry Division spotted hundreds of tanks, BMPs, and support vehicles from the Hammurabi Division of the Republican Guard attempting to escape across a causeway spanning the Hawr al-Hammar, a lake in the wetlands northwest of Basrah, and others headed toward the Americans. Enemy artillery fired on forward American units. General McCaffrey's division responded with a full-scale counterattack, destroying 185 enemy armored vehicles, 400 trucks, and 34 artillery pieces and capturing 3,000 prisoners, without suffering a single casualty. It was the last major battle of the Persian Gulf War.[5]

Although combat ended, violence did not. Because coalition forces had shattered the enemy army's communications network in the KTO, several Iraqi units in isolated posts who did not receive word of the cessation of hostilities fired on allied units. Other enemy soldiers knew of the cease-fire but refused to stop fighting, sometimes shooting artillery and antitank weapons at American troops. There were news reports of fire-fights in Kuwait City between Kuwaiti security forces and armed Palestinians. Terrorist activity remained a constant threat and sometimes became a reality. Patrolling UN military police units came under fire on a number of occasions. In one such incident, three marines were wounded in a "drive-by" shooting.[6]

Even after the deliberate violence abated, the tools of war still did their deadly work. The Iraqis had booby-trapped many of the vehicles they had abandoned throughout the theater and live land mines still blanketed the landscape. Unexploded coalition munitions exacerbated the danger. According to one source, 30–40 percent of U.S.-made Rockeye and BLU-75 submunitions had failed to detonate when they hit the ground.[7] These weapons formed a deadly carpet on the desert floor and became even more dangerous when wind-blown sand covered them up. Such ordnance wounded and killed dozens of coalition soldiers during postwar operations.[8]

Safwan

While coalition forces stood watch over the prostrate but still dangerous Iraqi army, allied military leaders prepared for a meeting to arrange a permanent cease-fire agreement. Generals Powell and Schwarzkopf considered using the battleship *Missouri*, where General Douglas MacArthur had accepted the surrender of the Japanese Empire on 2 September 1945, as the site for the talks with Iraqi representatives. The American leaders wanted Saddam to understand that the meeting was a surrender ceremony in everything but name. But, as British General de la Billiere observed, if the surrender talks had taken place on a U.S. warship—in essence, on American territory—the rest of the coalition would have felt "excluded."[9] Moreover, there was little time to prepare a shipboard ceremony. In the end Schwarzkopf chose a military landing strip near the Iraqi village of Safwan, located just north of the Kuwaiti border along the road from Kuwait City to Basrah, as the site for the talks. CINCCENT felt that having the "negotiations" on Iraqi soil under coalition guns would drive home to the Iraqi leaders the enormity of their defeat.

On 2 March 1991, the UN Security Council sent Iraq a set of conditions it would have to meet for the cease-fire to become permanent. In addition to the conditions President Bush had enumerated in his speech of 27 February, Baghdad would have to supply information on coalition troops listed as missing in action; provide a list identifying any storage sites set up in Kuwait for nuclear, chemical, or biological weapons; and agree to a demarcation line between the opposing forces, with one-kilometer buffer zones on either side, to prevent another battle like the one at Hawr al-Hammar. Iraqi units still on the coalition's side of the line would be allowed to pass through, provided they showed no hostile intent. Finally, the Security Council stipulated that coalition forces would not withdraw from Iraq until Baghdad signed a formal cease-fire agreement.[10]

Around 1100 on 3 March, nine U.S. Army Apache and Blackhawk helicopters descended from the sky, finally clear and sunny after weeks of cold rain and fog, and landed at Safwan airfield. The personal helicopter of Saudi King Fahd landed soon afterward. American tanks and artillery guarded the landing strip while attack helicopters and fighter jets patrolled the skies above. General Schwarzkopf and Saudi General Khalid Bin Sultan al-Saud, commander of all coalition Islamic forces, emerged from their helicopters and walked to a 12-foot-high tent erected for the occasion. There they awaited the arrival of the Iraqi delegation led by Lieutenant General Sultan Hashim Ahmad, Chief of Staff at the Ministry of Defense, and Lieutenant General Salah Abud Mahmud, commander of the largely destroyed III Corps. Shortly thereafter, the Iraqi officers arrived at the site in American humvees escorted by Abrams main battle tanks, Bradley fighting vehicles, and Apache attack helicopters.

Under the eyes of the coalition's assembled military leaders, the two parties, with their interpreters, took their seats opposite one another at a main table. A stern-faced Schwarzkopf declared each condi-

General Schwarzkopf, with Saudi General Sultan at his side, enumerates the cease-fire terms to the Iraqi generals in the tent at Safwan.

tion of the cease-fire. Having been granted authority by Saddam to do so, Ahmad accepted each point. Without much thought about the matter, Schwarzkopf agreed to Ahmad's request that armed Iraqi helicopters be allowed to operate in Iraqi air space after the cease-fire. The American general would soon regret this concession. Some 90 minutes later, Ahmad signed the cease-fire agreement and departed with his delegation.[11]

On 4 March, Iraq provided information on the location of its land and sea mines in and around Kuwait and began releasing coalition prisoners of war. The next day Iraq's Revolutionary Command Council "annulled the annexation of Kuwait" and agreed to return stolen Kuwaiti assets. On the 7th, Iraq began freeing Kuwaiti detainees.[12]

On 3 April, the UN Security Council passed Resolution 687, which laid out terms for a formal end to the Gulf War. Iraq had to accept the 1963 border with Kuwait; establish a demilitarized zone along the border to be monitored by UN observers; renounce terrorism; agree to service its foreign debt, particularly the vast sums it owed the other gulf states; and compensate Kuwait for war damage. Iraq also had to reveal the location of its nuclear, biological, and chemical weapons and ballistic missiles; assent to their destruction, removal, or neutralization under strict supervision by a UN Special Commission; and allow on-site inspection to verify their destruction. The country would be forbidden to develop or acquire any additional weapons of mass destruction. This marked the first time that the United Nations had taken concrete nuclear disarmament measures.[13]

On 6 April, Iraq's 250-member National Assembly voted to accept Resolution 687. Five days later the UN Security Council declared a formal cease-fire, ending the Gulf War.[14] Initially, Saddam seemed willing to comply with the terms of the cease-fire. In time, however, he would do so only when compelled.

The Prisoner Release

One requirement of the cease-fire agreement was the return of the 45 coalition service men and women (21 Americans, 12 British, 9 Saudis, 2 Italians, and 1 Kuwaiti) who had fallen into Iraqi hands during Desert Storm. All 21 American prisoners of war were eventually taken to the enemy capital. Many were imprisoned in a facility they dubbed the "Baghdad Biltmore." The American POWs included three Navy air crewmen, Lieutenants Jeffrey Zaun, Robert Wetzel, and Lawrence R. Slade, and five Marine aviators, Lieutenant Colonel Clifford Acree, CW04 Guy Hunter, Major Joseph Small, Captain Michael Berryman, and Captain Russell Sanborn.

American prisoners have been mistreated by their captors in every twentieth-century war, and the Persian Gulf War was no exception. Iraqi soldiers and guards often beat the men with rubber hoses, boards, sticks, and even hammers and shocked them with cattle prods or other electrical devices. The two American women POWs, Major Rhonda L. Cornum, USA, and Specialist Melissa A. Coleman, USA, were sexually abused during their captivity. The Iraqis forced Lieutenant Zaun and Lieutenant Colonel Acree to denounce allied "aggression" in the Middle East and broadcast their videotaped "condemnation" on television. When Air Force Major Jeffrey S. Tice refused to make a similar videotape, his captors wrapped wires around his head and jolted him with electricity, knocking chips out of his teeth. Fortunately for the coalition prisoners, the quick allied victory saved them from more abuse at the hands of Saddam's jailers.

Not all of the Iraqis mistreated their prisoners, however. A number of doctors treated wounded POWs with compassion and professional skill while common soldiers sometimes shared cigarettes with the captives.

On 28 February, a doctor entered Marine Major Small's cell and told him he would be going home soon. The major realized that the war was over when he heard Iraqis firing weapons into the air to celebrate what the doctor called Iraq's "victorious victory." Small said nothing, but he knew which side had really won.[15]

The Iraqis released the allied POWs on 4 and 6 March. The Americans and Italians were flown to hospital ship *Mercy,* then moored at Bahrain. Admiral Arthur greeted them upon their arrival. After a brief reception, the ex-POWs went below for hot showers, hot food, and a chance to telephone loved-ones at home. They received medical attention and debriefings over the next week.

On 9 March, the former POWs departed *Mercy* for Bahrain International Airport, where they boarded a Boeing 707 bound for the United States. Designated flight "Freedom Zero-One," the plane touched down at Andrews Air Force Base near Washington, D.C., the next day. Hundreds of cheering, flag-waving well-wishers lined the runway to welcome home the repatriated Americans. Defense Secretary Cheney and General Powell greeted them as they deplaned. After reunions with family and friends, the three Navy and five Marine Corps returnees went to the National Naval Medical Center in Bethesda, Maryland, for examinations and further treatment. The POWs had survived their ordeal because of rigorous training, personal initiative, com-

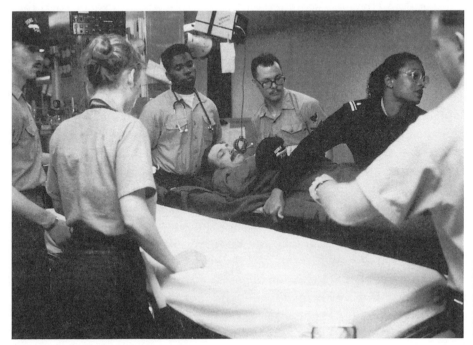

Navy medical personnel in hospital ship *Mercy* see to the care of Air Force Captain William Andrews, released by the Iraqis after the cease-fire.

mon sense, patriotism, and faith. All were glad to be home and proud to have served.[16]

Reconstruction of Kuwait

As the dust from Desert Storm began to settle, Kuwait's rulers faced the task of rebuilding their country. Much of the emirate had escaped the ravages of war, but where the opposing forces had fought, the landscape resembled a surrealistic junkyard. Thousands of burned-out tanks, armored personnel carriers, trucks, civilian automobiles, and other vehicles and mounds of Iraqi antitank rocket launchers and AK-47 rifles lay beside bomb-cratered roads. Personal property from thousands of Kuwaiti homes and businesses remained where the Iraqi looters had dropped it in their panicked flight from Kuwait City. Trenches, bunkers, gun emplacements, barbed-wire entanglements, land mines, gutted buildings, and piles of rubble scarred the beaches and countryside. Gaunt, starving camels, their coats stained and matted with oil, searched in vain for food. Sea mines, unexploded ordnance, sunken patrol boats with live ammunition still on board, shipwrecks, and corpses littered the ports, harbors, and seabed.

Saddam Hussein's scorched-earth exit from Kuwait exacerbated the devastation wrought by battle. Iraqi soldiers had attempted to destroy Kuwait's electric power and water supply systems and oil industry. More than 500 flaming oil wells spewed aloft flames and smoke, blotting out the sun and blackening the sand and everything on it with a thick coat of oil. Each day the fires consumed some five million barrels of petroleum and generated half a million tons of aerial pollutants. South of the capital and well into Saudi Arabia, as much as six million barrels of crude that the Iraqis had deliberately dumped into the Persian Gulf— probably the largest oil spill in history—blackened 300 miles of coastline and much of the wildlife it once nurtured.[17]

The magnitude of the physical destruction and environmental damage in Kuwait made it clear from the start that the international community would have to help the Emir restore his country's economic and social viability. With over $100 billion safely deposited in overseas accounts and huge reserves of oil in the ground, the Kuwaiti government could afford to rebuild. Still, the country needed the explosive ordnance disposal, civic action, and other specialized military units of the United States and its coalition allies to reconstruct civil authority in Kuwait and return the devastated nation to some semblance of its prewar economic status.

Courtesy of CDR John Griffith, RAN

A long-dead Iraqi swimmer discovered in the wire on Bubiyan Island by the men of Australian Commander John Griffith's Diving Clearance Team 3.

The Kuwaiti government in exile had begun planning for reconstruction soon after the Iraqi invasion. On 9 October 1990, Kuwait's ambassador to the United States had formally requested U.S. assistance in developing a recovery program. In mid-February, General Yeosock's Army Forces, Central Command established Task Force Freedom under Major General Robert S. Frix, USA, to direct the initial, emergency stage of restoring Kuwait and to coordinate the activities of coalition forces in that regard. Frix also prepared to transfer responsibility for the long-term restoration program to a follow-on Defense Department activity that would report to the Secretary of the Army, the executive agent for the Secretary of Defense. The general's command included the Army's 352d Civil Affairs Command and other Army Corps of Engineers, military police, medical, signal, intelligence, and explosive ordnance disposal units. The general also coordinated the efforts of Navy, Marine, Air Force, and British, Canadian, French, Australian, Saudi, Egyptian, and Kuwaiti EOD and salvage detachments.[18]

Task Force Freedom's various components began to arrive in Kuwait City on 28 February and immediately went to work supplying food, water, and medical care to needy Kuwaitis. Action teams soon repaired the electric power, water, communications, and transportation systems. Military police units and Kuwaiti authorities restored security to a city bristling with armed soldiers, resistance fighters, and a few Iraqi stragglers.[19]

UN naval forces had to deal with one of the largest tasks of the rebuilding effort, clearance of Kuwait's ports and restoration of their commercial operations. On 28 February, Schwarzkopf ordered the Navy to open a Kuwaiti port as soon as possible. Should hostilities flare up, the general wanted a port far forward to resupply his forces. On 1 March, Rear Admiral Taylor was charged with clearing the ports of Kuwait and opening them to maritime traffic.[20] The U.S. personnel under his direction included 25 divers, explosive ordnance disposal and salvage professionals, SEALs, and other specialists from the Navy's EOD Mobile Unit 2 and Mobile Inshore Undersea Warfare Units 202 and 108. He also exercised tactical control of similar Royal Australian Navy, Royal Navy, and French Navy units. The multinational team numbered approximately 140 men. The U.S. Naval Sea Systems Command's Office of the Supervisor of Salvage and Diving supported the port recovery and clearance effort. Salvage ship *Beaufort*, two commercial tugs, three supply boats, a barge, a mobile emergency recompression chamber, and 325 tons of equipment were employed in these operations.

USN DN-SC 92-00874

A diver of the U.S. Navy's Explosive Ordnance Disposal Mobile Unit 6 prepares to destroy an Iraqi LUGM sea mine with an explosive charge.

The first order of business was to reopen Ash Shuaybah. That port's capacity to accommodate deep-draft ships would enable the UN to provide food and water speedily to the distressed Kuwaiti population. The EOD teams cleared warehouses, wharfs, beaches, a refinery, and the waterfront area of booby traps, land mines, and unexploded coalition ordnance. They also removed five Silkworm antiship missiles from the Kuwaiti Girls Science High School! The harbor waters posed even greater dangers and difficulties. A thick layer of oil fouled the water's surface and drastically reduced visibility for divers working below, forcing them to feel their way around the sunken patrol boats, wrecked equipment, underwater obstacles, and numerous corpses.

Admiral Taylor saw the reopening of Ash Shuaybah as a chance to highlight the coalition's effort to restore Kuwait's international commerce. Even before work to clear the port was completed, he put out word that he was looking for a merchant ship to make the first postwar passage to Kuwait. Much to Taylor's surprise, the master of a Soviet merchantman volunteered his ship. Since the Cold War had just ended, the American admiral did not wish to let a Soviet ship make a solo triumphal entry into Ash Shuaybah, but he could not refuse the Soviet offer without provoking a diplomatic incident. Thinking quickly, he

USN DN-ST 91-09006

British EOD divers return to shore after an exhausting and hazardous day of clearing the detritus of war from a Kuwait harbor.

"volunteered" two Military Sealift Command ships which, together with the Russian ship, would form a convoy to Kuwait. Hence, on 12 March *LaSalle* and mine hunter HMS *Cattistock* led the three merchantmen, loaded with fresh water and supplies, safely through the Iraqi minefield and into Ash Shuaybah.

Meanwhile, the multinational group of divers and salvers began working in Kuwait's four other major commercial and naval installations, Ras al-Qulayah, North al-Ahmadi Pier, Ash Shuwaykh, and Mina ad-Doha. In succeeding weeks, they removed seven damaged or wrecked ships—including two Iraqi supertankers—and more than two dozen smaller vessels, and searched over 12 million square yards of muddy harbor floor. Farther out in the Persian Gulf, U.S. Navy salvers recovered three Tomahawk missiles and an SH-60B helicopter from the bottom. Ashore, the EOD teams recovered more than 80 tons of ordnance, including small-arms ammunition, grenades, artillery projectiles, mortar rounds, shoulder-fired rockets, demolition charges, and bombs. They also neutralized the sea mines that had washed ashore or had floated free from sunken Iraqi minelayers. The American, Australian, British, and French divers and salvers completed their port-clearing

USN DN-ST 91-06602

U.S. Ambassador Edward Gnehm, flanked by Rear Admiral Raynor A.K. Taylor, COMUS-NAVCENT, and Kuwaiti officials, gives thumbs-up to signal the opening to international shipping of the port of Ash Shuaybah.

U.S. Army heavy lift vessel *Algiers* raises a destroyed Iraqi *Osa II* missile boat from the bottom of the port of Ash Shuaybah.

mission on 23 April. Not one sailor lost his life during these dangerous operations.[21]

The U.S. Defense Reconstruction Assistance Office, led by Major General Patrick J. Kelly, USA, was established on 3 March and by the end of April had taken over responsibility for the $400 million long-range restoration program. This effort entailed contracting for permanent, rather than emergency repair of water and electrical systems; roads and bridges; commercial buildings, telecommunications centers, government facilities, and schools. By 1 December 1991 the coalition had restored Kuwait's electrical power system, water and sewage treatment plants, highway system, hospitals, police and fire stations, Kuwait International Airport, and 145 schools.[22]

Postwar Mine Countermeasures

While allied EOD specialists and salvers restored Kuwait's ports, multinational mine countermeasures forces cleared the shipping lanes farther out in the Persian Gulf. Begun during the war to support the right feint, MCM operations continued afterward as a vital part of the reconstruction effort, since most of the materials and supplies for that effort came by sea. Furthermore, the Iraqi mines had to be cleared before the owners and insurers of the world's supertankers would allow their ships to resume the oil trade on which the Kuwait economy depended.

This work was also dangerous. As Admiral Arthur told his sailors, "you won't find white flags flying from those mines."[23] Mine countermeasures ships from the Belgian, French, Dutch, Italian, German, and Japanese navies joined the U.S. and British MCM forces in conducting postwar operations.[24]

Coalition navies coordinated their postwar operations on the basis of two UN Security Council Resolutions. Resolution 686 of 2 March 1991 requested UN member states "to take all appropriate action to cooperate with the Government and people of Kuwait in the reconstruction of their country." Resolution 687 of 3 April 1991 lifted the embargo on Kuwait and tasked member states with reopening the emirate to normal commerce. These provisions sanctioned the clearing of mines from the northern gulf and the escorting of merchant ships through cleared channels into Kuwaiti harbors.[25]

The cooperative system of command and control established by coalition naval forces during the war had functioned well, and cooperation continued to be the rule after the war. Indeed, effective command and control in the northern gulf, particularly in the minefields, remained necessary to avoid accidents. Admiral Taylor and Commodore

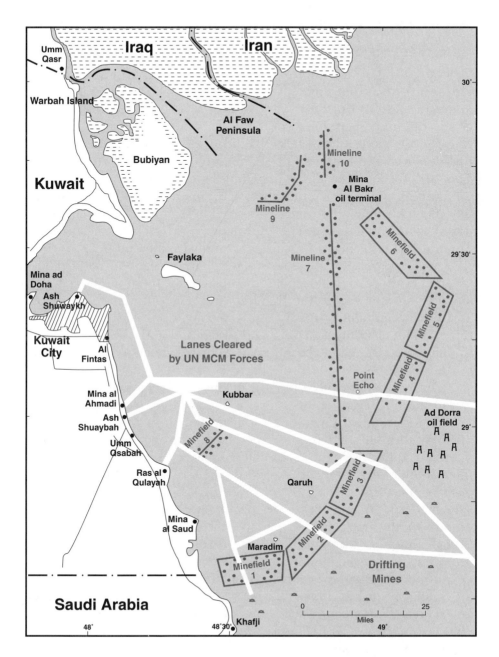

Reopening of Kuwait

Craig coordinated plans with the Belgian, Dutch, French, German, and Saudi mine-clearing commanders before their respective forces began MCM operations. Taylor convened frequent (at first, weekly) meetings of naval officers to improve coordination among the forces. The commanders decided early that Taylor would exercise tactical control in the northern gulf of the multinational mine clearing and other naval forces, including the Japanese mine-clearing units that arrived on 1 June. The Europeans organized their MCM forces into the European Task Unit, under the auspices of the Western European Union, but they did not chart a different operational course from the Americans.[26]

During the cease-fire talks, Baghdad informed the allies that they had deployed 283 bottom and 874 moored mines in offshore waters.[27] They also turned over a map providing comprehensive information on the position and characteristics of each mined area. The map showed how much wartime intelligence had erred in regard to the extent and location of the minefields. The information was such a revelation that Admiral Taylor likened it to "daylight coming in the window."[28]

At their monthly meeting in early March, coalition naval officers planned and coordinated operations to remove these mines as well as any drifting mines from the Iran-Iraq War. Each navy received its own area of responsibility.[29] Initially, the U.S. Navy and the Royal Navy concentrated on clearing, widening, and straightening the shipping lanes to Kuwaiti ports. Ultimately, coalition MCM forces aimed to clear the entire northern gulf.[30]

During the first three months of the mine-removal operation, the European mine clearing forces performed as would have been expected in a NATO conflict. Operating sophisticated ships and equipment, by mid-May the well-trained and experienced European seamen had destroyed or otherwise neutralized 750 sea mines. The Belgian and French mine hunters destroyed nearly 500 of them. The French mine hunter *Sagittaire* performed skillfully, neutralizing 145 mines in only 20 days. The U.S. and British forces destroyed fewer mines during the early months of the operation, in part because they were more concerned with clearing the existing lanes to the coast of Kuwait than systematically removing mines from identified minefields.[31]

The European MCM forces finished their share of the mine clearance task on 20 July 1991. The U.S. Navy and the Japanese Maritime Self-Defense Force completed their MCM operations on 10 September 1991. *Guardian* (MCM 5), the last remaining MCM ship in gulf waters, departed on 15 January 1992.

Clearing mines from the sea lanes of the Persian Gulf in less than a year was a major accomplishment. The allied units destroyed 1,288 mines, or virtually all mines thought to be in Persian Gulf waters (Table 6).

USN DN-SC 91-06606

Rear Admiral Taylor briefs the press about Iraqi mine concentrations being neutralized by the coalition clearance forces under his tactical control.

Courtesy of RADM R.A.K. Taylor, USN (Ret.)

The UN coalition's postwar mine clearance flotilla.

Table 6

NORTH ARABIAN GULF MINE STATISTICS

MINES DESTROYED, BY METHOD

Method	Destroyed	Notes
SMCM	1022	All nations. Destroyed using ROVs, divers, or influence systems.
Divers	145	All nations. Destroyed using shore- or ship-based divers. Includes floating mines.
EOD	95	All nations. Destroyed by EOD personnel. Includes beached mines.
AMCM	26	U.S. only. Destroyed by divers or influence systems.
TOTAL:	1288	

MINES DESTROYED, BY COUNTRY

Bahrain	1
Belgium	284
France	203
Germany	92
Italy	71
Japan	31
Kuwait	3
Netherlands	35
Saudi Arabia	49
United Kingdom	189
United States	248
beached mines	82*
TOTAL	1288

SOURCE: COMUSNAVCENT Briefing Slides, RADM Raynor A.K. Taylor Papers, OA; ltr, Taylor to Dudley, 29 Jan 1996, Authors' Files, OA.

*Destroyed by combined U.S., U.K., and Australian EOD teams, approximately one third for each team. French EOD personnel destroyed 10 other beached mines, which are included in the French total above.

The total included weapons believed left over from the Iran-Iraq War. No lives were lost, and only twice did unplanned mine detonations shake ships.

The allies could not be certain that they had destroyed every mine in the gulf's waters. Nevertheless, even the "weapons that wait" cannot last forever. Some 54 percent of the moored weapons and 7 percent of the bottom mines that the allies found proved to be inoperable, owing to water leakage, improper assembly, or improper installation. Similarly, any mines remaining in gulf waters will probably degrade and stop functioning over time. The international maritime industry understood that their ships could once again steam safely through gulf waters. By 1992 merchant shipping traffic in the gulf was booming and insurance rates had returned to prewar levels.[32]

Redeployment of Central Command Forces

While allied mine hunters and EOD experts cleared the way for Kuwait to resume international trade, U.S. forces departed the theater promptly, making good on President Bush's prewar promise to remove the American military presence from Saudi Arabia once the coalition had achieved its political objectives.[33] General Schwarzkopf designated 8 March 1991 as R-Day (retrograde day), when U.S. forces began withdrawing from the theater. Planners divided the withdrawal into two stages. These were not successive periods of time, but rather distinct types of operations conducted simultaneously. Stage I involved redeployment of U.S. naval, air, and ground forces. Stage II entailed removing all remaining ammunition and other bulk supplies.[34] The Navy played a paramount role in the redeployment of U.S. forces and materiel from the region. Military Sealift Command designated the operation "Desert Sortie." The Army named it "Desert Farewell" and the Air Force called it "Desert Calm." Irreverent military personnel dubbed the redeployment "Desert Scram."[35]

Because of their inherent mobility and self-supporting logistic capability, most naval units needed only to weigh anchor and steam out to sea to withdraw from the theater. At the end of Desert Storm, Admiral Arthur's forces included 6 aircraft carriers, 2 battleships, 2 command ships, 12 cruisers, 11 destroyers, 10 frigates, 4 mine warfare ships, 31 amphibious ships, 32 auxiliaries, 2 hospital ships, 3 submarines, and numerous military sealift ships. It was one of the largest naval armadas assembled since World War II. Some 82,278 Navy men and women had served on board these ships and at installations ashore. All were now veterans of the Persian Gulf War.[36]

Admiral Arthur established 10 March 1991 as R-Day for NAVCENT forces. In general, Navy crews returned on board their ships, while reservists and civilians flew home. Most of Arthur's fleet, including the *Saratoga*, *Midway*, *John F. Kennedy*, and *America* carrier battle groups, battleships *Wisconsin* and *Missouri*, hospital ships *Comfort* and *Mercy*, and the 13 Atlantic Fleet amphibious vessels departed the theater during March. By the end of April only 1,600 of the 6,800 naval reservists in-theater at the end of the war remained there. Most Coast Guard personnel had also been flown home by late spring.[37] Hence, less than two months after General Schwarzkopf ordered the withdrawal, only those combatants and support ships needed to secure U.S. interests in the region remained there.[38]

Redeployment of Central Command's Army, Marine, Air Force, and shore-based Navy units was much more demanding. To accomplish this evolution efficiently, CENTCOM component commanders and their counterparts in other unified and specified commands worked up a time-phased force deployment list to determine the sequence in which units would redeploy from the region. To ensure rapid reconstitution of combat formations in the United States, Europe, the Pacific, and else-

USN DN-ST 92-02330

Thoroughly cleaned M1A1 Abrams main battle tanks and plastic-encased CH-47 Chinook helicopters are ready for loading on board ships of the Navy's Military Sealift Command and return to the United States.

where, all U.S. services withdrew their people by unit rather than individually. Marines, for example, returned as elements of deployable air-ground task forces, ready for global contingency operations, like the disaster assistance in Bangladesh carried out by the 5th MEB and Amphibious Group 3 enroute to California.[39] General Schwarzkopf ordered planners to give priority to combat units, echoing his Desert Shield "shooters-first" deployment policy, but the actual sequence depended on the needs of a given service for a particular unit.[40]

But first, tanks, aircraft, equipment, ammunition, and supplies needed to be counted, segregated, dismantled, cleaned, labeled, packed up, and loaded on board ships. Even the lumber and crates used to ship equipment during Desert Shield were to be sent home. It was an unprecedented effort to clean up a theater of war before closing it down.[41]

Accordingly, U.S. forces disestablished their bases and put their areas of responsibility in trim before leaving the Arabian Peninsula. As General Pagonis put it, "we felt a moral obligation to clean up the huge mess we had made."[42] On average, units left 20 percent of their people behind to complete the dismantling of defensive emplacements, cantonments, and storage buildings and to prepare the unit's equipment for transportation. For example, the main body of Naval Mobile Construction Battalion 74 returned home to Gulfport, Mississippi, in May, but 109 sailors remained until mid-June to tear down the unit's camp, prepare equipment for transport, and load it onto ships. Marine bulldozers closed holes that were cut in the berm that defined the border between Saudi Arabia and Kuwait. Other marines policed up firing ranges, retrieved gear such as shovels and axes that had been discarded along roadsides during the land campaign, and even slit open sandbags, dumped out the sand, and disposed of the empty bags. They also destroyed ammunition, bunkers, and weapons that the Iraqis had abandoned in Kuwait and recovered enemy equipment for intelligence, training, and historical purposes.[43]

I MEF's 1st Force Service Support Group set up four "washrack units" to clean ammunition, equipment, vehicles, and aircraft in order to meet stringent U.S. Department of Agriculture standards set to prevent importation of crop-infesting insects into the United States. "We washed tanks, howitzers, bulldozers, and even the occasional grunt in desperate need of a shower," said Marine Captain William Sorfleet, the officer in charge of Wash-Down Site 1. More than 2,000 vehicles per day received a thorough scrubbing to remove all loose sand and dirt. Soldiers and marines even pulled engines out of tanks and other tracked vehicles to ensure that no parasite-ridden soil remained. U.S. logistics forces constructed a 4.8-million square-foot staging area to store washed equipment until it was shipped out. These men and women also jury-rigged an assembly line to shrink-wrap large equipment slated for shipment on open decks to protect it from the ravages of saltwater. Equipment cleaning was the largest in-theater operation during Desert Sortie.[44]

Admiral Arthur stressed the importance of safety during the retrograde operation. "We are surrounded by systems that do not have any sense of world events," he noted in a message to naval personnel. "Fuel oil leaks still cause fires, improperly maintained or flown aircraft still fall uncontrolled to the earth, improper conduct ashore can place you in harm's way, [and] frayed wiring or improperly grounded electrical equipment can still shock."[45]

For the same reasons, General Boomer adopted Schwarzkopf's phrase, "not one more life," as a theme for Desert Sortie. Boomer was especially concerned about accidents or casualties resulting from the mishandling of ordnance, which claimed the lives of 16 U.S. military personnel between 1 March and 24 July 1991. He cautioned his marines not to pick up souvenirs, possibly booby-trapped by the enemy, or coalition ordnance that might explode when jostled.[46]

While military personnel cleaned up after themselves in Kuwait and Saudi Arabia, the formations of I MEF, VII Armored Corps, and XVIII Airborne Corps withdrew from southern Iraq and Kuwait and converged on the ports and airfields of Saudi Arabia and Bahrain. Most of the soldiers and marines boarded MAC transport planes or chartered commercial airliners bound for the United States or other locations around the globe. Most U.S. Army units exited through the port of ad-Dammam, while most marines redeployed through al-Jubayl.[47]

The I Marine Expeditionary Force, 84,000 strong, began withdrawing from Kuwait to Saudi Arabia on 4 March. Major General John I. Hopkins' 7th Marine Expeditionary Brigade, the first Marine combat formation to deploy to Saudi Arabia, was the first to depart. By 16 April, when General Boomer and most of his staff departed the theater, I MEF personnel strength had dropped to 19,743 marines. Boomer turned over command of Marine affairs in the theater to Major General Norman E. Ehlert, who established a new headquarters, Marine Forces, Southwest Asia, to replace I MEF.[48]

Navy and Marine leaders considered it vital that the Maritime Prepositioning Force be quickly reconstituted for future contingencies. Rapidly deployable Marine units required not only vehicles, weapons, ammunition, and food, but also road-building equipment, copiers, fax machines, computers, video recorders, microwave ovens, and innumerable miscellaneous items of supply. To facilitate handling such a wide variety of paraphernalia, the 1st Force Service Support Group planned ship loads in advance, using an inventory system that included a computer database, bar-coded labels, and scanners. Leathernecks worked around the clock to ensure that equipment loaded back into the prepositioning ships was in combat-ready condition by draining fuel from vehicles, replacing filters, changing oil, and servicing optical sighting devices.

By July the Marines had loaded the five ships of Maritime Prepositioning Squadron 2, which then steamed for the staging base at Diego Garcia. In September and October, the eight ships of MPSRON 3 and MPSRON 1 secured their holds and headed for their bases, respectively at Guam and Saipan, and the U.S. East Coast.[49] Marine Forces, Southwest Asia was disestablished on 10 October 1991, when the last Marine combat service support units left Saudi Arabia.[50]

Like their Marine comrades, Army and Air Force personnel began departing the theater almost immediately after the cease-fire. By early June MAC had airlifted home 350,000 soldiers, "pumping" them through, to use General Pagonis' term, at the rate of 5,000 to 6,000 men and women per day. The pace slackened thereafter, and by November 1991 only about 8,000 U.S. ground troops remained in Saudi Arabia and Kuwait. During the same period almost 50,000 Air Force personnel departed the theater, leaving only about 5,000 in Saudi Arabia and Kuwait.[51]

The desert areas of the Persian Gulf quickly emptied of Army helicopters, armored vehicles, trucks, and equipment. During the first 120 days of Desert Sortie, U.S. forces loaded more than 117,000 wheeled and 12,000 tracked vehicles, 2,000 helicopters, and 41,000 containers of supplies onto sealift ships.[52]

Similarly, the Air Force's planes departed from air bases throughout the region. The F-15s of the 1st Tactical Fighter Wing, the first Air Force warplanes to reach Saudi Arabia, were the first to leave, departing the theater in mid-March for Langley Air Force Base in Virginia. Hundreds of CENTAF fighters, bombers, and other aircraft left during the summer. By November 1991 only 60–70 U.S. warplanes remained in Saudi Arabia and Kuwait.[53]

Military Sealift Command Empties the Desert

Even as the first U.S. combat units went home, Military Sealift Command began executing the second stage of Desert Sortie, which involved shipping out almost all remaining ammunition and supplies. Some of the materiel was slated to replenish stocks at U.S. military bases in Europe, Asia, and elsewhere around the world. Except for limited amounts that remained in Kuwait, the rest of the military supplies was shipped back to the United States.

With Congress even then considering major cutbacks in the Defense Department's post-Cold War establishment, American leaders did not underestimate the importance of preserving this materiel. Some of the most advanced weapons and equipment in the U.S. arsenal had been shipped to the Central Command theater. Unlike their predecessors in World War II, Korea, and Vietnam, officers at the helm during the Gulf War would not leave behind, sell for scrap, or dump in the ocean excess vehicles, equipment, or stocks of ammunition. "Hope you got a little sleep last night," General Boomer told his staff on the morning of 28 February 1991, "because now you have to manage getting this [Marine Expeditionary Force] redeployed back to [the United States]. The future of the Marine Corps is right here in this sand . . . equipment, ammunition; it's all here, it's all out of the barn right here in this dirt, and we have to pick it all up and get it all back in the barn."[54]

MSC, and to a lesser extent MAC, had delivered to the Central Command theater tens of thousands of vehicles and aircraft as well as the equipment, supplies, food, clothing, and much of the housing for more than 500,000 American service men and women. Between August 1990 and February 1991, Admiral Donovan's command had delivered 450 shiploads of cargo to the theater. It was a feat comparable to moving a city the size of Louisville, Kentucky, 8,500 miles to the Arabian Peninsula. Now the "city" had to be packed up and shipped home again. Although U.S. forces had consumed massive quantities of supplies and ammunition before and during the war, huge stockpiles remained. Approximately a third of a million short tons of ammunition, for example, sat in the desert, including 60 percent of all Marine Corps ammunition stocks.[55]

Soon after the war ended, Admiral Donovan turned off the tap that poured war materiel into the gulf. MSC had scheduled 145 shiploads of cargo to support Desert Storm, but less than half that amount had reached the theater by 28 February. Donovan cancelled the remaining shipments. Ships loading out cargo in the United States ceased operations, ships enroute to the theater reversed course, and ships offloading in Saudi Arabia began reloading. About 75 percent of the cancelled shipments consisted of ammunition.[56]

Multiservice logisticians then developed comprehensive plans for the loading, transportation, and delivery of cargo already in the gulf to destinations around the world. Joint combat service support teams operated in each of the major staging areas in the theater. One such team, stationed at Camp Tate near the port of Ras al-Mishab, comprised 665 Navy, Marine, civilian, and non-U.S. personnel. Following a detailed plan, this group inspected and repacked I MEF ammunition and loaded it onto break-bulk ships.

Loading a ship was labor-intensive, time-consuming, and often dangerous. Routinely, cranes lifted pallets of ammunition, some weighing as much as 6,000 pounds, from hardstands ashore and lowered them into ship holds. Forklift operators then positioned and stacked the material below. Finally, civilian carpenters used large amounts of wood, called "dunnage," to immobilize the munitions for rough voyages across the often storm-tossed seas.[57]

During the first 120 days of Desert Sortie, U.S. forces often loaded more than 20 ships each week. By mid-July they had stowed 903,000 short tons of materiel into 236 ships. As 1991 drew to a close, approximately 200 MSC-controlled vessels remained on the high seas, transporting cargo from the Central Command theater. By the year's end, only 30,000 short tons of equipment remained in Saudi Arabia.[58]

Redeployment of U.S. Army, Air Force, and Marine Corps unit equipment officially ended on 12 May 1992, when the U.S. merchant ship *Leslie Lykes* reached Bayonne, New Jersey. Since 11 March 1991, MSC had retrieved 456 ship-loads of cargo from the KTO—more than 1.9 million tons of equipment and supplies. Thus closed the book on one of the largest military sealifts in history.[59]

The Welcome Home

Long before these merchant vessels completed their mission, the American forces had come home to an exultant nation. Popular support for strong action against Saddam Hussein had remained high throughout Desert Shield and Desert Storm. American casualties, which since Vietnam had often determined the level of public support for overseas commitments, stayed remarkably low. Citizens approved of how quickly General Schwarzkopf's naval, air, and ground forces defeated Saddam's armed forces. Conscious of the poor reception accorded returning veterans of the Vietnam War, millions of Americans welcomed home Gulf War veterans as heroes.

Naval vessels steaming into the nation's ports received an enthusiastic greeting from fire boats spewing water, military bands playing patriotic tunes, and thousands of cheering, flag-waving family members, friends, and other well-wishers. As each transport plane disembarked its passengers at air facilities around the country, Americans were on hand to show their gratitude.

New York City sponsored a traditional ticker-tape parade for the returning forces and Washington staged the largest military extravaganza

USN DN-SC 92-00671

Lieutenants Robert Wetzel, Lawrence Slade, and Jeffrey Zaun (left to right) stand at attention as Admiral Frank B. Kelso, Chief of Naval Operations, presides at a ceremony honoring the dedication to duty of these naval aircrewmen shot down and imprisoned by Iraqi forces.

USN DN-SC 92-01265

U.S. Navy sailors enjoy a richly deserved ticker-tape victory parade through the streets of New York City.

USN DN-ST 91-11235

The faces of these *Thomas S. Gates* (CG 51) officers reflect the joy of returning home and the sense of professional accomplishment felt by naval personnel after their Gulf War experience.

since the end of World War II. Thousands of cities and towns around the country put on their own celebrations, often focused on local National Guard or Reserve units.

Most Gulf War veterans were grateful for the greeting and even more thankful to be home. Coastguardsman EM1 George Dotson, who had been on active duty with Port Security Unit 302 in the gulf since 14 November 1990, arrived home in Cleveland just in time to witness the birth of his daughter. The national outpouring of thanks surprised some returnees. When hospital ship *Comfort* reached Baltimore, Commanding Officer Captain Thomas J. Finger observed: "It's nice to see all these people here. We come and go all the time, and usually no one notices."

Celebration of the victory over Iraq enabled Americans to repair some of the damage done to the national psyche by the Vietnam War. U.S. forces "not only helped liberate Kuwait," President Bush told veterans at Sumter, South Carolina, "you helped this country liberate itself from old ghosts and doubts." Sergeant Major Wayne Smith of the 4th Marine Expeditionary Brigade hoped that "the Vietnam vets realize this celebration was for them just as much as it was for the ones who fought in the desert."[60]

After the military parade in Washington, Admiral Arthur paid his first-ever visit to the Vietnam Memorial. The sight of the more than 58,000 names engraved in black marble, identifying the American men and women killed during the war or who remain missing, moved him deeply. He paused to reflect on the meaning of the Vietnam War and Desert Storm. As he said later, the experience in the gulf showed that "we can do things right, when we decide to do them. And we did it right. We were lucky, too."[61]

The nation's welcome home for the Persian Gulf War veterans reaffirmed what most of them already felt. The Navy's report on the war summarized this understanding:

> The most significant contributor to our decisive victory was our motivated, dedicated, well-trained volunteers. Our people performed superbly, and validated the investments made in them over the past decades. Their courage, commitment and professionalism inspired unprecedented and well-deserved support from the American public and national leadership. . . . The men and women of the U.S. Armed Forces gave us victory.[62]

Reorganization of NAVCENT

As the fanfare subsided, Admiral Arthur returned to the gulf and took steps to refine the NAVCENT command structure. He especially wanted to improve its connection to the theater headquarters and the other U.S. armed services. Arthur and Admiral Taylor, his subordinate and then successor as COMUSNAVCENT, encouraged the Navy to take to heart the "lessons learned" from the Gulf War. They realized that during the war the naval command structure had not always served the Navy's or CINCCENT's best interests.

Accordingly, soon after the cease-fire, Arthur directed Taylor to investigate alternative approaches to the command set-up, so in future conflicts in the region U.S. naval forces could make an optimum contribution. Taylor was the right person to handle the job. Selected as a Navy Olmsted Scholar in 1967, he had studied international relations at the University of Grenoble in France and the American University in Washington. His studies included courses on the Arab Mahgreb of North Africa, which helped prepare him for duty in the Persian Gulf. In the late 1980s, he received a thorough education in unified command theory, structure, and doctrine during a tour as Director of Joint Operations (J-3) of the U.S. European Command in Stuttgart, Germany. Taylor had been an ardent advocate of "jointness" ever since.[63]

Courtesy of RADM R.A.K. Taylor, USN (Ret.)

Admiral Frank B. Kelso (right) confers with Rear Admiral Taylor during a visit to the Persian Gulf.

In reply to Arthur's directive, Taylor wrote a paper arguing that COMUSNAVCENT should be headquartered in Bahrain and "double-hatted" as Commander Middle East Force. He reasoned that the Middle East Force should be maintained as "an independent entity" because of its "historical legacy" and "legitimacy in the eyes of our gulf allies."[64]

Arthur carefully considered Taylor's "think piece." He concurred about the symbolic importance of the Middle East Force. "More than any U.S. force," he noted, "CMEF has provided both a symbol of our nation's constancy and strength in the region." And he certainly agreed that NAVCENT needed to be reorganized: "Desert Shield/Storm has shown the absolute need for a Navy component commander that has the staff, connectivity and seniority to command a large naval presence."

On 9 March, Arthur recommended to General Schwarzkopf that a "seasoned two-star rear admiral who has had prior battle group command experience" operate from *LaSalle* with "dual-hat" responsibility as COMUSNAVCENT and Commander Middle East Force. Should a Desert Storm-like crisis occur, the naval component headquarters could be shifted to Riyadh. Arthur then proposed to move the existing COMUSNAVCENT billet from Pearl Harbor to Norfolk, rename it "USNAVCENT Rear," and place a one-star admiral in command. Arthur chose Norfolk because it was one of the Navy's air logistics hubs, located in the same time zone as CENTCOM headquarters at Tampa, and was close to high-level Navy commands in Washington and Norfolk.[65]

Admiral Kelso, the Chief of Naval Operations, received Arthur's proposal carrying General Schwarzkopf's endorsement. Kelso agreed that a rear admiral with dual responsibilities would do as a "naval component forward" in peacetime. But he felt that in war, a rear admiral would not have enough "horsepower" to command a large naval force; only a three-star officer could serve effectively as CINCCENT's naval component commander. Since the Navy had no vice admirals to spare, Kelso concluded that CINCPACFLT or CINCLANTFLT (Commander in Chief, U.S. Atlantic Fleet) could provide one of their three-stars and staffs in a crisis like Desert Storm.[66]

Arthur viewed Kelso's response as backsliding. "As I see it," he wrote Vice Admiral Jeremy M. Boorda,[67] Chief of Naval Personnel,

> we are over-due on providing CINCCENT a component commander and staff with whom he can both deal daily, and have present at the table in battle if necessary—peace and war. If this is not done, then the lessons of the past 12 years of adhoc [*sic*] handling of crisis [*sic*] will be met with another bandaid fix.[68]

Arthur expressed his displeasure in even stronger terms to Schwarzkopf:

> [The] CNO has proposed to you that he wants to provide another three star fleet commander to plan and exercise with you and in case of a force buildup in SWA send him to command the forces. This misses the point entirely. You want a component commander not a fleet commander. Basically, what the CNO is really saying is that you don't need your own component commander. USCINCPAC has CINCPACFLT, USCINCLANT has CINCLANTFLT, USCINCEUR has CINCUSNAVEUR, but you must share. You know better than I that your AOR has had a very volatile past and the future looks like more of the same. Every time an increase in Navy force levels occurs the Navy has had to make an adjustment. JTFME and COMSEVENTHFLT as COMUSNAVCENT are the last two examples. During the Iran hostage extraction attempt CMEF was changed from reporting to CINCUSNAVEUR to CINCPACFLT. These arguments alone cry for a fix, and that fix requires a real live, functioning component commander.[69]

Despite the concerns of Arthur and Taylor, Kelso's views prevailed for another year and a half. When Vice Admiral Arthur stood down as the Central Command's naval component commander on 24 April 1991, Rear Admiral Taylor, who remained Commander Middle East Force, took on the added responsibility as COMUSNAVCENT. *LaSalle*, based in

Bahrain, became his headquarters. At the same time Rear Admiral Robert Sutton became Commander U.S. Naval Forces, Central Command Rear. The Navy moved his headquarters from Pearl Harbor to Tampa that summer.[70]

Despite Kelso's views, the long-term reorganization of NAVCENT would proceed on the course suggested by Taylor and Arthur. Another old hand in the Persian Gulf also played a role shaping this course, albeit unwittingly. That old hand was none other than Saddam Hussein.

Enforcing the Peace

When Desert Storm ended, Saddam seemed destined for a quick and ignominious exit from Iraq's political scene. His much vaunted army had been

USN DN-ST 91-09478

Kurds fleeing Saddam Hussein's brutal repression were forced to endure the hardships of winter encampment in the barren hills near the Iraqi border with Turkey.

decimated. What remained of his air force was confined to the ground. His navy now threatened only coalition divers. His country's bridges, airfields, electric power grid, water-pumping system, and other vital components of the economic infrastructure lay in ruins. Disease, hunger, and misery stalked his people. He was surrounded by foes, including many of his own countrymen.[71]

In March 1991, Kurds in northern Iraq and Shiites in the south rebelled against his regime. These uprisings constituted the greatest upheaval in modern Iraqi history. For a time the rebels seemed to be winning. Kurdish guerrillas claimed to have gained control of three northern provinces and the important oil center of Kirkuk, while Shiite Muslim militants held their own against Saddam's soldiers in Basrah and the holy Shiite cities Najaf and Karbala.[72]

But Saddam Hussein was to be the ultimate cat, landing on his feet after another disastrous war. In a 7 March briefing, General Boomer learned that the Iraqi army had recovered sufficient equipment from the KTO—600 tanks, 500 armored personnel carriers, and 65 artillery pieces—to equip three heavy divisions and four to six infantry divisions. Boomer's staff estimated surviving Iraqi forces at 26 divisions, 20 or 21 of which had never been deployed in the KTO.[73] Although it had been virtually impotent against Western forces, the Iraqi army whipped the lightly armed Kurds and Shiites. U.S. forces stood by, fettered by rules of engagement that disallowed unprovoked allied movement into unoccupied portions of Iraq. Refugees told tales of insurgents tortured with electricity and hung from the guns of T-72 tanks, apartment houses and private dwellings leveled by tank and mortar fire, and defenseless infants and children slaughtered by chemical weapons and napalm.[74]

Saddam's use of helicopter gunships against the Kurds and Shiites particularly outraged U.S. observers. During the talks at Safwan, Iraqi General Ahmad had asked that helicopter flights be permitted inside his country to transport government officials. Overland transport was nearly impossible, he explained, because coalition aircraft had destroyed most of Iraq's bridges and many of its roads. It had seemed a perfectly legitimate and innocuous request, so Schwarzkopf assented. He should have suspected that Saddam might use the helicopters to kill his own subjects.[75]

The brutal suppression of the rebellions precipitated the flight of nearly 1.5 million Iraqi civilians, primarily Kurds, from northern Iraq. Some 500,000 escaped into inhospitable mountain areas of Iraq, Iran, and Turkey, where in early April they died at a rate of 2,000 per day from dehydration, malnutrition, disease, and exposure to cold.[76]

Touched by the refugees' plight and conscious that Desert Storm had inspired the Kurds and Shiites to rebel against their oppressor, the United Nations acted. Security Council Resolution 688 authorized the use of force to ensure unhampered humanitarian assistance to Kurdish refugees in northern Iraq and Southern Turkey. Coalition military forces subsequently launched Operation Provide Comfort to aid the civilians in the mountains. The U.S. Army, Navy, Air Force, and Marine Corps as well as the British, Dutch, French, Italians, Spanish, Canadians, Germans, Luxembourgers, Belgians, and Australians dispatched forces to participate in this "armed relief effort," led by the U.S. European Command.

Elements of the combined task force, numbering some 20,000 people, including 11,000 U.S. service men and women, mostly from the Army, entered northern Iraq in mid-April. The coalition warned Baghdad not to resist the movement, not to fly aircraft in a "no-fly zone"[77] established north of the 36th parallel, and not to send troops into a "security zone" along the border with Turkey. Having just taken a beating and not inclined to risk another, Baghdad complied. Refugees fleeing to southern Iran and the occupied portion of southern Iraq also

USN DN-ST 92-03363

Amphibious assault ships *Wasp* (LHD 1) (foreground) and *Guadalcanal* (LPH 7) deployed to the harbor at Iskenderum, Turkey, in support of Operation Provide Comfort.

received food, tents, cots, blankets, water, clothing, and medical attention from U.S. and allied forces.[78]

From April to June 1991, a variety of naval forces participated in Provide Comfort. On 9 April, Amphibious Squadron 8, including *Guadalcanal* (LPH 7), *Austin* (LPD 4), and *Charleston* (LKA 13), cut short an amphibious exercise off Sardinia and sailed for Iskenderun, Turkey. The 24th Marine Expeditionary Unit (Special Operations Capable) carried food to the refugee camps in the mountains and conducted security operations in the vicinity of Zakho, Iraq. Contingency Marine Air-Ground Task Force 1-91 was airlifted in from Okinawa and carried out humanitarian relief operations at refugee and relocation camps along the Turkish border. The CH-53E Super Stallions of Navy Combat Support Helicopter Squadron 4 provided transport and cargo service from Incirlik Air Base to the Humanitarian Service Support Base at Silopi, which could not handle fixed-wing operations.

Two Navy special boat unit detachments conducted security patrols and formed a task unit to coordinate radio traffic among the various contingents. Two SEAL platoons conducted long-range reconnaissance missions into Iraq and served as on-call search and rescue units. Seabees from Naval Mobile Construction Battalion 133 supplied food, built roads, and constructed a new village for the Kurds. Navy and Marine Corps EOD detachments cleared minefields in northern Iraq and disposed of vast quantities of ammunition found there. Navy doctors, dentists, and corpsmen assigned to Marine units conducted medical civic action programs and offered medical services at refugee camps and the hospital at Zakho. Aircraft from *Theodore Roosevelt*'s Carrier Air Wing 8 flew tactical reconnaissance, air cover, and close air support for Combined Task Force Provide Comfort. Navy-Marine Liaison Team 10 carried out administrative support from Incirlik. Their combined efforts saved many lives. The last marines left northern Iraq on 15 June 1991. Amphibious Squadron 8 sailed for home four days later.[79]

The presence of coalition troops made the Kurds feel safe enough to return to their homes or to special "way station" camps set up near Zakho. By mid-June almost all of the refugees had left the squalid, mountaintop camps along the Turkey-Iraq border.

Following withdrawal of the remaining ground forces from northern Iraq in mid-July, the coalition established a U.S.-led Combined Task Force named Provide Comfort II in southeastern Turkey to continue pro-

A sailor of Navy Beachmaster Unit 2 and Kurdish refugees work together to erect a tent camp in northern Iraq.

Courtesy of Royal Australian Navy

As part of the continuing maritime interception operation, crewmen of Australian guided missile frigate HMAS *Darwin* prepare to board Iraqi merchant ship *Mansoura I.*

tecting the Kurds. Coalition air forces, including Mediterranean-based carrier air units, continued to patrol the no-fly zone in northern Iraq.[80]

While allied forces aided Iraqi civilians, chilling new facts came to light about Saddam's weapons program. In accordance with UN Security Council Resolution 687, Iraq admitted possession of approximately 1,000 tons of chemical weapons and intermediate chemicals; approximately 11,000 chemical-filled warheads, bombs, and shells; and a significant quantity of weapons-grade uranium. This disclosure, along with evidence uncovered by UN inspection teams, revealed the disturbing truth that the coalition had grossly underestimated the extent and nature of Iraq's past efforts to produce weapons of mass destruction. It became clear that before the Gulf War Saddam had invested enormous sums and devoted a large proportion of Iraq's scientific and technical resources, supplemented by secret foreign purchases, to develop nuclear weapons. Had the coalition not gone to war against Saddam Hussein, he might have had a nuclear weapon sooner than most observers had imagined possible.[81]

Not as frightening as the specter of a nuclear-armed Iraq, but still a matter of concern to the coalition, was the revival of Saddam's conventional military forces. In February 1992, just one year after Desert Storm,

a widely read defense journal reported that Saddam's army then numbered 400,000 men, almost twice the combined total active armed forces
for all six GCC states. The Iraqi forces were organized into 22 to 27 divisions, including at least four Republican Guard divisions. To equip these
units, Iraq could muster some 2,300 tanks, 5,500 other armored vehicles,
1,000 to 2,000 artillery pieces and heavy mortars, and 150 armed helicopters. Although not nearly so formidable as the force Saddam had
commanded in the summer of 1990, this post-Desert Storm Iraqi army
had the potential to develop a strong offensive capability if the UN lifted
the embargo.[82]

These developments made it clear to American policymakers that
military strength remained essential to keeping the peace in the Persian
Gulf region. According to one view, the bottom line of post-Desert
Storm U.S. policy in the gulf region was "the avoidance of a sudden, substantial, and potentially prolonged interruption of oil supplies with its
ultimate consequence of rising prices."[83] Toward these ends, Central
Command developed a postwar theater strategy resting on five pillars:
power projection, forward presence, combined exercises, security assistance, and readiness to fight.[84]

Courtesy of RADM R.A.K. Taylor, USN (Ret.)

Colonel Nasser al-Husainan, commander of Kuwaiti naval forces in the northern gulf
during the war, and his men receive recognition from Rear Admiral Taylor for their impressive performance.

Naval forces were crucial to this strategy. Maritime interception operations, an aspect of forward presence ongoing at this writing, helped prevent Saddam from resurrecting his unconventional weapons program and fully reconstituting his conventional forces. After the war naval forces under Commander U.S. Naval Forces, Central Command, in concert with other UN naval contingents, continued to monitor merchant shipping in the Persian Gulf and the Red Sea.[85] In 1992, for example, coalition ships intercepted 3,127 vessels and boarded 2,871 others, while diverting 157 merchantmen from their scheduled courses.[86] The effort focused on the Red Sea until 1994, when the Persian Gulf became the primary operational area. This refocus occurred because a UN ship inspection team was positioned ashore in al-Aqabah, Jordan, in September and because the Iraqis had cleared hazards to navigation from their ports and waterways and were attempting to smuggle goods out of the country.[87] On 27 May 1996, coalition forces had queried 22,554 ships, intercepted another 12,596, boarded 10,031, and diverted 552 ships from their intended destinations since the operations began in August 1990. As before, COMUSNAVCENT coordinated the effort and convened periodic meetings of coalition naval leaders to work out operating procedures.[88]

After the war Navy and Air Force staffs accorded planning for tactical air and Tomahawk land attack missile strikes a high priority. NAVCENT strike planners maintained close liaison with their counterparts in the carrier battle groups deployed to the region as well as with the Air Force's wing based in Dhahran. They continually reviewed and updated the CENTCOM-generated list of Iraqi military, political, and nuclear-biological-chemical targets.

Tomahawk missiles continued to be vital weapons in the American arsenal, so Admiral Taylor paid close attention to his forces' readiness to employ them. He required all TLAM-armed ships to have CENTCOM missions loaded into their computer files before they entered the theater. Whenever a new Tomahawk "shooter" arrived, Taylor interviewed the ship's commanding officer and tactical action officers to ensure their proficiency with the weapon and its role in current operations.

Taylor and his staff also took action to standardize the planning and targeting procedures followed by the Pacific Fleet and Atlantic Fleet cruise missile support offices in Honolulu and Norfolk. Thereafter, he received uniform strike information from these activities.[89]

Besides the maritime patrol, U.S. naval forces kept the peace by helping to build a collective security structure among America's Arab allies. Since Desert Storm, U.S. Middle East diplomacy has aimed at maintaining a military presence on and around the Arabian Peninsula. At any given time in the area, 75–80 aircraft were based on board a carrier, and more than 200 were deployed ashore in Kuwait, Bahrain, Qatar, and Saudi Arabia; 15–20 warships organized into carrier and amphibious task forces were in the region; and more than 15,000 U.S. military personnel stood ready afloat and ashore to enforce the UN mandate.[90]

American diplomats also encouraged the GCC states to improve their defensive capabilities, integrate their defense plans and programs, and involve external powers such as Egypt, Syria, Britain, and France. To help achieve these goals, the United States concluded defense agreements with Bahrain and Qatar for weapons sales, training, and joint exercises. The Kuwaiti government signed a 10-year security pact with the United States in September 1991, allowing U.S. forces to preposition military equipment and conduct exercises within Kuwait's borders. Although the leaders of these Muslim states routinely opposed the permanent basing of Western ground and air forces in their countries, they enthusiastically supported a strong U.S. military presence in the gulf and an increase in multinational cooperation.[91]

American policy objectives included improving the combat readiness of the region's armed forces as well as their ability to operate as part of a team with Western military units. Toward these ends, successive Commanders U.S. Naval Forces, Central Command and other CENTCOM leaders involved their commands and the GCC states' naval and air forces in a series of combined military exercises.[92] These exercises improved the coalition's ability to project power, promoted forward presence, honed naval combat skills, and fostered improved navy-to-navy relations.[93]

Unlike the huge "Reforger" (Reinforcement of Germany) exercises that NATO held in Europe, most of the exercises COMUSNAVCENT conducted were small, bilateral operations involving only a single ship or a handful of aircraft from the participating Arab country. Taylor likened them to building a wall of security around the region, one brick at a time. Ultimately, he hoped, they would lead to the creation of what he called a "GULFO," a collective security organization akin to NATO. Taking a cue from the Reforger series, he nicknamed the gulf region exercises "Remefer," which stood for "Reinforcement of the Middle East Force," to highlight that connection. In addition to improving the combat readiness of GCC military forces and their interoperability with Western forces, this "family" of exercises demonstrated both the determination and the growing capability of the GCC states to resist aggression.[94]

As during Desert Shield, the Americans had to adapt their training methods to the local situation. In one instance, a gulf nation offered to supply 20 trucks for a bilateral amphibious exercise. Taylor pressed his Arab counterpart to come up with 40 vehicles, which he believed to be

Courtesy of RADM R.A.K. Taylor, USN (Ret.)

Rear Admiral Taylor, Major General Ali Muhamad al-Mumin, Chief of the Kuwait Defence Staff, and other U.S. and Kuwaiti officers observe a postwar combined exercise.

the optimum number for a successful exercise. General Schwarzkopf, whose Vietnam and Middle Eastern experiences taught him patience and accommodation when dealing with allied officers, caught wind of Taylor's efforts and cautioned him to tread lightly. "Ray," he told the admiral, "take the twenty. You're in the art of the doable. You're not in the art of the right." Taylor learned that thinking too big could be counterproductive in a region where most countries had small, relatively inexperienced military forces that might be intimidated by the huge American military arm.[95]

U.S. naval forces and Arab forces conducted a broad range of exercises: replenishment at sea, aerial strike operations, amphibious landings, and equipment demonstrations.[96] American, Kuwaiti, Bahraini, and Qatari naval commandos also practiced together to improve their special skills.[97] On 3 January 1992, U.S. and Saudi forces launched Exercise Red Reef III, the largest such postwar bilateral activity. The training involved almost two weeks of live surface-to-surface and air-to-surface missile firings and amphibious training in the deep waters of the North Arabian Sea and the Persian Gulf. The Royal Saudi Naval Forces, designed for coastal patrol, had never before operated for such a long time on the open sea.[98] The following month, more than 70 U.S. Navy and

U.S. Air Force and Royal Saudi Air Force aircraft executed Exercise Indigo Anvil, the largest bilateral evolution in which the Royal Saudi Air Force had yet participated.[99]

In the year before the Gulf War, American and Arab naval forces carried out only two exercises in the gulf. But, during Admiral Taylor's tour as COMUSNAVCENT, they accomplished at least 125, a reflection of the changing nature of the U.S-Arab security relationship.[100]

The U.S. Navy also sponsored a Gulf Maritime Commanders Conference every three months involving a range of multilateral activities, including interception operations, command post exercises, port visits, development of common operating procedures, sharing of relevant information, and multilateral training programs in such subjects as submarine surveillance and antisubmarine warfare. With regard to the latter preparation, Colonel Ahmed Yousef al-Mullah, Commander Kuwait Naval Forces, observed in November 1993 that after the Gulf War he and other regional naval leaders were concerned about "offensive weapons acquisition programs" being undertaken by "our large non-Gulf Cooperation Council (GCC) neighbors." He stressed that "long-term regional security in the Arabian [Persian] Gulf is vitally dependent on building a strong maritime coalition [and] developing a cooperative, coalition-based strategy, on a defensive" basis.[101]

To support NAVCENT exercises, maritime interception, and other operations in the wake of Desert Storm, American naval leaders increased the resources and responsibilities of the Navy's shore-based logistic establishment in the gulf region.[102] During 1991 the Administrative Support Unit, Bahrain completed a 40,000-square-foot hangar and an office complex at Manama International Airport.[103] That September Admiral Taylor changed the name of the facility to Administrative Support Unit, Southwest Asia to reflect its broader, theater-wide duties.[104] The Navy also further developed the fleet logistics support sites at Hurghada in Egypt, Fujayrah and Jebel Ali in the UAE, and Bahrain.[105] In line with the increased logistic requirements of CENTCOM naval forces, on 1 September 1991 Taylor activated Task Force 153, which he identified as the focal point for Navy and Marine Corps logistics in the Middle East.[106]

Even with these steps to strengthen U.S. naval resources in the CENTCOM theater, the combat power of assigned fleet units was far from overwhelming. After Desert Storm, U.S. naval forces in the gulf usually consisted of command ship *LaSalle*, a carrier battle group, and a destroyer squadron. An amphibious squadron, with its embarked Marine expeditionary unit, operated on a "tether" to COMUSNAVCENT from Commander Seventh Fleet.[107] Taylor considered his fleet to be the first line of defense for America's interests in the gulf region. Indeed, he likened the Navy's role to that of the Army's light armored forces that defended the strategic Fulda Gap in Germany at the height of the U.S.-Soviet confrontation in Europe. As before the Gulf War, these "trip wire" forces would hold the line until reinforcements converged on the region from around the globe.[108]

Meanwhile, Saddam Hussein was steering Iraq toward another collision with the United States and its allies. Since the spring of 1991, the dictator had been playing what pundits called "nuclear cat and mouse," intermittently threatening and interfering with International Atomic Energy Agency and UN weapons inspection teams and backing down only after the coalition promised retaliation. Saddam compiled a notorious record of noncompliance with the Gulf War settlement. The Iraqi government resisted long-term monitoring of weapons programs, refused to accept UN terms for selling oil to pay for aid and reparations payments, failed to account for at least 600 Kuwaitis still held in Iraq, refused to return property stolen from Kuwait, and rejected the UN's demarkation of the border with Kuwait.[109]

The situation became even more ominous when the Iraqi dictator moved to crush Shiite resistance in southeastern Iraq. In May 1992, Saddam launched five or six Republican Guard and regular divisions

USN

An F-14 Tomcat of *Dwight D. Eisenhower*'s VF-143 flies past a destroyed Iraqi radar installation during Operation Southern Watch.

against an estimated 10,000 Shiite rebels and 200,000 civilians who had sought refuge in the trackless marshes near the confluence of the Tigris and Euphrates Rivers. By August, 60,000 Iraqi troops, supported by 70 aircraft, stood poised to butcher the Shiites, as Saddam's forces had done to the Kurds in previous years.[110]

To help stave off disaster for the lightly armed insurgents and unarmed refugees, the UN Security Council adopted Resolution 688, which forbade Saddam from using military aircraft against his own people. To support the resolution, on 26 August 1992 President Bush established a "no-fly zone" in southern Iraq, barring flights of Iraqi aircraft south of the 32d parallel. British Prime Minister John Major and French Foreign Minister Roland Dumas announced that their governments would join the United States in enforcing the restriction.

The next day, U.S. naval and air forces launched Operation Southern Watch. Navy Tomcats and Hornets from *Independence* and Marine Harriers from *Tarawa*, both ships operating in the Persian Gulf, along with Air Force F-117s, F-15s, F-16s, A-10s, and other aircraft began flying combat air patrols and reconnaissance missions over southern Iraq, ready to shoot down any Iraqi aircraft that ventured into the no-fly zone. Soon, British Tornados and French Mirages joined the American planes. Twenty-three U.S. naval vessels and more than 13,000 men and women were on hand in NAVCENT's area of responsibility to support Southern Watch. Baghdad threatened to ignore the ban, but, despite the rhetoric, Iraqi armed forces took no immediate counteractions.[111]

Marine General Joseph P. Hoar, who had succeeded Schwarzkopf as Commander in Chief, Central Command in September 1991, established a task force organization, designated Joint Task Force Southwest Asia (JTFSWA), to manage Southern Watch and to plan for other contingencies. Because CENTAF then operated the greatest number of U.S. aircraft in the theater, Hoar directed Lieutenant General Michael A. Nelson, his Air Force component commander, to lead the task force. Since the carrier battle group assigned to NAVCENT supplied almost as many tactical aircraft, Rear Admiral David N. Rogers, COMUSNAVCENT Rear, became Nelson's deputy. Although Air Force officers predominated in the 200-person JTFSWA staff, which also included U.S. Navy, U.S. Army,[112] Royal Air Force, and French air force officers, naval personnel participated fully in the planning and targeting functions. Navy captains also served as deputies of the key Intelligence (J-2) and Operations (J-3) staff positions.[113]

The task force staff employed an air tasking order "for every flying operation,"[114] and coordinated all air defense, air control, and rescue missions in the operational area; the fleet did not maintain separate control. Moreover, after the Gulf War the Navy dramatically improved the communications and data link systems on board the carriers, so working with the shore-based task force headquarters in refining the ATO presented no major problems.[115] Navy strike planners on board *LaSalle* and the carrier task force assigned to Central Command received the ATO via a Contingency Theater Automated Planning System (CTAPS) terminal. In contrast to the Desert Storm experience, the Navy's involvement in joint air operations and the ATO process did not generate anxiety among naval staff officers. "All the heartburn had finally gone away," Admiral Taylor later observed. "Nobody blinks an eyelash at it [now]."[116]

The Iraqis soon provided an opportunity to test the new JTFSWA organization. In early September 1992, Navy EA-6B Prowler aircraft and other sources detected a rise in Iraqi air defense activity within the no-fly zone and an increased tempo of Iraqi air operations above the 32d parallel. Allied forces responded to this threat with a show of force to preempt any Iraqi moves to disrupt Southern Watch. On the 9th, U.S., British, and French planes in combined formation for the first time flooded the air over southern Iraq. The threatening Iraqi military activity soon subsided.[117]

As the air patrol effort continued, on 16 September the *Ranger* battle group relieved *Independence* and her escorts on station in the central

USN

An F/A-18 Hornet of *Dwight D. Eisenhower*'s VFA-136 heads for a no-fly zone patrol over Iraq in Operation Southern Watch.

Persian Gulf. The next day aircraft from Carrier Air Wing 2 joined Southern Watch units operating over Iraq.[118] In early November, the Tomahawk-armed attack submarine *Topeka* (SSN 754) added a new dimension to the Navy's presence in the littoral areas of the world when she joined *Ranger*'s battle group. This deployment marked the first instance of a nuclear-powered U.S. submarine operating in the shallow waters of the Persian Gulf.[119]

Iraqi aggression against the Shiites and Operation Southern Watch precipitated another step in the evolution of NAVCENT. In October 1992, Admiral Kelso finally instituted the major command change recommended after the war by Arthur, Taylor, Schwarzkopf, and later, Hoar. A three-star flag officer would be permanently assigned as naval component commander to CINCCENT and he would be headquartered in the Central Command theater.[120]

On 19 October 1992, Vice Admiral Douglas Katz, who ably led the *America* carrier battle group during Desert Storm, succeeded Rear Admiral Taylor as COMUSNAVCENT. The change of command ceremony, held in Bahrain on board *LaSalle*, "the White Ghost of the North Arabian Coast," symbolized the Navy's recognition of the importance of tradition represented by the Middle East Force. It also signified the Navy's acknowledgement of the need for change, embodied in a fully developed CENTCOM naval component command organization.[121] Another step was taken on 1 July 1995, when the Defense Department established the U.S. Fifth Fleet with the mission to operate in the Central Command area of responsibility. After 1 January 1996 this AOR included the entire Arabian Sea and a portion of the Indian Ocean running south from Pakistan to near Diego Garcia and west from Diego Garcia to the coast of southern Kenya.[122]

Admiral Katz's NAVCENT received its baptism of fire toward the end of 1992, when Saddam once again stirred up trouble with military provocations in the gulf region. Diplomats and Middle East experts speculated about Saddam's motives for causing this friction. Some suggested that Saddam wanted to ensure that the world did not forget his country's "plight," or to improve the readiness of his armed forces, or to distract his destitute people with a foreign adventure. Many believed that he was "thumbing his nose" at his nemesis George Bush, who had lost the 1992 presidential election.[123]

Whatever Saddam's motives, trouble started brewing in late December, when the Iraqis positioned and activated antiaircraft missile batteries south of the 32d parallel. They also warned UN pilots flying over Iraq that they would shoot down any intruding planes. Then, the antiaircraft batteries fired on allied aircraft over both no-fly zones. On 6 January 1993, shortly before turning over power to newly elected

President William J. Clinton, George Bush delivered an ultimatum to Saddam: remove the missiles from the southern no-fly zone within 48 hours or suffer the consequences. The Iraqis replied by expropriating four Silkworm missiles and other military equipment from their former naval base at Umm Qasr, a portion of which had been ceded to Kuwait as part of the Gulf War settlement. They also refused permission for an aircraft carrying UN weapons inspectors to land in Baghdad.[124]

The allies responded quickly. On 13 January 1993, 35 U.S. Navy warplanes from the carrier *Kitty Hawk* (CV 63), which had arrived in the Persian Gulf on New Year's Day, along with 75 U.S. Air Force, British, and French aircraft, attacked four air defense command and control centers and two concentrations of SA-3 surface-to-air missiles in the southern no-fly zone. The Iraqis fired at least four missiles at American planes, but, to avoid HARM attack, did not activate their targeting radars. All of the missiles missed. The allies were no more successful. Because the allied aircraft released their cluster bombs, gravity bombs, and laser guided bombs from above 10,000 feet in anticipation of Iraqi antiaircraft fire, they only destroyed one mobile battery.[125]

The strike did not convince Saddam to yield. On 17 January, Iraqi antiaircraft artillery, missile batteries, and fighters once again threatened

To maintain the UN coalition's deterrent posture after Desert Storm, carrier *Nimitz* and command ship *LaSalle* steam in the ever-volatile Persian Gulf.

allied planes, this time in northern Iraq. The hostile aircraft repeatedly darted back and forth across the 36th parallel in an attempt to draw allied planes toward surface-to-air missile batteries just below the boundary. No allied airmen took the bait.

This time, the UN responded immediately. Later that day Aegis cruiser *Cowpens* (CG 63) and destroyers *Hewitt* (DD 966) and *Stump* (DD 978), operating in the Persian Gulf, and destroyer *Caron* steaming in the Red Sea, successfully launched 42 Tomahawk cruise missiles against a multibillion-dollar factory complex in Zaafaraniyah, about eight miles southeast of Baghdad. This facility contained computer-operated precision machine tools that had been used to enrich uranium for Iraq's nuclear weapons program. At least 30 Tomahawks got through, hitting every one of the targeted structures. The TLAMs destroyed four buildings, severely damaged two, and moderately damaged one. U.S. Air Force F-15Es also severely damaged the Tallil Station Air Operations Center with 2,000-pound bombs.[126]

Saddam had had enough. The next day, the eve of President Clinton's inauguration, Baghdad declared a cease-fire and informed the United Nations that it would no longer attempt to restrict flights of UN weapons inspectors inside Iraq.[127]

Only temporarily chastened, that spring Saddam sent an assassination team into Kuwait to kill former President Bush, who was then visiting the emirate. The National Command Authorities called on NAV-CENT to increase the pressure on the Iraqi dictator. On 26 June 1993, cruiser *Chancellorsville* (CG 62) in the Persian Gulf and destroyer *Peterson* (DD 969) in the Red Sea successfully launched 23 Tomahawks against an intelligence headquarters in the Iraqi capital. Even though three missiles, perhaps deflected by enemy fire, hit nearby residences, killing nine Iraqi civilians, the TLAMs scored at least 13 hits and severely damaged the targeted buildings. Without risking any pilots to death or capture, with their associated political costs, the Navy in the gulf once again enforced Washington's will to restrain Saddam.[128]

More than a year later, in the fall of 1994, Saddam began moving Republican Guard armored and other forces toward Iraq's border with Kuwait. On 6 October, American intelligence analysts concluded that Iraq would be capable of attacking Kuwait with five divisions in seven days. President Clinton immediately ordered the deployment of U.S. ground, air, and naval forces to the gulf in Operation Vigilant Warrior. On 7 October, he announced that U.S. forces would resist Iraqi aggression. The next day *Leyte Gulf* was in position to launch Tomahawks against Iraq. The *George Washington* (CVN 73) battle group, operating off Bosnia, immediately got underway and headed for the Middle Eastern trouble spot. After a fast transit of the Eastern Mediterranean and the Suez

Canal, the *Nimitz*-class, nuclear-powered carrier and her escorts joined the naval forces already in position in the theater. These forces were 10 surface ships and an attack submarine, with hundreds of Tomahawks among them, and the *Tripoli* amphibious ready group, with the 15th MEU(SOC) embarked. During this period 6,400 naval and 301 Air Force personnel reinforced the 6,600 sailors and marines and 4,000 Air Force men and women already in the Central Command area of responsibility. Army ground troops in the United States prepared for a trans-world air-lift and the Military Sealift Command's prepositioning ships at Diego Garcia and Guam set sail for the gulf with full loads of ammunition, equipment, and supplies.[129]

During the first days of the crisis, Marine forces constituted more than 50 percent of the American ground troops in the gulf. Moreover, during the first two weeks of the crisis, Navy and Marine Corps units accounted for 60 percent of the combat-ready U.S. aircraft in the region. These forces were not overwhelming, but their quick reaction to the Iraqi threat sufficiently convinced Saddam of American resolve. Hence, long before major U.S. land-based air (delayed by overflight and basing problems) and ground forces reached the theater, aerial intelligence sighted Iraqi trains carrying hundreds of armored vehicles headed away from the Kuwait border.[130]

Saddam Hussein's postwar provocations continued to upset the peace of the Persian Gulf region, but the quick and effective U.S. military response in each episode, routinely involving U.S. Naval Forces, Central Command, prevented a return to the unfavorable balance of power that existed in August 1990. The UN coalition's victory in Desert Storm, continuing vigilance, and readiness to resist Iraqi aggression in the postwar era paid huge dividends for stability in the Persian Gulf.

CHAPTER 8

Summary

MAINTAINING POLITICAL STABILITY AND THE free flow of oil to the global economy have been the overarching objectives of U.S. foreign policy in the Persian Gulf for almost half a century. The U.S. Navy has been one of the primary instruments of that policy, in both peace and war.

Prologue to the War

Between the establishment of the Middle East Force in 1949 and the outbreak of war in 1990, U.S. naval forces protected America's interests in the region and helped develop international support for U.S. foreign policy goals. The continuous, albeit limited, American military presence in the Persian Gulf demonstrated to potential aggressors that in any confrontation they faced the prospect of war with a superpower.

The Navy's extended presence in the region generated political support for the United States among the economically vital but militarily vulnerable states on the Arabian Peninsula. Local leaders recognized the value of having U.S. warships positioned between them and their often bellicose northern neighbors. They also came to consider naval forces that operated in international waters or required only minimal support facilities ashore as the most appropriate expression of U.S. ties to their countries. Their devout Muslim populations were not likely to accept large, predominantly Christian, and non-Arab air and ground forces operating from inland bases.

The U.S. Navy's performance during the Iran-Iraq War of 1980–1988 strengthened these relations. The carrier and battleship task forces that operated in the North Arabian Sea and the cruisers, destroyers, and mine countermeasures ships of Joint Task Force Middle East in the gulf were largely responsible for maintaining the flow of oil from the producing countries of the region. The fleet also prevented Iran's military power from advancing across the gulf. These positive actions helped dissipate the memory of Washington's lack of resolve during the Tehran hostage crisis and the Lebanese civil war in the early 1980s, when significant "doubt had developed about the reliability of the US security commitment."[1] The local Arab states would not forget this American constancy when Iraq threatened regional stability in 1990.

The Navy's long experience as a military shield in the gulf also fostered closer relations between the United States and its Western allies. Multinational operations during the "Tanker War" that involved naval units from the United States, Great Britain, France, Italy, Belgium, and the Netherlands enhanced a sense of joint responsibility for the protection of international shipping and maintenance of the Persian Gulf oil trade. Hence, America's traditional allies were well disposed to President Bush's August 1990 proposal for international military action against Iraq.

Not only did the Earnest Will tanker escort operation highlight growing American will to oppose threats to U.S. interests in the Persian Gulf but the Navy's increasing ability to support forceful action. More than four decades of preparing for war with the Soviet Union and engaging in Cold War operations had created a Navy of formidable fighting power. The experience had spurred development of the most advanced ships, aircraft, weapons, and equipment.

The Tomahawk land attack missile, intended originally to carry nuclear warheads deep into the USSR, was equally capable of delivering conventional munitions against other nations. *Missouri* and *Wisconsin* had been recommissioned in the 1980s because of their ability to employ cruise missiles, but the battleships' existing 16-inch guns were also ideal for bombardment missions. The sophisticated Aegis defensive system, designed to frustrate multidimensional Soviet attacks on the fleet, could handle lesser threats with great confidence. The Composite Warfare Commander concept, designed so carrier task force officers could control air strikes against distant Soviet targets and also defend their formation from enemy air, surface, and submarine attack, was also valid for combat against regional foes.

The Cold War experience had inspired the U.S. Navy and allied navies to develop common operational and tactical procedures and compatible weapons and communication systems. After decades of combined exercises around the globe, the British, Argentine, Australian, and other navies were adept at operating in conjunction with the American fleet. Having coordinated with Western European military authorities in the loading, transportation, and delivery of materiel to NATO armies numerous times during the Cold War, the Navy's

Military Sealift Command was reasonably well prepared to handle major transoceanic operations.

Equally important to the readiness of the U.S. Navy in 1990 was its combat experience in the regional wars in Korea and Vietnam and lesser hostilities in such places as Lebanon, Grenada, Libya, the Persian Gulf, and Panama. U.S. naval air forces had become skilled at projecting power ashore and sinking fast attack craft. Sailors and marines were no strangers to amphibious warfare during the Cold War and the gunners on board the *Iowa*-class battleships had honed the skills needed for accurate bombardment and naval gunfire support. U.S. naval forces also refined tactics and techniques for oceangoing patrol operations involving Navy, Coast Guard, and allied air and sea forces. The operations of naval special warfare, harbor defense, explosive ordnance disposal, and salvage units also reflected the Navy' experience in the regional conflicts of the Cold War.

The near loss of carrier *Forrestal* off Vietnam and frigates *Stark* and *Samuel B. Roberts* in the Persian Gulf to fire, missiles, and mines, respectively, reinforced the importance of thorough damage control training. Cruiser *Vincennes*' missile shootdown of an Iranian airliner had driven home in a few terrible minutes the vital importance of sound human judgment to fleet air defense. By August 1990 the officers and bluejackets manning the fleet's Aegis and NTU antiair warfare systems had been well trained in operating the equipment and coordinating their actions with Air Force E-3 AWACS units.

Great Britain's withdrawal of military forces from "east of Suez," Iran's revolutionary excesses, and the Soviet Union's maritime penetration of the Indian Ocean and invasion of Afghanistan prompted the Carter and Reagan administrations, and the Navy, to evaluate their resources for mounting military operations in the CENTCOM area. They were not heartened by the findings. There were no major U.S.-run ports, airfields, or logistic bases in the region and the distances from the East and West Coasts of the United States could hardly have been greater. Armed with this understanding, the defense establishment strengthened the Carter Doctrine and the Reagan Corollary during the 1980s by creating maritime prepositioning squadrons, with combat-loaded ships deployed in the Atlantic, Pacific, and Indian Oceans. Marine forces based around the globe would be airlifted into the theater to take possession of the weapons and supplies delivered by the MPS ships.

Deploying Marine rapid-reaction units to the combat arena was only one aspect of the sealift mission in a Persian Gulf conflict. The Navy was also responsible for transporting from the United States and other global sites an expeditionary army (minus the troops) of mechanized infantry, armored, and air assault divisions. The Navy then had to maintain the fighting forces in the field. To handle these tasks, the naval service administered the expenditure of over $7 billion worth of construction for the most modern ships, including the eight advanced, fast sealift ships. The Navy also worked with the Maritime Administration to ensure that the Ready Reserve Force fleet was prepared to sustain a major U.S. overseas conflict.

During the four decades of the Cold War that preceded the crisis with Iraq, the Navy developed a logistic support system that enabled its own combat forces to remain continuously deployed in waters far from the United States. Forward naval bases in the Western Pacific, the Mediterranean, and the Indian Ocean were important to this global establishment. The fleet, however, was not tied to shore bases, as it demonstrated during 1980s operations in the Indian Ocean and the Persian Gulf. A contingent of mobile logistic ships provided combatants, via underway replenishment, with the wherewithal to fight and remain on the line.

Navy Shortcomings

The Navy did not always take advantage of the Cold War experience, and this neglect hampered its effectiveness in the crisis with Iraq. The mine warfare operations in Korea and Vietnam did not set off alarm bells as they should have. The relative ease with which the Navy's MCM helicopters and surface units seemed to handle their duties masked the inadequacy of these platforms and their command and control establishment.

Throughout the Cold War, the Navy relied on its European allies to carry the burden of coastal mine countermeasures while it prepared for blue water combat. The British, Belgian, French, and other navies built and put to sea the most advanced ships and equipment and the most intensively trained sailors. To prepare for a global conflagration with the Soviet Union this made sense, but the Navy had to expect it would be committed to coastal operations in the post-Cold War era.

The damage by mines to merchant ship SS *Bridgeton* and frigate *Samuel B. Roberts* during 1987 and 1988 in the Persian Gulf briefly focused the Navy's attention on mine warfare. As a result, the fleet refined mine hunting and sweeping tactics and procedures, and tested some new equipment. These efforts and the success of American counter mine actions during the last months of the Iran-Iraq War, however, fostered a complacent attitude in the Navy about its mine countermeasures capability. Consequently, the Navy was little better prepared in 1990 to deal with sea mines than it had been in 1987.

The Navy's experience confronting the Soviet threat did not spur the service to adjust its post-Cold War relationship to the U.S. command structure. Enactment of the Goldwater-Nichols legislation in 1986 increased the operational control by theater commanders (whatever their service) over naval and other component forces, but the Navy resisted any weakening of its traditional autonomy. Naval leaders were steeped in Mahanian operational concepts that envisioned flag officers directing grand fleet actions at sea, as they had in the cataclysmic World War II battles of Midway, Philippine Sea, and Leyte Gulf. As embodied in the Maritime Strategy of the late 1980s, fleet commanders would control the aircraft and missiles they dispatched from their ships against the Soviet heartland.

Especially with regard to the Central Command, the Navy was not interested in long-term, fixed joint relationships. During Operation Earnest Will the naval command setup proved inadequate. To correct it, Washington combined the small staff of Commander Middle East Force with the new, still Navy-led, Joint Task Force Middle East. Soon after Iraq and Iran ceased their fire, however, the mission-oriented, short-term task force headquarters was disestablished.

The experience of the Iran-Iraq War and the prospect of further conflict in the Persian Gulf suggested that the Navy needed a more permanent and capable command function in the area and a stronger, more durable relationship with the theater headquarters. Naval leaders in Washington, however, resumed their reliance on the Middle East Force for routine gulf operations and kept the low-ranking and understaffed Commander Naval Forces, Central Command in Hawaii, far removed from both the Persian Gulf and CENTCOM headquarters in Tampa, Florida. The Navy expected that in the event of another conflict in the gulf the admirals leading the unified commands in the Atlantic and the Pacific would temporarily assign their naval forces to the Army or Marine general heading Central Command. In essence, the fleet's warships, especially its carriers, would remain under Navy control.

The Navy assigned few representatives to the staffs developing Operation Plan 1002 and taking part in Exercise Internal Look so the service was not fully attuned to Schwarzkopf's philosophy of command and his views with regard to a conflict in the CENTCOM theater. The Navy's reluctance to relinquish control of its forces to CINCCENT and to interact with the Tampa headquarters lessened the command's readiness to respond to Saddam's invasion of Kuwait.

Hardening the Shield

The U.S. Navy's presence in the Persian Gulf might have limited the scope of Saddam Hussein's aggressive activity in the waters of the gulf, but it certainly did not deter his attack on Kuwait. Ivory Justice, the July 1990 exercise ordered by Washington, involved only two American frigates, several Air Force aircraft, and a few jet fighters of the United Arab Emirates. It could not be called a show of force. A swift and simultaneous movement of the *Independence* carrier battle group and other naval forces toward the Strait of Hormuz might have made a difference. National security policymakers, including General Powell, however, did not want a spotlight on American military power. When their low-key approach to the crisis was coupled with Ambassador Glaspie's muted warning to Saddam, it was hardly surprising that the Iraqi generalissimo felt he had little to fear from American arms.

While the fleet's presence in the region did not deter Saddam's attack on Kuwait, it did make clear to the Iraqi dictator that further advances could cost him dearly. In hindsight, Saddam probably had no intention of invading Saudi Arabia, but the inveterate risk-taker might have launched such an attack if powerful U.S. naval and air forces were not close at hand. Within days of the invasion of Kuwait, carrier aircraft were in range to help defend the Arabian Peninsula.

On 15 August, just two weeks after Saddam's assault on Kuwait, three MPS ships disembarked at al-Jubayl the equipment and supplies of a Marine expeditionary brigade. The troops arrived by air the next day. This response was quick, but not as quick as it should have been. The movement forward of these U.S. naval forces needed the consent of no other nation and could have been ordered shortly after the Iraqi invasion of Kuwait. General Powell and others in Washington, however, concerned about Saudi sensitivities, waited until 7 August and the official start of Desert Shield to order the action.

On the 25th, the same day that General Hopkins declared his 7th MEB ready for combat, the troops, armored vehicles, and 30 days of ammunition and supplies of another MEB began arriving at al-Jubayl. In short order, these two brigades were ready to fight to hold open the ports and airfields into which streamed an increasing flood of Army troops and Air Force tactical squadrons. The speedy deployment of the Marine expeditionary brigades to the distant operational theater affirmed the soundness of the maritime prepositioning concept and the wisdom of devoting considerable sealift and airlift resources to the program.

During the tense days of August 1990, many observers concluded that Saudi Arabia was at great risk from a massive invasion by Iraqi armored forces and loss of oil wells and refineries in the eastern reaches of the country. There was much less appreciation of the serious threat posed by the Iraqi military machine to the sea lanes of the Persian Gulf and the Saudi and other GCC ports on its south shore. With 750 combat aircraft and approximately 165 naval vessels, 13 equipped with antiship missiles, the Iraqis had the ability to attack merchant ships in the waters of the gulf and to wreak havoc in the congested GCC harbors. Saddam's jets could have reached the shipping lanes of the central gulf and the coastal sites within minutes from their bases in Kuwait and Iraq. Denied use of these vital ports, the UN coalition could not have deployed an expeditionary army to the Arabian Peninsula as quickly as it did.

The Iranians possessed similar military resources and might have used the UN crisis with Saddam to close the Strait of Hormuz or, as they had during the Iran-Iraq War, threaten international shipping.

Neither Baghdad nor Tehran initiated hostilities of that sort during Desert Shield, and for many reasons might not have. But, the powerful naval force that the coalition rapidly concentrated in the Persian Gulf and contiguous waters could only have counseled Iraqi and Iranian caution. Land-based aircraft controlled by U.S. warships formed an aerial umbrella over the gulf. On the surface east of the Strait of Hormuz steamed American aircraft carriers protected by U.S., British, Canadian, Dutch, and Australian cruisers, destroyers, and frigates. Many of these warships were equipped with Aegis and other state-of-the-art radar systems, electronic countermeasures gear, surface-to-air missiles, and Phalanx close-in weapons systems. In coastal waters, GCC naval forces stayed on the lookout for fast craft or commercial vessels whose crews or passengers might have had hostile intent. Navy harbor defense, special warfare, and explosive ordnance disposal units, and Coast Guard port security units formed the final maritime line of defense in the key ports of Manama, al-Jubayl, and ad-Dammam.

The coalition's ability to counter enemy sea mines was a weak link in this defensive chain. Until mid-September, when British *Hunt*-class mine-hunting ships arrived on station, UN ships were vulnerable to Iraqi mines. The four-ship American MCM flotilla, carried to the gulf in a slow-moving vessel and shunted from port to port in search of an operating base was not ready for action until long after the Iraqi invasion of Kuwait.

The UN coalition was able to dispatch strong ground forces to Saudi Arabia because of the absence of any enemy opposition to seaborne movement. Friendly control of the sea, however, is not a given; it has to be established. Throughout August, fleet units deployed in the Mediterranean and the Western Pacific weighed anchor and converged on the Middle Eastern hot spot. By the end of the month Naval Forces, Central Command consisted of two carrier battle groups (which operated most of the 319 Navy and Marine aircraft then in the theater), a pair of battleships, and 25 other naval vessels, many of them armed with Tomahawk land attack missiles. British, French, and Arab surface combatants complemented this American fleet.

As some U.S. and allied warships steamed at flank speed for the Persian Gulf, other units replaced them in the Eastern Mediterranean, the Red Sea, and the North Arabian Sea. Even though some governments, the German in particular, were reluctant to involve their military forces in the confrontation with Iraq, no political commitment was required to demonstrate support for the UN stand by positioning naval forces in waters traversed by the ships of the allied expeditionary army.

These latter deployments were prudent, because the governments of Libya, Sudan, and Yemen, which fervently supported Saddam's stand against the West, had the ability to hazard the UN response to Iraq's invasion. The armed forces of these nations boasted more than 600 combat aircraft and a large number of missile-armed surface ships, submarines, and mine warfare vessels. These forces, or explosives-laden fast boats crewed by terrorists, could have attacked the sealift ships moving through the several constricted waterways around the Persian Gulf. But, with American and other combatants just off their shores, and carrier and land-based aircraft flying nearby, Qaddaffi and his ideological cohorts did not interfere with the UN sea line of communications.

Hence, U.S. and coalition naval forces helped ensure the success of allied fortunes in Desert Shield by helping to deter further Iraqi aggression on land and sea and by establishing control of the oceans that gave the coalition access to the Arabian Peninsula.

Increasing the Pressure on Saddam

The multinational embargo patrol, a naval blockade in all but name, proved to be a valuable weapon in the UN-U.S. arsenal. It did not compel Saddam to give up his Kuwait conquest, as its most fervent proponents hoped. But, the embargo patrol prevented the Iraqis from filling their war chest with imported aircraft, ships, missiles, ammunition, and the other necessities of combat.

Of equal importance, the patrol operation enabled the international community to employ *military force* against Saddam even if the UN member states were not yet ready to *wage war* against him. Most coalition governments readily allowed their navies to take part in offshore operations that involved minimal risk of casualties or political commitment.

The successful conduct of the embargo patrol during Desert Shield made it easier for participating Western governments to persuade citizens that their naval forces were engaged in a righteous international effort. In addition, the patrol demonstrated to the Arab world that only in a measured and discriminating fashion were Western and Christian military contingents likely to use force against other Arabs. Ultimately, it also allowed President Bush and other world leaders to argue that war was justified to liberate Kuwait, since the restrained application of military force represented by the embargo patrol failed to budge the Iraqi dictator. In short, the naval patrol helped the UN make the transition from peace to war.

Some analysts contend that U.S. forces operated as discrete national contingents during the gulf crisis, so the UN effort cannot be described as a truly multinational, combined military enterprise. While there may be merit to this argument with regard to ground and air forces, it is far from accurate with regard to naval forces. Most American leaders echoed Admiral Zlatoper's observation that the integration of the allied naval forces was a "major success [an] untold story."[2]

This was especially true of the embargo patrol. American leaders convened monthly conferences of the naval forces taking part in the patrol and suggested various operational approaches. After years of interaction, the Americans had learned how to lead NATO and other naval commanders while respecting their individual national requirements. Many of the participating navies followed U.S. direction, if allowed to do so by their home governments. With a few exceptions, cooperation and consensus among the naval contingents characterized command and control of the embargo patrol. That relationship worked well in the Persian Gulf crisis. The situation did not require absolute operational control of the forces involved.

Individual patrol sectors in the Red Sea, Arabian Sea, and Persian Gulf were the responsibility of one or more navies, but interception task groups routinely comprised ships and aircraft from several nations. Non-American officers often served as on-scene commanders. It was not unusual for U.S. and Australian frigates, British Royal Marines, or other UN naval forces to cooperate in combined, high-seas interception operations. The participants worked out common procedures for identifying, hailing, stopping, and boarding suspect merchant ships and limiting the risk of hostilities.

Normally, the presence of two or three warships, backed up by attack aircraft and armed helicopters loaded with combat-ready naval commandos and marines, was enough to stop a merchantman. But, the terms "vertical insertion" and "fast-roping" entered the lexicon of maritime patrol operations when the international team discovered that they could carry out their mission without the adverse political consequences associated with shooting up or sinking a ship that refused to stop for inspection. As the *Ibn Khaldoon* "peace ship" incident revealed, allied naval commanders had learned the importance of using minimal force to defuse antiwar demonstrations, which carried great potential for turning international opinion against the UN effort. The upshot of this effort was that a truly multinational force carried out the UN mandate and completely stopped Iraq's overseas commerce.

Conversely, the sea became a major highway over which flowed the war-making resources of a huge allied expeditionary army. As during the wars in Korea and Vietnam, sealift remained the only way to deploy large forces overseas quickly and efficiently and then to sustain them. In little more than seven months the Navy's Military Sealift Command deployed from the United States and elsewhere to the sands of Saudi Arabia 95 percent of the armored vehicles, attack helicopters, wheeled transport, heavy weapons, equipment, ammunition, and supplies for 10 combat divisions and many smaller formations.

The Navy's long-term preparation for the sealift mission bore fruit during Desert Shield. The specially designed fast sealift ships came on line as intended, loaded out Army armored vehicles and helicopters in American ports, sped across the Atlantic and the Mediterranean, and delivered their high-priority material to the operational theater. The ships returned to the United States and repeated the round-trip passage as many as seven times during Desert Shield. The saga of *Antares'* first Atlantic passage notwithstanding, the fast sealift ships proved to be the stars of the operation, carrying 10 percent of all Desert Shield cargo. More important, they accomplished their primary purpose, which was to put heavy Army units on the ground quickly.

The Ready Reserve Force fleet did its job but not without difficulty. The RRF lacked critical crewmen skilled in the operation of machinery in the older ships, some of which had not been adequately maintained. As a result, many of the crews had difficulty firing up the boilers of their ships, getting them to designated ports of embarkation on time, and keeping them in operation once underway. The RRF included plenty of older break-bulk freighters, but not enough roll on/roll off ships. Since the United States dominated the seas, however, foreign chartering firms did not hesitate to satisfy the American request for more ships. Foreign charters, faster to ports of embarkation and cheaper to operate than the American merchantmen, quickly made up the shortfall. Moreover, Japan, South Korea, and other maritime nations aided the sealift effort with their own merchant fleets.

Port operations in the United States, Europe, and Saudi Arabia that involved the joint Transportation Command, Navy and Army commands in the United States and overseas, and the governments and military forces of many European and Arab nations were anything but smooth. Some ships arrived late at ports of embarkation while others arrived ahead of their cargoes. At several sites the port groups took too long to load ships, stowed cargo improperly, or scattered the equipment of a single ground unit among a number of ships.

The combined efforts of many people helped alleviate most of these problems. The military and civilian officials responsible for the sealift effort exploited their previous preparation and training to break log jams quickly and decisively. These officials had anticipated supporting NATO forces battling the Warsaw Pact armies on the central German plain, but they adapted their plans and operations to the Desert Storm mission.

An important reason for the success of the sealift operation was that the UN coalition's European and Arab members made their sophisticated transportation establishments available. The Germans, Belgians, Dutch, and GCC countries put their highways, railroads, canals, and port facilities at the disposal of the U.S. logistic commands. Even former Warsaw Pact nations pitched in with resources. With an enormous capacity to unload and store cargo, Saudi ports easily handled the tanks, armored personnel carriers, and pallets of ammunition and supplies that the MSC ships disgorged at the end of their journey. Unfortunately, neither the Army nor the Marine logistic commands ashore had enough trucks to transport armored vehicles, troops, and supplies to the front. Once again, international support proved a godsend. The Saudis and Japanese supplied the coalition with hundreds of heavy equipment transporters, trucks, and other vehicles. This timely assistance enabled General Schwarzkopf's logisticians to complete the deployment of the half-million strong allied expeditionary force to the northern Saudi border in time for the G-Day offensive into Kuwait. Along with the Military Airlift Command, which flew American troops into the battle zone, MSC deployed a huge field army half way around the globe in little more than seven months.

Gearing Up for Battle

The Navy and the other U.S. armed services could have fought and beaten the Iraqis long before January 1991, but the task would have been harder and the cost higher. The Navy, like the other services, used the six months offered by Desert Shield to marshal powerful fleet units in the theater, fully arm and supply them, and bring active and reserve sailors and marines to fighting pitch.

Even with six months to prepare for war, the Navy experienced significant operational difficulties, especially in the area of command and control. In keeping with its previous insistence on providing the flag officer who would lead CINCCENT's naval forces in a major crisis in the gulf, in early August the Navy nominated the Pacific Command's Commander Seventh Fleet to be COMUSNAVCENT. With no viable alternative, the Secretary of Defense approved the proposal. An emergency did not develop, but precious time was lost before Admiral Mauz, his flagship, and much of his staff could deploy to the operational arena and get acclimated to the new operational environment.

During much of Desert Shield the Navy's top leadership saw the Persian Gulf, where the majority of the carriers would steam and where the commander of all CENTCOM naval forces hoisted his pennant, as its exclusive operational arena. Admirals Kelso and Mauz saw COMUSNAVCENT more as a fleet commander, executing a short-term mission than as General Schwarzkopf's component commander. Thus, Mauz remained on board his flagship in the gulf and continued to manage his Western Pacific responsibilities as Commander Seventh Fleet. He did not establish a close personal relationship with Schwarzkopf or Horner, his air commander. The representative whom Mauz posted to Riyadh late in Desert Shield lacked the rank and aviation background to have any real impact on Schwarzkopf or Horner. The small group of talented naval officers assigned to the CENTCOM staff and to the staff planning the air campaign were greatly outnumbered by their Air Force and Army counterparts.

Admiral Kelso and his staff in Washington were not convinced that the UN coalition would initiate hostilities in mid-January 1991. Hence, the CNO authorized the 1 December 1990 relief of Mauz by Arthur so the former could take up a new billet in the United States. This late change of command gave Admiral Arthur little time to get oriented to his forces, put his stamp on their direction, or prepare them for a war that most non-Navy observers believed close at hand. Arthur immediately appreciated the need for a closer, personal link with the theater commander. He also recognized that since the war against Iraq would be a joint campaign fought primarily on and over land, he needed to strengthen the Navy's presence on the staffs in Riyadh and better integrate naval forces into the campaign plan.

It was already too late. With the war liable to begin at any time, Arthur had no wish for his command to be caught in the middle of a headquarters shift or staff reorganization. Schwarzkopf and Arthur remained dissatisfied with the preparations made by Mauz and his staff for participation in the joint-service, multinational campaign. Fortunately for the Navy, Arthur, a combat-tested leader, possessed all the qualities needed to put Naval Forces, Central Command on a solid war footing.

U.S. naval forces trained intensively for combat operations during Desert Shield. Afloat forces carried out numerous antisurface, antiair, naval gunfire support, combat search and rescue, and amphibious exercises with other coalition units. Central Command put on the several highly publicized amphibious exercises to divert Iraqi attention from the desert flank and to prepare Navy and Marine units for actual amphibious operations, should they be necessary.

In some cases, ongoing operations added a strong dose of realism to this training. Formations of Iraqi aircraft went "feet wet" and briefly headed for the fleet on numerous occasions during Desert Shield. Aegis and NTU cruisers and Navy E-2C, Marine and Canadian F/A-18, and Air Force AWACs aircraft reacted quickly to the aerial threat. The routinely fast and coordinated response by strong UN antiair units during Desert Shield may have been one reason why the Iraqis launched only a single over-water attack during Desert Storm.

The Navy's training for participation in the Desert Storm air campaign, however, was a mixed bag. Officers and enlisted personnel of Admiral Mixson's Red Sea carriers, in theater for a long time and dependent on Air Force tanker and AWACs support for the overland approach to Iraq, worked with their Air Force counterparts to fit Navy operations into the joint air campaign plan. The *Saratoga* and *John F. Kennedy* attack, fighter, and electronic countermeasures aircraft rehearsed strike missions, large-scale aerial refueling missions, and other operations with comparable Air Force units. This interaction minimized wartime differences between Battle Force Yankee and the Air Force.

The carriers of Admiral March's Persian Gulf force were less well prepared to take part in the joint air campaign against Iraq. During much of Desert Shield, Battle Force Zulu air units carried out unilateral exercises in the North Arabian Sea. Since March's air units would approach their targets in southeastern Iraq and Kuwait primarily over water, they considered it more important to coordinate their operations with Navy aerial tankers and E-2C aircraft than with similar Air Force units. March had little face-to-face contact with the leaders and staff officers in Riyadh. Battle Force Zulu's lack of adequate training for coordinated, joint-service air operations complicated the Navy's participation in the air war.

While a sooner move of the carrier battle force into the Persian Gulf might have improved the coordination of air operations, naval leaders were rightly cautious about hazarding their capital ships in such a way. When asked just before Desert Shield about the feasibility of operating carriers in the gulf, commanding officers of ships that had made brief forays into those confined waters in the 1980s recommended against it. Admiral Mauz was concerned throughout Desert Shield about the threat from Iraqi missile-armed aircraft, fast attack vessels, and shore-based Silkworm missiles, and Iran's potential for mischief. As with Generals Powell and Schwarzkopf, the Vietnam experience had a marked influence on Mauz, Arthur, March, and numerous other naval commanders. They abhorred the waste of lives and resources that characterized the failed war in Southeast Asia and were determined to limit needless risks to their sailors, marines, ships, and aircraft. Moreover, they understood the impact that the loss of even one ship or helicopter loaded with marines could have on American sentiment and support for the administration's foreign policy. But, once these admirals decided that the threat was manageable and that the carriers could carry out flight operations in the obstacle-strewn gulf, they acted boldly. Mauz, for instance, not his superiors in Washington or Riyadh, pushed for the deployment of carriers *Independence* and *Midway* into the gulf during Desert Shield. Arthur followed suit. Eventually, four carriers launched aircraft from inside the Strait of Hormuz and just 185 miles southeast of Kuwait City.

Logistically supporting their forward-based combat forces in this distant region of the globe was not a big concern of these naval leaders. Backed up by facilities in the United States and overseas bases at Subic Bay, Naples, and Diego Garcia, naval logistic forces maintained a steady flow forward of personnel, fuel, ammunition, and supplies. The warships in the Central Command theater could count on the flotilla of U.S. and other coalition oilers, ammunition, stores, repair, and salvage ships, fleet resupply aircraft, and shore-based logistic support sites to keep them in the fight for the duration of the war. A dearth of precision guided munitions and slow mail delivery to some fleet units were exceptions to the generally positive performance of the logistic establishment.

By the start of hostilities, the Navy's medical establishment was ready to minister to the needs of the sailors and marines under Admiral Arthur and General Boomer. Staffed by hundreds of highly skilled and motivated healers, most of them naval reservists, the hospital ships *Mercy* and *Comfort*, three shore-based fleet hospitals, and several medical battalions stood ready for action. Thousands of hospital corpsmen lined up on the northern Saudi border alongside Marine infantrymen. Disease prevention teams cut short an outbreak of diarrhea among troops in the desert and other medical staffs sold most sailors and marines on the benefits of constant water consumption and good field hygiene. The Navy's medical contingent in the gulf lacked certain critical supplies, some chemical protective gear, and reliable field radios, but in general was geared up for war.

Desert Shield was not an easy time. More than 30 sailors involved in Desert Shield died as a result of mishaps, a reflection of the danger inherent even in peacetime naval operations. Other American sailors had to endure exhausting "port and starboard" watches, blistering heat and humidity, fouling sand, and sometimes rough seas to ready their ships, aircraft, and weapons for battle. Marines, Seabees, SEALs, corpsmen, and other personnel ashore enjoyed few creature comforts or diversions from the daily grind. Recognizing Arab and Muslim sensitivities, naval personnel accepted restrictions on their own political expression, religious observances, and social behavior.

Despite these hardships, the morale of America's sailors on the eve of Desert Storm was high. The naval establishment had, for the most part, trained them well for the coming fight, equipped them with the most modern weapons and equipment, and provisioned them with all manner of essential supplies. Most Navy men and women had confidence in themselves, their shipmates, and their leaders. Belief in the righteousness of the UN mission was widespread. Their common objective was to finish the enemy quickly and decisively and then return home to waiting families and friends. The Navy, along with the other U.S. and allied military services, was ready on 17 January 1991 to eject the Iraqis from Kuwait and destroy Saddam Hussein's war machine.

Littoral Combat in the Persian Gulf

Not for the first time in the twentieth century, the U.S. Navy fought the Persian Gulf War as part of a joint-service and multinational team that executed one of the most exceptional campaigns in military history. With Americans in the lead, coalition forces restored Kuwait to its government and people and severely limited Saddam Hussein's ability to threaten regional peace. The Navy and the other joint and combined forces reduced the Iraqi air force by more than half, eliminated the Iraqi navy as a fighting force, destroyed 4,200 tanks, armored personnel carriers, and artillery pieces, and killed, wounded, or captured perhaps 100,000 Iraqi troops.

Conversely, NAVCENT did not suffer the sinking of a single ship and lost only a half-dozen aircraft. Six naval air crewmen were killed in action. The Iraqis shot down seven Marine aircraft and killed or wounded 110 marines.[3]

The Air War

Naval power was fundamental to the success of the Desert Storm air offensive. The Navy's Tomahawk cruise missile, employed in many of the most critical strike operations of Desert Storm, added a new dimension to the traditional Navy mission of projecting power ashore. Battleships, cruisers, destroyers, and submarines positioned in the Persian Gulf, Red Sea, and Eastern Mediterranean launched these weapons. Without risking a single naval aviator, the fleet units were able to strike targets with reasonable accuracy hundreds of miles from the sea in heavily defended Baghdad. They were not super weapons. Needing greater penetration and explosive power during the Gulf War, the TLAMs did not always neutralize their targets. Moreover, the Iraqis were able to shoot down some of the missiles. Still, most of the successfully launched TLAMs survived to damage or destroy their targets.[4] Validated in war, the Navy's land attack missile significantly strengthened America's strike warfare arsenal.

Carrier squadrons, fighting alongside other American and coalition air units, brought devastating firepower to bear against the enemy's warmaking establishment in Baghdad and throughout Iraq. The air campaign severely damaged Saddam's national command-control-communications, power-generation, and integrated air defense systems; oil refining installations; airfields and aircraft shelters; and naval facilities. The coalition's air forces also leveled those Iraqi facilities that intelligence had identified as involved in the production of weapons of mass destruction.

The Navy made a special contribution to the air campaign by helping defeat Iraq's integrated air defense network in the early stages. Before the war the Navy's U.S.-based SPEAR intelligence group had suggested that the key to success would be neutralization of Iraq's radar-directed, surface-to-air missile system. This analysis was correct. Following up on this appreciation, General Horner used Navy tactical air launched decoys and Air Force-operated Navy drones to fool the enemy into thinking they were coalition aircraft. The Iraqis wasted scores of precious surface-to-air missiles on false targets. In addition, the Navy's HARM air-to-surface missiles destroyed many of those radars that dared to activate (unfortunately this equipment also included a few coalition radars). And, the Navy's carrier-based EA-6B Prowler electronic countermeasures aircraft proved to be "one of the real superstars of the conflict,"[5] protecting coalition strike aircraft by jamming Iraqi radar signals.

Other naval aircraft helped reduce the Iraqi army in Kuwait. As Commander Battle Force Zulu moved his carriers ever closer to the target areas, attacks on the enemy's field forces grew in intensity. Marine AV-8 Harriers and F/A-18 Hornets used Mavericks, and Navy A-6 Intruders used their FLIRs and 500-pound, laser guided bombs in "tank-plinking" strikes that by G-Day had severely mauled the enemy's armored forces. The naval services could have done greater damage to the enemy if they had had more precision guided munitions in the theater.

Not all missions, however, required this relatively expensive ordnance. General purpose bombs were the optimum weapons for reducing the battle worthiness of the enemy's field army.[6] Even though "ancient," the Korean War and Vietnam War vintage Mark 80 series of general purpose bombs, 5-inch Zuni and 2.75-inch rockets, fuel air explosives, and Walleyes proved almost as good as the Rockeyes for this mission. With A-6s dropping all manner of "dumb" bombs by night and F/A-18s, AV-8s, and other coalition aircraft by day, the helpless Iraqi troops got little respite from Horner's aerial onslaught. Navy and Marine aircraft also dropped leaflets as part of a sophisticated psychological warfare effort. Enemy morale and military effectiveness suffered badly from this constant attention.[7] By the last days of the war, carrier aircraft and both ship-based and shore-based Marine aircraft were launching numerous strikes against the Iraqi army as it fled from Kuwait City along the "highway of death."

Navy and Marine commanders, having digested the Vietnam and other Cold War experiences, generally employed their ordnance with precision and restraint. There were few civilian casualties and minimal destruction of non-military targets during the war. Aside from obvious humanitarian concerns, naval leaders understood how bombing inaccuracy might enrage the enemy population and generate domestic and international opposition to the UN mission.

As Lieutenants Fox and Mongillo demonstrated with their F/A-18s, Navy fighters were just as capable of shooting down enemy jets as Air Force F-16s and F-15s. Navy fighters did not score additional fixed-wing kills during the war, however. General Horner and his staff knew that the electronic gear on most Air Force fighters could differentiate between friendly and enemy aircraft, but they were not as confident about the Navy's IFF equipment. Naval leaders placed greater faith in their interceptors. Nevertheless, since there were more than enough Air Force units to handle those relatively small number of Iraqi fighters that elected to "dog fight," Horner wisely chose not to employ other coalition aircraft and risk accidental, or "blue-on-blue" shoot-downs.

If the Air Force was unsure about the Navy's IFF equipment, it had great confidence in Navy-designed weapons. The Sidewinder and Sparrow air-to-air missiles developed by the Naval Weapons Center at China Lake, California, performed especially well and figured prominently in the coalition's 38 aerial victories.[8]

As critics have observed, the A-7 and A-6 attack aircraft had made their operational debuts during the Vietnam War and hence lacked the more advanced avionics and weapons systems of the F-117.[9] These jets were reaching the end of their useful service lives. Despite that, they performed their various missions with marked effectiveness. The Navy's last two Corsair squadrons, whose deactivation was postponed for Desert Storm, did not lose a plane to enemy action and they employed with skill most of the weapons in the aerial arsenal, including precision guided munitions, general purpose bombs, and 20-millimeter guns.[10]

The venerable A-6 Intruder was clearly the naval services' "workhorse for strike warfare" during Desert Storm.[11] Navy and Marine A-6s carried 10,000 pounds of ordnance, much more than the F-117, operated in smoke-filled skies, bad weather, and at night, and flew long distances without aerial refueling. Their FLIR equipment was especially effective at nighttime spotting of stationary Iraqi vehicles. A-6Es were also vital because their laser designators helped other naval aircraft drop LGBs accurately.[12] The F/A-18 Hornet, even though its bomb-carrying capacity and range were inadequate for deep-strike missions, performed well in battlefield interdiction operations. The AV-8 could only operate effectively at low level, which made it vulnerable to enemy air defense weapons. The Harrier's ability to fly from unimproved airstrips and from assault ships close offshore, however, made it especially responsive to the requirements of Marine ground commanders.

Battle Force Zulu's four carriers were able to add their offensive punch to the air campaign in part because the air defense umbrella established by the coalition fleet allowed the capital ships to move close to the enemy's coast. U.S. naval leaders have concluded that a determined air assault on the fleet would probably have damaged or even sunk some coalition ships, especially in the early stages of Desert Shield when coalition air defenses in the gulf were not robust. By the start of Desert Storm, however, SAM-armed U.S. Aegis and NTU cruisers; British, Australian, Canadian, and Dutch warships; and Navy, Marine, Air Force, British, and Canadian early warning, patrol, and fighter aircraft saturated the northern gulf. The Iraqi air force had to test the defensive perimeter in the gulf only once to discover that the coalition's seaborne defenses were as impervious as those on land. The shootdown of two Iraqi Mirage jets on 24 January, while exposing some command and control shortcomings, highlighted the resiliency and depth of the allied air defenses.

Navy surface and air units and Air Force AWACS planes also monitored hundreds of aircraft flying over the gulf every day for the seven months of Desert Shield and Desert Storm. Of the 65,000 sorties monitored by allied forces, none involved a mid-air collision of coalition aircraft.

The Navy had its share of operational difficulties during the air campaign, but its battle commanders and staffs demonstrated true professionalism in diagnosing most problems and quickly correcting them. For instance, in the first days of Desert Storm, the carrier navy realized that its tactical approach to strike operations was wrong. Missions carried out at low level, in keeping with prewar training, resulted in the loss or damage of a number of planes. The Royal Air Force suffered as well in its low-level airfield attacks. Meanwhile, the allied onslaught had neutralized the enemy's air defenses above 10,000 feet, affording the coalition a virtual sanctuary at the higher altitudes.

Admiral Arthur, based on his own combat experience in Vietnam, recognized that the situation demanded an immediate change of course. A consummate wartime fleet commander, Arthur generally gave his subordinate officers the freedom they needed to fight their forces. But, as in this case, he did not hesitate to step in when decisive action was called for. He immediately advised his air wing commanders to forego the costly low-level tactic and employ their aircraft from the higher reaches of the Iraqi sky. Aircraft losses declined as a result.

So too did bombing effectiveness. Naval air crews had not been well trained for such missions and naval aircraft, electronic targeting systems, and aerial ordnance had not been configured for high-level strike operations. Many Rockeye bombs dropped from the higher altitudes, for instance, did not explode when they reached the ground.

Another hindrance to bombing effectiveness was the enemy's skill at cover and deception. Like the Communists in the Vietnam air war, the Iraqis positioned armored vehicles, trucks, and missile launchers made of wood at key locations; painted black "holes" in airfield runways; and employed ferries, pontoons, and earthen causeways to move supplies across the Euphrates and other critical rivers.

The Navy and the Air Force had a difficult time destroying the highway bridges between Baghdad and the front during the early weeks of the air campaign. Frequently, several strikes were required to knock out the durable, multi-span bridges. But, the Navy-Air Force experience benefited the later "bridge busting" operations of the Royal Air Force. By the end of Desert Storm the combined strike effort had eliminated 75 percent of the bridges between the Iraqi capital and southern Iraq. For the most part, the carrier forces were able to quickly adjust their tactics, aircraft, and weapons systems to the demands of the campaign.

The Navy and the Air Force also had difficulty tracking down Saddam's missile launchers that propelled high-explosive Scud warheads into the heart of Israel and Saudi Arabia. This massive search diverted aircraft from other vital missions and at the tactical level produced no tangible results—there is no evidence that coalition aircraft destroyed any Iraqi launchers.

Convinced that the allies were serious about locating and destroying the weapons, however, the Israelis stayed out of the war, and their decision had great strategic value. Saddam did not succeed in splitting the coalition of Christian and bitterly anti-Israeli Arab forces.

The Navy also suffered with the other services from the lack of accurate and timely battle damage assessments. Because of over compartmentalization, different service priorities, and the overwhelming volume of data available, the intelligence agencies in Washington and CENTCOM's J-2 in Riyadh were often unable to deliver timely information to naval forces on the line. Naval commanders in the Persian Gulf were also frustrated with the dearth of satellite intelligence on the basing and movement of aircraft on their northern flank in Iran. Moreover, the TARPS pods carried by a number of F-14 Tomcats provided the fleet with good tactical intelligence, but there were not enough of these specially equipped aircraft in the operational theater.

As in all of America's modern conflicts, interservice problems arose during the Persian Gulf War. From the first days of Desert Shield, General Schwarzkopf made it clear that he wanted General Horner and the Riyadh-based staff of the Joint Force Air Component Commander to control Air Force, Navy, and Marine Corps air units assigned to Central Command. Horner and most other Air Force officers, in keeping with their views on air power, were comfortable with this centralized control.

The Navy, because of its traditional stress on decentralized handling of air power, did not take easily to JFACC management. Some naval officers thought that the Air Force-heavy JFACC staff did not understand how to make optimum use of the Navy's primary strike weapons, the carrier planes and Tomahawk cruise missiles. Others feared that the Desert Storm experience would lead to greater Air Force control of carrier forces in the future and hurt the Navy's ability to compete for increasingly scarce defense dollars.

The Navy also had trouble working with the air tasking order, at least initially. Lacking compatible communications equipment, the carriers could not easily receive the lengthy Riyadh-generated document. Navy staff officers also found the large, daily menu of air strikes unwieldy. Moreover, Navy and Marine air staffs thought that the ATO would not be able to handle fast-changing battlefield situations. Carrier and shore-based naval air staffs, however, adapted their operations to the ATO process. They had to. Only the ATO could adequately handle the 2,500 daily sorties over Iraq, Kuwait, and the Arabian Peninsula. The Navy had no comparable mechanism. In fact, the battle groups and individual carriers were prompted to organize "strike cells" and refine the process by which they nominated targets to Riyadh. Horner also accommodated the needs of the naval services. The general, no air power ideologue, did not object to Admiral Arthur directing over-water operations, particularly the assault on the Iraqi navy and the air defense of the right flank. Horner also allowed Marine General Royal Moore to manage most of the missions in Kuwait of his 3d Marine Aircraft Wing.

Still, from the start friction dogged the Navy and Air Force staffs managing the air war. Mixson's Battle Force Yankee, having trained extensively with the Air Force in Desert Shield, worked reasonably well with the JFACC. Relations between Battle Force Zulu and Riyadh, however, were strained. The causes were many: the inadequacy of Battle Force Zulu's preparation for a joint air war, different service combat doctrines, parochialism on both sides, poor fleet-to-shore communications, the shortage of Navy officers in Riyadh with sufficient authority, and the small number of Navy personnel on the JFACC staff.

One particular source of irritation was Battle Force Zulu's dependence on Air Force aerial tankers for the strike missions into Iraq and portions of Kuwait. The Navy did not believe that the battle force carriers received their fair share of tanking support in the initial phase of the air war. One can rightly question allocation priorities when so many Air Force tankers were committed to refueling the B-52s (whose bomb drops were fairly inaccurate until late in the campaign) on their long round trips between Diego Garcia, Spain, and the United States. Another problem was that some of the Navy and Air Force aerial refueling equipment and fuel was incompatible. Both services, however, took successful steps to harmonize refueling operations.

In contrast to their staffs, Arthur and Horner had few disagreements. For the most part, Arthur's dealings with Schwarzkopf also remained cordial and professional. The one major exception was the latter's strong reaction to the fleet's sinking of Iraqi oil tankers. The admiral was justifiably concerned with the danger that these ships would pose to sailors and marines conducting any amphibious operations. The general, of course, knew there would be no amphibious assault on Kuwait. He feared that the Navy's actions might take the heat of international opinion off Saddam for his deliberate release of oil into the gulf and might cast the coalition as an ocean polluter. Again, with a few exceptions, accommodation and cooperation were much more typical of interservice relations than conflict. Despite their disagreements, Navy, Air Force, Marine, and Army commanders and staffs worked together to carry out a crushing air campaign.

The Maritime Assault on Kuwait

The maritime campaign mounted by the Navy in the northern Persian Gulf and the coastal reaches of Kuwait riveted the enemy's attention on the seaward flank. Believing that Saddam was especially concerned about a U.S. Marine assault on the coast of Kuwait, General Schwarzkopf directed his naval component commander to reinforce the Iraqi dictator's fears. Each phase of Admiral Arthur's maritime campaign focused on that objective.

The first stage, clearing enemy forces and defenses from the northern gulf, got off to a slow start. Horner had fully committed Battle Force Zulu to the air war ashore, and until *Theodore Roosevelt* arrived in the gulf Arthur and March lacked enough aircraft to search effectively for Iraqi combatants.

One measure taken against enemy naval vessels was short-lived. On the second day of the war, *Ranger* aircraft mined the approaches to the primary operating bases of the Iraqi navy. Even though the Iraqi command had already dispersed some of its combatants for protection along the coast and among the islands of the northern gulf, Arthur's forces had the ability, through intensive and repeated mine-laying activity, to stifle the movement of enemy naval vessels.[13] But U.S. naval officers have not always been enamored with the potential of offensive mine warfare. The admiral was also disturbed by the loss of a pilot and plane during the low-level mine-laying operation. Finally, he was concerned that there were "already too many mines in those waters,"[14] even though only American mines had been dropped there (presumably set for automatic self-sterilization). The upshot was that Arthur ruled out further mine-laying operations.

Arthur, however, did impress upon his principal subordinates the importance of the offensive antisurface mission and assigned the energetic "Zap" Zlatoper to direct operations. Zlatoper and his local area antisurface warfare officer, Captain G.T. Forbes, put together a hard-hitting, offensive campaign employing the most effective aircraft, weapons, and ships in his arsenal. Coalition ships with long-range radar, combat aircraft, and patrol planes searched the harbors, inland waterways, and seaways of the northern gulf for enemy naval combatants. Once they made contact, the allied patrol forces guided ship-based Army OH-58D Kiowa Warrior, British Lynx, and Navy LAMPS helicopters to prospective targets. These British-American teams then used their innovative hunter/killer tactics and advanced radars, mast-mounted sights, night-vision goggles, video cameras, and Sea Skua and Hellfire missiles to locate, identify, and destroy the Iraqi foes. Most operations routinely occurred after dark, because in the Gulf War the U.S. Navy, like the other American armed services, was supreme in nighttime warfare.

Coalition naval forces were the first to capture enemy troops when Commander Morral's American-Kuwaiti task unit seized the platforms in the ad-Dorra oilfield. The crews of *Nicholas* and *Istiqlal* found that most of their 23 Iraqi prisoners were in sad physical shape and eager to surrender. This impression was reinforced on 24 January when *Curts, Leftwich,* and *Nicholas* and their embarked SEAL and Army helicopter teams captured 75 Iraqi troops on and around Qaruh Island. Thus, even before the battle of Khafji there were clear signs that enemy troops were badly supported, demoralized, and unlikely to put up fierce resistance to UN ground forces. These operations also demonstrated to American commanders that Arab fighting men would be valuable members of the international team.

There was a little known but important maritime dimension to the battle of Khafji. U.S. and British naval aircraft eliminated the enemy boat force moving south along the coast toward the Saudi town and joined other coalition units in destroying the armored columns thrusting toward Khafji and the northern Saudi border.

Then, in the "Bubiyan Turkey Shoot," American, British, and Canadian aircraft bloodied the surviving vessels of the Iraqi fleet as they attempted to reach safety in Iranian territorial waters. The gulf experience laid to rest the old argument that small, fast, and highly maneuverable enemy missile craft would make littoral waters too dangerous for oceangoing navies. In a few short weeks, coalition naval forces destroyed or forced into Iranian hands over 140 enemy vessels, which included most of the larger units in the Iraqi navy and every one of its 13 missile-launching vessels. Naval strategist Colin Gray has aptly observed that "U.S. and other coalition naval forces enjoyed so absolute a control of the waters of the Persian Gulf in 1991 that the Mahanian term 'command' [of the sea] was not inappropriate." [15]

After clearing the enemy from the northern gulf, Admiral Arthur's forces proceeded to the next level of the effort to fix Iraqi eyes on the sea. Beginning in early February 1991 the Battle Force Zulu carriers, as scheduled in the ATO, intensified their air attacks on targets in Kuwait and Arthur moved the fleet ever closer to the hostile shore. Mine countermeasures forces cleared lanes through suspected minefields for battleships *Missouri* and *Wisconsin*, which the Iraqis probably expected to accompany an amphibious force. For several weeks before the ground assault into Kuwait, these ships signaled the coalition's naval presence by lofting their shells into Iraqi defenses ashore. Like the Tomahawk land attack missiles, the battleships' UAVs greatly improved the Navy's ability to project power ashore with precision and no risk to naval personnel.

Because of their especially thick protective armor, these ships could survive hits by enemy shells, bombs, missiles, and mines that would sink other less endowed surface combatants. Complementing the battleships' defenses was the firepower of their escorts, as demonstrated when British frigate *Gloucester*'s Sea Dart surface-to-air missiles destroyed an Iraqi Silkworm launched against *Missouri*.

Weeks before then, British and American MCM forces had worked to clear additional lanes and fleet staging areas in the suspected minefields off Kuwait. General Schwarzkopf's prewar order forbidding reconnaissance flights over the northern gulf compelled the fleet to operate with imprecise information about the outer boundaries and composition of the minefields. The Navy paid a price for this ignorance. Only several hours apart, *Tripoli*, ironically the mother ship for the six American MCM helicopters, and cruiser *Princeton* struck mines that severely damaged both ships. Damage control skills honed by American sailors since the Vietnam War enabled crewmen and experts flown out to the ships to keep them afloat and in position until relieved by other units.

Conventional wisdom has it that "1000 Iraqi sea mines deterred [the Navy] from launching an amphibious assault"[16] on Kuwait, but that appreciation is false. Schwarzkopf had long before ruled out a landing on the heavily fortified and defended coastline unless it was absolutely necessary. He did not want to destroy the commercial and residential facilities that crowded the shore south of Kuwait City. On 2 February 1991, Schwarzkopf made it clear to his chief subordinates that he would not order an amphibious landing on the coast of Kuwait. Neither Arthur nor Boomer pushed for a major landing, even though Marine Commandant Al Gray and his representatives pressed hard for it. Indeed, Arthur directed the use of an LPH, a ship that was critical to amphibious operations, as a mine countermeasures support platform.

Nor did the mines preclude a secondary mission, the amphibious seizure of Faylaka Island. Helicopters based on board the amphibious ships could have flown over the mines to deploy marines on the island. Ultimately, battleship bombardments, naval air strikes, and helicopter overflights were all that was needed to persuade the Iraqi garrison on Faylaka to surrender.[17] Had it been necessary for the MCM force to rapidly clear lanes through the minefields, however, there was great probability that ships in the MCM force and in the following amphibious flotilla would have been damaged or sunk. The presence of sea mines off the coast of Kuwait limited the battleships' ability to provide naval gunfire support. The relatively thin-hulled destroyers and frigates could not be used at all for that mission. Enemy mines also put two important warships out of action and delayed and complicated naval operations.

The American capability to execute mine countermeasures in the Persian Gulf was sadly deficient. *Avenger*, lead ship of the new class, had mechanical and magnetic signature problems, as did some of the older ocean minesweepers. The MCM staff in the gulf was an ad hoc group only recently formed. Inadequate planning for the MCM phase of an amphibious assault on the mainland caused British naval officers to question the soundness of American tactical leadership, the only significant instance of such dissatisfaction during Desert Storm. Tellingly, General Schwarzkopf, the theater commander, and his naval component commander, Arthur, asserted several times after the war that the Navy's MCM force just did not do the job that they wanted done.

Adapting the Cold War-era composite warfare commander concept to the handling of naval forces in offensive littoral operations led to some confusion among commanders about their responsibilities. Theoretically, Admiral March led all U.S. naval forces in the gulf, in keeping with the age-old principal of unity of command. But in practice he had to share command and control with Admiral Fogarty. March focused on the air war and Fogarty on the mine countermeasures, naval gunfire support, and amphibious aspects of the maritime campaign. March's battle leaders complained about the difficulty of getting timely authorization to attack enemy vessels. Fogarty's task group commanders were especially confused about which superior command was responsible for protecting their ships from enemy air attack. Needlessly complicating the command and control picture was the Navy's routine rotation of key commanders sometimes only days before the start of critical operations.

Despite the mined waters, in mid-February Admiral Arthur positioned the 31 ships of Admiral LaPlante's Amphibious Task Force, with General Jenkins' 4th and 5th MEBs and 13th MEU(SOC) embarked, in close proximity to the coalition front opposite Kuwait. This powerful and mobile force enabled the theater commander not only to threaten the length of Saddam's coastal flank but to reinforce coalition formations on land.

To convince the enemy that a landing was about to occur, the fleet increased its level of activity in the northern gulf on the day before the general offensive into Kuwait and for the next two days. Carrier aircraft and battleships rained bombs and shells on enemy troops on the mainland and on Faylaka Island. On successive days, attack aircraft and helicopters based in carriers and amphibious assault ships approached the hostile shore as if to inaugurate a landing.

Naval special warfare units simulated assaults on likely landing beaches. In these operations, Navy SEALs operated with the traditional derring-do that they first demonstrated in Vietnam. But, having learned from their Cold War experiences, the naval special warriors carefully planned and rehearsed their operations. They accomplished their hazardous missions without losing a man.

The amphibious deception worked to perfection. The enemy had wasted untold resources constructing bunkers and other fortifications and installing wire entanglements, minefields, and beach obstacles. The Iraqis also emplaced five antiship missile batteries and hundreds of artillery pieces on the coast. Of greatest importance, the enemy positioned seven divisions on that ultimately dormant front north and south of Kuwait City, delayed redeploying these critical forces until too late to influence the land battle, and ignored the exposed desert flank around which rumbled General Franks' armored behemoth. Franks observed that these Iraqi divisions were "effectively tricked out of the war."[18] In the words of two authorities on amphibious warfare, the fleet action was "strategic distraction at its most effective," and "Saddam Hussein bought it all the way."[19]

The gulf maritime campaign was truly a combined endeavor. In contrast to the embargo patrol units, with which Arthur employed a "cooperative" command system to carry on the work of the multinational patrol, COMUSNAVCENT directed the combat operations of British, Canadian, Australian, Dutch, and Kuwaiti naval forces in the gulf. The ships and aircraft of his coalition allies did not steam in a separate "foreign" flotilla but fought in fully integrated task groups that exploited national strengths. In short, these allied warships proceeded in tandem through the hazardous reaches of the northern gulf, and some of them together traded fire with the enemy.

As they had in almost every major American land campaign since the Meuse-Argonne Offensive in France during World War I, Marine and Army divisions fought side by side during the final assault into Kuwait. General Boomer's I MEF was an integral part of the coalition's huge ground army that liberated Kuwait. Nevertheless, the Marine formation was an expeditionary force that could neither deploy far from the sea nor fight without substantial Navy involvement. The naval services gave strong ship and shore-based aircraft support to the Marine divisions, in part because the latter lacked armored and artillery forces that were as powerful as the Army's. The Marines also counted on naval gunfire support, which the battleships provided, if only for a short time during the ground offensive. Much of their 16-inch fire was directed at targets in the enemy rear or in support of the Arab forces on the coastal road.

Integral to Marine operations in the land campaign was the 3d Naval Construction Regiment that, with Marine engineer units, established air strips, ammunition dumps, and logistic sites, opened roads through the desert, and braved enemy fire to widen lanes through the

Saddam Line. Also sharing danger with the Marines were Navy chaplains, medical corpsmen, and field hospital personnel, whose hard work and skillful planning had prepared them well for the desert war. Behind the lines and out to sea were the fleet hospitals, medical battalions, and hospital ships. They stood ready with advanced diagnostic and surgical equipment and well-trained professionals to handle thousands of wounded marines. Fortunately, they never had to.

The coalition offensive into Kuwait and southern Iraq completed the destruction of the Iraqi army begun on 17 January 1991. The air campaign had devastated Iraq's forces in the KTO and by the time of the coalition's ground offensive, communication between front line Iraqi units was problematic. Saddam's regular soldiers suffered badly from lack of food, warm clothing, and basic equipment and as a result, the morale of the officers and men had plummeted. When the coalition's mechanized juggernaut stormed across the Kuwait and Iraq borders on 24 February, it quickly rolled over the infantry divisions in the enemy's first line of defense.

The forces to the rear, however, including most of the Republican Guard divisions, still had lots of fight and military power in them, even though they had been a prime target of the air campaign. Contrary to the views of some critics, coalition ground forces had to beat their foe on the field of battle before they could claim victory. Had the coalition's ground forces not been so well equipped and skilled in their work, the Iraqis could have exacted a much higher price for allied success. The American armored, mechanized, and air mobile divisions had to demonstrate their overwhelming power before Saddam and his generals were induced to end the brutal occupation of Kuwait.

In sum, the UN coalition won the Persian Gulf War because George Bush orchestrated a masterful diplomatic offensive and Norman Schwarzkopf skillfully handled his responsibilities as the theater commander of a diverse, multinational expeditionary force. Just as important, U.S. and allied air, ground, and naval forces, despite the inevitable "frictions" of war, worked together to execute a well-crafted campaign plan. While husbanding the lives of the soldiers, sailors, airmen, and marines in their charge, General Schwarzkopf, Admiral Arthur, and their lieutenants brought overwhelming military power to bear against the invaders of Kuwait.

Maintaining Peace and Learning from the Gulf War Experience

The Navy was as critical to American interests in the Persian Gulf after Desert Storm as it had been in the 40 years before. Naval forces were involved in the UN efforts to restore the prewar overseas commerce of Kuwait and to withdraw speedily and efficiently the coalition's expeditionary units from the Arabian Peninsula. Moreover, the Navy played a prominent role in postwar efforts to limit Saddam's actions against the Shiites and Kurds in Iraq, assure his compliance with UN resolutions, and limit his ability to again threaten regional peace.

Even before the dust had settled over the Kuwaiti battleground, naval and other UN forces moved into Kuwait City and the country's main ports to restore their basic functions. U.S., Australian, British, and French EOD detachments worked long hours in harbors that were cluttered with lethal, unexploded ordnance, sunken vessels, and the other detritus of war. Despite this tough operating environment, the EOD units opened the ports in short order, and did so without a casualty.

Equally impressive was the coalition's operation to open Kuwait to international shipping and neutralize the Iraqi minefields. The Belgian, French, and British mine-hunting ships, under U.S. tactical control, starred in a gulf operation that also for the first time involved German and Japanese naval vessels. The troubles plaguing the U.S. MCM ships and helicopters during the war continued to hinder their operations in the months afterward. The Navy redoubled its efforts to provide the force with better equipment, including advanced sonars and remotely operated vehicles. Rear Admiral Raynor A.K. Taylor, the first postwar COMUSNAVCENT, concentrated on improving the training, readiness, and morale of the American MCM force. Taylor questioned the value to the operation of the helicopter units, but the overall American MCM performance improved steadily after June 1991 when the other navies departed the gulf. By early 1992 and the termination of the mine countermeasures program, U.S. naval forces had destroyed more than half of the 1,288 mines found in the gulf.

The withdrawal from the operational theater after the war of thousands of tanks, armored personnel carriers, and helicopters and tons of ammunition and other materiel was a monumental achievement of the Navy and the other American armed services.

Desert Storm was unlike previous wars when the American forces sold for scrap, destroyed, or simply abandoned mountains of weapons, equipment, and supplies. In response to President Bush's pledge to the Arab governments, Schwarzkopf, Boomer, and Taylor acted to erase the Western military presence from Saudi Arabia. They also endeavored to preserve America's expensive fighting machine, especially in the post-Cold War era of budgetary cutbacks. The men and women of Schwarzkopf's logistics commands planned carefully and worked hard to execute this massive retrograde movement. Ultimately, the American forces left the desert much as they had found it in August 1990.

In Operation Desert Sortie, the Navy redeployed to their home stations the ships and cargo of the maritime prepositioning squadrons. Very soon after the Gulf War, the U.S. military had reestablished America's global readiness posture. By the spring of 1992, MSC had transported from the theater in 456 ships a phenomenal 1.9 million tons of supplies and equipment.

The embargo patrol continued to symbolize international solidarity as a counter to Saddam's postwar actions. The UN Security Council could count on coalition navies, along with air forces, being available to enforce its cease-fire resolutions. While some coalition members balked at joining the United States in imposing the "no-fly" restrictions over Iraq during the post-cease-fire years, they maintained their involvement with the embargo patrol. The multinational operation also enabled the UN Security Council to enforce, on a daily and continuous basis, the measures taken by the body to destroy Saddam's capacity for chemical, biological, and nuclear war and to limit his ability to threaten his neighbors. Long after Desert Storm, Saddam continued to brandish a sword in Persian Gulf affairs, but the multinational embargo patrol helped ensure that the weapon stayed dull-edged. Air Force General Horner cogently observed after the war that the naval embargo was a "real victory story [because] that's the hammer lock we [continue to] have on the evil of Iraq." [20]

It took more than the maritime interception force to restrain Saddam's postwar actions, however. Time and again, U.S. naval and other American and allied forces were called on to curb his behavior. During Operation Provide Comfort, naval special warfare units, Seabees, and other naval forces, covered by carrier aircraft, operated in the UN protection zone in northern Iraq to bring humanitarian assistance to the Kurds and help protect them from the Iraqi army.

The fleet's presence also continued to assure America's gulf allies of U.S. constancy. Indeed, a prime function of Naval Forces, Central Command in the post-cease-fire period was to work for better collective security arrangements in the region, not just in relation to the Iraqi threat but the potential Iranian threat. Accordingly, the Navy exercised with GCC naval forces and trained them in the use of U.S. weapons, communications, and tactics.

It is clear that the presence in the Central Command theater of strong U.S. Navy and other UN forces, their rapid reinforcement, and their employment against Iraq during the 1993 and 1994 confrontations helped restrain the Iraqi dictator. The fleet's Tomahawk strikes against targets in or near Baghdad in January and June 1993, at the direction of President Bill Clinton, moderated Saddam's actions, if only temporarily. When he once again threatened the peace by moving Republican Guard divisions into southern Iraq in October 1994, it took the rapid deployment into the gulf of U.S. forces, naval forces in particular, to restore the status quo ante.

Critics of Washington's postwar policy with regard to Saddam pointed to the continuing need for force or the threat of force to maintain peace in the region. But in view of the possible alternatives—Saddam's eradication of the Kurdish and Shiite peoples, military adventures against neighboring states, or de-stabilization of the Middle Eastern oil industry—the messy, but relatively stable peace of the post-Gulf War era was clearly preferable. Since the UN coalition's objectives did not include deposing Saddam, the United States and its allies were compelled to threaten the use of force to maintain the postwar balance of power in the Persian Gulf region.

Maintaining stability in the Persian Gulf and other troubled regions has long been a mission of the U.S. Navy, and as a result of its Desert Shield and Desert Storm experience the naval service enhanced its ability to do so. After initial opposition, Admiral Kelso concurred in the Defense Department's 1992 decision to make Commander U.S. Naval Forces, Central Command a permanent, three-star admiral's billet. He also agreed the following year to the establishment ashore in Bahrain of the NAVCENT headquarters and improved logistic facilities. U.S. carrier, submarine, and surface forces in the gulf during the high-tension years of 1993 and 1994 were comparable in number to the Sixth Fleet and Seventh Fleet units that plied the waters of the Mediterranean and the Western Pacific. In the words of Vice Admiral John Scott Redd, COMUS-NAVCENT from September 1994 to August 1996, "if it looks like a fleet, acts like a fleet, and operates like a fleet, its a fleet!"[21] Consequently, on 1 July 1995 the Navy established the U.S. Fifth Fleet as CENTCOM's naval combat force.

The Navy improved its ability to work as part of a joint-services team, as demonstrated by its adaptation to the ATO process and integration into the staff of Operation Southern Watch, led by an Air Force general. Material improvements in ships, aircraft, weapons, and equipment following the Gulf War were legion, but a few examples should suffice: the fleet improved many of its communications and data link systems; developed, with its sister services, common aerial ordnance; greatly emphasized mine warfare with establishment of a Mine Warfare Command and completion of the technologically advanced *Avenger-* and *Osprey*-class ships;[22] equipped the SH-60B Seahawk/LAMPS III helicopters with Hellfire missiles, FLIR sets, machine guns, and a laser designator/range finder similar to that carried by the Air Force F-117;[23] and encouraged the Congress to fund construction of additional fast sealift ships.

In a larger sense, the Persian Gulf War stimulated the U.S. Navy to make the transition, rarely a comfortable process, from the Cold War to a new era of regional conflict with unknown enemies and uncertain allies. The 1992 White Paper *From the Sea* heralded the Navy's new post-Cold War strategy. Two years later that approach was further refined with promulgation of *Forward . . . From the Sea.* Both documents clearly embodied the experience of the Persian Gulf War and signaled the Navy's new focus away from the Soviet navy and open-ocean combat "toward power projection and the employment of naval forces from the sea to influence events in the *littoral regions* of the world—those areas adjacent to the oceans and seas that are within direct control of and vulnerable to the striking power of sea-based forces." [24] In that sense, the Persian Gulf War marked the opening of a new chapter in the history of the United States Navy.

Abbreviations

AAA	Antiaircraft Artillery
AAV	Assault Amphibian Vehicle
AAW	Antiair Warfare
AAWC	Antiair Warfare Commander
AD	Destroyer Tender
AE	Ammunition Ship
AFS	Combat Stores Ship
AGF	Auxiliary Command Ship
AH	Hospital Ship
AO	Oiler
AOE	Fast Combat Support Ship
AOR	Replenishment Fleet Tanker
AR	Repair Ship
ARCENT	Army Forces, Central Command
ASR	Armed Surface Reconnaissance
ASU	Administrative Support Unit
ASUWC	Antisurface Warfare Commander
ASWC	Antisubmarine Warfare Commander
ATF	Amphibious Task Force
ATO	Air Tasking Order
ATS	Salvage Ship
AWACS	Airborne Warning and Control System
BB	Battleship
BDA	Battle Damage Assessment
CA	Heavy Cruiser
CAFMS	Computer-Aided Force Management System
CAP	Combat Air Patrol
CAS	Close Air Support
CBU	Construction Battalion Unit
CEC	Civil Engineer Corps
CENTAF	Air Forces, Central Command
CENTCOM	Central Command

CENTO	Central Treaty Organization
CG	Guided Missile Cruiser
CGN	Nuclear Guided Missile Cruiser
CIA	Central Intelligence Agency
CINCCENT	Commander in Chief, Central Command
CINCLANTFLT	Commander in Chief, U.S. Atlantic Fleet
CINCPACFLT	Commander in Chief, U.S. Pacific Fleet
CIWS	Close-in Weapons System
CLF	Combat Logistics Force
CNA	Center for Naval Analyses
CNO	Chief of Naval Operations
COD	Carrier On Board Delivery
COMUS	Commander U.S.
CON/RO	Container Roll-On/Roll-Off Ship
CONREP	Connected Replenishment
CSAR	Combat Search and Rescue
CTAPS	Contingency Theater Automated Planning System
CTF	Commander Task Force
CTG	Commander Task Group
CV	Aircraft Carrier
CVA	Attack Aircraft Carrier
CVN	Nuclear-Powered Aircraft Carrier
CWC	Composite Warfare Commander
DD	Destroyer
DDG	Guided Missile Destroyer
DOD	Department of Defense
ECM	Electronic Countermeasures
EOD	Explosive Ordnance Disposal
EPW	Enemy Prisoner of War
EW	Electronic Warfare
FF	Frigate
FFG	Guided Missile Frigate
FLIR	Forward-Looking Infrared
FLSS	Forward Logistics Support Site
FROG	Free Rocket Over Ground
FSS	Fast Sealift Ship
FSA	Fire Support Area
FSCL	Fire Support Coordination Line
FSSG	Force Service Support Group
FSUC	Fire Support Unit Coordinator

GCC	Gulf Cooperation Council
GIUK	Greenland-Iceland-United Kingdom Gap
GPS	Global Positioning System
HARM	High-Speed Anti-Radiation Missile
HCS	Helicopter Combat Support Squadron
HET	Heavy Equipment Transporter
HMMWV	High-Mobility Multipurpose Wheeled Vehicle
IFF	Identification Friend or Foe
JCS	Joint Chiefs of Staff
JFACC	Joint Force Air Component Commander
JFC-E	Joint Forces Command East
JFE-N	Joint Forces Command North
JTFME	Joint Task Force Middle East
JSTARS	Joint Surveillance and Target Attack Radar System
JTFSWA	Joint Task Force Southwest Asia
KTO	Kuwait Theater of Operations
LAI	Light Armored Infantry
LAMPS	Light Airborne Multipurpose System
LASUW	Local Antisurface Warfare Commander
LAV	Light Armored Vehicle
LCAC	Landing Craft Air Cushion
LCC	Amphibious Command Ship
LCU	Landing Craft, Utility
LEDET	Law Enforcement Detachment
LGB	Laser Guided Bomb
LHA	Amphibious Assault Ship (general-purpose)
LHD	Amphibious Assault Ship (multipurpose)
LKA	Amphibious Cargo Ship
LPD	Amphibious Transport Dock
LPH	Amphibious Assault Ship (helicopter)
LSD	Landing Ship Dock
MAC	Military Airlift Command
MARCENT	Marine Forces, Central Command
MEB	Marine Expeditionary Brigade
MEU	Marine Expeditionary Unit
MCM	Mine Countermeasures Ship

MIRV	Multiple Independently Targeted Reentry Vehicle
MIUWU	Mobile Inshore Undersea Warfare Unit
MOPP	Mission-Oriented Protective Posture
MPS	Maritime Prepositioning Ship
MPSRON	Maritime Prepositioning Ship Squadron
MSC	Military Sealift Command
MSO	Minesweeper, Ocean
NAVCENT	Naval Forces, Central Command
NAVLOGSUPFOR	Naval Logistics and Support Force
NATO	North Atlantic Treaty Organization
NGFS	Naval Gunfire Support
NMCB	Naval Mobile Construction Battalion
NTU	New Threat Upgrade
OPAEC	Organization of Arab Petroleum Exporting Countries
OPEC	Organization of Petroleum Exporting Countries
OPLAN	Operation Plan
PIRAZ	Positive Identification Radar Advisory Zone
POW	Prisoner of War
PSHD	Port Security–Harbor Defense
PSU	Port Security Unit
RAN	Royal Australian Navy
RDJTF	Rapid Deployment Joint Task Force
RHIB	Rigid-Hull Inflatable Boat
RIO	Radar Intercept Officer
RNMCB	Reserve Naval Mobile Construction Battalion
RO/RO	Roll-On/Roll-Off
ROV	Remotely Operated Vehicle
R&R	Rest and Recreation
RRF	Ready Reserve Force
SAM	Surface-to-Air Missile
SEA	Sea Echelon Area
SEAD	Suppression of Enemy Air Defenses
SEAL	Sea Air Land Naval Commando
SOC	Special Operations Capable
SOCCENT	Special Operations Component, Central Command
SPEAR	Strike Projection Evaluation and Antiair Warfare Research
SRIG	Surveillance, Reconnaissance, and Intelligence Group

SSC	Surface Search Coordinator
SSN	Nuclear-Powered Attack Submarine
STWC	Strike Warfare Commander
SUCAP	Surface Combat Air Patrol
TALD	Tactical Air-Launched Decoy
TARPS	Tactical Area Reconnaissance Pod System
TERCOM	Terrain Contour Matching System
TLAM	Tomahawk Land Attack Missile
TPFDD	Time-Phased Force and Deployment Data
TRANSCOM	Transportation Command
UAE	United Arab Emirates
UAV	Unmanned Aerial Vehicle
USA	U.S. Army
USAF	U.S. Air Force
USCG	U.S. Coast Guard
USMC	U.S. Marine Corps
USNS	U.S. Naval Ship
USO	United Services Organization
USSR	Union of Soviet Socialist Republics
VA	Attack Squadron
VF	Fighter Squadron
VR	Transport Squadron
V/STOL	Vertical/Short Take-Off and Landing
WEU	Western European Union

Notes

Abbreviations

AVH   Naval Aviation History Branch, Naval Historical Center, Washington, DC.

IMEFB   I Marine Expeditionary Force Daily Command Briefings, U.S. Marine Corps Historical Center, Washington, DC.

AFPCD   U.S., Department of State, *American Foreign Policy: Current Documents* (Washington: Government Printing Office, 1982–).

CH   Contemporary History Branch, Naval Historical Center, Washington, DC.

CPGW   U.S. Department of Defense. *Conduct of the Persian Gulf War: Final Report to Congress* (Washington: Government Printing Office, 1992).

FRUS   U.S. Department of State. *Foreign Relations of the United States*. Washington: Government Printing Office, 1861–.

GWAPS   Cohen, Eliot A., director, *Gulf War Air Power Survey*, 5 vols. and a *Summary* (Washington: Government Printing Office, 1993).

NA   National Archives and Records Administration, College Park, MD

OA   Operational Archives, Naval Historical Center, Washington, DC.

OPDS   U.S., Congress, Senate, Armed Services Committee, *Operation Desert Shield/Desert Storm*, 102d Cong., 1st sess., 1991, S. Hrg. 102–326.

SH   Ships Histories Branch, Naval Historical Center, Washington, DC.

USNDS   U.S. Department of the Navy, *The United States Navy in "Desert Shield" "Desert Storm"* (Washington: Office of the Chief of Naval Operations, 1991).

Chapter 1

1. Ltr, Green to Schneller, 15 Oct 1993, Authors' Files, OA; USS *Taylor*, Command History 1990, SH.

2. *CPGW*, 19–20, 386–88; *USNDS*, 11–12.

3. Palmer, *On Course to Desert Storm*, 3–10.

4. Longrigg, *Oil in the Middle East*, 48, 372–73; Miller, *Search for Security*, 4–13, 55–63, 122–24, 141; Motter, *The Persian Corridor*; Palmer, *On Course to Desert Storm*, 14; Shwadran, *The Middle East, Oil, and the Great Powers*, 329; Yergin, *The Prize*, 178–95, 371–96.

5. Quoted in Yergin, *The Prize*, 393.

6. Yergin, *Shattered Peace*, 7–12, 168–70, 275, 322–24.

7. Palmer, *On Course to Desert Storm*, 21–25.

8. Quoted in *Congressional Quarterly, The Middle East*, 12.

9. Palmer, *On Course to Desert Storm*, 21–28; Yergin, *Shattered Peace*, 98, 161–64, 294.

10. *FRUS*, 1950, 5:1190–91.

11. Hourani, *A History of the Arab Peoples*, 342–52, 401–7; Rubin, "Pan-Arab Nationalism," 535–49; Sayigh, "The Gulf Crisis," 488–90.

12. Horwich and Mitchell, eds. *Policies for Coping With Oil-Supply Disruptions*, 67–68; Issawi, *Oil, the Middle East, and the World*, 65–66; McNaugher, *Arms and Oil*, 3.

13. Palmer, *On Course to Desert Storm*, 35–36.

14. *Congressional Quarterly, The Middle East*, 8, 15; Hourani, *A History of the Arab Peoples*, 411–15; Palmer, *On Course to Desert Storm*, 61–74; Shwadran, *The Middle East*, 89, 270–71; Yergin, *The Prize*, 451–558.

15. Cottrell, ed., *The Persian Gulf States*, 93–98; Center for Strategic Studies, *The Gulf*, 86–87; Hourani, *A History of the Arab Peoples*, 357; Issawi, *Oil, the Middle East, and the World*, 62; Yergin, *The Prize*, 565–66.

16. Center for Strategic Studies, *The Gulf*, 89–91; Hickman, "Soviet Naval Policy in the Indian Ocean," 42–52; Issawi, *Oil, the Middle East, and the World*, 54–64; Landis, *Politics and Oil*, 48–53; Noyes, *The Clouded Lens*, 52.

17. Quoted in Palmer, *On Course to Desert Storm*, 76.

18. McNaugher, *Arms and Oil*, 12; Noyes, *The Clouded Lens*, 54–57, 120–21; Palmer, *On Course to Desert Storm*, 75–88. The United States augmented the small Royal Saudi Navy and helped develop naval bases at al-Jubayl and Jiddah. Eilts, "The United States and Saudi Arabia," 29.

19. *Congressional Quarterly, The Middle East*, 26; Issawi, *Oil, the Middle East, and the World*, 20; Noyes, *The Clouded Lens*, xiii; Shwadran, *The Middle East*, 407, 431–43, 525, 532; Yergin, *The Prize*, 567–68.

20. *Congressional Quarterly, The Middle East*, 26–32; Cottrell et al., *Sea Power and Strategy in the Indian Ocean*, 81–82; Horwich and Mitchell, eds., *Policies for Coping With Oil-Supply Disruptions*, 4, 66; Issawi, *Oil, the Middle East, and the World*, 36–49; McNaugher, *Arms and Oil*, 3–9; Shwadran, *The Middle East*, 7; Yergin, *The Prize*, 592–635.

21. Cordesman and Wagner, *The Lessons of Modern War*, 3:22–34; Cottrell et al., *Sea Power and Strategy in the Indian Ocean*, 82; McNaugher, *Arms and Oil*, 5–13, 23; Noyes, *The Clouded Lens*, 112–13; Weimer, *The Strategic Petroleum Reserve*, 64–65; Yergin, *The Prize*, 637–45, 674–745.

22. Carter, *Public Papers of the Presidents: Jimmy Carter, 1980–1981* 1:171.

23. U.S., Department of State, *American Foreign Policy: Basic Documents, 1977–1980*, 55.

24. Quoted in Palmer, *On Course to Desert Storm*, 108.

25. Lehman, *Command of the Seas*, 383.

26. Palmer, *On Course to Desert Storm*, 91.

27. Quoted in Kitfield, *Prodigal Soldiers*, 237–40.

28. Stanley R. Arthur, Transcript of Naval Service, PERS-00F, 1 Aug 1992, Authors' Files, OA; Benson and Hines, *The United States Military in North Africa and Southwest Asia Since World War II*, 39–51.

29. U.S. Central Command, Command History, 1987, I–8, Post 1 Jan 1974 Command Files, OA.

30. U.S. Central Command, Command History, 1984, 13; Ibid., 1987, I–6–I–9, Post 1 Jan 1974 Command Files, OA; Palmer, *On Course to Desert Storm*, 103–19.

31. Palmer, *Guardians of the Gulf*, 114.

32. CENTCOM was based at Tampa because its predecessors, the Rapid Deployment Force and the Rapid Deployment Joint Task Force, had been based there.

33. Marolda and Fitzgerald, *From Military Assistance to Combat, 1959–1965*, 293–94.

34. The Navy called its prepositioning ships "Maritime Prepositioning Ships." The Army and Air Force termed their prepositioning vessels "Afloat Prepositioning Ships."

35. Browning, "MPS: Maritime Prepositioning Ships," 36–39; Cote and Sapolsky, "Lift Myths," 1–4; Lenton, "Maritime Aspects of Operation Desert Shield," 396; Mercogliano,

"United States Merchant Marine in the Persian Gulf War," 12–14; Phillips, "SWOs In Sealift," 20–23; *USNDS*, 13–15, 27–28.

36. Gibson and Calhoun, "Barely in Time," 72–80; Gibson and Shuford, "Desert Shield and Strategic Sealift," 6–11.

37. U.S., Congress, Senate, Committee on Armed Services, *Defense Organization: The Need for Change*, 157–87; Gruetzner and Caldwell, "DOD Reorganization," 136–45.

38. Fedyszyn, "A Maritime Perspective," 80–87; Senate Committee on Armed Services, *Reorganization of the Department of Defense*, 597–606; Trainor, "Regional Security: A Reassessment," 44.

39. Friedman, *Desert Victory*, 76–83.

40. Arthur, interview by Marolda and Schneller, 5, 6.

41. "Aspin's Major Factors of Desert Victory," 39–41; Gruetzner and Caldwell, "DOD Reorganization," 143–45.

42. Powell and Persico, *My American Journey*, 411; Kitfield, *Prodigal Soldiers*, 296–97.

43. Quoted in Hartmann, *Naval Renaissance*, 22.

44. Lehman, *Command of the Seas*, 99.

45. Yurso, "The Decline of the Seventies," 356; Korb, "The Erosion of American Naval Preeminence, 338; Korb, *The Fall and Rise of the Pentagon*, 34; Hartmann, *Naval Renaissance*, 11; Friedman, "Elmo Russell Zumwalt, Jr.," 370–71.

46. McDonald, "Thomas Hinman Moorer," 359; Korb, "The Erosion of American Naval Preeminence," 338.

47. Korb, *The Fall and Rise of the Pentagon*, 17; Ryan, *First Line of Defense*, 50, 66, figure 3.

48. Korb, "The Erosion of American Naval Preeminence," 338; Korb, *The Fall and Rise of the Pentagon*, 55; Lehman, *Command of the Seas*, 95, 97; Ryan, *First Line of Defense*, 72, 84; Hartmann, *Naval Renaissance*, 12, 19.

49. Hartmann, *Naval Renaissance*, 11; McDonald, "Thomas Hinman Moorer," 360.

50. Howarth, *To Shining Sea*, 531.

51. Love, *History of the U.S. Navy*, 679; Yurso, "The Decline of the Seventies," 325.

52. Howarth, *To Shining Sea*, 10; Love, *History of the U.S. Navy*, 678; Yurso, "The Decline of the Seventies," 356.

53. Korb, *The Fall and Rise of the Pentagon*, 34, 37; Hone, *Power and Change*, 99.

54. Hartmann, *Naval Renaissance*, 16; Korb, *The Fall and Rise of the Pentagon*, 42.

55. Yurso, "The Decline of the Seventies," 325. See also 355.

56. Hartmann, *Naval Renaissance*, 23.

57. Yurso, "The Decline of the Seventies," 356.

58. Korb, "The Erosion of American Naval Preeminence," 338.

59. Etzold, "The Navy and National Security Policy in the 1970s," 278–79; Lehman, *Command of the Seas*, 95; Siegel, *The Use of Naval Forces in the Post-War Era*, 1.

60. Lehman, *Command of the Seas*, 99. See also 117.

61. Love, *History of the U.S. Navy*, 674, 677, 678.

62. Lehman, *Command of the Seas*, 99. See also 96.

63. Korb, "The Erosion of American Naval Preeminence," 337.

64. Zumwalt, *On Watch: A Memoir*, 307. See also Howarth, *To Shining Sea*, 529.

65. Baer, *One Hundred Years of Sea Power*, 397–411; Hartmann, *Naval Renaissance*, 14–15; Korb, "The Erosion of American Naval Preeminence," 337; Lehman, *Command of the Seas*, 132; Muir, *Black Shoes and Blue Water*, 199; Ryan, *First Line of Defense*, 73, 85.

66. Quoted in Yurso, "The Decline of the Seventies," 356.

67. Quoted in Howarth, *To Shining Sea*, 531.

68. Quoted in Love, *History of the U.S. Navy*, 674.

69. Quoted in Love, *History of the U.S. Navy*, 679. The Soviet navy of the 1970s was decidedly not a "paper tiger" as at least one uninformed writer has characterized it. See Vistica, *Fall From Glory*, 54.

70. Friedman, *U.S. Aircraft Carriers*; Muir, *Black Shoes and Blue Water*, 199.

71. "AAW Master Plan," c.1988, Executive Summary, 6, 9, file 1, box 3, Woodall Papers, OA; Watkins, "The Maritime Strategy," 16.

72. Baer, *One Hundred Years of Sea Power*, 408; *CPGW*, 686–87; Polmar, *Ships and Aircraft of the U.S. Fleet*, 405.

73. Muir, *Black Shoes and Blue Water*, 232.

74. Kelley, "The Amphibious Warfare Strategy," 18–29.

75. "AAW Master Plan," c.1988, Executive Summary, 12, file 1, box 3, Woodall Papers, OA.

76. Watkins, "The Maritime Strategy," 12.

77. *CPGW*, 690–91; Francillon, *Grumman Aircraft*, 507–23; *GWAPS*, vol. 4, part 1, 107–108; Prezelin, *Combat Fleets*, 770; Spick, *An Illustrated Guide to Modern Fighter Combat*, 90–93.

78. Quoted in Spick, *Modern Fighter Combat*, 92.

79. "AAW Master Plan," c. 1988, Executive Summary, 13–15, file 1, box 3, Woodall Papers, OA.

80. Potter, *Electronic Greyhounds*, 190–93.

81. Bailey, *Aegis Guided Missile Cruiser*, 92–94; Polmar, *Ships and Aircraft of the U.S. Fleet*, 110–17; Prezelin, *Combat Fleets*, 787–90.

82. "AAW Master Plan," c.1988, Executive Summary, 13–15, file 1, box 3, Woodall Papers, OA.

83. Prezelin, *Combat Fleets*, 753.

84. Breemer, *Soviet Submarines*; Polmar and Noot, *Submarines of the Russian and Soviet Navies*.

85. Polmar, *Ships and Aircraft of the U.S. Fleet*, 110, 137–59.

86. *CPGW*, 715, 725; Potter, *Electronic Greyhounds*, 126–28.

87. Carson to the editor, *Proceedings* 118 (Nov 1992): 20; *CPGW*, 185–87; Lutz et al., *Antisurface Warfare*, 5–1; Peterson, "What's Happening With CWC?" 85; Powers, "Commanding the Offense," 60–63; Frank Schwamb et al., *Strike Warfare*, 1–36; Ward et al., *C3*, 1–12; Watkins, "The Maritime Strategy," 8–13.

88. A quarter of a century earlier, in the years after World War II, the Navy had followed a similar forward-based, offensive strategic approach toward the Soviet threat. See Palmer, *Origins of the Maritime Strategy*.

89. Baer, *One Hundred Years of Sea Power*, 433.

90. CNO, "Maritime Strategy, Revision IV," 23 Feb 1989, file 1, box 3, Woodall Papers, OA; Baer, *One Hundred Years of Sea Power*, 407, 418–44; Friedman, *U.S. Maritime Strategy*; Hattendorf, "Evolution of the Maritime Strategy, 1977–1987"; Kelley, "The Amphibious Warfare Strategy," 26; Langdon and Ross, 12; Watkins, "The Maritime Strategy," 4–12.

91. CNO, "Maritime Strategy, Revision IV," 23 Feb 1989, file 1, box 3, Woodall Papers, OA; Baer, *One Hundred Years of Sea Power*, 407, 418–44; Friedman, *U.S. Maritime Strategy*; Grove, *Battle for the Fiords*; Hattendorf, "Evolution of the Maritime Strategy"; Kelley, "The Amphibious Warfare Strategy," 26; Watkins, "The Maritime Strategy," 4–12; Wood, "Fleet Renewal and Maritime Strategy in the 1980s."

92. Grove, *Battle for the Fiords*; Langdon and Ross, *Superpower Maritime Strategy in the Pacific*, 12; Muir, *Black Shoes and Blue Water*, 231.

93. Baer, *One Hundred Years of Sea Power*, 441; House Armed Services Committee, *The 600-Ship Navy and the Marine Corps*; Hartmann, *The Naval Renaissance*; Lehman, "The 600-Ship Navy."

94. Baer, *One Hundred Years of Sea Power*, 430, 441–42.

95. LaPlante, interview by Marolda and Schneller, tape 3, side 2.

96. Powell and Persico, *My American Journey*, 315.

97. Karsh and Rautsi, *Saddam Hussein*, 66–69, 138–94; al-Khalil, *Republic of Fear*, 259–73.

98. Hiro, *The Longest War*, 4.

99. This discussion of the Tanker War and Operation Earnest Will is based on Cordesman, *The Lessons of Modern War* 3:90–92, 277–90, 375–81, 530–46, 567–73; McDonald, "The Convoy Mission," 36–44; O'Rourke, "The Tanker War," 30–34; Palmer, *On Course to Desert Storm*, 103–34.

100. Palmer, *On Course to Desert Storm*, 121–34. During this period, the Air Force dispatched AWACS aircraft to Saudi Arabia to bolster the country's air defenses. West, "A Lasting Friendship," 36.

101. Crowe, *The Line of Fire*, 189. See also Less interview by Crist, Grieve interview by Crist, and Office of the Chief of Naval Operations, "Arabian Gulf Lessons Learned Report: April–November 1987, 13 Apr 1988, 17, collection of David B. Crist.

102. Palmer, *On Course to Desert Storm*, 121–34.

103. "COMUSNAVCENT Fact Sheet," in Seventh Fleet, Command History 1990, Post 1 Jan 1990 Command Files, OA; Palmer, *On Course to Desert Storm*, 124–26.

104. Crowe, *The Line of Fire*, 187.

105. In contrast, General Colin Powell, soon to become Chairman of the Joint Chiefs of Staff, spoke for many Army officers when he observed in his memoir that "the job clearly belonged to a soldier or Marine, not a sailor" because the navies in the area were "few, weak, and insignificant" and because "CENTCOM had been designed as a rapid deployment task force to fight land battles in the desert region." Powell and Persico, *My American Journey*, 383. Moreover, Powell saw the mission of the Navy's carrier-centered fleet more in terms of protecting sea lanes than maintaining a presence and projecting power ashore in the littoral regions of the world. *Ibid*, 438, 452.

106. CINCPAC, Admiral Ronald Hays, helped improve the command situation in the Central Command theater when he agreed to relinquish operational control of a Pacific Command carrier battle group to Crist when it came within 48 hours steaming time (at 14 knots) of the Strait of Hormuz. George B. Crist, interview by David B. Crist; Hayes, interview by Crist; and msg, Crist to Crowe, 0519Z 14 Jan 1987, subj: Joint Task Force Headquarters, collection of David B. Crist.

107. Bernsen, interview by Crist; and Howe, interview by Crist, collection of David B. Crist; Crowe, *The Line of Fire*, 187–88.

108. Levinson and Edwards, *Missile Inbound*.

109. Melia, *"Damn the Torpedoes"*, 121–23; Palmer, *On Course to Desert Storm*, 129–31; David Crist, "A Low-Intensity Conflict at Sea: U.S. Marine Corps Operations in the Persian Gulf, 1987–1988," unpublished paper presented at the U.S. Naval Academy Symposium, Oct 1997.

110. Lehman, *Command of the Seas*, 394–95.

111. Palmer, *Guardians of the Gulf*, 150–62.

112. *AFPCD*, 1989, 365.

113. Ibid., 363–64; Blacker, "The Collapse of Soviet Power in Europe," 88–102; Mandelbaum, "The Bush Foreign Policy," 5–22.

114. *CPGW*, 33, 349–50.

115. Powell and Persico, *My American Journey*, 111.

116. Ibid., 148.

117. Ibid.

118. Ibid.

119. Weinberger's pronouncement on the use of American forces overseas stipulated the following: "(1) Commit only if our or our allies' vital interests are at stake. (2) If we commit, do so with all the resources necessary to win. (3) Go in only with clear political and military objectives. (4) Be ready to change the commitment if the objectives change, since wars rarely stand still. (5) Only take on commitments that can gain the support of the American people and the Congress. (6) Commit U.S. forces only as a last resort." Powell and Persico, *My American Journey*, 303.

120. Ibid., 434. See also 416, 464.

121. Ibid., 475. See also Schwarzkopf, *It Doesn't Take a Hero*; Horner in Miller, ed., *Seeing Off the Bear*, 140.

122. Sharp, interview by Marolda and Schneller, tape 1, side 1.

123. Ibid.

124. Adler, *The Generals*; CPGW, 33, 349–52; GWAPS, vol. 5, part 1, 18; Hallion, *Storm Over Iraq*, 128; Horner in Miller, ed., *Seeing Off the Bear*, 141; Mackenzie, "A Conversation with Chuck Horner," 57–60; Motter, *The Persian Corridor*, 461–80; Schwarzkopf, *It Doesn't Take a Hero*; Sharp, interview by Marolda and Schneller, tape 1, side 1.

125. al-Khalil, *Republic of Fear*, 261.

126. Halliday, "The Gulf War and its Aftermath," 227; Palmer, *Guardians of the Gulf*, 150–62.

127. Devlin, "The Baath Party," 1396–1407; Friedman, *Desert Victory*, 15–26; Karsh and Rautsi, *Saddam Hussein*, 208; al-Khalil, *Republic of Fear*, 5, 38, 65, 70, 110–11; Muslih and Norton, "The Need for Arab Democracy," 6–7; Palmer, *Guardians of the Gulf*, 150–62.

128. House Committee on Armed Services, *Crisis in the Persian Gulf: Sanctions, Diplomacy, and War*, 41–51.

129. Palmer, *Guardians of the Gulf*, 150–62. See also Sifry and Serf, eds., *The Gulf War Reader*, 66; de la Billiere, *Storm Command*, 24–25, 74.

130. Chubin, "Gulf Regional Security After the Crisis," 204–6; Copley, "Saddam Hussein Gently Wakens the Dreamers of the Era of Universal Peace," 26; Karsh and Rautsi, *Saddam Hussein*, 136.

131. Mylroie, "Why Saddam Hussein Invaded Kuwait," 126.

132. CPGW, 3–4, 15–16; Karsh and Rautsi, "Why Saddam Hussein Invaded Kuwait," 19–21; Oberdorfer, "Missed Signals in the Middle East," 21–23; Palmer, *Guardians of the Gulf*, 150–62.

133. Quoted in Karsh and Rautsi, "Why Saddam Invaded Kuwait," 20–21.

134. Bengio, ed., *Saddam Speaks*, 37–49; Oberdorfer, "Missed Signals," 22.

135. Bengio, ed., *Saddam Speaks*, 48.

136. Quoted in Sifry and Cerf, eds., *The Gulf War Reader*, 125.

137. Kaplan, "Tales From the Bazaar," 52.

138. AFPCD, 1990, 438–39; Eilts, "The Persian Gulf Crisis," 14; Farouk-Sluglett and Sluglett, *Iraq Since 1958*, 100, 123; Haley, "Saddam Surprises the United States," 166, 172, 174; Inman, Nye, Perry, and Smith, "Lessons from the Gulf War," 61; *Los Angeles Times*, 23 Feb 1992, 1; Oberdorfer, "Missed Signals," 21–22; Palmer, *Guardians of the Gulf*, 150–62; *Triumph Without Victory*, staff of *U.S. News and World Report*, 13–20.

139. AFPCD, 1990, 444; Palmer, *Guardians of the Gulf*, 152.

140. Bengio, ed., *Saddam Speaks*, 59–60.

141. Oberdorfer, "Mixed Signals," 23.

142. *AFPCD*, 1990, 438–42 (emphasis added).

143. Bennet, "Sand Trap," 26; Blair, *At War in the Gulf*, 9; House Committee on Armed Services, *Crisis in the Persian Gulf: Sanctions, Diplomacy, and War*, 7; Karsh and Rautsi, "Why Saddam Invaded Kuwait," 21–22; Oberdorfer, "Missed Signals," 36; Sayigh, "The Gulf Crisis," 502.

144. Quoted in Palmer, *Guardians of the Gulf*, 159–60.

145. Karsh and Rautsi, "Why Saddam Invaded Kuwait," 24–26; Oberdorfer, "Missed Signals," 37–38; Palmer, *Guardians of the Gulf*, 150–62.

146. Palmer, 150–62

147. Quoted in Karsh and Rautsi, "Why Saddam Invaded Kuwait," 24–25.

148. *CPGW*, 4-6; Karsh and Rautsi, "Why Saddam Invaded Kuwait," 26; *Triumph Without Victory*, 21.

149. al-Khalil, *Republic of Fear*, 120; Prados, *Iraq and Kuwait*; Watson, ed., *Military Lessons of the Gulf War*, 15–16.

150. *CPGW*, 8; Oberdorfer, "Missed Signals," 37; *Triumph Without Victory*, 21–31.

151. *CPGW*, 8–12.

152. *The New York Times*, 25 Jul 1990, A1; Gordon and Trainor, *The Generals' War*, 19; Palmer, *Guardians of the Gulf*, 157, 200; USS *Reid*, Command History 1990, SH; USS *Taylor*, Command History 1990, SH.

153. *AFPCD*, 1990, 448–50.

154. Given the tenor in Washington, there was little that a CENTCOM staff officer could have done to change the direction of U.S. policy, but Admiral Sharp later concluded that the "most unsuccessful aspect of my tour with Central Command . . . was the inability to deter Saddam Hussein from attacking Kuwait." He added that in 1996 the United States and CENTCOM were better prepared for "signalling our intentions when someone begins to threaten our vital interests." Sharp, interview by Marolda and Schneller, tape 2, side 2. See also Powell and Persico, *My American Journey*, 462; Gordon and Trainor, *The Generals' War*, xii, 17–18.

155. Oberdorfer, "Missed Signals," 38–39; Palmer, *Guardians of the Gulf*, 150–62; *Triumph Without Victory*, 22–24.

156. Quoted in Gordon and Trainor, *The Generals' War*, 22.

157. House Committee on Armed Services, *Crisis in the Persian Gulf: Sanctions, Diplomacy, and War*, 7; Chubin, "Gulf Regional Security," 204; Oberdorfer, "Missed Signals," 40; Palmer, *Guardians of the Gulf*, 150–62.

158. Oberdorfer, "Missed Signals," 40; Palmer, *Guardians of the Gulf*, 150–62; *Triumph Without Victory*, 31–32.

159. Sharp, interview by Marolda and Schneller, tape 1, side 1.

160. Brooks, interview by Marolda and Schneller, tape 2, side 1.

161. Schubert and Kraus, eds., *Whirlwind*, ch. 3; Gordon and Trainor, *The Generals' War*, 25–28; Oberdorfer, "Missed Signals," 40; Palmer, *Guardians of the Gulf*, 150–62; Feely quoted in *Triumph Without Victory*, 30; see also 33–34.

162. Palmer, *Guardians of the Gulf*, 150–62; *Triumph Without Victory*, 25–26.

163. *CPGW*, 3; Scales, *Certain Victory*, 45.

164. *CPGW*, 3–4; Dunnigan and Bay, *From Shield to Storm*, 23; Nordwall, "Tethered Aerostat," 21; *The Military Balance, 1990–1991*, 108–9; Watson, ed., *Lessons of the Gulf War*, 15.

165. There is a large body of work on the causes of the Persian Gulf War. Interpretations range widely, with authors variously blaming Saddam Hussein, George Bush, or both for the war. For a sample of this literature, see the sources cited throughout this chapter, as well as Brown and Schneller, *A Select Bibliography of United States Naval Forces in Desert Shield and Desert Storm*.

166. Dunnigan and Bay, *From Shield to Storm*, 28; Indyk, "Watershed in the Middle East," 71–72; Karsh and Rautsi, *Saddam Hussein*, 216; Palmer, *Guardians of the Gulf*, 150–62; Quandt, "The Middle East in 1990," 53.

167. *CPGW*, 20; Gordon and Trainor, *The Generals' War*, 48; *The Military Balance 1991–1992*, 117–18; Palmer, *Guardians of the Gulf*, 150–62; *Triumph Without Victory*, 9–10, 40–74.

168. George Bush, "Remarks to Department of Defense Employees," *Weekly Compilation of Presidential Documents* 26 (20 Aug 1990), 1256. See also Linn, "Crisis in the Persian Gulf," 10–14; Palmer, *Guardians of the Gulf*, 150–62.

169. According to Sharp, after a Camp David meeting around this time, Powell told Sharp and others from MacDill that "on the basis of what I heard, after you all left [Camp David], I think you can just go back [to Tampa] and stand down. I don't think anything is going to happen." Sharp, interview by Marolda and Schneller, tape 2, side 1 (see also tape 1, side 1); Swain, *"Lucky War"*, 22.

170. Friedman, *Desert Victory*, 55; Palmer, *Guardians of the Gulf*, 150–62; *Triumph Without Victory*, 67–76.

171. George Bush, "Remarks and an Exchange with Reporters on the Iraqi Invasion of Kuwait," 5 Aug 1990, *Weekly Compilation of Presidential Documents* 26 (13 Aug 1990), 1208–9.

172. *AFPCD*, 1990, 471; Senate Committee on Armed Services, *Crisis in the Persian Gulf Region: U.S. Policy Options and Implications*, 8–23; Palmer, *Guardians of the Gulf*, 150–62; Sharp, interview by Marolda and Schneller, tape 2, side 1; *Triumph Without Victory*, 82–86.

173. George Bush, "Address to the Nation Announcing the Deployment of United States Armed Forces to Saudi Arabia," 8 Aug 1990, 1216–18; and "The President's News Conference," 8 Aug 1990, *Weekly Compilation of Presidential Documents* 26 (13 Aug 1990), 1223.

174. Ron Cole, JCS Joint Staff Historian, telephone conversation with Schneller, 19 Mar 1992; msg, CJCS, 091332Z Aug 1990, Authors' Files, OA; Schwarzkopf, *It Doesn't Take a Hero*, 309–10.

CHAPTER 2

1. Senate Committee on Armed Services, *Crisis in the Persian Gulf Region: U.S. Policy Options and Implications*, 654.

2. Sharp, interview by Marolda and Schneller, tape 2, side 1.

3. *CPGW*, 33–34, 39–43, 381, 490–97; Palmer, *On Course to Desert Storm*, 107.

4. Schwarzkopf took seriously a defector's report that the Iraqis had a plan for an attack into Saudi Arabia. Gordon and Trainor, *The Generals' War*, 65.

5. *CPGW*, 34–37.

6. Compilation, "Iraq Invasion of Kuwait" and "OP. Desert Shield," 22 Aug 1990, OA; Grove, ed., *Britain's Gulf War*, 54; Jacobs, "Arabian Gulf Navies in Crisis," 343–48; *CPGW*, 33–41; *USNDS*, B-2–B-5.

7. U.S. Naval Forces, Central Command, Command History 1990, 13, Post 1 Jan 1990 Command Files, OA; *USNDS*, A-2.

8. At least one carrier steamed in the Mediterranean at any one time during Desert Shield, including carriers deploying to the CENTCOM AOR through the Mediterranean. *Saratoga* alternated between the Red Sea and Eastern Mediterranean. By 6 January 1991, she had transited the Suez Canal five times. *USNDS*, A-12.

9. Commander Sixth Fleet, Command History 1989, 14–15, Post 1 Jan 1974 Command Files, OA.

10. Collins, "Military Geography of Iraq and Adjacent Arab Territory," 2; Friedman, *Desert Victory*, 104–5; Grove, *Operation Granby*, 55–56; Marolda, "A Host of Nations," 6; *The Military Balance, 1989–1990* 107, 113–14, 117–18; Palmer, *Guardians of the Gulf*, 167; Preston, "Allied MCM in the Gulf," 53. According to one source, during the latter half of 1990 the Libyans converted several Iraqi transport planes into aerial tankers. Gordon and Trainor, *The Generals' War*, 104.

11. *CPGW*, 35–36; Gordon and Trainor, *The Generals' War*, 54–55; *GWAPS, Summary Report*, 3; Jamieson, "Lucrative Targets," 5, 6; Scales, *Certain Victory*, 50–51.

12. Gordon and Trainor, *The Generals' War*, 30; see also 28–29, 36, 39, 52.

13. Ibid., 50.

14. Sharp, interview by Marolda and Schneller, tape 1, side 2.

15. JULLS Long Report 92049–40158 (00023), 22 Sep 1990, Naval History Documentation Team, CAPT L. Douglas, USNR, USCENTCOM Documents re: Desert Shield/Storm, acc. #917152, OA.

16. *CPGW*, 34; Palmer, *Guardians of the Gulf*, 171.

17. Schubert and Kraus, eds., *Whirlwind*, chs. 3–4; *CPGW*, 34–37, 381–87; Scales, *Certain Victory*, 51; *USNDS*, A-2, A-3.

18. There were also 529 Air Force aircraft in the CENTCOM area at that time. Davis, *Strategic Air Power in Desert Storm*, 15.

19. She operated as an aircraft ferry but might have been available in a crisis.

20. Compilation, "Iraq Invasion of Kuwait" and "OP Desert Shield," 22 Aug 1990, Authors' Files, OA; Jacobs, "Arabian Gulf Navies in Crisis," 343–48; *CPGW*, 33–41. Naval leaders remembered the April 1989 tragedy that had befallen *Wisconsin*'s sister ship, *Iowa* (BB 61), when an explosion in the center gun of turret II had killed 47 officers and men. To help prevent a similar tragedy if *Wisconsin* was called upon to engage Iraqi forces, the Chief of Naval Operations, Admiral Frank B. Kelso II, demanded that her guns be certified "safe to fire." Accordingly, Commander Naval Surface Force, U.S. Atlantic Fleet, Vice Admiral Joseph S. Donnell III, ordered Captain Peter W. Bulkeley to proceed to the Middle East at the head of a small team. In late August, Bulkeley's group was helicoptered from Seeb, Oman, out to the battleship, then in the Gulf of Oman enroute to the Persian Gulf. They spent six days inspecting *Wisconsin*'s guns, ammunition, and fire control equipment, as well as the training records of each gunner and the firing procedures used in each turret. At the end of the month, based on Bulkeley's recommendation, Admiral Kelso certified *Wisconsin*'s 16-inch naval rifles "safe to fire." Bulkeley, interview by Marolda and Schneller, 22–31.

21. Arthur and Pokrant, "Desert Storm at Sea," 83; Moore Jr., "Marine Air: There When Needed," 66; Zimmeck, "A War of Logistics," 1-13–1-17, 1-28.

22. *CPGW*, 380–81; Graham, "Maritime Prepositioning Enters the 1990s," 82–84; Norton, "Sealift," 44; Palmer, *Guardians of the Gulf*, 163–92; Simmons, "Getting Marines to the Gulf," 53–54; Sinagra, "Maritime Prepositioning System," 28–29; *USNDS*, A-2–A-3; Zimmeck, "A War of Logistics," 1-13–1-17, 1-28.

23. Senate Committee on Armed Services, *Crisis in the Persian Gulf Region: U.S. Policy Options and Implications*, 24.

24. Hallion, *Storm Over Iraq*, 146–47.

25. *CPGW*, 190–91; Friedman, *Naval Institute Guide to World Naval Weapons Systems*, 79–81; Palmer, *On Course to Desert Storm*, 114.

26. Quoted in Palmer, *Guardians of the Gulf*, 216.

27. *CPGW*, 190; Friedman, *Desert Victory*, 209; Friedman, *Guide to World Naval Weapons Systems*, 89–90; Liebman, "We Need Armed Helos," 84–86; Prezelin, ed., *Combat Fleets of the World 1990/91*, 261–64.

28. *CPGW*, 190; Liebman, "We Need Armed Helos," 84–86.

29. Cordesman and Wagner, *The Lessons of Modern War* 2:102, 532.

30. Msg, USCINCCENT, 0155Z, 17 Aug 1990, attached to Sitrep #19, CNO Desert Shield Situation Reports, OA.

31. *CPGW*, 639–46; Simpson, *Chemical and Biological Weapons in the Persian Gulf Area*.

32. Sharp, interview by Marolda and Schneller, tape 1, side 2.

33. *CPGW*, 31–42.

34. Ibid., 31–42.

35. Boomer, "Special Trust and Confidence Among the Trail-Breakers," 48. Admiral Sharp believed that there was no good reason why Saddam would not invade, so he anticipated attack until about mid-September. Sharp, interview by Marolda and Schneller, tape 2, side 1.

36. *CPGW*, 31–42, 334–37; Hopkins, "This Was No Drill," 58.

37. The mining of U.S. merchant ships in port during the Vietnam War hampered the logistical effort.

38. IMEFB, 2 Sep 1990.

39. *CPGW*, 523–29; IMEFB, 5 Dec 1990.

40. Bosco, "Making Things Happen in the Persian Gulf," 35; Bosco, "Port Harbor Security," 25–26; *CPGW*, 399–400; U.S. Coast Guard, "Desert Shield/Desert Storm Chronology," 19 Jun 1992, U.S. Coast Guard Historian's Office; *USNDS*, 42; Commander U.S. Naval Forces, Central Command, Command History 1990, 7–8, Post 1 Jan 1990 Command File, OA; United States Special Operations Command, "10th Anniversary History," 16 Apr 1997, 32, Authors' Files.

41. Ltr, Sutton to Marolda, 12 Apr 1996, Authors' Files, OA. Communist swimmers sank a number of merchant ships in the harbors of South Vietnam. The effectiveness of the enemy's campaign was limited, however, by the efforts of Navy and Coast Guard harbor defense forces in Operation Stable Door. Marolda, *By Sea, Air, and Land*, 149–53. See also Rear Admiral Robert Sutton, Biographical Sheet, in Commander U.S. Naval Forces, Central Command, Command History 1990, Post 1 Jan 1990 Command Files, OA.

42. Bosco, "Making Things Happen in the Persian Gulf," 35; Bosco, "Port Harbor Security," 25–26; Commander U.S. Naval Forces, Central Command, Command History 1990, 7–8, Post 1 Jan 1990 Command Files, OA; *CPGW*, 399–400; U.S. Coast Guard, "Desert Shield/Desert Storm Chronology," 19 Jun 1992, U.S. Coast Guard Historian's Office; *USNDS*, 42.

43. *GWAPS, Summary Report*, 34. See also Pokrant, *A View*, 2–5.

44. Ltr, Mauz to Marolda, 12 Jun 1996, Authors' Files, OA.

45. Quoted in *Triumph Without Victory*, 101. See also *CPGW*, 31, 37–38; Friedman, *Desert Victory*, 61–63.

46. Gordon and Trainor, *The Generals' War*, 56. Air Force General Charles Horner also believed that "there really was very little to stop them other than air power." Quoted in Jamieson, "Lucrative Targets," 4.

47. Scales, *Certain Victory*, 85.

48. Sharp, interview by Marolda and Schneller, tape 1, side 2.

49. Gordon and Trainor, *The Generals' War*, 63, 99; Scales, *Certain Victory*, 86.

50. Ltr, Fogarty to Marolda, 5 Mar 1996, Authors' Files, OA.

51. Mann, *Thunder and Lightning*, 130.

52. Hopkins, "This Was No Drill," 59.

53. Ibid.

54. Walter E. Boomer, remarks made at the Society for Military History Conference, Quantico Marine Corps Base, 11 Apr 1992.

55. Ibid.

56. *CPGW*, 384–87; Jones, "MPS and Desert Storm," 47–48; Simmons, "Getting Marines to the Gulf," 53–59.

57. de la Billiere, *Storm Command*, 48.

58. Friedman, *Desert Victory*, 321–22; Griffis et al., *Amphibious Operations*, vi, 2; LaPlante, interview by Marolda and Schneller, tape 1, side 1.

59. *CPGW*, 384–87; Jones, "MPS and Desert Storm," 47–48; Simmons, "Getting Marines to the Gulf," 53–59; Swain, *"Lucky War"*, 39.

60. Sharp, interview by Marolda and Schneller, tape 1, side 2.

61. Brown et al., *Training*, 4–12; Commander U.S. Naval Forces, Central Command, Command History 1990, 7, 8, 11, 13, Post 1 Jan 1990 Command Files, OA; ltr, Grieve to Marolda, 26 Mar 1996, Authors' Files, OA; LaPlante, interview by Marolda and Schneller; Melia, *"Damn the Torpedoes,"* 127; Passarelli et al., *Mine Countermeasures*, 2-1, A-1; *USNDS*, 42.

62. Ltr, Mauz to Marolda, 12 Jun 1996, Authors' Files, OA.

63. LaPlante, interview by Marolda and Schneller, tape 2, side 1.

64. On 1 January 1991, Captain Grieve's designation became CTG 151.4 as part of a reorganization of Navy forces within the Persian Gulf. He still reported to Rear Admiral Fogarty (CTF 151).

65. Brown et al., *Training*, 4-12; Commander U.S. Naval Forces, Central Command, Command History 1990, 7, 8, 11, 13, Post 1 Jan 1990 Command Files, OA; ltrs, Grieve to Marolda, 26 Mar 1996, and Mauz to Marolda, 12 Jun 1996, Authors' Files, OA; LaPlante, interview by Marolda and Schneller; Melia, *"Damn the Torpedoes,"* 127; Passarelli et al., *Mine Countermeasures*, 2-1, A-1; *USNDS*, 42.

66. Sharp, interview by Marolda and Schneller, tape 1, side 2; see also tape 2, side 1.

67. Grove, *Operation Granby*, 59. See also 54–49.

68. Kitfield, *Prodigal Soldiers*, 366–69. Admiral March expressed the similar view that the "only way that the Navy was going to play in the game was if we were inside." March, interview by Marolda and Schneller, tape 1, side 1.

69. Kitfield, "Navy Blues," 28.

70. Msg, *Independence* to COMUSNAVCENT, 1200Z, 6 Oct 1990, file 1, box 14, Woodall Papers, OA.

71. Withern, "In Harm's Way," 14–15.

72. *CPGW*, 38–40, 65, 388; *Triumph Without Victory*, 143–44; *USNDS*, A-2–A-7; ltr, Zimmeck to Shulimson, n.d., Authors' Files, OA.

73. Sutherland, interview by Marolda; *CPGW* 350–52; Nickel et al., *Logistics*, 2–3.

74. Arthur, interview by Marolda and Schneller, 5, 47, 48.

75. Ltr, Mauz to Marolda, 12 Jun 1996, Authors' Files, OA.

76. Sharp, interview by Marolda and Schneller, tape 1, side 2.

77. *CPGW*, 350–52.

78. Msg, Eyes Only, CINCCENT to CNO, 311200Z Mar 1991, USCENTCOMFWD, CinC's File, folder 61, box 2, RG 518 (CENTCOM Records), National Archives (NA). See also msg, Personal, Schwarzkopf to Powell, info to CINCs, 051630Z Apr 1991, US-CENTCOMFWD, CinC's File, folder 60.

79. "COMUSNAVCENT Fact Sheet," Seventh Fleet, Command History 1990, and "Rear Admiral Robert Sutton, U.S. Navy," in U.S. Naval Forces, Central Command,

Command History 1990, Post 1 Jan 1990 Command Files, OA; ltr, Sutton to Marolda, 12 Apr 1996, Authors' Files, OA.

80. U.S., Department of Defense, *Conduct of the Persian Gulf War: Final Report to Congress* 1:IV-1–2 (working paper dated 10 Oct 1991), OA.

81. Commander in Chief, U.S. Pacific Command, Command History 1990, 1:4, Post 1 Jan 1990 Command Files, OA.

82. Ibid., 13; *CPGW*, 552.

83. Only hours after the Americans met with King Fahd, Schwarzkopf gathered his chief staff officers around his bed in the Riyadh hotel where they were staying. When the discussion turned to naval matters, Admiral Sharp suggested that despite some early bumps in the command and control of naval forces during Operation Earnest Will, the Joint Task Force Middle East structure under Rear Admiral Less had functioned fairly well. He reasoned that because the Navy would be playing a major role in the theater with multi-carrier operations, the COMUSNAVCENT billet should be filled by a three-star *"fleet commander."* The consideration that Schwarzkopf might need a three-star naval *component commander* with him at CENTCOM headquarters in Riyadh was not raised. Sharp, interview by Marolda and Schneller, tape 1, side 2. Sutton subsequently served as one of Mauz's deputies.

84. *CPGW*, 350–51, 552–53; Stanik, *Swift and Effective Retribution*; "Transcript of Naval Service for Vice Admiral Henry Herrward Mauz, Junior, U.S. Navy," 1 Aug 1989, Biographical Files of Naval Officers, OA.

85. Arthur, interview by Marolda and Schneller, 8-9; Pokrant, *A View*, 2-1.

86. Ltr, Mauz to Marolda, 12 Jun 1996, Authors' Files, OA.

87. Ibid.

88. *CPGW*, 543–59; Perla, *Summary*, 34–35; *USNDS*, A-5.

89. Commander U.S. Seventh Fleet/Commander U.S. Naval Forces, Central Command, Command History 1990, section II, 4–5, Post 1 Jan 1990 Command Files, OA; *CPGW*, 552-53; ltr, Sutton to Marolda, 12 Apr 1996, Authors' Files, OA; Shepko et al., *Maritime Interception Operations*, 6; Ward et al., *C3*, 1-1–1-10.

90. In international law, a formal blockade is an act of war, a step the UN coalition was not yet ready to take.

91. *CPGW*, 320–21; Palmer, *Guardians of the Gulf*, 175; *USNDS*, 20–21.

92. Blair, *At War in the Gulf*, 12–25; *CPGW*, 26–29.

93. The UN Security Council adopted twelve resolutions during Operation Desert Shield. For texts of the resolutions and votes by members of the council, see Browne, *Iraq-Kuwait* or *CPGW*, 319–31.

94. Maritime Interception Operations, Concept of Operations, in CENTCOM J-5 After Action Report, USCENTCOMFWD, J-5 Strategic Planning File, Vol. I, tab G, box 1, RG 518 (CENTCOM Records), NA.

95. Utz, *Cordon of Steel*.

96. Marolda, *By Sea, Air, and Land*, 143–61, 313–29; Marolda, *Crucible of War*, 222; Schreadley, *From the Rivers to the Sea*, 75–101,

97. *CPGW*, 57–58.

98. Maritime Interception Operations, Concept of Operations, in CENTCOM J-5 After Action Report, USCENTCOMFWD, J-5 Strategic Planning File, vol. I, tab G, 5, box 1, RG 518 (CENTCOM Records), NA.

99. Operation Order 002, Revision 2, 011604Z Sep 1991, encl 2 of CENTCOM J-5 After Action Report, USCENTCOMFWD, J-5 Strategic Planning File, vol. I, tab G, box 1, RG 518 (CENTCOM Records), NA. See also Schwarzkopf, *It Doesn't Take a Hero*, 321–22;

CPGW, 57; Carroll, *Maritime Interception Force Operations*, 27; Gordon and Trainor, *The Generals' War*, 64; *USNDS*, A-3.

100. Bowman, *Persian Gulf War*, compilation, "Iraq Invasion of Kuwait and OP. Desert Shield," 22 Aug 1990; *CPGW*, 20, 49–53; *USNDS*, C-2.

101. Perla, *Summary*, 3.

102. Ltr, Mauz to Marolda, 12 Jun 1996, Authors' Files, OA; Multi-National Naval Commander's Conference, encl 5 of J-5 After Action Report, USCENTCOMFWD, J-5 Strategic Planning File, vol. I, tab G, box 1, RG 518 (CENTCOM Records), NA; Marolda, "A Host of Nations," 271.

103. *CPGW*, 49–53, 502–4; Gimblett, "Preliminary Research Results," 4; Gimblett, "Canadian Coordination of the Persian Gulf Combat Logistics Force," in Haydon and Griffiths, *Multinational Forces*, 232–33; Morin and Gimblett, *Operation Friction, 1990–1991: The Canadian Forces in the Persian Gulf*, 60–61.

104. Craig, *Call for Fire*, 168.

105. Ltr, Mauz to Marolda, 12 Jun 1996, Authors' Files, OA; Multi-National Naval Commander's Conference, encl 5 of J-5 After Action Report, USCENTCOMFWD, J-5 Strategic Planning File, vol. I, tab G, box 1, RG 518 (CENTCOM Records), NA.

106. Ltr, Mauz to Marolda, 12 Jun 1996. See also Mauz in *Twelfth International Seapower Symposium*, 70; Horner, *The Gulf Commitment*, 72, 104; C.J. Oxenbould, RAN, "Australians Going to War in the 1990s," presentation at Australian War Memorial, 6 Nov 1991, 17; and Richard H. Gimblett, Directorate of History, National Defence Headquarters, "Preliminary Research Results: Canadian Naval Operations in the Persian Gulf, 1990–1991," 5 Mar 1992, 4, Authors' Files, OA; *Gulf News*, 17 Oct 1990, 3.

107. Msg, Personal, Schwarzkopf to Powell, info to CINCs, 051630Z Apr 1991, US-CENTCOMFWD, CinC's File, folder 60, box 2, RG 518 (CENTCOM Records), NA.

108. Delery, "Away, the Boarding Party!" 66; *CPGW*, 50–53; *USNDS*, 20–23.

109. Carroll, *Maritime Interception Force Operations*, 13, 25–29; Shepko et al., *Maritime Interception Operations*, 1.

110. Friedman, *Desert Victory*, 70–71.

111. *CPGW*, 49–53, 353, 502–4.

112. Horner, *The Gulf Commitment*, 103; ltr, P. C. van Royen, Director, Institute for Maritime History, Ministry of Defence to Dr. Marolda, 17 Oct 1997, re "Dutch participation in Gulf War, 1990–1991," Authors' Files.

113. Captain Douglas Bauer, USNR, Trip Report, "Desert Storm: An Historical Odyssey, 28 Feb–3 Apr 1991," Jun 1991, 115, OA. See also Eduardo Alfredo Rosenthal, "The Argentine Navy in the Persian Gulf," 5; Admiral Molina Pico, Argentine Navy, in *Twelfth International Seapower Symposium*, 70.

114. Department of the Navy, "1992 Posture Statement," Feb–Mar 1992, 8.

115. HMAS *Darwin*, Report of Proceedings, Oct 1990, 5, Authors' Files, OA.

116. Brooks, interview by Marolda and Schneller, tape 2, side 1; Brian Shellum, *A Chronology of Defense Intelligence in the Gulf War: A Research Aid for Analysts* (Washington: Defense Intelligence Agency, 1997), 16, 27.

117. Burgess, "Orions of Arabia," 15; *CPGW*, 334–37, 502–4; Vallance, "Royal Air Force Operations in the Gulf War," 35.

118. Carroll, *Maritime Force Interception Operations*, 13; *CPGW*, 54–55; Delery, "Away, the Boarding Party!" 67.

119. HMAS *Success*, Report of Proceedings, Sep 1990, 7, Authors' Files, OA.

120. Horner, *The Gulf Commitment*, 88. See also HMAS *Darwin*, Report of Proceedings, Sep 1990, 5, Authors' Files, OA.

121. Ltr, Mauz to Marolda, 12 Jun 1996, Authors' Files, OA.

122. Delery, "Away, the Boarding Party!" 67–68; "Severing Saddam's Lifeline: Maritime Interception Controls the Flow to Iraq," *All Hands* 68 (Desert Storm Special Issue), 11; *USNDS*, 22.

123. *CPGW*, 57-58; Horner, *The Gulf Commitment*, 86-87; HMAS *Darwin*, Report of Proceedings, Sep 1990, 5; and HMAS *Success*, Report of Proceedings, Sep 1990, 4, Authors' Files, OA.

124. Quoted in *CPGW*, 55.

125. *CPGW*, 53–57, 62, 334–37, 502–4.

126. Msg, CTG 150.2, 060931Z Sep 1990, MIF file #1, Naval History Documentation Team (CAPT W.R. McClintock, USNR), acc. #917150, OA.

127. Burgess, "Orions of Arabia," 15; *CPGW*, 56–57.

128. Ltr, Mauz to Marolda, 12 Jun 1996, Authors' Files, OA.

129. *CPGW*, 53–57, 62, 502–4.

130. Ibid., 58, 502–4.

131. Delery, "Away the Boarding Party!" 71; *CPGW*, 58–59; Herndon, "Amphibious Forces and the Gulf War," 79–80; HMAS *Darwin*, Report of Proceedings, Oct 1990, 5–6, Authors' Files, OA; Horner, *The Gulf Commitment*, 94–96.

132. Carroll, *Maritime Interception Force Operations*, 25; *CPGW*, 54–60.

133. House Committee on Armed Services, *Crisis in the Persian Gulf War: Sanctions, Diplomacy, and War*, 856; *OPDS*, 180; Palmer, *Guardians of the Gulf*, 175.

134. "Breakbulk" ships carry cargo that is not packed into containers.

135. Norton, "Sealift," 43–44; Rost et al., *Sealift*, 3–5, 10–13; Hansford Johnson, interview by Matthews and Smith, 4, U.S. Transportation Command.

136. *CPGW*, 417–18; Donovan, "Surge and Sustainment," 42; Prina, "Conflict Spotlights Sealift, Shipbuilding Deficiencies," 46; Rost et al., *Sealift*, 10.

137. The FSS were: *Algol* (T-AKR 287), *Altair* (T-AKR 291), *Antares* (T-AKR 294), *Bellatrix* (T-AKR 288), *Capella* (T-AKR 293), *Denebola* (T-AKR 289), *Pollux* (T-AKR 290), and *Regulus* (T-AKR 292). Matthews and Holt, *United States Transportation Command History*, 145.

138. To deliver this amount of cargo by C-5A Galaxy airlift aircraft would require some 230 flights. Gordon and Trainor, *The Generals' War*, 43.

139. *CPGW*, 378–79; Gibson and Shuford, "Desert Shield and Strategic Sealift," 12; Frederick and Nagy, "So Where Were All the RO/Ros?" 125; Johnson, "Presentation to the Committee on Merchant Marine and Fisheries;" Matthews and Holt, *United States Transportation Command History*, 43; Norton, "Sealift," 44; Rost, et al., *Sealift*, 4–5, 8–9, 22–28; *USNDS*, 28.

140. Matthews and Holt, *United States Transportation Command History*, 43.

141. The travails of *Antares* were a staple at the daily CINC's briefing during August at CENTCOM Headquarters in Tampa, Florida. Edward J. Marolda, memo, "CENTCOM MORNING BRIEF, 0815 31 AUG 90," Authors' Files, OA.

142. Hansford Johnson, interview by Matthews and Smith, 10–11, 27, U.S. Transportation Command.

143. Ackley, "Sealift and National Security," 43; *CPGW*, 378; "Lessons Learned Or Lost?" 2; Hansford Johnson, interview by Matthews and Smith, 10, U.S. Transportation Command; Norton, "Sealift," 44–46; Rost et al., *Sealift*, 5, 11; Senate Committee on Armed Services, *Crisis in the Persian Gulf Region: Policy Options and Implications*, 78; *USNDS*, 30.

144. Matthews and Holt, *United States Transportation Command History*, 48–49; Rost et al., *Sealift*, 14.

145. Rost et al., *Sealift*, 9, 11, 25, 31.

146. Ibid., 5, 31; *CPGW*, 46; Norton, "Sealift," 43–44.

147. Rost et al., *Sealift*, 21.

148. See for instance, Kesteloot, "Sealift After the Storm," 37–40; Collar, "Desert Storm and Its Effect on U.S. Maritime Policy," 67.

149. Cote and Sapolsky, "Lift Myths," 3.

150. Ltr, Sutton to Marolda, 12 Apr 1996, Authors' Files, OA.

151. Johnson, "Presentation to the Committee on Merchant Marine and Fisheries"; Norton, "Sealift," 42, 46; Rost et al., *Sealift*, 3; Verrico, "Getting It There Vital to Victory," 6.

152. *CPGW*, 394, 402–3; Evans, "From the Gulf," 77; Suit, "The Logistics of Air Power Projection," 12.

153. Matthews and Holt, *United States Transportation Command History*, xi; Rost et al., *Sealift*, 6, 21.

154. Matthews and Holt, *United States Transportation Command History*, 95, 182.

155. Quoted in "Strategic Sealift—Desert Storm 1990–91," *Navy Talking Points* (Winter 1991).

156. Johnson, "Presentation to the Committee on Merchant Marine and Fisheries"; Norton, "Sealift," 42, 46; Rost et al., *Sealift*, 3; Verrico, "Getting It There Vital to Victory," 6.

157. Hansford Johnson, interview by Matthews and Smith, 10, U.S. Transportation Command.

158. Hooper, *Mobility, Support, Endurance*, 1–7; Marolda, *By Sea, Air, and Land*, 239–40; Marolda, *Crucible of War*, 224; Palmer, *On Course to Desert Storm*, 83–103, 101–34.

159. Nickel et al., *Logistics*, 2-1.

160. Compilation, "Iraq Invasion of Kuwait and 'OP. Desert Shield,'" 22 Aug 1990, Authors' Files, OA; *USNDS*, 30.

161. Nickel et al., *Logistics*, 5-2–5-3.

162. Ibid., 5-9, 5-10, 5-15; Mixson, interview by Ramsdell, 17–18.

163. Nickel et al., *Logistics*, 5-4, 5-5, 5-16.

164. Bosco, "Making Things Happen in the Persian Gulf," 34; Nickel et al., *Logistics*, 5-9, 5-10.

165. "Combat Logistics," 44.

166. HMAS *Success*, Report of Proceedings, Nov 1990, 1, Authors' Files, OA.

167. HMAS *Sydney*, Report of Proceedings, Feb 1991, 2, Authors' Files, OA.

168. HMAS *Brisbane*, Report of Proceedings, Feb 1991, 2, Authors' Files, OA.

169. Bosco, "Making Things Happen in the Persian Gulf," 33; *CPGW*, 394, 399–400; Nickel et al., *Logistics*, 2-5, 4-2–4-6, 5-1, 5-2, 5-4.

170. Nickel et al., *Logistics*, 4-3.

171. Graham et al., *Medical*, 17–18; Matthews and Holt, *United States Transportation Command History*, 143.

172. *CPGW*, 451–70; Engbrecht, "Fleet Hospital," 29–30; compilation, "Iraq Invasion of Kuwait and OP. Desert Shield," 22 Aug 1990, Authors' Files, OA; Roberts, "The Untold Story in the Gulf," 9–11; *USNDS*, 15–16.

173. *CPGW*, 451–70; Engbrecht, "Fleet Hospital," 29–30; "Iraq Invasion of Kuwait and OP. Desert Shield"; Roberts, "Navy Medicine and the Marines," 9–11; *USNDS*, 15–16, Zimmeck, "A War of Logistics," 1-32–1-33, 1-37.

174. Ltr, Zimmeck to Shulimson, n.d., Authors' Files, OA; *The Washington Post*, 23 Jan 1993. See also Hyams et al., "Diarrheal Disease during Operation Desert Shield," 1423.

175. Bove et al., "Fleet Hospitals," 77; *CPGW*, 454–61; Graham et al., *Medical*, 1, 19–21, 32; "Persian Gulf Service Station," 36–39, Zimmeck, "A War of Logistics," 1-32–1-33, 1-37.

176. *CPGW*, 442–44; Naval Mobile Construction Battalions 5, 7, 40, Command Histories, 1990-91; and Seabee Command Historian informational sheet, 1 May 1991, Post 1 Jan 1990 Command Files, OA; Nickel et al., *Logistics*, 9-1-9–9; *USNDS*, 32–33; Zimmeck, "A War of Logistics," 2-11.

177. Brabham, "Training, Education Were the Keys," 52.

178. Huddleston, "Commentary on Desert Shield," 32; "Iraq Invasion of Kuwait and 'OP. Desert Shield."

179. *CPGW*, 400–401, 448.

180. Ibid., 382–87; "The Forces of Desert Storm," 34; Friedman, *Desert Victory*, 297–300; Horner, "Desert Shield/Desert Storm," 6; Perla, *Summary*, 18; Simmons, "Getting Marines to the Gulf," 59.

181. Senate Committee on Armed Services, *Crisis in the Persian Gulf Region: U.S. Policy Options and Implications*, 661.

CHAPTER 3

1. Schubert and Kraus, eds., *Whirlwind War*, ch. 5.

2. *CPGW*, 91–92; *GWAPS, Summary*, 33-35; Putney, "From Instant Thunder to Desert Storm," 40.

3. Apparently, Warden did not think involving officers from the other services was necessary or even desirable. Reynolds, *Heart of the Storm*, 28.

4. Warden authored the influential *The Air Campaign* and taught air power theory at the Air War College, Maxwell Air Force Base, Alabama.

5. *CPGW*, 91–92; *GWAPS, Summary*, 91–92; Morocco, "From Vietnam to Desert Storm," 68–73; Palmer, *Guardians of the Gulf*, 199; Palmer, "The Storm in the Air," 25–26; Putney, "From Instant Thunder to Desert Storm," 41.

6. Schwarzkopf, *It Doesn't Take a Hero*, 318. General Peter de la Billiere, overall commander of British forces in the theater, later said Schwarzkopf told him that "the trouble" with Brent Scowcroft, the President's national security advisor, was that he was "an airman and the worst kind of airman. He's a *strategic* airman!" Billiere, *Storm Command*, 86.

7. Quoted in Putney, "From Instant Thunder to Desert Storm, 41.

8. Quoted in Putney, "From Instant Thunder to Desert Storm," 42. See also Gordon and Trainor, *The Generals' War*, 84, 137.

9. Gordon and Trainor, *The Generals' War*, 98; Mandeles, et al., *Managing Command and Control*, 10–13; Powell and Persico, *My American Journey*, 476; Putney, "From Instant Thunder to Desert Storm," 42.

10. *GWAPS, Summary*, 37; *CPGW*, 91–92. The Air Force's Tactical Air Command also opposed the plan. Mann, *Thunder and Lightning*, 1–3, 29; Reynolds, *Heart of the Storm*, 121–31.

11. Horner in Miller, ed., *Seeing Off the Bear*, 146. See also Putney, "From Instant Thunder to Desert Storm," 44, 47.

12. Reynolds, *Heart of the Storm*, 133.

13. *CPGW*, 93; *GWAPS, Summary*, 37–38; Mandeles et al., *Managing Command and Control*, 15; Palmer, *Guardians of the Gulf*, 201.

14. Davis, *Strategic Air Power in Desert Storm*, 13; Gordon and Trainor, *The Generals' War*, 90; Mann, *Thunder and Lightning*, 63.

15. *CPGW*, 91–94.

16. When later discussing Air Force Chief of Staff Michael Dugan's public contention that air power alone could win the war, Powell implied that like Dugan the object of some air power theorists was little more than a "grab for Air Force glory." Powell and Persico, *My American Journey,* 477. See also *GWAPS, Summary,* 38, 44; Palmer, *Guardians of the Gulf,* 96–98.

17. *GWAPS, Summary,* 38, 44; Palmer, *Guardians of the Gulf,* 180.

18. Powell and Persico, *My American Journey,* 489.

19. Gordon and Trainor, *The Generals' War,* 96–98.

20. Ltr, Mauz to Marolda, 12 Jun 1996, Authors' Files, OA.

21. Ibid.

22. Kitfield, *Prodigal Soldiers,* 361–62.

23. Palmer, *Guardians of the Gulf,* 182–83; Powell and Persico, *My American Journey,* 498–99; Schwarzkopf, *It Doesn't Take a Hero,* 353–62.

24. According to one source, Powell considered giving the embargo one or even two years to work on Saddam. Gordon and Trainor, *The Generals' War,* 131.

25. Schwarzkopf, *It Doesn't Take a Hero,* 320. See also Palmer, *Guardians of the Gulf,* 201–2; Palmer, "The Storm in the Air," 27.

26. Sharp, interview by Marolda and Schneller, tape 2, side 1.

27. Purvis, interview by Marolda, 1; Scales, *Certain Victory,* 109; Schwarzkopf, *It Doesn't Take a Hero;* Swain, *"Lucky War",* 76–78; Schubert and Krause, eds., *Whirlwind War,* ch. 5.

28. *CPGW,* 65–67; Scales, *Certain Victory,* 124; Swain, *Lucky War,* 78.

29. Purvis, interview by Marolda, 19. See also Sharp, interview by Marolda and Schneller, tape 2, side 1.

30. *CPGW,* 65–67; Morocco, "From Vietnam to Desert Storm," 68; Powell and Persico, *My American Journey,* 485; Schwarzkopf, *It Doesn't Take a Hero,* 356–61; Schubert and Kraus, eds., *Whirlwind War,* ch. 5.

31. *CPGW,* 67–68.

32. Purvis, interview by Marolda, 8. See also 5–7, 18, 47, 52, 65–67; Schubert and Kraus, eds., *Whirlwind War,* ch. 5.

33. Purvis, interview by Marolda, 48. See also Gordon and Trainor, *The Generals' War,* 176; Scales, *Certain Victory,* 128. Several times that fall, Mauz tried unsuccessfully to get CINCCENT to reach a decision on the employment of the ATF. Pokrant, *A View,* 3-12. Admiral Sharp doubted that Schwarzkopf gave serious thought to a landing for fear of heavy losses. Sharp, interview by Marolda and Schneller, tape 2, side 1. General de la Billiere, who was in the confidence of Schwarzkopf and his immediate staff, later observed that in that period, "nobody liked the idea of an amphibious landing at the head of the Gulf." de la Billiere, *Storm Command,* 84. See also *CPGW,* 212–13; Gordon and Trainor, *The Generals' War,* 292; Schwarzkopf, *It Doesn't Take a Hero,* 356–61.

34. Ltr, Mauz to Marolda, 12 Jun 1996, Authors' Files, OA.

35. LaPlante, interview by Marolda and Schneller, tape 2, side 1.

36. Ibid.

37. In December General Trainor briefed the I MEF staff on the performance of the Iraqi armed forces during the Iran-Iraq War. Impressed, General Boomer told his staff that Trainor was "probably more knowledgeable than most of these guys floating around here who claim to be experts on this subject." IMEFB, 7 Dec 1990. General Alfred M. Gray, Commandant of the Marine Corps, consistently pressed for a major amphibious assault. Gordon and Trainor, *The Generals' War,* 134, 173–77.

38. Trainor, "Still go-ing," 33. See also Trainor, "Amphibious Operations in the Gulf War," 57–60.

39. Pokrant, *A View*, 3-14. Until Schwarzkopf rejected the proposal, Mauz considered reducing the ATF from 13 amphibious ships to 9. Ibid., 3-14–3-15.

40. Msg, Personal, Schwarzkopf to Powell, info to CINCs, 051630Z Apr 1991, US-CENTCOMFWD, CinC's File, folder 60, box 2, RG 518 (CENTCOM Records), NA.

41. Swain, *Lucky War*, 83.

42. *CPGW*, 387-89; Schubert and Kraus, eds., *Whirlwind War*, ch. 5.

43. According to Pokrant, *A View*, 4-3, "the decision came as a surprise" to Admiral Mauz, who "originally believed that [because of the lack of land-based aerial tankers] 6 CVBGs were more than could be efficiently employed" against Iraq.

44. *CPGW*, 67–69, 386–89; Gordon and Trainor, *The Generals' War*, 153–54; Simmons, "Getting Marines to the Gulf," 59–60.

45. George Bush, "The President's News Conference on the Persian Gulf Crisis," *Weekly Compilation of Presidential Documents* 26 (8 Nov 1990), 1790.

46. *CPGW*, 77–78, 387–89; *USNDS*, 16.

47. 8 Rodney et al., *Reserve Manpower*, 1–16.

48. *CPGW*, 387–89; *USNDS*, A-8–A-11; Walters, "The Year in Review: 1990," 16; Walters and Burgess, "The Year in Review: 1991," 18.

49. The Navy had ordered the force home in November, but kept it in the Western Pacific pending President Bush's decision to double the forces assigned to Central Command. After Bush's announcement, the personnel of Amphibious Squadron 5 and the 13th MEU(SOC) received liberty in the Philippines.

50. *CPGW*, 213-14, 523-30; Johnson, interview by Partin, 13, 28, USCENTCOMFWD, J-3 JOC, box 5, Planning Files, CENTCOM Records, RG 518, NA; ltr, Quinn to Head, History Writing Unit, 11 Jan 1996, Authors' Files, OA; IMEFB, 5 Dec 1990; U.S. Special Operations Command, "10th Anniversary History," 33, Authors' Files.

51. Brame, "From Garrison to Desert Offensive in 97 Days," 31. See also Schubert and Kraus, *Whirlwind War*, ch. 5.

52. Pokrant, *A View*, appendix C, 2. See also Craig, *Call for Fire*, 192, 212.

53. *CPGW*, 523-30; Rodney et al., *Reserve Manpower*, 8-9; U.S. Coast Guard, Desert Shield/Desert Storm Chronology, 19 Jun 1992, U.S. Coast Guard Historian's Office, Washington, DC; Wilder, interview by Bauer, Oral Histories, OA.

54. Quoted in Coast Guard Liaison Officer, Manama, Bahrain, Operation Desert Shield and Storm After Action Report, 10 Jun 1992, U.S. Coast Guard Historian's Office, Washington, DC.

55. Quoted in Bosco, "Port Harbor Security," 25.

56. Coast Guard Liaison Officer, Manama, Bahrain, Operation Desert Shield and Storm After Action Report, 10 Jun 1992, U.S. Coast Guard Historian's Office, Washington, DC.

57. Nickel et al, *Logistics*, 1-1, 4-3, 5-6–5-7, 5-16, 5-17; Palmer, *On Course to Desert Storm*, 38, 39, 82-84, 88.

58. Arthur, interview by Marolda and Schneller, 12-13; Nickel et al, *Logistics*, 5-6, 5-7; Pokrant, *A View*, 4-25.

59. Ltr, Sutton to Marolda, 12 Apr 1996, Authors' Files, OA.

60. Mobley, interview by Ramsdell, 16. See also Nickel et al, *Logistics*, 4-25–4-29; Rodney et al., *Reserve Manpower*, 10.

61. Gawlowicz, "Persian Gulf Service Station," 36-39.

62. "Combat Logistics," 44; Nickel et al., *Logistics*, 5-18–5-22.

63. Nickel et al., *Logistics*, 5-18–5-19, 8-3–8-5.

64. LaPlante, interview by Marolda and Schneller, tape 1, side 2; Nickel et al., *Logistics,* 5-20–5-22, 8-8; Schwarzkopf, *It Doesn't Take a Hero,* 369; Morin and Gimblett, *Operation Friction,* 91.

65. LaPlante later related that when Bush visited flagship *Nassau* for Thanksgiving Day, the admiral was so impressed with the ability of the President's party to communicate with agencies in the United States via INMARSAT that he asked for and received a similar linkup, thanks to Vice Admiral Gerald Tuttle's command. LaPlante, interview by Marolda and Schneller, tape 2, side 2.

66. Nickel et al., *Logistics,* 1-3–1-5, 4-1–4-6, 4-16–4-20, 4-21–4-24, 5-17, 6-9.

67. LaPlante, interview by Marolda and Schneller, tape 2, side 2.

68. Pokrant, *A View,* appendix C, 31. Admiral March expressed similar sentiments. March, interview by Marolda and Schneller, tape 2, side 1.

69. Nickel, et al., *Logistics,* 5-1.

70. HMAS *Success,* Report of Proceedings, Jan 1991, 2, Authors' Files, OA.

71. Ibid., 3.

72. On occasion, disagreement rather than cooperation characterized coalition naval relations. Admiral March related that the French naval commander "got a little pissed when I put an Australian [sic] in charge" of the underway replenishment duty, but the "French admiral was kind of restricted [by his government] on what he could do." In short, "the French really weren't players." March, interview by Marolda and Schneller, tape 2, side 2.

73. Miller and Hobson, *The Persian Excursion,* 11, 56–57, 92, 94, 155–59, 180; Gimblett, "Canadian Naval Operations"; Morin and Gimblett, *Operation Friction,* 179–210; Gimblett, Canadian Coordination of the Persian Gulf Combat Logistics Force," 233–39; Cairns in *Twelfth International Seapower Symposium,* 101–2; HMAS *Success,* Report of Proceedings, Jan 1991, 3, 5–6, Authors' Files, OA.

74. At the same time, NMCB 4, one of the earliest battalions to deploy to the gulf, returned to the United States.

75. Ltr, M.R. Johnson (CEC), USN to Marolda, 27 and 29 Mar 1996; and Commander Naval Construction Battalions, U.S. Pacific Fleet, Naval Construction Force, Operation Desert Shield/Desert Storm After Action Report, ser CB30/067, 23 Jan 1992, Authors' Files; Karen Fedele, "The Seabees Go to War," 3–13; Zimmeck, "A War of Logistics," 3-15–3.16. *CPGW,* 442–43; NMCB 74 and NMCB 40, Command Histories, 1990 and 1991, Post 1 Jan 1990 Command Files, OA; Nickel et al., *Logistics,* 9-1–9-9; *USNDS,* 32.

76. Rodney et al., *Reserve Manpower,* v, 3–5.

77. Horner, *The Gulf Commitment,* 75–76, 150–51; Morin and Gimblett, *Operation Friction,* 50.

78. Quoted from IMEFB, 28 Nov 1990.

79. IMEFB, 28 Nov, 8, 12, 19, 22, and 31 Dec 1990.

80. Graham et al., *Medical,* 5–8, 29, 31; Mercogliano to Marolda and Schneller, 28 Feb 1996, Authors' Files, OA; Zimmeck, "A War of Logistics," 2-33–2-35.

81. Hattendorf, ed., *Eleventh International Seapower Symposium,* 108–9. See also Schubert and Kraus, eds., *Whirlwind War,* ch. 5.

82. The dry cargo consisted of high-priority items like Patriot missiles, tank and aircraft parts, chemical warfare protective gear, medical equipment, and specialized ordnance. Matthews and Holt, *United States Transportation Command History,* 17–18, 109.

83. Bond, "Troop and Materiel Deployment Missions," 94; *CPGW,* 375–77.

84. The four were VR 55, VR 57, VR 58, and VR 59. Matthews and Holt, *United States Transportation Command History,* 15–17.

85. Rost et al., *Sealift*, 3, 7, 14; Hattendorf, ed., *Eleventh International Seapower Symposium*, 69.

86. Brame, "From Garrison to Desert Offensive in 97 Days," 30.

87. Rost et al., *Sealift*, 5, 7, 9; Hansford Johnson, interview by Matthews and Smith, 26–27, U.S. Transportation Command.

88. Brame, "From Garrison to Desert Offensive in 97 Days," 30.

89. Hattendorf, ed., *Eleventh International Seapower Symposium*, 109; Matthews and Holt, *United States Transportation Command History*, 68.

90. Hattendorf, ed., *Eleventh International Seapower Symposium*, 108.

91. Schubert and Kraus, eds., *Whirlwind War*, ch. 5.

92. Brame, "From Garrison to Desert Offensive in 97 Days," 28-29; Swain, *Lucky War*, 164. See also Schubert and Kraus, eds., *Whirlwind War*, ch. 5.

93. Brame, "From Garrison to Desert Offensive in 97 Days," 28–29. See also Schubert and Kraus, eds., *Whirlwind War*, ch. 5.

94. Matthews and Holt, *United States Transportation Command History*, 56.

95. Quoted in Bond, "Troop and Materiel Deployment Missions," 95. See also Rodney et al., *Reserve Manpower*, 8–10.

96. Pagonis, *Moving Mountains*, 71.

97. Swain, *Lucky War*, 165. See also *ibid.*, 78, 105, 160.

98. Brame, "From Garrison to the Offensive in 97 Days," 31–35; IMEFB, 14 Jan 1991; Gordon and Trainor, *The Generals' War*, 194; Pagonis, *Moving Mountains*, 123, 203–5; Scales, *Certain Victory*, 75, 80; Schubert and Kraus, eds., *Whirlwind War*, ch. 5.

99. Apparently, there were limits to the forces Schwarzkopf wanted in theater. When British General de la Billiere suggested the aircraft carrier HMS *Ark Royal* be deployed to the gulf, Schwarzkopf observed wryly that he "already had more ships in the Gulf than water to float them on." de la Billiere, *Storm Command*, 115. See also *CPGW*, 77–78; Grove, ed., *Britain's Gulf War*, 44–48.

100. Matthews and Holt, *United States Transportation Command History*, xi.

101. Ltr, Mauz to Marolda, 12 Jun 1996, Authors' Files, OA. According to one historian, this was "probably [Schwarzkopf's] most important briefing of the war from the standpoint of transmitting the commander's intent." Swain, *"Lucky War"*, 90.

102. Smith, letter to the editor in *Proceedings* 121 (Feb 1995), 15. Ltr, Mauz to Marolda, 12 Jun 1996, Authors' Files, OA; Kitfield, *Prodigal Soldiers*, 366–67.

103. Ltr, Mauz to Marolda, 12 Jun 1996, Authors' Files, OA. In contrast, Admiral March later remarked, "my one complaint about Mauz and Arthur is that they should have been in Riyadh. . . . I would have had just as good communication with him in Riyadh as I did to his flagship." March, interview by Marolda and Schneller, tape 1, side 2. Admiral Sharp, the top naval officer on Schwarzkopf's staff, also felt that it "clearly would have been a tremendous advantage" having COMUSNAVCENT and his staff in the Saudi capital. He added that "when the *Blue Ridge* went to sea, it cut off all land lines to them and it was not easy to communicate with them." Sharp, interview by Marolda and Schneller, tape 2, side 2.

104. Msg, Personal, Schwarzkopf to Powell, info to CINCs, 051630Z Apr 1991, US-CENTCOMFWD, CinC's File, box 2, folder 60, RG 518 (CENTCOM Records), NA.

105. Wages to COMUSNAVCENT, "End of Tour Report," 5 Mar 1991, 6-7; and report, Ramsdell to Director Naval Historical Center, 14 May 1991, Authors' Files, OA.

106. Arthur, interview by Marolda and Schneller, 9. Admiral March was not concerned about Mauz's late replacement by Arthur. He later observed that since the staff would remain in place, there would be no disruption. "Our training structure, our com-

mand structure is predicated on routine [turnover.]" March, interview by Marolda and Schneller, tape 2, side 1.

107. Arthur, interview by Marolda and Schneller, 9; Perla, *Summary*, 35.

108. Schwarzkopf, *It Doesn't Take a Hero*, 437.

109. IMEFB, 15 Dec 1990, 12.

110. Kitfield, *Prodigal Soldiers*, 374–75.

111. Craig, *Call For Fire*, 196. The British had similar problems. Craig took charge of the Royal Navy's forces only two days after the American change of command and the commodore was also "surprised by the absence of [British] war plans against an enemy who would, on past record, think nothing of attacking us at any time." *Ibid.*, 175.

112. Msg, CINCCENT to CNO, 301800Z Mar 1991, USCENTCOMFWD, CinC's File, box 2, folder 61, RG 518 (CENTCOM Records), NA.

113. Arthur, interview by Marolda and Schneller, 11. Despite the drawbacks, March still thought Arthur "should have been in Riyadh [where] he could have done more good things there keeping Schwarzkopf smoothed over and played against Horner and some of the other senior component commanders." March, interview by Marolda and Schneller tape 1, side 2. See also Kitfield, *Prodigal Soldiers*, 375.

114. Admiral Arthur remained dual-hatted as the Pacific Fleet's Commander Seventh Fleet. Shepko et al., *Maritime Interception Operations*; CPGW, 552–53; Gee, interview by Ramsdell, 7.

115. Hendrickson, interview by Ramsdell, 20.

116. March, interview by Marolda and Schneller, tape 2, side 1.

117. Brown et al., *Training*, 2-4, 3-1; Commander Carrier Group 7, Desert Storm 17 Jan–19 Mar 1991, Battle Force Zulu ASUWC Briefing, in Zlatoper to Marolda, 23 Mar 1996, 24, Authors' Files, OA; *DSDSLL*, 52–53; Gee, 3, 4, 6, Hendrickson, 6, 11, Mixson, 2–6, Mobley, 15, and White, 1–4, 11–15, 26, interviews by Ramsdell.

118. HMAS *Sydney*, Report of Proceedings, Dec 1990, 3, 6, Authors' Files, OA.

119. Brown et al., *Training*, 3-6; Richards and Taylor, interview by Marolda, 2, 29, 55, 69.

120. Hunt, interview by Marolda, 4, 6, 11, 12, 22; Richards and Taylor, interview by Marolda, 35–37, 55–57; Horner, *The Gulf Commitment*, 146.

121. Brown et al., *Training*, 3-9, 4-12; ltr, Grieve to Marolda, 26 Mar 1996, Authors' Files, OA; Richards and Taylor, interview by Marolda, 2, 69.

122. General Glosson's direct, often back channel contacts with Rear Admiral McConnell, the J-2, proved to be especially useful to planning and conducting the air war. Mandeles et al., *Managing Command and Control*, 22, 103.

123. Brooks, interview by Marolda and Schneller, tape 1, side 1.

124. Ibid.

125. Ibid.

126. Ibid.

127. LaPlante, interview by Marolda and Schneller, tape 2, side 1.

128. Brooks, interview by Marolda and Schneller, tape 2, side 1.

129. *GWAPS, Summary*, 126. See also Brooks, interview by Marolda and Schneller, tape 2, side 2; and Gordon and Trainor, *The Generals' War*, 103–6, 110. The GAO report, *Operation Desert Storm*, 107, emphasizes that "elimination of [Iraq's] integrated coordinated air defense" was a "form of air supremacy."

130. Ltr, Perla to Pokrant, 19 Jan 1996, Authors' Files, OA.

131. Gordon and Trainor, *The Generals' War*, 115–17; Holliday et al., *TLAM Performance*, 12.

132. Brooks, interview by Marolda and Schneller, tape 1, side 2.

133. Ibid., tape 1, side 2. Schwarzkopf concurred, stating that "current imagery collection, production and dissemination do not totally satisfy the requirement for near-real time imagery in support of combat operations." See msg, Personal, Schwarzkopf to Powell, info to CINCs, USCENTCOMFWD, CinC's File, box 2, folder 60, RG 518 (CENTCOM Records), NA.

134. March, interview by Marolda and Schneller, tape 2, side 1.

135. Brooks, interview by Marolda and Schneller, tape 2, side 2.

136. Msg, Personal, Schwarzkopf to Powell, info to CINCs, 051630Z Apr 1991, USCENTCOMFWD, CinC's File, box 2, folder 60, RG 518 (CENTCOM Records), NA.

137. Brooks, interview by Marolda and Schneller, tape 2, side 1.

138. Ibid., tape 1, sides 1–2.

139. Richards and Taylor, interview by Marolda, 52, 92; Marolda, "Crucible of War," 228–29; Marolda, *By Sea, Air, and Land*, 80–81.

140. Cangelosi, interview by Marolda and Schneller, tape 1, side 1.

141. Regarding this air support, Captain Hunt observed that "the Marine Corps was our right hand through Desert Shield. They were right there all the time. They never left." Hunt, interview by Marolda, 28–29.

142. Morin and Gimblett, *Operation Friction*, 106. See also 105.

143. Ltr, Mauz to Marolda, 12 Jun 1996, Authors' Files, OA. See also Thomas Marfiak in *Twelfth International Seapower Symposium*, 118.

144. Ltr, Mauz to Marolda, 12 Jun 1996, Authors Files, OA.

145. Quoted in Morin and Gimblett, *Operation Friction*, 110.

146. IMEFB, 5 Sep, 9 Oct, 1 and 7 Nov 1990.

147. Richards and Taylor, interview by Marolda, 19. See also Hunt interview by Marolda, 2, 62.

148. Hunt, interview by Marolda, 3–10; IMEFB, 15 and 16 Nov, 4 Dec 1990, 12 Jan 1991; Richards and Taylor, interview by Marolda, 26.

149. Hunt interview by Marolda, 10; Richards and Taylor, interview by Marolda, 34, 60–61.

150. Cangelosi, interview by Marolda and Schneller, tape 1, side 2.

151. March, interview by Marolda and Schneller, tape 2, side 1. See also Pokrant, *A View*, 3-1.

152. Arthur, interview by Marolda and Schneller, 25-26.

153. Hunt, interview by Marolda, 4–6.

154. IMEFB, 7 Nov 1990.

155. Ibid., 7 and 9 Nov 1990.

156. Hunt, interview by Marolda, 9.

157. Ibid., 51–52, 59–60; Richards and Taylor, interview by Marolda, 63.

158. IMEFB, 30 Nov 1990; see also 11 Sep; 24 Oct; 19, 28, and 29 Nov; 4, 6, and 21 Dec 1990; Shellum, *A Chronology of Defense Intelligence in the Gulf War*, 16, 22.

159. IMEFB, 29 Nov 1990.

160. Ltr, Mauz to Marolda, 12 Jun 1996, Authors' Files, OA; msg, CHINFO to distribution, 0401Z, 10 Nov 1990, file 1, box 1, Woodall Papers, OA; IMEFB, 9 Jan 1991. See also IMEFB, 27 Dec 1990 and 10 Jan 1991; Pokrant, *A View*, 4-21.

161. Pokrant, *A View*, 4-5.

162. Ltr, Taylor to Dudley, 29 Jan 1996, Authors' Files, OA.

163. Arthur, interview by Marolda and Schneller, 35–36.16

164. Hunt, interview by Marolda and Schneller, 23–24; Richards and Taylor, interview by Marolda, 44–45, 48.

165. Purvis, interview by Marolda, 11–12.

166. Already that fall the ATF had carried out two limited-scale amphibious exercises outside the gulf, off Oman. Pokrant, *A View*, 3–12.

167. *CPGW*, 214. See also Commander U.S. Naval Forces Central Command, Command History 1990, 15, Post 1 January 1990 Command Files, OA; Pokrant, *A View*, 4–5.

168. LaPlante, interview by Marolda and Schneller, tape 2, side 2.

169. IMEFB, 10 Dec 90. See also Boatman, "USMC Assault Practice," 687; Boomer, "Special Trust," 48; *CPGW*, 213–14; Simmons, "Getting Marines to the Gulf," 56.

170. LaPlante, interview by Marolda and Schneller, Oral Histories, OA, tape 2, side 2.

171. Ibid., tape 2, side 2. The previous two exercises in the series took place off Ras al-Madrakah, Oman, from 29 September to 5 October and from 30 October to 8 November.

172. Arthur, interview by Marolda and Schneller, 39.

173. LaPlante, conversation with Marolda, 21 Mar 1994, at TRANSCOM Conference on the Lessons Learned from the Gulf War; LaPlante, interview by Marolda and Schneller.

174. IMEFB, 15 Dec 1990, 30.

175. *CPGW*, 58–59, 502–3.

176. Not only did the coalition force display no hostility, but a medical team from the amphibious transport dock ship *Trenton* treated one woman who exhibited heart attack symptoms. The woman was transferred to a hospital in Muscat, Oman. *CPGW*, 59–60; HMAS *Sydney*, Report of Proceedings, Jan 1991, Authors' Files, OA, 10; Horner, *The Gulf Commitment*, 133–37; Mercer, interview by Bauer, 9.

177. *CPGW*, 59–60.

178. Mercer, interview by Bauer, 1, 12.

179. *CPGW*, 60–61.

180. Quoted in Phillips, "Desert Storm," 8. See also Friedman, *Desert Victory*, 68.

181. Hattendorf, ed., *Eleventh International Seapower Symposium*, 43.

182. Quoted in Phillips, "Desert Storm," 8. See also Arthur, interview by Ramsdell, 19–20.

183. Quoted in Hattendorf, ed., *Eleventh International Seapower Symposium*, 43.

184. Pokrant, *A View*, 4–14.

185. LaPlante, interview by Marolda and Schneller, tape 2, side 2.

186. Powell and Persico, *My American Journey*, 492.

187. McCausland, "How Iraq's CBW Threat Affected Coalition Operations," 12–15; Livingstone, "Iraq's Intentional Omission," 29–30; Hunt, interview by Marolda, 81–84

188. Hunt, interview by Marolda, 82–84. There were others, for the most part officers, however, who felt that the mobility of ships at sea or armored forces ashore, intensive training, and the protective clothing of coalition personnel would limit the effectiveness of Iraqi chemical attacks. See LaPlante, interview by Marolda and Schneller, tape 3, side 1; Craig, *Call For Fire*, 214; Powell and Persico, *My American Journey*, 468, 503.

189. Arthur, interview by Marolda and Schneller, 15.

190. Gee, interview by Ramsdell, 14-15. A few days later, a truck carrying *Midway* crewmen on liberty in Abu Dhabi, United Arab Emirates, flipped over, killing two bluejackets.

191. Quoted in David Evans, "From the Gulf," 79.

192. U.S. Central Command, *Troop Information Handbook*.

193. Msg, CTG 150.6 to TG 150.6, 1259Z, 11 Sep 1990, LaPlante Papers, OA.

194. Ibid.

195. Claborn, "Pest Control in the Desert," 56. See also U.S. Central Command, *Troop Information Handbook*.

196. "Recollections of War," 14.

197. Moskos and Wattendorf, "Troops in Desert Shield."

198. Ibid.

199. *The Washington Post*, 18 Aug 1990, A16.

200. U.S. Central Command, *Troop Information Handbook*.

201. "Gen. Schwarzkopf Addresses Issues," 24. See also Schwarzkopf, *It Doesn't Take a Hero*, 312.

202. Schwarzkopf, *It Doesn't Take a Hero*, 335-38; Schubert and Kraus, eds., *Whirlwind War*, ch. 4.

203. LaPlante, interview by Marolda and Schneller, tape 2, side 2.

204. Mobley, interview by Ramsdell, 14.

205. Ltr, Mauz to Marolda, 12 Jun 1996, Authors' Files, OA; IMEFB, 15 Nov 1990; "Shelter From the Storm," 16–18; Senate Committee on Armed Services, *Crisis in the Persian Gulf Region: U.S. Policy Options and Implications*, 673.

206. *CPGW*, 489–90.

207. Schwarzkopf, *It Doesn't Take a Hero*, 378. See also IMEFB, 23 Nov 1990 for a description of how the President's visit to I MEF headquarters boosted the morale not only of the assembled Marines but Mr. Bush himself.

208. Schwarzkopf, *It Doesn't Take a Hero*, 397. See also Doll, "Comedian Entertains Front-line Marines," 19; LaPlante, interview by Marolda and Schneller, tape 2, side 2.

209. Norman, "*Wisconsin* Hosts Desert Shield Sports Festival," 22–23.

210. Hunt, interview by Marolda, 87–88.

211. *CPGW*, 329–30.

212. The Senate voted 52-47 in support of the resolution authorizing force; the House voted 250–183.

CHAPTER 4

1. Indeed, because TLAMs could not be recalled, the allies had irrevocably committed themselves to armed conflict. Palisano recorded these words on an audio tape for his family. Quoted in McWilliams, *This Ain't Hell*, 56. See also *Paul F. Foster*, Command History 1991, SH.

2. "Hard Rain," 15. These carrier battle groups were the cutting edge of an allied fleet of 150 naval vessels from 14 nations. The U.S. Navy made the largest contribution, deploying 108 aircraft carriers, battleships, cruisers, destroyers, frigates, submarines, amphibious ships, and logistic support ships. At the outset of the war, 34 U.S. ships were operating in the Persian Gulf, 35 in the Gulf of Oman and North Arabian Sea, 26 in the Red Sea, and 13 in the Mediterranean. *CPGW*, 85–86; Friedman, *Desert Victory*, 318–23; Schneller, "Persian Gulf Turkey Shoot;" *USNDS*, A-13.

3. Oxenbould, "Australians Going to War in the 1990s," 12–13. According to Admiral March, he had not been authorized to inform the other coalition navies of H-Hour, but said "screw it" and told them anyway. He reasoned that the Dutch and other commanders in his escort force needed to know when Tomahawk missiles and aircraft would go screaming over their ships in the early hours of 17 January. March, interview by Marolda and Schneller, tape 1, side 2.

4. *CPGW*, 68–69.

5. Ibid., 97–98; Humphries, "Operations Law," 31.

6. U.S., Department of Defense, *Conduct of the Persian Gulf Conflict*, 1-1, 1-2, 2-6; *CPGW*, 101.

7. *CPGW*, 100–101; McPeak, Defense Department Briefing; *OPDS*, 234.

8. *CPGW*, 76, 187–90.

9. Arthur, interview by Marolda and Schneller, 53–54.

10. *CPGW*, 187–91; Schwamb et al., *Strike Warfare*, 1-34.

11. CO Log I, 17 Jan 1991 entry, folder 1, box 1, Woodall Papers, OA; *CPGW*, 115–21; Froggett, "Tomahawk in the Desert," 71–72; Gerken to the editor, *Proceedings* 118 (Sep 1991): 16; *GWAPS, Summary*, 200, and vol. 5, part 1, 386; Halliday et al., *TLAM Performance During Desert Storm*, vol. 1, 16; Hallion, *Storm Over Iraq*, 171; Hewish, "Tomahawk Enhances Navy Role in Land Warfare," 458; *Jane's Weapon Systems 1987–1988*, 486–87; MacDonald, "Rounding Up the Storm," 10; McWilliams, *This Ain't Hell*, 65–67, 73–74; *OPDS*, 208, 216; Schwamb, *Strike Warfare*, 8-3–8-6; *USNDS*, 47, A-15.

12. GAO, *Operation Desert Storm: Evaluation of the Air Campaign*, 105; Morocco, "Allied Strategists," 60; Morocco, "U.S. War Plan," 16.

13. Ninety of these were Navy and Marine Corps planes. *CPGW*, 85–86, 105–7, 114–15; Schwamb, et al., *Strike Warfare*, 1-50.

14. *CPGW*, 154; Hallion, *Storm Over Iraq*, 147; Luti, "Battle of the Airwaves," 50; Mazarr et al., *Desert Storm*, 93.

15. McPeak, "Defense Department Briefing."

16. Luti, "Battle of the Airwaves," 50.

17. *CPGW*, 115–16.

18. *GWAPS*, vol. 2, part 1, 120–24; During the first night's strikes, the F-117s were able to hit just over half of their targets. Foul weather prevented some pilots from releasing their ordnance. Gordon and Trainor, *The Generals' War*, 220.

19. According to an official Air Force history, some of the missiles "dispensed spools of carbon fibers" that caused "massive short circuits and automatic shut downs" of the electric power system. Davis, *Strategic Air Power in Desert Storm*, 26. See also Gordon and Trainor, *The Generals' War*, 216.

20. *CPGW*, 115–21; *GWAPS*, vol. 2, part 1, 143; Hallion, *Storm Over Iraq*, 166–71.

21. Coyne, "Plan of Attack," 46; Hallion, *Storm Over Iraq*, 169–70; *New York Times*, 17 January 1991. Later that morning, a B-52 bomber formation completed an arduous 18-hour transit from Barksdale, Louisiana, to fire 39 conventionally armed, air-launched cruise missiles against targets in Iraq. Although a historic first, the mission's results were mixed. For technical reasons, the bomber crews could not release four of the weapons, and CENTCOM could not determine precisely how much damage the remainder inflicted on the enemy. Moreover, the Air Force, which had not been enthusiastic about the cruise missile program, expended over half of the weapons in its inventory in that one operation. And, since American political leaders were concerned that the nations of the coalition would object to planes landing on their soil with cruise missiles (which could also carry nuclear warheads), the bomber crews endured an 18-hour trans-Atlantic return flight involving multiple aerial refuelings. In contrast, TLAM-armed ships of the fleet operated in international waters, so the Navy needed only General Schwarzkopf's permission to sustain an extended cruise missile campaign. Davis, *Strategic Air Power in Desert Storm*, 28; Gordon and Trainor, *The Generals' War*, 63, 205–6, 223; *GWAPS, Summary*, 224.

22. Quoted in "Desert Storm's Hard Rain," 8, and Hallion, *Storm Over Iraq*, 172. See also Attack Squadron 72, Command History 1991, AVH.

23. Gordon and Trainor, *The Generals' War*, 217–19; *GWAPS, Summary*, 58–59.

24. *CPGW*, 89–90, 119–20; Hallion, *Storm Over Iraq*, 173; Mixson, "Where We Must Do Better," 38; Morocco, "Allied Strategists," 60–61.

25. Gordon and Trainor, *The Generals' War*, 113, 114, 217.

26. *Triumph Without Victory*, 224.

27. Unfortunately, at least six HARMs damaged coalition ground radars or ships, including *Jarrett*, *Nicholas*, and the Saudi warship *Abu Obdaidah*, the latter killing at least one Saudi sailor and wounding others. *DSDSLL*, 69; Morral, interview by Marolda and Schneller, tape 2, side 1; Pokrant, *A View*, 1-23, 5-9; Fulghum,"Navy, Marine Decoy Gliders," 64; Fulghum, "U.S. Decoys," 21; Luti, "Battle of the Airwaves, 50–51.

28. *CPGW*, 115–26; Hallion, *Storm Over Iraq*, 166; Quilter, *With the I Marine Expeditionary Force*, 49; Schwamb et al., *Strike Warfare*, 1-42, 1-43, 1-52.

29. Perla, *Summary*, 43; Schwamb et al., *Strike Warfare*, 1-41, 1-50; *OPDS*, 180.

30. *CPGW*, 124; Friedman, *Desert Victory*, 357–58; Hallion, *Storm Over Iraq*, 175.

31. Quoted in "Desert Storm's Hard Rain," 8. See also Attack Squadron 72, Command History 1991, AVH.

32. Quoted in Mackenzie, "A Conversation With Chuck Horner," 60. See also *CPGW*, 124; Friedman, *Desert Victory*, 357–58; Hallion, *Storm Over Iraq*, 175; Keaney, "Surveying Gulf War Airpower," 27.

33. Hurley, "Saddam Hussein and Iraqi Air Power," 9.

34. Fox and Mongillo, interview by Ramsdell, 3–5.

35. *CPGW*, 123; Mazarr et al., *Desert Storm*, 108; *OPDS*, 261–62; Rose, "Saratoga MiG Killers," 13–14.

36. Fox and Mongillo, interview by Ramsdell, 10–11. According to one source, "all bombs missed" their targets. Ltr, Pokrant to Marolda and Schneller, 26 Jan 1996, Authors' Files.

37. Chambers et al., *Anti-Air Warfare*, 1-1; *GWAPS*, vol. 2, part 1, 145 and vol. 5, part 1, 345, 352.

38. Quoted in *GWAPS*, vol. 2, part 2, 123. Admiral Sharp also believed that the air defense division of labor was reasonable. See Sharp, interview by Marolda and Schneller, tape 2, side 2.

39. Horner, interview by Carpenter, 4–5, Authors' Files.

40. March, interview by Marolda and Schneller, tape 2, side 1. One study suggests that Glosson was "perhaps, the most despised senior officer in theater to some Third Army commanders." Swain, *"Lucky War"*, 182. Another history relates that some Army ground force commanders found "his posturing . . . insufferable" and even Air Force officers regarded the general as "ambitious, aggressive, fiercely energetic, and arrogant." Mandeles, *Managing Command and Control*, 133; see also 137, 144.

41. Arthur, interview by Marolda and Schneller, 22. Indeed, one source suggests that Glosson had no intention of accommodating the Navy. See Atkinson, *Crusade*, 151–52. See also *DSDSLL*, 83.

42. The mining of Haiphong and other harbors on the coast of North Vietnam during 1972 virtually ended the enemy's use of the sea for military resupply. Marolda, *Operation End Sweep*, xi–xiv.

43. Arthur, interview by Marolda and Schneller, 35. Admiral March could not recollect the details of the mining operation. See March, interview by Marolda and Schneller, tape 2, side 1.

44. *CPGW*, 193–94.

45. Lutz et al., *Anti-Surface Warfare*, 4-18–4-20.

46. *CPGW*, 124–26.

47. The submarine can hardly be described as a "weapons system that was essentially irrelevant" to Desert Storm, as did Gordon and Trainor in *The Generals' War*, 237.

48. Muir, *Black Shoes and Blue Water*, 94–96. See also *GWAPS*, vol. 2. pt. 1, 156–57.

49. Msg, COMUSNAVCENT 190630Z Jan 1991, "VADM Arthur's Personal Desert Shield/Storm Message File," CNA. See also Arthur, interview by Marolda and Schneller, 3–5. U.S., British, and French air units also suffered losses as a result of their early preference for low-level tactics. Gordon and Trainor, *The Generals' War*, 221; Horner in Miller, ed., *Seeing Off the Bear*, 148–49.

50. Friedman, *Desert Victory*, 353–54; Perla, *Summary*, 60; *USNDS*, A-16.

51. *CPGW*, 115–21; Hallion, *Storm Over Iraq*, 171, 175–76; Quilter, *With the I Marine Expeditionary Force*, 49; *USNDS*, A-15, A-16.

52. Msg, COMCRUDESGRU EIGHT to COMUSNAVCENT, 152236Z Mar 1991, VADM Arthur's Personal DESERT SHIELD/STORM Message File, CNA.

53. *GWAPS, Summary*, 146; Horner in Miller, ed., *Seeing Off the Bear*, 142.

54. *GWAPS, Summary*, 147 and vol. 1, part 2, 417–18; Horner, interview by Carpenter, *Shield and Sword* Resource Files, 1-11; Horner in Miller, ed., *Seeing Off the Bear*, 140; Sharp, interview by Schneller and Marolda, tape 1, side 1; Ward et al., *C3*, viii.

55. Moreover, Admiral Arthur and General Boomer managed the resources for fleet air defense and close air support for their respective commands. Mandeles, *Command and Control*, 24; McNamara, *Air Power's Gordian Knot*, 126.

56. Johnson, interview by Ramsdell, 24–25.

57. One source notes that Horner feared that use of TLAMs would be an "expensive waste of effort." Reynolds, *Heart of the Storm*, 124. Admiral Arthur later observed that the JFACC unnecessarily limited TLAM launches because the staff "never understood" that the missiles would not fly at the same altitudes as coalition aircraft endangering the latter. Pokrant, *A View*, App. C, 11. See also ltr, Ramsdell to Director Naval Historical Center, 14 May 1991, Authors' Files; Cohen, "The Mystique of U.S. Air Power," 117.

58. Wages to COMUSNAVCENT, "End of Tour Report," 5 Mar 1991, 3, Authors' Files. General Horner also observed efforts on the part of some marines to "frustrate the JFACC," but General Boomer did not let the marines hamper operations. See Horner, interview by Carpenter, 1, Authors' Files; Mann, *Thunder and Lightning*, 58–59.

59. Perla, *Summary*, 35; Mandeles, *Managing Command and Control*, 27–33; Jamieson, "Lucrative Targets," 28, 125.

60. Quoted in McNamara, *Air Power's Gordian Knot*, 132.

61. Palzkill, "Making Interoperability Work," 51–52.

62. Boomer, interview by Carpenter, 5, Authors' Files.

63. Stanbridge, interview by Ramsdell, 5.

64. Pokrant, *A View*, 1-20; Mixson, interview by Ramsdell, 10, Authors' Files, OA.

65. Arthur, interview by Marolda and Schneller, 27.

66. Santoli, *Leading the Way*, 220. See also Horner in Miller, ed., *Seeing Off the Bear*, 140.

67. Mandeles et al., *Command and Control*, 143, makes the apt point that the "Air Force was the only organization with a concept of theater-wide air war and the institution to support it." See also Perla, *Summary*, 52–55; ltr, Ramsdell to Director Naval Historical Center, 14 May 1991, Authors' Files, OA; Schwamb et al., *Strike Warfare*, 2-11–2-12.

68. Msg, CTF 154 to COMUSNAVCENT, "Desert Shield/Desert Storm Quicklook," 081422Z Mar 1991, COMUSNAVCENT N3 Desert Shield/Storm Working Papers and Message Files, OA, CNA. March later held a different view about the Navy's supposed inability to conduct multicarrier strike operations. He labeled such conclusions a "bunch of bullshit [because] we had four flag officers on those four carriers and they knew the job." March, interview by Marolda and Schneller, tape 1, side 2. See also *DSDSLL*, 98, 100.

69. *CPGW*, 98–100, 102–3; Humphries, "Operations Law," 31–32; Muir, "A View From the Black Hole," 85–86; Perla, *Summary*, 35; Ramsdell, "Impressions of the Desert Storm Carriers," 11; Schwamb et al., *Strike Warfare*, 2-2, 2-7, 2-8, 2-16, 2-23.

70. Schwamb et al., *Strike Warfare*, 2-4; Ward et al., *C3*, 1-9, 1-25.

71. Pokrant, *A View*, 4-6.

72. Perla, *Summary*, 35.

73. Ramsdell, interview by Carpenter, 4, Authors' Files.

74. Bien, "From the Strike Cell," 58–60; Schwamb et al., *Strike Warfare*, 2-16. March felt that it was Bien "who kept things going for us." March, interview by Marolda and Schneller, tape 2, side 1.

75. Ibid.

76. Ibid., tape 1, side 2. March added that he also had "very little communication with Washington," which was "probably why I ended up a two star instead of a three star; plus I pissed off a few folks" by favoring the F/A-18 over the A-6. Ibid., tape 1, side 1.

77. The seven aviators included four commanders and three lieutenant commanders. The two intelligence officers were lieutenants. Another former Navy air wing commander joined the cell halfway through the war.

78. The Navy deployed 20 percent of the total number of coalition aircraft and flew 19 percent of the combat sorties during Desert Storm. See Schwamb et al., *Strike Warfare*, 1-17.

79. Muir, "A View from the Black Hole," 86.

80. Jamieson, "Lucrative Targets," 126.

81. *GWAPS*, vol. 1, part 2, 172–74; Schwamb et al., *Strike Warfare*, 2-16.

82. Wages to COMUSNAVCENT, "End of Tour Report," 5 Mar 1991, 2–3, Authors' Files.

83. March, interview by Marolda and Schneller, tape 2, side 1.

84. Mandeles et al., *Managing Command and Control*, 130. The JFACC's naming of an over-water CAP station after Brigadier General Billy Mitchell, who believed air power would doom all navies, was less than tactful. Chambers et al., *Antiair Warfare*, 3-54.

85. Memo, Commander Carrier Strike Force Seventh Fleet/COMCARGRUFIVE to COMUSNAVCENT, 21 Feb 1991, Miscellaneous DESERT SHIELD/DESERT STORM Working Papers from VADM Arthur's Personal Files, CNA; Muir, "A View From the Black Hole," 86.

86. Ltr, Mauz to Marolda, 12 Jun 1996, Authors' Files.

87. Arthur, interview by Ramsdell, 17, Authors' Files. See also Johnson, interview by Ramsdell, 33.

88. *CPGW*, 98–103, 214–15; Humphries, "Operations Law," 31–32; Muir, "A View From the Black Hole," 85–86; Perla, *Summary*, 35; Ramsdell, "Impressions of the Desert Storm Carriers," 11; Schwamb et al., *Strike Warfare*, 2-2, 2-7, 2-8, 2-16, 2-23; Ward et al., *C3*, 1-17.

89. Arthur, interview by Ramsdell, 9; Bien, "From the Strike Cell," 59; March, interview by Marolda and Schneller, tape 2, side 1.

90. Some of the Air Force units that possessed CAFMS had difficulty operating it. Indeed, one Air Force staff officer alluded to "an information management nightmare" in the employment of the systems. See Vriesenga, *From the Line in the Sand*, 78; see also 16.

91. Gordon and Trainor, *The Generals' War*, 312; *GWAPS, Summary*, 149; *GWAPS*, vol. 1, part 2, 117–18; 154–55; Ward, *C3*, x. In earlier wars, the Air Force sent each unit only that portion (fragment or "frag") of the daily order that applied to it. But since most air units possessed networked computers, the JFACC sent the entire ATO to each one during the Gulf War. Individual units then scrolled to and printed the relevant portions.

92. Msg, COMCRUDESGRU 8 to COMUSNAVCENT, 152236Z Mar 1991, VADM Arthur's Personal Desert Shield/Storm Message File, CNA.

93. Schwamb et al., *Strike Warfare*, 2-28.

94. Horner, interview by Carpenter, Authors' Files, 6. Arthur considered Mixson a "good warrior" and "really extraordinary." Arthur, interview by Marolda and Schneller, 54–55, OA.

95. Memo, Commander Carrier Strike Force Seventh Fleet/COMCARGRUFIVE to COMUSNAVCENT, 21 Feb 1991, Miscellaneous DESERT SHIELD/DESERT STORM Working Papers from VADM Arthur's Personal Files, CNA; Wages to COMUSNAVCENT, "End of Tour Report," 5 Mar 1991, 1-10, Authors' Files; Muir, "A View From the Black Hole," 86; Pokrant, *A View*, 1-22; Schwamb et al., *Strike Warfare*, 1-10, 2-28–2-30, 9-6; *USNDS*, A-13. A-32.

96. March, interview by Ramsdell, 5–6. Horner observed that March's battle group "never really bothered to integrate" and that problems with the Navy generally originated in the Persian Gulf. Horner, interview by Carpenter, 6, Authors' Files. See also Arthur, interview by Marolda and Schneller, 29-30; Brown et al., *Training*, 3-2. After the war, Admiral Zlatoper called for joint training to be put "on the front burner." See Commander Carrier Group 7, Desert Storm, 17 Jan–19 Mar 1991, Battle Force Zulu ASUWC Briefing, in ltr, Zlatoper to Marolda, 23 Mar 1996, 18, Authors' Files.

97. March, interview by Marolda and Schneller, tape 1, side 2.

98. Memo, Commander Carrier Strike Force Seventh Fleet/COMCARGRUFIVE to COMUSNAVCENT, 21 Feb 1991, Miscellaneous DESERT SHIELD/DESERT STORM Working Papers from VADM Arthur's Personal Files, CNA; Wages to COMUSNAVCENT, "End of Tour Report," 5 Mar 1991, 1-10, Authors' Files; Muir, "A View From the Black Hole," 86; Pokrant, *A View*, 1: 22; Schwamb et al., *Strike Warfare*, 1-10, 2-28–2-30, 9-6; *USNDS*, A-13, A-32.

99. Quick elimination of these missile-firing vessels and the Silkworm antiship missile sites on the coast of Kuwait would have allowed the carriers to operate closer to shore and to increase the Navy's contribution to the strategic air campaign. McNamara, *Air Power's Gordian Knot*, 127.

100. Palzkill, "Making Interoperability Work," 50–51.

101. *CPGW*, 97–98; Bien, "From the Strike Cell," 59; Schwamb et al., *Strike Warfare*, 2-7, 9-1.

102. Arthur, interview by Ramsdell, 9.

103. Wages to COMUSNAVCENT, "End of Tour Report," 5 Mar 1991, 5, Authors' Files, OA. See also McNamara, *Air Power's Gordian Knot*, 131. According to one director of the Air Force-commissioned Gulf War Air Power Survey, "commanders [of all services] changed one fifth of all missions during the few hours between the time staffs printed the centralized air tasking order and the time aircraft took off." Cohen, "The Mystique of U.S. Air Power," 113.

104. *GWAPS* Summary, 154; *CPGW*, 102-3; Mandeles, *Command and Control*, 132; Hallion, *Storm Over Iraq*, 155; Quilter, *With the I Marine Expeditionary Force*, 50; Wages to COMUSNAVCENT, "End of Tour Report," 5 Mar 1991, 8–10, Authors' Files.

105. Davis, *Strategic Air Power in Desert Storm*, 16. See also Mandeles et al., *Managing Command and Control*, 47.

106. Marolda, *By Sea, Air, and Land*, 99–101.

107. Bien, "From the Strike Cell," 59; Liebman, "Navy Tankers," 82–83; *CPGW*, 170–73; Perla, *Summary*, 65–66; Schwamb et al., *Strike Warfare*, xiv, 7-6–7-7, 35; Wages to COMUSNAVCENT, "End of Tour Report," 5 Mar 1991, 8–10, Authors' Files. Most allied air forces also used the basket configuration for their tankers.

108. Schwamb et al., *Strike Warfare*, 7-35. Battle Force Zulu's dependence on land-based tankers declined as Admiral Arthur moved the carriers farther north in the

Persian Gulf. Once the carriers arrived in their northernmost operating areas on 14 February, Navy KA-6s provided virtually all aerial refueling for Battle Force Zulu's strikes.

109. Vriesenga, *Line in the Sand*, 137–40.

110. Sharp, interview by Marolda and Schneller, tape 1, side 2.

111. *GWAPS*, vol. 1, part 2, 55–57.

112. Arthur, interview with Ramsdell, 17. March also "had the highest regard for Horner, but the one-stars he had working for him were real pricks." March, interview by Marolda and Schneller, tape 2, side 1.

113. Horner, interview by Carpenter, 1, Authors' Files. Boomer added that he and Horner told their subordinates, "don't worry about dotting every "i" or crossing every "t" in terms of doctrine. Leave the component commanders, the commanders on the battle-field, the flexibility to maneuver and work this out." Boomer, interview by Carpenter, 3, Authors' Files. On the other hand, Horner made it clear to the Canadians that he would determine how their CF-18 aircraft would fit into his air campaign. According to Horner, Commodore Summers told the CF-18 squadron commander that the Canadian aircraft could only cover Canadian ships. Horner and Summers "had a rather difficult conversa-tion," but the general "outranked him by two stars," so the Canadian finally agreed to using CF-18s for general air defensive duties. Hoping also to employ the planes in strike operations, Horner solicited the intercession of Mary Collins, the Canadian Associate Minister of National Defence, who was visiting Riyadh at the time. The following day, "the Canadian squadron was on the operational plan–dropping bombs." Horner in Miller, ed., *Seeing Off the Bear*, 145.

114. Wages to COMUSNAVCENT, "End of Tour Report," 5 Mar 1991, 1.

115. Arthur, interview by Marolda and Schneller, 24–25, 37.

116. March, interview by Marolda and Schneller, tape 1, side 2.

117. Pokrant, *A View*, 5-10–5-11.

118. Quoted in Atkinson, *Crusade*, 148.

119. Pokrant, *A View*, 5-11–5-12; Arthur, interview by Marolda and Schneller, 19–21.

120. Pokrant, *A View*, 5-13.

121. Arthur, interview by Marolda and Schneller, 21, 38.

122. Ibid., 38.

123. Ibid.

124. Commander Carrier Group 7, Desert Storm, 17 Jan–19 Mar 1991, Battle Force Zulu ASUWC Briefing, in ltr, Zlatoper to Marolda, 23 Mar 1996, 24, Authors' Files; *DSD-SLL*," 73. Air Force aircraft, especially the F-16, also had accuracy problems from medium and high altitudes. See Jamieson, "Lucrative Targets," 107.

125. Quilter, *With the I Marine Expeditionary Force*, 107.

126. *DSDSLL*, 110. See also Ibid., 54, 72–73, 108, 114–15; ltr, Pokrant to Dudley, 26 Jan 1996, Authors' Files; Cassara critique, 22 Aug 1996, Authors' Files; Quilter, *With the I Marine Expeditionary Force*.

127. *DSDSLL*, 110. See also Ibid., 54, 72, 73, 108, 114–15.

128. Quoted in *GWAPS*, vol. 2, part 1, 189.

129. Schwarzkopf, *It Doesn't Take a Hero*, 417–18.

130. de la Billiere, *Storm Command*, 216.

131. Ibid., 209.

132. During the Gulf War the Iraqis fired Scuds exclusively from mobile launchers. Postwar intelligence indicated that they possessed approximately 36 of them. *GWAPS*, vol. 2, part 1, 181 and vol. 2, part 2, 333.

133. Gordon and Trainor, *The Generals' War*, 239–40, 497; *GWAPS*, vol. 2, part 1, 191; Mahnken, "America's Next War," 179.

134. Mackenzie, "A Conversation With Chuck Horner," 62; *GWAPS, Summary*, 17.

135. *GWAPS*, vol. 2, part 2, 331; and vol. 2, part 1, 190. The allies launched approximately 1,000 additional "Scud patrol" sorties against mobile launchers, but when the aircraft involved failed to locate any, they were diverted to other targets. U.S. and British special operations forces also hunted for the elusive launchers. Gordon and Trainor, *The Generals' War*, 245–46.

136. Historian Thomas C. Hone has argued persuasively that Horner and his staff might have been more effective in dealing with the problem if they had approached the Scud threat the same way the Navy handled the German U-boat menace in the Atlantic during World War II in a comprehensive, multidimensional, multiresource approach. See Mandeles et al., *Managing Command and Control*, 71–73.

137. *GWAPS*, vol. 2, part 1, 198.

138. Quoted in *GWAPS*, vol. 2, part 1, 196.

139. Cohen, "The Mystique of U.S. Air Power," 121; *CPGW*, 89–90, 125–30, 166–68; *GWAPS*, vol. 2, part 1, 179–91; and vol. 2, part 2, 330–40; Hallion, *Storm Over Iraq*, 177–88; Lenhart and Masse, *Persian Gulf War*; Schwamb et al., *Strike Warfare*, 5-33; Chambers et al., *Antiair Warfare*, 3-1.

140. Gay, interview by Ramsdell, 3–5.

141. Ibid., 8–13; and Mobley, interview by Ramsdell, 3–5; Schwamb et al., *Strike Warfare*, 1-10–1-12.

142. Schwamb et al., *Strike Warfare*, 1-10–1-12, 1-36, 1-44.

143. *OPDS*, 212.

144. Ibid.; Perla, *Summary*, 14.

145. *CPGW*, 534; msg, USS *Saratoga* to COMUSNAVCENT, 091709Z Mar 1991, Desert Storm Engagement Message File, CNA; U.S. Air Force 16th Special Operations Wing, Command History, 375–78, Authors' Files; Vriesenga, *From the Line in the Sand*, 177–85.

146. *CPGW*, 533–34; Gordon and Trainor, *The Generals' War*, 262; *GWAPS*, vol. 5, part I, 641–49; U.S. Air Force 16th Special Operations Wing, Command History, 374–75, Authors' Files.

147. By far the largest contingent was that of the U.S. Air Force, whose 1,100 planes represented almost half of the coalition's total. The Navy contributed 400 aircraft, the Marines 200, and allied air forces 600. The Navy averaged approximately 400 sorties per day, the Marines about 250, and the Air Force about 1,500. Perla, *Summary*, 46–47.

148. *DSDSLL*, 101.

149. Perla, *Summary*, 46–50, 58.

150. *CPGW*, 89–90, 123–24; Schwamb et al., *Strike Warfare*, 4-11–4-12.

151. Rosenthal, "The Argentine Navy in the Persian Gulf," 11.

152. Johnson, interview by Ramsdell, 20.

153. March, interview by Marolda and Schneller, tape 2, side 2.

154. Arthur, interview by Marolda and Schneller, 17. Fleet defense was decidedly not, as some Air Force officers and writers have suggested, a "ruse" designed by Navy leaders to free themselves from the ATO process. See Mandeles et al., *Command and Control*, 131.

155. Quoted in Craig, *Call For Fire*, 217. See also Miller, *Persian Excursion*, 100.

156. Chambers, *Antiair Warfare*, 2-2; Naval Surface Warfare Center, *Desert Storm: Analysis of Aegis Operations*, 2, 5.

157. Marfiak in *Twelfth International Seapower Symposium*, 119.

158. At times, non-U.S. naval forces directed American air defense units. For instance, in January and February Australian and other coalition naval commanders exercised tactical control of U.S. Navy F/A-18s and F-14s flying CAP stations in the gulf. See HMAS *Sydney*, Report of Proceedings, Jan 1991, 8, Authors Files.

159. Chambers et al., *Antiair Warfare*, 1-1, 2-2, 3-51–3-53; *CPGW*, 196-99; msg, USS WORDEN to USCINCCENT, 192212Z Mar 1991, Desert Storm Engagement Message File, CNA; Perla, *Summary*, 86. 160. Chambers et al., *Anti-Air Warfare*, 2-16; *CPGW*, 196–99.

160. Chambers et al., *Anti-Air Warfare*, 2–16; *CPGW*, 196–99.

161. To facilitate air control and deconfliction, AAW ships received the daily ATOs by helicopter. Converting the complex and unwieldy ATO into a database format that ships could use took an average of three hours each night. USS *Mobile Bay*, "Draft Tacmemo: Battle Force Anti-Air Warfare Commander (BF AAWC) for Multiple Carrier Battle Force Operations for AEGIS Cruisers," May 1991, folder 6, box 9, Woodall Papers, OA; Chambers et al., *Antiair Warfare*, 1-1; *CPGW*, 197–98; DiRita, "Exocets, Air Traffic, & the Air Tasking Order," 60–61; ltr, P.C. van Royen, Director, Institute for Maritime History, Ministry of Defence, to Dr. Marolda, re "Dutch Participation in Gulf War, 1990–1991," Authors' Files.

162. Msg, *Mobile Bay* to SECDEF, 230650Z Jan 1991, file 5, box 12, Woodall Papers, OA; Stephen R. Woodall, comments re *Shield and Sword* mss, 25 Jan 1996, Authors' Files.

163. USS *Mobile Bay*, "Draft Tacmemo: Battle Force Anti-Warfare Commander (BF AAWC) for Multiple Carrier Battle Force Operations for AEGIS Cruiser," May 1991, folder 6, box 9, Woodall Papers, OA; *CPGW*, 196–99.

164. Msg, *Mobile Bay* to CTF 154, 042020Z Mar 1991, folder 3, box 13, Woodall Papers, OA.

165. Arthur, interview by Marolda and Schneller, 15–16; Pollock, "Persian Gulf AAW—A SWO Perspective," 25–27; and Hardesty, "24 January 1991 F-1 Shootdown/C3 Failure," 28–29, in folder 6, box 9, Woodall Papers, OA; Chambers et al., "Antiair Warfare," *Vector* (Feb), 3-54–3-57; Gordon and Trainor, *The Generals' War*, 263–65.

166. Richards and Taylor, interview by Marolda, 87.

167. Hardesty, "24 January 1991 F-1 Shootdown/C3 Failure," 28–29, in folder 6, box 9, Woodall Papers, OA; Khaled, *Desert Warrior*, 358–60.

168. Admiral March implied that the fleet's antiair warfare resources were not enlisted earlier because the JFACC headquarters in Riyadh and the AWACS commander "basically wanted the Saudis to get the shot." March, interview by Marolda and Schneller, tape 2, side 1.

169. Commanding Officer *Mobile Bay* to COMUSNAVCENT, 6 Mar 1991, folder 9, box 9, Woodall Papers, OA; Chambers et al., *Antiair Warfare*, 3-56–3-57.

170. Pollock, "Persian Gulf AAW—A SWO Perspective," 25–27 in folder 6, box 9, Woodall Papers, OA

171. Naval Surface Warfare Center, *Desert Storm: Analysis of Aegis Operations*, 5.

172. Woodall comments re *Shield and Sword* mss, 25 Jan 1996, Authors Files. See also msg, *Curts* to CTF 154, 280830Z Jan 1996, Authors Files.

173. DiRita, "Exocets, Air Traffic, & the Air Tasking Order," 59–60.

174. Keaney, "Surveying Gulf War Airpower," 27–28.

175. March, interview by Marolda and Schneller, tape 1, side 2.

176. Admiral Brooks later observed that intelligence had revealed that the Iranian's were as surprised as the UN coalition when Saddam's air force began to bolt. Brooks, interview by Marolda and Schneller, tape 1, side 2. Surprised or not, Tehran was not prepared to make common cause with Saddam. Iranian air defense units shot up some Iraqi aircraft as they flew overhead. Moreover, Horner related that American fighters shot down Iraqi aircraft 20–30 miles inside Iran and these actions apparently elicited no hostile response from Tehran. Horner in Miller, ed., *Seeing Off the Bear*, 150–51.

177. Quoted in Horner, *The Gulf Commitment*, 177.

178. One observer believed that Admiral March worried excessively over enemy air attack; that he was "profoundly concerned that one of the carriers was going to take battle damage." Ramsdell, interview by Carpenter, 8. See also Arthur, interview by Marolda and Schneller, 17–18; Hallion, *Storm Over Iraq*, 194; IMEFB, 26 Jan 1991.

179. Cohen, "The Mystique of U.S. Air Power," 111; *CPGW*, 128–29; Hallion, *Storm Over Iraq*, 195; Horner, "Desert Shield/Desert Storm," 7; Hurley, "Saddam Hussein and Iraqi Air Power," 4–13; Jamieson, *Lucrative Targets*, 62. U.S., Department of the Air Force, *Reaching Globally, Reaching Powerfully*, 32–35.

180. *CPGW*, 123–24.

181. Ibid., 187–90.

182. *CPGW*, 188–91; Schwamb et al., *Strike Warfare*, 1-34. In the Red Sea, Rear Admiral Douglas J. Katz, Commander Cruiser Destroyer Group 2, handled the job of antisurface warfare commander.

183. The position of the Iraqi boats was 29 45 N 48 49 E, in the vicinity of the Iraqi minefields.

184. Morral, interview by Marolda and Schneller, tape 1, side 1; Morral, interview by Wright, 5, Center of Military History; U.S. Special Operations Command, "10th Anniversary History," 33, Authors' Files.

185. Green, Silvernell, Lattimore, and Hicks, interview by Wright, Center of Military History; Walker, interview by Wright, 6, Center of Military History; Frank Colucci, "Warriors at Sea," 6–11.

186. Simpson, interview by Wright, 37; see also 40; Green, Silvernell, Lattimore, and Hicks, interview by Wright, 8, 16, 25, 38-42; group interview by Wright, 8–11, 31, 35, 53; and Morral, interview by Wright, 2, 5, Center of Military History; Report re Attack on Iraqi Oil Platforms and USS *Nicholas*, 9 Jul 1991, 1–10, Authors' Files.

187. Morral, interview by Marolda and Schneller, tape 1, side 2; Morral, interview by Wright, 5.

188. Report of Oil Platform Attack and USS *Nicholas*, Jul 1991, 17, Authors' Files.

189. Morral later observed that "if I had detected any sincere attempt by forces to surrender, I would not have . . . engaged them." Morral, interview by Marolda and Schneller, tape 1, side 2.

190. Responding to the request of a *Nicholas* crewman, in July 1991 the Navy organized a fact-finding group headed by Rear Admiral Douglas A. Katz to look into the circumstances related to the 18 January attack on the ad-Dorra platforms. The Katz group, whose findings were endorsed by Commander Naval Surface Force, U.S. Atlantic Fleet and Commander U.S. Atlantic Fleet, concluded that Morral "was remiss in not pursuing the matter [of the white flags] further with his crew and with higher authority [and indeed] suppressing reports to higher authority." They considered these actions a "significant lapse of judgment." Morral admitted that "in retrospect, common sense told him he should have reported the information." Report of Iraqi Platform Attack by USS *Nicholas*, Jul 1991, 10–25, 36, Authors' Files.

The Katz group, however, stressed that Morral was fully justified in ordering the attack and complied with the Law of Naval Warfare, the Law of Land Warfare, Navy regulations, and the existing rules of engagement. They pointed out that Morral had been granted permission to attack the Iraqi-occupied platforms; that hostile fire had emanated from the site; that the LAMPS crew was not sure if any Iraqis wanted to surrender (only one Iraqi EPW later stated that he had tried to give up and other prisoners on *Nicholas* were uncooperative if not surly); the possibility that the white flags might be used as a ruse; that only a command authority on the platforms, as on a ship, could surrender that combatant unit; and finally that "each platform had the potential capability to instantaneously summon potent over-the-horizon strike aircraft and missiles" against the three vulnerable coalition ships. Ibid., 31–38. Not only did the naval leadership conclude that Morral had acted properly in the ad-Dorra event, but awarded him the Silver Star Medal for his direction of the operation.

191. Morral, interview by Wright, 6; Green, Silvernell, Lattimore, and Hicks, interview by Wright, 8, 16, 25, 38–42; and Group interview by Wright, 8–11, 31, 35, 53, Center for Military History; Report of Attack on Iraqi Platforms, Jul 1991, 10–27, Authors' Files.

192. During this period, Morral had a large white cross painted on top of the superstructure of *Istiqlal* to prevent a "friendly fire" incident. For, coalition aircraft were even then attacking patrol boats of the same class that the Iraqis had captured when they stormed into Kuwait. Morral, interview by Schneller, tape 1, side 1.

193. Morral, interview by Marolda and Schneller, tape 1, side 2.

194. Simpson interview by Wright, 43, Center of Military History. Morral related that he and Simpson, who had "done a superb job," worked well together and added in jest, "not once [during their association] did he mention the fact that we [the Navy] lost the Army-Navy game this year." Ibid., 13. Morral also praised the OH-58 crewmen, whose "stressful, dangerous, nighttime job" left no "margin for error." Morral, interview by Marolda and Schneller, tape 1, side 2. For their part, the Army aviators considered Morral a true "warrior" and a naval officer who appreciated "what our aircraft can do for his ability to project his power and also defend himself." Walker, interview by Wright, 10, Center of Military History.

195. Morral, interview by Marolda and Schneller, tape 1, side 2; Morral, interview by Wright, 7, Center of Military History; Report of USS *Nicholas* Attack on Iraqi Platforms, Jul 1991, 10–27, Authors' Files.

196. A second Arabic speaker in *Nicholas*'s crew, a Jordanian American, also assisted with interpreting duties. Morral, interview by Wright, 8, Center of Military History. Report of USS *Nicholas* Attack on Iraqi Platforms, Jul 1991, 28, identifies the two Arabic speakers as SH3 Abulail and FC3 Daoud.

197. Morral, interview by Marolda and Schneller, tape 1, side 1.

198. Morral emphatically denied postwar rumors that Iraqi EPWs were mistreated on board the Kuwaiti patrol boats. He observed that at least one U.S. naval officer was always on board each vessel and that these Americans reported that the Kuwaitis "treated them [Iraqi EPWs] humanely." In fact, Morral lavished praise on Kuwaiti sailors, whom he characterized as "outstanding" and "willing to put it on the line." At his recommendation, two Kuwaiti officers were awarded Bronze Star medals. Morral also dismissed any suggestion that any of his crewmen mishandled EPWs. Morral, interview by Schneller, tape 1, side 1; Morral, interview by Wright, 8. The Katz group, in Report of *Nicholas* Attack on Iraqi Platforms, Jul 1991, 38, stressed that "enemy prisoners of war were treated fairly and humanely in full compliance with the Geneva Convention on Prisoners of War." Further, the captain and crew of "*Nicholas* made extraordinary efforts to attend to the medical, physical, and comfort needs of the EPWs," for which they should be "commended."

199. The sources for this section were Commander Carrier Group 7, Command History 1991; and SEAL Team ONE, Command History 1991, Post 1 Jan 1990 Command Files, OA; Morral, interview by Marolda and Schneller; Morral, interview by Schneller; *CPGW*, 192–94; and Rodrique and Ruby, "Taking Down the Oil Platforms," 53.

200. Morral, interview by Marolda and Schneller, tape 1, side 2. See also Bell, *Naval Special Warfare*, 16; U.S. Special Operations Command, "10th Anniversay History," 35.

201. Msg, Bill to Hunt, Putnam, and Woodall, 202025Z Jan 1991; and Bill to Woodall and Woodall to Bill, 20 Jan 1991, file 8, box 14, Woodall Papers, OA.

202. Lutz et al., *Antisurface Warfare*, v.

203. Naval units from these latter nations did, however, free other units for offensive operations by defending coalition combatants and merchantmen in the gulf and patrolling the southern coastline,

204. Arthur, interview by Marolda and Schneller, 31–32; *CPGW*, 188–93.

205. Commander Carrier Group 7, Command History 1991, Post 1 Jan 1990 Command Files, OA; *CPGW*, 188–91.

206. March, interview by Marolda and Schneller.

207. USS *Mobile Bay*, "Draft Tacmemo: Battle Force Anti-Air Warfare Commander (BF AAWC) for Multiple Carrier Battle Force Operations for AEGIS Cruisers," May 1991, folder 6, box 9, Woodall Papers, OA; Commander Carrier Group 7, Command History 1991, Post 1 Jan 1991 Command Files, OA; *CPGW*, 188–91; Schwamb et al., *Strike Warfare*, 1-34.

208. Even as late as 27 January, Captain Forbes expressed concern that there were insufficient "shooters" dedicated to ASUW. Msg, COMDESRON 7 to CTG 154.3, 271620Z Jan 1991, file 8, box 14, Woodall Papers, OA. See also Hunt, interview by Marolda, 16.

209. Msg, COMDESRON 7 to CTG 154.11, 210808Z Jan 1991, file 8, box 14, Woodall Papers, OA.

210. Msg, CTG 154.3 to COMDESRON 7, 231045Z Jan 1991, file 8, box 14, Woodall Papers, OA.

211. Commander Carrier Group 7, Command History 1991, Post 1 Jan 1990 Command Files, OA; *CPGW*, 188–91; Lutz et al., *Antisurface Warfare*, v.

212. Commander Carrier Group 7, Command History 1991, Post 1 Jan 1990 Command Files, OA; *CPGW*, 191; Lutz et al., *Antisurface Warfare*, v; McWilliams, *This Ain't Hell*, 109.

213. Zlatoper, "The War at Sea," 2.

214. Some commanders suggested arming the Orions with Harpoon antiship missiles and Rockeye cluster bombs. Admiral Arthur decided against the proposal because he was not confident the Harpoons would be able to discriminate between hostile and friendly ships in the close quarters of the northern gulf, and Rockeye detonations might damage the thin-skinned patrol planes. Chambers et al., *Antiair Warfare*, 1-1; *CPGW*, 191–98; Liebman, "We Need Armed Helos," 84–85; Lutz, *Antisurface Warfare*, 3-10, 3-12; Zlatoper, "The War at Sea," 2. In at least one instance, an F-14 strafed Iraqi surface craft. See Commander Carrier Group 7, Desert Storm, 17 Jan–19 Mar 1991, Battle Force Zulu ASUWC Briefing, in ltr, Zlatoper to Marolda, 23 Mar 1996, 62, Authors' Files.

215. Morral, interview by Marolda and Schneller, tape 1, side 1.

216. Admiral Arthur thought that the U.S. Navy's disinclination to have its own missile-armed attack helicopters was "dumber than dirt," since the "daggum Lynx with the Sea Skua was just absolutely deadly." Arthur, interview by Marolda and Schneller, 32.

217. After the war Zlatoper and Morral called for development of a U.S. Navy armed helicopter. See Commander Carrier Group 7, Desert Storm, 17 Jan–19 Mar 1991, Battle Force Zulu ASUWC Briefing, in ltr, Zlatoper to Marolda, 23 Mar 1996, Authors' Files, OA; Morral, interview by Marolda and Schneller, tape 1, side 2; Brown, *The Royal Navy and the Falklands War*, 82, 362; *CPGW*, 191–93; Liebman, "We Need Armed Helos," 84–85; Craig, "Gulf War," 12–14; Watson et al., *Military Lessons of the Gulf War*, 128; Zlatoper, "The War at Sea," 2; Pokrant, *A View*, app. C, 6, 17.

218. Almond, *Desert Score*, 351–54. The Hellfire could also operate with infrared and radio frequency seekers.

219. Simpson, interview by Wright, 9, Center of Military History.

220. Woodall comments re *Shield and Sword* mss, 25 Jan 1996, Authors' Files.

221. Msg, COMDESRON 7 to CTG 154.3, 271620Z Jan 1991, file 8, box 14, Woodall Papers, OA.

222. Msg, COMDESRON 7 to CTG 154.3, 221931Z Jan 1991, file 8, box 14, Woodall Papers, OA.

223. CO's Log, 26 and 29 Jan 1991 entries, file 1, box 10, Woodall Papers, OA; Woodall comments re *Shield and Sword* mss, 25 Jan 1996, Authors' Files. See also Lutz, *Antisurface Warfare*, 5-10.

224. Woodall comments re *Shield and Sword* mss, 25 Jan 1996, Authors' Files, OA.

225. Msg, CTG 154.11 to CTF 154, 231857Z Jan 1991, file 8, box 4, Woodall Papers, OA.

226. Atwal, "Through Sea, Sand, and Storm," 17; *CPGW*, 191–93; Cordesman and Wagner, *The Lessons of Modern War*, 2: 102, 532; *DSDSLL*, 66; Friedman, *Desert Victory*, 209, 361; Hunt, interview by Marolda, 15–16; Liebman, "We Need Armed Helos," 84–85; Lutz, *Antisurface Warfare*, 3-1, 4-14; Slade, "The FAC's End Approaches," 12–13; *USNDS*, A-18–A-25; Zlatoper, "The War at Sea," 2. Dates of engagements and identities of enemy vessels are uncertain because several craft were reported disabled or sunk on multiple occasions.

227. Perla, *Summary*, 77; Pokrant, *A View*, 5-24.

228. Arthur felt he was hindered throughout the war in the use of Navy SEALs, because most of the men were under SOCCENT's operational control, not his. Griffis et al., *Amphibious Operations*, 18–19; Pokrant, *A View*, 5-24.

229. Also on the 24th, at night, a LAMPS/OH-58 team from *Nicholas* discovered four armed Iraqi patrol boats off the coast of Kuwait. The Army helicopters reportedly sank or heavily damaged all four of the enemy vessels. Morral, interview by Wright, 11, Center of Military History.

230. Craig, *Call for Fire*, 233; 24 Jan 1991 entry, CO's Logbook, file 1, box 10, Woodall Papers, OA; USS *Curts* (FFG 38), Command History 1991, SH; USS *Leftwich* (DD 984), Command History 1991, SH; Carver interview by Wright, 7, Center of Military History; Lutz et al., *Antisurface Warfare*, A-2, B-1, C-1, C-2; msg, *Curts* to CTF 151, 242330Z Jan 1991, file 5, box 12, Woodall Papers, OA; Montgomery, "When the Liberation of Kuwait Began," 51; Sitrep for 25–26 Jan 1991, Middle East Force CTF 151 Daily Sitreps, OA; Perla, *Summary*, 77. The sources disagree as to whether the second Iraqi vessel was a patrol boat, minesweeper, or minelayer.

231. *CPGW*, 194.

232. Pokrant, *A View*, 5-24.

233. Msg, CTU 156.1.1 to COMUSNAVCENT, 311030Z Jan 1991, file 5, box 12, Woodall Papers, OA; *CPGW*, 219; Griffis et al., *Amphibious Operations*, 18–19; Pokrant, *A View*, 5-24.

234. Arthur, interview by Marolda and Schneller, 19-21; Pokrant, *A View*, 5-10–5-11, 5-18.

235. Quoted in Pokrant, *A View*, 5-12. See also Canby, "After the Storm," 16.

236. Badolato, "Pollution as Ammunition," 69; "CG Heads Oil-Assist Team to Assess Persian Gulf Damage," 4; Mazarr, et al., *Desert Storm*, 111.

237. "CG Heads Oil-Assist Team," 4.

238. Richards and Taylor, interview by Marolda, 73–74.

239. Scales, *Certain Victory*, 190.

240. de la Billiere, *Storm Command*, 250; Gordon and Trainor, *The Generals' War*, 268–70; *GWAPS*, *Summary*, 19.

241. Craig, *Call for Fire*, 239; de la Billiere, *Storm Command*, 251; *CPGW*, 130–33, 195–96; Gordon and Trainor, *The Generals' War*, 268–88, 499–500, footnote 3; Jamieson,

Lucrative Targets, 112–20; Marolda, "A Host of Nations," 265–66; Mitzelfelt, "Trapped Recon Teams," 30; Perla, *Summary*, 77; Quilter, *With the I Marine Expeditionary Force*, 60–62; Schwarzkopf, *It Doesn't Take a Hero*, 424–27; Swain, *Lucky War*, 191. Except for a corporal slightly injured by shell fragments, the Marine reconnaissance detachment escaped from Khafji unscathed.

242. The employment of FLIR by carrier- and shore-based Navy and Marine A-6 Intruders proved particularly effective against both heat-emitting warships and armored vehicles. *DSDSLL*, 54; Cassara, critique, 22 Aug 1996, Authors' Files.

243. Cassara, critique, 22 Aug 1996, Authors' Files; *CPGW*, 193–96; Lutz, *Antisurface Warfare*, 4–6; McWilliams, *This Ain't Hell*, 109–12; Wilhelm, "Live by the Sword," 68–69; Morin and Gimblett, *Operation Friction*, 169–70.

244. de la Billeire, *Storm Command*, 255; Commander Carrier Group 7, Command History 1991, Post 1 Jan 1990 Command Files, OA; *CPGW*, 195–96; Middle East Force/CTF 151 Daily Sitreps, 310528Z Jan to 010528Z Feb 1991, OA; Zlatoper, "The War at Sea," 2.

245. Msg, COMDESRON 7 to *Mobile Bay*, 050910Z Mar 1991, file 9, box 9, Woodall Papers, OA.

246. *CPGW*, 195–96. After the war, Captain David J. Grieve, COMUSMCMGRU, argued that because Iraqi mines prevented the Navy from using the water as it pleased, it did not really control the sea. Ltr, Grieve to Marolda, 26 Mar 1996, Authors' Files.

CHAPTER 5

1. *CPGW*, 243–44, 251–56, 265; Hammick, "Iraqi Obstacles and Defensive Positions," 989; Quilter, *With the I Marine Expeditionary Force*, 15–18; *Triumph Without Victory*, 296; Watson, *Military Lessons*, 90–91.

2. Quoted in Hiro, *Desert Shield to Desert Storm*, 319.

3. Hallion, *Storm Over Iraq*, 209.

4. *OPDS*, 362; *CPGW*, 75–76, 100–101, 112–13, 227–28.

5. Palmer, "The Storm in the Air," 24–31; Scales, *Certain Victory*, 176.

6. Quoted in Hallion, *Storm Over Iraq*, 209; U.S., Department of the Air Force, *Reaching Globally, Reaching Powerfully*, 40.

7. American ground commanders, especially the Vietnam veterans, generally favored B-52s over other Air Force aircraft because of the psychological impact a massive bomber strike had on enemy troops. But, the B-52s, which normally dropped their unguided, "dumb bombs" from high altitude to avoid enemy air defenses, destroyed only insignificant amounts of Iraqi army materiel. Inaccurate targeting, at least until mid-February, compounded the problem. B-52 strikes were also used to breach Iraqi frontline fortifications, but Horner observed that he was "not sure it did any good at all." One must question the utility of using these long-range bombers in a battlefield bombing role, especially since the Air Force had to devote 40 percent of its best tankers and 25 percent of its theater refueling effort to support the operation of B-52s from air bases located thousands of miles from the battlefield. Davis, *Strategic Air Power in Desert Storm*, 29; Gordon and Trainor, *The Generals' War*, 201, 318; Jamieson, *Lucrative Targets*, 104–6, Horner quote from 152.

8. *CPGW*, 174–75; Johnson, "Roles and Missions."

9. Schwamb et al., *Strike Warfare*, 1-46, 1-51.

10. March, interview by Marolda and Schneller, tape 1, side 1.

11. *OPDS*, 213. Admiral March later remarked that had the war lasted longer, he would have deployed five or six carriers into the gulf. March, interview by Marolda and Schneller, tape 2, side 2.

12. Schwamb et al., *Strike Warfare*, 1-47, 1-55–1-56.

13. Ibid., 1-46.

14. Perla, *Summary*, 50; Schwamb et al., *Strike Warfare*, 1-46, 1-55.

15. March, interview by Marolda and Schneller, tape 2, side 1.

16. Bridges outside the KTO were Phase I targets.

17. *DSDSLL*, 94–95; ltr, Pokrant to Dudley, 26 Jan 1996, Authors' Files.

18. *CPGW*, 134–38, 158; *GWAPS, Summary*, 97–99; Jamieson, *Lucrative Targets*, 82–84; Schwamb et al., *Strike Warfare*, 6-25, 6-33–6-49; GAO, *Operation Desert Storm*, 151.

19. *CPGW*, 142, 158; *GWAPS, Summary*, 94–95; Jamieson, *Lucrative Targets*, 83–84; Schwamb et al., *Strike Warfare*, 6-35–6-36, 6-40.

20. *CPGW*, 134–35, 142; *GWAPS, Summary*, 97–99.

21. Adolph, "PSYOP," 16–17; *CPGW*, 139–40.

22. ohnson, *PSYOP*, 50–51.

23. Ibid., 16–17; *CPGW*, 139–40.

24. *CPGW*, 135–36; *GWAPS, Summary*, 52; Jones, "Close Air Support," 63; Pokrant, *A View*, C-3; U.S., Department of the Air Force, *Reaching Globally, Reaching Powerfully*, 37–38; Schwamb et al., *Strike Warfare*, 2-23–2-24, 4-12, 6-9, 6-16.

25. *OPDS*, 213; Schwamb et al., *Strike Warfare*, 4-12, 5-4, 6-18–6-22; Wilhelm, "Live by the Sword," 69.

26. *CPGW*, 138–40; Major Mace Carpenter, USAF, conversation with Schneller, 22 Mar 1994; Jamieson, "Lucrative Targets," 93.

27. Wilhelm, "Live by the Sword," 69.

28. *CPGW*, 248–49; Perla, *Summary*, 104–5; Schwamb et al., *Strike Warfare*, 6-14; *USNDS*, A-36.

29. *CPGW*, 112–14, 343.

30. Schwarzkopf, *It Doesn't Take A Hero*, 431.

31. Gordon and Trainor, *The Generals' War*, 190.

32. Winnefeld et al., *A League of Airmen*, 151; *GWAPS, Summary*, 49–51.

33. *CPGW*, 112–14, 339–43; Freedman and Karsh, *The Gulf Conflict*, 368–72.

34. "BDA" appears variously as the acronym for "bomb," "battle," or "battlefield" damage assessment, all of which mean essentially the same thing.

35. *GWAPS*, vol. 2, part 2, 32; Jamieson, "Lucrative Targets," 110; Mandeles, *Managing Command and Control*, 91–115; Swain, *Lucky War*, 187.

36. Commander Carrier Group 7, Desert Storm, 17 Jan–19 Mar 1991, Battle Force Zulu ASUWC Briefing, in ltr, Zlatoper to Marolda, 23 Mar 1996, Authors' Files; Schwamb et al., *Strike Warfare*, 6-28.

37. IMEFB, 1 Feb 1991; U.S., Department of Defense, *Conduct of the Persian Gulf Conflict*, 25-1.

38. U.S., Department of Defense, *Conduct of the Persian Gulf Conflict*, 25-1; *CPGW*, 113–14, 140–42, 175–76, 339–43; Freedman and Karsh, *The Gulf Conflict*, 368–72; Glosson, "Impact of Precision Weapons," 8.

39. Msg, COMCARGRU 2 to COMUSNAVCENT, 142016Z Mar 1991, COMUSNAVCENT N3 Desert Shield/Storm working papers and message files, CNA.

40. Msg, CTG 154.12 to COMUSNAVCENT, 090800Z Mar 1991; and msg, CTG 154.11 to COMUSNAVCENT, 141745Z Mar 1991, COMUSNAVCENT N3 Desert Shield/Storm working papers and message files, CNA.

41. de la Billiere, *Storm Command*, 278; *CPGW*, 175–76; Freedman and Karsh, *The Gulf Conflict*, 368–72; Lewis, "JFACC," 12; Scales, *Certain Victory*, 187–88; House Committee on Armed Services, Oversight and Investigations Subcommittee, *Intelligence*, 18–19.

42. Msg, Personal, Schwarzkopf to Powell, info to CINCS, 051630Z Apr 1991, US-CENTCOMFWD, CinC's File, box 2, folder 60, RG 518 (CENTCOM Records), NA.

43. *OPDS*, 341. Admiral Brooks suggested that one problem with BDA was the inability of Washington to get carrier pilot debriefings in a timely fashion. Brooks, interview by Marolda and Schneller, tape 2, side 2.

44. Schwarzkopf, *It Doesn't Take A Hero*, 432.

45. *CPGW*, 113–14, 140–42, 175–76, 339–43; Freedman and Karsh, *The Gulf Conflict*, 368–72; *GWAPS, Summary*, 105–106.

46. Quoted in de la Billiere, *Storm Command*, 273.

47. Quoted in Morocco et al., "Soviet Peace Plan," 22.

48. *CPGW*, 144–45, 159–60; Freedman and Karsh, *The Gulf Conflict*, 372–73; Winnefeld et al., *A League of Airmen*, 148–51; Lewis, "JFACC," 15.

49. Fifteen other launch attempts proved unsuccessful because of equipment failures. Holliday, *TLAM Performance*, 15; Schwamb et al., *Strike Warfare*, 8-3–8-6.

50. Arthur, interview by Marolda and Schneller, 24–25; Gordon and Trainor, *The Generals' War*, 327; *DSDSLL*, 90.

51. *CPGW*, 141; Heidenrich, "The Gulf War," 117–19.

52. Heidenrich, "The Gulf War," 117.

53. *CPGW*, 141; Gordon and Trainor, *The Generals' War*, 324–27; Hallion, *Storm Over Iraq*, 199; Humphries, "Operations Law," 35–36; Mazarr et al., *Desert Storm*, 121.

54. Quoted in Hallion, *Storm Over Iraq*, 199.

55. Ibid.

56. Ibid., 199–200.

57. Msg, CTF 151 to COMUSNAVCENT, sitrep for 250528Z Jan to 260528Z Jan 1991, Middle East Force/CTF 151 Sitreps, OA; *CPGW*, 199–202; Gawlowicz, "Mine Countermeasures," 23; Passarelli et al., *Mine Countermeasures*, 5-2–5-3.

58. *CPGW*, 190, 212–14; Hammick, "Iraqi Obstacles and Defensive Positions," 989; *OPDS*, 207; Santoli, *Leading the Way*, 312; Watson, *Military Lessons of the Gulf War*, 92.

59. *CPGW*, 213–15; Griffis et al., *Amphibious Operations*, 12.

60. *CPGW*, 215–16; Griffis et al., *Amphibious Operations*, 47.

61. Australian Clearance Diving Team 3, Report of Proceedings, 11 May 1991, Authors' Files.

62. LaPlante, interview by Marolda and Schneller, tape 3, side 2.

63. Ltr, Grieve to Marolda, 26 Mar 1996, Authors' Files.

64. Ltr, Sutton to Marolda, 12 Apr 1996, Authors' Files.

65. LaPlante, interview by Marolda and Schneller, tape 2, side 1.

66. Ltr, Grieve to Marolda, 26 Mar 1996; and ltr, Brown to Director Naval Historical Center, 3 Jan 1996, Authors' Files; LaPlante, interview by Marolda and Schneller, tape 2, side 1; HM 14, Command History 1991, 10 Mar 1992, OA.

67. Ltr, Grieve to Marolda, 26 Mar 1996, Authors' Files; Pokrant, *A View*, 5-17, 5-19.

68. Craig, *Call for Fire*, 227, 236–38; ltr, Grieve to Marolda, 26 Mar 1996, Authors' Files.

69. Craig, *Call for Fire*, 236–38; Pokrant, *A View*, 5-17; HM 14, Command History 1991, 10 Mar 1992.

70. Craig, *Call for Fire*, 236–38; de la Billiere, *Storm Command*, 256–59; ltr, Grieve to Marolda, 26 Mar 1996.

71. *CPGW*, 212–21; Griffis et al., *Amphibious Operations*, xiv, 24.

72. *OPDS*, 207.

73. Boomer, interview by Carpenter, 5, Authors' Files, OA; Gordon and Trainor, *The Generals' War*, 292–94.

74. Griffis et al., *Amphibious Operations*, 24–26. The planned raid on Faylaka Island was also referred to as "Operation Desert Dagger."

75. Quoted in *CPGW*, 217. Italics added for emphasis.

76. Bulkeley, interview by Marolda and Schneller, 31–32, 55; *CPGW*, 216–17; Commander Destroyer Squadron 22, Command History 1991, OA; ltr, Grieve to Marolda, 26 Mar 1996; Griffis et al., *Amphibious Operations*, 27; *OPDS*, 382–85; Passarelli et al., *Mine Countermeasures*, 7-1; Schwarzkopf, *It Doesn't Take a Hero*, 437; Craig, *Call for Fire*, 270.

77. The commander of the 4th Squadron, 17 Cavalry, the Army unit that operated OH-58D helicopters from fleet frigates, complained in mid-February that "sometimes you really don't know who you work for. . . . Who tells us what to do? I'm often confused." Simpson, interview by Wright, 27, Center of Military History. His executive officer also found the Navy's command organization "weird." He observed that since Fogarty's force was a "bureaucratic command . . . they do not do a lot of operational planning [and never were] a true battle staff." Walker, interview by Wright, 2, Center of Military History.

78. March, interview by Marolda and Schneller, tape 1, sides 1-2; Craig, *Call for Fire*, 257.

79. LaPlante, interview by Marolda and Schneller, tape 1, side 1.

80. Craig, *Call for Fire*, 207. Admiral LaPlante also related that March showed only minimal interest in prospective amphibious operations. LaPlante, interview by Marolda and Schneller, tape 1, side 2.

81. Craig, *Call for Fire*, 197.

82. Ibid., 250. See also 265.

83. Sharing the danger in these waters were Saudi combatants, including missile corvette *Tabuk* (FSG 618) and fast attack craft HMS *Abdul Aziz* (PCFG 515) and HMS *Faisal* (PCFG 517). *CPGW*, 208–12; Horne et al., *Naval Gunfire Support*, 1; *OPDS*, 209; *USNDS*, H-2–H-5; Stillwell, *Battleship Missouri*, 314, 316.

84. Stillwell, *Battleship New Jersey*, 201–41; Marolda, "Crucible of War," 227–28.

85. David S. Bill, telephone conversation with Marolda, 10 Apr 1996, Authors' Files; *CPGW*, 208–12; *OPDS*, 209; Stillwell, *Battleship Missouri*, 308, 316; Santoli, *Leading the Way*, 290; *USNDS*, H-2–H-5. The UAVs were then called remotely piloted vehicles (RPVs).

86. *CPGW*, 200–208; msg, COMDESRON 22 to USCINCCENT, 041456Z Mar 1991, Desert Storm Engagement Message File, CNA; Craig, *Call for Fire*, 245–47; Passarelli et al., *Mine Countermeasures*, 2-5.

87. Bulkeley, interview by Marolda and Schneller, 43-49; Commander Destroyer Squadron 22, Command History 1991, OA; Craig, *Call for Fire*, 251.

88. Msg, COMDESRON 22 to USCINCCENT, 041456Z Mar 1991, Desert Storm Engagement Message File, CNA; Bulkeley, interview by Marolda and Schneller, 49; ltr, Grieve to Marolda, 26 Mar 1996, Authors' Files; HM 14, Command History 1991, 10 Mar 1992, OA.

89. "Aegis at War," briefing slides, file 8, box 5, Woodall Papers, OA; msg, *Mobile Bay* to COMNAVSURFGRU WESTPAC, 101845Z Feb 1991, file 5, box 12, Woodall Papers; Bulkeley, interview by Marolda and Schneller, 59.

90. Bulkeley, interview by Marolda and Schneller, 59–64.

91. Ltr, Grieve to Marolda, 26 Mar 1996, Authors' Files; Taylor, interview by Marolda and Schneller, 72–74, 297.

92. The Royal Navy mounted camera systems in two helicopters to look for moored mines during Desert Storm, so technically, they also had an AMCM capability.

93. *CPGW*, 203–5; Passarelli et al., *Mine Countermeasures*, 2-1; HM 14, Command History 1991, 10 Mar 1992.

94. Ltr, Grieve to Marolda, 26 Mar 1996, Authors' Files.

95. HM 14, Command History 1991, 10 Mar 1992, OA; Fursdon, "Iraqi Mines," 145; Taylor, interview by Marolda and Schneller, 285–86; Ward et al., *C3*, 7-3.

96. *Atherstone* (M-38), *Cattistock* (M-31), *Dulverton* (M-35), *Hurworth* (M-39), and *Ledbury* (M-30). *CPGW*, 203–6; Fursdon, "Iraqi Mines," 142–46.

97. Bauer, "Desert Storm," 70; Fursdon, "Iraqi Mines Know No Ceasefire," 145; Passarelli et al., *Mine Countermeasures*, 1-5; Taylor, interview by Marolda and Schneller, 270.

98. Quoted in Bauer, "Desert Storm," 70.

99. For descriptions of mine warfare in the Cold War and in Vietnam, see Melia, *"Damn the Torpedoes"*; Marolda, *By Sea, Air, and Land*; Marolda, ed., *Operation End Sweep*; Marolda, "Crucible of War," 229.

100. Almond, *Desert Score*, 263–65; *CPGW*, 203–205; ltr, Grieve to Marolda, 26 Mar 1996, Authors' Files; Passarelli et al., *Mine Countermeasures*, 1-4, 2-2–2-6; Taylor, interview by Marolda and Schneller, 270–71.

101. Arthur, interview by Marolda and Schneller, 44.

102. *OPDS*, 325. The mine threat had an unanticipated impact on the provision of medical support. Schwarzkopf later remarked that fear of mines and air attack kept the hospital ships *Mercy* and *Comfort* so far from the front that no more than 100 patients were being cared for on the ships at any time during Desert Storm. This situation was exacerbated by the ships' dependence on the relatively slow helicopters, rather than fixed-wing aircraft, for the transport of casualties. See msg, Personal, Schwarzkopf to Powell, info to CINCs, 051630Z Apr 1991, USCENTCOMFWD, CinC's File, box 2, folder 60, RG 518 (CENTCOM Records), NA.

103. Ltr, Mauz to Marolda, 12 Jun 1996, Authors' Files. See also Bell, *Naval Special Warfare*, 18.

104. Bulkeley has concluded that the intelligence on Iraqi minefields captured by coalition forces on Qaruh did show the actual location of minefields but was not passed on to him or Grieve before they steamed into trouble. The authors have found no other information to support his contention. See Bulkeley interview, by Marolda and Schneller, Authors' Files.

105. Almond, *Desert Score*, 263–65; Arthur, interview by Ramsdell, 14–15; Bulkeley interview by Marolda and Schneller, 64; *CPGW*, 200–208; ltr, Grieve to Marolda, 26 Mar 1996; ltr, Mauz to Marolda, 12 Jun 1996; Passarelli et al., *Mine Countermeasures*, 2-5, 2-6, 5-3, 5-10; Preston, "Allied MCM in the Gulf," 47; IMEFB, 26 Jan 1991; Taylor, interview by Marolda and Schneller, 240, 254–55; map showing early Feb 1991 intelligence estimate of Iraqi minefields and postwar map showing actual location of the minefields, R.A.K. Taylor Papers, OA.

106. Bulkeley, interview by Marolda and Schneller, 65–67; *CPGW*, 206–7; Martin, "We Still Haven't Learned," 64; msg, COMDESRON 22 to USCINCCENT, 041456Z Mar 1991, Desert Storm Engagement Message File, CNA.

107. Quoted in Evans, "*Princeton* Leaves the War," 70. Admiral Taylor finds it an "enormous irony for Captain Hontz to see merit in being out in front of the minesweepers—in fact, unbelievable. In the Annals of naval history, this is one for the How not to do it section." Ltr, Taylor to Dudley, 29 Jan 1996, Authors' Files. Admiral March thought Hontz was "pushing his luck." March, interview by Marolda and Schneller, tape 1, side 1.

108. Rigorous damage control training had been a central feature of the fleet's readiness efforts during the 1970s and 1980s. Many sailors of that era viewed a training film that analyzed how the carrier *Forrestal* had almost been lost to fire and explosion off Vietnam because of inadequate damage control practices. In contrast, swift and effective action by damage controlmen was widely credited with saving frigates *Stark* and *Samuel B.*

Roberts from sinking during Operation Earnest Will. Naval Imaging Command, "Trial by Fire," training video; OPNAV Summary Report A-34, Authors' Files, OA; Marolda, "Crucible of War," 226–27; Palmer, *Guardians of the Gulf*, 1–38.

109. Bauer, "Desert Storm," 67, 71, 75; de la Billiere, *Storm Command*, 271; Bulkeley, interview by Marolda and Schneller, 68; *CPGW*, 206–7; Gawlowicz, "Mine Countermeasures," 22; ltr, Grieve to Marolda, 26 Mar 1996; Giusti, "Mine Reading," 17; msg, COMDESRON 22 to USCINCCENT, 041456Z Mar 1991, Desert Storm Engagement Message File, CNA; *OPDS*, 183; Martin, "We Still Haven't Learned," 64; Thompson, "Tripoli Keeps on Ticking," 14.

110. de la Billiere, *Storm Command*, 271; msg, COMDESRON 22 to USCINCCENT, 041456Z Mar 1991, Desert Storm Engagement Message File, CNA; ltr, Grieve to Marolda, 26 Mar 1996; Stillwell, *Battleship Missouri*, 320.

111. Quoted in *CPGW*, 205.

112. Bauer, "Desert Storm," 83; de la Billiere, *Storm Command*, 271; Boatman, "Gulf Mines Almost Sank U.S. Cruiser," 866; *CPGW*, 205–207; Evans, "*Princeton* Leaves the War," 70, 72; Gawlowicz, "Mine Countermeasures in the Gulf," 22; Preston, "Allied MCM," 55; "Take a Hit," 13; *USNDS*, A-34.

113. Bauer, "Desert Storm," 62, 69; *CPGW*, 206–7; Preston, "Allied MCM," 54; "Threading Past Danger With Friends," 12. Even during the short period when *Princeton*'s defensive systems were not operating, she was not a "sitting duck" as Michael Gordon and Bernard Trainor contend. The AAW defenses on guided missile cruiser *Horne* (CG 30) and British guided missile destroyer *Manchester* (D 95) operating nearby covered the stricken cruiser. Furthermore, the Iraqis could not have known that American ships had struck mines. Bauer, "Desert Storm," 82; Gordon and Trainor, *The Generals' War*, 345; Truver, "Lessons from the *Princeton* Incident," 740–41.

114. *CPGW*, 205–7; ltr, Taylor to Dudley, 29 Jan 1996.

115. *CPGW*, 205–7; Preston, "Allied MCM," 56; Miller, *Persian Excursion*, 87.

116. Bulkeley, interview by Marolda and Schneller, 69–75; ltr, Grieve to Marolda, 26 Mar 1996; Passarelli et al., *Mine Countermeasures*, 5-9.

117. *CPGW*, 202–9; msg, COMDESRON 22 to USCINCCENT, 041456Z Mar 1991; HM 14, Command History 1991, 10 Mar 1992, OA.

118. HM 14, Command History 1991, 10 Mar 1992, OA.

119. *CPGW*, 207; Stillwell, *Battleship Missouri*, 320; Taylor interview, by Marolda and Schneller, 61–66.

120. Passarelli et al., *Mine Countermeasures*, A-18–A-21.

121. Bauer, "Desert Storm," 73; Passarelli et al., *Mine Countermeasures*, 5-14–5-16; Snaza, "Lucky *Foster*," 10.

122. Ltr, Grieve to Marolda, 26 Mar 1996. Because of the dense smoke from oil fires ashore, the men of HM 14 routinely flew their exacting, low-level sweeping missions "in conditions of near zero visibility." HM 14, Command History 1991, 10 Mar 1992, OA.

123. Quoted in Pokrant, *A View*, C-15.

124. Msg, COMDESRON 22 to USCINCCENT, 041456Z Mar 1991, Desert Storm Engagement Message File, CNA. See Chapter 6 for details of the bombardment.

125. IMEFB, 21 Feb 1991.

126. Admiral Sharp handled, at Schwarzkopf's direction, the integration of the Arab forces into the campaign plan. The flag officer, dressed like everyone else in a desert camouflage uniform, related that "all the Arabs called me general because all I talked to them about were ground operations." Sharp, interview by Marolda and Schneller, tape 2, side 1. See also *CPGW*, 234–35; Friedman, *Desert Victory*, 261–96.

127. Quilter, *With the I Marine Expeditionary Force*, 21, 33–34, 37–38.

128. *CPGW*, 243–45, 251–52, 265; Quilter, *With the I Marine Expeditionary Force*, 15; *Triumph Without Victory*, 296; Watson, ed., *Military Lessons of the Gulf War*, 90–91.

129. Quoted in Summers, *On Strategy II*, 280.

130. Cureton, *With the 1st Marine Division*, 24; Mroczkowski, *With the 2d Marine Division*, 10–13; Quilter, *With the I Marine Expeditionary Force*, 20–21, 33–34, 37–38, 41–42.

131. Krulak, "CSS in the Desert," 31–32; NMCB 5, NMCB 40, and NMCB 74 Command Histories, Post 1 Jan 1990 Command Files, OA; Quilter, *With the I Marine Expeditionary Force*, 43; Roberts, "The Untold Story in the Gulf," 8–15; ltr, M.R. Johnson (CEC), USN to Marolda, 27 and 29 Mar 1996, Authors' Files; Commander Naval Construction Battalions, U.S. Pacific Fleet, Naval Construction Force Operation Desert Shield/Storm After Action Report, ser CB30/067, 23 Jan 1992, Authors' Files; Fedele, "The Seabees Go To War," 3–13; Zimmeck, *A War of Logistics*, 3-21–3-32, 4-4–4-6.

132. Blackwell, *Thunder in the Desert*, 154–57; Hammick, "Iraqi Obstacles and Defensive Positions," 991; Quilter, *With the I Marine Expeditionary Force*, 46.

133. Quilter, *With the I Marine Expeditionary Force*, 54–55, 78, 81.

134. Krulak, "CSS in the Desert," 32–37; Melson et al., *Anthology and Annotated Bibliography*, 159; Quilter, *With the I Marine Expeditionary Force*, 54–56; Roberts, "The Untold Story in the Gulf," 8-15; Zimmeck, *A War of Logistics*, 5-7–5-11.

135. Commander Naval Construction Battalions, U.S. Pacific Fleet, Naval Construction Force Operation Desert Shield/Storm After Action Report, ser CB30/067, 23 Jan 1992, Authors' Files; Fedele, "The Seabees Go to War," 3–13.

136. IMEFB, 19 Mar 1991. See also ltr, M.R. Johnson (CEC), USN to Marolda, 27 and 29 Mar 1996; and Commander Naval Construction Battalions, U.S. Pacific Fleet, Naval Construction Force Operation Desert Shield/Storm After Action Report, ser CB30/067, 23 Jan 1992, Authors' Files; Fedele, "The Seabees Go To War," 3-13; Zimmeck, *A War of Logistics*, 3-21–3-32, 4-4–4-6.

137. *CPGW*, 245; Quilter, *With the I Marine Expeditionary Force*, 69.

138. Cordesman, "The Gulf War."

139. *CPGW*, 140–41, 227–28, 245–46; Hallion, *Storm Over Iraq*, 227–28; Schubert and Kraus, eds., *Whirlwind War*, chap. 7, "Preparing for the Storm;" Scales, *Certain Victory*, 145.

140. Freedman and Karsh, *Gulf Conflict*, 370–72; Mazarr et al., *Desert Storm*, 120–21; Schwarzkopf, *It Doesn't Take a Hero*, 433–35.

141. Gordon and Trainor, *The Generals' War*, 196.

142. George Bush, "Remarks to the American Association for the Advancement of Science," 15 Feb 1991, *Weekly Compilation of Presidential Documents* 27 (18 Feb 1991), 173–74.

143. Freedman and Karsh, *Gulf Conflict*, 374–85; Hiro, *Desert Shield to Desert Storm*, 364–79; Palmer, *Guardians of the Gulf*, 224–27.

144. Marlin Fitzwater, "Statement by Press Secretary Fitzwater on the Persian Gulf Conflict," 22 Feb 1991, *Weekly Compilation of Presidential Documents* 27 (25 Feb 1991), 201; Freedman and Karsh, *Gulf Conflict*, 374–85.

CHAPTER 6

1. *CPGW*, 227–28, 239–40, 268; *OPDS*, 209; Simmons, "Getting the Job Done," 94.

2. *CPGW*, 267, 277; Quilter, *With the I Marine Expeditionary Force*, 46–47, 73–75.

3. Because forces from several different Marine divisions and expeditionary brigades made up his division, Myatt organized the units as armored or mechanized task forces

and gave them colorful names like Grizzly, Taro, Ripper, Papa Bear, Shepherd, Troy, and X-Ray.

4. Cureton, *With the 1st Marine Division in Desert Shield and Desert Storm*, 54–59; Curtis, "The Tip of the Spear," 23; Fulghum, "UAVs," 59; Mroczkowski, *With the 2d Marine Division*, 31–43; *OPDS*, 66–67; Quilter, *With the I Marine Expeditionary Force*, 75–76.

5. Ltr., Commanding Officer 1st ANGLICO to Commanding Officer 1st SRIG, 1 Oct 1991, Authors' Files, OA; *CPGW*, 208–12; Horne et al., *Naval Gunfire Support*, 1-2; Quilter, *With the I Marine Expeditionary Force*, 83–88.

6. Quoted in *OPDS*, 220. Despite the impression conveyed by Michael Gordon and Bernard Trainor, neither General Jenkins nor General Boomer exercised operational control of amphibious operations. That authority rested with Admiral Arthur as CO-MUSNAVCENT. LaPlante and Jenkins, who worked especially well together, shared the direction of the Amphibious Task Force. LaPlante, interview by Schneller and Marolda, tape 1, side 1; and tape 2, side 2. See also Gordon and Trainor, *The Generals' War*, 338, 368–69, 415.

7. Arthur, interview by Marolda and Schneller, 40–41; *CPGW*, 209–20; Gordon and Trainor, *The Generals' War*, 306, 339, 345; Griffis et al., *Amphibious Operations*, 31; press release, n.d., "DESRON-22: Messages on Desert Saber, Slash, Dagger, Storm, 1991," acc. 917062, OA; msg, USS *Missouri* to USCINCCENT, 032045Z Mar 1991, COMUSNAV-CENT Desert Shield/Desert Storm Message Files on Jamming, NGFS, ICRC, Drawdown, Airspace, C7F, Borders, Bastion, Submarines, NOTACK, and Blue on Blue, CNA.

8. Msg, CTF 156 to TG 156.1, 151817Z Feb 1991, LaPlante Papers, OA.

9. *USNDS*, H-5.

10. Despite the great danger in this operation and many others like it, Captain Ray Smith's Naval Special Warfare Task Group Central did not lose a single man during Desert Shield and Desert Storm. This was a testament to Smith's determination that his naval commandos would not be improperly employed, as some SEALs believed had occurred in Operation Just Cause in Panama. According to his subordinate, Captain Tim Holden, Smith's approach was as follows: "We're going to do missions that make a difference in the war. We're not going to do missions just to keep busy. We're going to do missions with a high probability of success. And we're going to do missions where people have a good chance of coming back. No suicide operations." Quoted in Santoli, *Leading the Way*, 207–8.

11. Army General Franks praised the "very well-planned and . . . well-executed Navy and Marine amphibious deception maneuver." Clancy and Franks, *Into the Storm*, 252. See also IMEFB, 23 Feb 1991; Dockery, "SEALs," acc. 917239, 36–37, OA; Dwyer, "SEALs," 98; *OPDS*, 390; Waller, *The Commandos*, 324–34; U.S. Special Operations Command, "10th Anniversary History," 34, 35, 37, Authors' Files.

12. "Mother of All Surrenders," 28–29; Quilter, *With the I Marine Expeditionary Force*, 14, 74–75, 83–86.

13. Boomer was not as optimistic as Michael Gordon and Bernard Trainor suggest with regard to the enemy's capability and desire to fight. Indeed, even they acknowledge that the Marines "faced armored and mechanized divisions and a formidable concentration of Iraqi artillery at the Al Jaber airfield" and that "American intelligence had flatly predicted that the Iraqis would use chemical weapons." Gordon and Trainor, *The Generals' War*, 355; see also 295, 306. Army General Franks was also convinced the enemy would employ chemical warfare. See Clancy and Franks, *Into the Storm*, 276.

14. IMEFB, 21 and 23 Feb, 3 Mar 1991; Quilter, *With the I Marine Expeditionary Force*, 15, 35, 46–47; Cureton, interview by Schneller, Authors' Files. Regarding the strengths and weaknesses of the Iraqi army, see Scales, *Certain Victory*, 116–17.

15. Curtis, "The Tip of the Spear," 22; *CPGW*, 265; Quilter, *With the I Marine Expeditionary Force*, 14, 74–80; Zumwalt, "Tanks! Tanks! Direct Front!" 75–77.

16. Quoted in *OPDS*, 69.

17. Cureton, *With the 1st Marine Division*, 87. See also Quilter, *With the I Marine Expeditionary Force*, 88–90.

18. *CPGW*, 265–67; Keys, "Rolling With the 2d Marine Division," 79; Mroczkowski, *With the 2d Marine Division*, 43; Quilter, *With the I Marine Expeditionary Force*, 78–83.

19. Although the source of the chemical agent remains unclear, it had probably been present in the area since before G-Day. Mroczkowski, *With the 2d Marine Division*, 45.

20. Ibid.; Quilter, *With the I Marine Expeditionary Force*, 86–88.

21. Quilter, *With the I Marine Expeditionary Force*, 78–83.

22. Curtis, "The Tip of the Spear," 25; *CPGW*, 265–67; Murray Hammick, "Iraqi Obstacles and Defensive Positions," 989; Myatt, "The 1st Marine Division in the Attack," 75; Quilter, *With the I Marine Expeditionary Force*, 90–91.

23. Quoted in Curtis, "The Tip of the Spear," 20.

24. Cureton, interview by Schneller, Authors' Files.

25. *CPGW*, 248–49; Cureton, *With the 1st Marine Division*, 68; Mazzara, "Artillery in the Desert, 1991: Report # 2," 36; Peterson, "Intelligence," 19; Quilter, *With the I Marine Expeditionary Force*, 80–83.

26. Ltr, Quinn to Head, History Writing Unit, 11 Jan 1996, Authors' Files.

27. Doctrinally, if the ground commander nominated a target beyond—in this case, north of—the FSCL, the mission was called "battlefield air interdiction." If the mission was flown against targets designated by the ATO under JFACC control, it was simply "interdiction." See Jones, "Close Air Support," 64.

28. *CPGW*, 146, 266–68; Kurth, "Whiskey With a Kick," 34; Moore, "Marine Air," 63; Murray, *GWAPS*, vol. 2, part 1, 296, 301–2, 310–13, 322; Quilter, *With the I Marine Expeditionary Force*, 80–86; *OPDS*, 213–14; *USNDS* 38, H-5; *GWAPS*, vol. 2, part 2, 231–33, 242.

29. Quoted in *Washington Post*, 17 Mar 1991, A22.

30. Quoted in Curtis, "The Tip of the Spear," 25.

31. McCain and Shyles, eds., *The 1,000 Hour War: Communication in the Gulf*, 107.

32. The complete text of Schwarzkopf's briefing appears in Summers, *On Strategy II*, 268–94.

33. Quoted in *Washington Post*, 28 Feb 1991, A30.

34. de la Billiere, *Storm Command*, 301.

35. *OPDS*, 71–72.

36. Welch, interview by Roberts, 1, Oral Histories, OA.

37. Curtis, "The Tip of the Spear," 25; McPeak, Defense Department Briefing; "Mother of All Surrenders," 26; *OPDS*, 82; Quilter, *With the I Marine Expeditionary Force*, 88–91.

38. The JFC-E was divided into four combat formations and reserve and support units: (1) Force Abu Bakr: 2d SANG Brigade; (2) Force Othman: Royal Saudi Land Forces 8th Mechanized Brigade, Kuwait Al-Fatah Brigade, Oman Motorized Infantry Battalion, and Bahrain Infantry Company; (3) Task Force Omar: Royal Saudi Land Forces 10th Mechanized Brigade, UAE Motorized Infantry Battalion; (4) Task Force Tariq: Royal Saudi Marine Battalion Task Force, Senegalese Infantry Battalion, and Moroccan 6th Mechanized Infantry Regiment; (5) reserve and support units: Qatar Mechanized Infantry Battalion, 1st East Bengal (Bangladesh) Infantry Battalion, Combat Aviation Battalion (Kuwait/UAE), Royal Saudi Land Forces 14th Field Artillery Battalion, Royal Saudi Land Forces 18th Field Artillery Battalion, and Royal Saudi Land Forces Engineer Force 5 Saif Allah. *CPGW*, 237; Friedman, *Desert Victory*, 290–91.

39. Kleinsmith, interview by Marolda and Schneller. See also ltr, Commanding Officer 1st ANGLICO to Commanding Officer 1st SRIG, 1 Oct 1991; "Operation Desert Storm: Naval Gunfire Lessons Learned: Communications," undated 1st ANGLICO document, Authors' Files.

40. Ltr, Commanding Officer 1st ANGLICO to Commanding Officer 1st SRIG, 1 Oct 1991, Authors' Files; *CPGW,* 267.

41. Ibid.; Bauer, "Desert Storm," 30, 53–61, OA; *CPGW,* 199–212, 516–18; Cureton, interview by Schneller; Horne et al., *Naval Gunfire Support,* 1-2; Kleinsmith, interview by Marolda and Schneller; Mazzara, "Supporting Arms in the Storm," 44–45; *OPDS,* 210; Quilter, *With the I Marine Expeditionary Force,* 83–88.

42. *CPGW,* 220–21; Griffis et al., *Amphibious Operations,* 40–42; "Interview: BGEN Peter J. Rowe, USMC," 129–30; Quilter, *With the I Marine Expeditionary Force,* 90–91; "Greater Gators," 33.

43. Schwarzkopf, *It Doesn't Take A Hero,* 452–53.

44. Curtis, "The Tip of the Spear," 25; *CPGW,* 265–67; Hammick, "Iraqi Obstacles and Defensive Positions," 989; Myatt, "The 1st Marine Division in the Attack," 75; Quilter, *With the I Marine Expeditionary Force,* 90–91.

45. Quoted in IMEFB, 24 Feb 1991.

46. *CPGW,* 260–64; Scales, *Certain Victory,* 198–220.

47. Quilter, *With the I Marine Expeditionary Force,* 88.

48. *CPGW,* 243–44, 264–65.

49. Quoted in Scales, *Certain Victory,* 201.

50. Scales, *Certain Victory,* 200–206, 226.

51. *CPGW,* 260–64; Scales, *Certain Victory,* 254–55.

52. Bauer, "Desert Storm," 31; Craig, "Gulf War," 14; Griffis et al., *Amphibious Operations,* 32–33; press release, n.d., "DESRON-22: Messages on Desert Saber, Slash, Dagger, Storm, 1991," acc. 917062, OA; *CPGW,* 199, 208–21, 268–69; USS *Missouri* (BB 63), Command History 1991, SH; Stillwell, *Battleship Missouri,* 320; "Victory at Sea," 23; Ward et al., *C3,* 4-6.

53. After the war, analysts determined that the Iraqis probably fired the Silkworms on a compass bearing toward the ships, without radar or infrared guidance. Msg, COMDESRON 22 to USCINCCENT, 041456Z Mar 1991, Desert Storm Engagement Message File, CNA; msg, CTU 151.11.2 to CTF 151, 25132?Z Feb 1991, Authors' Files, OA; de la Billiere, *Storm Command,* 290; Bulkeley, interview by Marolda and Schneller, 82–89; press release, n.d., "DESRON-22: Messages on Desert Saber, Slash, Dagger, Storm, 1991," acc. 917062, OA; *CPGW,* 199, 268–69; Griffis et al., *Amphibious Operations,* 32–33; USS *Missouri* (BB 63), Command History 1991, SH; Stillwell, *Battleship Missouri,* 322-25; Ward et al., *C3,* 4-6–4-10. According to one source, the Silkworm was four miles from *Missouri* when *Gloucester* shot it down. *DSDSLL,* 9.

54. Msg, COMDESRON 22 to USCINCCENT, 041456Z Mar 1991, Desert Storm Engagement Message File, CNA; msg, CTU 151.11.2 to CTF 151, 25132?Z Feb 1991, Authors' Files; de la Billiere, *Storm Command,* 290; Bulkeley, interview by Marolda and Schneller, 82–89; press release, n.d., "DESRON-22: Messages on Desert Saber, Slash, Dagger, Storm, 1991," acc. 917062, OA; *CPGW,* 199, 268–69; Griffis et al., *Amphibious Operations,* 32–33; USS *Missouri* (BB 63), Command History 1991, SH; Stillwell, *Battleship Missouri,* 322–25; Craig, *Call for Fire,* 275; Ward et al., *C3,* 4-6–4-10.

55. IMEFB, 25 Feb 1991; Cureton, *With the 1st Marine Division,* 90–91.

56. *Washington Post,* 28 Feb 1991, A30; *CPGW,* 275–76, 283; Cureton, *With the 1st Marine Division,* 91–103; Kitfield, *Prodigal Soldiers,* 411; Quilter, *With the I Marine Expeditionary Force,* 91–95.

57. Mroczkowski, *With the 2d Marine Division,* 53; Zumwalt, "Tanks! Tanks! Direct Front!," 74–80.

58. *CPGW,* 273–76; Quilter, *With the I Marine Expeditionary Force,* 92–95; Mroczkowski, *With the 2d Marine Division,* 55–59.

59. Scales, *Certain Victory,* 247.

60. Although controversy surrounds the timing, direction, and speed of the VII Corps' advance, a detailed analysis of this issue is beyond the scope of this work. For fuller discussions, see Clancy and Franks, *Into the Storm;* Schwarzkopf, *It Doesn't Take A Hero,* 455–83; Swain, *Lucky War,* 333–34; Burton, "Pushing Them Out the Back Door;" Dietrich, "From Valhalla With Pride;" Swain, "Compounding the Error;" Griffith, "Mission Accomplished;" and letters to the editor of *Proceedings* by John H. Cushman (Jul 1993): 17; Paul E. Funk, M. Thomas Davis, and Bruce B.G. Clarke (Sep 1993): 22–26; William B. McDaniel and Charles D. McFetridge (Oct 1993): 24; James G. Burton (Nov 1993): 19–25; William S. Lind (Dec 1993): 23–24; and Kenneth F. McKenzie, Jr. and David C. Nilsen (Jan 1994): 23–24.

61. Scales, *Certain Victory,* 244–45; Swain, *Lucky War,* 225.

62. Gordon and Trainor, *The Generals' War,* 369; Quilter, *With the I Marine Expeditionary Force,* 97.

63. Bengio, ed., *Saddam Speaks,* 207.

64. Bush, "Address to the Nation on the Iraqi Statement on Withdrawal From Kuwait," *Weekly Compilation of Presidential Documents* 27 (26 Feb 1992), 214.

65. LaPlante, interview by Marolda and Schneller, tape 3, side 1; *CPGW,* 220–21; Friedman, *Desert Victory,* 232; press release, n.d., "DESRON-22: Messages on Desert Saber, Slash, Dagger, Storm, 1991," acc. 917062, OA; *OPDS,* 199.

66. Quoted in Lionetti, "Air Defense," 16.

67. Quoted in Smith, ed., *The Media and the Gulf War,* 204.

68. Only 28 of these 1,400 wrecks were tanks or other armored vehicles. The bulk of the destroyed vehicles lay on a 2.5-mile stretch of highway between al-Jahra and Basra.

69. Smith, ed., *The Media and the Gulf War,* 205; Commander Carrier Group 7, Command History 1991, Post 1 Jan 1990 Command File, OA; *CPGW,* 282–83; *GWAPS,* vol. 2, part 2, 254; Quilter, *With the I Marine Expeditionary Force,* 97–98; *USNDS,* A-41.

70. *CPGW,* 283; Cureton, *With the 1st Marine Division,* 103–19; Myatt, "The 1st Marine Division in the Attack," 74; Quilter, *With the I Marine Expeditionary Force,* 98–101; *Washington Post,* 28 Feb 1991, A30.

71. *The Koran* 28, 83–84, quoted in Mroczkowski, *With the 2d Marine Division,* 66.

72. *CPGW,* 282–83; Quilter, *With the I Marine Expeditionary Force,* 98–100; Mroczkowski, *With the 2d Marine Division,* 59–68.

73. Ltr, Commanding Officer 1st ANGLICO to Commanding Officer 1st SRIG, 1 Oct 1991, Authors' Files.

74. Chip Beck, telephone conversation with Robert J. Schneller, 2 Sep 1992; Beck, "The Gulf War," 2–9; Beck, "Operation Desert Storm War Diary," 65, Authors' Files; *CPGW,* 283, 289, 531–33; Keene, "The Storm is Over,"41–42; Quilter, *With the I Marine Expeditionary Force,* 103; J.M. Shotwell, "The Ride into Kuwait City," *Leatherneck* 74 (May 1991), 21.

75. *CPGW,* 289; Quilter, *With the I Marine Expeditionary Force,* 103–6; Schubert and Kraus, eds., *Whirlwind War,* chap. 8.

76. Quoted in Shotwell, "The Ride into Kuwait City," 20.

77. Barnes, "When Freedom Came," 42; Beck, "The Gulf War," 9; Curtis, "The Tip of the Spear," 27; *CPGW,* 289; Quilter, *With the I Marine Expeditionary Force,* 103–6; *Washington Post,* 28 Feb 1991, A28.

78. *CPGW,* 289; Shotwell, "The Ride into Kuwait City," 21.

79. Myatt, "The 1st Marine Division in the Attack," 76. See also *OPDS*, 202–3; "Greater Gators," 33.

80. Naval aircraft also interdicted the enemy's flight from offshore positions when several A-6Es sank two boats speeding from Faylaka Island loaded with Iraqi secret policemen. *CPGW*, 289; Quilter, *With the I Marine Expeditionary Force*, 104–6; *USNDS*, 39, A-43.

81. The battle is also often referred to as the Battle of 73 Easting, the grid designation on coalition maps where the enemy's main body was positioned.

82. Scales, *Certain Victory*, 252, 261–65.

83. Quoted in letter to the editor, *Naval War College Review* 46 (Summer 1993): 130.

84. Scales, *Certain Victory*, 290. See also Clancy and Franks, *Into the Storm*, 341; Gordon and Trainor, *The Generals' War*, 412; Swain, *The Lucky War*, 338. Other analysts dispute this conclusion, contending that because General Franks excluded Horner's strike units from the immediate battle area, Republican Guard divisions were able to escape from southern Iraq. See Jamieson, "Lucrative Targets," 180–82; Lewis, "JFACC," 15.

85. Quoted in Scales, *Certain Victory*, 294. See also 291–300.

86. *CPGW*, 276–89; Quilter, *With the I Marine Expeditionary Force*, 99–100.

87. Blackwell, *Thunder in the Desert*, 208; Summers, *On Strategy II*, 282; *Triumph Without Victory*, 401; Scales, *Certain Victory*, 308–10.

88. O'Neill and Kass, "The Persian Gulf War," 224; Schwarzkopf, *It Doesn't Take A Hero*, 468–69; U.S., Department of Defense, *Conduct of the Persian Gulf Conflict*, 1-1, 1-2, 25-1; *Washington Post*, 28 Feb 1991, A27, A34. Senior participants in White House decision making discounted the influence of the press in Bush's decision to end the war. Thomas A. Keany and Eliot A. Cohen point out that most of the media coverage of the "Highway of Death" occurred after Bush announced his decision to end hostilities in the evening of 27 February. See *GWAPS, Summary*, 251–52.

89. *OPDS*, 322–23.

90. Schwarzkopf, *It Doesn't Take A Hero*, 469–70. See also Gordon and Trainor, *The Generals' War*, 423.

91. Keys, "Rolling With the 2d Marine Division," 80. Richard Swain concludes that "it is hard to envision a defeat more nearly total than that imposed south of the Euphrates. Such yearning after the perfect is simply moonshine!" Swain, *Lucky War*, 335. See also de la Billiere, *Storm Command*, 304–5; Gordon and Trainor, *The Generals' War*, 439.

92. Arthur, interview by Marolda and Schneller, 49. In contrast, March felt that "we stopped the war too soon [and] left him with too much armor." March, interview by Marolda and Schneller, tape 2, side 2. See also Gordon and Trainor, *The Generals' War*, 424, 429–30; Swain, *Lucky War*, 291.

93. Bush, "Address to the Nation on the Suspension of Allied Offensive Combat Operations in the Persian Gulf," 27 Feb 1991, *Weekly Compilation of Presidential Documents* 27 (4 Mar 1991), 224–25.

94. Schwarzkopf, *It Doesn't Take a Hero*, 470.

95. Bush, "Address to the Nation on the Suspension of Allied Offensive Combat Operations in the Persian Gulf," 27 Feb 1991, *Weekly Compilation of Presidential Documents* 27 (4 Mar 1991), 224–25.

96. IMEFB, 1 Mar 1991; Blackwell, *Thunder in the Desert*, 208; *CPGW*, 283–88.

97. *GWAPS*, vol. 2, part 2, 259–62. The equipment figures are based on a CENTCOM estimate of 1 March 1991. The source cited questions the accuracy of these totals but offers no concrete alternative figures because of the difficulty in "attribution of equipment destruction to a particular weapons system" during the coordinated air-ground action.

CHAPTER 7

1. O'Neill and Kass, "The Persian Gulf War," 221.

2. *USNDS*, A-43–A-61.

3. Msg, CTG 151.11 to distribution, 281325Z Feb 1991, DESRON 22 Type, Post 1 January 1990 Command Files, OA.

4. M.K. Snyder, letter to the editor, *Proceedings* 121 (May 1995): 34; *USNDS*, 43, A-44; IMEFB, 4 Mar 1991.

5. Blackwell, *Thunder in the Desert*, 209–10; Scales, *Certain Victory*, 312–14; Schwarzkopf, *It Doesn't Take A Hero*, 478–79; Swain, *Lucky War*, 304; *Triumph Without Victory*, 402; *USNDS*, A-43.

6. IMEFB, 11 and 29 Mar 1991; McMichael, "Aftermath in Kuwait," 18.

7. Hammick, "To the Victor the Spoiled Land," 992.

8. McMichael, "Desert Demolitions," 14–15.

9. Quoted in de la Billiere, *Storm Command*, 312. See also Schwarzkopf, *It Doesn't Take a Hero*, 473–74.

10. de la Billiere, *Storm Command*, 312–19; *CPGW*, 330–31; Kindsvatter, "VII Corps in the Gulf War," 5; Schwarzkopf, *It Doesn't Take A Hero*, 479–80.

11. General Horner argues persuasively that Schwarzkopf was unfairly criticized for his handling of the cease-fire agreement, since the State Department should have had "*their* campaign plan!" ready for the end of hostilities. Horner in Miller, ed., *Seeing Off the Bear*, 147. Shortly after the war, Schwarzkopf made the same point when he told Powell that with the close of combat, "some of the necessary follow-on actions were not ready for implementation" and that in the future, "documents for war termination need to be drafted and coordinated." Msg, Personal, Schwarzkopf to Powell, info to CINCs, 051630Z Apr 1991, USCENTCOMFWD, CinC's File, RG 518 (CENTCOM Records), box 2, folder 60, NA. See also de la Billiere, *Storm Command*, 312–19; Gordon and Trainor, *The Generals' War*, 446; Kindsvatter, "VII Corps in the Gulf War," 3–5; Scales, *Certain Victory*, 322–23; Schwarzkopf, *It Doesn't Take a Hero*, 480–91.

12. Hashim, "Iraq, the Pariah State," 11; "The Month in Review," *Current History* 90 (May 1991): 235; *USNDS*, A-45.

13. Ekeus, "The Iraqi Experience and the Future of Nuclear Nonproliferation," 68; O'Neill and Kass, "The Persian Gulf War," 230–31; "United Nations Security Council Resolution 687, 3 Apr 1991 (excerpts)," *Survival* 33 (May/Jun 1991): 274–78; *USNDS*, A-59.

14. "Four Months in Review," *Current History* 90 (Sep 1991): 283; Hashim, "Iraq, the Pariah State," 11; *USNDS*, A-60–A-61.

15. IMEFB, 6 Mar 1991; Berens, "POWs," 37; Dorr, "POWs in Iraq," 24–25; U.S., Department of Defense, *Conduct of the Persian Gulf Conflict*, 12-4; Marechal-Workman, "*Mercy* Returns," 20; *New York Times*, 5 Mar 1991 A1, A10; 6 Mar 1991 A14; and 29 Jun 1992 A1, A13.

16. Bashore, "A Hero's Welcome," 24–29; Dorr, "POWs in Iraq," 24; Hoffmeier, "POWs Start Home Aboard *Mercy*," 22; U.S., Department of Defense, *Conduct of the Persian Gulf Conflict*, 12-4; *USNDS*, A-45; *The New York Times*, 11 Mar 1991, A11.

17. Canby, "After the Storm," 10; Craig, *Kuwait*, 14–16; McMichael, "Aftermath in Kuwait," 17–20.

18. Defense Reconstruction Assistance Office, Completion Report, 20 Nov 1991; and U.S. Army Corps of Engineers draft history excerpts, U.S. Army Corps of Engineers History Office; Frix and Davis, "Task Force Freedom and the Restoration of Kuwait," 3–10.

19. Craig, *Kuwait*, 19; Frix and Davis, "Task Force Freedom and the Restoration of Kuwait," 3–10; McDonnell, "Rebuilding Kuwait," 51; Yeosock, "H + 100," 58.

20. CNO, Navy Command Center, NDDC, Operations Briefing Notes for CNO, 1 Mar 1991, Post 1 Jan 1990 Command File, OA; ltr, Taylor to Dudley, 29 Jan 1996, Authors' Files.

21. Bosco, "Hunting Mines," 28; Covey, "Offering a Helping Hand in Iraq," 106–9; Fiske, "Salvage in Combat," 65–69; Hammick, "To the Victor the Spoiled Land," 992–93; Horner, *The Gulf Commitment*, 170, 193–96; Nagle, "Having a Blast in the Persian Gulf," 104–7; Passarelli et al., *Mine Countermeasures*, 2-8, C-2; Rankin and Smith, "Australian Divers Clear Mines," 74; Resing, "Clearing the Way," 40–41; Taylor, interview by Marolda and Schneller, 89–92; *USNDS*, A-48; Australian Clearance Diving Team 3, Report of Proceedings, 11 May 1991, Authors' Files.

22. Defense Reconstruction Assistance Office, Completion Report, 20 Nov 1991; and U.S. Army Corps of Engineers draft history excerpts, U.S. Army Corps of Engineers History Office; Frix and Davis, "Task Force Freedom and the Restoration of Kuwait," 3–10.

23. Msg, COMUSNAVCENT to NAVCENT, 031420Z Mar 1991, Authors' Files.

24. The forces included Belgian mine hunters *Dianthus, Iris, Myosotis*, support ship *Zinnia*; French mine hunters *Orion, Sagittaire, Aigle, Pegase, Loire*, support ship *Pluton*; German mine hunters *Paderhorn, Schleswig, Marburg, Koblenz*; Italian mine hunters *Milazzo, Vieste, Castagno, Platano*; Japanese mine hunters *Hatsushima, Yurishima, Hikoshima, Awashima, Sakushima*, support ship *Hayase*, oiler *Tokiwa*; Dutch mine hunters *Haarlem, Harlingen, Zierikzee*; British mine hunters *Ledbury, Dulverton, Atherstone, Cattistock, Hurworth*, support ship *Herald*; U.S. mine hunters *Avenger, Guardian*, minesweepers *Adroit, Impervious, Leader*, 6 MH-53E helicopters. Preston, "Allied MCM in the Gulf," 48; Passerelli et al., *Mine Countermeasures*, 2-4, C-1; ltr, P. C. van Royen, Director, Institute for Maritime History, Ministry of Defence, to Dr. Marolda, 17 Oct 1997, re "Dutch Participation in Gulf War, 1990–1991," Authors' Files.

25. *CPGW*, 330–31; ltr, Taylor to Dudley, 29 Jan 1996, Authors' Files.

26. Ibid.; Giusti, "Mine Reading," 17; Passarelli et al., *Mine Countermeasures*, 2-8, C-1, C-2; Taylor, interview by Marolda and Schneller, 63; Preston, "Allied MCM in the Gulf," 56.

27. Brown and Foxwell, "Report from the Front," 735; Passarelli et al., *Mine Countermeasures*, C-5.

28. Taylor, interview by Marolda and Schneller, 255.

29. The mines were emplaced in six roughly rectangular boxes (identified as MF-1 to MF-6) and in four mine lines (identified as ML-7 to ML-10). Responsibility for clearing these areas was divided as follows: MF-1 and MF-2, Belgium and France; MF-3, Germany and the Netherlands; MF-4, United Kingdom; MF-5, United States and Japan; MF-6, Italy and Germany; ML-7, Germany, Italy, and the United States; ML-8, Belgium and France; ML-9, United States; ML-10, United States and Japan.

30. Msg, CTF 151 to COMUSNAVCENT 160812Z Mar 1991, COMUSNAVCENT N3 Desert Shield/Storm Working Papers and Message Files, CNA; Brown and Foxwell, "Report from the Front," 735–38; Commander U.S. Naval Forces Central Command Press Release No. 92-0003, "Active Mine Countermeasures End in Arabian Gulf," in Commander U.S. Naval Forces Central Command, Command History 1992, Post 1 Jan 1990 Command Files, OA; memo, Commander R. F. Duncan, USCG, to Professor R. J. Grunwalt, 26 Sep 1991, Authors' Files; Nagle, "Having a Blast in the Persian Gulf," 104–7; Passarelli et al., *Mine Countermeasures*, C-2, C-8; *Washington Post*, 9 Sep 1992, A26; Preston, "Allied MCM in the Gulf."

31. Preston, "Allied MCM in the Gulf," 56–58.

32. Commander U.S. Naval Forces, Central Command Press Release No. 92-0003, "Active Mine Countermeasures End in Arabian Gulf," in Commander U.S. Naval Forces Central

Command, Command History 1992, Post 1 Jan 1990 Command Files, OA; Passarelli et al., *Mine Countermeasures*, C-5, C-7; ltr, Taylor to Dudley, 29 Jan 1996, Authors' Files.

33. Non-U.S. coalition naval, air, and ground forces also left the region promptly.

34. Pagonis, *Moving Mountains*, 150–51.

35. Canedy et al., *TRADOC Support*, 8, 30; "Fast Sealift Ships Begin Operation Desert Sortie," 1; Holland, interview by McClintock, 21, Oral Histories, OA; Pagonis and Raugh, "Good Logistics is Combat Power," 34; Pagonis, *Moving Mountains*, 12, 97, 119–120; Quilter, *With the I Marine Expeditionary Force*, 107–112.

36. Memorandum for the CNO: Sitrep #44," 1 Mar 1991, Chief of Naval Operations Desert Storm Situation Reports, OA; *USNDS*, A-46–A-48.

37. "Flyers Provide Comfort," 4; "Last Storm CVs Return," 4; *New York Times*, 8 Nov 1991, 4; Rodney et al., *Reserve Manpower*, 11; *USNDS*, A-43–A-61.

38. These units included carrier *Nimitz* (CVN 68), which relieved *Ranger* in the North Arabian Sea in late April; *Forrestal* (CV 59), which replaced *Theodore Roosevelt* in the Red Sea in June; and successive marine expeditionary units (11th, 13th, 15th, 22d). "Last Storm CVs Return," 4; Quilter, *With the I Marine Expeditionary Force*, 107–12.

39. A devastating cyclone struck Bangladesh on 29–30 April. The disaster relief mission, begun on 10 May, involved over 7,000 U.S. service men and women. Siegel, *A Chronology*, 53; Siegel, *Requirements*, 61–70; Stackpole, "Angels From the Sea," 110–16.

40. Miles, "Personnel Issues After Desert Storm," 22; Pagonis, *Moving Mountains*, 150–51; Quilter, *With the I Marine Expeditionary Force*, 107–12; Schwarzkopf, *It Doesn't Take A Hero*, 467.

41. IMEFB, 7 Mar 1991; Pagonis, *Moving Mountains*, 156–58.

42. Pagonis, *Moving Mountains*, 156.

43. IMEFB, 5, 22, 25, and 26 Mar 1991; Naval Mobile Construction Battalion 74, Command History 1991, Post 1 Jan 1990 Command Files, OA; Quilter, *With the I Marine Expeditionary Force*, 107–12; "Success Behind the 'Storm' Front," 787; Zimmeck, "A War of Logistics," 7-7–7-16.

44. "Heading Home," 15; Pagonis, *Moving Mountains*, 13–14, 156–58.

45. Msg, COMUSNAVCENT to NAVCENT 031420Z Mar 1991, Authors' Files.

46. IMEFB, 6 and 11 Mar 1991; Mark, *Iraq's Invasion of Kuwait*, 9; Quilter, *With the I Marine Expeditionary Force*, 110; Schwarzkopf, *It Doesn't Take A Hero*, 474.

47. Miles, "Personnel Issues After Desert Storm," 22; "Success Behind the 'Storm' Front," 787.

48. Quilter, *With the I Marine Expeditionary Force*, 107–12.

49. Moore, "Head 'Em Up," 7; "MPF Loadout Completed," 36–39; Quilter, *With the I Marine Expeditionary Force*, 107–12; Headquarters Marine Corps, Logistics Plans, Policies, & Strategic Mobility Div., Logistics Plans & Operations Branch, "Initial Logistics Guidance in Support of USMC SWA Redeployment," 18 Mar 1991; and "Sourcing Requirements," "G-4 Ground Ordnance Brief," and "Redeployment-Reconstitution System Support: Mission Statement," undated briefing slides, file "Item 2," Retrograde/Reconfiguration Messages, Briefs, and Memos, CNA.

50. Quilter, *With the I Marine Expeditionary Force*, 107–12.

51. Kindsvatter, "VII Corps in the Gulf War," 3; *New York Times*, 8 Nov 1991, 4; *GWAPS*, vol. 5, part 1, 57, 61; Yeosock, "H + 100," 58.

52. Karr and Terao, "Ammunition Retrograde from SWA," 47; Pagonis, *Moving Mountains*, 157–58; "Redeployment Going Even Better than Deployment," 3; "The Right Word Getting Out," 12.

53. Kindsvatter, "VII Corps in the Gulf War," 3; *New York Times*, 8 Nov 1991, 4; David Rosmer, USCENTAF Command Historian, telephone conversation with Schneller, 7 Feb 1995; Yeosock, "H + 100," 58.

54. IMEFB, 28 Feb 1991.

55. U.S., Department of Defense, *Conduct of the Persian Gulf Conflict*, 7-1; Hill, "Depot Operations," 19; Pagonis, *Moving Mountains*, 12–13, 150–51, 156–57; Quilter, *With the I Marine Expeditionary Force*, 107–12; "Redeployment Going Even Better than Deployment," 3.

56. Tiernan, "A History of the Military Sealift Command," 49.

57. Moore, "Still in the Sand," 18–19; "The Right Word Getting Out," 14; Zimmeck, "A War of Logistics," 7-7–7-16.

58. Karr and Terao, "Ammunition Retrograde from SWA," 47; Pagonis, *Moving Mountains*, 157–58; "Redeployment Going Even Better Than Deployment," 3; "The Right Word Getting Out," 12.

59. Deyerle, "Last Desert Storm Shipment Returns Home," 5; James K. Matthews and Cora Holt, TRANSCOM History Office, "Final Desert Sortie Airlift and Sealift Statistics," facsimile message sent to Schneller, 9 Feb 1993, Authors' Files; COMUSNAVCENT Public Affairs, "MSC Closes the Book on Operation Desert Storm," 8 May 1992, draft of a press release in Commander U.S. Naval Forces Central Command, Command History 1992, Post 1 Jan 1990 Command Files, OA. Military Sealift Command ceased recording Desert Sortie statistics when *Leslie Lykes* arrived in the United States. Redeployment of Desert Storm materiel had not ended as of 7 February 1995. James K. Matthews, TRANSCOM Command Historian, telephone conversations with Schneller, 1 and 9 Feb 1993; David Rosmer, CENTAF Command Historian, telephone conversation with Schneller, 7 Feb 1995.

60. Finger quoted in Christine MacKinnon, "Crowd of 3,000 Greets Comfort's Return," 6; Bush quoted in *The Washington Post*, 18 Mar 1991, A19; Smith quoted in Stroschen and LaPointe, "Operation Welcome Home," 15–16. See also "A Capital Celebration Honors Operation Desert Storm Vets," 20–23; Delaney, "New Baby," 6; Schwarzkopf, *It Doesn't Take a Hero*, 492–93.

61. Arthur, interview by Marolda and Schneller, 56–57.

62. *USNDS*, i.

63. Taylor, interview by Marolda and Schneller, 4–12, 98.

64. Msg, COMIDEASTFOR to COMUSNAVCENT 030548Z Mar 1991, COMSEVEN-THFLT/NAVCENT N3 Operations Folder, CNA. See also CENTCOM J-5, "Orientation and Background Book for RADM P.D. Smith," Mar 1991, USCENTCOMFWD J-5, Strategic Planning File, box 2, RG 518 (CENTCOM Records), NA.

65. CENTCOM J-5, "Orientation and Background Book for RADM P.D. Smith," Mar 1991, USCENTCOMFWD J-5, Strategic Planning File, box 2, RG 518 (CENTCOM Records), NA; msg, COMUSNAVCENT to USCINCCENT, 090944Z Mar 1991, COMUS-NAVCENT Plans Officer DESERT SHIELD/STORM Love Boat, Long Range Plans, Long Range Force Levels, NAVCENT Manpower, CTF-156, and Combined Oplan for the Defense of Saudi Arabia Working Papers and Message Files, CNA.

66. Msg, CNO to CINCCENT, 091302Z Apr 1991, COMUSNAVCENT Plans Officer DESERT SHIELD/STORM Love Boat, Long Range Plans, Long Range Force Levels, NAVCENT Manpower, CTF-156, and Combined Oplan for the Defense of Saudi Arabia Working Papers and Message Files, CNA.

67. Admiral Boorda later received a fourth star and in June 1994 became Chief of Naval Operations.

68. Msg, COMUSNAVCENT to CNO, 231736Z Apr 1991, COMUSNAVCENT N3 Desert Shield/Storm Working Papers and Message Files, CNA.

69. Msg, COMSEVENTHFLT to USCINCCENT, 261720Z Apr 1991, COMUSNAV-CENT N3 Desert Shield/Storm Working Papers and Message Files, CNA.

70. Msg, COMIDEASTFOR to COMSEVENTHFLT, 261358Z Apr 1991, Desert Shield/Storm Command/Organization Message File, CNA; *The Washington Times*, 5 Nov 1992, B-6.

71. Dawisha, "The United States in the Middle East," 1; *The Washington Post*, 28 Feb 1991, A31.

72. "Heavy Fighting in Iraq Continues," 426; Mylroie, "Iraq Since the Gulf War."

73. IMEFB, 7 Mar 1991.

74. "Heavy Fighting in Iraq Continues," 426; Kindsvatter, "VII Corps in the Gulf War," 7; *Triumph Without Victory*, 399; IMEFB, 1 Apr 1991.

75. Schwarzkopf, *It Doesn't Take A Hero*, 488–89.

76. Sharp, "NEPMU-7 Supports Operation Provide Comfort," 10; Shaw and DiMattio, "Provide Comfort," 32.

77. This no-fly zone and the one later established south of the 32d parallel were created as allied initiatives and not directly supported by any UN resolution. *The Washington Post*, 14 Jan 1993, A17. See also Siegel, *Requirements*, 49–60.

78. Copson, *Persian Gulf Conflict*, 3, 10–11; Cushman, "Joint, Jointer, Jointest," 80–85; Elmo, "Food Distribution During Operation Provide Comfort," 8; Jones, "Operation Provide Comfort," 99-107; Pagonis, *Moving Mountains*, 154–55; Ripley, "Operation Provide Comfort II," 1056.

79. Blackstone, "Special Boat Unit Supports Operation Provide Comfort," 35; ltr, Brown to Director, Naval Historical Center, 3 Jan 1996, Authors' Files; Cushman, "Joint, Jointer, Jointest," 80–85; Hughes, "Flying Workhorses Over Iraq," 23; Jones, "Operation Provide Comfort," 99–107; Ripley, "Operation Provide Comfort II," 1055; Siegel, *Requirements*, 49–60; Sharp, "NEPMU-7 Supports Operation Provide Comfort," 12.

80. Ripley, "Operation Provide Comfort II," 1055–56; *The Washington Post*, 14 Jan 1993, A18.

81. Blix, "Verification of Nuclear Nonproliferation, 57–59; Hashim, "Iraq, the Pariah State," 14; O'Neill and Kass, "The Persian Gulf War," 231; "Playing Cat and Mouse," 58; *The Washington Post*, 26 Jul 1991, A1.

82. Bruce, "How Saddam Is Picking Up the Pieces," 284; *The Military Balance 1992–1993*, 105, 110–11, 113, 118–20, 125. The sources differ on the figures for Iraq; the figures from Bruce are quoted here.

83. Johar and Bahgat, "View From Kuwait," 175.

84. Peay, "The Five Pillars of Peace in the Central Region," 35.

85. Some allied navies refer to postwar MIF operations as "MIF II." See Smith, ed., *Peacekeeping*, 207.

86. Commander U.S. Naval Forces, Central Command, Command History 1992, 2-3-16–2-3-17, Post 1 Jan 1990 Command File, OA.

87. The nations that provided naval forces for the maritime interception operations from 1990 to 1994 were Argentina, Australia, Belgium, Canada, Denmark, France, Greece, Italy, Netherlands, New Zealand, Norway, Saudi Arabia, Spain, United Kingdom, and United States. From 1994 to 1995 ships from Belgium, Canada, Italy, New Zealand, United Kingdom, and United States continued the operation. Throughout this period Bahrain, Kuwait, the UAE, and Saudi Arabia allowed the interception force to divert suspected merchant ships to their ports for inspection. Redd in *Thirteenth International History Symposium*, 119–22.

88. CENTCOM PAO, telephone conversation with Schneller, 29 Sep 1994; Copson, *Postwar Issues for Congress*, 11; Cruger, "Assignment: Red Sea," 8–13; R. F. Duncan,

"Middle East Trip Report, or, How I Spent My Summer Vacation," unpublished memo, Authors' Files; Taylor, interview by Marolda and Schneller, 171.

89. Stanik, interview by Schneller, 1-4; Joseph T. Stanik, telephone conversation with Robert J. Schneller, 20 Feb 1996; ltr, Stanik to Dudley, 10 Jan 1996, Authors' Files; Taylor, interview by Marolda and Schneller, 221–22.

90. Admiral Sharp, the head CENTCOM planner, developed a plan for the postwar prepositioning of equipment in the gulf states and the rotation of Navy and Air Force air units into and out of the theater. See Sharp, interview by Marolda and Schneller, tape 2, side 2; Thomas, "Standup of the Fifth Fleet"; *Washington Post*, 31 Jul 1996.

91. Dawisha, "The United States in the Middle East," 3–4; Hollis, "What Price Renewed Conflict in the Middle East?" 52; "Iran Eyes Purchase of Two More Russian Subs," 20–21; Meacham, "A New Middle East Security Equation," 43; Metz, ed., *Persian Gulf States*, xxviii, 92; John E. Peterson, Office of the Deputy Prime Minister for Security and Defence, Sultanate of Oman, conversation with Schneller at the Defense Intelligence Agency College, 12 Jan 1993; Royal United Services Institute for Defence Studies, London, ed., *RUSI and Brassey's Defence Yearbook, 1992*, 148–50, 153–56; Simon, "US Strategy in the Persian Gulf," 81–97; Starr, "Saudi Rejects US Basing Move," 549; Tripp, "The Gulf States and Iraq," 43–61.

92. U.S. naval forces also trained in the region with Egyptian, French, and even Russian units. Commander U.S. Naval Forces Central Command, Command History 1992; and Commander, U.S. Naval Forces Central Command Press Release No. 92-019, 2-3-1–2-3-15, Post 1 Jan 1990 Command Files, OA.

93. Peay, "The Five Pillars of Peace in the Central Region," 38.

94. Taylor, interview by Marolda and Schneller, 110–30, 152–54.

95. Ibid.

96. Commander U.S. Naval Forces Central Command, Command History 1992, 2-3-1–2-3-15, Post 1 Jan 1990 Command File, OA.

97. Carpenter, "An Exercise in Patience," 21–31.

98. Commander U.S. Naval Forces Central Command, Command History 1992, 2-3-1–2-3-2, Post 1 Jan 1990 Command File, OA.

99. Ibid., 2-3-3.

100. Commander, U.S. Naval Forces Central Command Press Release No. 92-020, in Commander U.S. Naval Forces Central Command, Command History 1992, Post 1 Jan 1990 Command File, OA. See also Redd in *Thirteenth International Seapower Symposium*, 119.

101. Al-Mullah in *Twelfth International Seapower Symposium*, 59–60.

102. Commander U.S. Naval Forces Central Command, Command History 1992, 2-4-1, Post 1 Jan 1990 Command File, OA.

103. COMUSNAVCENTREAR, Command History 1991, 11, Post 1 Jan 1990 Command Files, OA.

104. Kevin Stephens, "CTF 153 Stands Up," proposed press release in Commander U.S. Naval Forces Central Command, Command History 1992, Post 1 Jan 1990 Command File, OA; Taylor, interview by Marolda and Schneller, 150.

105. Commander U.S. Naval Forces Central Command, Command History 1992, 2-4-1, Post 1 Jan 1990 Command File, OA.

106. Kevin Stephens, "CTF 153 Stands Up," proposed press release in Commander U.S. Naval Forces Central Command, Command History 1992, Post 1 Jan 1990 Command File, OA; Taylor, interview by Marolda and Schneller, 150.

107. Copson, *Post-War Issues for Congress*, 12; Taylor, "Naval Special Warfare," 19. NAVCENT also dispatched units to support Operation Restore Hope, the humanitarian relief effort in Somalia.

108. Stanik, interview by Schneller, 13 Sep 1994, 7.

109. "Catalogue of Non-Compliance," 8; Metz, ed., *Persian Gulf States*, xxii, 94; Milhollin, "The Iraqi Bomb," 47.

110. Bruce, "Campaign Against Shiites Hardens," 967; Starr, "Air Forces Join to Hold 'No-Fly Zone,'" 5.

111. "Allies Flying Over Iraq to Enforce U.N. Sanctions," 26; Gregory, "Persian Gulf War Allies Launch Operation Southern Watch," 7; "The Month in Review," *Current History* 91 (Oct 1992): 351; "Naval Air Extends Security and Helping Hand," 4; Stanik, interview by Schneller, 12 Aug 1994, 2; "U.S. Navy Planes Begin 'Operation Southern Watch,'" 5; *The Washington Post*, 27 Aug 1992, A27.

112. The combat forces assigned to JTF-SWA included shore-based Army Patriot surface-to-air missile batteries.

113. Nelson and Katz, "Unity of Control," 60.

114. Nelson and Katz, "Unity of Control," 60; Stanik, interview by Schneller, 12 Aug 1994, 2.

115. Nelson and Katz, "Unity of Control," 63. See also Armistead, "Crossdecking," 70.

116. Taylor, interview by Marolda and Schneller, 164. See also Stanik, interview by Schneller, 12 Aug 1994, 1–2.

117. Commander U.S. Naval Forces Central Command, Command History 1992, 2-3-10, Post 1 Jan 1990 Command File, OA.

118. Ibid., 2-3-10–2-3-11.

119. "U.S. Nuclear Submarine to Enter Gulf," draft of a press release in Commander U.S. Naval Forces Central Command, Command History 1992; *Washington Times*, 5 Nov 1992, B6.

120. Taylor, interview by Marolda and Schneller, 100–107, 130–40.

121. Commander U.S. Naval Forces Central Command, Command History 1992, Post 1 Jan 1990 Command File, OA.

122. *Daily Press*, 8 Feb 1996, 2; Thomas, "Standup of the Fifth Fleet."

123. *The Washington Post*, 12 Jan 1993, A1, A13; 14 Jan 1993, A1, A17; and 17 Jan 1993, A43; John E. Peterson, Office of the Deputy Prime Minister for Security and Defence, Sultanate of Oman, conversation with Schneller at the Defence Intelligence Analysis Center, Washington, DC, 12 Jan 1993.

124. Fulghum, "Allies Strike Iraq for Defying U.N.," 22–24; Peterson, conversation with Schneller at the Defence Intelligence Analysis Center, 12 Jan 1993; *The Washington Post*, 12 Jan 1993, A1, A13; 14 Jan 1993, A1, A17; and 17 Jan 1993, A43.

125. Fulghum, "Allies Strike Iraq for Defying U.N.," 22–24; *The Washington Post*, 14 Jan 1993, A17, A18; 15 Jan 1993, A26; and 17 Jan 1993, A43.

126. Holliday et al., *Tomahawk Weapon System Performance During January and June 1993 Strikes Against Iraq* 1:3–4; *The Washington Post*, 18 Jan 1993, A1, A22, A24; Locke and Werrell, "Speak Softly," 33. Despite their success in shooting down one Tomahawk, which struck the al-Rashid Hotel, the Iraqis could hardly take comfort from what one source describes as a "propaganda coup." Gordon and Trainor, *The Generals' War*, 460.

127. *The Washington Post*, 20 Jan 1993, A1.

128. Holliday et al., *Tomahawk Weapon System Performance During January and June 1993 Strikes Against Iraq* 1:4–5; USS *Chancellorsville* (CG 62), Command History 1993; and USS *Peterson* (DD 969), Command History 1993, SH; Locke and Werrell, "Speak Softly," 33; Nelson and Katz, "Unity of Control," 61.

129. Hoffman, "The U.S. Marine Corps in Review," 132–33; Peay, "The Five Pillars of Peace in the Central Region," 32; Reason, "Naval Forces First to the Fight," 16–17; Truver, "The U.S. Navy in Review," 121.

130. Ibid.; Rosas, "MSC," 37; Friedman, "World Naval Developments in Review," 144.

Chapter 8

1. Eilts, "The United States and Saudi Arabia," 30.

2. COMCARGRU7 (Battle Force Zulu ASUWC), Report, Desert Storm, 17 Jan–19 Mar 1991, in ltr CINCPACFLT to Marolda, 23 Mar 1996, 17, Authors's File.

3. Five I MEF hospital corpsmen, three *Princeton* sailors, and one *Saratoga* naval air officer received battle wounds. *GWAPS*, vol. 5, part 1, 641; CAPT John Quinn, USMC, U.S. Marine Corps Historical Center, telephone conversation with Schneller, 13 Jul 1995. Marine casualties as of 7 May 1991.

4. Schwamb, *Strike Warfare*, 8-25.

5. *DSDSLL*, 115.

6. According to one source, 92 percent of the munitions expended during the war were unguided. See GAO, *Operation Desert Storm*, 29.

7. *DSDDLL*, 78, 82, 115.

8. *GWAPS*, 58.

9. Although clearly a superior attack plane, the F-117 hit rate was estimated to range between 41 and 60 percent. See GAO, *Operation Desert Storm*, 1.

10. GAO, *Operation Desert Storm*, 31–32, makes the valid point that "older, less costly, and less technologically advanced aircraft and weapon systems made substantial contributions to the air campaign as did the newer, more technologically advanced systems."

11. *DSDSLL*, 54.

12. Ibid., 54–57.

13. In a similar operation during the Linebacker II Campaign of the Vietnam War, Navy-laid sea mines trapped 27 Communist ships in the North Vietnamese port of Haiphong for almost a year. Marolda, *Operation End Sweep*, xi.

14. Arthur, interview by Marolda and Schneller.

15. Colin S. Gray, *The Navy in the Post-Cold War World: The Uses and Value of Strategic Sea Power*, 14.

16. "China Develops Cunning Sea Mines," *Parade Magazine* (19 Mar 1995), 10. See also William V. Kennedy, "Ground the Airborne?" *The Washington Post*, 8 May 1997, who contends that when *Tripoli* and *Princeton* ran afoul of mines, "the invasion was called off" and the press duped into "believing that the invasion was only a 'feint'."

17. Making the same point are Alexander and Bartlett, *Sea Soldiers of the Cold War*, 165.

18. Clancy and Franks, *Into the Storm*, 516.

19. Ibid., 164.

20. Horner, interview with Carpenter, 9.

21. Jeffrey H. Thomas, "The Fifth Fleet Stands Again," *Pull Together*, Spring/Summer 1997, 9.

22. Department of the Navy, "1992 Posture Statement" (Feb–Mar 1992), 32.

23. William T. Laurie, "Seahawks fight fire with fire: Hellfire/FLIR key to littoral warfare success," *Surface Warfare* (Jan/Feb 1995), 18.

24. Department of the Navy, *Forward . . . From the Sea*, 1994.

Bibliography

Archival and Special Collections

Center for Naval Analyses. Alexandria, VA.
Naval Forces Central Command Papers, 1990–1991.
COMSEVENTHFLT/NAVCENT N3 Operations Folder, 12 June 1990–1 June 1991.
COMUSNAVCENT N3 (CAPT R.L. Johnson Jr.) DESERT SHIELD/STORM Working Papers and Message Files.
COMUSNAVCENT Plans Officer DESERT SHIELD/STORM CVBG, VP/VQ, Redeployment, Physical Security, and DS Personnel Working Papers and Message Files.
DESERT STORM Engagement Message File.
Miscellaneous DESERT SHIELD/DESERT STORM Working Papers from VADM Arthur's Personal Files.
VADM Arthur's Personal DESERT SHIELD/STORM Message File.

Marine Corps Historical Center. Washington, DC.
I Marine Expeditionary Force Daily Command Briefings.

National Archives and Records Administration. College Park, MD.
Central Command Records (RG 518).
CINC's File.
J-5 Strategic Planning File.
Plan Files.

Naval Historical Center. Washington, DC.
Naval Aviation History Branch. Command Histories.

Operational Archives Branch.
Authors' Files.
Articles.
Manuscripts.
Johnson, Richard Denis. "PSYOP, The Gulf Paper War: Psychological Warfare Operations Against the Iraqi Military and Civilian Establishments Between November 1990 and February 1991."
Mercogliano, Salvatore R. "United States Merchant Marine in the Persian Gulf War."

Oral Histories.

Boomer, LGEN Walter E., USMC. Interview by Mason P. Carpenter, n.d.

Horner, LGEN Charles A., USAF. Interview by Mason P. Carpenter, 27 December 1993.

Ramsdell, CAPT Steven U., USN. Interview by Mason P. Carpenter, 21 January 1994.

Bauer, Douglas. "Desert Storm: An Historical Odyssey, 28 February–3 April 1991." Account of naval surface operations during the war.

Biographical Files of Naval Officers.

Chief of Naval Operations Desert Shield Situation Reports.

Chief of Naval Operations Desert Storm Situation Reports.

Oral Histories.

Arthur, ADM Stanley R., USN. Interview by Edward J. Marolda and Robert J. Schneller, 25 January 1995.

Arthur, VADM Stanley R., USN. Interview by Steven U. Ramsdell, 6 March 1991.

Brooks, RADM Thomas A., USN (Ret.). Interview by Edward J. Marolda and Robert J. Schneller, 11 March 1996.

Bulkeley, CAPT Peter W., USN. Interview by Edward J. Marolda and Robert J. Schneller, 14 March 1996.

Cangelosi, CDR Diana, USN. Interview by Edward J. Marolda and Robert J. Schneller, 30 May 1996.

Cureton, LCOL Charles H., USMC. Interview by Robert J. Schneller, 10 August 1992. (no transcript)

Fox, LCDR Mark I., USN, and LT Nick Mongillo, USN. Interview by Steven U. Ramsdell, 1 March 1991.

Gay, CAPT John, USN. Interview by Steven U. Ramsdell, 28 February 1991.

Gee, RADM George N., USN. Interview by Steven U. Ramsdell, 2 March 1991.

Hendrickson, CAPT Dean M., USN. Interview by Steven U. Ramsdell, 2 March 1991.

Holland, CAPT Donald L., USN. Interview by William R. McClintock, 24 July 1991.

Hunt, CAPT William C., USN. Interview by Edward J. Marolda, 22 August 1991.

Kleinsmith, CAPT Douglas, USMC. Interview by Edward J. Marolda and Robert J. Schneller, 15 September 1992. (no transcript)

Johnson, CAPT Robert L., USN. Interview by Steven U. Ramsdell, 6 March 1991.

LaPlante, VADM John B., USN. Interview by Edward J. Marolda and Robert J. Schneller, 18 March 1996.

Longworth, CDR Mike, USN. Interview by Steven U. Ramsdell, 15 February 1991.

March, RADM Daniel P., USN (Ret.). Interview by Edward J. Marolda and Robert J. Schneller, 9 April 1996.

March, RADM Daniel P., USN. Interview by Steven U. Ramsdell, 16 February 1991.

Mercer, LCDR Gary, USN. Interview by Steven U. Ramsdell, 3 March 1991.

Mixson, RADM Riley D., USN. Interview by Steven U. Ramsdell, 27 February 1991.

Mobley, CAPT Joseph S., USN. Interview by Steven U. Ramsdell, 2 March 1991.

Morral, CAPT Dennis G., USN (Ret.). Interview by Edward J. Marolda and Robert J. Schneller, 6 June 1996.

Morral, CAPT Dennis G., USN (Ret.). Interview by Robert J. Schneller, 25 July 1996.

Purvis, COL Joseph N., USA. Interview by Edward J. Marolda, 19 August 1991.

Richards, CDR William, USN, and LCDR Jeffrey Taylor, USN. Interview by Edward J. Marolda, 22 August 1991.

Sharp, RADM Grant A., USN (Ret.). Interview by Edward J. Marolda and Robert J. Schneller, 20 March 1996.

Stanbridge, CAPT Harry, USN. Interview by Steven U. Ramsdell, 28 February 1991.

Stanik, LCDR Joseph, USN. Interview by Robert J. Schneller, 12 August and 13 September 1994.

Taylor, RADM Raynor A.K., USN. Interview by Edward J. Marolda and Robert J. Schneller, 2–3 August 1993.

Welch, SSGT Ryan, USA. Interview by Michael Roberts, 27 February 1991.

White, CAPT A. Hardin, Jr., USN. Interview by Steven U. Ramsdell, 28 February 1991.

Wilder, CAPT Frederick, USCG. Interview by Douglas C. Bauer, 11 March 1991.

Papers of VADM John B. LaPlante, USN (Ret.).

Papers of RADM Raynor A.K. Taylor, USN (Ret.).

Papers of CAPT Stephen R. Woodall, USN (Ret.).

Post 1 January 1974 and Post 1 January 1990 Command Files.

Records of the Naval History Documentation Team.

Tiernan, Harold S. "A History of the Military Sealift Command During Operation Desert Shield and Desert Storm."

Ship's History Branch. Command Histories.

Private Collection. David B. Crist.

Bernsen, RADM Harold J., USN (Ret.). Interview by David B. Crist. Norfolk, VA, 10 August 1995.

Crist, GEN George B., USMC (Ret.). Interview by David B. Crist. Beaufort, SC, 5 February 1994.

Crist, GEN George B. Message to ADM William J. Crowe, 140519Z August 1987, Subj: Joint Task Force Headquarters.

Grieve, CAPT David, USN (Ret.). Interviews by David B. Crist. Newport, RI, 11 May 1995; 14 Aug 1995.

Hays, ADM Ronald J., USN (Ret.). Telephone Interview by David B. Crist, 6 August 1996.

Howe, ADM Jonathan T., USN (Ret.). Interview by David B. Crist. Jacksonville, FL, 8 August 1996.

Less, VADM Anthony, USN (Ret.). Interview by David B. Crist. Falls Church, VA, 28 November 1994.

Office of the Chief of Naval Operations. "Arabian Gulf Lessons Learned Report: April–November 1987, 13 April 1988.

U.S. Army Center of Military History. Washington, DC.

Carver, CW3 Dudley C.A., USA. Interview by MAJ Robert K. Wright Jr., USA. Manama, Bahrain, on board *Curts,* 13 February 1991.

Green, CW2 Robert, USA, 1LT David L. Silvernell, USA, CW2 Jim Lattimore, USA, CW4 Patrick H. Hicks, USA. Interview by MAJ Robert K. Wright Jr., USA. Manama, Bahrain, 12 February 1991.

Group interview with members of Troop B, 4th Squadron, 17th Cavalry Regiment. Interview by MAJ Robert K. Wright Jr., USA. Manama, Bahrain, mid-February 1991.

Morral, CDR Dennis G., USN. Interview by MAJ Robert K. Wright Jr., USA. Manama, Bahrain, on board *Nicholas,* 13 February 1991.

Simpson, LCOL Bruce, USA. Interview by MAJ Robert K. Wright Jr., USA. Manama, Bahrain, 13 February 1991.

Walker, MAJ Sam S. III, USA. Interview by MAJ Robert K. Wright Jr., USA. Manama, Bahrain, 13 February 1991.

U.S. Coast Guard Historian's Office. Washington, DC.

Desert Shield/Desert Storm Chronology, 19 June 1992.

Coast Guard Liaison Officer, Manama, Bahrain. Operation Desert Shield and Storm After Action Report, 10 June 1992.

U.S. Transportation Command. Scott AFB, IL.
Johnson, GEN Hansford T., USAF. Interview by James K. Matthews and Jay H. Smith, 15, 24, and 31 July 1992.

Secondary Sources

Published Reports and Books

Adler, Bill. *The Generals: the New American Heroes.* New York: Avon Books, 1991. Popular, instant biographical sketches of Generals Colin Powell and H. Norman Schwarzkopf Jr.; has been supplanted.

Alexander, Joseph H., and Merrill L. Bartlett. *Sea Soldiers in the Cold War: Amphibious Warfare, 1945–1991.* Annapolis: Naval Institute Press, 1995. An operational history of amphibious warfare in the Cold War, principally as executed by the two superpowers and their allies and surrogates.

Almond, Denise L., et al., eds. *Desert Score: U.S. Gulf War Weapons.* Washington: Carroll Publishing Co., 1991. Reference work on individual weapons and weapons systems used in the Gulf War.

Anderson, M. *Desert Shield/Desert Storm: Lessons Learned.* China Lake, CA: Naval Weapons Center, 1991. Classified report analyzing the performance of naval aircraft and weapons.

Atkinson, Rick. *Crusade: The Untold Story of the Persian Gulf War.* Boston: Houghton Mifflin Co., 1993. Entertaining journalistic political and military account of the Gulf War.

Baer, George. *One Hundred Years of Sea Power: The U.S. Navy, 1890–1990.* Stanford, CA: Stanford University Press, 1994. A masterful history of U.S. naval strategy and operations in the modern period.

Bailey, Dennis M. *Aegis Guided Missile Cruiser.* Osceola, WI: Motorbooks International, 1991. Popular, illustrated description of Aegis cruiser.

Baldwin, Sherman. *Ironclaw: A Navy Carrier Pilot's Gulf War Experience.* New York: William Morrow & Co., 1996.

Barlow, Jeffrey G. *Revolt of the Admirals: The Fight for Naval Aviation, 1945–1950.* Washington: Naval Historical Center, 1994. A reevaluation of the "revolt of the admirals" based on an examination of formerly classified Navy, Air Force, and Joint Chiefs of Staff documents.

Bell, Robert S. *Desert Storm Reconstruction Report Volume XII: Naval Special Warfare.* Alexandria, VA: Center for Naval Analyses, 1991. CNA produced numerous analytical reports on aspects of U.S. naval operations during the Gulf War. Although based on classified documents, "sanitized" versions of these reports have been released.

Bengio, Ofra, ed. *Saddam Speaks on the Gulf Crisis: A Collection of Documents*. Tel Aviv: The Moshe Dayan Center for Middle Eastern and African Studies, the Shiloah Institute, Tel Aviv University, 1992. Collection of speeches and addresses by Iraqi president Saddam Hussein between February 1990 and February 1991.

Benson, Lawrence R., and Jay E. Hines. *The United States Military in North Africa and Southwest Asia Since World War II*. Tampa, FL: United States Central Command Office, 1988.

de la Billiere, Peter. *Storm Command: A Personal Account of the Gulf War*. London: Harper Collins, 1992. Well-written, dispassionate, and informative memoir by overall commander of British forces involved in Desert Shield and Desert Storm.

Blackwell, James. *Thunder in the Desert: the Strategy and Tactics of the Persian Gulf War*. New York: Bantam Books, 1991. Deputy Director, Center for Strategic and International Studies and CNN analyst describes the military operations, with numerous drawings, maps, and charts.

Blair, Arthur H. *At War in the Gulf: A Chronology*. College Station, TX: Texas A&M University Press, 1992. Daily chronology from 2 August 1990 through 28 February 1991 tracks selected military and diplomatic developments.

Borowski, Harry R., ed. *Military Planning in the Twentieth Century: Proceedings of the Eleventh Military History Symposium, 10–12 October 1984*. Washington: Office of Air Force History, 1986. Thomas H. Etzold's chapter, "The Navy and National Security Policy in the 1970s," is especially perceptive.

Bowman, Steven R. *Persian Gulf War: Summary of U.S. and Non-U.S. Forces*. Washington: Congressional Research Service, Library of Congress, 1991.

Breemer, Jan. *Soviet Submarines: Design, Development and Tactics*. London: Jane's, 1979. Provides detailed, accurate information on the undersea vessels of the USSR.

Brown, Alan, Lester Gibson, and Alan Marcus. *Desert Storm Reconstruction Report Volume XIII: Training*. Alexandria, VA: Center for Naval Analyses, 1991.

Brown, David. *The Royal Navy and the Falklands War*. London: Arrow Books, 1989. Operational history by the head of the Naval Historical Branch of the British Ministry of Defence.

Brown, R.A., and Robert J. Schneller. *A Select Bibliography of United States Naval Forces in Desert Shield and Desert Storm.* Washington: Naval Historical Center, 1993. Annotated.

Brown, Ronald J. *With the Marines in Operation Provide Comfort: Humanitarian Operations in Northern Iraq, 1991.* Washington: History and Museums Division, Headquarters, U.S. Marine Corps, 1995. A thorough description of the operation and the naval and other forces involved.

Browne, Marjorie Ann, comp. *Iraq-Kuwait: U.N. Security Council Resolutions—Texts and Votes.* Washington: Congressional Research Service, Library of Congress, 1990.

Canedy, Susan, et al. *TRADOC Support to Operations Desert Shield and Desert Storm: A Preliminary Study.* Fort Monroe, VA: Office of the Command Historian, United States Army Training and Doctrine Command, 1992.

Carroll, Timothy J. *Desert Storm Reconstruction Report Volume VII: Maritime Interception Force Operations.* Alexandria, VA: Center for Naval Analyses, 1991.

Carter, James E. *Public Papers of the Presidents of the United States: Jimmy Carter.* 12 vols. Washington: Government Printing Office, 1977–1982.

Center for Strategic Studies. *The Gulf: Implications of British Withdrawal.* Washington: Center for Strategic and International Studies, 1969. Examines British pull-out from the Persian Gulf announced in 1968 and completed by 1972.

Chambers, Charles E., et al. *Desert Storm Reconstruction Report, Volume III: Antiair Warfare.* Alexandria, VA: Center for Naval Analyses, 1991.

Clancy, Tom, with General Fred Franks Jr. (Ret.). *Into the Storm: A Study in Command.* New York: G.P. Putnam's Sons, 1997.

Cohen, Eliot A., director. *Gulf War Air Power Survey,* 5 vols. and a *Summary* volume. Washington: Government Printing Office, 1993. The definitive study of air power in the Gulf War.

Cole, Ronald H., et al. *The History of the Unified Command Plan, 1946–1993.* Washington: Joint History Office, Office of the Chairman of the Joint Chiefs of Staff, 1995. Brief overview of the joint planning process, previously classified, and a short history of CENTCOM.

Collins, John M. *Military Geography of Iraq and Adjacent Arab Territory.* Washington: Congressional Research Service, Library of Congress, 1990.

Congressional Quarterly. The Middle East: U.S. Policy, Israel, Oil, and the Arabs, 4th ed. Washington: *Congressional Quarterly,* 1979. Brief introductory summary for the uninformed.

Copson, Raymond W. *Persian Gulf Conflict: Post-War Issues for Congress.* Washington: Congressional Research Service, Library of Congress, 1991.

Cordesman, Anthony H., and Abraham R. Wagner. *The Lessons of Modern War.* 4 vols. Boulder, CO: Westview Press, 1990–1996. Good, detailed comparative analyses of weapon performances, but gives short shrift to the human element.

Cottrell, Alvin J., ed. *The Persian Gulf States: A General Survey.* Baltimore: The Johns Hopkins University Press, 1980. Examines history, economics, culture, and art; poor on the region's dramatic socio-political changes of the past century.

Cottrell, Alvin J., et al. *Sea Power and Strategy in the Indian Ocean.* Beverly Hills, CA: Sage Publications, 1981. Articles on naval policy and strategy by Geoffrey Kemp and retired admirals Robert J. Hanks and Thomas H. Moorer.

Craig, Chris. *Call for Fire: Sea Combat in the Falklands and the Gulf War.* London: John Murray, 1995. Written by the Royal Navy's Senior Naval Officer Middle East during the Gulf War.

Craig, Theodore. *Kuwait: Background, Restoration, and Questions for the United States.* Washington: Congressional Research Service, Library of Congress, 1991.

Crowe, William J., Jr. with David Chanoff. *The Line of Fire: From Washington to the Gulf, the Politics and Battles of the New Military.* New York: Simon and Schuster, 1993. Memoir by former Chairman of the Joint Chiefs of Staff.

Cureton, Charles H. *U.S. Marines in the Persian Gulf, 1990–1991: With the 1st Marine Division in Desert Shield and Desert Storm.* Washington: History and Museums Division, Headquarters, U.S. Marine Corps, 1993. Excellent operational study.

Dalton, John H., J.M. Boorda, and Carl E. Mundy, *Forward . . . From the Sea.* Washington: Department of the Navy, 1994. Son of *From the Sea;* an updated statement on littoral warfare.

Davis, Richard G. *Strategic Air Power in Desert Storm.* Washington: Air Force History and Museums Program, n.d. A brief introduction to the subject.

Duncan, Stephen M. *Citizen Warriors: America's National Guard and Reserve Forces and the Politics of National Security.* Novato, CA: Presidio Press, 1997.

Dunnigan, James F., and Austin Bay. *From Shield to Storm: High-Tech Weapons, Military Strategy, and Coalition Warfare in the Persian Gulf.* New York: William Morrow & Co., 1992. Hastily produced hodgepodge.

Farouk-Sluglett, Marion, and Peter Sluglett. *Iraq Since 1958: From Revolution to Dictatorship.* New York: I.B. Tauris, 1990. Good general history.

Freedman, Lawrence, and Efraim Karsh. *The Gulf Conflict, 1990–1991: Diplomacy and War in the New World Order.* Princeton: Princeton University Press, 1993. Analysis of the Gulf War in the context of international relations.

Friedman, Norman. *Desert Victory: The War for Kuwait.* Annapolis: Naval Institute Press, 1991. This first full-length analysis of the war to treat the Navy's contribution contains separate chapters on the embargo, the air campaign, and the maritime campaign, and an appendix on naval forces in the embargo and the war.

_____. *Naval Institute Guide to World Naval Weapons Systems.* Annapolis: Naval Institute Press, 1989. Basic reference work.

_____. *U.S. Aircraft Carriers.* Annapolis: Naval Institute Press, 1983. Presents technical information and analysis of the Navy's primary warship.

Garrett, H. Lawrence, III, Frank B. Kelso II, and Carl E. Mundy, *Department of the Navy 1992 Posture Statement.* Washington: Department of the Navy, February–March 1992.

Gehring, Stephen P. *From the Fulda Gasp to Kuwait: U.S. Army, Europe and the Gulf War.* Washington: Department of the Army, 1998.

Gordon, Michael R., and Bernard E. Trainor. *The Generals' War: The Inside Story of the Conflict in the Gulf.* New York: Little, Brown and Company, 1995. Written from a high-command perspective, this is the best one-volume study of military aspects of the war.

Graham, Amy, A. Dale Burns, and Linda Keefer. *Desert Storm Reconstruction Report, Volume XI: Medical.* Alexandria, VA: Center for Naval Analyses, 1991.

Gray, Colin S. *The Navy in the Post-Cold War World: The Uses and Value of Strategic Sea Power.* University Park, PA: The Pennsylvania State University Press, 1994. Reflects on sea power theory as it relates to the Cold War.

Griffis, Henry S., et al. *Desert Storm Reconstruction Report, Volume V: Amphibious Operations.* Alexandria, VA: Center for Naval Analyses, 1991.

Grove, Eric. *Battle for the Fiords: NATO's Forward Maritime Strategy in Action.* With Graham Thompson. Annapolis: Naval Institute Press, 1991. Describes how allied naval forces operated in Exercise Teamwork '88.

Grove, Eric, ed. *Britain's Gulf War: Operation Granby.* London: Harrington Kilbride, 1991. Brief, well-illustrated account of British involvement in the war.

Hagan, Kenneth J. *In Peace and War: Interpretations of American Naval History, 1775–1978.* Westport, CT: Greenwood Press, 1978. Lawrence J. Korb's contribution, "The Erosion of American Naval Preeminence, 1962–1978," is an insightful overview of one of the Navy's periodic "dark ages."

Hallion, Richard P. *Air Warfare and Maritime Operations.* Fairbairn, Australia: Air Power Studies Centre, 1996. Presents interesting, if questionable, conclusions regarding air power's impact on naval operations in the world wars, Korea, Vietnam, and the Gulf War.

_____. *Storm over Iraq: Air Power and the Gulf War.* Washington: Smithsonian Institution Press, 1992. The author, later selected as the Air Force historian, discusses the development of air power from Vietnam to the Gulf, argues that air power won the Gulf War, and is highly critical of the Navy's aircraft carriers.

Hartmann, Frederick H. *Naval Renaissance: The U.S. Navy in the 1980s.* Annapolis: Naval Institute Press, 1990. An overview of the Navy's growth and rejuvenation during the late Carter and Reagan administrations.

Hattendorf, John B, ed. *Eleventh International Seapower Symposium: Report of Proceedings of the Conference, 6–9 October 1991.* Newport, RI: Naval War College Press, 1992.

_____. *Thirteenth International Seapower Symposium: Report of Proceedings of the Conference, 5–8 November 1995.* Newport, RI: Naval War College Press, 1992. Naval officers from many nations provided insight on coalition naval operations during Desert Shield and Desert Storm.

Haydon, Peter T., and Amy L. Griffiths, eds. *Multinational Naval Forces.* Halifax: Center for Foreign Policy Studies, Dalhousie University, 1995. An article by Richard H. Gimblett discusses Royal Canadian Navy operations in the Gulf War.

Head, William, and Earl H. Tilford Jr., eds. *The Eagle in the Desert: Looking Back on U.S. Involvement in the Persian Gulf War.* Westport, CT: Praeger, 1996. A collection of thirteen essays assessing political questions, logistic support, the allied victory, and air, ground, and naval operations.

Hiro, Dilip. *Desert Shield to Desert Storm: The Second Gulf War.* New York: Routledge, 1992. An instant history written from the Arab point of view, based on uneven sources; fair on diplomatic context, not so good on military matters.

_____. *The Longest War: The Iran-Iraq Military Conflict.* London: Paladin, 1990. An analysis of the war and its political consequences, concluding that Iraq's self-declared victory was elusive.

Holliday, Mary Robin, et al. *TLAM Performance During Operation Desert Storm: Assessment of Physical and Functional Damage to the TLAM Aimpoints: Volume I: Overview and Methodology.* Alexandria, VA: Center for Naval Analyses, 1994. A report prepared by CIA and DIA analysts.

Hone, Thomas C. *Power and Change: The Administrative History of the Office of the Chief of Naval Operations, 1946–1986.* Washington: Naval Historical Center, 1989. A perceptive analysis of the CNO's progressive loss of operational and administrative authority during the Cold War.

Horne, Gary E., et al. *Desert Storm Reconstruction Report, Volume XIV: Naval Gunfire Support.* Alexandria, VA: Center for Naval Analyses, 1991.

Horner, David. *The Gulf Commitment: The Australian Defence Force's First War.* Melbourne: Melbourne University Press, 1992. An excellent study of Australia's military role in Desert Shield and Desert Storm, including postwar operations.

Horwich, George, and Edward J. Mitchell, eds. *Policies for Coping With Oil-Supply Disruptions.* Washington: American Enterprise Institute for Public Policy Research, 1982. Collection of papers by professionals from government, industry, and academia.

Hourani, Albert. *A History of the Arab Peoples.* Cambridge: Belknap Press, 1991. The definitive general survey.

Howarth, Stephen. *To Shining Sea: A History of the United States Navy, 1775–1991.* New York: Random House, 1991. A solid, balanced appraisal of the more-than-200-year history of the U.S. naval service.

Issawi, Charles. *Oil, the Middle East, and the World.* New York: The Library Press, 1972. Brief study on why the Middle East dominates the world's oil industry.

Jane's Weapon Systems 1987–1988. London: Jane's Publishing Co., 1988.

Karsh, Efraim, and Inari Rautsi. *Saddam Hussein: A Political Biography.* New York: The Free Press, 1991. Excellent study of Saddam's motivations, rise, and dictatorship.

Khalid Bin Sultan. *Desert Warrior: A Personal View of the Gulf War by the Joint Forces Commander,* with Patrick Seale. New York: Harper Collins, 1995. Written in response to General Schwarzkopf's autobiography, this work presents some alternative views on command decisions during Desert Storm.

al-Khalil, Samir. *Republic of Fear: The Politics of Modern Iraq.* Berkeley: University of California Press, 1989. Excellent study of the inner workings of Saddam Hussein's government.

Kitfield, James. *Prodigal Soldiers: How the Generation of Officers Born of Vietnam Revolutionized the American Style of War.* New York: Simon and Schuster, 1995. With interviews as his principal source, a journalist examines some of the strategic, social, and doctrinal developments in the services during the period between the Vietnam and Persian Gulf Wars.

Korb, Lawrence J. *The Fall and Rise of the Pentagon: American Defense Policies in the 1970s.* Westport, CT: Greenwood Press, 1979. An informative, provocative interpretation of the Defense Department's difficulties in the post-Vietnam years.

Landis, Lincoln. *Politics and Oil: Moscow in the Middle East.* New York: Dunellen Publishing Co., 1973. Describes Soviet economic policy, strategic concerns with oil, and the history of Moscow's involvement in the Middle East from 1917 to 1973.

Langdon, Frank C., and Douglas A. Ross, eds. *Superpower Maritime Strategy in the Pacific.* London and New York: Routledge, 1990. This collection of essays provides U.S., Soviet, and other perspectives on the Maritime Strategy.

Lehman, John F., Jr. *Command of the Seas.* New York: Charles Scribner's Sons, 1988. Memoir by President Ronald Reagan's Secretary of the Navy.

Lenhart, Warren W., and Todd Masse. *Persian Gulf War: Iraqi Scud Ballistic Missile Systems.* Washington: Congressional Research Service, Library of Congress, 1991.

Levinson, Jeffrey L., and Randy L. Edwards. *Missile Inbound: The Attack on the Stark in the Persian Gulf.* Annapolis: Naval Institute Press, 1997. A description of U.S. naval operations during a critical phase of the Iran-Iraq War.

Longrigg, Stephen H. *Oil in the Middle East: Its Discovery and Development,* 2d ed. New York: Oxford University Press, 1961. This history of the development of the Middle Eastern oil industry focuses on the interaction of local governments, peoples of the Middle East, and oil companies.

Love, Robert W., Jr. *History of the U.S. Navy: Vol: 1: 1942–1991.* Harrisburg: Stackpole Books, 1992. A detailed, informative interpretation of modern U.S. naval history.

Love, Robert W. Jr., ed. *The Chiefs of Naval Operations.* Annapolis: Naval Institute Press, 1980. Comprehensive biographical essays of the men who led the U.S. Navy from World War I through the post-Vietnam period.

Lutz, Jeffrey, et al. *Desert Storm Reconstruction Report, Volume VI: Antisurface Warfare.* Alexandria, VA: Center for Naval Analyses, 1991.

Mandeles, Mark D., Thomas C. Hone, and Sanford S. Terry. *Managing "Command and Control" in the Persian Gulf War.* Westport, CT: Praeger, 1996. Based primarily on the command and control volume of the Air Force-commissioned Gulf War Air Power Survey. An insightful treatment of a complex issue.

Mann, Edward C., III. *Thunder and Lightning: Desert Storm and the Airpower Debates.* Maxwell AFB, AL: Air University Press, 1995.

Maritime Strategy and the Balance of Power: Britain and America in the Twentieth Century. New York: St. Martin's Press, 1989. Discusses how the globe's two naval powers operated in a century of warfare.

Mark, Clyde R. *Iraq's Invasion of Kuwait: A Review of Events.* Washington: Congressional Research Service, Library of Congress, 1991.

Marolda, Edward J. *By Sea, Air, and Land: An Illustrated History of the U.S. Navy and the War in Southeast Asia.* Washington: Naval Historical Center, 1994.

Marolda, Edward J., ed. *Operation End Sweep: A History of Minesweeping Operations in North Vietnam.* Washington: Naval Historical Center, 1993.

Marolda, Edward J., and Oscar P. Fitzgerald. *From Military Assistance to Combat, 1959–1965.* Washington: Naval Historical Center, 1986. Comprehensive analysis of the U.S. Navy's involvement in the Vietnam conflict from 1959 to 1965.

Matthews, James K., and Cora J. Holt. *United States Transportation Command History: Desert Shield/Desert Storm, Volume I, 7 August 1990–10 March 1991.* Scott AFB, IL: USTRANSCOM Office of History, 1992. Thorough, comprehensive study of TRANSCOM's role in the Gulf War.

Mazarr, Michael J., Don M. Snider, and James A. Blackwell Jr. *Desert Storm: The Gulf War and What We Learned.* Boulder, CO: Westview Press, 1993. Solid, balanced study of the military aspects of the war.

McCain, Thomas A., and Leonard Shyles, eds. *The 1,000 Hour War: Communication in the Gulf.* Westport, CT: Greenwood Press, 1994. This fine collection includes essays on communication issues in press-military relationships, communication practices unique to the Gulf War, and issues and images on television.

McNamara, Stephen J. *Air Power's Gordian Knot: Centralized Versus Organic Control.* Maxwell AFB, AL: Air University Press, 1994. Addresses the issue of the JFACC and close air support using cases from World War II, Korea, Vietnam, and Desert Storm.

McNaugher, Thomas L. *Arms and Oil: U. S. Military Strategy and the Persian Gulf.* Washington: The Brookings Institution, 1985. Well-written analysis of U.S. strategy in the gulf and the threats faced by the GCC states.

McWilliams, Barry. *This Ain't Hell . . . But You Can See It From Here: A Gulf War Sketchbook.* Novato, CA: Presidio, 1992. Cartoons and anecdotes from the war.

Melia, Tamara Moser. *"Damn the Torpedoes" A Short History of U.S. Naval Mine Countermeasures, 1777–1991.* Washington: Naval Historical Center, 1991. Touches lightly on Persian Gulf operations during the Tanker War and Gulf War.

Melson, Charles D., Evelyn A. Englander, and David A. Dawson, comps. *U.S. Marines in the Persian Gulf, 1990–1991: Anthology and Annotated Bibliography.* Washington: History and Museums Division, Headquarters, U.S. Marine Corps, 1992. This reference work contains 26 articles drawn from U.S. Naval Institute *Proceedings, Marine Corps Gazette, Field Artillery,* and *The Washington Post;* messages and briefings from senior officers; task organization; and chronology in addition to the bibliography.

Metz, Helen Chapin, ed. *Persian Gulf States: Country Studies.* Washington: Government Printing Office, 1994. Prepared by the Library of Congress, this fine reference work describes and analyzes the political, economic, social, and national security systems and institutions of Kuwait, Bahrain, Qatar, the UAE, and Oman.

The Military Balance, 1990–1991. London: International Institute for Strategic Studies, 1990. Provides statistical summaries of the world's military forces.

The Military Balance, 1992–1993. London: International Institute for Strategic Studies, 1992.

Miller, Aaron David. *Search for Security: Saudi Arabian Oil and American Foreign Policy, 1939–1949.* Chapel Hill, NC: University of North Carolina Press, 1980. Focused on the origins of the "special relationship" between the United States and Saudi Arabia.

Miller, Duncan E., and Sharon Hobson. *The Persian Excursion: The Canadian Navy in the Gulf War.* Nova Scotia: The Canadian Peacekeeping Press, 1995. A summary history of the Canadian navy's involvement in embargo patrol, air patrol, and logistic operations in the Persian Gulf.

Miller, Roger G., ed. *Seeing Off the Bear: Anglo-American Air Power Cooperation During the Gulf War.* Washington: Air Force History and Museums Program, 1995. These proceedings of the Joint Meeting of the Royal Air Force Historical Society and the Air Force Historical Foundation contain General Horner's insightful banquet address.

Moore, Molly. *A Woman at War: Storming Kuwait With the U.S. Marines.* New York: Charles Scribner's Sons, 1993. Thinly documented but well-received journalistic account written from the perspective of LGEN Walter E. Boomer.

Morin, Jean H., and Richard H. Gimblett. *Operation Friction, 1990–1991: The Canadian Naval Forces in the Persian Gulf.* Toronto: Dundurn Press, 1997. The official history of the Canadian Department of National Defence.

Motter, T.H. Vail. *The Persian Corridor and Aid To Russia.* Washington: Office of the Chief of Military History, Department of the Army, 1952. This "Green Book" details the Army's operations in Iran during World War II.

Mroczkowski, Dennis P. *U.S. Marines in the Persian Gulf, 1990–1991: With the 2d Marine Division in Desert Shield and Desert Storm.* Washington: History and Museums Division, Headquarters, U.S. Marine Corps, 1993. Excellent operational study.

Muir, Malcolm, Jr. *Black Shoes and Blue Water: Surface Warfare in the United States Navy, 1946–1986.* Washington: Naval Historical Center, 1996. A comprehensive appraisal of the development of surface ships and their weapons systems through the Cold War, Korea, and Vietnam periods.

Nickel, Ronald, et al. *Desert Storm Reconstruction Report Volume IX: Logistics.* Alexandria, VA: Center for Naval Analyses, 1991.

Noyes, James H. *The Clouded Lens: Persian Gulf Security and U.S. Policy.* Stanford, CA: Hoover Institution, 1979. Former Deputy Assistant Secretary of Defense for Near Eastern, African, and South Asian Affairs examines U.S. policy in the region.

Pagonis, William G. *Moving Mountains: Lessons in Leadership and Logistics From the Gulf War.* Boston: Harvard Business School Press, 1992. Part logistics study, part autobiography, and part management primer, this book provides a readable account of what is normally considered a dry topic.

Palmer, Michael A. *Guardians of the Gulf: A History of America's Expanding Role in the Persian Gulf, 1833–1992.* New York: The Free Press, 1992. Diplomatic, military, and economic history of the United States' involvement in the gulf, with a concise treatment of Desert Shield and Desert Storm.

_____. *On Course to Desert Storm: The United States Navy and the Persian Gulf.* Washington: Naval Historical Center, 1992. Why, how, and when the U.S. Navy became a presence in the Persian Gulf, covering the period 1833–1988.

Passarelli, Ralph, et al. *Desert Storm Reconstruction Report Volume IV: Mine Countermeasures.* Alexandria, VA: Center for Naval Analyses, 1991.

Perla, Peter P. *Desert Storm Reconstruction Report, Volume I: Summary.* Alexandria, VA: Center for Naval Analyses, 1991. Based on the other 13 CNA reconstruction reports, this volume summarizes the Navy's role in the conflict.

Pokrant, Marvin A. *A View of Desert Shield and Desert Storm As Seen From COMUSNAVCENT.* Alexandria, VA: Center for Naval Analyses, 1991.

Polmar, Norman. *Ships and Aircraft of the U.S. Fleet*, 14th ed. Annapolis: Naval Institute Press, 1987. A standard, accurate reference source on the subject.

Polmar, Norman, and Jurrien Noot. *Submarines of the Russian and Soviet Navies, 1718–1990.* Annapolis: Naval Institute Press, 1991. An informative history of the submarine design and development process in Russia.

Potter, Michael C. *Electronic Greyhounds: The Spruance-Class Destroyers.* Annapolis: Naval Institute Press, 1995. A history of the development of the *Spruance, Kidd,* and *Ticonderoga* classes of surface warships.

Powell, Colin. *My American Journey.* With Joseph E. Persico. New York: Random House, 1995. Powell, Chairman of the Joint Chiefs of Staff during the Persian Gulf War, candidly describes his role in the joint arena and high-level direction of the war effort.

Prados, Alfred B. *Iraq and Kuwait: Conflicting Historical Claims.* Washington: Congressional Research Service, The Library of Congress, 1991. Iraq-Kuwait territorial dispute.

Prezelin, Bernard, ed. *Combat Fleets of the World 1990/91: Their Ships, Aircraft, and Armament.* Translated by A.D. Baker III. Annapolis: Naval Institute Press, 1990. Organized alphabetically by country, this valuable reference lists characteristics of most types of ships, planes, and weapons in service in the world's navies.

Quilter, Charles J., II. *U.S. Marines in the Persian Gulf, 1990–1991: With the I Marine Expeditionary Force in Desert Shield and Desert Storm.* Washington: History and Museums Division Headquarters, U.S. Marine Corps, 1993. Excellent operational study.

Quinn, John T., II. *U.S. Marines in the Persian Gulf, 1990–1991: Marine Communications in Desert Shield and Desert Storm.* Washington: History and Museums Division, Headquarters, U.S. Marine Corps, 1996. A detailed study of Marine communications during the war by an official historian.

Readings in American Naval Heritage. New York: American Heritage Custom Publishing Group, 1996. Edward J. Marolda's essay, "Crucible of War: The U.S. Navy and the Vietnam Experience," relates how the naval service's Vietnam experience influenced its readiness for the Gulf War.

Record, Jeffrey. *Hollow Victory: A Contrary View of the Gulf War.* Washington: Brassey's, 1993. Collection of negative interpretations of political, military, and strategic issues surrounding the war.

Reynolds, Richard T. *Heart of the Storm: The Genesis of the Air Campaign Against Iraq.* Maxwell AFB, AL: Air University Press, 1995.

Rodney, David, Robert W. Downey, and Jonathan Geithner. *Desert Storm Reconstruction Report, Volume X: Reserve Manpower.* Alexandria, VA: Center for Naval Analyses, 1991.

Rost, Ronald F., John F. Addams, and John J. Nelson. *Sealift in Operation Desert Shield/Desert Storm: 7 August 1990 to 17 February 1991.* Alexandria, VA: Center for Naval Analyses, 1991.

Royal United Services Institute for Defence Studies, London, ed., *RUSI and Brassey's Defence Yearbook, 1992.* London: Brassey's, 1992. Overview of international relations focused on defense issues.

Ryan, Paul B. *First Line of Defense: The U.S. Navy Since 1945.* Stanford, CA: Hoover Institution Press, 1981. A conventional account of the Navy's role in national security affairs after World War II.

Santoli, Al. *Leading the Way: How Vietnam Veterans Rebuilt the U.S. Military, An Oral History.* New York: Ballantine Books, 1993. Includes interviews with naval participants in the Gulf War.

Scales, Robert H., Jr., director. *Certain Victory: The United States Army in the Gulf War.* Washington: Office of the Chief of Staff, United States Army, 1993. First rate history of Army operations.

Schwamb, Frank, et al. *Desert Storm Reconstruction Report, Volume II: Strike Warfare.* Alexandria, VA: Center for Naval Analyses, 1991.

Schubert, Frank N., and Theresa L. Kraus, general eds. *The Whirlwind War: The United States Army in Operations Desert Shield and Desert Storm.* Washington: Center of Military History, 1995. An official history of Army operations in the Gulf War.

Schwarzkopf, H. Norman, Jr., with Peter Petre. *It Doesn't Take a Hero.* New York: Bantam Books, 1992. This candid, provocative, and well-written autobiography has become the focus of much debate and criticism.

Shepko, Michael, Sandra Newett, and Rhonda M. Alexander. *Maritime Interception Operations.* Alexandria, VA: Center for Naval Analyses, 1991.

Shwadran, Benjamin. *The Middle East, Oil, and the Great Powers.* New York: Wiley, 1973. Dated but still useful survey.

Siegel, Adam B. *A Chronology of U.S. Marine Corps Humanitarian Assistance and Peace Operations.* Alexandria, VA: Center for Naval Analyses, 1994.

_____. *Requirements for Humanitarian Assistance and Peace Operations: Insights from Seven Case Studies.* Alexandria, VA: Center for Naval Analyses, 1995.

_____. *The Use of Naval Forces in the Post-War Era: U.S. Navy and U.S. Marine Corps Crisis Response Activity, 1946–1990.* Alexandria, VA: Center for Naval Analyses, 1991. A detailed analysis of more than 200 crises and other international activities in which the Navy and Marine Corps participated during the Cold War.

Sifry, Micah L., and Christopher Serf, eds. *The Gulf War Reader: History, Documents, Opinions.* New York: Times Books, 1991. Collection of documents, articles, speeches, congressional testimony, and related material.

Simpson, Michael M. *Chemical and Biological Weapons in the Persian Gulf Area: Health Effects and Protections.* Washington: Congressional Research Service, Library of Congress, 1991.

Smith, Hedrick, ed. *The Media and the Gulf War: The Press and Democracy in Wartime.* Washington: Seven Locks Press, 1992. Includes Senate hearings, lawsuit briefs, and newspaper articles criticizing the media's performance and the Pentagon's rules.

Smith, Hugh, ed. *Peacekeeping: Challenges for the Future.* Canberra: Australian Defence Studies Centre, Australian Defence Force Academy, 1993.

Spick, Mike. *An Illustrated Guide to Modern Fighter Combat.* London: Salamander Books, 1987. Reference work describing selected fighter aircraft, weapons, and tactics from around the world.

Stanik, Joseph T. *"Swift and Effective Retribution:" The U.S. Sixth Fleet and the Confrontation with Qaddafi.* Washington: Naval Historical Center, 1996. A detailed account of how the Navy executed President Reagan's policies to restrain Libyan leader Muammar Qaddafi's support for international terrorism.

Stewart, George, Scott M. Fabbri, and Adam B. Siegel, *JTF Operations Since 1983.* Alexandria, VA: Center for Naval Analyses, 1994.

Stillwell, Paul. *Battleship Missouri: An Illustrated History.* Annapolis: Naval Institute Press, 1996. An amply illustrated narrative history of the most well-known U.S. Navy battleship, including her service in the Gulf War.

Summers, Harry G., Jr. *On Strategy II: A Critical Analysis of the Gulf War.* New York: Dell, 1992. This account focuses on the post-Vietnam U.S. military renaissance.

Swain, Richard M. *"Lucky War:" Third Army in Desert Storm.* Fort Leavenworth, KS: U.S. Army Command and General Staff College Press, 1994. A partisan appraisal of U.S. Army activities in the Gulf War, particularly ground and air operations in Saudi Arabia, Kuwait, and Iraq.

Swartz, Peter M., Jan S. Breemer, and James J. Tritten, comps. *The Maritime Strategy Debates: A Guide to the Renaissance of U.S. Naval Thinking in the 1980s.* Revised edition. Monterey, CA: Naval Postgraduate School, 1989. An excellent annotated bibliography of commentary on maritime strategy issues.

Triumph Without Victory: The Unreported History of the Persian Gulf War. By the staff of *U.S. News & World Report.* New York: Times Books, 1992. Well-written instant history, based on more than 600 interviews. Good on nuts-and-bolts military aspects, but evidence does not support conclusion that coalition victory was not decisive.

U.S. Central Command. *Troop Information Handbook.* Tampa, FL: United States Central Command, 1990.

U.S. Congress. House. Committee on Armed Services. *Defense Organization: The Need for Change.* 99th Cong., 1st sess., 1985. S. Rpt. 99-86. Committee on Armed Services staff study calling for reorganization of the Department of Defense (background to Goldwater-Nichols legislation).

———. *Reorganization of the Department of Defense.* 99th Cong., 1st sess., 1985. S. Hrg. 99-1083. Hearings on proposal to reorganize Department of Defense (background to Goldwater-Nichols legislation).

———. *Crisis in the Persian Gulf: Sanctions, Diplomacy, and War.* 101st Cong., 2d sess., 1990. H. Hrg. 101–57. Features testimony by 34 witnesses, including Secretary of Defense Richard Cheney, Joint Chiefs of Staff Chairman General Colin Powell, and Admiral Robert F. Dunn.

———. Oversight and Investigations Subcommittee. *Intelligence Successes and Failures in Operations Desert Shield/Storm.* 103d Congress, 1st sess., 1993. Committee Print No. 5. Brief study of the collection, dissemination, and analysis of intelligence.

U.S. Congress. Senate. Committee on Armed Services. *Crisis in the Persian Gulf Region: U.S. Policy Options and Implications.* 101st Cong., 2d sess., 1990. S. Hrg. 101-1071. Features testimonies of Secretary

Cheney, General Powell, James R. Schlesinger, General David F. Jones, Admiral William J. Crowe, Henry Kissinger, James Webb, Edward N. Luttwak, and others.

_____. *Operation Desert Shield/Desert Storm.* 102d Cong., 1st sess., 1991. S. Hrg. 102-326. Postwar analyses by Vice Admiral Stanley R. Arthur, Major General James M. Myatt, General H. Norman Schwarzkopf, and others.

U.S. Department of the Air Force. *Reaching Globally, Reaching Powerfully: The United States Air Force in the Gulf War.* Washington: Department of the Air Force, 1991. Brief, early (September 1991) study supplanted by the Gulf War Air Power Survey.

U.S. Department of Defense. *Conduct of the Persian Gulf War: An Interim Report to Congress.* Washington: Government Printing Office, 1991. Discusses many operational and social aspects of the war in the format of answers to questions raised by members of Congress. Most sections end with lists of "accomplishments" and "shortcomings." The *Final Report* listed below has not entirely supplanted the *Interim Report* in content.

_____. *Conduct of the Persian Gulf War: Final Report to Congress.* Washington: Government Printing Office, 1992. This important official unclassified source on the war embodies the consensus view of the services. Its narrative covers the Iraqi invasion of Kuwait through the coalition ground campaign, with separate chapters on maritime interception operations and the maritime campaign. Appendixes analyze selected topics such as intelligence, preparedness of U.S. forces, deployment, logistics, medical support, reserves, special operations, legal issues, women in the theater of operations, and weapons systems.

U.S. Department of the Navy. *The United States Navy in "Desert Shield" "Desert Storm."* Washington: Office of the Chief of Naval Operations, 1991. This indispensable reference work provides an overview of naval operations, with a section on initial "lessons learned"; includes 16 appendixes and a chronology.

U.S. Department of State. *American Foreign Policy: Basic Documents, 1977–1980.* Washington: Department of State, 1983.

_____. *American Foreign Policy: Current Documents.* Washington: Government Printing Office, 1982–.

_____. *Foreign Relations of the United States.* Washington: Government Printing Office, 1861–.

U.S. General Accounting Office. *Operation Desert Storm: Evaluation of the Air Campaign.* Washington: GAO, 1997.

Vistica, Gregory L. *Fall From Glory: The Men Who Sank the U.S. Navy.* New York: Simon and Schuster, 1995. Although the author interviewed scores of key figures in the U.S Navy during the 1980s and 1990s, the work is seriously flawed by the inaccurate and distorted treatment of the sources.

Vriesenga, Michael P. *From the Line in the Sand: Accounts of USAF Company Grade Officers in Support of Desert Shield/Desert Storm.* Maxwell AFB, AL: Air University Press, 1994. Presents accounts of Air Force personnel in the Gulf War, including their interaction with the Navy.

Waller, Douglas C. *Commandos: The Inside Story of America's Secret Soldiers.* New York: Simon and Schuster, 1994. Presents the accounts of Navy SEAL and other special operations personnel during Desert Storm.

Ward, Robert W., et al. *Desert Storm Reconstruction Report, Volume VIII: C3/Space and Electronic Warfare.* Alexandria, VA: Center for Naval Analyses, 1992.

Warden, John A., III. *The Air Campaign.* Washington: National Defense University Press, 1988. This book provided the theoretical underpinning for Instant Thunder and Phase I of the Desert Storm campaign plan.

Watson, Bruce W. ed. *Military Lessons of the Gulf War.* Novato, CA: Presidio Press, 1991. Collection of 16 essays addressing diplomacy, naval and military operations, logistics, electronic warfare, terrorism, and other topics.

Weekly Compilation of Presidential Documents. Published by the Office of the Federal Register. National Archives and Records Administration. Washington: Government Printing Office, various dates.

Weimer, David Leo. *The Strategic Petroleum Reserve: Planning, Implementation, and Analysis.* Westport, CT: Greenwood Press, 1982. Comprehensive and objective review of the development of policy for the Strategic Petroleum Reserve.

Winnefeld, James A., Preston Niblack, and Dana J. Johnson. *A League of Airmen: U.S. Air Power in the Gulf War.* Santa Monica, CA: RAND Corp., 1994. Survey of air power focusing on the U.S. Air Force.

Woodward, Bob. *The Commanders.* New York: Simon and Schuster, 1991. According to the author, he had extensive contact with General Colin Powell. Much of the coverage is not documented.

Yergin, Daniel. *The Prize: The Epic Quest for Oil, Money, and Power.* New York: Simon and Schuster, 1991. The definitive general history of the geopolitics of oil.

_____. *Shattered Peace: The Origins of the Cold War.* New York: Penguin Books, 1990. Sophisticated revisionist account of how the Cold War began.

Zumwalt, Elmo R., Jr. *On Watch: A Memoir.* New York: Quadrangle, 1976. The autobiography of a major U.S. naval leader, who discusses the state of the Navy in the troubled post-Vietnam years.

Articles and Papers

Ackley, Richard T. "Sealift and National Security." U.S. Naval Institute *Proceedings* (hereafter *Proceedings*) 118 (July 1992): 41–47.

Adolph, Robert B., Jr. "PSYOP: Gulf War Force Multiplier." *Army* 42 (December 1992): 16–22.

"Allies Flying Over Iraq to Enforce U.N. Sanctions." *Aviation Week & Space Technology* 137 (31 August 1992): 26. Southern Watch.

Armistead, Edwin L. "Crossdecking Is Key to Link-11." *Proceedings* 121 (January 1995): 70–71. Discusses improvements in joint and Navy communications since Desert Storm.

Arthur, Stanley R., and Marvin Pokrant. "Desert Storm at Sea." *Proceedings* 117 (May 1991): 82–87. Overview on Navy's role.

"Aspin's Major Factors of Desert Victory." *Sea Power* 34 (August 1991): 39–41. Summarizes preliminary results of studies by six House Armed Services Committee teams.

Atwal, Kay, and Michael Gething. "Through Sea, Sand, and Storm." *Defence* 22 (September 1991): 15–22. Contributions of naval helicopters.

Badolato, Ed. "Pollution as Ammunition." *Proceedings* 117 (October 1991): 68–70. Argues that the United States could have curbed Iraq's environmental terrorism during the war.

Barnes, Edward. "When Freedom Came," *Life* 1 (special weekly edition, 11 March 1991). Liberation of Kuwait.

Bashore, Sherri E. "A Hero's Welcome." *All Hands* 68 (June 1991): 24–29.

Beck, Chip. "The Gulf War: A Department Officer on Active Military Duty Tells His Story." *The State* 343 (April 1991): 2–9. Account of re-opening the U.S. Embassy in Kuwait City.

Bennet, James. "Sand Trap: US Diplomacy Did Work: It Got Us Into War." *The Washington Monthly* 23 (April 1991): 25–28.

Berens, Robert J. "POWs: Quiet Heroism in Ambiguity." *Army* 9 (September 1992): 34–39.

Bien, Lyle G. "From the Strike Cell." *Proceedings* 117 (June 1991): 58–60. Lessons learned from the air war by a key participant.

Blacker, Coit D. "The Collapse of Soviet Power in Europe." *Foreign Affairs: America and the World 1990/91* 70 (1991): 88–102.

Blackstone, J. "Special Boat Unit Supports Operation Provide Comfort." *Full Mission Profile* (Fall 1992): 35.

Blix, Hans. "Verification of Nuclear Nonproliferation: The Lesson of Iraq." *The Washington Quarterly* 15 (Fall 1992): 57–65.

Boatman, John. "Gulf Mines Almost Sank U.S. Cruiser." *Jan's Defence Weekly* 15 (25 May 1991): 866.

_____. "USMC Assault Practice." *Jane's Defence Weekly* 14 (13 October 1990): 687. Amphibious exercise "Camel Sand."

Bond, David F. "Troop and Materiel Deployment Missions Central Elements in Desert Storm Success." *Aviation Week and Space Technology* 134 (22 April 1991): 94–95.

Boomer, Walter E. "Special Trust and Confidence Among the Trail-Breakers." *Proceedings* 117 (November 1991): 47–50. Interview with LGEN Walter E. Boomer, Commander I Marine Expeditionary Force; discusses Marine operations ashore during the war.

Bosco, Lee. "Hunting Mines in Nil-Vis." *All Hands* 68 (July 1991): 27–31.

_____. "Making Things Happen in the Persian Gulf: Logistics Command Proves No Desert Storm Puzzle Is Too Tough." *All Hands* 68 (June 1991): 32–35.

_____. "Port Harbor Security: Interservice Coalition Kept Ships Safe." *All Hands* 68 (August 1991): 24–27.

Bove, Alfred A., T.G. Patel, and Raphael F. Smith. "Fleet Hospitals: Full-Service Care." *Proceedings* 118 (October 1992): 77–79.

Brabham, James A. "Training, Education Were the Keys." *Proceedings* 117 (November 1991): 51–54. Interview with BGEN James A. Brabham, Commander 1st Force Service Support Group during the war; gives insights on Marine logistics.

Brame, William L. "From Garrison to Desert Offensive in 97 Days." *Army* 42 (February 1992): 28–35. Moving the VII Corps from Europe.

Brown, David K., and David Foxwell. "Report from the Front: MCM and the Threat Beneath the Surface." *International Defense Review* 24 (July 1991): 735–738.

Bruce, James. "Campaign Against Shiites Hardens." *Jane's Defence Weekly* 17 (6 June 1992): 967.

_____. "How Saddam Is Picking Up the Pieces a Year After Storm." *Jane's Defence Weekly* 17 (22 February 1992): 284.

Burgess, Richard R. "Orions of Arabia: Patrol Squadrons in Desert Shield/Storm," *Naval Aviation News* 73 (September–October 1991): 14–16.

Burton, James G. "Pushing Them Out the Back Door." *Proceedings* 119 (June 1993): 37–42. Discusses the VII Corps's advance into Iraq.

Canby, Thomas Y. "After the Storm." *National Geographic* 180 (August 1991): 2–35. Photographic essay featuring dramatic illustrations of the Kuwaiti oil well fires.

"A Capital Celebration Honors Operation Desert Storm Vets." *Army* 41 (August 1991): 21–23.

Carpenter, John D. "An Exercise in Patience," "Bravo Platoon in Bahrain," and "Next Stop, Qatar." *Full Mission Profile* (Fall 1992): 21–31. Naval special operations in CENTCOM area of responsibility after the Gulf War.

"Catalogue of Non-Compliance," *Jane's Defence Weekly* 18 (8 August 1992): 8. Iraq's record of compliance with the Gulf War cease-fire terms.

"CG Heads Oil-Assist Team to Assess Persian Gulf Damage." U.S. Coast Guard Commandant's *Bulletin* (March 1991).

"China Develops Cunning Sea Mines." *Parade Magazine* (19 March 1995): 10.

Chubin, Shahram. "Gulf Regional Security After the Crisis." *International Defense Review* 24 (March 1991): 204–206.

Chubin, Shahram, and Charles Tripp. "Domestic Politics and Territorial Disputes in the Persian Gulf and the Arabian Peninsula." *Survival* 35 (Winter 1993): 3–27.

Claborn, David. "Pest Control in the Desert." *Marine Corps Gazette* 75 (August 1991): 56–58.

Cohen, Eliot A. "The Mystique of U.S. Air Power." *Foreign Affairs* 73 (January–February 1994): 109–124. Article based on the Gulf War Air Power Survey.

Collar, Leo L. "Desert Storm and Its Effect on U.S. Maritime Policy." *Defense Transportation Journal* 47 (June 1991): 67–68.

Colucci, Frank. "Warriors at Sea." *U.S. Army Aviation Digest* (November–December 1992): 5–11.

"Combat Logistics: The Power Behind the Punch." *All Hands* 68 (Desert Storm Special Issue): 43–45.

Copley, Gregory. "Saddam Hussein Gently Wakens the Dreamers of the Era of Universal Peace." *Defense and Foreign Affairs Strategic Policy* 18 (September 1990): 8–9, 26–30. Iraqi invasion of Kuwait in the context of the end of the Cold War.

Cordesman, Anthony. "The Gulf War and the Revolution in Military Affairs." Lecture delivered at the Woodrow Wilson Center, Smithsonian Institution, Washington, DC, 27 September 1994.

Cordesman, Anthony H. "Rushing to Judgement on the Gulf War." *Armed Forces Journal International* 128 (June 1991): 66–72.

Cote, Owen, and Harvey M. Sapolsky. "Lift Myths." *Breakthroughs* 1 (Spring 1991): 1–4. Discussion of sealift.

Covey, Dana C. "Offering a Helping Hand in Iraq." *Proceedings* 118 (May 1992): 106–9. Describes the Navy's role in explosive ordnance disposal (EOD) and in humanitarian medical assistance in southern Iraq.

Coyne, James P. "Plan of Attack." *Air Force Magazine* 75 (April 1992): 40–46. Development of the plan for the air campaign against Iraq.

Craig, C.J.S. "Gulf War: The Maritime Campaign." *RUSI Journal* 137 (August 1992): 11–16.

Cruger, J. King. "Assignment: Red Sea." *All Hands* 69 (April 1992): 7–15. Postwar maritime interception operations.

Cushman, John H. "Joint, Jointer, Jointest." *Proceedings* 118 (May 1992): 75–85. Operation Provide Comfort.

Dawisha, Adeed. "The United States in the Middle East: The Gulf War and Its Aftermath." *Current History* 91 (January 1992): 1–5.

Dean, Michael. "Desert Storm's First Purple Heart." *Navy Medicine* 82 (January–February 1991): 11.

Delaney, Marshalena. "New Baby, Thankful Wife, and Grateful Nation Greet EM1 Dotson." *The Coast Guard Reservist* 38 (May–June 1991): 6.

Delery, Tom. "Away, the Boarding Party!" *Proceedings* 117 (May 1991): 65–71. The multinational Maritime Interception Force in enforcing the embargo of Iraq.

Devlin, John F. "The Baath Party: Rise and Metamorphosis." *American Historical Review* 96 (December 1991): 1396–1407.

Deyerle, Leta. "Last Desert Storm Shipment Returns Home." *Command Post* (29 May 1992): 5.

Dietrich, Steve E. "From Valhalla With Pride." *Proceedings* 119 (August 1993): 59–60. Discusses the VII Corps's advance into Iraq.

DiRita, Larry. "Exocets, Air Traffic, & the Air Tasking Order." *Proceedings* 118 (August 1992): 59–63. Aegis cruisers in Desert Shield and Desert Storm; critique of the air tasking order system.

Doll, Kevin. "Comedian Entertains Front-line Marines." *Marines* 20 (February 1991): 19–20.

Donovan, Francis R. "Surge and Sustainment." *Sea Power* 33 (November 1990): 39–45. Initial deployment of sealift ships; based on testimony by Vice Admiral Francis R. Donovan, Commander Military Sealift Command during the war, before House Merchant Marine Subcommittee on 26 September 1990.

Dorr, Robert F. "POWs in Iraq Survived Thanks to Training, Courage, Faith." *Naval Aviation News* 73 (September–October 1991): 24–25.

Dwyer, John B. "SEALs in Desert Storm." *Proceedings* 118 (July 1992): 95–98.

Eilts, Hermann F. "The Persian Gulf Crisis: Perspectives and Prospects." *Middle East Journal* 45 (Winter 1991): 7–22.

———. "The United States and Saudi Arabia: A Half-Century Overview." *Middle East Insight* (Special Edition, Saudi Arabia, 1995): 14–30.

Ekeus, Rolf. "The Iraqi Experience and the Future of Nuclear Nonproliferation." *The Washington Quarterly* 15 (Fall 1992): 67–74.

Elmo, David S. "Food Distribution During Operation Provide Comfort." *Special Warfare* 5 (March 1992): 8–9.

Engbrecht, R.J. "Fleet Hospital: Supporting the Troops in the Middle East." *Leatherneck* 73 (November 1990): 29–30.

Evans, David. "From the Gulf." *Proceedings* 117 (January 1991): 77–80. Impressions of military operations in Saudi Arabia during the first four months of Desert Shield.

Evans, Frank. "*Princeton* Leaves the War." *Proceedings* 117 (July 1991): 70–72. Account of *Princeton*'s 18 February 1991 mine strike, based on commanding officer's recollection.

"Fast Sealift Ships Begin Operation Desert Sortie." *Sealift* (June 1991): 1.

Fedele, Karen. "The Seabees Go to War." *Navy Civil Engineer* (Summer 1991).

Fedyszyn, T.R. "A Maritime Perspective." *Proceedings* 111 (July 1985): 80–87. Perspective on the Joint Chiefs of Staff (background to Goldwater-Nichols legislation).

Fiske, R.P. "Salvage in Combat." *Proceedings* 118 (September 1992): 65–69. Naval salvage operations during and after Desert Storm.

Fitzgerald, Chris. "That Was No Rambo—That Was a Hellfire." *Proceedings* 122 (November 1996): 76–77. Argues that arming LAMPs helicopters with Hellfire missiles is valid.

"Flyers Provide Comfort to Kurds, Bangladeshis." *Naval Aviation News* 73 (July–August 1991): 4.

"The Forces of Desert Storm." *Air Force Magazine* 74 (March 1991): 34–40. Lists major Air Force units deployed.

Frederick, T.J., and P.N. Nagy. "So Where Were All the RO/ROs?" *Proceedings* 118 (May 1992): 124–27. Performances of the Fast Sealift Ships and other roll-on/roll-off (RO/RO) ships used during Desert Storm; lessons for design and acquisition of new RO/ROs.

Friedman, Norman. "World Naval Developments in Review." *Proceedings* 121 (May 1995): 143–44.

Frix, Robert S., and Archie L. Davis. "Task Force Freedom and the Restoration of Kuwait." *Military Review* 72 (October 1992): 2–10.

Froggett, Steve. "Tomahawk in the Desert." *Proceedings* 118 (January 1992): 71–75. Describes effectiveness and limitations of sea-launched cruise missiles in the Gulf War.

Fulghum, David A. "Allies Strike Iraq for Defying U.N." *Aviation Week and Space Technology* 138 (18 January 1993): 22–25.

_____. "UAVs Pressed Into Action To Fill Intelligence Void." *Aviation Week and Space Technology* 135 (19 August 1991): 59–60.

Fursdon, Edward. "Iraqi Mines Know no Ceasefire." *Navy International* 96 (May 1991): 142–46. Postwar mine countermeasures operations.

Gawlowicz, Joe. "Persian Gulf Service Station: USS *Acadia* on Station, Serving the Fleet on the Edge of Desert Storm." *All Hands* 68 (April 1991): 36–39. Naval logistics.

_____. "Mine Countermeasures in the Gulf." *All Hands* 68 (July 1991): 20–23.

"Gen. Schwarzkopf Addresses Issues." *Marines* 19 (December 1990): 24–25. Desert Shield personnel issues including rotation, uniforms, etc.

Gibson, Andrew E., and William M. Calhoun. "Barely in Time: The Successful Struggle to Create the Transportation Command." *Naval War College Review* 43 (Autumn 1990): 72–80.

Gibson, Andrew E., and Jacob L. Shuford. "Desert Shield and Strategic Sealift." *Naval War College Review* 44 (Spring 1991): 6–19.

Gimblett, Richard H. "Preliminary Research Results: Canadian Naval Operations in the Persian Gulf, 1990–1991." Unpublished paper. 5 March 1992.

Giusti, James. "'Mine Reading'—Avoiding the Pain." *Surface Warfare* 16 (May–June 1991): 16–22. MCM in the gulf during and after Desert Storm.

Glosson, Buster C. "Impact of Precision Weapons on Air Combat Operations." *Airpower Journal* 7 (Summer 1993): 4–10.

Graham, Paul S. "Maritime Prepositioning Enters the 1990s." *Proceedings* 117 (June 1991): 82–84. Maritime Prepositioning Ship unloading operations.

"Greater Gators: Amphibious Forces Kept Saddam Guessing," *All Hands* 68 (Desert Storm Special Issue): 32–33.

Gregory, Melissa. "Persian Gulf War Allies Launch Operation Southern Watch." *Navy News* (2 September 1992): 7.

Griffith, Ronald H. "Mission Accomplished—In Full." *Proceedings* 119 (August 1993): 63–65. Discusses the VII Corps' advance into Iraq.

Gruetzner, James K., and William Caldwell. "DOD Reorganization." *Proceedings* 113 (May 1987): 136–45. Brief history of reform movement behind the Goldwater-Nichols legislation.

Haley, P. Edward. "Saddam Surprises the United States: Learning from 'The Revolution of August 2.'" *Armed Forces & Society* 22 (Winter 1995/96): 159–85. Critique of U.S. policy toward Iraq before the invasion of Kuwait.

Halliday, Fred. "The Gulf War and Its Aftermath: First Reflections." *International Affairs* 67 (April 1991): 223–34.

Hammick, Murray. "Iraqi Obstacles and Defensive Positions." *International Defense Review* 24 (September 1991): 989–91.

———. "To the Victor the Spoiled Land." *International Defense Review* 24 (September 1991): 992–94. Postwar explosive ordnance disposal in Kuwait.

"Hard Rain: Desert Storm Brings Nasty Weather." *All Hands* 68 (Desert Storm Special Issue): 14–19. Carrier operations during Desert Storm.

Hartley, Douglas. "A Port in a Storm." *Defense & Diplomacy* 9 (March–April 1991): 35–36. Perspective on Gulf War from Dubai by a former U.S. diplomat.

Hashim, Ahmed. "Iraq, the Pariah State." *Current History* 91 (January 1992): 11–16. A significant proportion of Iraq's military power survived the war.

Hattendorf, John B. "Evolution of the Maritime Strategy, 1977–1987." *Naval War College Review* 41 (Summer 1988): 3. A thoughtful, informed analysis of the Maritime Strategy's development.

"Heading Home Means Leaving Saudi Soil—All of It—Behind." *Leatherneck*, 74 (June 1991): 15. Equipment cleaning.

"Heavy Fighting in Iraq Continues." *Jane's Defence Weekly* 15 (23 March 1991): 426. Shiite rebellion.

Heidenrich, John D. "The Gulf War: How Many Iraqis Died?" *Foreign Policy* 90 (Spring 1993): 108–125.

Herndon, Charles M., Jr. "Amphibious Forces and the Gulf War." *Marine Corps Gazette* 77 (February 1993): 74–80.

Hewish, Mark. "Tomahawk Enhances Navy Role in Land Warfare." *International Defense Review* 24 (May 1991): 458.

Hickman, William F. "Soviet Naval Policy in the Indian Ocean." *Proceedings* 105 (August 1979): 42–52.

Hill, Richard D. "Depot Operations Supporting Desert Shield." *Military Review* 71 (April 1991): 17–28.

Hoffman, Frank G. "The U.S. Marine Corps in Review." *Proceedings* 121 (May 1995): 131–35.

Hoffmeier, Donna. "POWs Start Home Aboard *Mercy*." *Public Affairs Communicator* 3 (July–August 1991): 5, 22.

Hollis, Rosemary. "What Price Renewed Conflict in the Middle East?" *RUSI Journal* 137 (October 1992): 50–55. Postwar diplomatic issues.

Hopkins, John I. "This Was No Drill." *Proceedings* 117 (November 1991): 58–62. Interview with MGEN John I. Hopkins, USMC, Commander 7th Marine Expeditionary Brigade and Deputy Commander I Marine Expeditionary Force during Operations Desert Shield and Desert Storm; insights on battlefield intelligence, defense of Saudi Arabia, and equipment performance.

Horner, Charles A. "Desert Shield/Desert Storm: An Overview." *Air Power History* 38 (Fall 1991): 5–9. By Central Command's Air Force component commander.

Huddleston, Craig. "Commentary on Desert Shield." *Marine Corps Gazette* 75 (January 1991): 32–33. Early lessons learned.

Hughes, E.H. "Flying Workhorses Over Iraq." *Leatherneck* 74 (October 1991): 23. Marine helicopters in Provide Comfort.

Humphries, John G. "Operations Law and the Rules of Engagement in Operations Desert Shield and Desert Storm." *Airpower Journal* 6 (Fall 1992): 25–41.

Hurley, Matthew M. "Saddam Hussein and Iraqi Air Power." *Airpower Journal* 6 (Winter 1992): 4–16. Excellent study.

Hyams, Kenneth C., et al. "Diarrheal Disease during Operation Desert Shield." *New England Journal of Medicine* 325 (14 November 1991): 1423–28.

Indyk, Martin. "Watershed in the Middle East." *Foreign Affairs, America and the World 1991/92* 71 (1992): 70–93. Assessment of impact of Gulf War on diplomacy.

Inman, Bobby R., Joseph S. Nye Jr., William J. Perry, and Roger K. Smith. "Lessons from the Gulf War." *The Washington Quarterly* 15 (Winter 1992): 57–74.

"Interview: BGEN Peter J. Rowe, USMC." *Proceedings* 118 (May 1992): 128–31. Commander 5th MEB discusses strategic amphibious deception operations during Desert Storm and disaster relief operations in Bangladesh.

"Iran Eyes Purchase of Two More Russian Subs." *Aviation Week & Space Technology* 137 (9 November 1992): 20–21.

Jacobs, Gordon. "Arabian Gulf Navies in Crisis." *Navy International* 95 (October 1990): 343–49.

Jamieson, Perry D. "Lucrative Targets: The U.S. Air Force in the Kuwaiti Theater of Operations." Washington: Air Force History and Museums Program 1995. An unpublished, but cleared for public release, draft of an official Air Force history of the Gulf War. The work is based on a wealth of primary materials and interviews with participants.

Johar, Hasan, and Gawdat Bahgat. "View From Kuwait: Oil and Democracy: The American Dilemma in the Persian Gulf Region." *Comparative Strategy* 14 (April–June 1995): 173–83. A view of post-Desert Storm U.S. policy in the Persian Gulf region.

Johnson, Dana J. "Roles and Missions for Conventionally Armed Heavy Bombers–An Historical Perspective." Prepared for the U.S. Air Force. Rand Note N-3481-AF, 1994.

Johnson, Hansford T. "Presentation to the Committee on Merchant Marine and Fisheries, Subcommittee on Merchant Marine, U.S. House of Representatives," 23 April 1991.

Jones, Brian W. "Close Air Support: A Doctrinal Disconnect." *Airpower Journal* 6 (Winter 1992): 60–71.

Jones, Ernest J. "MPS and Desert Storm." *Marine Corps Gazette* 75 (August 1991): 47–50.

Jones, James L. "Operation Provide Comfort: Humanitarian and Security Assistance in Northern Iraq." *Marine Corps Gazette* 75 (November 1991): 98–107.

Kaplan, Robert D. "Tales From the Bazaar." *Atlantic Monthly* (August 1992): 37–61. Provides context for U.S. policy toward Iraq on the eve of the invasion of Kuwait.

Karr, Kennard G., and Richard G. Terao. "Ammunition Retrograde from SWA." *Ordnance* 9 (May 1992): 44–47.

Karsh, Efraim, and Inari Rautsi. "Why Saddam Hussein Invaded Kuwait." *Survival* 33 (January–February 1991): 18–30.

Keany, Thomas A. "Surveying Gulf War Airpower." *Joint Forces Quarterly* (Autumn 1993): 25–36.

Keene, R.R. "The Storm is Over." *Leatherneck* 74 (April 1991): 37–43.

Kelley, P.X. "The Amphibious Warfare Strategy." *Proceedings* 112 (January 1986 special supplement): 18–29. Unclassified summary of the amphibious portion of the Maritime Strategy.

Kesteloot, Robert W. "Sealift After the Storm: A Plan to Revitalize the U.S.-Flag Fleet." *Sea Power* 34 (June 1991): 37–41.

Keys, William M. "Rolling With the 2d Marine Division." *Proceedings* 117 (November 1991): 77–80. Interview with Commanding General 2d Marine Division during Desert Shield and Desert Storm; provides insights on ground war.

Kindsvatter, Peter S. "VII Corps in the Gulf War: Post-Cease-Fire Operations." *Military Review* 72 (June 1992): 2–19.

Kitfield, James. "Navy Blues." *Government Executive* 24 (April 1992): 26–28. Naval aviation in the Gulf War, jointness, and postwar reduction of the Navy.

Krulak, Charles C. "CSS in the Desert." *Military Review* 73 (July 1993): 22–25. Overview of decision making and logistical preparation for the ground war.

Kurth, Michael M. "Whiskey With a Kick." *Amphibious Warfare Review* 9 (Summer 1991): 33–34. Marine Cobra helicopters in Desert Storm.

"Last Storm CVs Return." *Naval Aviation News* 73 (September–October 1991): 4.

Laurie, William T. "Seahawks Fight Fire With Fire: Hellfire/FLIR Key to Littoral Warfare Success." *Surface Warfare* 20 (January/February 1995): 18–21. Discusses enhancements in capabilities and mission of SH-60B helicopters made since Desert Storm.

Lenton, H.T. "Maritime Aspects of Operation Desert Shield." *Navy International* 95 (September 1990): 396–398.

"Lessons Learned or Lost?" *News Briefs: American Maritime Officers' Service* 10 (Summer 1991): 2. Sealift.

Lewis, Richard B.H. "JFACC Problems Associated with Battlefield Preparation in Desert Storm." *Airpower Journal* 8 (Spring 1994): 4–21.

Liebman, Marc E. "Navy Tankers Are Needed Now!" *Proceedings* 118 (September 1991): 82–85. The Gulf War pointed up the inadequacy of naval aerial refueling aircraft.

———. "We Need Armed Helos." *Proceedings* 118 (August 1991): 84–86. Proposals for U.S. naval helicopters in light of antisurface warfare in the northern Persian Gulf.

Linn, Tom. "Crisis in the Persian Gulf." *Amphibious Warfare Review* 8 (Fall/Winter 1990): 10–14. Implications of possible disruptions to the flow of oil from the Middle East as a result of Iraqi action.

Lionetti, Donald M. "Air Defense: No 'Road to Basra.'" *Army* 41 (July 1991): 16–26. Lessons from Desert Storm for ground force air defense.

Livingstone, Neil C. "Iraq's Intentional Omission." *Sea Power* 34 (June 1991): 29–30. Discusses why Iraqi forces never launched a chemical attack on coalition forces.

Locke, Walter M., and Kenneth P. Werrell. "Speak Softly and . . ." *Proceedings* 120 (October 1994): 30–35. Outlines the Tomahawk's advantages over manned aircraft in attacks on Iraq, 1991–1993.

Luti, William J. "Battle of the Airwaves." *Proceedings* 118 (January 1992): 49–55. Suppression of enemy air defenses during Desert Storm.

MacDonald, Scot, et al. "Rounding Up the Storm." *Surface Warfare* 16 (July/August 1991): 8–17. Highlights of Navy surface ship actions.

Mackenzie, Richard. "A Conversation with Chuck Horner." *Air Force Magazine* 74 (June 1991): 57–64.

MacKinnon, Christine. "Crowd of 3,000 Greets Comfort's Return." *Sealift* (May 1991): 6.

Mahnken, Thomas G. "America's Next War." *The Washington Quarterly* 16 (Summer 1993).

Mandelbaum, Michael. "The Bush Foreign Policy." *Foreign Affairs: America and the World 1990/91* 70 (1991): 5–22.

Marechal-Workman, Andree. "*Mercy* Returns With a Shipload of Memories." *Navy Medicine* 82 (May–June 1991): 19–20.

Marolda, Edward J. "A Host of Nations: Coalition Naval Operations in the Persian Gulf War." In *Perspectives on Warfighting, Number Three: Selected Papers From the 1992 (59th Annual) Meeting of the Society for Military History*, edited by Donald F. Bittner. Quantico, VA: Command and Staff College Foundation, 1994.

Martin, James M. "We Still Haven't Learned." *Proceedings* 117 (July 1991): 64–68. Argues that the *Tripoli* and *Princeton* incidents indicate that the Navy was unprepared for mine warfare.

Mazzara, Andrew F. "Artillery in the Desert, 1991: Report # 2." *Marine Corps Gazette* 75 (June 1991): 35–36. Second of three-part series on operations and lessons of Marine artillery in the war.

_____. "Supporting Arms in the Storm." *Proceedings* 117 (November 1991): 41–45. Analyzes contributions of various fire support arms during Desert Storm.

McCausland, Jeffrey D. "How Iraq's CBW Threat Affected Coalition Operations." *Defense & Foreign Affairs Strategic Policy* 20 (September 1992): 12–15.

McDonald, Wesley. "The Convoy Mission." *Proceedings* 114 (May 1988): 36–49. Earnest Will.

McDonnell, Janet A. "Rebuilding Kuwait." *Military Review* 73 (July 1993): 50–61.

McKillip, J.D. "Iraqi Strategy During the Gulf War: An Alternative Viewpoint." *Military Review* 75 (September–October 1995): 46–51. Speculation based on secondary sources.

McMichael, William H. "Aftermath in Kuwait." *Soldiers* 46 (June 1991): 17–20. Immediate postwar scene in Kuwait.

_____. "Desert Demolitions." *Soldiers* 46 (June 1991): 13–26. Postwar destruction of Iraqi equipment and ordnance in Kuwait and occupied Iraq.

McPeak, Merrill A. Defense Department Briefing, 15 March 1991.

Meacham, Jim. "A New Middle East Security Equation." *Defense & Diplomacy* 9 (October–November 1991): 43–46.

Miles, Donna. "Personnel Issues After Desert Storm." *Soldiers* 46 (June 1991): 22–23.

Milhollin, Gary. "The Iraqi Bomb." *The New Yorker* (1 February 1993): 47–56.

Mitzelfelt, Brad. "Trapped Recon Teams Called for Air and Artillery Fire on Their Position and Helped Clear Khafji." *Leatherneck* 74 (March 1991): 30.

Mixson, Riley D. "Navy's Version of Carrier Contribution to Desert Shield/Desert Storm." *Armed Forces Journal International* 129 (February 1992): 44.

_____. "Where We Must Do Better." *Proceedings* 118 (August 1991): 38–39. Five areas where naval aviation should be improved.

Montgomery, Glenn. "When the Liberation of Kuwait Began." *Proceedings* 117 (April 1991): 51. The skipper of *Curts* discusses his role in the Qaruh Island operation.

Moore, James E. "Head 'Em Up, Move 'Em Out." *Marines* 20 (July 1991): 7. Marine retrograde operations.

_____. "Still in the Sand." *Leatherneck* 74 (October 1991): 18–19. Marine retrograde operations.

Moore, Royal N., Jr. "Marine Air: There When Needed." *Proceedings* 117 (November 1991): 63–70. Interview with Commanding General Third Marine Aircraft Wing, who commanded I MEF's combat aviation during Desert Shield and Storm.

Morocco, John D. "Allied Strategists Altered Battle Plans to Compensate for Dugan's Comments." *Aviation Week & Space Technology* 134 (22 July 1991): 60–61.

_____. "From Vietnam to Desert Storm." *Air Force* 75 (January 1992): 68–73. Air power lessons learned in Vietnam and applied in the gulf.

_____. "U.S. War Plan: Air Strikes to Topple Hussein Regime." *Aviation Week & Space Technology* 133 (24 September 1990): 16–18.

Morocco, John D., et al. "Soviet Peace Plan Weighed As Gulf Ground War Looms." *Aviation Week & Space Technology* 134 (25 February 1991): 20–22.

Moskos, Charles, and John Wattendorf. "Troops in Desert Shield." *Inter-University Seminar on Armed Forces and Society Newsletter* (9 March 1991): 1–2. Glimpse of living conditions, morale, and motivations of U.S. troops deployed in the Saudi desert.

"Mother of All Surrenders: Marines Lead the Charge from Khafji to Kuwait." *All Hands* 68 (Desert Storm Special Issue): 26–31.

"MPF Loadout Completed." *Marine Corps Gazette* 75 (November 1991): 36–39. Reconstitution of maritime prepositioning squadrons.

Muir, Daniel J. "A View from the Black Hole." *Proceedings* 117 (October 1991): 85–86. Problems in joint aerial strike planning.

Muslih, Muhammad, and Augustus Richard Norton. "The Need for Arab Democracy." *Foreign Policy* 83 (Summer 1991): 3–19.

Myatt, J.M. "The 1st Marine Division in the Attack." *Proceedings* 117 (November 1991): 71–76.

Mylroie, Laurie. "Iraq Since the Gulf War." Paper presented at the Defense and Arms Control Studies Program, Center for International Studies, Massachusetts Institute of Technology, 21 April 1993.

_____. "Why Saddam Hussein Invaded Kuwait." *Orbis* 37 (Winter 1993): 123–34.

Nagle, R.J. "Having a Blast in the Persian Gulf." *Proceedings* 118 (October 1992): 104–7. Naval explosive ordnance disposal.

"Naval Air Extends Security and Helping Hand." *Naval Aviation News* 75 (November–December 1992): 4–5. Naval aviation in Southern Watch and miscellaneous relief operations.

Nelson, Michael A., and Douglas J. Katz. "Unity of Control: Joint Air Operations in the Gulf—Part Two." *Joint Forces Quarterly* (Summer 1994): 59–63.

Neves, Juan Carlos. "Interoperability in Multinational Coalitions: Lessons from the Persian Gulf War." *Naval War College Review* 48 (Winter 1995): 50–62.

Nordwall, Bruce D. "Tethered Aerostat Alerted Kuwait to Iraqis Heading Across Border." *Aviation Week and Space Technology* 133 (24 September 1990): 21–22.

Norman, Kevin M. "*Wisconsin* Hosts Desert Shield Sports Festival." *All Hands* 68 (April 1991): 22–23.

Norton, Douglas M. "Sealift: Keystone of Support." *Proceedings* 117 (May 1991): 42–49. Importance of rapid logistical support in first 120 days of Desert Shield.

Oberdorfer, Don. "Missed Signals in the Middle East." *Washington Post Magazine* (17 March 1991): 19–41. Prewar U.S.-Iraqi diplomacy.

O'Keefe, Sean C., Frank B. Kelso, and Carl E. Mundy. "From the Sea: A New Direction for the Naval Services." *Marine Corps Gazette* 76 (November 1992): 18–22. Full text of Navy-Marine Corps White Paper, prepared by the Secretary of the Navy, Chief of Naval Operations, and Commandant of the Marine Corps, defining a new vision for the Navy and Marines; emphasizes the post-Cold War shift from a blue-water, global threat to littoral, regional challenges such as the Gulf War.

O'Neill, Bard E., and Ilana Kass. "The Persian Gulf War: A Political-Military Assessment." *Comparative Strategy* 11 (April–June 1992): 213–40.

O'Rourke, Ronald. "The Tanker War." *Proceedings* 114 (May 1988): 30–35.

Oxenbould, C.J. "Australians Going to War in the 1990s." Presentation at Australian War Memorial, 6 November 1991.

Pagonis, William G., and Harold E. Raugh, "Good Logistics Is Combat Power: The Logistics Sustainment of Operation Desert Storm." *Military Review* 71 (September 1991): 28–39.

Palmer, Michael A. "The Storm in the Air: One Plan, Two Air Wars?" *Air Power History* 39 (Winter 1992): 24–31.

Palzkill, Dennis. "Making Interoperability Work." *Proceedings* 118 (September 1991): 50–54.

Peay, J.H. Binford, III. "The Five Pillars of Peace in the Central Region." *Joint Forces Quarterly* (Autumn 1995): 32–39. General Peay discusses post-Desert Storm American military policy in the Central Command region.

Peterson, C.B. "What's Happening With CWC?" *Proceedings* 107 (June 1981): 85. Discussion of composite warfare commander organization.

Peterson, Harries-Clichy, Jr. "Intelligence: Fix It or Forget It." *Marine Corps Gazette* 76 (March 1992): 18–20. Problems.

Pope, John R. "U.S. Marines in Operation Desert Storm." *Marine Corps Gazette* 75 (July 1991): 62–69. Overview.

Porteous, Holly. "Playing Cat and Mouse Over Iraq's Nuclear Secrets." *Jane's Defence Weekly* 15 (13 July 1991): 58.

Powers, Robert Carney. "Commanding the Offense." *Proceedings* 111 (October 1985): 59–64. Discussion of the composite warfare commander concept.

Phillips, Mark D. "SWOs In Sealift." *Surface Warfare* 16 (July/August 1991): 20–23.

Preston, Antony. "Allied MCM in the Gulf." *Naval Forces* 12 (April 1991): 48–69.

Price, Chris, and Sherri E. Bashore. "Shelter From the Storm: Navy Hotline Provides Information During Times of Crisis." *All Hands* 68 (April 1991): 16–20.

Prina, L. Edgar. "Conflict Spotlights Sealift, Shipbuilding Deficiencies." *Sea Power* 33 (October 1990): 46–49.

Putney, Diane T. "From Instant Thunder to Desert Storm." *Air Power History* 41 (Fall 1994): 38–50. Excellent study of the evolution of the air campaign.

Quandt, William B. "The Middle East in 1990." *Foreign Affairs: American and the World 1990/1991* 70 (1991): 49–69.

Rankin, A.G., and R. G. Smith. "Australian Divers Clear Mines." *Proceedings* 117 (July 1991): 74. Postwar EOD.

Reason, J. Paul. "Naval Forces First to the Fight." *Surface Warfare* 19 (November–December 1994): 15–17.

"Recollections of War." *Widener: The Magazine of Widener University* (October 1991).

"Redeployment Going Even Better Than Deployment." *Sealift* (August 1991): 3.

Resing, David C. "Clearing the Way." *Proceedings* (October 1994): 40–41. Postwar Navy explosive ordnance disposal.

"'The Right Word Getting Out:' Interview with MSC Commander Vice Adm. Francis R. Donovan." *Sea Power* 35 (July 1992): 11–19.

Ripley, Tim. "Operation Provide Comfort II: Western Force Protects Kurds." *International Defense Review* 24 (October 1991): 1055–57.

Roberts, Michael D. "The Untold Story in the Gulf: Navy Medicine and the Marines." *Navy Medicine* 83 (March/April 1992): 8–15.

Rodrique, George, and Robert Ruby, "Taking Down the Oil Platforms." *Proceedings* 117 (April 1991): 53. Account of *Nicholas* recapturing Dorra oil field drilling rigs in the Persian Gulf.

Rosas, Sylvia. "MSC: Logistical Support for Dual Contingencies." *Surface Warfare* 19 (November/December 1994): 36–37.

Rosenthal, Eduardo Alfredo. "The Argentine Navy in the Persian Gulf." *Boletin del Centro Naval* No. 763 (Winter 1991): 255–68.

Rouleau, Eric. "America's Unyielding Policy Toward Iraq." *Foreign Affairs* 74 (January/February 1995): 59–72. French view of postwar U.S. policy.

Rubin, Barry. "Pan-Arab Nationalism: The Ideological Dream as Compelling Force." *Journal of Contemporary History* 26 (September 1991): 487–507.

Sayigh, Yezid. "The Gulf Crisis: Why the Arab Regional Order Failed." *International Affairs* 67 (July 1991): 487–507.

Schneller, Robert J., Jr. "Persian Gulf Turkey Shoot: The Destruction of Iraqi Naval Forces During Operation Desert Storm." Paper given at the 1993 meeting of the Society for Military History, Kingston, Ontario, Canada. May 1993.

Sharp, Trueman W. "NEPMU-7 Supports Operation Provide Comfort." *Navy Medicine* 83 (January–February 1992): 10–13.

Shaw, Marjie, and J.D. DiMattio. "Provide Comfort: Navy-Marine Corps Team Gets New Image." *All Hands* 68 (September 1991): 30–32.

Shotwell, J.M. "The Ride into Kuwait City." *Leatherneck* 74 (May 1991): 20–21.

Simmons, Edwin H. "Getting Marines to the Gulf." *Proceedings* 117 (May 1991): 50–64. Deployment and operations of Marines in the war.

_____. "Getting the Job Done." *Proceedings* 117 (May 1991): 94–96. Marines in Desert Storm.

Simon, Steven. "US Strategy in the Persian Gulf." *Survival* 34 (Fall 1992): 81–97.

Sinagra, Tony. "Maritime Prepositioning System Works during Operation Desert Shield." *Leatherneck* 73 (November 1990): 28–29.

Slade, Stuart. "The FAC's End Approaches." *Naval Forces* 12 (November 1991): 12–13. Predicts that the Third World market for fast attack craft will shrink because of poor performance of the Iraqi navy.

Snaza, Gregg L. "Lucky *Foster* and Forbes' Forces." *Surface Warfare* 16 (July–August 1991): 10. Contains an account of the destruction of Iraqi navy from the local antisurface warfare commander's point of view.

Stackpole, H.C. "Angels From the Sea." *Proceedings* 118 (May 1992): 110–116. Bangladesh relief effort.

Stanik, Joseph T. "Welcome to El Dorado Canyon." *Proceedings* 122 (April 1996): 57–62. Detailed account of the 1986 Navy-Air Force strike on Libya.

Starr, Barbara. "Air Forces Join to Hold 'No-Fly Zone.'" *Jane's Defence Weekly* 18 (5 September 1992): 5. Southern Watch.

_____. "Saudi Rejects US Basing Move." *Jane's Defence Weekly* 17 (4 April 1992): 549.

Steele, Dennis. "A Capital Celebration Honors Operation Desert Storm Vets." *Army* 41 (August 1991): 20–23.

Strike Fighter Squadron 87. "Aircraft-Yes, Tactics-Yes, Weapons-No." *Proceedings* 118 (September 1991): 55–57. The Navy lacked adequate numbers of precision-guided munitions during the war.

Stroschen, Valerie A., and Thomas J. LaPointe. "Operation Welcome Home." *Marines* 20 (July 1991): 14–16.

"Success Behind the 'Storm' Front." *Jane's Defence Weekly* 15 (11 May 1991): 783–87.

Suit, William. "The Logistics of Air Power Projection." *Air Power History* 38 (Fall 1991): 9–20.

Swain, Richard M. "Compounding the Error." *Proceedings* 119 (August 1993): 61–62. Discusses the VII Corps' advance into Iraq.

"Take a Hit and Keep on Tracking." *Surface Warfare* 16 (May/June 1991): 12–15. Account of *Princeton* mine strike.

Taylor, R.A.K. "Naval Special Warfare Within the NAVCENT AOR." *Full Mission Profile* 1 (Fall 1992): 19–20.

Thomas, Jeffrey H. "The Fifth Fleet Stands Again." *Pull Together* 36 (Spring/Summer 1997): 6–10.

Thompson, Harry F. "Tripoli Keeps on Ticking." *Surface Warfare* 17 (January/February 1992): 14–15.

"Threading Past Danger With Friends." *Surface Warfare* 16 May/June 1991): 12. Account of *Tripoli*'s egress from mined waters following her mine strike.

Trainor, Bernard C. "Amphibious Operations in the Gulf War," *Marine Corps Gazette* 78 (August 1994): 56–60.

_____. "Regional Security: A Reassessment." *Proceedings* 118 (May 1992): 38–44.

_____. "Still Go-ing . . . Amphibious Warfare." *Proceedings* 118 (November 1992): 30–33. Discussion of why the Marines did not launch an amphibious assault during the Gulf War.

Tripp, Charles. "The Gulf States and Iraq." *Survival* 34 (Fall 1992): 43–61.

Truver, Scott C. "Exploding the Mine Warfare Myth." *Proceedings* 120 (October 1994): 36–43.

_____. "Lessons from the *Princeton* Incident." *International Defense Review* 24 (July 1991): 740–41.

_____. "The U.S. Navy in Review." *Proceedings* 121 (May 1995): 120–25.

"U.S. Navy Planes Begin Operation Southern Watch." *Bluejacket* (3 September 1992): 5.

Vallance, Andrew. "Royal Air Force Operations in the Gulf War." *Air Power History* (Fall 1991): 35–38.

Verrico, John. "Getting It There Vital to Victory." *Surface Warfare* 16 (May–June 1991): 6–7.

"Victory at Sea." *All Hands* 68 (Desert Storm Special Issue): 20–25.

Walters, Judith A. "The Year in Review: 1990." *Naval Aviation News* 73 (July–August 1991): 10–20.

Walters, Judith A., and Richard R. Burgess. "The Year in Review: 1991." *Naval Aviation News* 74 (July–August 1992): 10–25.

Watkins, James D. "The Maritime Strategy." *Proceedings* 112 (January 1986 Supplement): 2–17.

West, John C. "A Lasting Friendship Despite a Clash of Cultures." *Middle East Insight* (Special Edition, Saudi Arabia, 1995): 32–36.

Wilhelm, Ross M. "Live by the Sword, Die by the Swordsmen: Intruders at the Eye of Desert Storm." *The Hook* 19 (Summer 1991): 66–70. Desert Storm operations of *Ranger*'s CVW-2.

Withern, J.D. "In Harm's Way: Carrier Battle Group Operations Inside the Persian Gulf." Unpublished student paper. 1991. Naval War College, Newport, RI.

Yeosock, John J. "H + 100: An Army Comes of Age." *Army* 41 (October 1991): 44–58. Brief account of Third Army operations in Desert Shield/Storm.

Yurso, Joseph F. "The Decline of the Seventies." In *Naval Engineering and American Seapower*, edited by Randolph W. King. Baltimore: The Nautical and Aviation Publishing Company of America, Inc., 1989. An insightful analysis of the Defense Department's troubles as a result of the Vietnam War.

Zlatoper, Ronald J. "The War at Sea During Desert Storm." *The Hook* 19 (Fall 1991): 2–5.

Zimmeck, Steven M. "U.S. Marines in the Persian Gulf, 1990–1991: A War of Logistics: Combat Service Support in Desert Shield and Desert Storm." Draft manuscript. Marine Corps Historical Center, 1997.

Zumwalt, J.G. "Tanks! Tanks! Direct Front!" *Proceedings* 118 (July 1992): 72–80. Account of operations of Bravo Company, 4th Tank Battalion, 4th Marine Division during Desert Storm.

Index

Aba-al-Ayala, Mahdi, 217
Abrams main battle tank. *See* Vehicles,
    tanks
Abu Dhabi, 11, 77
Abu Obdaidah (Saudi Arabia), 418n.27
Acadia (AD 42), 106, 126, 127
Acree, Clifford, 312
ad-Dammam, Saudi Arabia, 71–72, 74,
    78, 123–24, 126, 134–35, 203,
    328, 361
ad-Dorra oilfield, 214–17, 224, 260, 264,
    266, 425n.190
Adelaide (Australia), 91, 95
Aden, Gulf of, 81, 88, 151
Administrative Support Unit (ASU),
    Bahrain, 16, 72, 83, 101, 104,
    129, 218, 346
Afghanistan, 12, 24, 32, 40, 357
Africa, Horn of, 89
Ahmad, Sultan Hashim, 310–11, 311
    (photo), 338
Aircraft
    aerial refueling, 50, 66, 172, 191
        (photo), 195, 203, 366–67,
        417n.21, 421n.107
        KA-6, 190, 421n.108
        KC-135, 50, 190–91, 191 (photo)
        tankers, 66, 110, 184, 219
    attack, 27, 42, 55, 67
        A-6 Intruder, 27, 79, 144, 167, 174,
            181, 183, 191 (photo), 192, 195,
            199, 221, 224, 228 (photo), 230,
            231 (photo), 240, 286, 297, 302,
            420n.76
        A-7 Corsair II, 169 (photo), 174,
            175 (photo), 199, 201 (photo),
            302
        A-10 Thunderbolt, 79, 187, 199,
            286, 348
        AV-8 Harrier, 79, 195, 235, 240–41,
            250, 294, 348
        OV-10 Bronco, 257
    bombers, 24, 27, 31, 42, 55, 67, 110,
        132, 172

B-1B, 25
B-52, 132, 172, 234, 237, 429n.21,
    429n.7
    Backfire, 31
    GR-1 Tornado, 236, 348
cargo
    C-2, 126
    C-9, 125, 132
electronic countermeasure/air early
    warning, 267
    E-2C Hawkeye, 28, 179–79, 204–5,
        230, 367
    E-3 Airborne Warning and Control
        Systems (AWACS), 63, 146, 174,
        199, 203, 357
    EA-6B Prowler, 27, 167, 174
        (photo), 191 (photo), 199, 202,
        297, 349
    EF-111 Raven, 174
    EP-3, 146
    S-3 Viking, 29, 221
    F-4G Wild Weasel, 174
fighters, 42, 55, 62, 67, 110, 267
    CF-18 (Canada), 130, 146–47, 204,
        422n.113
    F-14 Tomcat, 28, 95, 145–46, 167,
        176, 180–81, 199, 204, 207–8,
        244, 347 (photo), 348, 423n.158,
        427n.214, 243 (photo)
    F-15 Eagle, 63, 176, 180–81, 187,
        209, 240, 329, 348, 352
    F-16 Falcon, 79, 172, 187, 218,
        237–38, 286, 296, 348
    F-111, 187, 227, 240
    F-117, 145, 170, 173, 246, 348
    F/A-18 Hornet, 27, 65, 79, 95, 146,
        148, 172, 174, 176, 178–79, 180
        (photo), 181,183, 204, 206–8,
        221, 229, 237, 240, 286, 302, 349
        (photo), 349 (photo), 358, 366,
        420n.76, 423n.158
helicopters, 29, 36–38, 52, 73–76
    (photo), 77, 93 (photo), 94–95,

100–102, 104, 110, 121, 24–26, 128, 130, 184, 188, 199, 204, 224, 254, 259, 279, 285, 292, 329, 338, 364

AH-1 Sea Cobra, 196, 226, 252

AH-6 Sea Bat, 37

AH-64 Apache, 110, 290, 302, 310

CH-46 Sea Knight, 104, 126, 226, 299 (photo), 308

CH-47 Chinook, 326 (photo)

CH-53 Sea Stallion, 226, 250, 299 (photo)

CH-53E Super Stallion, 339

Cobra, 79, 229, 286, 294

Desert Duck, 218

HH-60, 121

Lynx H.A.S. Mk. III, (U.K.) 77, 93 (photo), 95, 215, 220–21, 229, 231, 260

MH-53E Sea Dragon, 36, 75, 76 (photo), 252–53, 261

OH-58D Kiowa Warrior, 213 (photo), 213–14, 216, 221, 223–25, 426n.194, 428n.229, 432n.77

Pave Low, 199

SH-3 Sea King, 77, 94, 125 (photo), 163

SH-60B Seahawk LAMPS Mark III, 29, 94, 213–16, 221, 224, 260, 428n.229

Squirrel (Australian), 83 (photo)

UH-60 Blackhawk, 29, 131, 310

Iraqi aircraft

F-1 Mirage, 36, 147, 205, 207, 209

Mi-8/17 HIP, 204

MiG-21, 178–79

MiG-23, 147, 174

MiG-25, 174

MiG-29, 179, 209

Su-24, 209

patrol and reconnaissance, 90 (photo), 267

Atlantique (France), 89

Nimrod (U.K.), 89, 221

P-3 Orion, 89, 90, 221, 427n.214

RA-3B, 145

RA-5C, 145

RF-8, 145

tankers. *See* Aircraft, aerial refueling

transports, 63, 101, 104, 110, 131–32

C-130 Hercules, 270, 272, 274

C-141 Starlifter, 50, 75

MC-130, 121, 126, 145, 237, 328, 329

unmanned aerial vehicles (UAVs), 149, 257–58, 258 (photo), 260, 294

vertical/short take-off and landing (V/STOL), 79, 241, 250

Airlift operations. *See* Logistics

Air tasking order, 168, 170, 183–92, 189–92, 194, 238–40, 302, 349–50, 437n.27

difficulties with, 420n.91, 421n.103, 424n.161

"Air Tet," 209

al-Ahmadi, Kuwait, 250, 318

al-Ansari, 217

al-Aqabah, Jordan, 86, 87, 151, 152, 343

al-Burqan, Kuwait, 283, 294

Al Fao (Iraq), 91–92

al-Faw Peninsula, Iraq, 117, 229

al-Fintas, 292, 293

al-Firdos bunker bombing, 246–47

Algeria, 11, 151

Algiers (U.S. Army), 319 (photo)

al-Hamas, Ibrahim, 245

al-Hammar, Hawr, Iraq, 309, 310

al-Husainan, Nasser, 214–18, 342 (photo)

al-Jaber, Kuwait, 181, 269, 283, 436n.13

al-Jahra, Kuwait, 269, 277, 285, 296, 299

al-Jubayl, Saudi Arabia, 42–43, 101, 105–7, 130, 203, 234, 267, 360–61

cargo unloading at, 134

defense of, 64–65, 70–71, 74–75, 77–78

Fleet Hospital 5, 156

naval construction forces in, 129

port security–harbor defense units in, 123–24

al-Khanjar, Saudi Arabia, 272, 273 (photo)

al-Kibrit, Saudi Arabia, 270, 272, 289

al-Kut, Iraq, 205

al-Manaqish oilfield, 227, 233, 273, 284

al-Mishab, Ras, Saudi Arabia, 234, 267, 270, 289, 330

al-Mullah, Ahmed Yousef, 346

al-Mumin, Ali Muhammad, 345 (photo)

al-Qaddafi, Muammar 62, 63 (photo), 362

al-Qaim, Iraq, 243

al-Qulayah, Ras, Kuwait, 117, 223, 226, 227, 318

al-Rashid Hotel, Baghdad, 173, 447n.126

al-Rumaila, Kuwait, 48, 72

Al Sanbouk (Kuwait), 64, 122, 213

al-Saud, Khalid Bin Sultan, 70, 310

al-Shamrani, Ayedh, 207

Altair (T-AKR 291), 98

al-Wafrah, Kuwait, 233, 270, 272–74, 282, 289

Al Wasitti (Iraq), 95

America (CV 66), 121, 136 (photo), 137, 140, 176, 235, 280, 302, 326, 350

Amiriya, 246

Amman summit, 45–46

Amnesty International, 164

Amphibious Construction Battalion 1, 64

Amphibious Group 2, 75

Amphibious Group 3, 121, 122, 289, 327, 339, 344–45

Amphibious operations, 16, 23, 28, 31, 79, 154, 192, 357, 367
    assault amphibian vehicle (AAV), 64, 65 (photo)
    Bubiyan Island, 116–18, 247, 297
    casualty concerns, 117–18, 409n.33
    Faylaka Island, 297
    in Kuwait, 52, 149–151, 237–38, 280, 294, 300
    in Saudi Arabia, 121–23
    intelligence for, 143, 244
    logistics support for, 127, 250
    Maradim Island, 226
    mine warfare, 77, 141, 263

Amphibious Squadron 5, 75, 121–22, 224, 410n.49

Amphibious Squadron 8, 339, 340

Amphibious task force (ATF), 75, 105–6, 110, 125, 126, 139, 150, 156, 189, 220, 250, 289, 344, 409n.33, 436n.6

Amuriyah (Iraq), 95, 192

Anderson, John, 286

Anderson, Michael, 174

Andrew J. Higgins (T-AO 190), 127

Andrews, William, 313 (photo)

Angola, 24

Antares (T-AKR 294), 98, 406n.141

Antiair warfare, 146, 188, 203, 208, 264, 424n.161, 434n.113

Antietam (CG 54), 60 (photo), 146–47

Antisurface warfare, 146, 219, 220, 222

Aqabah. *See* al-Aqabah, Jordan

Arab-American Oil Company, 235

Arab Cooperation Council, 45–46

Arabian Peninsula, 42, 54, 60–61, 64–66, 75, 95–96

Arabian Sea, 350, 363

Arab-Israeli Six Day War, 9

Arab "Marshall Plan," 48

Arab Shipbuilding and Repair Yard, 126

Argentina, 86, 88, 202, 219, 346, 445n.87

Ark Royal (U.K.), 412n.99

Armilla Patrol, 61

Armstrong, Douglas M., 255, 258–59

Arnett, Peter, 173, 247

Arthur, Stanley R., 182 (photo), 325, 367, 381
    air war, 168, 181–92, 194, 202–3, 227
    amphibious operations, 150, 168, 210–12, 224, 234, 252–55, 268, 277–80, 292, 297, 375–78, 436n.6
    antisurface warfare, 232, 376–80, 427n.216
    on bombing altitude, 183, 373, 419n.49, 419n.57
    carrier operations, 209, 235, 421–22n.108
    on cease-fire/troop withdrawal, 305, 313, 325–28
    command and control, 366–67, 413n.13
    command responsibilities, 16–17, 80
    composite warfare commander concept, 170
    fleet defense, 423n.154
    fleet hospital placement, 130
    on Harpoon missiles, 427n.214
    intelligence provided to, 145, 190, 226
    interservice rivalry, 184–88, 192, 194, 421n.96
    mine warfare, 149, 181, 219, 224–26, 247, 256, 263, 268, 320, 376–79
    NAVCENT reorganization, 137–39, 334–37, 350, 412–13n.106
    postwar assessments, 127, 190, 263, 268, 334, 379
    on Schwarzkopf, 194
    on terrorism, 123

Artus (U.K.), 260

Ash Shuaybah, 181, 250–54, 279, 292, 317–18

as-Salman, 290

A-Team, 95

Athabaskan (Canada), 128, 266

Atherstone (U.K.), 77

Atlantic Ocean, 24, 31

Austin (LPD 4), 339

Australia, 141, 167, 356
    amphibious operations, 250
    antisurface warfare, 219
    carrier support, 205, 210, 361, 416n.3
    combat air patrol 423n.158
    humanitarian relief operations, 338–39
    maritime interception, 88–89, 91–92, 95, 363, 445n.87

medical support, 130, 260
refueling operations, 128
replenishment, 411n.72
Avenger (MCM 1), 75, 76 (photo), 142, 262–63, 266
Avenger-class, 384
"Axis Sally," 157
Azerbaijan, Republic of, 7
Aziz, Tariq, 48, 165, 275
Azores, 18
az-Zubayr, 88, 181, 231

Baath Party, 44, 49, 173, 218
Baba Gurgur (Iraq), 86
Bab al-Mandab, 88
Baghdad. *See* Iraq
"Baghdad Betty," 157
Baghdad Biltmore, 312
Baghdad Pact, 9
Baghdad Radio, 297
Bahrain, 146, 202–3, 235, 267, 269, 336–37
   Administrative Support Unit (ASU), 16, 72, 83, 101, 104, 129, 218, 346
   fleet hospital placement, 130, 313
   Kuwait liberation, 301, 318
   port security and harbor defense, 123–24
   postwar exercises, 344–45, 445n.87
   Scud attacks, 197
   ship repair, 126, 129
Bahrain International Airport, 313
Baker, James, 161, 165
Baldomero Lopez (T-AK 3009), 65 (photo)
Ball, John R., 218
Baltic Sea, 31
Bangladesh, 269, 327
Barbey (FF 1088), 3, 61
Barksdale, Louisiana, 417n.21
Bartram, Dave, 128 (photo)
Bases
   Abd al-Aziz Naval Base, 234
   Ali al-Salem Air Base, 301
   Andrews Air Force Base, 313
   al-Khanjar, 273 (photo)
   Diego Garcia, 4, 60, 82, 234, 267–68, 329, 350, 352
   Humanitarian Service Support Base, Silopi, Turkey, 339
   Incirlik Air Base, 339–40
   Langley Air Force Base, VA, 329
   Lonesome Dove base, 234, 271 (map)
   MacDill Air Force Base, FL, 16, 17, 35–36, 43, 111, 400n.169
   Naples, Italy, 368

   Scott Air Force Base, IL, 18
   Shaikh Isa Air Base, 129, 176
   Subic Bay, 368
Basrah, Iraq, 48, 68, 92, 181, 236, 297, 302, 309–10, 337
Battleaxe (U.K.), 64, 95
Battle damage assessment, 181, 243, 431n.43
Battle Force Yankee (CTF 155)
   air campaign, 135–37, 169–70, 183, 183, 186–90, 188–89, 194, 198, 202–4, 204, 210, 212, 219, 235, 243, 243–44, 255, 367, 421n.96, 421–22n.108
   command structure, 139, 139, 170
   intelligence, 145
   Iranian threat, 147
   operational area, 176–77, 176–78
Battle Force Zulu (CTF 154)
   air campaign, 169–70, 183, 186–90, 194, 202–4, 210, 212, 219, 222, 236, 240, 243–44, 255, 367, 421n.96, 421–22n.108
   command structure, 139
   intelligence, 145
   Iranian threat, 147
   operational area, 176–77, 235
Battle of Bubiyan Channel, 231. *See also* Bubiyan Turkey Shoot
Battle of Medina Ridge, 303
Battle of the Marne, 134
Battle of Wadi al-Batin, 302
Bayonne, NJ, 331
Beaufort (ATS 2), 126, 266, 316
Beaumont, Texas, 99
Bedouins, 119, 270
Belgium, 133
   humanitarian relief operations, 338–39
   in Tanker War, 33, 356
   logistics, 365
   maritime interception, 86, 88, 445n.87
   mine warfare, 320–24, 358, 442n.29
Belknap-class cruisers, 208
Bernsen, Harold J., 36
Berryman, Michael, 312
Bever, Lynn, 108
Bien, Lyle, 186–88, 421n.107
Bill, David S., III, 218, 253, 255
Biological weapons. *See* chemical/biological weapons
Bitburg, Germany, 132
Black Hole team, 113, 144, 187
Black Sea, 31
Blanzola, Cheryl, 156–57

Blue (DD 744), 81
Blue Ridge (LCC 19), 82, 89, 129, 137–38,
    163, 181, 242, 250–51, 254,
    412n.103
Blue-water operations, 23, 80, 218
Bomb damage assessment (BDA),
    242–44, 258, 417n.21
Boomer, Walter E., 71 (photo), 368. *See
    also* United States, Armed Forces,
    Marine Corps
  air campaign, 114, 148, 185, 190, 257
  amphibious operations, 254, 378,
    436n.6
  on Arthur, 137–38
  casualty concerns, 328
  chemical weapons concerns, 282
  command responsibilities, 74, 82
  doctrine, 422n.113
  ground campaign, 118, 130, 134,
    149–51, 269–70, 277, 282,
    294–300
  on Iraqi military, 70, 74. 402n.35,
    409n.37
  Kuwait liberation, 380–81
  on redeployment, 330, 382
  Seabees, 107–8, 273–74
Boorda, Jeremy M., 336
Bosnia, 352
Brabham, James A., 74
Brazen (U.K.), 93, 95, 152, 163, 229
Brazil, 269
Brewton (FF 1086), 60 (photo), 91–92
Bridgeton (SS), 36
Brisbane (Australia), 104, 128, 142
    (photo), 167, 209, 210 (photo)
Briscoe, Brad, 295
Brooks, Dennis M., 35–36
Brooks, Thomas, 51, 89, 142–43, 145,
    424n.176, 431n.43
Brown, Harold, 23
Bubiyan Island, 48–49, 117, 194, 207,
    212, 228–30, 247, 297, 315
Bubiyan Turkey Shoot, 228–30, 377
Bulgaria, 40
Bulkeley, Peter, 259 (photo), 259–60,
    264–67, 294, 308, 401n.20,
    433n.104
Bunker Hill (CG 52), 141, 146, 163, 203,
    204 (photo), 207–8
Burke, Delta, 163
Burns, Ken, 154
Burqan. *See* al-Burqan
Bush, George W. (and Bush administra-
    tion), 55 (photo)
  air war plans, 245–46

  casualty concerns, 164
  cease-fire, 305, 307, 310, 351, 440n.88
  chemical weapons concerns, 284
  ground war plan, 116–17
  Iraq embargo, 85, 164
  Israeli relations, 196–97
  Kuwait liberation, 301, 305, 363
  media influence to end war, 440n.88
  oil spill concerns, 194, 227
  Persian Gulf policy, 4, 40, 54–56
  postwar Iraqi relations, 348–51, 356
  prewar Iraqi relations, 46–47, 50–51,
    400n.169
  redeployment, 325, 382
  on Saddam, 297
  Saddam's assassination plot, 352
  Soviet policy, 40
  troop deployment, 64, 110–11,
    120–21, 153–54, 167–68, 410n.49
  troop morale, 161, 333
California (CGN 36), 14 (photo), 132,
    155
Camp Lejuene, NC, 121
Camp Stethem, 108
Camp Tate, 330–31
Camp Tom Orr, 129
Canada, 141, 266, 361
  air campaign, 146, 204, 234, 422n.113
  amphibious operations, 150
  humanitarian relief operations,
    338–39
  Kuwait reconstruction, 315
  logistics, 128–29
  maritime interception, 86–88, 445n.87
  medical support, 130
Cangelosi, Diana, 147
Cape Cod (AD 43), 127
Cardiff (U.K.), 215–16, 220, 229
Caribbean Sea, 24
Caron (DD 970), 226, 352
Carriers. *See* Ships, aircraft carriers
Carter, James E., 13, 16, 22–23, 27
Carter Doctrine, 13, 25, 357
Carver, Dudley C.A., 224–25
Cassara, Richard, 229–30
Casualties, U.S., 41, 143–44, 174, 197,
    280, 307, 328, 331, 433n.102
  Marine, 295 (photo), 409n.33
  Navy, 36–37, 126–27, 154, 181, 190,
    265–66, 401n.20, 409n.33
  preparations for, 105–7, 129–30, 368
Casualties, coalition, 119, 128, 164, 362,
    418n.27
Casualties, Iranian, 32, 36, 38, 302, 357

Casualties, Iraqi, 32, 115, 186–87, 225, 298, 304–7, 315 (photo), 352, 368
Cattistock (U.K.), 77, 318
Cease-fire, 304, 313, 440n.88, 441n.11
  conditions, 275–76, 305–12
  Iraqi non-compliance, 347, 351
  Palestinian/Kuwait linkage, 275–76
  Tanker War, 38
Central Command, 17–19, 40
  air war plans, 113–16, 167–68, 184, 343
  amphibious operations, 118, 367
  chemical/biological weapons, 69, 116
  command structure, 35–36, 38, 41, 78–83, 113, 350, 366–67, 397n.106
  ground war plans, 115–16, 242, 304, 397n.205
  intelligence provided to, 52, 69, 119, 143, 145–46, 242, 245, 268
  Iraqi equipment destruction, 440n.97
  on Iraqi forces, 67, 69–70, 73–74, 306
  maritime campaign, 43, 64–65, 77–83, 121, 149, 440n.8
  maritime interception, 85–89, 91–96
  postwar policies, 342, 359, 446n90
  redeployment of forces, 307, 325–34
  Soviet threat, 40–42
  theater (map), 6
  troop deployment, 42, 52, 56–57, 59–61, 64–65, 97, 102–4, 110, 133, 135
  on U.S. foreign policy, 399n.154
  war planning, 52, 59–61, 116–19
Central Intelligence Agency (CIA), 51–52, 54, 141, 143, 187, 242, 244, 252
Central Treaty Organization (CENTO), 9
Chancellorsville (CG 62), 352
Charleston (LKA 13), 339
"Checkmate" group, 112, 145
Chemical/biological weapons, 32, 45, 47, 69, 107, 112–13, 116, 130, 154, 165, 246, 270, 282–34, 289, 293, 311–12, 338, 341, 343, 367–68, 383, 436n.13, 437n.19
  chemical protective gear, 280, 411n.82, 415n.188
Cheney, Richard B., 55 (photo), 161, 313
  bombing missions curtailed, 247
  casualty concerns, 280
  command and control, 366
  Dugan's firing, 114
  Kuwait reconstruction, 315
  Reserves, 99, 121

  troop deployment, 4, 50, 120
  war plan briefings, 52, 54–56, 59, 113, 116
China, 37, 49, 86, 448n.16
Christensen, Ernest E., Jr., 219
CINCCENT, 115, 116, 118, 129–30, 137, 180, 186, 252, 304, 310, 336, 366
Civil War, United States, 116
Clarey, Stephen S., 84, 289
Clark, Greg, 155
Clemenceau (France), 64
Cleveland, OH, 123
Clinton, William J., 351–52, 383
Close air support (CAS) missions, 285–86, 340
CNN (Cable News Network), 173, 199–200, 247
Cold War, 7, 23, 40, 172, 356–59
Cole, Ray, 283
Coleman, Melissa A., 312
Collins, Mary, 422n.113
Colombo, Sri Lanka, 91
Combat air patrol, 65, 176, 180, 181, 200, 203–4, 205, 230, 307, 348, 423n.158
  Navy, 423n.158
  Whiskey 1, 146
  Whiskey 2, 146–47
  Whiskey 4, 207
Combat Logistics Force (CLF), 102–4, 124–25
Combat search and rescue (CSAR), 121–22, 125, 231, 339, 366
Comfort (T-AH 20), 97, 105–6, 106 (photo), 128, 129–30, 326, 333, 368, 433n.102
Command and control, coalition
  air defense communications, 146–47
  air power, 114–15
  antisurface warfare, 218
  maritime interception, 86–88, 363
  mine warfare operations, 320, 322
  multidimensional naval attacks, 18–20, 24, 35–36, 38, 255, 366–67
  naval commander rotations, 259, 379
  in Operation Earnest Will, 404n.83
  rotation of U.S. commanders, 256
Command and control, Iraqi
  coalition attacks on, 113, 173–74, 183, 208, 234, 258, 280, 282, 351, 358
Communications, Iraqi, 27, 43, 113, 236–37, 244, 309
Communications, U.S., 62, 85, 87, 147, 159–61, 205, 288, 339, 362
  amphibious operations, 292

coalition compatibility, 19, 129, 356
Contingency Theater Automated
    Planning System (CTAPS), 349
countermeasures, 27, 43
improvements in, 348–49
Kuwaiti, 296
medical support, 130
Mobile Communication Team, 122
problems with, 127, 200, 203, 222,
    264–65
U.S. Armed Forces Radio and
    Television Service, 159
Composite warfare commander (CWC)
    concept, 30, 31, 168–69, 170, 218,
    222, 356
Computer-Aided Force Management
    System (CAFMS), 188, 420n.90
Congress, U.S., 38, 151
appropriations, 22, 31, 330
authorizes military force against Iraq,
    165, 398n.119
Cheney address to, 59
on service rivalries/cooperation, 19
Constellation (CVA 64), 20
Construction Battalion Units 411 and
    415, 107–8
Contingency Theater Automated
    Planning System (CTAPS), 349
Coontz (DLG 9) (photo), 25
Cordner, L. G., 104
Cornhusker State, 133
Cornum, Rhonda L., 312
Coronado (AGF 11), 79
Costen, William, 181
Courier, 127
Cowpens (CG 63), 352
Craig, Chris, 138, 253–59, 413n.111
Crist, George B., 35–36, 397n.106
Crooks, Richard, 101
Crowe, William J., Jr., 33, 35–36, 114
Cuba, 24, 85
Cubi Point Naval Air Station,
    Philippines, 105
Culligan, Robert, 218
Cunard Princess, 161
Curts (FFG 38), 213, 224–26, 260, 377
Cuxhaven, Germany, 133
Czechoslovakia, 40

Damage control training, 413n.111
Darwin (Australia), 91–93, 95, 341
    (photo)
Dasman Palace (Kuwait), 52
David R. Ray (DD 971), 3, 61
D-Day, 249
Deconfliction, 203, 205, 424n.161

Defense Department U.S., 122, 315, 330,
    350
Defense Intelligence Agency, 142, 148,
    242, 244, 268, 306
Defense Logistics Agency, 18
Defense Mapping Agency, 170
DeGolyer, Everette Lee, 7, 8, 11
De la Billiere, Peter, 74, 196, 408n.6,
    409n.33, 412n.99
Delaney, William, 286
Denmark, 86–88, 101, 219, 445n.87
Deptula, David, 234
Dhahran, Saudi Arabia, 70, 343
    defense of, 78
    troop deployment to, 63, 77
Diana (Spain), 152
Dietz, Thomas, 280
Direct Support Command, 270, 287
DiRita, Larry, 208
Djibouti, 64, 89
Dmitriy-Furmanov (Soviet Union), 152
Doha, Qatar, 146
Dokman, William, 104 (photo)
Dongola (Cyprus), 86
Donnell, Joseph S., III, 401n.20
Donovan, Francis R., 97–99, 132–35, 330
Dotson, George, 333
Douhet, Giulio, 112
Dubai, 11, 126
Duffy, Philip F., 35
Dugan, Michael A., 114, 170, 172,
    409n.16
Dulverton (U.K.), 77
Dumas, Roland, 348
Dupleix (France), 64
Dwight D. Eisenhower (CVN 69), 4, 5, 22,
    61, 64, 73, 347

Eastern Mediterranean, 362, 369
East Germany, 40, 133
Egypt, 132, 344
    3d Egyptian Mechanized Division,
        134–35, 269, 290
    4th Egyptian Armored Division,
        134–35
    coalition support, 124, 134, 140
    in Kuwait reconstruction, 301, 315
    U.S. Navy, peacetime training in, 155
Ehlert, Norman E., 328
Eisenhower, Dwight D., 42
Electronic countermeasures, 27, 174
Electronic warfare (EW), 174, 203
Embargo, 225, 122
    command and control, 363
    goals of, 82–83
    humanitarian nature of, 83, 151

Iraqi evasion attempts, 91–95, 151–53
rules of engagement, 87, 89, 93
success of, 64, 96, 151–53
UN authorization for, 83, 85–87, 91
England (CG 22), 3, 61, 85
Engstad, Philip, 146
Environmental Protection Agency, 227
Ethiopia, 24
Euphrates River, 236, 292, 303, 348
European Task Unit, 322
Exercises, 140–41
Imminent Thunder, 150
Indigo Anvil, 346
Internal Look 90, 43, 52, 81, 359
Ivory Justice, 50–51, 360
Red Reef III, 345
"Reforger" (Reinforcement of
Germany), 131, 344
"Remefer," 344
Sea Soldier III, 150
Sea Soldier IV, 150
Team Spirit, 97
Explosive Ordnance Disposal, 260–63,
314–20, 325, 340, 357, 361
Mobile Unit 2, 315–16
Mobile Unit 5, 71–72
Mobile Unit 6, 316 (photo)
Mobile Units 3 and 9, 72

Fahd, King, 51–56, 59, 227, 310, 404n.83
Fallon, NV, 139
Family Service Centers, 161
Faw Peninsula. *See* al-Faw Peninsula
Faylaka Island, 219
amphibious operations, 254–61,
279–80, 297
bombing of, 260–61, 266–67, 268, 279
intelligence on, 254
Iraqi defense of, 268, 308
Feely, John, 52
Fife (DD 991), 128, 152
Fifth Eskadra (Soviet Union), 24
Finger, Thomas J., 333
Fintas. *See* al-Fintas
Firdos. *See* al-Firdos bunker bombing
Fire support area (FSA), 251, 259
Fire support coordination line (FSCL),
285–86, 302, 437n.27
"Five-Day War," 304
Fleet Coordinating Group, 83, 139, 186
Fleet Hospitals, 367
5, 105, 107–8, 109 (photo), 129–30,
156, 295 (photo), 295
6 and 15, 130–31
"Flying Dutchman," 133–34

Fogarty, William, 258
as Commander Middle East Force, 85
as Commander Maritime Intercep-tion
Force, 83–84, 88, 92, 139
combat air patrol missions, 146–47
command and control, 255, 379,
432n.77
exercises, 50
mine countermeasures, 77, 251, 259,
266–67
Forbes, G. T., 219–20, 222, 224, 232
Forcier, Jean-Yves, 128 (photo)
Ford, Gerald, 22, 23
Forrestal (CV 59), 190, 443n.38
Fort Dix, NJ, 130
Fort Stewart, GA, 77
Forward logistics support sites (FLSSs),
105
Forward-looking infrared system (FLIR),
196, 224, 240
Fox, Mark I., 178–80 (photo), 181
France, 12, 61, 344, 362
6th Light (Daguet) Armoured
Division, 135, 269, 290
air campaign, 143, 219, 348–49, 351
amphibious operations, 150
ground war, 269, 274, 277, 290
humanitarian relief operations,
338–39
Kuwait reconstruction, 315–16
logistic operations, 411n.72
maritime interception, 54, 86–89,
445n.87
mine countermeasures, 320–24, 358,
442n.29
sealift, 135
Tanker War, 33, 356
Franke, Kelly, 125 (photo)
Franks, Frederick M., Jr., 133, 290–91,
296–97, 302–3, 436n.13
"Freedom Zero-One," 313
Friendly fire, 189, 208, 216–17, 300
Frix, Robert S., 315
Frost, David E., 219
Fujayrah, UAE, 105, 126, 346
Fulda Gap, Germany, 347

Gallagher, John, 91
Gates, Robert, 116
Gaza Strip, 85
G-Day, 56–57, 273–74, 279–83, 285, 288,
290, 292, 365, 437n.19
Gee, George N., 84, 141 (photo), 154,
183, 188, 203

General Headquarters, Iraq. *See* Republican Guard.
Geneva, Switzerland, 165
George Washington (CVN 73) battle group, 352–33
Germany, 40, 62, 107, 131–34, 362, 365
  humanitarian relief operations, 338–39
  mine countermeasures, 320, 442n.29
Gibraltar, 23
"Glasnost," 40
Glaspie, April, 51, 360
Global Positioning System (GPS), 142, 196, 261
Globokar, Susan, 108 (photo)
Glosson, Buster C., 113, 144–45, 181, 192, 241–42, 418n.40
Gloucester (U.K.), 128, 220, 229, 293–94
Gnehm, Edward, 318 (photo)
Golan Heights, 275
Goldsborough (DDG 20), 91–93
Goldwater, Barry, 19
Goldwater-Nichols Department of Defense Reorganization Act of 1986, 19–20, 142
Gorbachev, Mikhail, 40, 275
Gordon, Michael, 409n.33, 434n.113, 436n.6 and n.13
Gray, Alfred M., Jr., 134, 161, 251, 378, 409n.37
Great Bitter Lake, Egypt, 56
Great Wheel, 274. *See* Left hook plan
Greece, 7, 47, 86–88, 445n.87
Green, Kevin P., 3
Greenland–Iceland–United Kingdom (GIUK) gap, 30
"Green water" war, 168
Grenada, 19, 42, 153, 357
Grieve, David J., 253, 255, 433n.104
  amphibious operations, 258–59
  mine countermeasures, 75, 77, 141–42, 251, 264–67
Griffith, John R., 250, 303, 315
Ground war, 50, 69, 269–74, 277–80, 282–304, 397n.205, 429n.7
  casualty estimates, 115
  Iraqi combat effectiveness, 241–45
  naval support for, 70, 73, 116–20, 151, 168, 233–36, 247, 256, 269, 279–80, 288–89, 292–94, 297–98, 300–302
  troop deployment, 55–56, 61, 63–65, 70, 133–35
Guadalcanal (LPH 7), 339 (photo)
Guam, 18, 63, 297, 329, 352

Gulf Cooperation Council (GCC), 72–73, 82, 101, 222, 227, 256, 342–46, 361, 365
Gulf Maritime Commanders Conference, 346
GULFO, 344
Gulfport, MS, 327
Gulf War Air Power Survey, 198, 421n.103
Gyroscopic inertial guidance systems, 170

Haifa, Israel, 154, 255
Haiphong, Vietnam, 448n.13
Hamas, Ibrahim. *See* al-Hamas, Ibrahim
Hammurabi Division, 309
Handshoe, David Lee, 91
"Hanoi Hanna," 157
Harbor Defense Command (CTG 161.9), 72
Hardisty, Huntington, 81–82
Harry W. Hill (DD 986), 127
Hart, Alan, 295–96
Hart, Basil Liddell, 30
Hassayampa (AO 145), 20
Hawaii, 41, 343, 359
Hawr al-Hammar. *See* al-Hammar, Hawr
Hays, Ronald, 397n.106
Hayward, Thomas B., 27, 30
Heidenrich, John G., 246
Hendrickson, Dean M., 139–40
Heng Chung Hai (China), 86
Herald (U.K.), 77, 262
Hercules mobile base, 38
Hewitt (DD 966), 352
H-Hour, 170, 173, 416n.3
Highway 8, 290
"Highway of Death" ("Highway to Hell"), 297–98, 300, 440n.88
Hill, Stephen P., 230
Hitt, John, 302
Hoar, Joseph P., 348, 350
Holden, Tim, 436n.10
Holland, 89, 128
Holliman, John, 173
Holloway, James L., III, 20–21, 23, 25, 27, 30
Holy war. *See* Jihad
Hone, Thomas C., 423n.136
Hontz, Edward B., 264–66, 433n.107
Hope, Bob, 163
Hopkins, John I., 64–65, 74, 151
Hormuz, Strait of, 78–79, 361, 397n.106
  coalition forces in, 33, 35, 43, 88, 129, 151
Horne (CG 30), 121, 434n.113

Horner, Charles, 115 (photo), 137, 173,
    366, 413n.113
  air campaign, 73, 82–83, 111–14, 146,
    168, 178, 181, 184–90, 207, 212,
    220, 229, 234, 236, 246, 366,
    370–71, 424n.176, 429n.7
  defends Schwarzkopf on cease-fire,
    441n.11
  doctrine, 422n.113
  embargo success, 383
  interservice rivalries, 192, 374–75,
    419n.57, 421n.96
  route packages, 138
  Scud hunt, 423n.136
Humanitarian relief operations, 307,
    339–40
Hungary, 40
Hunt, William, 147–48, 154, 415n.188
Hunt-class mine hunters (U.K.), 77,
    262–64, 361
Hunter, Guy, 312
Hurghada, Egypt, 124, 132, 346
Hurworth (U.K.), 77
Husainan, Nasser. *See* al-Husainan,
    Nasser
Hussein, King (Jordan), 45–47, 51, 87
Hussein, Saddam, 4, 32, 68, 337, 368. *See
    also* Iraq
  Amman speech, 45–46
  background, 43–44
  Bush assassination plot, 352
  Bush characterization of, 50, 164,
    175–76, 297
  Glaspie meeting, 51, 360
  hostage release, 164
  human rights violations, 44–47, 84–85,
    164–65
  international economic demands,
    45–46, 48, 275
  jihad threats, 84–85
  military miscalculations, 45, 47, 69,
    196, 304
  Schwarzkopf on, 304
  terrorist threats, 51, 227, 311
  on United States, 46
  U.S./global opinion of, 46–47, 51,
    53–54, 59, 62, 84, 160, 164, 275,
    304–5, 353, 383
  "window of opportunity," 70, 74, 79
  world power dreams, 45–46
Ibn Khaldoon (Iraq), 151
"Ice Cube," 296
"Ice Tray," 296
Identification Friend or Foe, 180–81, 208
Imperial Iranian Gendarmerie, 41

Impervious (MSO 449), 75, 262–63, 266
Inchon, 117, 250
Independence (CV 62), 3, 50, 61, 64, 95,
    121, 137, 348–50, 368
Independence battle group, 4, 73, 78–79,
    81, 360
Indian Ocean, 4, 15, 35, 64, 350, 357
  Soviet naval presence in, 9, 24
  U.S. naval presence in, 14, 16, 35, 102,
    358
Intelligence, U.S., 119, 142–45, 348
  1st Surveillance, Reconnaissance and
    Intelligence Group, 227, 242, 300
  air campaign, 143, 170, 172, 185,
    191–92, 203, 352
  on chemical weapons, 69, 107, 246
  collection methods, 242–44, 414n.133
  collection problems, 145–46
  for amphibious operations, 143, 219,
    252, 254, 268
  on Iraqi equipment, 244–45, 274, 327
  on Iraqi air force, 178, 209, 424n.176
  on Iraqi infantry, 49, 226, 277
  on Iraqi mine warfare, 219–20,
    223–24, 263–64, 322, 433n.104
  on Iraqi threat to Kuwait, 52, 352–53
  Joint Intelligence Center, 142
  Joint Intelligence Liaison Element, 89
  Military Intelligence Board, 142,
    145–46
  Office of Naval Intelligence, 142–43
  Operational Intelligence Center, 89
  on Scuds, 197, 422n.132
Internal Look 90, 43, 52, 81
International Atomic Energy Agency, 347
Interservice cooperation, 23
  air tasking order, 188, 191–92, 234
  intelligence gathering, 143
  logistics operations, 18–19, 65–66
  troop deployment, 131
Interservice rivalries, 117, 190, 255,
    421n.96
  aerial refueling, 191–92
  air tasking order, 187–88, 190–92
  command and control, 18–20, 35–36,
    38, 114–15
  Navy/CENTCOM relations, 80–83,
    145
Iowa (BB 61) (photo), 26, 28, 401n.20
Iowa-class battleships, 256
Iran, 117, 205, 338, 361, 368. *See also*
    Iran-Iraq War
  aircraft losses, 39, 302, 357, 424n.176
  casualties, 32, 36–88, 302, 357
  hostage crisis, 19, 356

Imperial Iranian Gendarmerie, 41
Iraqi aircraft in, 209, 231, 424n.176
jihad threats, 149
oil industry, 7, 32–33, 37–38, 39
    (photo), 67, 149
Revolutionary Guard, 32
Tanker War, 33, 36–38, 61–62
threat to U.S. fleet, 147, 149, 189, 222,
    256
U.S. foreign policy, 5, 7, 9, 11, 17, 40,
    46
Iran Ajr (Iran), 37 (photo)
Iranian Exclusion Zone, 78
Iran-Iraq War, 32, 43, 69, 146, 361,
    409.37
    chemical warfare, 32, 154
    mine warfare, 260, 322, 325
    Navy role in, 355, 359
Iraq. *See also* Hussein, Saddam
    air assault on, 171 (map)
    casualties, 32, 186, 285, 298, 304,
        306–7, 352, 368
    cease-fire, 275, 311, 347–48, 350–52
    chemical/biological weapons, 45, 47,
        69, 107, 112, 113, 116, 130, 154,
        165, 246, 270, 274, 280, 283–84,
        341
    command and control, 113, 172–75,
        183, 208, 234, 258, 280, 282, 351,
        358
    communications network, 113, 183,
        195, 198, 309
    economy and debt, 43, 45–46, 48, 51,
        53, 58, 275, 311, 337, 347
    electric power facilities, 113, 143, 168,
        173, 183, 337, 417n.19
    embargo, 54–55, 83–95, 83–96, 115,
        153, 164, 342, 362–33
    foreign nationals, 85, 305, 312, 347
    General Headquarters, 49
    global disapproval of, 96, 153
    human rights violations, 44–45, 47,
        84–85, 164, 183, 338
    Israeli relations, 47–48
    National Assembly, 312
    nuclear weapons, 45, 47, 113, 154,
        168, 172, 196, 198, 341
    oil faciities/industry, 7, 32, 43, 48, 54,
        69, 88, 113, 183, 198, 214–17,
        220
    oil spill, 227, 314
    psychological warfare, 157–58
    Revolutionary Command Council,
        275, 311
    targets in, 170–76, 185–86, 188–89,

        193–99, 202, 219–21, 245–47,
        302, 417n.21
    terrorism, 123, 142, 227, 308–9, 311
    U.S. prewar diplomacy, 9, 46–47, 51
    Vietnam War lessons, 237
Iraq, armed forces of, 286. *See also*
        Republican Guard
    10th Armored Division, 302
    1st Mechanized Division, 269
    5th Mechanized Division, 227
    3d Armored Division, 227, 269
    6th Armored Division, 269
    440th Marine Brigade, 308
    45th Infantry Division, 290
    48th Infantry Division, 290
    5th Mechanized Division, 227, 250,
        269
    air campaign, 52, 69–71, 114, 172,
        175–76, 181, 189, 195, 202,
        205–8, 206 (map), 209, 143
        146–47
    aircraft losses, 178, 204, 207, 209
    amphibious attacks, 52
    artillery, 285, 292, 306, 351–52
    coalition attacks on, 167–70, 174–76,
        178–81, 183, 198–99, 198–200,
        202–3, 209, 219–24, 229–232
    equipment destruction, 286, 440n.97
    ground divisions, 271 (map)
    III Corps, 269, 295, 310
    in Kuwait, 48–49, 51–54, 56, 73, 79, 81,
        113, 116, 118, 225–26, 241–42,
        247–50, 249 (photo), 251
        (photo), 254, 277, 292–304, 360,
        361, 428n.272
    in Saudi Arabia, 74, 202, 227
    intelligence on, 67, 172, 185, 191, 192,
        209, 222–23, 225–26
    IV Corps, 269
    Khafji attack, 149, 227–29, 256–67
    leadership assessment, 286–87
    military facilities, 112, 173–74, 176,
        183, 192, 195, 198, 201 (photo),
        209, 279, 289, 292, 352
    military power, 42, 49, 66–71, 73–74,
        88, 118 361
    mine warfare, 68, 75, 148, 181, 192,
        205, 212, 219, 223–26, 231, 233,
        235, 247–57, 277, 282
    missile warfare, 154, 197–98, 202, 214,
        217, 220, 223, 229, 368, 447n.126
    oil platform warfare, 212, 215–17, 220,
        266, 425n.90, 426n.198, 426n.198
    performance assessment, 208, 210,
        218, 220, 223

radar systems, 113, 153
Saddam Line, 233–34, 272, 277
Scud missiles, 197, 422n.132, 423n.135
Stark attack, 3, 36, 67
supergun, 47
troop deployment, 52, 54
troop morale/desertion, 217, 237,
    245, 279, 282, 286, 289, 298, 304,
    308–9, 409n.37, 436n.13
Isfahan, Iran, 38
Iskenderum, Turkey, 339
Islam, 55
Islamic coalition forces, 310
Israel, 275
    Iraq threat to, 45, 47–48, 112
    Patriot antimissile deployments to,
        197–98
    Scud attacks on, 196
    U.S. diplomacy towards, 46, 196–97
    Yom Kippur War, 11, 24
Istiqlal (Kuwait), 64, 122, 213–18, 377
Italy, 47, 141
    combat air patrol, 205, 219
    humanitarian relief operations,
        338–39
    in Tanker War, 33, 356
    maritime interception, 47, 86–88,
        445n.87
    mine countermeasures, 320–21, 324,
        442n.29
    troop deployment, 132
Iwo Jima (LPH 2), 126–27, 162 (photo),
    297

Jaber. See al-Jaber
Jackson, David, 263
Jacob Van Heemskerck (Netherlands), 128,
    212 (photo)
Jahra. *See* al-Jahra
Japan, 54, 85, 101, 132, 364–65
    mine countermeasures, 320–24,
        442n.29
Japanese Maritime Self-Defense Force,
    322
Jarrett (FFG 33), 37, 213, 260, 292–93,
    418n.27
Jason (AR 8), 126
Jebel Ali, United Arab Emirates, 126, 346
"Jedi Knights," 115–16
Jenkins, Harry W., Jr., 84, 117–18, 139, 150,
    226, 250, 252–53, 279–80, 292,
    379, 436n.6, 436n.6
Jeremiah, David E., 50, 153
Jiddah, Saudi Arabia, 126, 132
Jihad, 84–85, 149

Jillian, Ann, 163
John A. Bole (DD 755), 81
John F. Kennedy (CV 67), 78–79, 102, 136
    (photo), 140, 172–74, 176, 326,
    367
Johnson, Hansford T., 96–97, 99, 101–2
Johnson, Jesse, 122
Johnson, Lyndon Baines, 21–22
Johnson, Michael, 107, 143, 272
Johnson, Robert L., 184, 202
Johnston, Robert B., 116
Joint Chiefs of Staff, 114, 118, 153
    caution on ground war, 50
    on Iraqi threat to Kuwait, 33, 52, 81
    Powell as chairman, 31, 40–41
    role of chairman, 20
Joint Force Air Component Commander
    (JFACC)
    air tasking orders, 184–85, 187, 189–90
    interdiction operations, 437n.27
    on Khafji battle, 229
    service rivalries, 189
Joint Forces Command East (JFC-E), 269,
    277, 279, 288–90, 292, 300,
    437n.38
Joint Forces Command North (JFC-N),
    269, 277, 290, 296, 300
Joint Surveillance and Target Attack
    Radar System (JSTARS), 297
Joint Task Force Middle East (JTFME), 3,
    4, 9, 16, 35–36, 38, 43, 50, 61, 72,
    79–80, 83, 113, 355–56, 359,
    404n.83
Joint Task Force Southwest Asia (JTF-
    SWA), 348–50
Jones, Devon, 199–200
Jordan, 9, 24, 45, 51–53, 86, 152
Joseph Strauss (DDG 16), 39
Joshua Humphreys (T-AO 188) (photo), 94
Jouett (CG 29), 60 (photo)
Jubayl. *See* al-Jubayl, Saudi Arabia
Jupiter (U.K.), 64

Kaiss, Albert L., 256, 294
Kansas City (AOR 3), 127
Karbala, Iraq, 337
Katz, Douglas A., 350, 425n.90
Kelly, John H., 47
Kelly, Patrick J., 320
Kelly, Paul X., 138
Kelso, Frank B., II, 81, 83, 135, 137–38,
    332 (photo), 335–37, 350, 366
Kendall, David W., 230
Kennedy, John F., 85

Keys, William M., 270, 279, 283–85, 295–96, 300, 305
Khafji, 123, 256, 257
  casualties in, 409n.33
  Iraq attack on, 227, 229
  mine warfare near, 149
Khalid Bin Sultan al-Saud. *See* al-Saud, Khalid Bin Sultan.
Khanaqin (Iraq), 86
Khanjar. *See* al-Khanjar
Khomeini, Ayatollah Ruhollah, 12, 46. *See also* Iran
Khruschev, Nikita, 85
Kibrit. *See* al-Kibrit
Kill boxes, 238–40, 239 (map), 285, 297
King Fahd International Airport, 274
Kingston, Robert, 138
Kirkuk, Iraq, 337
Kissinger, Henry, 24
Kitty Hawk (CVA 63), 20
Kleinsmith, Douglas, 288–89
Knowles, Brian G., 300
Kola Peninsula, Russia, 31
Korea, 220, 330, 357
  mine warfare, 263, 358
  mistreatment of captured aviators, 183
Korea, Republic of, 7–8, 98, 101, 114
Korean War, 22, 74, 99–101, 107, 285
Krulak, Charles C., 270, 272, 287
Kubbar Island, 224, 263
Kurds, 8, 69, 307, 337–40
Kurile Islands, 30
Kut. *See* al-Kut, Iraq
Kuwait, 67, 196, 198
  air campaign, 139, 146–50, 168–70, 176, 190, 202, 205, 210–31, 233–57, 262, 269, 282–86, 290–95, 367–81
  allied ground campaign, 38, 226, 247, 268–75, 277–80, 282–86, 289–91, 294–98
  American Embassy in, 300–301
  amphibious operations, 116–18, 150–51, 210, 219–20, 247, 250–60, 263, 268, 289, 292–93, 301, 374–80
  and Iraqi armed forces, 3–4, 48–56, 83–85, 111–16, 153, 163–65, 227, 229, 233–34, 241, 247–58, 250, 269–76, 292, 294–305, 360–61
  enemy troop evacuation, 297–300, 302, 304, 306, 371
  industrial facilities, 33, 85, 183, 252, 254, 269–70, 272, 283, 314–15, 378

Kuwaiti Girls Science High School, 317
  liberation of, 189, 277, 291 (map), 301–6, 369, 380
  marines, 122
  military facilities, 85, 181–83, 256–58
  mine warfare, 148, 219, 223–25, 233, 245, 247–56, 258–59, 283, 289, 297, 305, 311, 314, 317–18, 376–78
  navy, 122, 346
  oil industry, 7, 11, 33, 48, 52, 54, 88, 192, 226–27, 314
  postwar maritime interception, 343n.87
  reconstruction, 314–21, 382
  support to coalition forces, 101, 132
  U.S. diplomacy, 50–51, 194, 344
Kuwait City, 178, 235, 265, 309–10
  air campaign, 176–78, 301
  coalition ground campaign, 269–70, 277, 283, 288, 294–304
  industrial facilities, 269, 277, 294–96
  Iraqi armed forces in, 250, 269–70, 292, 294–305
  Kuwait International Airport, 277, 283, 294–95, 298–301, 320
  liberation, 291 (map), 300–306, 306 (photo)
  military facilities, 269, 279, 301
  police headquarters, 301
Kuwait Theater of Operations (KTO), 113, 168, 176, 190, 202, 233–34, 243, 276

Landing Force (CTF 158), 139, 150
LaPlante, John B.
  amphibious operations, 31, 117–18, 127, 139, 143, 154, 156, 226, 250–53, 280, 292–93, 379–80, 436n.6, 253 150
  on chemical weapons, 415n.188
  interservice rivalries, 255
  troop morale/discipline, 160
La Salle (AGF 3), 3, 61, 71, 72 (photo), 82, 113, 129, 147, 163, 267, 318, 335–37, 346, 349–50
Lautenbacher, Conrad C., 186
Law of Land Warfare, 425n.90
Law of Naval Warfare, 425n.90
Leader (MSO 490), 75, 262, 266
Lebanon, 9, 19, 40, 46, 108, 143, 275, 356–57
Ledbury (U.K.), 77

Leenhouts, John, 173–74, 178, 201 (photo)
Left hook plan, 234, 247, 254, 274, 296
Leftwich (DD 984), 224–26, 377
Lehman, John F., 13, 19, 21 (photo), 23, 31, 38, 256
LeMay, Curtis, 112
Lend Lease program, 5
Leno, Jay, 162 (photo), 163
Leslie Lykes, 331, 444n.59
Less, Anthony, 36, 43, 404n.83
Leyte Gulf (CG 55), 208, 352, 359
Libya, 11, 53, 62, 82, 362, 401n.10
Logistics, 138
    administrative support for, 43, 61, 77, 80–83, 97–98, 102–4, 108–110, 127, 128–29, 219–20, 287
    airlift, 17–18, 36
    bases, 358
        al-Khanjar, 273 (photo)
        al-Kibrit, 270, 272, 289
        shore-based sites, 367
    British systems, 42, 61–63, 66 (photo), 96–97, 105, 116, 121, 131–32, 184
    ground campaign, 119, 250–52, 285
    Iraqi logistical operations, 49, 73, 279
    maritime prepositioning, 17–19, 50, 63, 66, 105
    redeployment, 325, 327–31
    replenishment at sea, 102–4, 106 (photo), 148, 345, 367, 411n.72, 429n.7
    roll on/roll off vessels, 8, 64, 70, 88, 97–98, 100, 364
    sealift, 18, 41–2, 61–63, 70, 77–78, 96–102, 99 (photo), 104, 116, 122, 132, 318, 318, 326 (photo), 352, 357–58, 364–66, 444n.59
    supplies, 65–66, 70, 97–98, 101–5, 196
    Task Forces 63 and 73, 102
    underway replenishment, 127, 129, 358, 411n.72
Lombardi, Vince, 124
London (U.K.), 292
Long, Robert L.J., 16, 30
Long Beach, CA, 121
Louisiana, 234
Louisville (SSN 724), 183
Louisville, KY, 330
Luck, Gary E., 73, 296
Luti, William J., 172
Luxembourg, 132, 338–39
Lynch, Thomas C., 73, 84

MacArthur, Douglas, 309–10
McCaffrey, Barry, 303, 309

McClellan, George B., 116
McEwen, Bruce, 265
McKee (AS 41), 127
Mackley, Paul, 240
McNamara, Robert S., 17
Macdonough (DDG 39), 163
McPeak, Merrill A., 153, 172
McRaney, Gerald, 163
McSwain, Donald W., 187
Madani, Yousef, 59–60
Madura (SMIT), 126
Mahan, Alfred Thayer, 27, 359, 377
Mahmud, Salah Abud, 310
Major, John, 348
Manama, Bahrain, 361
Manama International Airport, 346
Manaqish. *See* al-Manaqish
Manchester (U.K.), 434n.113
Manifah oilfield, 207
Mansoura I (Iraq), 341 (photo)
Maradim Island, 224–27, 263
March, Daniel P., 84, 139
    air campaign, 367, 424n.168
    on air tasking orders, 185, 188–89
    command concerns, 412n.103, 413n.113, 420n.76, 421n.96
    command responsibilities, 141, 170, 186–87, 212
    on Glosson, 181, 418n.40
    intelligence gathering, 145, 192, 226
    on Iraqi threat, 202–3, 209
    logistics, 128, 411n.72
    on Tomahawk missiles, 416n.3
Marfiak, Thomas F., 146, 203–4, 208
Maritime Administration, 97, 358
Maritime Interception Force (CTF 152), 139
Maritime interception operations, 137, 151–53, 164
    fast roping, 94, 300, 363–64
    in temporary cease-fire, 307–8, 343, 445n.87
Maritime prepositioning, 17–19, 50, 63–66, 105, 121, 132, 252, 357
    Maritime Prepositioning Force, 328–9
    Maritime Prepositioning Squadrons 1, 2, and 3, 329
Maritime Strategy, 359
Martin, Steve, 163
Marvin Shields (FF 1066), 128
Masirah, Oman, 89, 95
Masirah Island, 126, 127
Mattis, Jim, 285
Mauz, Henry H., Jr., 71 (photo)
    air defenses, 146
    amphibious operations, 117–18

casualty concerns, 144
and CENTCOM, 80, 83
command and control, 114–15, 138, 147
command responsibilities, 3
carrier operations, 72, 81–85, 123, 137, 255, 412n.103, 412–13n.106
embargo operations, 86–87, 91–94
on Iraqi threat, 73, 135
on Iraq mine operations, 263
on mine warfare, 75, 77
service rivalry, 187
Mecca, Saudi Arabia, 55, 157, 160, 164
Medical support, casualties treated
by Navy units, 125
corpsmen, 106–7, 340, 367
dentists, 106–7, 340
doctors, 340
equipment, 411n.82
fleet hospitals/ships, 105, 107–8, 109 (photo), 129–31, 156–57, 197, 260, 270, 295, 325, 333, 360, 367, 381, 433n.102
for Kurds and Shiites, 338–39
for POWs, 426n.198
naval hospital, 273
Navy Medical Research Institute, 107
Navy reservists, 105–6, 367
nurses, 106, 156–57
Medina, Saudi Arabia, 55, 157, 164
Medina Armored Division, 303
Mediterranean Sea, 31, 102, 358, 416n.2
Mediterranean Strike Group (CTG 150.9), 139
Merchant Marine Academy, 99
Merchant mariners, 97, 99–100, 106
Mercy (T-AH 19), 97, 105, 129–30, 313, 433n.102
Mexico, Gulf of, 24
Middle East, 8–10, 18, 41, 42, 52
Middle East Force (U.S. Navy), 125, 138–39, 267, 350, 355, 359
Middle Shoals Buoy, 37
Midway (CV 41), 121, 128, 140, 150, 207, 219, 226, 255, 280, 302, 359, 368
air operations from, 199
battle group, 79, 110
Carrier Air Wing 5, 176
in KTO, 235
in northern gulf, 212
not under JFACC control, 189
Military Airlift Command (MAC), 17, 18, 42, 61–63, 66 (photo), 96–97, 105, 121, 131–33, 184, 365. *See also* Logistics

Military Sealift Command, 17, 18, 77–78, 96–102, 116, 122, 132–35, 318, 325, 327–31, 352, 357–58, 360, 364–65, 444n.59. *See also* Logistics
Military Traffic Management Command, 18, 96–97
Military Traffic Management Command Europe, 133
Miller, Duncan E., 129
Mina ad-Doha, 318
Mina al-Ahmadi, 226–27
Mina al-Bakr, 88, 192
Mina al-Saud, 280
Mina Sulman, Bahrain, 72, 137
Mine clearing, coalition (table), 122, 141–42, 212, 248 (map), 255, 258–59, 282, 442n.29
Mine countermeasures, coalition, 75–77, 125, 210, 219–20, 252–55, 260–68, 307–8, 358–59, 432n.92
postwar operations, 320–25, 324 (table)
Mine warfare, coalition, 181, 192
Mine warfare, Iraq, 68, 118, 148–49, 181, 192, 205, 223–26, 231, 233, 235, 245, 247–51, 256–59, 277, 321
Mishab. *See* al-Mishab
Mission-Oriented Protective Posture (MOPP), 69, 284
Mississippi (CGN 40), 151, 152
Missouri (BB 63), 26, 33, 103 (photo), 121, 142, 256–57, 259, 266–68, 279, 289, 292–94, 294, 309–10, 326, 356, 377–78
Mitchell, Billy, 112
Mixson, Riley D., 185–88, 198, 367, 375
battle damage assessment, 243
command responsibilities, 84, 139, 140 (photo), 170
Mobile Bay (CG 53), 128, 142, 203, 205, 207–8, 218, 220, 222, 226, 424n.161
Mobile Communication Team, 122
Mobile Inshore Undersea Warfare Units (MIUWUs), 72, 123–24
Unit 108, 316
Unit 202, 123, 316
Mobley, Joseph S., 126, 160–61
Mongillo, Nick, 178–79
Montgomery, Glenn H., 225
Moore, Royal N., Jr., 74, 114, 285–86, 375
Morocco, 269
Moron, Spain, 132
Morral, Dennis G., 213–18, 221, 377, 425n.90, 426n.194, 426n.198

Moskos, Charles, 157
Mubarek, Hosni, 46–47, 50–51, 73. *See also* Egypt
Mullah, Ahmed Yousef. *See* al-Mullah, Ahmed Yousef
Mumin, Ali Muhammad. *See* al-Mumin, Ali Muhammad
Muscat, Oman, 91
Mutla Ridge, 269, 277, 299–300
Myatt, James M., 74, 270, 279, 283, 294, 298–300, 435–36n.3

Najaf, Iraq, 337
Naples, 367
Nassau (LHA 4), 161, 241, 297
Nasser, al-Hussainan. *See* al-Hussainan, Nasser
National Assembly (Iraq), 312
National Command Authorities, 61, 86, 352
National Oceanic and Atmospheric Administration, 227
National Security Agency, 142
National Security Council, 52
NATO, 18, 23–24, 62, 87–89, 129, 131, 133, 141, 153, 322, 344, 363, 365
Naval Air Station, Point Mugu, CA, 175
Naval Supply Center, Norfolk, VA, 102
Naval War College, 30
Nelson, Michael A., 348
Netherlands, 141
　air defense, 205, 219, 361, 416n.3
　humanitarian relief operations, 338–39
　in sealift, 133, 365
　in Tanker War, 33, 356
　maritime interception operations, 87, 445n.87
　mine warfare, 320–24, 442n.29
New Hampshire, 123
New Jersey (BB 62), 26
New Orleans (LPH 11), 121
Newsweek, 150
New York (SMIT), 126–27
New York, New York, 331
New Yorker magazine, 247
New Zealand, 88, 445n.87
Nicholas (FFG 47), 128, 163, 213, 215–18, 224–25, 418n.27, 425n.90, 426n.198, 428n.229
Nichols, William, 19
Niger, 269
Night-vision technology, 215, 221, 225, 302

Nimitz (CVN 68), 14 (photo), 22, 27, 443n.38
Nimitz-class carrier, 352–53
Nimrod patrol plane (U.K.), 89, 221
Nixon, Richard M. (Nixon administration), 10, 21–24
Nixon Doctrine, 10–11
Noble, Richard M., 231 (photo)
Noble Star, 105
Noriega, Manuel, 41
Normandy, 273
North Africa, 8
North Arabian Sea, 35, 50, 55, 103, 121, 127, 189, 203, 362, 416n.2
North Korea, 7–8
Norway, 31, 86, 88, 130, 219, 445n.87
Nuclear weapons, 22, 45, 47, 113, 154, 165, 304, 310–12, 341, 343, 347, 352, 356, 383, 417n.21

Oceanographic research, 97
O'Connell, Edward P., 191–92
Ogden (LPD 5), 95, 309
Oil
　American dependence on, 5, 7–9, 12, 13, 16–17
　embargo/sanctions, 54, 83–96
　importance of, 355–56
　Iraqi oil industry, 84, 88, 96, 113
　Kuwaiti oil industry, 33, 48
　Persian Gulf industry, 5, 7–11, 32, 45, 67, 69, 78, 141
　release into Gulf, 226
　Saudi Arabian industry, 70, 73, 117, 207
　Tanker War, 32–40
Okean exercises (Soviet Union), 24–25
Okinawa (LPH 3), 226, 292
"Old Breed" Marines, 270, 294, 298
Oldendorf (DD 972), 152
Oliver Hazard Perry (FFG 7), 29
Olna (U.K.), 260, 264
Omaha Beach, 249
Oman, 301
Oman, Gulf of, 9, 11, 140, 269
　coalition forces in, 33–35, 43, 61, 81, 89, 104, 151, 203
　Midway operations in, 189
　naval blockade in, 88, 95
　U.S. fleet in, 416n.2
One corps vs. two corps, 116, 118
Operation Plan 1002-88, 184
Operation Plan 1002-90, 42–43, 52, 54–60, 81, 97, 184
　objectives of, 56, 59–61

Time-Phased Force and Deployment
        Data (TPFDD), 42
Operations
    Crescent Shield, 57
    Desert Calm, 325
    Desert Dagger/Slash, 279–80
    Desert Farewell, 325
    Desert One, 31
    Desert Saber, 251–52
    Desert Scram, 325
    Desert Slash, 254
    Desert Sortie, 325–34
    Earnest Will, 33, 35–36, 38, 79, 155,
        213–14, 263, 356, 359, 404n.83,
        413n.111
    El Dorado Canyon, 82
    Instant Thunder, 112–13
    Just Cause, 436n.10
    Linebacker II, 448n.13
    Market Time, 85
    Praying Mantis, 38
    Provide Comfort, 338–39, 340
    Provide Comfort II, 340–41
    Rolling Thunder, 112
    Southern Watch, 347–50
    Stable Door, 402n.41
    Urgent Fury, 42
    Vigilant Warrior, 352
Orangeleaf (U.K.), 61
Ordnance, 68, 209
    20-lb. demolition charges, 280
    ammunition, 21, 64, 70, 71, 73, 77, 85,
        97–98, 100, 103, 107–9, 111, 153,
        164, 203, 222, 226, 270, 285, 314,
        327, 328, 330, 331, 340, 360, 367,
        401n.20
    antiaircraft artillery (AAA), 172, 173,
        174, 183
    bombs, 21, 25, 29, 31, 69, 179, 185–88,
        194–99, 227, 297, 309, 318
        Beluga bomblet dispenser, 67
        cluster, 223, 351
        GBU-12 laser guided, 240
        laser guided (LGBs), 195–96, 230,
            236, 246–47, 351
        Mark 83, 229
        Mark 84 general purpose, 79
        Rockeye, 69, 195–96, 309, 427n.214
        Skipper laser guided, 228 (photo)
    grenades, 318
    guns, 28
        5-inch, 28, 256
        16-inch, 26, 257 (photo), 356
        23mm antiaircraft, 217
        25mm chain gun, 148, 213

        40mm antiaircraft, 217
        50-caliber machine gun, 148, 214,
            225, 257 (photo)
        76mm, 224
        antiaircraft, 172, 174, 288
        M-60 machine gun, 123
        machine gun, 297
    howitzer
        D-20 152mm, 269
        GCT self-propelled, 49
        GHN-45 towed, 49
    mines, coalition, 29
        aerial, 297
        Mark 36 Destructor, 181
    mines, Iraqi, 33, 68, 71, 77, 100, 118
        antiboat/antipersonnel, 249
        chemical contact, 249
        influence, 253, 261–62
        land, 250, 309
        LUGM-145, 249, 265–66, 316
            (photo)
        magnetic, 261
        Manta acoustic/magnetic, 249, 265
        moored, 253, 261–62
        Myam, 247
        Siegeel acoustic influence, 249, 253
        Soviet M-08, 247, 249
        UDM acoustic influence, 249, 253
    missiles, coalition
        air-to-surface, 345
        antiship, 24, 27
        cruise missiles, 24, 27, 170, 356,
            417n.21
        free rocket over ground (FROG),
            240, 269
        Harpoon, 27, 29, 39, 427n.214
        HAWKS, 172
        Hellfire, 214, 216, 221, 223,
            427n.218
        high-speed anti-radiation (HARMs),
            24, 27, 174, 175, 199, 351,
            418n.27
        Maverick, 79, 194, 196, 240, 260
        Patriot, 77–78, 198, 411n.82
        Pershing II theater, 25
        Phoenix air-to-air, 28, 180
        Sea Dart surface-to-air, 294, 378
        Sea Skua air-to-surface, 221, 223,
            427n.216
        Sidewinder, 178–79, 196, 204, 207
        Sparrow air-to-air, 178–79
        standoff land attack, 195
        surface-to-air, 361
        Tomahawk (TLAM), 26–28, 64, 112,
            144–45, 167, 169 (photo), 170, 181,

183, 184, 192, 193 (photo), 245–46,
308, 318, 343, 350, 352, 356, 362,
368–89, 417n.21, 447n.126
missiles, Iraqi, 260, 286
AA-6 air-to-air, 67
AA-7 air-to-air, 67
AM-39 Exocet, 67
antiship, 100, 202
AS-30L laser guided smart, 67
ballistic, 304
Exocet, 3, 36, 67, 189, 202, 208, 229,
253, 424n.161
Franco-German Roland, 172
Magic air-to-air, 67
point-defense, 176
R-530 air-to-air, 67
SA-2, 6, 8, 9, 13, 14, 16 surface-to-
air, 172
SA-3 surface-to-air, 172, 351
SA-7 surface-to-air, 172, 225–26
Silkworm, 33, 37, 67, 69, 146, 214,
220, 229, 242, 247, 249, 253, 258,
264
Styx antiship, 62, 67
missiles, Libyan
Ottomat antiship, 62
mortars, 133, 226, 318
precision guided munitions, 367
rocket launcher, 152, 288, 314
rocket-propelled grenade launcher,
225
rockets, 69, 269, 297
2.5-inch, 214
small arms, 318
submunitions
BLU-75, 309
supergun, 47
torpedoes, 28, 29, 63
Organization of Arab Petroleum
Exporting Countries (OAPEC),
11
Organization of Petroleum Exporting
Countries (OPEC), 48
Osa II missile boat, 67–68, 230, 319
(photo)
Osirak nuclear facility, 47
Osmond, Marie, 163
Osprey-class, 384
Overseas Valdez, 104
Oxenbould, C. J., 167, 209, 416n.3

"Pachyderm Palace," 129
Pacific Command, 14, 16, 19, 35, 41, 64,
80–81

Pacific Fleet, 14, 20, 30, 35, 121, 126, 137,
343
Pagonis, William G., 134, 327, 329
Pahlavi, Muhammad Reza. *See* Shah of
Iran
Pakistan, 9, 14, 269, 350
Palestine, 8, 53, 275, 309
Palestine Liberation Organization, 53
Palisano, Joseph, 167
Panama, 41, 153, 357, 436n.10
Pan-Arab nationalism, 8
Parker, J. W., 212, 219
Parkison, "Chip," 295
Paul F. Foster (DD 964), 167, 170, 219
Pearl Harbor, Hawaii, 335, 337
Peninsula Shield, 57
Pentagon, 82, 112, 142, 145
Peterson (DD 969), 352
"Phantom army," 273
Philadelphia, PA, 127
Philippines, 122, 410n.49
Philippine Sea, 359
Pittsburgh (SSN 720), 183, 193
Point Echo, 264, 266
Pointer Sisters, 163
Poland, 40, 130, 197
Pollock, Kevin E., 207–8
Popular Army, Iraqi. *See* Republican
Guard
Portland (LSD 37), 292
Port Security and Harbor Defense, 124
Port Security–Harbor Defense
(PSHD) groups, 72
Port Security Unit (PSU) 301, 72
PSU 302, 72, 123–24, 333
PSU 303, 72
Portsmouth (VA) Naval Hospital Surgical
Team 2, 106
Port Zayed, Abu Dhabi, 77
Powell, Colin
casualty concerns, 280
caution on use of military force,
40–42, 50, 54–55, 63, 360
cease-fire, 309–10, 4441n.11
and CENTCOM, 81, 397n.105
on Dugan, 409n.16
embargo, 96
maritime interception, 91, 96
maritime prepositioning, 66
military philosophy, 154, 368
photos of, 55, 119, 162, 313
plans, 54–55, 111–14, 116, 118–20,
234, 304
on Schwarzkopf, 42
Tomahawk missiles, 144, 192

troop deployment, 50, 52, 57, 110
troop morale, 31, 161
Primakov, Yevgeny, 275
Princeton (CG 59), 264, 265–66, 267, 378, 434n.113, 448n.16
Prisoners of war, American, 183, 199–200, 312–14
Prisoners of war, coalition, 275, 305, 311–13
Prisoners of war, enemy, 217–18, 225, 226, 229, 245, 286–89, 294, 298, 306, 426n.198
Protecteur (Canada), 128
Psychological warfare, 237–38, 283, 429n.7
Pugh, John, 225
Purvis, Joseph H., 115–17, 119, 409n.33
Push CAS system, 285–86

Qaddafi, Muammar. *See* al-Qaddafi, Muammar 62, 63 (photo), 362
Qaim. *See* al-Qaim
Qaruh Island, 224, 263, 285, 377, 433n.104
Qatar, 7, 11, 61, 141, 229, 269, 301, 344–45
Quayle, Dan, 161
Quincy (CA 71), 56

Radar
    Iraqi, 143, 172, 226
        active, 67
        air defense, 113
        bombing of, 256
        deflectors, 222
        early warning, 153
        fire-control, 223
        infrared, 67. 438n.53
        installation, 347
        targeting, 293
    U.S., 123, 361
        active-radar seeker, 28, 67
        air-to-ground, 179
        combat air patrol, 205, 207–8
        computer-assisted, 28
        decoys, use of, 175
        electronic, 28
        fire control, 28
        friendly destruction of, 418n.27
        high resolution, 29
        infrared, 29, 93, 427n.218
        Joint Surveillance and Target Attack Radar System (JSTARS), 297
        point defense system, 28

positive identification radar advisory zone (PIRAZ), 146
RAM Panels, 142 (photo), 210 (photo)
    search, 28, 29, 67
    shipboard, 28, 266
    SPY-1A phased array, 28
    thermal-imaging system, 295
    warning receivers, 214
Ramsdell, Stephen U., 186
Ranger (CV 61), 121, 140, 167, 189, 192, 199, 203, 204, 212 (photo), 219, 231, 235, 302, 350, 376, 443n.38
    Air Wing 2, 176, 297
    VA-155, 181, 229–30, 240, 297
Rapid Deployment Joint Task Force (RDJTF), 16
Ras al-Mishab. *See* al-Mishab
Ras al-Qulayah. *See* al-Qulayah
Rashid Hotel. *See* al-Rashid Hotel, Baghdad
Ras Tannurah, Saudi Arabia, 205
R-Day, 325–26
Ready Reserve Force (RRF), 18, 97–99, 358, 364
Reagan, Ronald (and Reagan administration), 40, 357
    CINCENT strengthened, 19–20
    Iraq policy, 33, 46
    military build-up under, 25–26, 31
    Saudi Arabian policy, 13
Reagan Corollary, 13
Reasoner (FF 1063), 60 (photo), 95
Reconnaissance
    1st Surveillance, Reconnaissance, and Intelligence Group (SRIG), 300
    2d Force Reconnaissance Group, 300
    Armed Surface Reconnaissance (ASR), 221
    for amphibious operations, 250
    in Khafji, 123
    in Kuwait Theater of Operations, 236
    Kuwait City liberation, 277
    of oil platform, 213–15
    postwar, 339–40, 348
    Surface Combat Air Patrol (SUCAP), 221–22
    Surface Search Coordinator (SSC), 221–22
    Tactical Air Reconnaissance Pod System (TARPS), 145, 243 (photo), 244
    Team Piglet 2-1, 300
Red Cross, 161
Redeployment operations, 325–34, 443n.38

"Red" forces, 52
Regulus (T-AKR 292) (photo), 96
    (photo), 183
Regulus land attack missile program, 183
Reid (FFG 30), 3, 50, 61, 86
Reid, James A., 91
"Remefer" (Reinforcement of the Middle
    East Force), 344
Repair and salvage, 126–27
Repose (AH 16), 105–6
Republican Guard, 342, 352
    against Shiites and Kurds, 347–48
    air attacks on, 168, 240, 240, 269,
        302–4
    air defenses, 172, 176
    Hammurabi Division, 309
    in Kuwait, 52, 113, 115–16, 202, 234,
        237, 277, 303–4
    Medina Armored Division, 303
    strength, 49, 67
    Tawalkalna Mechanized Division, 302
Reserve forces, 100, 124, 326, 365
    Air Force, 110
    Civil Reserve Air Fleet, 132
    Coast Guard, 72, 123
    in welcome home celebrations, 333
    Marine, 287
    National Guard, 121
    Navy, 72, 77, 105–6, 123, 129, 130,
        132–33, 157
    temporarily assigned active duty per-
        sonnel, 77, 97
Reveille Counterattack, 296
Revolutionary Command Council, 275,
    311
Revolutionary Guard. *See* Iran
Richards, William, 147, 207
Richmond K. Turner (CG 20), 205
Rickover, Hyman G., 22–23
Ritchie, C. A., 104
Riyadh, Saudi Arabia, 119, 366,
    412n.103, 413n.113
    briefings, 112, 135–36, 280
    Scud attacks on, 197
Robert G. Bradley (FFG 49), 3, 61, 86, 86
Roberts, John, 294
Rogers, David N., 348
Romania, 40
Roosevelt, Franklin Delano, 7, 56
Rowe, Peter J., 289
Rules of engagement, 87, 89, 93–94,
    180–81, 338, 425n.90
Rumaila. *See* al-Rumaila
Russell, Terodney, 104 (photo)

Sabah, Sheik Jabir Ahmed, 48, 53. *See also*
    Kuwait
Sacramento (AOE 1) (photo), 103
Saddam Line, 233–34, 272, 277, 279, 282,
    284, 288
Safwan, 310, 338
Sagittaire (France), 322
Sahand (Iran), 39 (photo)
Saipan, 329
Saito, Christopher, 240
Sakhalin island, Russia, 30
Salvage operations, 126, 315
Sampson (DDG 10), 151
Samuel B. Roberts (FFG 58), 37, 141, 357,
    358, 413n.111
Sanborn, Russell, 312
Sanctuary (AH 17), 106
San Diego, CA, 121
San Diego Naval Hospital Surgical Team
    1, 106
San Jacinto (CG 56), 170
Saratoga (CV 60), 64, 78, 126, 136
    (photo), 139–40, 154, 155
    (photo), 160–61, 174, 191, 229,
        255, 326, 367, 400n.8
    air wings, 188
    Attack Squadron 35, 183
    Carrier Air Wing 17, 176, 200
    Fighter Squadron 103, 199
Satellites, 24, 49, 209, 243, 277
Saud, Abdul Aziz Ibn, 7
Saud, Khalid Bin Sultan. *See* al-Saud,
    Khalid Bin Sultan
Saudi Arabia
    coalition defense, 42–43, 51–61,
        65–78, 107–113, 119–22, 131–35,
        137–53, 176, 202, 226–27, 229,
        234–35, 304
    culture/religion, 157–59
    host nation support, 101–2, 105,
        122–23, 219, 269, 300, 315, 344,
        445n.87
    oil industry, 7, 88, 117, 205, 226–27,
        314, 361
    Royal Saudi Air Force, 113
    Royal Saudi Navy, 140–42
    Scud attacks on, 197–98
    U.S. prewar policy, 5, 7–11, 13, 33
Savannah, GA, 135
Sawahil (Kuwait), 122
Schwarzkopf, H. Norman, 5
Schwarzkopf, H. Norman, Jr., 41–42, 86,
    94, 158–59, 163, 331, 359, 381
    air campaign, 83, 111–15, 168, 181,
        184, 187, 210, 408n.6

amphibious operations, 75, 118,
149–51, 252, 254–56, 258, 280,
292, 409n.33
Bush briefings, 54–55, 111
casualty concerns, 118, 129–30
cease-fire, 304–5, 309–11, 338, 441n.11
chemical warfare concerns, 270, 289
command and control, 13, 86–88,
335–36, 350, 366
ground campaign, 56–57, 59–61,
64–65, 70, 116–20, 134–35, 137,
168, 194, 234, 241–42, 266,
269–70, 274, 290, 296, 434n.126
in Kuwait, 48, 51–52, 54, 302, 316–17,
376
interservice rivalries, 145, 374–75
in Vietnam, 345, 367–68
Iraqi army assessment, 286
logistics/troop deployments, 97,
101–3, 109–10, 123
maritime campaign, 78–79, 81, 86–88,
91, 96, 122, 138, 153, 404n.83,
412n.103, 412n.99, 413n.113,
414n.133, 417n.21
mine warfare concerns, 263–64, 289,
378–79, 433n.102
photos of, 55, 119, 311
redeployment, 325–28, 365, 382
Tomahawk missiles, 144, 192, 246
Scoles, John, 253
Scott (DDG 995), 86
Scowcroft, Brent, 116, 408n.6
Scud missiles, 45, 196
coalition attacks on, 168, 173, 196–98,
307
launchers, 197–98, 242, 305, 422n.132,
423n.135
Seabees, 279, 339–40, 368
Camp Tom Orr, 129
Construction Battalion Units 411 and
415, 107–8
infrastructure improvements, 105,
107–8, 157, 254, 285
logistics operations, 64, 270, 273
(photo)
Naval Mobile Construction Battalions
(NMCBs) 4, 5, 7, and 40, 107–8
Sea Island Ocean Terminal (Kuwait), 192
Sea Isle City, 37
Sea-Land Corporation, 18, 98
SEAL delivery vehicle (SDV), 263
Sealift. *See* Logistics
SEAL teams, 94 (photo), 121
amphibious operations, 224, 250, 280,
436n.10

embargo operations, 94–95, 151
harbor patrol, 71–72, 122–23
in Kuwait liberation, 301
mine warfare operations, 37, 260
search and rescue, 212–13, 217–18,
339
Teams 1 and 5, 122
Sea Plan 2000, 30
Seeb, Oman, 89, 401n.20
Sembach, Germany, 132
Senate Armed Services Committee, 244
Senegal, 269
Shah of Iran. *See* Muhammad Reza
Pahlavi
Shamrani, Ayedh. *See* al-Shamrani, Ayedh
Sharp, Grant
air campaign, 192
integration of Arab forces, 434n.126
intelligence, 51
maritime campaign, 42–43, 64–65, 73,
75–77, 80, 86, 404n.83, 412n.103
postwar equipment prepositioning,
446n.90
Saudi defense plans, 54–55, 70, 119,
402n.35
on U.S. foreign policy, 399n.154,
400n.169
Shatt-al-Arab, 49, 231
Shaw, Bernard, 173
Sheehan, John J., 251
Shiites, 8, 12, 108, 307, 337–39, 350
Ship Repair Unit, Bahrain Detachment
(CTG 151.12), 126
Ships and craft, 3, 4
aircraft carriers
aerial refueling, 190–91
air campaign, 55, 111, 167, 176–81,
209, 235, 240, 255, 341, 343–44,
348–50, 361, 366–67, 416n.2,
421n.99, 425n.178
amphibious operations, 150, 189
carrier on board delivery (COD),
126, 145
in Iran-Iraq War, 355–56
intelligence for, 143–45
Iranian threat, 147
logistics, 103, 125–27, 129
Powell on, 397n.105
prewar gulf presence, 43, 61–62,
121, 400n.8
redeployment, 325
amphibious ships and craft, 23, 24, 31,
64, 75, 78, 121, 231, 234, 250,
292, 325, 416n.2

landing craft air cushion (LCAC), 28, 68, 250, 289

landing craft utility (LCU), 250

landing helicopter assault ship, 241

Polnocny C-class tank landing ships (Iraqi), 68

transport dock ship (LPH), 14, 253

battleships, 34, 28, 31, 60, 64, 67, 78, 81, 103 (photo), 121, 142, 163, 192, 246, 253-54, 257, 259, 292-93, 296, 325, 355, 362, 369, 416n.2, 418n.27

command ship, 61, 71, 163, 325, 346

cruisers, 3, 14, 31, 56, 61–62, 64, 85, 121, 126, 146, 151, 163, 203, 204 (photo), 205, 221, 246, 253, 260, 296, 325, 355, 361, 366, 369, 416n.2, 434n.113

destroyers, 3, 14, 22, 25 (photo), 28–29, 31, 38, 39, 61, 64, 86, 88, 121, 127–28, 151, 152, 163, 167, 221, 231, 246, 253, 260, 296, 325, 346, 352, 355, 361, 369, 416n.2

frigates, 3, 14, 25, 28, 31, 37–38, 50, 60 (photo), 61, 64, 68, 89, 91, 121, 128, 141, 146, 151, 163, 213, 260, 325, 360–61, 363, 369, 416n.2, 432n.77

hospital ships, 105, 106 (photo), 129, 197, 260, 313, 325, 367, 433n.102

hydrographic survey, 97

merchant, 38, 65, 86–89, 91, 92 (photo), 93–95, 100, 129, 132, 135, 151–52, 203, 317–18, 331, 341 (photo), 343, 364

mine warfare, 36, 62, 68, 75, 76 (photo), 77, 149, 192, 224, 231, 260, 266, 292–93, 316, 318, 322, 325, 362

missile craft, 61, 64, 67–69, 146, 189, 220, 229–31

  FPB 57 (Iraqi), 30, 67, 229

  Osa II missile boat (Iraqi), 67–68, 230, 319 (photo), 319

roll-on/roll-off vessels, 8, 64, 70, 88, 97–98, 100, 364

small boats and craft

  Mark III patrol boats, 37

  rigid-hull inflatable boats (RHIBs), 91, 217

  Sea Raider utility craft (photo), 72 (photo)

  S.O. 1 patrol boat (Iraqi), 68

  whaleboat, 91, 217, 224

  Zhuk patrol boat (Iraqi), 68

  Zodiac rubber assault craft, 280, 280

submarines, 22–25, 27, 31, 38, 62, 183, 246, 323 (photo), 325, 352, 355, 362, 369, 416n.2

support ships,

  aviation support, 260

  cargo, 18, 22, 88, 97, 100

  fast sealift, 77, 96 (photo), 97–99, 132, 325, 364

  fleet tender, 106

  oilers, 20, 96, 102–3, 121, 127, 260, 367

  repair, 126, 250, 367

  replenishment tanker, 128

  salvage, 126, 127, 266

  seaplane tender, 14

  stores, 97, 102–4, 125, 367

  tugs, 97, 99, 125, 126, 127, 142,

Sigonella, Sicily, 132

Simpson, Bruce E., 213, 217, 426n.194

Sinai Peninsula, 178

Six Day War, 9

Slade, Lawrence R., 199–200, 31–32, 332 (photo)

Small, Joseph, 312–13

Smith, Leighton W., Jr., 131

Smith, Maurice, 135–36, 187

Smith, Ray, 122, 436n.10

Smith, Wayne, 333

Smith, William D., 153

Snedeker, Mark, 257–58

Sorfleet, William, 327

South China Sea, 102

South Korea, 97, 101, 132, 364

South Yemen, 9

Soviet Union, 5, 7–9, 11, 18, 23–25, 27, 31, 40, 54, 79, 143, 148, 168, 356–57

  arms for Iraq, 49, 68

  in Tanker War, 32–33

  U.S. relations, 28–30, 85, 358–39, 396n.69

Soyster, Harry E., 142

Spain, 86, 88, 98, 125, 219, 234, 338–39, 445n.87

"Special Middle East Support Agreement," 100

Special Operations Component, Central Command (SOCCENT), 122

Speicher, Michael Scott, 174, 208

Spica, 104

Spruance-class ships, 22, 29

Stalin, Joseph, 7, 44

Stanbridge, Harry, 185–86

Stark (FFG 31), 3, 36 (photo), 67, 141, 202–3, 357, 413n.111
State Department, 46–47, 50–52, 101, 441n.11
Stethem, Robert Dean, 108
Strategic Air Command, 184
Strategic Defense Initiative, 25
Strategies, 448n.16
    amphibious deception, 118, 150, 294, 301, 366
    forward-based, offensive strategic approach, 396n.88
    global containment, 7, 13–14
    left hook plan, 234, 247, 254
    maritime, 25–31
    "phantom army," 273
    postwar, 342
    "route package," 138, 185
    "shooters first," 61, 75, 109–10, 327, 327
Strike Projection Evaluation and Antiair Warfare Research (SPEAR), 144
Studeman, William O., 142
Stump (DD 978), 352
Stuttgart, Germany, 334
Subic Bay, 367
Success (Australia), 91, 104, 128
Sudan, 53, 61–63, 362
Suez Canal, 4–5, 61, 63, 121, 126, 152, 400n.8
Suez Crisis, 9
Suffren (France), 64
Suisun Bay, CA, 99
Suitland, MD, 143, 145
Sullivan, Francis J., 83
Summers, K. J., 128 (photo), 128–29, 219, 422n.113
Sumter, SC, 333
Sunnis, 8
Sununu, John, 54
Super Servant III (Netherlands), 75, 76 (photo)
Suppression of Enemy Air Defenses (SEAD), 174–76, 185, 198–99, 202
Sutton, Robert, 124, 402n.41
    command responsibilities, 81, 83, 139, 337
    fleet hospital placement, 130
    logistics, 83, 105–6, 125–27, 139, 252
    navy war planning, 43, 72, 77
Sweigart, Frank, 297
Switzerland, 54
Sydney (Australia), 104, 128, 151, 209
Sylvania (AFS 2), 103–4

Sylvester, John B., 300
Syria, 9, 11, 45, 61, 134–34, 143, 269, 301, 344

Tabriz, Iran, 38
Tactical air-launched decoys (TALDs), 175
Tactical Air Reconnaissance Pod System (TARPS), 145, 243 (photo), 244
Tadmur (Iraq), 93 (photo)
Takrit, Iraq, 44
Talil Station Air Operations Center, 352
Tampa, FL, 52, 337, 359, 400n.169
Tanajib, 234–35
Tanker War, 32–40, 34 (map), 61, 88, 141, 356. *See also* Iran-Iraq War
Tarawa (LHA 1), 121, 197, 289, 348
Task Forces
    118, 213–14
    126, 8
    151, 255, 267
    152, 267
    153, 346, 346
    154, 219
    amphibious task force (AFT), 75, 125–26, 150, 156, 220
    Freedom, 315–16
    Grizzly, 279, 435–36n.3
    Marine air-ground, 31, 74
    Mike, 280
    Papa Bear, 283, 298, 435–36n.3
    Ripper, 283, 286, 298, 435–36n.3
    Shepherd, 283, 298, 301, 435–36n.3
    Taro, 279, 435–36n.3
    Troy, 273, 435–36n.3
    X-ray, 435–36n.3
Task groups, 259, 308
    150.3, 72
    151.11, 255, 263
    mine countermeasures, 260, 266–67
Task units
    150.3.1, 77
    150.4.1, 77
Tawalkalna Mechanized Division (Iraq), 302
"Taxicab Army," 134
Taylor, Raynor A.K., 346, 349
    amphibious operations, 344–45
    Kuwait port reconstruction, 316–18
    mine warfare, 267, 322, 324. 149, 382, 433n.107
    NAVCENT reorganization, 334–37, 350
    on Tomahawk missiles, 343
    photos of, 318, 323, 335, 342, 345

Terra Nova (Canada), 128
Terrorism, 51, 63, 108, 123, 142, 227, 308–9, 311
Texas, 132
Theodore Roosevelt (CVN 71), 121, 140, 189, 207–8, 220, 255, 280, 302, 443n.38, 199
  Air Wing 8, 340
  Attack Squadron 65, 224
Thomas S. Gates (CG 51), 333
Thornton, Michael, 154
Threat Condition 1, 52
Tice, Jeffrey S., 312
Ticonderoga (CG 47), 29 (photo)
Tigris River, 44, 236, 348
Tiran, Strait of, 88
"Tokyo Rose," 157
Tonkin, Gulf of, 102, 190
Topeka (SSN 754), 350
Top Gun, 186
Trainor, Bernard E., 118, 409n.33, 409n.37, 434n.113, 436n.6 and n.13
Transportation, Department of, 18, 97, 100
Tripoli (LPH 10), 121, 253, 255, 259–60, 264–67, 268 (photo), 353, 448n.16
Truman, Harry S., 7–8
Truman Doctrine, 7
Tulfah, Khayrallah, 44
Turkey, 7–9, 47, 88, 132, 188, 338, 340
Turner, Charles, 181
Turner, Stansfield, 27
Tutwiler, Margaret, 50–51
Twentynine Palms, CA, 63
Twin Pillars policy, 10–11

Umm Gudair oilfield, 270, 272
Umm Qasr, Iraq, 83, 176, 181, 183, 231, 351
United Arab Emirates, 48, 360
  ground campaign, 269, 301
  maritime campaign, 33, 50–51, 61, 105, 123, 126, 141, 260, 445n.87
  postwar maritime interception, 445n.87
United Kingdom, armed forces of, 5, 61, 344
  1st Armoured Division, 135, 269, 303
  4th Armoured Brigade, 135
  7th Armoured Brigade, 135
  air campaign, 202, 205, 223, 234, 236, 260, 348–49, 351
  flight altitude, 419n.49
  ground campaign, 274
  explosive ordnance disposal, 317 (photo), 250, 260
  humanitarian relief operations, 338–39
  in Kuwait, 277, 299, 315
  in Tanker War, 33, 356
  maritime campaign, 64, 128, 141, 150, 219, 229, 356, 361–63
  maritime interception, 47, 54, 87, 363, 445n.87
  mine warfare, 77, 259–60, 262–63, 292, 322, 358, 432n.92, 442n.29
  Persian Gulf policy (prewar), 7, 9
  redeployment, 357
  Royal Air Force, 113, 229
  Scud hunt, 423n.135
United Nations, 61, 86–87, 304, 309
  Article 51, 55–56
  diplomatic pressure, 121, 151, 153, 163
  Iraqi sanctions, 56, 83–84, 115, 164
  Kuwait reconstruction, 315, 317
  Saudi Arabia defense, 59
  Tanker War cease-fire, 38
  weapons inspections, 347, 351
United Nations Security Council, 91, 153
  cease-fire conditions, 305, 310
  Resolution 660, 53–54, 275
  Resolution 661, 54, 83, 87
  Resolution 662, 85, 276
  Resolution 664, 85
  Resolution 665, 86, 87
  Resolution 678, 165
  Resolution 686, 320
  Resolution 687, 311–12, 320, 341
  Resolution 688, 338, 348
United Nations Special Commission, 312
United States. *See also* Bush, George
  coalition country relations, 53, 61–64, 86–87, 96, 100–101, 344
  Department of Agriculture, 327
  Egypt relations, 50, 55–56, 63
  in Tanker War, 33–40
  in Vietnam War, 5, 7–11, 13, 43, 70
  Iran relations, 7, 10–12, 16, 17, 19, 33–40, 79
  Iraq relations, 33, 36, 42–43, 46–47, 51, 53, 67, 151
  Israel relations, 46
  oil importance, 3–5, 7–13, 16
  Persian Gulf policy, 9–11, 113, 355
  postwar Middle East diplomacy, 343–34
  Saudi Arabia defense, 54–57, 59–78

Soviet Union relations, 7, 9, 12–14,
17–18, 23–25, 27–31, 40, 54, 356,
358–59
Syria relations, 11
war preparations, 17–20, 25, 96, 110
United States, Armed Forces
Air National Guard, 110
Air Force,
tactical fighter wings, 63, 79, 170,
329
A-10 Thunderbolt, 199
"Checkmate" group, 112
Gulf War Air Power Survey,
421n.103
Joint Air Force Component
Commander, 83
Joint Surveillance and Target Attack
Radar System (JSTARS), 297
Ninth Air Force, 63, 88, 183–85,
187–88
Seventh Air Force, 186
Army,
1st Armored Division, 133–34,
296–97, 303
1st Battalion, 6th Infantry
Regiment, 23d Infantry Division,
41
1st Brigade. *See* Tiger Brigade
1st Cavalry Division, 79, 110
2d Armored Cavalry Regiment, 302
3d Armored Cavalry Regiment, 79,
110, 290
11th Aviation Brigade, 302–3
12th Aviation Brigade, 79
21st Theater Army Area Command,
133
24th Infantry Division
(Mechanized), 41–42, 77, 79, 98,
110, 290–92, 303, 309
82d Airborne Division, 63–64, 73,
79, 110, 290
101st Airborne Division (Air
Assault), 290
352d Civil Affairs Command, 315
air war planning, 112–13
armor and weapons deployment,
109–10
B Troop, 4th Squadron, 17th
Aviation Regiment, 213–14, 224,
432n.77
Corps of Engineers, 227, 315
School for Advanced Military
Studies, 115
Special Forces, 122

Tiger Brigade, 269, 284–85, 287,
296, 299
VII Corps, deployment of, 120,
131–35, 269, 274, 277, 290, 292,
296, 304, 439n.60
XVIII Airborne Corps, 73, 269, 274,
277, 290, 296, 304, 328
Coast Guard. *See also* Port Security and
Harbor Defense
harbor defense, 72, 123–14, 402n.41
in Iraqi embargo operations, 91, 95
and oil spill, 227
in Vietnam coastal patrol, 85
law enforcement
detachments(LEDETs), 91, 213,
217
oceangoing patrol operations, 357
port security units, 123–24, 361
Reserve forces, 72
Marine Corps, 46, 107, 134
1st Air/Naval Gunfire Liaison
Company (ANGLICO), 288
1st Battalion, 7th Marines, 285
1st Force Service Support Group
(FSSG), 108, 328–29
1st Marine Division, 74, 79, 270,
272–74, 277, 279, 282–85,
294–96, 298–99
1st Surveillance, Reconnaissance
and Intelligence Group, 227, 242,
300
2d Air/Naval Gunfire Liaison
Company (ANGLICO), 288
2d Force Reconnaissance Company,
300
2d Force Service Support Group,
121
2d Marine Aircraft Wing, 121
2d Marine Division, 121, 269–74,
279, 284, 294–96, 298–99
2d Medical Battalion, 273
3d Marine Aircraft Wing, 285
4th Marine Expeditionary Brigade,
116–18, 151, 250, 333
5th Marine Expeditionary Brigade,
118, 121–22, 250, 289, 327
6th Marines, 283
7th Marine Expeditionary Brigade,
64–65, 74, 328, 360
7th Marines, 286
8th Marines, 295
11th Marine Expeditionary Unit,
443n.38
13th Marine Expeditionary Unit
(SOC), 118, 121–22, 224, 250,

292, 308–9, 326, 410n.49,
443n.38
15th Marine Expeditionary Unit
(SOC), 352, 443n.38
22d Marine Expeditionary Unit,
443n.38
24th Marine Expeditionary Unit
(SOC)
Company B, 4th Tank Battalion, 295
I Marine Expeditionary Force, 118,
252, 269, 270, 273, 277, 285,
288–90
Marine Air Ground Task Force 1-91,
339
Marine Air Group 11, 129, 146, 176
Marine expeditionary brigades, 8,
60, 64–65
Marine Forces, Southwest Asia, 328
Navy-Marine Liaison Team 10, 340
Navy support for ground war, 256
"Old Breed," 270, 294, 298
Reserves, 287
Navy,
"600-ship Navy," 21, 31
3d Naval Construction Regiment,
107, 272, 279
Administrative Support Unit,
Bahrain, 129
Bureau of Personnel, 161
Family Service Centers, 161
Joint Intelligence Liaison Element,
89
Mobile Inshore Undersea Warfare
Unit 202, 123, 316
Naval Beach Group 2, 252
Naval Cargo Handling Battalions 3
and 13, 252
Naval Inshore Undersea Warfare
Group 2, 123
Naval Mobile Construction
Battalion 5, 271 (photo), 272,
327, 340
Navy Combat Support Helicopter
Squadron 4, 339
Navy-Marine Liaison Team 10, 340
Navy Medical Research Institute,
107
Office of Information, 161
Office of Naval Intelligence, 142–43
Reserve Naval Mobile Construction
Battalions (RMNCBs), 4, 5, 24,
74, 129
Seventh Fleet, 30, 80–82, 102, 137,
182, 186, 242, 346, 366

Ship Repair Unit, Bahrain
Detachment (CTG 151.12), 126
Sixth Fleet, 9, 11, 24, 62, 82, 102
Special Warfare Development
Group, 122
Strategy and Concepts Branch (OP-
603), 82
Supervisor of Salvage, 227, 316
Swimmer Delivery Vehicle Team 1,
122
transport squadrons (VRs), 132
United States Armed Forces Radio and
Television Service, 159
United States European Command, 334,
338
United States Marine Forces, Central
Command (MARCENT), 190
United States Merchant Marine
Expeditionary Medal, 100
United States Naval Academy, 23, 81
United States Organization (USO), 163
United States Pacific Fleet (CINC-
PACFLT), 16
Unruh, Jerry L., 73, 78, 84

Vail, David, 267
Valley Forge (CG 50), 266
Vandergrift (FFG 48), 3, 61
Vehicles, 119, 121, 132–33
BMP armored personnel carriers, 49,
299, 302, 309
Bradley armored fighting vehicles, 25,
98, 296, 299, 302, 310
Fuchs ("Fox") reconnaissance vehicles, 283–84
heavy equipment transporters (HETs),
134
high-mobility multipurpose wheeled
vehicles (HMMWVs), 285, 296,
310
Iraqi armored vehicles, 283, 285, 286,
295–96, 302
light armored vehicles (LAVs), 64,
285, 299 (photo)
tanks, 134, 233, 250, 294, 309–10, 314
Abrams main battle tank, 25, 74, 96
(photo), 98, 285, 296, 299, 302,
303 (photo), 310, 326 (photo)
M60A1 tanks, 74, 282–85, 282
(photo)
Tatra military tractor trailers, 133
TOW-equipped, 294–95
Vencedora (Spain), 89
Vietnam Memorial, 334

Vietnam War, 24, 99, 103, 134, 181, 220, 330–31, 333–34, 402n.41
  casualties, 190
  lessons learned, 72, 86, 105–7, 112, 114, 116, 138, 143–44, 146, 165, 183–85, 221, 237, 240, 254, 257, 345, 357, 367, 413n.111, 429n.7
  Linebacker II Campaign, 448n.13
  maritime patrol operations, 17, 85
  mine warfare, 263, 358
  Navy budget, 22–23, 31
  Navy morale, 20–21
  Operation Stable Door, 402n.41
  Powell in, 41
  River Squadron 5, 81
  Rolling Thunder Campaign, 112
  Schwarzkopf in, 41
  South Vietnamese Airborne Brigade, 41
  Tet Offensive, 300
Vincennes (CG 49), 38, 203
Viorst, Milton, 247
Vladivostok, 30
VQ-1 Detachment Echo, 146, 147
Vulcan (AR 5), 126

Wadi al-Batin, 274, 290, 302
Wafrah. *See* al-Wafrah
Wages, Brian E., 184, 187, 192
Wainwright (CG 28), 205
Warbah Island, 48
Warden, John A., III, 112–13, 145
Warsaw Pact, 18, 30, 131, 133, 134, 365
Wash-Down Site I, 327
Wasp (LHD 1), 28, 339 (photo)
Watkins, James D., 27–28, 31
Weapons development project, 183
Weapons of mass destruction, 154, 312, 341, 343, 347, 351
Weapons systems, 23, 85
  Aegis, 28–29, 128, 138, 142, 146, 204, 356–57, 361, 366
  antiair, 213, 215
  Contingency Theater Automated Planning System (CTAPS), 349
  Forward-Looking Infrared (FLIR), 196, 240
  Global Positioning System (GPS), 196
  new threat upgrade antiair warfare systems, 357
  Phalanx, 142 (photo), 210 (photo), 361
  Terrain contour matching (TERCOM) systems, 170

Phalanx close-in weapons system (CIWS), 28
Webster, William, 54
Weinberger, Caspar, 41, 165, 398n.119
Weinberger Doctrine, 41
Welch, Ryan, 287–88
Western European Union (WEU), 87, 322
West Germany, 40
Westmoreland, William C., 80
Wetzel, Robert, 183, 312, 332 (photo)
Whidbey Island (LSD 41), 28
Wilson, Harold, 9
Wimbrown mobile base, 38
Wisconsin (BB 64), 26, 64, 79, 103 (photo), 142, 155, 162 (photo), 163, 218, 253, 256, 257 (photo), 258, 260, 279, 288–90, 294, 298, 326, 356, 377, 401n.20
Wolfowitz, Paul, 54
Woodall, Stephen R., 203, 205, 208, 218, 222, 255
Worden (CG 18), 146–48, 154, 163, 205, 207, 208
World War I, 32, 134, 154, 249, 274
World War II, 5, 7–8, 12, 21, 30, 40, 42, 114, 170, 220, 249, 273, 302, 330, 359, 396n.88, 423n.136
  veterans in Gulf War, 99
Wright, Timothy W., 83, 186

Yellowstone (AD 41), 126
Yemen, 24, 45, 53, 86, 362
Yeosock, John, 137, 274, 315
Yokosuka, Japan, 79, 121, 140
Yom Kippur War, 11, 24
York (U.K.), 61–62, 64
Yugoslavia, 68

Zaafaraniyah, Iraq, 352
"Zagros Gateguard," 209–10
Zagros Mountains, Iran, 209
Zakho, Iraq, 339–40
Zanoobia (Iraq), 91, 92 (photo), 93
Zaun, Jeffrey, 183, 312, 332 (photo)
Zlatoper, Ronald J., 219–22, 363, 376, 421n.96
Zuiderkruis (Netherlands), 144
Zuluf oilfield, 149
Zumwalt, Elmo R., Jr., 24, 27